THE MINERS' WELFARE FUND
1921 – 1952

First published by Unicorn
an imprint of the Unicorn Publishing Group LLP, 2020
5 Newburgh Street
London W1F 7RG

www.unicornpublishing.org

The publisher has made every effort to contact the current copyright holders
to the pictures included in this book. Any omission is unintentional, and the
details should be addressed to the Unicorn Publishing Group to be rectified in
any reprint.

10 9 8 7 6 5 4 3 2 1

ISBN 978-1-913491-30-7

Design by Unicorn Publishing Group

Printed in Wales by Gomer Press Ltd

THE GREATEST PIECE OF
SOCIAL REFORM OF ITS TIME

THE MINERS' WELFARE FUND 1921–1952

SARAH A.M. TURNER

UNICORN

*For Nanny
and Great Nan*

CONTENTS

'*There was no precedent for such a fund*'

Viscount Chelmsford, Chairman, The Miners' Welfare Committee
First Conference of District Welfare Committees, 28.11.1922

'*In providing systematically for all the workers of an industry out of sums subscribed by every component unit, the Miners' Welfare Fund is unique in this country and probably in the whole world*'.

Fifteenth Annual Report of the Miners' Welfare Committee, 1936

PREFACE

As a child, I was aware that my maternal grandfather, Thomas Albert Bennett, had worked for an organisation which was involved with coal miners and convalescent homes. My grandfather worked for the Miners' Welfare Committee and Commission, which provided a breadth of social reform which went far beyond what I had expected when beginning to research this book. Throughout the 31 years that the Miners' Welfare Committee and Commission existed, it worked towards materially improving the working and living conditions of coal miners and their families. My grandfather was born in Islington, London, in 1887, the third of four children. His father, Thomas Bennett, was a coachman and gardener and his mother, Elizabeth Emma Bennett, was a trained nurse.

When my grandfather was twelve, his father died. His two older sisters were already working as a sales assistant and machinist, respectively. His mother chose to return to nursing, working as what was known as a 'monthly' nurse, which necessitated her nursing patients in their own homes. She could sometimes be away from the family home for months at a time.

My grandfather passed his Bookkeeping and Accountancy examination in 1906, and came third in the examinations held by Society of Incorporated Accounts and Auditors in 1910, while employed as a Clerk by Mr W J Wincey of Finsbury Pavement, London. By 1918, he was working in the Coal Mines Department in the Board of Trade, had married Grace Laughton, with whom he had two children, and had become an Associate of the London Association of Accountants Limited. In 1925, he moved his family and mother from London to Gerrards Cross in Buckinghamshire.

He was first mentioned in the Annual Reports of the Miners' Welfare Committee in 1933, the same year he was awarded an MBE in the King's Birthday Honours. He became Assistant Secretary to the Miners' Welfare Committee and Secretary to the Miners' Welfare National Scholarship Scheme Selection Committee in 1934, Acting Joint Secretary to the Miners' Welfare Commission in 1946, and Secretary on 1st January 1948.

After he retired, he was elected in 1955 as District Councillor for Gerrards Cross to Eton Rural District Council, where he was also elected as Vice-Chairman on the Public Works Committee 1959-1964. In October 1964, he resigned from the District Council following the death of his wife, in August 1964. He died in 1973.

The Archives for the Miners' Welfare Committee are held at the National Archives at Kew. They consist of an incomplete set of minutes, agenda papers, and 11 annual reports. However, supplemented by minutes of the Safety in Mines Research Board held in the National Archives at Kew, newspaper articles held by the Durham Mining Museum, annual reports and the memorandum agreement held in the archives of the National Union of Mines Workers in Barnsley and parliamentary debates recorded in Hansard, it has been possible to compile this history of the many achievements of the Miners' Welfare Committee and Commission.

ONE

THE MINERS' WELFARE FUND IS CONCEIVED
1919–1920

The rationale for the establishment of a fund to improve the social and living conditions among the miners in this country developed slowly, over a period of approximately two years, during which time periods of industrial unrest, political manoeuvring and a Royal Commission to inquire into the position of and conditions prevailing in the coal industry all played their part in its inception.

In the opening month of 1919, The Miners' Federation of Great Britain (MFGB) put forward a series of demands on wages, hours and mines nationalisation. In the previous summer, the MFGB Annual Conference had decided on a wage demand, a reduction of the working day from a nominal eight hours to a nominal six and a demand for State ownership of mines. They had waited until the November Armistice to put forward these demands, and then had to wait until the General Election of December 1918. Thus, it was not until 9th January 1919 that the Miners' Federation's demand for 30% upon their total earnings (exclusive of the war wage) was put forward to the Coal Controller.

In January 1919, the disbandment of vast war-time armies was a preoccupation not only of the soldiers but the whole country. The possible plight of the ex-soldiers who had previously worked in the mines was of concern to the mining communities. Consequently, when the MFGB Special Conference met on 14th January at Southport, the delegates prioritised a series of demobilisation demands, coupled with those of a Six Hour Act and the nationalisation of the mines. The demand for a 30% advance was reaffirmed but only after an extra day's discussion, as there was a strong feeling that a 50% wage advance should be pushed for for. It was finally decided to demand:

a. Full maintenance for demobilised and unemployed miners
b. An amendment of the so-called 'Eight Hours Act' to read 'six' for 'eight' (which really meant a seven hours day)
c. Nationalisation of all mines and minerals (which by the decision of an earlier conference included control by the workers as a part of any scheme of nationalisation);
d. 30% advance on earnings, exclusive of war wage (3s).[1,2]

On the morning of 31st January, all these demands were discussed between the representatives of the Miners' Federation, the Minister of Labour, Sir Robert Horne, the Home Secretary, Rt Hon Edward Shortt KC, the President of the Board of Trade, the Rt Hon Sir Albert Stanley MP, and the Coal Controller, Sir Guy Calthorp. The President of the Miners' Federation, Robert Smillie, pointed out that no reply whatsoever had yet been given to the wages demand put forward on 9th January. Sir Robert Horne stated that the questions at issue would be put forward before the Cabinet for the decision of the Government.[3]

At a meeting of the War Cabinet on the afternoon of 31st January 1919, Sir Robert Horne reported that he had met with the representatives of the coalminers with regard to their demands for a six-hour day. The deputation had also demanded exceptionally favourable demobilisation terms; that miners returning from the forces should receive full wages until they obtained employment, and also that the men turned out of the mines to make way for the returning miners from the forces should receive similar treatment until found work. In addition, they asked for an advance of 30% on their wages, and nationalisation of the mines. The delegates had said that, unless a reply on the wages issue was received by Monday, trouble would ensue. It was pointed out to them, however, that the whole wage question was closely connected with that of a six-hour day, and the position would be considered by the Government as rapidly as possible. A reply would be given, if possible, by the end of the next week.[4]

By 4th February 1919, a joint memorandum on the 'Miners' claim for advances in wages and reduction of hours etc' had been produced by the Home Secretary, the President of the Board of Trade and the Minister of Labour for the War Cabinet to consider. The demands for increased wages and a reduction in hours were far-reaching in character and, if conceded, would involve huge increases in the price of coal. It was estimated that the wage demand alone would amount to about £40 million per annum, and that probably about 3/6 or 3/- per ton would have to be added to the price of coal on an annual output of about 250 million tons. It was impracticable to estimate what additional cost would be involved by the adoption of the reduced working hours, but it was clear that the concession would still further greatly increase the price of coal.

However, the miners' last increase in wages of 1/6d per day had been in June 1918, and then other trades (engineering, shipbuilding, explosives) had received, by arbitration, an increase of 3/6d a week immediately after the miners' increase in wages. In December 1918, these same trades had again, by arbitration, received a further 5/- a week as there had been a marked increase in the cost of living. It seemed, therefore, that the miners were at least 5/- per week behind.

The authors of the memorandum were concerned about the effects the increase of price of coal would have on the export trade of British coal, the cost of iron and steel and in consequence shipbuilding, the position of the railways (already deeply in debt due to wage increases given to the railwaymen) and the small consumers of coal (those who bought coal by the hundredweight) who would be forced into a lower standard of life.

A proper enquiry into the facts and circumstances of the miners' case was seen as the way in which the demands could be made. The effect upon the attitude of other trades arising from treating the miners differently had to be considered. It could not be expected that important trades would continue to have course to arbitration if the miners, by 'direct action', could secure from the Government any terms they liked to submit.

It was suggested that the miners should be offered, at once, whatever amount by way of additional war wage was due to them, on the grounds of the increase in the cost of living since they received their last advance. With regard to their other demands, they should be informed that the Government intended to establish at once a strong representative committee, on which the miners would nominate their own representatives, to enquire into the matters raised. The terms of reference would be sufficiently wide to enable the committee to enquire into the wages and the question of the organisation of the mines. The committee could be asked to report on the future organisation of the coal industry, but the committee would first be asked to present an interim report on the matter of wages and hours of work.

The demands for demobilised miners were seen as extravagant. It was concluded that the scheme which was applicable to the rest of the country must be equally applied to the miners.[5]

On 7th February 1919, the War Cabinet discussed the joint memorandum, and a note by the Acting Secretary of the War Cabinet with reference to the joint memorandum.

The Minister of Labour proposed that the Government should take a clear stand. As regarded demobilisation, there was no room for discussion. It was impossible to concede preferential treatment to the miners over the rest of the workers of the country. Regarding wages, the demand was for an additional 30%. This would have a crippling effect on industry. However, the miners had a reasonable claim for consideration. Their last advance had been in June 1918, when the Prime Minister had promised them that wages would be reconsidered if the cost of living rose. The Minister of Labour suggested that two alternatives should be made to the miners:

(i) An increment of 1s a day.
(ii) That their claims should be examined by the Interim Court of Arbitration, which had succeeded the Committee on Production.

What he proposed was that they should be empowered to offer the miners a full and impartial inquiry into the whole question of their wages. He suggested a possible membership of the Committee of Inquiry which included representatives of both the Miners' Federation and the mine owners. This Committee would also go into the question of hours. He further suggested that the Committee should submit, as soon as possible, an interim report on the question of wages and hours and that it should then consider the further and wider question of joint control or the nationalisation of mines. The mine owners themselves had asked for a full inquiry into the whole mechanism of the coal industry and into the question of profits.

As a promise had been made to the Miners' Federation to give a reply to their present claims by the end of the week, the Minister of Labour suggested that representatives of the Federation should be invited the following Monday to a conference when the views of the Government would be communicated to them. It was firstly suggested that this could be a verbal communication but, after further discussion, it was decided that the verbal message should at once be followed by a printed memorandum.[6]

On 10th February, Sir Robert Horne met with members of the Miners' Federation and he read to them the memorandum containing the reply of the Government to the miners' proposals. Robert Smillie, remarking that the Government's reply did not come within measurable distance of the miners' demands, stated it would be submitted to the Federation Conference.

A Miners' Special Conference met two days later at Southport, on February 12th and 13th, to receive the report of the negotiators. Meanwhile, on the evening of 11th February, the Prime Minister, David LLoyd George, delivered a threatening speech in the House of Commons, the purpose of which appeared to be to intimidate the Conference. It had the reverse effect, with the Conference unanimously carrying the motion that 'this Conference rejects the terms offered by the Government as being no answer to our claims'. It was further decided to take a ballot of the membership on the question of a stoppage.[7]

On Friday, 21st February, in response to an invitation, the Executive Committee of the Miners' Federation met the Prime Minister at 10, Downing Street. The Prime Minister asked that the miners should delay the expiry of the strike notices (which were dated for 15th March) for a fortnight and should participate in a Commission which would be bound to present an interim report by 31st March.

Robert Smillie, in reply, reminded the Government that the miners' claim had been lodged as far back as 9th January. He showed that the claim, having been reduced to the lowest possible amount, was just and fair from every point of view. He dwelt on the miners' housing conditions and the conditions of their working life. He then pointed out that, if the mines were handed back to the mine owners, the miners would have no right to a voice on the working conditions in the mines or the commercial side. Finally, he said that the wages and hours claim, on which information was already in the hands of the Government, should be dealt with immediately and need not stand over until a Commission reported. The Prime Minister refused this, and again said that these matters must be remitted to the Commission. He suggested that the miners might serve on such a Commission. The Executive Committee then agreed to call a Conference to consider whether the miners should participate.

Meanwhile, the result of the Strike Ballot had become known, and Mr Lloyd George had agreed that the interim report of the Commission should be published on 20th March. The ballot showed a five to one majority in favour of a stoppage.[8]

The Coal Industry Commission Bill establishing a Royal Commission was debated in the House of Commons on 24th and 25th February 1919 and in the House of Lords on 26th February.[9] The Act gave wide powers 'to constitute a Commission to inquire into the position of, and conditions prevailing, in the Coal Industry'. The Commissioners were to inquire in particular as to:

(a) the wages and hours of work in the various grades of colliery workers, and whether and, if so, to what extent, and by what method, such wages should be increased and hours reduced; regard being had to a reasonable standard of living amongst the colliery workers, and to the effect of such changes on the economic life of the country;

(b) any equality between different grades of colliery workers as regards wages, hours of work, and other conditions, and whether and, if so, to what extent any of these inequalities are unjustifiable and capable of remedy;

(c) the cost of production and distribution in the coal industry, or any industry commonly carried on in connection therewith or as ancillary or incident thereto, and the general organisation of the coalfield and the industry as a whole;

(d) selling prices and profits in the coal industry, or any industry commonly carried on in connection therewith or as ancillary or incidental thereto;

(e) the social conditions under which colliery workers carry on their industry;

(f) any schemes that may be submitted to or formulated by the Commissioners for the future organisation of the coal industry, whether on the present basis, or on the basis of joint control, nationalisation, or any other basis;

(g) the effect of the present incidence of, and practice in regard to, mining royalties and wayleaves upon the coal industry and the cost of coal, and whether any and what changes in these respects are desirable;

(h) the effect of proposals under the above heads upon the development of the coal industry and the economic life of the country.[10]

The Conference of the MFGB met on the 26th February in London and adjourned after a day's discussion. Strong arguments had been pressed against participation, on the grounds that if the report was adverse, the miners' case would be prejudiced. The next day it was decided to participate, but only on strict conditions as to the miners' representation. It was also agreed to postpone the strike notices until 22nd March, Lloyd George having promised that an interim report should be ready by 20th March. Eventually, an understanding was reached that the miners should appoint four representatives directly and the other two representatives on the workers' side should be agreed upon between the miners and the Government, but formally nominated by the latter. Accordingly, around the 1st March, the Commission was made up as follows:

Hon. Mr Justice Sankey (in the chair)

Workers' side:
  Appointed by the Miners Federation:
  Mr Robert Smillie
  Mr Herbert Smith
  Mr Frank Hodges
  Sir Leo Chiozza Money
  Agreed between the Government and the Miners' Federation:
  Mr R. H. Tawney
  Mr Sidney Webb

Employers' side:
  Government nominees:
  Mr Arthur Balfour
  Sir Arthur Duckham
  Sir Thomas Royden
  Representatives of Coal-owners:
  Mr Evan Williams
  Mr R. W. Cooper
  Mr J. T. Forgie.[11]

The Coal Industry Commission held its first meeting on 3rd March 1919 when it decided on its course of procedure. By what came to be seen as a sound strategy on the workers' side of the Commission, it was decided to call Government witnesses first, thereafter representatives of industries immediately dependent on the coal industry, then the coal-owners' witnesses, and finally the miners' witnesses. The public examination of witnesses began on 4th March and concluded on 17th March. The Commission sat every day except Sunday and met several times in private and, after 17th March, deliberated entirely in camera until the report was ready.

The second witness to be called was Mr Arthur Lowes Dickinson, Financial Adviser to the Coal Mines Department, who gave evidence over a period of two days. The revelations disclosed by him of profiteering by the coal industry during the war caused immediate revulsion in the general public, and support erred in favour of the miners and against the mine owners. By evidence of the witnesses who followed, it became clear that the private ownership and distribution of coal had not merely meant swollen profits, wrung out of the low wages paid to the miners and high prices paid by the public, but had also seriously hampered the national effort during the war by its inefficiency and wastefulness.[12]

By the end of the first week, under cross-examination of the workers' side, it had become obvious that the case for private ownership was labouring heavily. This applied not merely to the ownership of mines and minerals but to the private control of distribution, both wholesale and retail. To a certain amount of surprise, the public, and perhaps some of the miners, learned that nationalisation provided the only really adequate method by which to preserve and raise the miners' standard of living, besides being the only effective safeguard for the consumers.[13]

The witnesses for the Miners' Federation were examined on the Friday and Saturday, 14th and 15th March. These were:

	Subject
W. Straker (Northumberland)	Nationalisation
J. Robertson (Scotland)	Standard of life (Housing, Health, Education, Accidents etc)
J. Potts (Yorkshire)	Hours and Output
Vernon Hartshorn, MP (South Wales)	Wages[14]

In each case, the miners' point of view was ably stated and sustained under severe cross-examination from the coal-owners side of the Commission. Mr Straker, who had submitted a draft provision indicating the sort of control of the industry which the miners desired as part of any national scheme, was kept in the witness box all day[15], while Mr Robertson's evidence on the abominable housing conditions in mining villages undoubtedly made a very deep impression both on the Commission and the public, and was reflected in recommendation

XXI of the Commission's Interim Report which stated:

> 'Evidence has been placed before the Commission as to the housing accommodation of the colliery workers in various districts. Although it is true that there is good housing accommodation in certain districts- and to some extent- there are houses in some districts which are a reproach to civilisation. No judicial language is sufficiently strong or sufficiently severe to apply to their condemnation.'[16]

The public sessions closed on Monday, 17th March, with evidence from the co-operative societies being taken on 15th and others on 17th March. The effect of their evidence was to reinforce the impression of the opening sessions, that private ownership in production and distribution of coal was characterised by wastefulness and extravagance.[17]

It was found impossible to present a unanimous report and eventually, on 20th March, three reports were announced; a Majority Report, a Report signed by the Chairman, and a Report signed by the coal-owners. The Majority Report was signed by Messrs R Smillie, Frank Hodges, Herbert Smith, Sir Leo Chiozza Money, Messrs R H Tawney and Sidney Webb[18].

The following is a summary of their conclusions:

1. We find that the miners' claim for an advance in the standard of life is justified and that the percentage of rise of wages asked for, namely 30% (on earnings apart from the war wage) is not excessive.
2. We find justified the claim to a substitution in the Coal Mines Regulation Act of 1908 of six for eight (making the future working day underground vary from six-and-a-half hours in some mines to eight-and-a-half in others and averaging 7 hours). A corresponding shortening of the working day should apply to surface workers.
3. We find justified the miners' claim for a more efficient organisation of their industry-the individual ownership of collieries being officially declared to be 'wasteful and extravagant' whilst the method of retail distribution is unnecessarily costly; and in view of the impossibility of tolerating any unification of all the mines in the hands of a Capital Trust we think that, in the interest of the consumer as much as that of the miners, nationalisation ought to be, in principle at once determined on.
4. As to the claims in respect of miners demobilised from the Army, we think that it would be better for these to be dealt with along with the cases of men in other industries.[19]

The Sankey Report was signed by the Honourable Mr Justice Sankey, and the three Government nominees: Mr Arthur Balfour, Sir Arthur Duckham and Sir Thomas Roydon.

Their recommendations as to hours and wages were:

I. We recommend that the Coal Mines Regulation Act 1908, commonly called the Eight Hours Act, be amended by the substitution, in the clauses limiting the hours of work underground, of the word 'seven' for the word 'eight' as and from July 16th, 1919, and subject to the economic position of the industry at the end of 1920, by the substitution of the word 'six' for the word 'eight' as and from July 13th, 1921. Certain adjustments must be made in the hours of classes of underground workers specifically mentioned in the Act.

II. We recommend that as from July 1919, the hours of work of persons employed on the surface at or about collieries shall be forty-six and a half working hours per week exclusive of mealtimes, the details to be settled locally.

III. We recommend an increase of wages of two shillings per shift or per day worked in the case of the classes of colliery workers, employed in coal mines, whose wages have in the past been regulated by colliery sliding scales. In the case of workers under 16 years of age, the advance is to be one shilling.

IV. We recommend the continuation of the Coal Mines Control Agreement, 1918, subject to certain suggestions indicated in our report.[20]

The Sankey Report had something to say as to how the appalling housing conditions of the miners could be addressed:

'It is a matter for careful consideration whether 1d per ton should not be at once collected on coal raised and applied to improving housing and meanities of each particular colliery district. A 1d per ton on present output means about £1,000,000 a year'.[21]

However, their recommendation, which proved of greatest importance and was to have tremendous repercussions, dealt with nationalisation and control of industry by the workers:

'Even upon the evidence already given, the present system of ownership and working in the coal industry stands condemned and some system must be substituted for it, either nationalisation or a method of unification by national purchase and/or by joint control'.[22]

The Coal-owners' report, signed by Messrs R. W. Cooper, J. T. Forgie and Evan Williams, was confined solely to wages and hours of labour.[23]

On Thursday, 20th March, the three reports were presented to Parliament. That evening Bonar Law announced that the Government had adopted the Sankey Report 'in spirit and letter' but, if a strike took place, the Government would use all the resources of the State without hesitating.

The Miners' Conference, held in London on 21st March, recommended the Districts (whose strike notices expired the following day) to continue working until Wednesday, 26th March, while the Executive negotiated with the Government with a view to securing a modification of the Sankey proposals.

On Saturday, 22nd March, various points were urged before Mr Bonar Law, who promised that he would give a reply by Tuesday, 25th March.[24]

On Tuesday morning, 25th March, Mr Bonar Law gave the War Cabinet an outline of what he proposed, with the War Cabinet's approval, to say to the miners that afternoon. The miners had intimated that they would strike unless the Government gave concessions beyond the Sankey Report. The matter they pressed was of working hours, and that they wished to reduce the working hours from eight to seven in July, and six unconditionally in July 1920. He proposed to say that the Government could not go beyond the Sankey Report but that if there were any points which required interpretation, the Government would be quite willing to submit these points to Justice Sankey for his ruling.[25]

In the afternoon of 25th March, Mr Bonar Law met with the representatives of the Miners' Federation and told them that he could not make any substantial change to the Sankey Report.

At the Federation Conference on 26th March, it was decided to take a ballot of the members as to the acceptance of the Government proposals; meanwhile, the District was to continue to work. The Executive Committee met afterwards and decided that the ballot should be held on 9th and 10th April and the results would be in the hands of the Secretary by 14th April.

When the result of the MFGB ballot was declared on 15th April, it showed 693,084 votes for accepting the Government's terms and only 76,992 against. The Special Conference meeting the next day ordered the withdrawal of the strike notices.[26]

With the acceptance of the Government terms, the Commission, which had been suspended for a month, was able to meet again and entered on its second stage which lasted from 24th April to 23rd June. The second stage took up a comprehensive investigation into schemes for 'nationalisation or a method of unification by national purchase and/or by joint control'.

In the interval between the two stages of the inquiry, Sir Thomas Royden resigned owing to ill health, and Sir Allan Smith (Chairman of the Engineering Employers' Federation) was appointed in his stead. A few days later, after the second stage had begun, Mr J. T. Forgie resigned for health reasons and his place was taken by Sir Adam Nimmo (who had resigned his official post as advisor to the Coal Controller).

During the second stage, evidence was taken over twenty-eight days, and 116 witnesses were examined. These witnesses included expert economists, royalty owners, Home Office witnesses, witnesses as to the working of nationalisation abroad or in the Colonies, technicians, coal owners, miners, miners' wives, industrial consumers, managers and administrators.

The evidence for the Miners' Federation was presented on 23rd, 27th, 28th and 30th May. Mr H. Slesser, Standing Counsel to the Miners' Federation, submitted a draft parliamentary bill, embodying the miners' scheme for the nationalisation of mines and minerals. This was supported by Mr Straker and Mr Winstone of the MFGB, while evidence on the conditions of the miners' life was given by Mrs Hart, Mrs Andrews and Mrs Brown, miners' wives from Lancashire, South Wales and Scotland respectively. In addition, in accordance with the precedent set by several previous Commissions, notably the Poor Law Commission of 1906-09 and the Commission on Ecclesiastical Discipline, two members of the Commission, Mr Sidney Webb and Sir Leo Chiozza Money, went into the witness box and submitted plans for systems of ownership and management in substitution for the existing system.

The miners' own scheme was presented by Mr Straker as part of the draft parliamentary bill of the Miners' Federation. It was based on vesting all powers in a National Mining Council, consisting of the Minister of Mines for the time being and twenty whole-time members, ten appointed by the Government and ten by the Miners' Federation.

By 20th June, four reports were presented. The report of the Chairman, Mr Justice Sankey, was supported in the main by six commissioners (Sir Leo Chiozza Money, Messrs Robert Smillie, Herbert Smith, Frank Hodges, R. H. Tawney and Sidney Webb) who, however, presented conclusions separately. A third report was that of Sir Adam Nimmo, KBE, Sir Allen M. Smith KBE, and Messrs Arthur Balfour, R. W. Cooper and Evan Williams. Sir Arthur Duckham KCB, MICE was the only signatory to the fourth report.

All four reports agreed on two points; firstly, on recommencing the State ownership of all seams of coal and hence the royalties; and secondly in recommending, in view of the overwhelming evidence of the extreme wastefulness of the system by which coal was distributed to household consumers, that the machinery of local authorities and the co-operative movement should be utilised for the purpose of distribution.

The Chairman's report recommended that the principle of state ownership of coal mines be accepted. It further recommended that some scheme for local administration be immediately set up with the aid of the local Controller's department, and legislation passed to acquire coal mines for the state after the scheme had been worked for three years from the date of the report (during which time coal control would be continued), fair and just compensation being paid to the owners.

After dealing with the method of purchase and carrying on the coal mines, the Chairman proceeded to outline a scheme of administration which, due to time constraints on the Chairman, were only suggestions for the use of Parliament not as recommendations.[27]

It appeared that the Government, who had received the four reports on 20th June, were bound by their previous adoption of the previous Sankey Report. Constitutionally, they were not bound to accept the reports of the Royal Commissions but, when a specific pledge had been given, it was certain that the refusal to accept the Chairman's report, or the report of the six members, would be regarded as a breach of faith. Furthermore, the fact that seven of the Commissioners, including the Chairman, were agreed on nationalisation, made a strong presumption in favour of adoption of that principle.[28] However, this was not how it played out.

The Government was extremely concerned about public opinion. The popularity of the miners' cause put limits on its ability to manoeuvre. On 8th July, the cabinet agreed a strategy to exploit the poor state of public finances to paint the miners' demands as excessive and damaging to the national economy. On 9th July, a 6s rise in the price of coal was announced in the House of Commons to come into effect on 15th July, the day before the first Sankey Award became operative. It was explained that the price rise was needed to pay for the concessions which had been made to the miners. It was emphasised that not only would it harm the consumer, but it would also damage industry, reduce exports and increase unemployment.[29]

The Executive Council of the MFGB had managed to defend its 'wait and see' policy and keep their members invested in the Sankey process. However, it was questioned how long it would be able to resist pressures for action, in the form of widespread disgruntlement in the collieries, over the practical implications of the Sankey Award which came into effect on Wednesday, 16th July. On the same day, a month-long Yorkshire miners' strike began. These grievances, in conjunction with the coal output crisis and the 6s increase in the cost of a ton of coal, were responsible for a growing dissatisfaction with Sankey, and let loose a new wave of unrest which touched every major coalfield to engulf the Federation. In the week following the MFGB Annual Conference in Keswick, approximately 200,000 miners went on strike in Scotland, the North-East, Lancashire, Nottinghamshire, Derbyshire, the Midlands, South Wales and Kent over issues arising from the Sankey Commission (interpretation of reduction in hours and piece rate adjustments). With the Yorkshire strike included, the movement at its peak involved about 400,000 miners or about half of the Federation's total membership. Although outside Yorkshire the strikes were brief affairs, they were a highly important component of the general crisis in the days immediately before the Government's final decision on nationalisation.[30]

The Parliamentary Coal Committee, an organisation of mine-owner MPs, circulated a memo in the first half of July calling for steps to be taken 'to protect our great industries against the organised revolutionary and predatory forces of direct action and against the nationalisation of the mines'. Three hundred and five MPs signed the memo and presented it to Lloyd George in mid-July.[31]

On 23rd July 1919, the War Cabinet discussed the desirability of making a statement regarding nationalisation of mines. The Prime Minister had a meeting arranged the next day to meet Mr Smillie, and suspected that Mr Smillie would ask if the Government was able to give any information regarding nationalisation. The Prime Minister therefore thought that it would be wise to make a statement on the subject before the recess. This was generally agreed, since, if a strike was to come, the best month in which to have it was August.[32]

The policy of saying nothing was spun out until 18th August, when the Prime Minister announced in the House of Commons the Government's conclusions to the Sankey Reports and to the evidence of the Commission.

'The Government accepts the policy of State purchase of mineral rights in coal on which subject all the Reports of the Royal Commission were perfectly unanimous. The Government have been deeply impressed by the evidence tendered to the Commission with respect to the unsatisfactory social conditions under which miners have been compelled to carry on their industry in some parts of the country. They hold that a reasonable standard of living should be secured to the miners and their families; that the deplorable housing conditions which, in some of the coalfields of the country, should be remedied as rapidly as possible and that every effort should be made to improve the comfort and amenities of the miners and their families.'

The Prime Minister proposed that a fund should be raised from a deduction from the purchase value of coal to improve the social conditions and the conditions of life among the miners of the country.

As to the future organisation of the coal industry, the Prime Minister said 'that the Government accepted in the letter and the spirit of the Interim Report of Mr Justice Sankey's Commission. In their Report there is a recommendation in favour of the unification and reorganisation of the industry. In his Final Report, Mr Justice Sankey proceeded with his interpretation of that principle. We accept the principle, but we cannot accept Mr Justice Sankey's final interpretation'.[33]

In 1920, the Government introduced the Ministry of Mines Bill which primarily dealt with the future organisation of the coal industry, but also provided the owners of coal mines would pay one penny per ton for the next five years upon the tonnage of coal raised and that this fund would be devoted to the purpose of improving the social welfare of the mining community.[34]

In August 1920, the Ministry of Mines Bill was amended to the Mining Industry Bill. The Ministry of Mines became a Department of Mines and amendments were made in the House of Commons relating to the decentralisation of the betterment fund.[35]

The Mining Industry Act 1920 dated 16th August 1920, 'provided for the better administration of mines, and to regulate the coal industry and for other purposes connected with the mining industry and the persons employed therein'. Section 20 of the Act provided for the establishment of a fund for the improvement of social conditions of colliery workers. The 'fund would be applied for such purposes connected with social wellbeing, recreation, and with conditions of living of workers in or about coal mines and with mining education and research as the Board of Trade, after consultation with any Government Department concerned may approve'.

The owners of every coal mine would before 31st March 1921, and before the 31st March in each of the subsequent five years, pay into the fund a sum equal to one penny a ton of the output of the mine during the previous calendar year.

The duty for allocating the money credited to the fund would be vested in a committee consisting of five persons, appointed by the Board of Trade, of which one should be appointed by the Board of Trade after consultation with the Mining Association of Great Britain, and another after consultation with the Miners' Federation of Great Britain. The Committee should have the assistance of three assessors appointed by the Ministry of Health, the Board of Education and the Secretary for Scotland respectively. The assessors would have the right of attending meetings of the Committee and of taking part in the deliberations but not of voting.

The Committee would take into consideration any scheme submitted by a district and, before allocating any money for a local purpose, they should consult the district committee concerned. Twenty-five coal districts were named in Part I of the Second Schedule of the Act, and the Committee was charged with allocating, for the benefit of these districts, sums equal to four fifths of the contributions from the owners of coal mines in those districts respectively.

The Committee could also invite a local authority to submit a scheme. They could also allocate money, in whole or in part, for the provision of pithead baths but only on the understanding that section seventy-seven of the Coal Mines Act 1911 would apply to such accommodation and facilities.[36]

Thus, the Betterment Fund was born but, as will be seen in the next chapter, it would soon be renamed the Miners' Welfare Fund.

TWO

FIRST QUINQUENNIUM
1921–1926

The members of the first Committee of the Betterment Fund were appointed in January 1921. The Chairman, Lord Gorell CBE, MC was joined by Mr A. Leslie Wright, representing the Mining Association, Rt. Hon. William Brace, Professor E. L. Collis MA, MD, and Sir William Walker. Mr W. R. Davies was appointed as the Committee's assessor representing the Board of Education, and Dr G. S. Buchan representing the Ministry of Health. The Acting Secretary to the Committee was Mr W. G. Nott Bower.[1]

At the time of his appointment, Ronald Gorell Barnes, 3rd Baron Gorell, was a member of the House of Lords sitting on the Liberal benches. In July 1921, he was appointed as Under-Secretary for Air in the coalition government of David Lloyd George, at which time a new Chairman had to be appointed.[2]

The Rt. Hon. William Brace had been a Welsh trade unionist and a Liberal-Labour member of Parliament for South Glamorganshire from 1906–1918. He was sponsored by the Miners' Federation of Great Britain, which was affiliated to the Labour Party, but he took the Liberal whip. During the First World War he held the post of Under-Secretary of State for the Home Department. In 1916, he was made a Privy Councillor. When the South Glamorganshire seat was abolished in 1918, he was elected as the Labour party MP representing the new Abertillery seat. He resigned from the House of Commons in 1920 in the wake of a bitter dispute within the miners' union, and he took up the position of Labour Advisor to the Ministry of Mines.[3]

Professor Edgar Leigh Collis had qualified from St Thomas' Hospital in 1896. In 1908, he had joined the staff of the Factory Department of the Home Office as a medical inspector of factories where he became a leading authority on pneumoconiosis. In the First World War, he was appointed a member of the Health of Munition Workers Committee and, in 1917, he became Director of Welfare and Health in the Ministry of Munitions. In 1918, he became a member of the newly set up Industrial Fatigue Research Board and, in 1919, he was appointed Talbot Professor of Preventive Medicine at the Welsh National School of Medicine at Cardiff, where he continued to take an active interest in the improvement of workers' conditions in coal mines and in miners' welfare. [4]

Sir William Walker had been an Inspector of Mines firstly in Durham, then in York and Lincoln District, and then in Edinburgh. In 1907, he was elected president of the Midland Institute of Mining Engineers and was a member of the committee instituted by the Royal Commission on Mines to inquire into and report on the prevention of accidents from falls of ground in shafts and by haulage in mines. In 1916, he took up the position of Deputy Inspector of Mines at the Home Office. In 1917, he was promoted to acting Chief Inspector, and during 1919–20 was Chief Inspector.[5]

From the start, the Fund did not bear any part of the salaries either of the Secretary or of the other officers of the Mines Department who were concerned with it, nor the cost of accommodation and ordinary supplies of stationery and furniture. These expenses were borne by Public Funds on the Votes of the Governments concerned and with the support of the Mines Department.[6]

1921 was not an auspicious time to launch a Fund whose income was derived from a levy on coal output, and which would have to rely on the good working relationship between the owners and mineworkers to achieve the Fund's objectives.

A slump in the British economy hit the country at the end of 1920. Britain passed into a chronic depression of trade and rapid unemployment. In February 1921, the Government decided to bring forward the decontrol of the mining industry financially from 31st August 1921 as prescribed in the Coal Industry Act 1920 to 31st March 1921. This decision ended the discussions the mine owners and the MFGB were having over the settlement of both wages and 'profit sharing'. The Coal Mines (Decontrol) Act was given Royal assent on 24th March 1921. From the beginning of March 1921 onwards notices, were posted throughout the coalfields that all contracts of service (including those of pump men and other 'safety men') would end on 31st March 1921. The mineworkers expected a reduction in wages because of the trade slump and the fall in the cost of living but the reductions demanded by some District Associations of coal-owners amounted to a halving of wages of certain grades. The Government refused to intervene, and the coal-owners universal lockout of the mines started on 1st April 1921. The same day, 'a state of emergency' was declared under the Emergency Powers' Act 1920. The Government, coal-owners and miners entered a three-month period of recriminations and heated negotiations. The final meeting with the coal-owners took place on 27th June at the Board of Trade where the Executive Committee of the MFGB provisionally agreed to the terms of a wage settlement with the Government and the owners. After an overwhelming vote in favour of resumption, the mines returned to work at the beginning of July 1921 However, the effect of the National Wages Agreement of July 1921 was that coalmining, from being for a short time one of the best paid trades, fell to being one of the worst paid.[7]

The first meeting of the Betterment Fund Committee took place on 3rd February 1921. The meeting was opened by the Secretary for Mines, the Rt. Hon. William Clive Bridgeman. Most of the meeting was taken up with discussing the scope of the Fund; education, recreation, health and safety and research. The Committee were aware of mining education schemes such a mining institutes in Staffordshire, the Treforest and Crumlin Schools in Wales (supported by the tonnage contribution of the coalmine owners), and the University Extension work undertaken by Sheffield University, but an investigation into education in the mining areas was needed to inform the Committee. To gain information on recreational facilities, it was decided to initally approach the Inspectors of Mines and Ministry of Agriculture. It was thought that mortality and morbidity statistics were inadequate but the Committee were unable to proceed much further with health and safety as the Mines Department were in the process of setting up the Mining Dangers Research Board in accordance with the recommendation of the Eskmeals' Committee.[8]

The Committee also considered the title of the Fund. The title was considered both cumbersome and, at the same time, not altogether descriptive of the objectives of the Fund. They therefore suggested to the Secretary for Mines that the 'Miners' Welfare Fund' was a more convenient and appropriate designation. Mr Bridgeman expressed considerable objection to the change in name and asked the Committee to reconsider but they persisted with their request and a letter from the Mines Department was sent out on 28th February to all coal owners and miners' associations confirming the change in name.[9]

From the end of March 1921, the unsettled conditions in the coal industry made it impossible for the Committee to make any progress save in the direction of preliminary investigations.[10] Having held two meetings in February 1921, the third meeting was not held until 27th July 1921. At this meeting, the Committee were able to hear Mr G. H. Winstanley, Inspector for the Board of Education, give a report on the education in mining areas of England and Wales. (A report from Scotland was still awaited). Mr Winstanley referred to the segregation of those engaged in mining, to the consequent narrowness of outlook, to the effect of the destructive character of mining operations, to the peculiar characteristics of miners and to their special need of good educational influences.

In his review of the existing education facilities, he described the 4 levels available to miners in a typical mining county. At level 1, there were many part-time evening classes giving instruction in subjects such as English, practical arithmetic, drawing and mining sciences. The minimum age at which a young miner could sit for the statutory examination for a Mine Manager was 23, and he could not practice as a Mines Manager before he was 25. Hence, many, though not all, pit boys postponed attendance at local classes for some years. At level

2, in any well-organised county area, there would be district schools available offering further education facilities. At level 3, came the mining colleges such as Treforest and the mining departments of such technical colleges as those in Stoke-on-Trent, Wigan and other large towns in mining districts. Finally, at level 4, there were the mining departments at certain university institutions, and in some mining counties, there were scholarships by means of which a mining student was occasionally enabled to proceed to a university course in mining, or perhaps in some subject other than mining.

He then went on to highlight several examples of good practice that the Committee could consider.

The experiment of the Staffordshire Education Authority in establishing small technical schools in mining villages in South Staffordshire had proved very successful. The pre-war cost of building in such cases was about £1,700–£2,000.

Although not every area had appointed an Organiser, these Organisers had banded together into an Association and met periodically to exchange views and experiences, so their value was becoming very considerable.

Derbyshire Education Authority had responded to a suggestion made in the Board of Education Paper 1, and had instituted a scholarship for miners which was to be solely for the study of mining subjects.

To further inform the Committee on mining education, a decision was taken to communicate with Local Authorities, institutions (such as the Treforest and Crumlin schools) not controlled by Local Education Authorities, the University Grants Committee and the universities in respect of both Extension Courses and Tutorial Classes.[11]

In September 1921, Viscount Chelmsford GCSI GCIE, PC was appointed as Chairman of the Committee following Lord Gorell's appointment as Under-Secretary of State for Air. Frederic John Napier Thesinger, 1st Viscount Chelmsford had been Governor of Queensland (1905–1909), Governor of New South Wales (1909–1913) and Viceroy and Governor-General of India (1916–1921).[12]

In October 1921, the MFGB nominated Mr Herbert Smith to replace Mr Brace. Herbert Smith was the Vice-President of the MFGB.[13]

The final meeting of 1921 took place on 5th October and considered a letter from the Secretary for Mines proposing the setting up of Special Joint District Committees in each District. The Mining Industry Act 1920 stipulated that the Committee, before allocating any money for a local purpose, should consult with the District Committee to be established under Part II of the Act. As it would be some time until District Committees could be put in place, Mr Bridgeman had suggested inviting coal owners' and the colliery workers' associations in each district to set up a special ad hoc joint committee to whom the central

Lord Chelmsford

Herbert Smith

Welfare Committee could refer all local applications for grants from the Fund for preliminary consideration and report.[14]

On 22nd October 1921, letters were sent out from the Mines Department by the Under-Secretary for Mines, Mr E. A. Gowers, to all coal owners' and workmen's associations asking for their co-operation in appointing special joint committees at the earliest possible date. Enclosed with the letter was a memorandum which had been prepared by the Miners' Welfare Committee, dealing with the scope of the Fund and the method of its administration. Once a local committee had been established in a district, they were asked to notify the Mines Department so that the Central Welfare Fund Committee could establish direct relations with the local committee and give them particulars of the sum which was available in their district and the applications for grants which had already been received.[15]

Mr Gowers followed up on the progress being made in November when he wrote to each District enquiring as to the position with regard to the establishment of a Joint Welfare Committee, as Mr Bridgeman was anxious that the allocation of money from the Fund should not be delayed in any district by reason of the fact that no local advice was available to the Central Committee.[16]

The duty of allocating money credited from the Fund from the one penny per ton of output was vested in the Central Committee subject to two provisos; firstly that the objects to which the Committee allocated should be such as the Board of Trade might approve and, secondly, that a sum equal to four-fifths of the contribution from the coal owners in each district should be allocated for the benefit of that district and would be designated 'Districts Funds'.

The other one fifth of the contributions was designated as the General Fund. Although the General Fund was not subject to any restrictions as regard to allocation, the applications for assistance from the General Fund fell into two main categories: research regarding health and safety problems of coalmining and, secondly, education. The allocation of money in either of these categories called for specialist knowledge and administrative experience. The Committee therefore looked to obtain the advice from the Safety in Mines Research Board, the Medical Research Council and the University Grants Committee respectively, in conjunction with that of the assessors and government departments concerned.[17]

The Committee were required by the Mining Industry Act 1920 to take into consideration any scheme submitted by a District Committee and, before allocating any money for a local purpose, must consult with the District Committee concerned. The Miners' Welfare Committee, being a statutory body, could only allocate the moneys standing to the credit of the Fund to the objects defined by the Act and to no other. The objects of the Fund being 'Such purposes connected with the social well-being, recreation and conditions of living of miners in or about coal mines and with mining education and research as the Board of Trade, after consultation with any Government Department concerned, may approve'.

The Welfare Committee would rely upon the District Committees to represent the requirements of their Districts as a whole. Applications for grants for local purposes could be made either direct to the Miners' Welfare Committee who would refer the applications to the Welfare Committees in their District for their observations or through the appropriate District Welfare Committee. In the case of an application from a local government authority, the application would be more speedily considered if the District Welfare Committee was consulted before making a submission to the Miners' Welfare Committee. District Welfare Committees were asked to pay special attention to the suitability of each application having regard to the equitable distribution of the total sum available for all the localities and objects in the district. It had to be understood that no individual colliery or group of collieries had a prescriptive right to the return of the actual amount contributed by its owners to the Miners' Welfare Fund.

As the Fund was not a permanent one, allocations as a rule would be made for capital rather than revenue purposes. Where a scheme involved annual expenditure on maintenance, the responsibility for such annual expenditure was the applicants. However, in certain cases, the Miners' Welfare Committee were prepared to consider schemes for investment of moneys granted from the Fund to provide partial endowment in perpetuity.[18]

In allocating the Fund, the Welfare Committee gave the greatest possible choice of objects. In their October 1921 memorandum to District Committees, they had suggested several purposes to which grants might be made under the headings of education, recreation, public health and well-being. However, they were prepared to consider any other proposals which seemed to come within the intentions of the 1920 Act.[19]

One of the very few applications to be turned down was from the Lancashire and Cheshire Welfare District Committee, who had applied for a grant from their four-fifths allocation to augment the wages of miners on short time. There were 8,500 adult miners in the District earning less than 34/- a week. The proposal was to give nothing to single men without dependents, but to make up the wages of married men to 35/- a week. This was to be only a temporary one. A deputation from the District Committee headed by Sir Thomas Ellis and Mr Stephen Walsh MP attended the 17th January 1922 Committee meeting having previously been informed by the Welfare Committee, acting on the advice of the Solicitors to the Mines Department, that this was not a purpose within the scope of Section 20 of the Act. The President of the Board of Trade had received a deputation from the District Committee after the first refusal of their application, and had raised no objection to the Welfare Committee hearing the application again. After hearing the deputation, the Welfare Committee discussed the matter and decided that there were no grounds to justify any variation of their previous decision. They remained convinced that to divert any portion of the Fund to the augmentation of wages would be contrary both to the intention of Parliament and to the best interests of the mining industry.[20]

Although the Welfare Committee made its first allocations from the Fund in February 1922, the progress made in the distribution of the District Fund varied considerably. Out of the twenty-five District Committees, seven (The Lothians, Durham, Cumberland, Lancashire and Cheshire (except for the wage augmentation), South Staffordshire, Bristol and Kent) had made no recommendations by the end of 1922.

Just over three quarters of the money allocated from the District Fund was made under the heading of recreation. Numerically, by far the largest class of District scheme sanctioned in 1922 was recreation and sports grounds. These were naturally popular since the initial outlay and maintenance were comparatively small. Next in popularity were the institute or village hall-type scheme which provided a place for social gatherings. Many of the institutes were equipped with libraries. In some cases, the recreation grounds were combined with institutes or developed in other cases to cater not only for

East Kirby Miners' Institute (Derbyshire)

the working miners themselves, but also their wives and children and for old people of the community.

The Welfare Committee did not bring any pressure to bear upon District Committees to employ experts in the preparation of their schemes, but the Welfare Committee did realise that the planning and organisation of industrial welfare schemes, except in a few cases, could not be carried out successfully by the District Committees. This conviction was strengthened by the opinions of the two District Committees in South Wales and Lanarkshire, who had already availed themselves of the assistance of the Industrial Welfare Society's organisers.

There were only two applications for pithead baths; Linton and Ellington, owned by the Ashington Coal Company in Northumberland, and Old Roundwood Colliery in West Yorkshire for a cycle store and drying room.

The most costly and ambitious District scheme was the Convalescent Home in Ayrshire, involving the total outlay of £50,000, of which £20,000 was allocated for the purchase and equipment of Kirkmichael House, and the remaining £30,000 was to be invested to produce, in perpetuity, an income equal to half the total maintenance costs of the home. The other half would be contributed by the workmen themselves by means of levy of 1d per week. The allocation of £50,000 was payable in five annual instalments, the first of which was paid in 1922. The coal owners advanced the balance of the purchase money to enable the scheme to proceed.

A number of grants were made to existing hospitals and Accident Homes for either structural extensions or endowment purposes. Several District Committees chose to establish trust funds, the income from which was devoted to the purchase of admission tickets for hospitals and convalescent homes.

Some Districts also chose to take steps to assist the development of mining education in their own localities. Warwickshire, Leicestershire and South Derbyshire recommended grants towards the extension of county mining schools, and Cannock Chase invested a sum to provide an Educational Sustenance Fund to assist local students with their travelling and maintenance expenses.[21]

Of more long-term importance to mining education, the Welfare Committee took the decision in April 1922 to invite the University Grants Committee to appoint a special Sub-Committee 'To inquire into the existing facilities for education in Coal Mining at the Universities and Technical Schools in Britain and to recommend the principles upon which such public or other funds may from time to time be available should be applied to meet the educational requirements of the Coal Mining Industry'. Sir Dugald Clark KBE was appointed as the Chairman of the Sub-Committee and the other members were Sir Frances Ogilvie CB, Sir Thomas Holland KCSI, KCIE, Mr G. H. Winstanley (Board of Education) and Mr J. T. Ewen OBE (Scottish Board of Education).[22]

Kirkmichael House, Ayrshire District Miners' Convalescent Home

The Welfare Committee were prepared to devote a substantial proportion of the General Fund to national research purposes, so when the Safety in Mines Research Board recommended a scheme for a new central research station to replace that at Eskmeals in Cumberland in January 1922, the Welfare Committee provisionally allocated £500,000 for this purpose. This proposal was subsequently withdrawn. However, £10,000 was awarded to the Explosives in Mines Research Committee which was set up in September 1922 to investigate the characteristics of individual explosives and £12,000 was allocated to enable the Safety in Mines Research Board to proceed with research into safety lamps and coal dust dangers, pending the development of the Board's plans for a complete research organisation for the coal mining industry.[23]

At the end of November 1922, a special meeting was held in London to which representatives of the Joint District Welfare Committees of Coal-Owners and Workmen were invited. This meeting gave the Central Committee the opportunity to come face to face with those who were carrying out the very important work in the districts. The Central Committee knew the initial administrative machinery was faulty, but they knew that District Committees had valuable suggestions. The Committee were indebted to some districts for their criticism, and special mention was made of Mr Finlay Gibson, South Wales District, who had put in an enormous amount of work at the end of 1921 and the beginning of 1922, continually seeing Viscount Chelmsford and the Secretary in London regarding the machinery.

The meeting enabled the Central Committee to discuss with the representatives of the District Committees the constitution of the local committees, representation on District Committees, bank loans, Trust Deed forms, schemes liability for income tax and local authority assisted schemes for over 60's. The latter was raised by Leicestershire, who were proposing to devote the whole of the money available to form the nucleus of a Pension Fund for men unable or fit to work on reaching the age of 60. There would appear to have been very bad feeling among the Leicestershire miners towards the Fund, but the pension scheme had the support of the 4,000 miners in the District. The Old Age Pension only came into effect at the age of 70, and there was a need for something to bridge the period from 60 years of age to 70. The Central Committee were not empowered to approve such a scheme, but Leicestershire were given the opportunity to raise this matter with the Secretary for Mines.[24]

With more settled conditions in the Coal Mining Industry in 1923, the Central Committee were able to make marked progress in the distribution of the Fund, making 50% greater number of approved allocations over the previous two years. £1,030,000 was allocated in 1923, in comparison to only £525,000 in the preceding two years.[25]

During 1923, the Welfare Committee sought to refine their policy in allocating District Funds. The Committee had previously recommended that, where land was purchased or money was invested in connection with a scheme to which a grant had been made from the Fund, the property should be secured by a Trust Deed. After consultation with the Charity Commissioners and the Legal Advisors to the Mines Department, a model form of combined Conveyance and Trust Deed was drawn up and circulated to the District Committees on 31st October 1922. It was intended that the Deed should be modified to suit circumstances but, it was recognised that there might be occasions (particularly in the case of Endowment Funds) when it would be unsuitable as it stood. In such cases, the District Committee could consult their own legal advisors and draw up deeds suitable for the particular purpose.[26]

Early in 1923, the Committee suggested that some form of commemorative inscription should be placed in schemes in each District to indicate that the scheme had been established by means of a grant from the Miners' Welfare Fund. Several designs submitted by the Industrial Welfare Society were considered and a simple design selected. The District Committees, however, preferred something more ambitious than the monogram for large schemes. It was therefore concluded that the simple design of commemorative tablets would be financed by the General Fund and more elaborate designs from the District Funds.[27]

Commemorative Plaque

Liability of Welfare schemes for the payment of income tax had been raised at the First Conference of District Committees in November 1922. The Committee took up the question with the Mines Department and the Board of the Inland Revenue. Schemes were exempt from tax under Section 37 of the Income Tax Act 1918 until, once an allocation had been made and payments in respect of it commenced, the right to exemption of income derived therefrom depended upon the circumstances of each group. A circular setting out the classification of entitlement to exemption of schemes, having been approved by the Board of Inland Revenue, was issued for the information of District Committees at the beginning of June 1923. Income tax liability in respect of income derived from Miners' Welfare grants varied according to the objects to which the grants were applicable. The Committee therefore made arrangements for the Secretary of the Miners' Welfare Committee to take up on behalf of any District Welfare Committee with the Board of Inland Revenue any case in which an assessment for income tax had been made and an entitlement to exemption was considered to exist.[28]

By the end of 1923, out of the twenty-five District Committees, only Lancashire had made no formal recommendation for the allocation of their District Fund, but this District was well advanced in developing its proposal to devote the whole of the money available to them for the erection and endowment of a convalescent home.

Recreational types of schemes were again the most popular type of scheme in 1923, followed by institutes (or village halls). Together these represented 85% of the total number of schemes approved from the Districts Fund. The Central Committee believed the initial success of these schemes could be best achieved by the appointment of trained welfare supervisors. This belief was supported by the District Representatives at the 1923 General Conference. Many colliery companies had made an appointment of a Welfare Supervisor but the District Committees were very slow in setting aside a sufficient capital sum to Provide an annual salary for a trained Supervisor.

Although the Committee continued with their policy of not making any attempt to enforce the services of the Industrial Welfare Society onto the District Committees, they fully realised the importance of having a centre to which enquiries could be directed particularly for Local Welfare Committees so that they could secure the best possible assistance with individual schemes. The Committee therefore took up the offer of the Industrial Welfare Society to establish such a centre as an experiment. £2,000 was allocated from the General Fund to meet the cost of the first year's work and £1,966 was also reimbursed in respect of similar work undertaken in the previous year.

The Centre was put in the charge of Commander B. T. Coote RN and it commenced active operations at 82, Victoria Street, SW1 in March 1923. Those District Committees that made use of the facilities spoke very highly of Cdr Coote's services, so the Committee had no hesitation in continuing with the Centre for a further year.

However, in October 1923, Mr Hyde, Director of the Industrial Welfare Society, wrote to the Committee to point out that the special branch established to deal with the Miners' Welfare Fund was becoming unable to cope with the ever increasing calls made upon it, and that the system by which South Wales and Lanark had District Organisers of their own, not connected with Cdr Coote's Office, made unification of the work almost impossible. It was suggested that the whole work being undertaken on behalf of the Miners' Welfare Fund should be centralised in one department and controlled from one office. Lord Chelmsford took the decision to arrange a meeting with a deputation from the Society on 20th January 1924 to discuss the Society's proposal. In the interim, the Society was asked to provide an approximate estimate of the cost of the scheme. Mr Hyde duly provided an estimate of £4,165 per annum. This did not include the cost of the District Organisers in South Wales and Lanark.[29]

The deputation had to cancel their attendance at the January 1924 meeting, due to illness of some of their members. In their absence, the Chairman suggested that an equally efficient service might be obtained at a lower cost by asking the Mines Department to find a place for the necessary advisory staff.

The deputation finally attended the April meeting of the Committee, where they presented their proposals and Cdr Coote presented charts showing the expansion of the work done by his special branch. After the deputation had withdrawn, the Committee discussed the options and finally decided that it would be preferable and more economical to have their own staff for the work, provided they could offer them sufficiently attractive prospects of permanency. It was therefore decided to consult the Secretary for Mines as to whether room could be found for the necessary staff in the Mines Department and, if so, on what terms could they invite Cdr Coote to work directly under them.

In June 1924, the Mines Department confirmed that, subject to Treasury approval, it would be possible to provide accommodation in the Department for Cdr Coote and his staff after March 1925, on the understanding that the rate of pay and conditions of service were assimilated to those of the Civil Service (subject to an arrangement regarding Cdr Coote's part-time service in connexion with the Duke of York's camp) and that salaries and expenses were paid from the Welfare Fund. The Committee instructed the Secretary to ask the Mines Department to proceed at once with the necessary arrangements for taking over Cdr Coote and his staff.[30]

Health schemes, which included pithead baths and convalescent homes, continued to represent a small percentage in number (13%) but, in monetary terms, assumed a much greater importance than this percentage would appear.

The Committee regarded it as a matter of concern that the coal industry had so little washing and drying accommodation available at the Pithead. They felt that this situation was largely because the majority of individual workmen were unaware of the many advantages to be obtained from the provision of the facilities, enabling them to cleanse themselves at the pithead instead of their own homes. The provision of the necessary accommodation throughout the country would have involved expenditure on a scale outside the scope of the Fund, and the Committee would not have been disposed to approve of the Fund being used in this way. However, they did feel that the Fund could be properly employed to stimulate the provision of the pithead baths during what they called the educational period.

By the end of 1923, six pithead bath schemes had been initiated with allocations from the Welfare Fund. There were three in Northumberland at Linton and Ellington, Newbiggin and Benwell. The others were at Wath Main and Nunnery Collieries in the South Yorkshire District and at Chislet Colliery in Kent.

The most ambitious scheme of the six was the one which had been planned at the Linton and Ellington collieries owned by the Ashington Coal Company with a grant of £20,000.

In several cases, a substantial contribution towards the capital cost had been made by the colliery concerned and, in other cases, the sites had been provided free of charge.[31]

Kent District Welfare Committee, having been pressed by the men's representatives to expedite the scheme at Chislet, had signed the contract before they had approval from the Central Committee for the allocation for the scheme

Linton and Ellington Pithead Baths

OPPOSITE: Plan of the interior (as designed by the Ashington Coal Co Ltd)

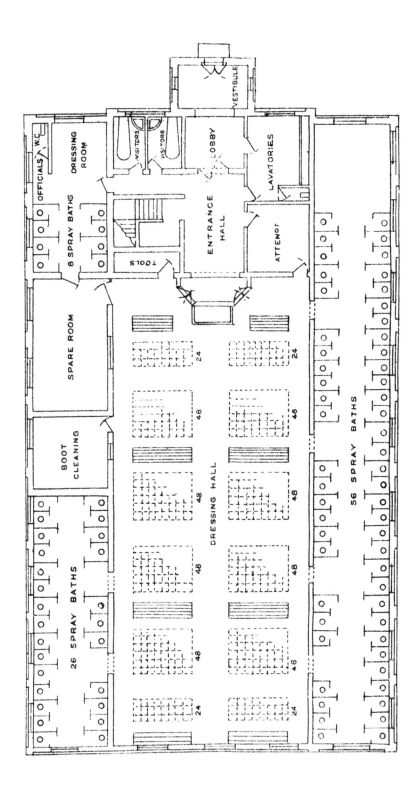

(£2,500 representing half the total cost of £5,000). The Chairman did sanction the allocation of £2,500, but Kent District Welfare Committee were warned that steps must be taken in future not to incur expenditure in anticipation of the decision of the Central Committee.[32]

On 13th October 1923, the South Wales District Convalescent Home at Talygarn was opened by Mr Evan Williams, President of the Mining Association of Great Britain. It was considered to be the outstanding feature of 1923 involving a total expenditure which was likely to exceed £250,000. The house and grounds cost nearly £16,500 and a further £10,000 had been spent on alterations and furniture and equipment. The cost of maintenance had provisionally been estimated to exceed £12,500 per annum. The whole of this amount was to be provided from the Miners' Welfare Fund by the investment of a sufficient capital sum which was to be completed by annual instalments of which the first amounting to £60,000 had already been paid. In deference to representatives of the South Wales District Committee, the Central Committee had departed from their normal practice of expecting some part at least of the cost of the maintenance to be met by guaranteed contributions from the workmen and/or the employers.

A third convalescent home was very nearly ready for occupation in Nottinghamshire District. The total outlay from the Fund for the Mansfield and

Talygarn Convalescent Home (South Wales)

District Convalescent Home at Berry Hill Hall was in the neighbourhood of £30,000, of which £15,000 represented the cost of the property and its adaptation and equipment. The balance of £15,000 was to be invested to meet the cost of maintenance, the rest of the annual maintenance costs were guaranteed by weekly contributions from the workmen.

Convalescent homes were already been planned in Warwickshire, North Staffordshire and Lancashire and Cheshire.

Other District Committees chose to establish trust funds, the proceeds from which were used to purchase admission tickets to established convalescent homes. West Yorkshire District had two such schemes, the Wakefield and District Convalescent Home Scheme (£14,000) and the Western Yorkshire Mineworkers Convalescent Scheme (£30,000).

The report of the Sub-Committee of the University Grants on Mining Education was submitted to the Central Committee at the end of 1922 (see Chapter 7, Education for full details). The Sub-Committee compared the existing Educational System to a ladder of five rungs. They recommended that the lower rungs should be provided solely by local resources, and that assistance from the General Fund should be confined to the higher rungs. Local resources could come from the District portion of the Miners' Welfare Fund or from the local Education Authorities. The Central Committee were clear that they were not prepared to make allocations from the General Fund to any area until they were satisfied that ample provision was made for the lower rungs.

Copies of the Report were sent out to the Education Authorities concerned and to the District Committees. Most of the District Committees appeared to believe educational schemes should be paid for out of the General Fund. The Central Committee only had a sum available which was unlikely to exceed £475,000 and was clearly insufficient to meet the needs of the higher rungs. The Central Committee were not prepared to make hasty decisions. They wanted to have all the facts before them so that they could get full value from the money available, by making grants in those places where they were most required.

However, a few allocations were made for education in 1923. The most important allocation made from the Districts Fund was the Educational Sustenance Fund for £5,500 provided by the Cannock Chase District Welfare Committee in co-operation with the Staffordshire County Council to assist Miners to attend technical institutes or universities. Two allocations were made from the General Fund; £827 (one fifth of the total cost) for a three-year course of non-vocational lectures in South Yorkshire, West Yorkshire and Derbyshire, whose District Funds would contribute the appropriate proportion of the remaining four-fifths of the cost and £5,933 to Warwickshire County Education Committee for an extension and equipment for the County Mining School at Nuneaton.

With the proposal to replace the Experimental Research Station at Eskmeals in Cumberland with a new station still under consideration and the Committee having made the decision to allocate no more than £500,000 from the General Fund for Research purposes during the statutory period of the Fund, the Committee still needed to respond to applications for funding made by the Safety in Mines Research Board.

The Committee had been criticised for being ready to allocate a considerable sum for the purpose of transferring the Experimental Station from Eskmeals and of endowing it when transferred on the grounds that a totally new research laboratory was not required because the universities were the best places for most of the research in mining. Large-scale experiments were undertaken at Eskmeals which were totally unsuitable for a university. It had been hoped that these types of experiments would cease to be required, but mining disasters had occurred during the year and so the experiments would have to continue.

The Safety in Mines Board were responsible for either controlling or subsidising work being carried out at the universities of Sheffield, Birmingham, Manchester, Leeds and London and any research work on problems relating to health and safety in coal mines was admitted by the Central Committee as being a proper charge on the Welfare Fund.

The Central Committee decided to contribute to research by means of allocations from the General Fund in three different ways:

(i) Towards experimental work carried out by staff employed directly by the Safety in Mines Research Board.
(ii) Towards experimental problems delegated to ad hoc committees by the Board or by the Medical Research Council.
(iii) Towards experimental work carried out by an independent research body or by an independent investigator working at a university.

It was also agreed in 1923 that the Safety in Mines Research Board would present, at the beginning of each financial year (1st April–31st March), an estimate of the total cost of their whole programme, such an estimate being split into the various sub-headings according to the different lines of investigation.

£23,000 was allocated in 1923 for plant and equipment at Eskmeals, most of which would be available for transfer, if necessary, to the new research Station site. Ten separate allocations were made to fund research work carried out by the Safety in Mines Research Board (totalling £3,221.19s.7d up to 31st March 1923). The Explosives in Mines Research Committee received £18,000 to cover the costs of their research to 31st March 1924, and a further £16,500 was allocated for general maintenance for the year ending 31st March 1924.[33]

The Second Conference of Representatives of District Committees was held on 27th November 1923 in London. As the Mining Industry Act had only established the Welfare Fund until 31st December 1925, Lord Chelmsford took the opportunity to urge the District Committees to put their heads together and see whether they could make a suggestion to the Secretary for Mines that the Fund should continue in some form. There was a growing opinion that the Fund should continue. In October 1923, at the opening of the convalescent home at Talygarn, Mr Evan Williams, President of the Mining Association of Great Britain, had said that he was quite sure that there was today 'not a coal owner in the country who regretted the levy'. He went on to say that the coal owners 'were proud that the mining industry had led the way, as they had in welfare matters, and hoped that they would continue to do so'.[34]

The Committee was reappointed in January 1924 for a further year. Shortly after the reappointment of Committee, Lord Chelmsford was appointed First Lord of the Admiralty, so his place was taken by Sir William Walker. Mr E. W. Ravenshear had replaced Mr W. G. Nott-Bower as Secretary to the Committee at the end of 1923.

In 1924, the Fund accrued nearly £1,250,000 (including interest). Although only 475 allocations were made, in comparison to 502 in 1923, the amount allocated in 1924 was £1,078,550 compared with £1,032,500 in 1923.

In 1924, recreational schemes continued to comprise 85% of the total number of schemes approved from the Districts Fund, although in monetary terms, the proportion was 66.7%. However, these types of schemes had broadened to include contributions to colliery bands, libraries and swimming pools and baths, the latter being erected generally in co-operation with a local authority, though sometimes forming part of institutes.

Recreational schemes were usually managed by a joint committee of owners and workmen, and maintained by a weekly levy from the workmen concerned if the normal receipts from games etc. were not enough. About 15% of the total number, however, had been handed over for management and maintenance to local authorities.

There were several large allocations for recreational schemes. Examples include £12,250 for the erection of public swimming baths at Blantyre in Lanarkshire, which would be built and maintained by Lanarkshire County Council. £8,500 had been allocated for the Cambuslang Institute (total £10,000), on the understanding that the balance would be raised locally. The Institute provided the usual recreational facilities, but also included baths and a gymnasium.

In Northumberland District, £8,710 was allocated for building the Wallsend 'G' and Rising Sun Institute, and £7,000 towards the Cowpen and Crofton

Institute. The latter included the provision of bowling greens and tennis courts. Nearly half of cost of this scheme, estimated to cost about £13,700, had been agreed to be raised by the workmen concerned.

In South Yorkshire District, the Brodsworth Main Miners' Welfare Scheme (allocation £10,126) comprised a public hall and library, together with a recreation ground and pavilion with facilities for tennis, football and cricket. Contributions had been made by the colliery company and workmen concerned towards the total cost of £12,000, the site having been given free.

In Nottinghamshire District, an allocation of £14,000 had been made towards the cost of building swimming baths and laying out of three recreation grounds at Sutton-in-Ashfield. The scheme would be maintained by Sutton Urban District Council, who were contributing the sites of the recreation grounds (valued at £4,350) and a sum of £3,000 in cash.

In North Wales District, an allocation of £8,000 had been made towards the cost of building an Institute at Rhos; the estimated cost would be £13,000.

Supplementary allocations were also made generally to extend buildings already erected, purchase additional land to provide further recreational facilities, or to continue development of recreational grounds. Examples included a further sum of £6,750 for extending the hall and four separate recreation grounds at Bolton upon Dearne. The original allocation had been £8,500, and the original total cost was £13,110: six acres of land had been given by the Wath Main Colliery Company, and over twenty acres and £1,500 in cash by Bolton Urban District Council, who managed and maintained the scheme.

In South Wales, £2,500 had been added to the original allocation of £5,000 made to the Ton Pentre Recreation Association to enable them to build a Boys' Club. The Shotts Institute in Lanarkshire had its original allocation of £9,000 raised to £12,000. The scheme had already cost over £14,000, towards which £2,000 had been raised by local effort. The Institute included a large swimming bath.

By 1924, there were seven endowed convalescent home schemes; Kirkmichael (Ayrshire), Talygarn (South Wales), Mansfield (Nottinghamshire), Higham Grange (Warwickshire), Horton Lodge (North Staffordshire), Weston-Super-Mare (Cannock Chase) and Blackpool (Lancashire and Cheshire).

The Warwickshire Miners' Convalescent Home at Higham Grange near Nuneaton was opened by HRH, the Duke of York on 29th May 1924. The house, together with 136 acres of land, was purchased for £9,000, and £4,500 was spent on repairs, alterations and equipment. £20,000 had been invested to provide part of the maintenance, the balance being raised by a levy of one penny per week from each workman employed in the coalfield, together with a contribution of £500 per annum from the owners. There was accommodation for 50 patients.

The Shotts Institute

The North Staffordshire Home of Rest for Miners was at Rudyard, where Horton Lodge with about nine and a half acres of land was purchased for £6,200. Repairs, alterations and equipment had cost £9,800, and £45,000 had been invested in an endowment fund yielding two thirds of the maintenance costs, the rest being provided by contributions from the owners and workmen in equal proportions. There was accommodation for 40 patients.

A suitable house capable of extension had been acquired for £3,000 in Weston-Super-Mare for the Cannock Chase and Pelsall Miners' Convalescent Home. £2,500 had been spent on repairs, alterations and equipment and £44,000 had been placed in an endowment Fund. The District's convalescent ticket fund (£2,000) was available to meet the cost of maintenance. The present home provided for twenty-four patients.

The Lancashire and Cheshire Miners' Convalescent Home at Blackpool fronted the sea in a seven-and-a-half-acre site which had cost £8,000. The new building had been planned to provide accommodation for 100 patients initially with the opportunity for further extension. The building was still in progress and was expected to cost over £100,000. £115,000 had already been allocated for this scheme. Both sides of the industry in the district wanted the whole of the District Fund to be applied to this scheme so that the sum available for the endowment would probably exceed £100,000.

At Holmside and South Moor, Durham, where the owners had given a site on which a cottage hospital was being erected by the local welfare committee for a total of £16,000; an additional allocation of £1,000 had been approved for purchasing a motor ambulance. There would be 26 beds, of which half would be available for female patients, as free medical services had been offered by the local doctors. Half of the annual maintenance costs of £2,000 would be met by the owners.

West Yorkshire had received an allocation of £15,000 to establish a third ticket fund scheme, the South Kirkby and Hemsworth Miners' Convalescent Scheme.

The Coal Mines (Washing and Drying Accommodation) Bill was introduced by the Secretary for Mines, Mr E. Shinwell, in July 1924. This Bill made the provision of pithead baths compulsory at all collieries. Mr Shinwell had in consequence asked the Central Committee to make no further allocations for pithead baths from the Welfare Fund. However, the Bill lapsed in November with the change in Government, leaving the Committee in the position of again being able to make allocations for pithead baths.

Practically all the 1924 allocations for pithead baths fell in the first six months. There were six new schemes, of which five were in South Yorkshire District at Orgreave, Treeton, Barnsley Main, Tinsley Park and Robroyd. The sixth was at Boldon Colliery in Durham. The total amount allocated during the year was £45,860. Substantial contributions towards the capital cost continued to be made by the owners of the collieries concerned. In 1924 this amounted to £10,975 in cash alone, apart from the value of the sites and, in four of the six new schemes, the owners had undertaken the whole of the maintenance costs.[35]

In February 1924, the Committee received a memorandum from the Under Secretary for Mines regarding the expenditure of the Safety in Mines Research Board for 1923/24. Expenditure had increased unexpectedly after August 1923, but the Board had not become aware of this until January 1924. The accountancy system had been overhauled, but the Secretary for Mines hoped that the Committee would be willing to grant them a further £5,500 to cover the Board's expenditure in the present financial year, to avoid the only other alternative – curtailment of work already embarked on by the board.

The Estimates of the Safety in Mines Research Board 1924/25, which included not only the cost of research for 1924/25, but also the costing of the transfer large scale experimental station from Eskmeals to a proposed site near Buxton, was due for consideration by the Committee; a special meeting was arranged for 21st March 1924. This meeting was attended by Sir Richard Redmayne and Mr Stedman (representing the Board), and Mr Foley and Mr Starky (representing the Mines Department). The Chairman pointed out that the Committee had never promised to the Board an allocation of half the General Fund, whatever the total might be. They had definitely set aside the sum of £500,000 to include all research for which allocations had been made or would be made, on the assumption that the General Fund would amount to £1,000,000 in all in the statutory 5 ½ years, but this was dependent on the output of coal which could be affected by a prolonged stoppage. He accordingly advised the Board to frame their programmes of work in the future on the basis that the total allocation was limited to £500,000. If the period of the Fund was extended, the Board would be able to expect further assistance. At the end of the special meeting, the Committee allocated £30,000 for the 'Establishment of proposed Experimental Station near Buxton' and £31,500 for 'Research Expenditure during the Financial Year 1924/5'.[36]

During 1924, only six allocations were made from the Districts Fund for mining education, the total amount being £4,850. Three of these allocations represented schemes proposed by the district committees concerned for lower rung educational schemes to take the place of previous allocations for educational schemes which, as a result of the Sub-Committee's report on Mining Education, were now considered as higher rung schemes and therefore to be funded from the General Fund.

On the other hand, a significant amount of the Committee's time in 1924 was spent on the allocation of money from the General Fund earmarked for Education. The Sub-Committee appointed by the University Grants Committee to consider education had made recommendations on which the Central Committee based their scheme of allocating the sums available for Mining Education. The Sub-Committee recommended the division of authorities concerned with education of miners into geographical groups (which would roughly correspond with the principal coalfields) and to set aside for each group its proportion of the estimated available total, calculated on the basis of working miners resident in each group when the distribution was made. It was further recommended that the authorities should be regarded as falling into two main groups, one of which would consist of the County Councils and County Borough Education Authorities, and the other of the universities, university colleges and technical colleges of university standard. To the first of these groups, the Sub-Committee recommended the assignation of 70% of the money and to the second 30%. Financial assistance from the General Fund should be confined to the senior and advanced courses. These courses, together with those conducted by the authorities in the second group (see above), were referred to as the 'higher rungs'. The preliminary and junior courses, which were described as the 'lower rungs', were regarded as suitable for assistance from the Districts Fund. However, before any grant could be made from the General Fund for the higher rungs, the preliminary and junior courses in the area had to be co-ordinated and efficient.[37]

With several applications for Mining Education having already been received by December 1923, Lord Chelmsford and Mr Winstanley met on 4th December to discuss preliminary allocations for presentation at the next Committee meeting in February 1924.

They suggested setting aside £30,000 (later increased to £35,000) for contingencies, and the approximate amounts available for each district from the remaining £440,000 based on the number of wage earners at 1st December 1923. The twenty-five districts were placed into eight main geographical groups, some of which had to be subdivided. Each geographical group had named districts and educational authorities within it.[38]

During 1924, nearly all the education authorities had submitted applications of some kind, but the standard of application varied so that it was only possible to make provisional allocations to those who had submitted the most comprehensive and economical schemes.

In dealing with individual applications, the Committee received advice from their Assessors, Mr G. H. Winstanley, in the case of England and Wales, and Professor T. Hudson Beare, in the case of Scotland, who was assisted by Mr J. T. Ewen OBE, HM Inspector. In the case of the universities, the University Grants Committee was consulted.

The Committee also benefitted from special reports published by the Board of Education, in which a detailed survey had been made of the existing facilities for mining education, in particular coalfields (Durham, North Wales, South Wales, Lancashire, Yorkshire, Warwickshire, North Staffordshire and the Forest of Dean), followed by recommendations for attaining internal co-operation and high efficiency.

The Committee, having made the decision to restrict allocations to equipment and buildings, needed to devise the machinery for securing the expert investigation in detail of the schemes proposed, and for ensuring the sums allocated would be devoted to the purposes for which they had been assigned. The procedure to be followed was worked out to first meet the case of the local authorities in England and Wales, and was the result of detailed discussion with the Mines Department and the Board of Education.

If there was a *prima facie* case for making an allocation, the Committee would make a provisional allocation. In the case of allocations for equipment, all the detailed list of equipment would be scrutinised by the Committee's assessors and, if they gave their approval, the allocation was confirmed. In the case of allocations for buildings, the education authorities had to submit plans and specifications in full detail to the Board of Education. In addition to the approval of the Board, the education authority had to complete a form of undertaking between the Board of Trade and themselves to secure the right of the Board of Education to supervise the constructional work, to secure the completion of the building by a pre-determined date, and to secure the use in perpetuity of the building for the purpose for which the grant had been made.

By the end of 1924, £195,121.15s had been allocated in England and Wales and £33,670 in Scotland. The total of confirmed allocations for mining education in England and Wales was £33,918.15s.6d and £4,670 which included £807 for non-vocational lectures.[39] (see Chapter 7. Education for a full description of the allocations)

In 1925, Lord Chelmsford was restored to the Chair of the Committee. Sir William Walker had to resign through ill health, and was replaced by Sir Arthur Lowes Dickinson.

Although the Committee made 593 allocations, an increase of 118 on the number in 1924, the amount paid out in 1925 was £948,082 against £1,015,915 in 1924.[40]

One of the most important developments during the year was the establishment of the Advisory Branch, to undertake the work which had for the previous three years been performed by the Industrial Welfare Society on agency terms. The Secretary for Mines had semi-official negotiations with the Society in January 1925, with the view to transferring Cdr. Coote and his staff and these negotiations had been completed in time for the transfer of Cdr. Coote and his staff to the Mines Department under the direct control of the Committee and the Secretary for Mines, effective from 25th March 1925.[41]

As one of Cdr. Coote's sub-ordinates had resigned shortly before the transfer, the opportunity was taken to appoint an assistant with architectural qualifications to the vacancy. This appointment led to an expansion in the scope of work undertaken and, with calls upon the staff in the Advisory Branch increasing rapidly, a further appointment was made, bringing the number of Advisory Branch staff to eight. Despite this, the annual cost of the Branch to the Fund was under £2,700 as compared with the annual rate of over £3,250 charged by the Industrial Welfare Society.

From 25th March 1925, Cdr Coote. attended Committee meetings as an advisor and, in this capacity, he was able to comment on all the recommendations received from district welfare committees and suggest improvements. These were put forward as constructive suggestions for improvement, rather than rigid requirements which had to be accepted before the recommendation could be approved.

The Committee continued to encourage district committees to appoint welfare organisers. South Wales, Lanarkshire, Fife and the Forest of Dean had already appointed their own welfare organisers. The Committee saw no reason for the appointment of district organisers to be confined to larger districts. Two or more smaller district could combine with a view to sharing the services of such an organiser.

In connexion with the importance that the Committee placed on trained leadership, Cdr. Coote was sent to America to attend, at the invitation of the Playground and Recreation Association of America, their Twelfth Annual Congress which was held at Ashville, North Carolina in September and October. At the same time, he was able to visit some of the principle recreation developments in America.

The report of his visit was presented to the Committee at the end of October. The main conclusion, which Cdr. Coote intended to explain at the Annual Conference of District Committees in November, was the need for the appointment of trained organisers and leaders if the full value was to be obtained from recreational schemes of all types.[42]

Although forms of Conveyance and Trust Deeds had been available for the use of District Committees since October 1922, and a new model form which complied with the Mortmain and Charitable Uses Act 1888 had been issued in June 1924, in 1925 the Committee had become aware that the model form had been followed without due regard to local conditions and, even worse, in March 1925, they found out that South Yorkshire District Committee had been using a form of Trust Deed, drawn up by a firm of local solicitors, which was very different from the Committee's model. Acting on local legal advice, the South Yorkshire District Committee had assumed that the Welfare schemes did not come within the scope of the Mortmain and Charitable Uses Act 1888. The Charity Commission considered that many of the South Yorkshire Deeds already executed did not create valid trusts, and the Mines Department had consequently written officially to the District Welfare Committee to say that, in their opinion, the deeds should be re-executed.[43]

With still no prospect of the life of the Fund being extended, the Committee in May 1925 had to reject a proposal made by Nottinghamshire District Committee to use a proportion of their district fund (£2,000 a year) to meet directly the cost of treating cases of spinal injuries at the National Hospital, Queen's Square, London instead of investing a lump sum of £40,000 for this purpose. However, as the Bill to extend the life of the Fund had its second reading on 6th July 1925, the Committee did agree to an allocation of £200 to be expended on the medical treatment of special accident cases at their July meeting pending the outcome of the passage of the Bill.[44]

In June 1925, the Committee received a deputation from South Wales District Committee to discuss the question of allocations being made from their District Fund to maintain schemes which, owing to the closure of many collieries due to the depression in the coal industry, had lost their usual means of support.

Garth Recreation Ground, Bridgend in 1923

Garth Recreation Ground, Bridgend in 1924

They proposed a sum of £8,000–£10,000, which remained unallocated in their District Fund, to keep schemes open to the end of the year. The Committee reluctantly agreed to a scheme for giving temporary assistance of a limited amount to the worst cases, subject to very strict conditions. As there was a possibility of a general stoppage, the Committee communicated their decision to all districts stating that similar arrangements might be recommended, but no other district appeared to regard any immediate action necessary.[45]

During 1925, 471 allocations were made for recreational schemes, of which 135 were new schemes. Recreational schemes remained the most popular for funding from the Districts Fund.

Although the Committee was disappointed that the provision for 10-16 year-olds was not being fully realised in many districts, South Wales had built a permanent camp at St Athan's, which could be used during the summer months to give a week's holiday to boys or girls in batches of 100 a time. The initial cost of establishing the camp was about £5,500, of which £4,500 was found from the district fund. The camp was situated in 9 acres with permanent buildings of timber and corrugated iron comprising three sleeping huts, a hut for a kitchen and dining area, a hut for recreation and canteen and huts for staff, offices and stores. The weekly cost of maintenance was estimated to be £77, to which each boy or girl under 14 contributed 15s and those over that age paid an extra 1s for each year in excess of 14.

Recreation grounds schemes in hilly districts were after a few years coming to fruition. Extensive levelling was costly, but several schemes in South Wales had overcome the difficulties imposed by the natural features. Terracing had been used at Eldon and Murton in Durham and Bridgeness and Carriden in Lanarkshire. In Durham, the recreation ground at Dawdon included a suspension bridge forming an approach across the dene to the main entrance. The cost of the bridge was £2,900 but was cheaper than filling up the dene with a culvert, which was estimated to cost over £5,000.

Of the larger schemes, £5,200 was added to the £13,000 already granted for the recreation ground at Castleford, West Yorkshire for particularly developing the junior section of the ground. The scheme was one of the most comprehensive and, when finished, was predicted to be one of the finest in the country. The main pavilion provided facilities for gymnastics and social functions in the winter months.[46]

There were no further schemes proposed for convalescent homes. However, in Fife District, a mansion house near Culross had been made available through the generosity of the Fife Coal Company. The Company was also prepared to adapt and equip the building, but the expectation was that a grant would be made from the district fund to partially endow the scheme.

The Suspension Bridge at Dawdon

CASTLEFORD PAVILION
(WEST YORKSHIRE)

Pavilion at Castleford Recreation Ground

A house in Troon had been given as a convalescent home for the wives and daughters of miners by Mr Robert L. Angus, Chairman of Ayrshire District Welfare Committee. It would be managed as a whole with Kirkmichael House. £4,000 from the District Fund was allocated for adapting and equipping the house.

Allocations were made to Kirkmichael House, Ayrshire, (£3,500) to extend the accommodation, to the scheme at Blackpool (£11,500) to meet the estimated cost of professional fees connected with the planning and execution of the building, to the Miners' Home of Rest at Horton Lodge, North Staffordshire (£1,500), for recreational facilities, to the scheme at Weston-Super-Mare, Cannock Chase District (£18,000), to increase the accommodation from 24 to 40 patients, and to increase the endowment fund to Talygarn, South Wales (£65,526) for further adaptation and equipment, addition to the endowment fund, nucleus of a reserve fund to meet depreciation, and a grant for the deficit on maintenance.

In order to provide a uniform basis for comparing relative costs of maintaining the various convalescent homes which had been established, the Committee obtained copies of the system of accounts prepared by King Edward's Hospital Fund for use by the London Hospitals, and asked the district committees concerned to follow the system as closely as possible in preparing their accounts each year. The system included a model statistical table for indicating the cost per patient of various groups of expenditures.

All the existing schemes involving the purchase of tickets of admission to existing convalescent institutes had their funds increased; West Yorkshire's three schemes by £12,000, the Wakefield and District Miners' Convalescent Scheme by £6,000, and the South Kirkby and Hemsworth Miners' Convalescent scheme by £6,000. A ticket-fund scheme was established during 1925 in South Staffordshire district with an allocation of £3,000.[47]

There were only 5 new schemes for pithead baths: two in South Yorkshire at Maltby Main and Dodworth Colliery, two in Northumberland district at Linton and Backworth Collieries, and one in Nottinghamshire district at Harworth Colliery.

At the end of 1925, the position in regard to the approved scale of allowances for members of district welfare committees came to a conclusion, with the daily allowance of 5s for workmen members who lost wages as a result of attending meetings being accepted, with the majority of district welfare committees voting against any increase in the rate.[48]

In 1923, it had become apparent that there were disparities between District Committees in how allowances in respect of out-of-pocket expenses were paid and, after the issue had been raised at the Second Conference of Representatives of District Committees, the Central Committee undertook to give further consideration to this matter. Since the issue of the original circular on subsistence allowances in February 1922, the interpretation of what could be claimed had become confused. The practice regarding the payment of expenses had been inconsistent and operated inequitably. Four districts (Nottingham and Derby, Lothians, Warwickshire, Lancashire and Cheshire) were found to have obtained special privileges and were paying far more than the other districts. The Committee took a decision at the July 1924 meeting that no inclusive allowances should be allowed, but third-class travel expenses and 5/- per meeting would be allowed. This information was sent out in a circular to all districts in August 1924. Following the Third Conference of District Committees, a further referendum on this subject was issued to district welfare committees.[49]

The Safety in Mines Research Board had presented their estimates for the financial year 1925/26 which commenced on 1st April 1925, covering researches in progress and planned and included health recommended by the Health Advisory Committee, which amounted to £51,470. The Committee had made an allocation of £50,000 to meet this expenditure, the balance representing the amount remaining from the Government grant of £6,030 after the cost of statutory testing. The Committee had observed that the cost of statutory tests and of research work in connection with such testing was increasing leaving less money available for general research. They were therefore of the opinion that a much greater proportion of the necessary research should be met from public funds. In September 1925, a Royal Commission on the Coal Industry, under the Chairmanship of the Rt Hon Sir Herbert Louis Samuel GBE, was set up to 'inquire into and report upon the economic position of the Coal Industry, and the conditions affecting it and to make any recommendations for the improvement thereof'. In the light of this, the Committee felt unable to proceed further until the Royal Commission had reported.[50]

Although the amount spent by the districts on education had increased, it continued to be regrettably small (£11,309 compared with £4,850 in 1924) but the recommendations had come from eleven districts compared with four in 1924.[51]

However, the Committee was able to increase the amount earmarked for higher rung educational building and equipment from £475,000 to £500,000. The total of the General Fund over the whole of the original statutory period of five and a half years had been expected to be about £1,000,000, and this figure had nearly been reached by the end of December with still the amount due in March 1926 in respect of the output for 1925 to be added. The cost for miscellaneous services would be met from the excess over the million.

During 1925, the Committee had given considerable attention to the possibility of establishing a scholarship scheme on a national basis, and had discussed in some detail the principles on which such a scheme would be founded. There would be an ample sum available for the endowment of the scheme, but the Committee had to wait until the total 1925 output had been confirmed. It was the intention that the scholarship should be of a sufficient amount to enable the holders (either working miners or their sons or daughters) to enjoy the full benefit of university life, and to exercise complete freedom of choice as to the course they would pursue. The Committee hoped that the scheme would be in operation before the end of 1926.

Provisional allocations for mining education for approved purposes amounted at the 31st December 1925 to a total of £271,165. Of this total, allocations amounting to £57,775 had been confirmed at that date. These totals compared with £228,792 and £37,792 respectively in 1924. The Committee were disappointed with the slow progress but the conversion of a provisional allocation to a confirmed allocation did involve a considerable amount of local work and subsequent correspondence. (See Chapter 7 for a full description of the allocations.)[52]

On 22nd December 1925, the Mining Industry (Welfare Fund) Act 1925 received Royal Assent, extending the Fund for a further five years and increasing the number of Committee members by two, one of whom was to be appointed by the Board of Trade after consultation with the Mining Association of Great Britain, and one appointed after consultation with the Miners' Federation of Great Britain. The last contribution under the original Act of 1920 would be due in March 1926, but so much remained to be done.[53]

THREE

SECOND QUINQUENNIUM
1926–1931

During 1926, the number of members of the Central Committee was increased twice. In January, Mr Andrew K. McCosh (nominated by the Mining Association of Great Britain) and Mr Arthur J. Cook (nominated by the Miners' Federation of Great Britain) joined the Committee under the provision of the Mining Industry (Welfare Fund) Act 1925. At the end of the year, a further addition resulting from Section 15 of the Mining Industry Act 1926, under which Sir Granville C. H. Wheler Bart MP (nominated by the Mining Association of Great Britain) and Mr William Pallister Richardson (nominated by the Miners' Federation of Great Britain) became members of the Central Committee.

The activity of the Fund in 1926 was well maintained in comparison to with previous years, with 588 allocations made (5 less than 1925) with the total sum allocated of £1,283,200, more than double the corresponding sum in 1925. The money accruing to the Fund was, however, owing to the increasing depression in the industry, over £100,000 less than in the previous year and amounted to only £1,108,380.

As 1926 was regarded as the end of the original period of the Miners' Welfare Fund as established under Section 20 of the Mining Industry Act 1920, the Committee undertook a review of the previous 5½ years. A total sum of nearly £5,500,000 had been contributed to the output levy, to which was added interest in temporary investments amounting to £430,706. During the whole of the first period, this interest had been distributed at the end of each year between the District Funds and the General Fund, in equal proportion to the average balance of each during the year.

The Central Committee had left the district committees to decide how they would make their recommendations as to how their district funds would be allocated, and this had led to considerable variation between districts as to the type of scheme supported and the manner in which the available funds had been proportionately distributed among the applicants. Recreation accounted for approximately 85% of the schemes and for two-thirds of the money, and health for approximately 13% of the schemes and one third of the money. On the other hand, education had been practically ignored. Some districts devoted all their attention to recreation and others only dealt with health. Ayr, Lancashire and North Staffordshire had devoted the whole of their district funds each to a convalescent home.

The development of welfare at places of work had been conspicuously absent. There had been a few pithead baths schemes, pithead shelters and cycle sheds, but there had been no recommendations made for the amelioration of actual working conditions. In this respect, the development of welfare in collieries had followed quite different lines from those under the Factory, Police etc (Miscellaneous Provisions) Act of 1916. No suggestions had been submitted for dealing with the supply of drinking water, or the provision of meals at the pithead or underground.

There had been misunderstandings between the Central Committee and the District Committees, and contact between the District Committees and the Local Committees had not been sufficiently close or effectively maintained. The Central Committee saw the appointment of District Organisers to overcoming these difficulties. There were too few staff in the Advisory Branch to maintain contact with nearly 1,100 different schemes. The need for better co-operation between District Committees and Local Committees was a special topic at the Conference of Representatives from District Committees in November 1926, where the Advisory Branch presented an outline of what ought to be the sequence of events every time a new scheme was started or an old one extended. By the end of 1926, there were District Organisers in only five Districts (South Wales, Lanarkshire, Fife, Forest of Dean and South Yorkshire) and it was hoped that more would follow.

The Central Committee had issued a questionnaire on recreational schemes to all Local Committees at the end of 1925, in the hope of gaining interesting material for a detailed review of progress. The returns came in more slowly than expected due to the stoppage, and some were incorrectly filled in; those that had been correctly filled in, supplemented by reports on many of the schemes which had been actually visited, revealed a catalogue of problems that needed addressing. The necessity for supplying local committees with facilities for obtaining advice on technical matters cropped up everywhere. There were fundamental problems with the design and construction of both indoor and outdoor schemes, and it was evident that the local committees required advice on the keeping of their accounts and estimating their maintenance costs. The local committees were also unaware that a complete plan from the outset of a scheme, which might take ten to fifteen years to complete, additional facilities being added from time to time as funds became available, was more economical than using patchwork methods.

In the first quinquennium, nine convalescent homes had been established, providing the districts of Ayrshire, Cannock Chase, Derbyshire, Lancashire, North Staffordshire, South Wales, South Yorkshire, Warwickshire and for the Mansfield area of Nottinghamshire. There were wide variations in the capital expenditure per bed of these schemes with the Lancashire scheme, which was a new build, being the most expensive at £1,130 in comparison to South Yorkshire at £325. The cost per patient week calculated on the basis recommended by the King Edward's Hospital Fund showed substantial variations between the six Homes fully in operation with Ayrshire the lowest (£2.8s.1d) and the highest in the case of Mansfield (£3.15s.9½d). However, occupancy levels did impact on these costings.

Despite the observations made on the first quinquennium, the Committee proposed in the second quinquennium to make no substantial departure from the system already in operation. The only important variation in policy would be the decision to relax to some extent the rigid rules which applied to expenditure of a non-capital nature.[1]

The number of allocations for recreation during 1926 was 454 of which 79 were new schemes. The proportion of recreational schemes in total number remained unchanged at 85%. The Committee continued to promote developments for children with details of Evening Play Centres being included in the 1926 Annual Report of the Miners' Welfare Fund. The first fully equipped children's playground in Scotland, at Newtongrange Park in the Lothians district, was opened by Lord Chelmsford on 11th September 1926.

There were few new schemes of comparatively large size in 1926. In Fife, an allocation of £18,000 was made for building a large institute at Cowdenbeath. A central site was purchased for £1,300 and a building on two floors was under construction, containing a reading room and games room for men, similar accommodation for women, a billiards room with eight tables, several committee rooms, a library, adequate storage and other conveniences, and quarters for the caretaker. Two of the rooms on the ground floor would be capable of conversion (by removing a folding partition) into a hall with seating accommodation for 300 persons. Another allocation for £10,000 was made for similar building at Methil, near Buckhaven, on a site of one-fifth of an acre taken on feu at 30s per annum. The institute, once built, would include a reading room and a games room, together forming a hall when required accommodating 250 persons, a ladies' room large enough for 100 persons, two committee rooms, a billiards room with three tables, slipper and shower baths and caretaker's quarters.

In West Yorkshire, one of the allocations was £7,500 for the purchase of a site and the erection of swimming baths for the Clayton West and Emley Moor area near Huddersfield. The other scheme also involved an allocation of £7,500 for the erection of an institute at Hunslet Carr near Leeds, which would provide a large

The children's Playground at Newtongrange Park

hall seating up to 500 persons, ample lavatory accommodation for both sexes
at each end, a billiards room with three tables, a large games lounge, a reading
room and library, two committee rooms divided by a folding partition so as
to be capable of use as a small hall when required, a secretary's room, kitchen,
cloakroom and lavatory, and ample space for storage. The preliminary plans for
both were drawn up by staff in the Advisory Branch, prior to locally appointed
architects taking over the schemes under the supervision of the advisory staff.[2]

During 1926, Commander Coote and the Secretary to the Central
Committee undertook visits to several Districts. In February 1926, Mr
Ravenshear and Cdr. Coote met with Mr R. Clive and Mr Alf Smith (Joint
Secretaries, South Yorkshire District Welfare Committee). The meeting had
been arranged to discuss the necessity of furnishing to the Miners' Welfare
Committee any detailed particulars of the recommendations (particularly of
those for supplementary grants) which had recently been made by the South
Yorkshire District Welfare Committee. The District Welfare Committee were
most unwilling to furnish information which the Central Committee normally
required before approving an allocation, contending that these detailed
questions should be left entirely to them, and that the Central Committee
was wasting time asking for information which they said had already been
most carefully gone into. A typical example of misleading information was
a supplementary grant of £568, which was solely described as 'Addition to
Institute and Recreation Ground – Caretaker's House' which turned out to
be additional room or rooms added to the Institute which had actually been
completed for some time, the cost being met by raising a bank loan. The real

purpose of the proposal was for a grant to pay off the bank overdraft.

The discussion then merged more generally into the question of the value to South Yorkshire of the Committee's Advisory Branch. No advice of any kind was wanted at all in South Yorkshire. They needed no help or assistance either for economy or improvement.

The District Welfare Committee had made no use of the Advisory Branch, but a few local committees in South Yorkshire had taken advantage of the assistance that the Advisory Branch could give to schemes to their benefit.

What was clearly needed in South Yorkshire was a District Organiser. They duly appointed one towards the end of 1926. Mr W. A. Bates had been Vice-Chairman of the South Yorkshire Committee since its inception, and he commenced his duties on the 1st November 1926. The Central Committee asked him to call at the London office to discuss the various problems which would confront him in his work, and the best means of affecting close co-operation with the Central Advisory Branch. Mr Bates' letter of appointment included the statement that 'The Supervisor [is] to devote his whole time to his duties and to sever his connection with public and political bodies with which he is at present associated'.[3]

At the Central Committee's meeting on 18th May 1926, Cdr. Coote and the Secretary reported on their visit to several schemes in Warwickshire, Staffordshire, and Shropshire. The visit had provided further evidence of the great need for every District to have a District Organiser to make regular visits to schemes. One man with a car stationed in Chasetown (Staffordshire) could quite easily deal with the five Districts of North Staffordshire, South Staffordshire, Cannock Chase, Warwick and Shropshire, and the expense would be very small between the five Districts.[4]

In September 1926, Cdr. Coote and the Secretary spent three and a half days visiting 32 schemes in South Wales, and 6 in the Forest of Dean.

South Wales had made much more progress in comparison with other Districts, so a high standard was expected. However, faults in construction, development and supervision were apparent. The Advisory Branch was only in constant touch with a few schemes they visited, so the other schemes they discovered were very eager for advice on all kinds of points.

Mr Mason, the South Wales District Organiser was still employed by the Industrial Welfare Society. He had frequently consulted the Advisory Branch when it was part of the Society, but little or no use had been made of it once the Committee took over in April 1925.

Most schemes had children's playgrounds, but their condition was nearly in every instance unsatisfactory. It was questionable whether the great attention given to bowls and tennis was justified, so long as those who were not interested in bowls and tennis were not catered for efficiently. Mr Finlay Gibson, Secretary,

Monmouth and South Wales Coal Owners' Association, was obsessed with the idea of starting Challenge Cup Leagues for these games, which Cdr. Coote and the Secretary saw as further killing the enthusiasm of the mediocre players.

Having visited the 32 schemes, Cdr. Coote and the Secretary believed the Committee were justified more than ever in asking for plans, specifications and details of all developments in South Wales before approving future allocations.

Mr Mason had no organised method of visiting local committees, and several places had not seen him that year. Mr Mason did not possess the expert knowledge for examining specifications and tenders. It was quite unnecessary to employ architects for dealing with recreational schemes visited.

Cdr. Coote and the Secretary had found it unpleasant to have to expose these inefficiencies, but they felt that the problem lay in Mr Mason's continued connection with the Industrial Welfare Society, which attempted to ignore the existence of the Advisory Branch.[5]

Lord Chelmsford had subsequently met with Mr Nicholas and Mr Morrell, Chairman and Vice Chairman of the South Wales District Committee on 22nd October 1926. Lord Chelmsford protested the attitude adopted by the South Wales District Committee in attempting to ignore the authority of the Miners' Welfare Committee. It had been necessary to enquire more fully into the details of the schemes. Local committees were not getting the advice, assistance and encouragement they ought to get.

The Chairman also dealt with the question of equipment allocations and made it clear that the Committee must be furnished with the quarterly statements of purchases which they had originally asked for, or some equivalent information. The District Welfare Committee had refused to supply these, while continuing to incur expenditure without the Committee's authority. Until the information for the June and September quarters had been supplied, no more allocations for equipment would be made by the Central Committee. Unfortunately, this was not the last of this matter.[6]

At the end of October 1926, Mr R. Whitfield Parker (Advisory Branch) visited 17 schemes in Lanarkshire. The majority, large and small, had caretakers and the cleanliness and cheerfulness (or otherwise) was normally reflected in the caretaker in charge. Three institutes had provided a room for women. The lavatory accommodation in most buildings was inadequate and in a lot of cases very poor. The urinals were the worst feature. Many of them were just cement-rendered, and it was hardly possible to describe the state of the floor in such cases; the smell was dreadful. The small hall (holding 250) at Fenn and Draffin had only 1 WC for the two sexes, and when the hall was used for dances, the men used the side and back of the hall, which was in a disgusting mess. In almost all the schemes, the games rooms were much too small. The atmosphere

South Yorkshire Miners' Convalescent Home

in the rooms used most often was usually pretty foul, and it was unusual to find a window open. The balance sheets of many of the Institutes had a variety of ways of making them out, so a model method was needed.[7]

During 1926, two new convalescent schemes were established for the Derbyshire and South Yorkshire districts, and further allocations were made to five of the seven established schemes.

The Derbyshire scheme involved a new building at Skegness to take the place of the scheme, which had been operating there for some years under the Derbyshire Miners' Association in premises which had become inadequate. The Association gave a site of 4 acres (valued at £2,000) for free, and were also contributing a sum of £5,000 from the building fund that had accumulated. The cost of the building was estimated at £50,000, and the furniture and equipment at £10,000. An allocation of £110,000 was made, the balance of which would be invested in an endowment fund. The income would be made up to a total of approximately £10,000 per annum by payment of ½d per week from each workman in the district and a charge of 5s per patient admitted. The building would accommodate 124 male patients, 30 female patients and 15 staff.

The South Yorkshire scheme followed the more usual practice of purchasing and adapting an existing country house. The Low Hall, Scalby, near Scarborough,

Lancashire and Cheshire Miners' Convalescent Home

was bought for £9,500. The cost of incidentals, adaptation and equipment came to £3,500, and £60,000 was allocated for investment in an endowment fund. There would be 40 patients from the outset, with ample scope for subsequent extension.

£7,118.5s.7d was allocated to meet the cost of completing the adaptation of Kirkmichael House, Ayrshire. During the 1926 stoppage, £1,930 was also allocated to keep the home open as the weekly contribution in the district was not available. A further allocation of £150,000 was made to Lancashire and Cheshire district for the building at Blackpool in order to increase the accommodation by 28 beds to a total of 132. £1,500 was added to the Cannock Chase District scheme at Weston-Super-Mare to meet the additional expenditure on the connection with an adjoining house and £7,500 was added to the endowment fund. A further allocation of £2.950.13s.2d was made to the scheme at Mansfield to improve the accommodation for patients, and provide extra facilities for indoor and outdoor recreation. £6,450 was allocated to Talygarn, South Wales to meet further capital charges including the redemption of the tithe rent. £20,000 was also added to the endowment fund.

With the relaxation of the rule of spending on non-capital items, allocations of £500 and £2,000 were made to Nottinghamshire and Derbyshire districts respectively for the special treatment of serious colliery accident cases. The object of these two schemes was to provide funds for treating cases of serious spinal and cranial injuries which, generally, could not be treated locally.

In South Yorkshire, £13,400 was allocated towards the erection of a casualty and outpatient department at Beckett Hospital, Barnsley. This was to be maintained by the Hospital Committee, on which colliery owners and workmen were represented, who were also finding £3,000 from their capital fund to make up the balance of the cost.

In South Wales, a further allocation of £4,000 was allocated to the Order of the Hospital of St John for the provision of 4 more motor ambulance centres in connection with their ambulance transport service in the coalfield. An allocation of £7,000 was made towards the cost of building a cottage hospital at Treherbert. The total cost was expected to be about £25,000; the balance was expected to be met by substantial contributions from the colliery owners and workmen in the area.

A supplementary allocation of £2,635 was made to the cottage hospital scheme at Holmside and South Moor in Durham making a total of just over £24,000.

In South Derbyshire, an allocation of £12,000 was made for establishing an ambulance service covering the whole district, which was likely to be of particular benefit as most of the mining centres were some distance from the nearest infirmary in Burton.

In the first statutory period, the General Fund had reached a total of £1,210,401, which was over £200,000 in excess of the figure on which the original estimates were based. The £500,000 set aside for research had been allocated, and the greater part of the £500,000 set aside for education for the purpose of buildings and equipment had already been assigned for definite schemes. £16,700 had been accounted for by miscellaneous services, consisting mainly of expenditure on technical staff and £150,000 had been provided for the scholarship scheme. The balance had temporarily been absorbed into an allocation for experimental pithead installations, since the provision made in Part III of the Mining Industry Act 1926 had extended the duties of the Fund to the general establishment of pithead baths. The greater part of the £45,000 for the experimental pithead baths would eventually be met from the new baths fund with only the cost of the experiment being charged finally to the General Fund.

In the next Quinquennium, a further £250,000 was assigned to educational building and equipment. It was expected that at least £250,000 from the General Fund would need to be added to the new Baths Fund. The Committee had agreed to finance annual research programmes and they were expecting something in the neighbourhood of £180,000 was likely to be absorbed unless the State contribution was substantially increased. The available total in the second period was hardly likely to be as much as £1,000,000, as this period was six months shorter than the first and all receipts in the future would be assigned to the Baths Fund.

The year 1926 saw the completion of the original research scheme, which the Miners' Welfare Fund undertook to finance in the period covered by the Act of 1920, involving the establishment of new research accommodation in place of the unsuitable research accommodation at Eskmeals. Partial execution of this scheme had been achieved, with an allocation of £30,000 in 1924 to establish a station for large scale experimental work at Harpur Hill near Buxton. Early in 1926, the Safety in Mines Research Board were able to submit their final detailed proposals for completing the scheme by erecting laboratories for small-scale work at Sheffield, on a site which they had agreed to lease from the university. The cost of the building and equipment was estimated at £28,000, of which £250 (in respect of preliminary expenses) had already been provided. This brought the capital expenditure in connexion with research to £72,592.6s.9d.

The amount allocated up to 31st March 1926 to finance year-by-year researches was £133,911.12s.5d, leaving a balance of £294.496.0s.10d from the £500,000 originally set aside to provide future maintenance of the scheme. The Board had submitted estimates for 1926/27 amounting to a net total of £51,500. This left a sum of £255,622.9.6d available for permanent investment. This sum was handed over in the form of a 5% War Loan to two trustees appointed by the Secretary for Mines, under a simple declaration of trust which provided that it should be kept invested under the title of 'The Mining Research (Safety and Health) Endowment Fund' and that the income should be applied 'in or towards defraying the expenses of and incidental to the work of research into the causes of mining dangers (including dangers to health) and means for preventing such dangers carried on under the direction of the Safety in Mines Research Board'.

The income from the endowment fund in 1926 was about £12,670, to which was added the balance of the annual grant from the Treasury which was then £2,000 per annum. The income would fall short of the scale which had been adopted in the previous four years. The Committee believed that the Treasury should substantially increase their contribution, but the Committee saw the importance of an uninterrupted programme of work to the welfare of mineworkers. They were, without prejudice, prepared to consider the estimates during the second statutory period and, if satisfied with the proposed research, make annual allocations to cover the deficit between the approved estimates and the income available from the endowment fund and the grants from the Treasury.

In 1926, the Committee set aside a further sum of £250,000 for senior and advanced courses of instruction in mining from the General Fund in the second quinquennium. A total sum assigned by the end of 1926 for definite schemes was £433,000.10s.9d, an increase of £162,000.

The number of educational schemes recommended by District Welfare Committees in 1926 was a disappointing 7, involving a total sum of only £3,712. Non-vocational lectures of various kinds accounted for the greater part of the money allocated. The experimental programme of lectures by the Industrial Health Education Society financed in 1925 by the General Fund had been justified, as a recommendation to continue the programme (at the expense of the funds from the districts concerned) had come from Fife, Lanarkshire and Northumberland.[8]

In February 1926, preliminary draft proposals for the Scholarship Scheme from the University Grants Committee, the Board of Education and the Adult Education Committee of the Board of Education were put forward to the Committee. The Committee decided to appoint a sub-committee (Lord Chelmsford, Professor Collis and Mr Winstanley) to go fully into the question of the Scholarship Scheme, in consultation with the Government Departments concerned. The first meeting of the sub-committee was held on 18th March, to which representatives of the Board of Education and of the Scottish Education Department were invited. The Ministry of Agriculture and Fisheries also attended, to give the sub-committee the benefit of the wide experience they had gained during the previous five years in the administration of their scheme for agricultural workers. At the March meeting, the draft scheme was revised and then circulated to Departmental representatives. The revised draft scheme was presented to the Committee in July 1926. Two difficulties arose in drafting the scheme; whether awards should be available to students intending to take diploma courses, and whether Scotland should have a separate scheme. It was decided to confine the scheme to degree courses only and, since the possible number of Scottish awards based on the proportionate assigned to Scotland would translate into 1½ scholarships annually, a combined national scheme would be adopted.

The Secretary for Mines appointed the Under-Secretary for Mines (Sir E. A. Gowers KBE,CB), Principal Assistant Secretary in charge of Technical Instruction at the Board of Education (Mr W. R. Davies CB) and the Secretary of the Scottish Education Department (Dr G. Macdonald CB) as 'The Trustees of the Miners' Welfare National Scholarship Endowment Fund', into which the Committee had invested £150,000. The Trust was held under a simple declaration of trust which required the trustees to apply its income 'in or towards defraying the expenses of and incidental to the provision of University Scholarships… for workers in or about coalmines in Great Britain and their sons and daughters in accordance with the recommendations of the Selection Committee appointed by the trustees'.

The Trustees appointed as the first members of the Selection Committee;

Lord Chelmsford (Chairman), Sir Theodore Morrison, Alderman William Jenkins MP, Mr R. H. Tawney and Mr Winstanley. They held their first meeting shortly before the end of 1926.

Miners would normally apply for scholarships through the authorities responsible for continuation classes, university extension courses etc., while the sons and daughters of miners would normally be studying at secondary schools and would apply through them. The candidates would be selected mainly on the recommendation of those who knew them as students and by personal interview. However, the Selection Committee had been instructed to have regard to the personality and the character of the candidates, and their capacity and attainments in other fields.

In fixing the endowment fund at £150,000, it was believed that enough income would be available to enable ten scholarships to be awarded annually. It was assumed that approximately half the awards would extend on average for four years. 35 scholarships would probably be running concurrently when the scheme was in full operation.

The object of the scheme was to afford an opportunity for working miners and their sons and daughters to enjoy the full advantages of university life, for the purpose not only of attaining educational distinction but also to associate on equal terms with fellow students. The awards were to consist of three parts; an initial grant for outfit, a grant sufficient to cover all the fees of the approved course, and an allowance to cover maintenance which might also include something towards the cost of living during the vacations.[9]

No new schemes for pithead baths were recommended during 1926 by district welfare committees, but additional grants had to be made to seven schemes in South Yorkshire and one in Northumberland owing to the actual cost of the installations being in excess of the original estimates. These supplemental allocations amounted to £4,907, and further sums amounting to approximately £3,500 were contributed by the colliery companies concerned.

While the progress in pithead construction from the District Funds in 1926 was disappointing, the responsibility for the general establishment of the pithead baths became the responsibility of the Miners' Welfare Fund during 1926. This was one of the recommendations of the Royal Commission on the Coal Industry (1925), and to meet the extra cost to the Fund, a special levy on mineral rights would be added to the Fund. Effect was given to this recommendation by Part III of the Mining Industry Act 1926. Provision was made in the Act for the collection by the Inland Revenue Department of a special levy on the rental value of the rights to work coal and mineral wayleaves in connection with coal equal to 1s in the pound. The first rent was due in 1927 in respect of the financial year 1926–27, and the annual revenue was estimated at about £250,000 in a normal year. The receipts would be paid into the Welfare Fund, but would be separately accounted for by the Board of Trade. The baths established under the Act were relieved of the necessity to comply with the regulations prescribed under the Act of 1911.

The design followed by all existing pithead baths in Great Britain up to 1926 was based on typical installations erected in the principal coal-mining centres on the Continent, particularly those in France and Belgium. The building consisted essentially of a large and lofty hall surrounded by enclosed shower bath cubicles. The hall was used for both undressing and dressing, and was equipped with a system of ropes or chains by which either clean or dirty clothes were suspended in the roof of the building.

The continental design was open to criticism on many points: the height of the building made it cost-excessive; clean clothes were not properly isolated from dirty clothes under the overhead chain and hook system; fine dust constantly fell from the suspended clothes, soiling the floor, the bathers and the clean clothes; bathers had to push past bundles of dirty clothing to get back to dress, getting their feet and bodies covered with coal dust, and had to handle their pit clothes after washing. The removal of coal dust and vermin from clothing was difficult, dirt accumulated in places where it was difficult to remove, the hall was often overcrowded with lack of seating accommodation and proper lavatory accommodation. Ample ventilation and light were frequently overlooked, and the cost of maintenance was higher than it needed to be, due to the high consumption of water and excessive expenditure of time on cleaning due to the design.

A new design had to be produced with the object of overcoming the shortcomings of the Continental style of pithead bath. The new design consisted of three sections: one for pit clothes, one for bathing, and one for clean clothes. The bathing section consisted of shower-bath cubicles. The pit clothes and clean clothes sections (referred to as 'dirty and 'clean') were each equipped with lockers, one for each man. The dirty lockers would be constructed to dry and fumigate the pit-clothes, as well as to confine dirt from them to a controllable area, while the clean lockers would also be capable of drying clothes if wet owing to a rainy day. There would always be enough seating accommodation, as each man would have the space in front of his locker. Adequate lavatory accommodation, a first aid room for dressing minor injuries, arrangements for boot-cleaning and greasing, and arrangements for supplying drinking water to fill water bottles were included. There would be no difficulty in adding provision for a canteen, laundry and the repair of clothes and boots if desired.

The Committee devoted a great deal of their time during 1926 to discussing all aspects of pithead baths' design, capital outlay, maintenance and management, starting with a special meeting in June 1926. Cdr. Coote had enlisted the assistance of the principal manufacturing firms concerned, and the Committee were able to inspect and test sample fittings of various types. 12 pits where the continental type of installation was in use were visited by Cdr. Coote who then had produced a report on how the features of the new design differed from the continental type which had been recommended by the Departmental Committee which had sat in 1912/13 to consider what should be prescribed under Section 77 of the Coal Mines Act 1911.

The advantages and disadvantages of the new design could only be ascertained if this type of installation were erected. The Committee therefore decided to proceed at once with the erection of 4 experimental installations: Letham in Scotland, Mainsforth in Durham, Pooley Hall in Warwickshire and Llwynypia in South Wales. The Collieries were approached but the prolonged stoppage prevented any considerable progress being made.

In order that progress might not be further delayed pending the collection of the royalties' levy, the Committee decided to meet the cost of the four experimental installations in the first place from the General Fund.

It was clear from the wording of Section 17(1) of the 1926 Act that the Committee could not effectively carry out the duty imposed on them for building the pithead baths by simply awaiting independent applications from the more progressive collieries without regard to the relative urgency of individual cases. The definite recommendations of the Royal Commission in this connection were:

a) That collieries with a probable life of less than 15 years should be excluded
b) That preference should be given where double shifts were worked.

The District Welfare Committees would play an important part in drawing up a programme of more urgent cases that could be built for the funds available for the first five years.

The total cost of giving effect to the provisions of the Act was assumed to lie between £4,000,000 and £10,000,000 (the lower and upper figures quoted by the Royal Commission). The royalties' levy was estimated to produce an annual revenue of about £250,000, which was insufficient by itself to achieve the desired object within a reasonable period. The Committee therefore proposed to give preference, other things being equal, to schemes which District Welfare Committees were prepared to assist. Preference would also be given where colliery owners were prepared to fund part of the capital required.

However, some definite predetermined increase of the amount available under the Act for the provision of baths was essential, if the Committee were to adequately carry out the duty imposed on them. They decided to add to the

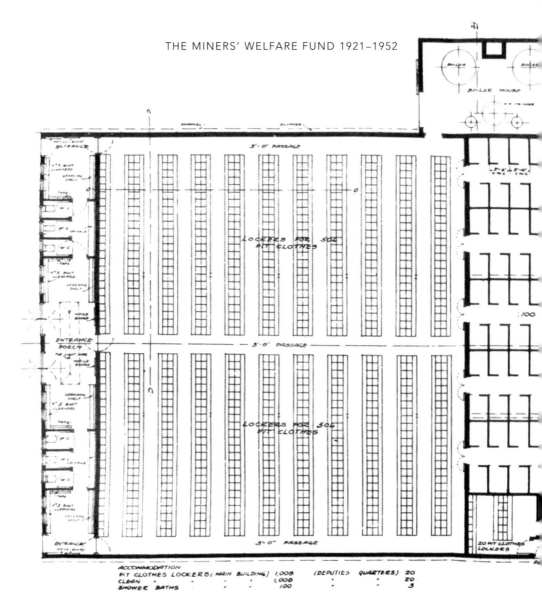

Baths Fund a sum equal to not less than one-fifth of its annual income from the existing General Fund (about £50,000 pa), and also such sums as accrued from time to time in the form of interest on the temporary investment of the Fund as a whole. During the previous five years, this interest had been divided between the District and General Funds in the proportion of the average monthly balance of each. This division would cease on 31st December 1926. These measures would raise the total income available for baths to an average of £400,000 per annum.

The Committee produced a set of provisional regulations under which grants would be made from Baths Fund covering how collieries would be chosen, the

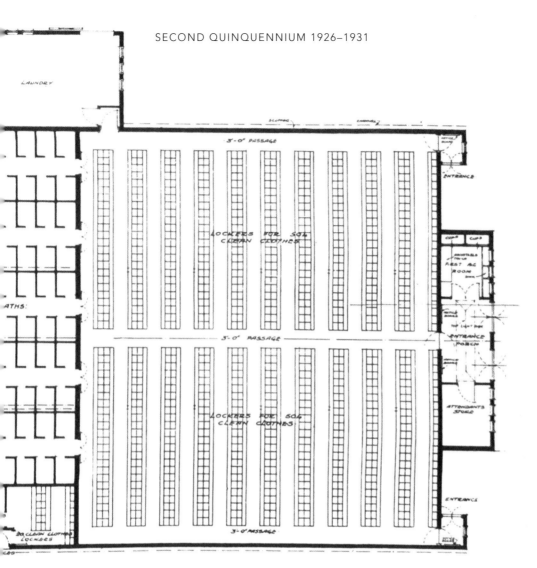

Specimen Design for Experimental Installation

design and construction of the installation, Trust Deeds and the management and method of maintenance of the installations to be erected. A copy of these regulations and a form for districts to submit a classified list covering every pit in their District was sent out to every District Welfare Committee in October 1926. It was hoped that the completed lists would be returned no later than 1st February 1927.[10]

Before leaving 1926, some reference needs to be made to the turmoil that existed throughout this year in the mining industry. With falling coal prices in 1925, at the end of June, the colliery owners sent the MFGB a notice of termination of the National Wages Agreement which had been in force since

18th June 1924. This notice was to run for the month of July terminating at midnight on 31st July 1925. On 1st July, the owners sent the Miners' Federation their proposals for a new wages agreement which included an immediate reduction in wages, the guarantee of a minimum wage to disappear and a guarantee of profits to take its place. July was taken up with meetings between the owners, the government, the MFGB and the TUC, but no progress was made, with the whole of the last week of discussions being conducted in the light of the transport and railway unions resolution not to handle coal. With no further progress being made, the embargo on coal movements was put in force on 30th July. On 31st July, the Prime Minister met the Special Committee of the Trades Union Congress General Council, together with the Executive of the Miners' Federation and explained that the owners had agreed to suspend notices, that an enquiry would take place and that, in the meantime, the Government would guarantee financial assistance to the coal industry up to 1st May 1926.

The Royal Commission on the Coal Industry was given royal warrant on 5th September 1925. Under the Chairmanship of the Rt Hon Sir Herbert Louis Samuel GBE, it was to inquire into and report upon the economic position of the Coal Industry and the conditions affecting it and to make any recommendation for improvement thereof. The Royal Commission's Report was completed on 6th March 1926 and published on 10th March. It recommended a reduction in the miners' wages. Subsequent negotiations between the coal owners and the miners broke down in April, when it became clear that the owners were in favour of the longer working day, district agreements on wages, and a reduction in wages. The owners in most districts posted notices to end existing contracts, and stated employment on the existing terms would cease on 30th April 1926. This was a lockout, which would not end until the last day of November 1926.

This seven months of inactivity in the coal industry not only impacted on the income of the Fund but also on the welfare schemes to a varying extent. Only four Districts applied for special assistance from the Fund but, while many schemes had doubtless been temporarily financed by colliery owners, the Committee feared that a great number of schemes had become burdened with heavy debt.

The stoppage (a term used by the Government for the lockout) made no difference to the central administration of the Fund, and many of the District Welfare Committees continued to meet periodically and find common ground for agreement, even during such a prolonged industrial dispute. Some District Committees did suspend their meetings, however, resulting in the holding up of applications from local committees and a temporary suspension of progress with new schemes.[11]

Mr R. Whitfield Parker's report on his visit to 17 institutes in Lanarkshire in October 1926 (see p61 above) was considered at the Committee's meeting on 18th January 1927. Two meetings later, on 23rd March 1927, Cleanliness, Ventilation etc. of Buildings was an agenda item. By 1927, there were nearly 500 buildings that had been established through the Miners' Welfare Fund, so the Committee was extremely anxious that these schemes were maintained to a set standard. All District Committees were subsequently sent a circular on the subject in April 1927 itemising the features which characterised best practice. These features covered cleanliness, room décor, heating and ventilation, lavatory construction and maintenance, and provision for women.

In April 1927, Cdr. Coote and Mr Ravenshear visited schemes in Leicestershire (3 recreation grounds and one institute), Nottinghamshire (11 recreation grounds, 4 institutes, 1 swimming bath and 1 convalescent home) and Derbyshire (23 recreation grounds, 4 institutes, 1 swimming bath and 1 hall) between 25th and 29th April. In Nottinghamshire, the recreation grounds were well developed, as far as they had gone. Most of the institutes obtained considerable revenue from the sale of intoxicants.

In both Derbyshire and Nottinghamshire there were 'Visiting Committees', consisting of owners' and workers' representatives, appointed by the District Committee to investigate new applications and to keep in touch with schemes already established. Both Districts expressed the opinion that this practice made it unnecessary to appoint a District Organiser. This view was more strongly held in Nottinghamshire; with justification, as their schemes had produced better results than Derbyshire. However, Cdr. Coote and Mr Ravenshear believed both Districts would benefit from the appointment of a District Organiser.

Leicestershire had no system of visiting, and had declined to send a representative to a meeting which Lord Chelmsford had proposed to hold to discuss the possibility of a joint appointment of a District Organiser to serve several small Districts in the South Midlands.

The sale of intoxicants at Welfare Schemes had been an agenda item at the 4th Conference of District Committees on 17th November 1925. Following Cdr. Coote's report on Leicestershire, Derbyshire and Nottinghamshire, the Committee asked the Secretary to investigate.

The Licenced Institutes were found to be almost wholly in the Midlands. Out of 100 institutes in the Districts of South Yorkshire, West Yorkshire, Nottinghamshire, Derbyshire, South Staffordshire, Warwick and South Wales, information was available for 81 schemes. 33 of the 81 were licenced. 24 of the schemes known to be licenced were in Nottinghamshire and Derbyshire where the information covered 39 of the 56 existing Institute schemes. In October 1927, a circular was issued to District Committees asking them to consider the issue, and to let them know whether grants should not be recommended in future for schemes to hold a licence, or to prohibit the taking out of a licence by other schemes.[12]

At the end of September 1927, Cdr. Coote and Mr Ravenshear spent a week in Yorkshire, visiting 11 schemes in West Yorkshire and 35 in South Yorkshire. Both Districts had been given a fortnight's notice of the programme.

Most of the schemes in West Yorkshire did not correspond as accurately as had been expected with the information provided by the District Welfare Committee in support of the applications. Whether this indicated lack of control by the District Welfare Committee, or merely failure to report changes which they had in fact approved, was not known. West Yorkshire still did not have a District Organiser.

In South Yorkshire, the policy of the District Welfare Committee prevented close co-operation between Mr Bates, the District Organiser, and the Advisory Branch; thus losing the value of the appointment of an Organiser. Mr Bates had no previous technical experience and, if he were to function successfully, he needed to rely to a considerable extent on those through whom he could obtain it.

The most successfully managed outdoor schemes in South Yorkshire seemed to be those where the Surveyor of the Council was in charge.[13]

In March 1927, the Committee had to decide as to how to manage the situation that was escalating between the Central Committee and South Wales District Committee.

On 25th January, the District Committee wrote to the Central Committee informing them that their District Organiser, Mr Mason, would not be attending the next District Organisers' Conference pending their meeting with the Secretary for Mines. Despite a reply which stressed the importance and value of the Conferences, the District Committee refused to change their decision.

At their meeting on 3rd March 1927, the Committee decided to make certain inquiries and impose certain conditions on several allocations recommended by the South Wales District Committee. In each case, the District Committee had subsequently refused to supply the information asked for, or to comply with the conditions imposed. This seemed very unfair to the Local Committees concerned.

At the same meeting, the committee decided to invite the South Wales District Welfare Committee, with their Secretaries and District Organiser, to a meeting on 29th March 1927 at the Board of Trade. The Committee believed the whole position regarding the administration of the Miners' Welfare Fund had been misunderstood by the District Committee. The Committee had no wish to enter into further controversy by correspondence. The District Committee wrote back to say they had written to the Secretary of Mines regarding the difficulties that had arisen, and asking that their position be clearly defined.

On 11th March 1927, a letter from Mr Finlay A. Gibson, Secretary to the Monmouthshire and South Wales Coal Owners' Association, had been published in The Times in which it was claimed that the growth in the size of the Central Committee staff was leading to increasing interference in the work of the local committees. The letter went on to make the erroneous statement that 'men in the provinces have no business experience or capabilities and, therefore, cannot be trusted to do the work that has been delegated to them under an Act of Parliament'.

Lord Chelmsford replied to this letter, pointing out that the duties of the Central Committee had substantially increased since the Mining Industry Act of 1926, and explaining that Parliament imposed the sole responsibility of allocation of the Fund to the Central Committee. The Central Committee had recently invited the District Committee to a joint meeting, but they had declined.

Mr Gibson had also published, on 11th March, a long article severely criticising the Miners' Welfare Committee in three principal papers in South Wales. The Western Mail had added a leader on the same subject.

While dealing with pithead bath matters in South Wales, Cdr. Coote, Mr Forshaw, Chief Architect, and Mr Rayner, Chief Quantity Surveyor, took the opportunity to visit the Great Western and Tymawr Institute on 9th March. £845.10.2d had been allocated to this scheme for equipment. This equipment had been supplied by two firms which had been used in practically every scheme requiring furniture. Cdr. Coote had never had any success in obtaining a catalogue from them to ascertain the quality of their furniture supplied. Cdr. Coote found that the quality of both the linoleum and the furniture at the Institute was not only inferior in most cases but also priced far higher than its value. Library books had been supplied by the Industrial Welfare Society, despite the Miners' Welfare Committee writing to the District Committee on 19th January 1927 refusing the application for funding. Circular 97 of 26th May 1926 had explained that no grants would be made for the purchase of books, as better facilities could be provided by the Public Library Authorities.

At the next meeting of the Committee, on 23rd March 1927, it was reported that the District Welfare Committee had met with the Secretary for Mines. They had also agreed to meet with the Central Committee on 29th March.

At the meeting on 29th March, it was agreed to appoint a small sub-committee to go into questions of detail, and to consider the best means of securing full co-operation in order that future recommendations might be dealt with in such a way as to satisfy the Committee's requirements. Four representatives of the South Wales District Welfare Committee would attend a meeting on 4th April at the Mines Department.

The sub-committee met on 4th April, and Lord Chelmsford sent a letter to the District Welfare Committee after the meeting setting out the Miners' Welfare Committee's position and the responsibilities in the administration of the District's portion of the Miners' Welfare Fund. The letter then described, in some detail, what the Miners' Welfare Committee wanted to be included in applications for grants. It was recommended that the District Welfare Committee should sever the connection between Mr Mason and the Industrial Welfare Society, and to engage him as a direct servant of the Fund. It was also proposed that the District Welfare Committee modify its system of apportioning the District Fund, from that collectable from the previous year's output to estimated receipts of the whole statutory period. In this way, local committees would not go in for more ambitious and expensive developments than they could afford.

The sub-committee had a further meeting on 11th May 1927. The District Welfare Committee had agreed to take Mr Mason over from the Industrial Welfare Society and to refrain from further articles in the press. The Miners' Welfare Committee had undertaken not to publish any statement unless further difficulties arose.[14]

The experimental pithead bath construction would be a major development for the Committee during 1927. At their January meeting, Cdr. Coote introduced Mr Forshaw (the architect) and Mr Rayner (the quantity surveyor) as new members of the Committee's staff for pithead bath work, and reported on the progress made so far.

At Mainsforth in Durham, the site was ready for survey. At Letham in Scotland, the company had agreed to provide the site and part of the maintenance costs and were consulting with workmen at an early date. At Llwynypia, the pit was not yet fully working and the Company had deferred consulting the workmen.

The Committee considered sketch plans for Pooley Hall in Warwickshire, which employed 1,249 men as of the 14th December 1926. The Company had asked for slate for the roof, but this was not accepted. 'Robertson protected asbestos sheeting' was proposed as an experiment, subject to a guarantee from the makers. There was concern about preventing drifting snow and rain entering the building via the flat roof. It was accepted that 80 cubicles ought to be enough for 640 men.

Arrangements had been made for the Government Analyst to test the proposed water supply for purity. The colliery was using canal water for their water supply, which was passed through a Neckar water-softening plant, but this water might need further filtration to bring it up to the purity levels laid down by the Miners' Welfare Committee. The water would be heated in a calorifier in the bath house, and steam would be supplied directly from the colliery boilers. The pithead bath effluent would be discharged back into the canal, the Colliery officials having agreed to accept full responsibility for the discharge.

A first aid room and a boot-cleaning room had been included on the plan, and the company was proposing to provide a covered way from the shaft and a new lamp room as part of the bath buildings.[15]

By March 1927, all four experimental sites had run into difficulties. At Pooley Hall, the colliery company had more than once changed their minds as whether provision should be made for 800 or 900 miners. At Mainsforth, the company intended to employ 600 more men (2000 in all) in a year's time, so the decision was taken that the plans should be drawn to facilitate future extension and would be constructed on two storeys. At Letham, the men were unwilling to share the maintenance, so there was a risk of this scheme falling through. An unsuitable site had been offered at Llwynypia, so the Secretary was instructed to consult with the South Wales District Welfare Committee with a view to a more suitable alternative being selected.[16]

It was reported at the May meeting of the Committee that the Ocean Coal Company in South Wales had accepted the offer to erect an experimental installation at Treorchy. There were further delays in Durham in connection with the tenure of the site. Lanarkshire District Welfare Committee had suggested Auchengeich, Bedlay or Robroyston as alternative sites to take the place of Letham. Cdr. Coote had arranged to visit these places the following week, and Mr McCosh (a member of the Central Committee) had agreed to accompany him. Tenders for Pooley Hall were also considered at this meeting.

On 24th May 1927, Cdr. Coote and Mr Forshaw visited four sites in Lanarkshire (Mr McCosh visited 3 with them) to select a site for the Pithead Bath experimental installation. Robroyston was ruled out as there was a probability of an increase in its personnel soon. There was little difference between the other three collieries: Auchengeich, Bedlay, and Dalziel and Broomside. Cdr. Coote and Mr Forshaw arrived at Dalziel and Broomside 'just as the Morning Shift were leaving and we were struck by the very wet and dirty state of the men's clothes, some of them were thoroughly soaked and had to travel several miles to their homes. We were informed that about 200 men out of 434 employed underground came up in this state every day'. Cdr. Coote and Mr Forshaw considered that Dalziel and Broomside was the most deserving, but it was left to the District Committee to make the final decision.[17]

As there were several questions arising regarding pithead baths which needed more time for consideration than generally available, it was proposed to hold a special meeting on 6th July 1927. At this meeting, it was reported that work had begun at the end of June at Pooley Hall with the work to be completed by 31st March 1928. There had been further correspondence on the site at

Mainsforth but the Committee were prepared to accept the original site in the Colliery Yard without requiring any special contribution from the company. At Treorchy, the company had guaranteed to maintain the baths if the men were unwilling to contribute so the Committee authorised Cdr. Coote to proceed with the plans. Cdr. Coote was also authorised to proceed with the preliminary negotiations with the Glasgow Steel and Iron Co. Ltd, the owners of the Dalziel and Broomside Colliery.

Cdr. Coote gave the Committee a summary of the progress made, and the steps taken since the previous special pithead bath meeting in June 1926. The estimated costs of £10 per man at Pooley Hall had been exceeded by 50%. Savings on professional fees at Pooley Hall of between £800 and £1,000 were deemed possible if the number of central architectural staff was increased. The Committee were reluctant to make permanent architectural staff appointments until they had progressed further with the experimental installations, but they did authorise the temporary employment of two Architectural Draughtsmen, one Junior Assistant Quantity Surveyor and one Senior Assistant Quantity Surveyor at an estimated cost of £900pa, in order that remaining experimental installations could be dealt with simultaneously.[18]

In September, with all 4 experimental installations making progress and the return of the majority (21 out of 25) of the survey forms on the collieries from the District Committee, the Central Committee turned its attention to the future development of the Pithead Baths Programme. The apportionment of the money would be based on the number of workmen employed and partly on the source of the money. The first period for building the bath would run to the end of 1931, and the programme would be based on the sum expected to be available during that time. The Committee had devised a priority order based on such factors as contribution from the colliery owners or district funds, exceptionally hot or wet conditions, and size to determine which collieries could be dealt with in the first period up to the limit available. The District Committees would be made aware of this method of prioritising and invited to suggest some other order. Durham and Lanark Committees subsequently expressed the opinion that the classification was impractical. Small collieries and those with a probable life of between 15 and 20 years were not definitely excluded from the programme if some modified form of planning and construction could be devised.

It was estimated that, up to 31st December 1931, the total amount available for the bath programme, assuming continuance of normal conditions (i.e. no stoppage), and after allowing for the probable cost of the 4 experimental installations, would be £1,860,000. If the planning and construction during the 4 years was administered by a central technical staff, as in the case of the experimental installations, the cost of administration would be approximately

£60,000, leaving at least £1,800,000 for the baths themselves. Engaging outside professional assistance, using recognised professional fees, would cost at least £160,000.[19]

By October 1927, a fully-costed proposal for pithead baths technical staff (architects, quantity surveyors and support staff) had been produced, including annual increments and accommodation needed for a staff of this size. The maximum cost was estimated at £87,000 over four years. Outside professional services would cost an extra £110,000. The proposal was accepted by the Committee on the understanding that their prior sanction would be obtained as and when required.[20]

As it was probable that considerable progress would have been made with the preparation of the priority lists before the January 1928 meeting, and recruitment would take two to three months, in November 1927 the Committee authorised the appointment of an assistant architect Grade I and five assistant architects Grade II, who would be in charge of the five sections into which it was proposed to distribute the work; only four of the latter posts were to be actually filled, pending the completion of the South Wales returns, and two typist-clerks.

Tenders for Broomside were considered in November 1927. The cost per man per cubicle was higher than Pooley Hall, so adjustments were made to the height of the building and equipment, reducing the figure to £11,545 12s 9d for the bath house which included provision for 26 women. The canteen was to be provided by the Colliery Owners.[21]

In April 1927, the Committee received a statement from Messrs Pearson and Dorman Ltd, whose Welfare Organiser had been appointed one of the joint secretaries of the recently reconstituted Kent Welfare Committee. The Kent Coalfield was in a state of rapid development, and it was felt that it should receive special treatment from the Miners' Welfare Fund. The Company had provided figures to show a rapid increase in output from two of their collieries amounting to 2,946,494 tons in total by the end of 1930, equating to £9,820 for welfare purposes at the end of 1930. There were no welfare schemes in the District, and miners were being recruited from areas where welfare facilities were already available. The Company had already spent or advanced considerable sums to meet immediate needs, but they could not continue.

There was only £2,653 unallocated of the Kent District Fund, and the only possible answer was for the District Welfare Committee to repay instalments from the proceeds of future years; which had been followed by many Districts. The Company and the District Committee were informed accordingly.

The District Committee had then made a request for a deputation to consider the situation in the Kent coalfield, and the Committee understood they would be making a request for an advance of £50,000 for pithead baths and for recreation grounds at each of the four Kent Collieries, except for the bath at Chislet, where there was a bath already.

The Chairman and Mr Herbert Smith met with the Kent deputation on the 18th July 1927, a report of which was made at the July Committee meeting. It was agreed that Cdr. Coote should visit Kent and he then spent 2 days in the District at the end of August. After the visit, Cdr. Coote was in full sympathy with the claim put forward for a credit of £50,000, but this was impracticable based on the estimated receipt during the statutory period of the Fund.

Cdr. Coote proposed that, together with the existing balance of the District Fund, £10,000 should be advanced on account of the District Fund and £25,000 from the Baths Fund; which would provide a bath at Tilmanstone, one at Snowdon, and an extension to the one already built at Chislet. Betteshanger did not need to be considered until it was in full production, which was not likely to be during this period of the Fund.

At the November 1927 meeting, the Committee agreed to the advance from the General Fund of £10,000. There was a strong case for providing baths at Tilmanstone and Snowdon, which were both very hot collieries. £25,000 could be provided without causing any detriment to other districts.[22]

Pithead welfare was not confined just to pithead baths; it also included the provision of drinking water and hot meals. This was considered by the Committee in October 1926. Drinking water was to be provided in the experimental pithead baths, but the Committee had to give further consideration to the matter in May 1927, in the light of the observations made by the Secretary for Mines after consulting with the Mines Inspectors over the supply of drinking water and hot meals underground. In July 1927, Cdr. Coote produced plans of a proposed canteen estimated to cost £500 in brick and £400 in timber, including fittings, but assuming a free site. The Industrial Canteen Caterers would be prepared to undertake the full responsibility of running such a place, for an experimental period of 6 months. It was agreed that Cdr. Coote would ask the District Organiser to recommend one colliery each in South Wales, Lanarkshire and South Yorkshire where workmen were prepared to co-operate in order that the experiment might be tried at the cost of the General Fund.

By November, very little progress had been made in the three districts in identifying a site. South Yorkshire's suggestions for suitable sites had been rejected by the General Manager of the colliery companies concerned. Lanarkshire had suggested that the experiment should be tried in connection with the new pithead bath at Broomside, but the owners at Broomside were considering making this addition.[23]

By October 1927, the situation with the Advisory Branch had become one of acute congestion. Cdr. Coote had 13 lay outs waiting to be done, dating from

23rd June to 6th October, and 12 to be completed on receipt of plans. In the Recreation Ground Section, Captain J. D. O'Kelly had 13 schemes outstanding, so with his two assistants fully occupied, he had to ask contractors to submit their own designs, which could be quite unsuitable. Mr R. W. Parker had previously submitted a memorandum on the backlog in the Building Section. The situation had now become critical with 23 different schemes requiring attention, 6 dating back to May and June. 2 schemes had been given to [local] architects with the consent of the local committees. Plans were required immediately for 4 schemes being developed under Captain O'Kelly and this was on top of schemes under construction. In the light of this evidence, the Chairman authorised the recruitment of two additional draughtsmen.[24]

In March 1927, The Committee had become a little perturbed that the revised estimates for establishing and endowing the Blackpool Convalescent Home now amounted to practically the whole of the receipts from seven years' output. Lancashire and Cheshire District Welfare Committee had made no indication that they were planning facilities for recreation that would benefit those miners who were fortunate not to require convalescent treatment, but might derive some benefit from the operations of the Fund.

The Committee invited a deputation of the District Welfare Committee to attend the April meeting of the Committee consisting of Colonel Pilkington, Mr Greenall MP, Mr Stephen Walsh MP, Mr McGurk, Mr Ratcliffe-Ellis and one other.

The Chairman explained that, while they desired to give District Committees complete autonomy to a point in deciding what to do with District Funds, they felt bound to draw the District Committee's attention to the view that it was not consistent with the intentions of the Act to confine the benefits of the Fund to one particular object.

The District Committee wished to see the Scheme through, which had originally been agreed upon unanimously. It was now nearly finished, and they anticipated a balance of between £250,000 and £300,000 in the first ten years and it was their intention to devote this to recreation.[25]

In April 1927, the Committee had to allocate £700 to meet a deficit at Horton Lodge Convalescent Home (North Staffordshire). This was largely due to the fact that the Trustees had not yet been able to recover income tax deducted from their endowment income, owing to the scheme being described in the Trust Deed as a 'Home of Rest' instead of a 'Convalescent Home'. Every effort had been made to persuade the Inland Revenue Department to admit the claim for exemption, but the final decision was held up pending the judgement on a somewhat similar case before the Courts.[26]

The Safety in Mines Research Board estimates for 1927/28 were considered at the Committee's March 1927 meeting. Sir Edward Troup attended the meeting to explain any point which might arise out of the estimates amounting to £38,700. The Committee had previously decided not to set aside in the second quinquennium any definite sum for Research but had agreed to consider each year the Board's estimates. The Committee had a balance of £40,000 not definitely assigned, so the estimates for 1927/28 were agreed. It was considered to be not a propitious time for approaching the Treasury for a larger state contribution, but it was decided to approach the Secretary for Mines to make a formal application at the first convenient opportunity, since the Committee remained firmly of the opinion that the Fund was being asked to find too large a share of the Board's income.[27]

In July, the preliminary Report of awards for the Scholarship Scheme was made to the Committee. Eleven scholarships had been granted. 2,253 applications had been received, of which 1,196 were A candidates (working miners) and 1,055 from B candidates (children of miners). A remarkable proportion of the candidates were from Wales. 37 A candidates were selected for personal interview and eight awards were made. 22 B candidates were selected for personal interview and three awards were made, one of which was a girl. A compassionate grant from the Welfare Fund was recommended for a fourth good candidate (Miss McManus) to enable her to complete her degree course.

The standard among both A and B candidates who were personally interviewed was very high. Recommendations for awards bore in mind the instruction in the scheme that, other things being equal, A candidates should have preference to B candidates. 6 out of the 8 A candidates intended to study economics at their chosen university. 2 of the B students had places at Oxford University. The third candidate had been attending Cardiff University College at her father's expense. She was awarded the scholarship to complete her medical degree course. She thought that there was a useful sphere in the mining districts of South Wales for female medical practitioners. 9 of the 11 successful candidates attended the July Committee meeting.[28]

In September 1927, the Committee were made aware that the coal owners who controlled the School of Mines in South Wales were prepared to hand over the school to the education authorities of South Wales for an advanced technical institution, in connection with the Joint Scheme of Education for Miners in the Coalfield under a scheme, if the Board of Education would agree to make one, under the Endowed Schools Acts or the Charitable Trusts Acts. The Chairman suggested that he should discuss the proposal with the Board of Education, the education authorities and the owners, but it was unlikely that there would be money available from the Fund for maintenance.

A deputation attended the September 1927 meeting of the Committee in support of an application for extensions to Manchester College of Technology, providing 20 rooms with two-thirds devoted to mining and fuel, and allowing an increase in numbers of students from 50 or 60, of whom 3 might be taking full-time degree courses, to 150 and 10 respectively. All the degree work was administered by the University. £10,000 was allocated, with the proviso that the full accommodation proposed was provided.[29]

The Lothians District Welfare Committee had held no effective meeting since 8th February 1926. A meeting was called on 10th March 1927, but no business was transacted owing to a difference of opinion as to who should be chairman. Consequently, several supplementary allocations to meet excess costs of schemes which had been agreed by the District sub-committee had been prevented from coming forward for approval. In one of these cases, the Institute at Wallyford, legal proceedings were threatened.

The Chairman decided to allocate the sum necessary to avoid legal proceedings, without waiting for a formal recommendation. The notification of the allocation was accompanied by a letter from the Chairman, in which he pointed out that the Central Committee could not condone the situation in the Lothians District and hoped the difficulties could be settled. Enquiry was made as to what steps were being taken to hold a further meeting.

The Chairman offered to preside over a meeting of representatives from the two sides, to see if the differences could be adjusted in order that the District Welfare Committee could function again.

The workmen accepted the offer without condition, but the owners wished to have an opportunity to confer with Lord Chelmsford before accepting the offer. Lord Chelmsford could not agree to meet the owners separately unless he met the workmen separately on the same day, but he was prepared to follow this procedure if it was agreed in advance that a joint meeting would be held later in the day should he consider it desirable.

While waiting for a reply from the owners, a third local committee had made a complaint that they could not get their application dealt with.

Lord Chelmsford and Mr Ravenshear eventually met the Lothians' coal owners at the North British Station Hotel, Edinburgh at 11am on Thursday, 27th March 1928. Ten owners including Mr John Clark, Mr Ramsey, Mr Hamilton and Mr Brown and their Secretary were present.

The owners stated that they had made up their minds not to sit under the chairmanship of a workman. Lord Chelmsford proposed that the Miners' Welfare Committee, with the consent of the Secretary for Mines, should appoint a neutral chairman. The owners, after a private discussion, reluctantly accepted this proposal. Lord Chelmsford then proposed a joint meeting with the workmen in the afternoon to discuss the compromise. The owners were still unwilling to meet the workmen, but agreed to stand by in another room.

In the afternoon, Lord Chelmsford met the workmen, were represented by Mr Andrew Clarke, Mr Murray, Mr Burnside and 2 others. The workmen were not prepared to accept an independent chairman, as it would reflect badly on the District and there was no guarantee that the owners would meet them under a neutral chairman if they would not meet them under the chairmanship of Lord Chelmsford. They urged Lord Chelmsford to bring about a joint conference. The owners refused, as joint meetings had already been offered but on unacceptable conditions and they produced the correspondence in support of this.

After conferring again with the workmen then the owners, a joint meeting was held with Lord Chelmsford presiding. It was apparent that there had been misunderstandings. Both the owners and the workmen agreed to a joint conference of six from each side to discuss their differences.[30]

A great deal of the Committee's time in 1928 was taken up with pithead welfare, pithead baths and canteens. Cdr. Coote's and Mr Forshaw's visit to the continent to look at pithead baths in Germany, France and Belgium between 21st November and 12th December 1927, coupled with their visits to 20 pithead baths in Great Britain, lead to modifications in the design of the experimental pithead baths which were aimed at improving the design and the saving of costs of future installations.

Bad weather and closure for the Scottish New Year holiday had led to delays in the construction of Pooley Hall and Broomside respectively, but it was hoped that the bath house at Pooley Hall would be ready by April 1928. The Colliery Owners at Broomside had decided not to proceed with the canteen. The drawings for Treorchy and Mainsforth had been modified as a result of Cdr. Coote's and Mr Forshaw's visit to the continent. The shell of the building was to be compressed, thus reducing the cost. Double lockers were proposed, with seating accommodation reduced to provide enough for the largest shift only, and in the clean locker section only. A percentage of unscreened showers would be introduced, but arranged so that they were capable of being screened if it was found that they would not be used, as the miners were only using the enclosed cubicles available.

Out of the 25 districts, only Ayr, Nottingham, Lancashire and Lothians had not returned their reply to the District priority classifications of collieries by January 1928. Ayr had not held a meeting since the list had been sent to them in October 1927. By February 1928, priority lists had been agreed with all Districts except Lothians, Ayr, South Yorkshire, Nottingham, Cannock Chase and Somerset. In those cases where it had been possible to proceed to the next stage of making offers to individual colliery companies, the position had not proceeded very far. By 14th February 1928, 69 offers had been made at various dates; 14 definite replies had been received, of which 5 were acceptances.

With the opening of Pooley Hall fixed for 14th April 1928 and no firm numbers attending, the Committee authorised between £45 to £60 for refreshments.

With the main programme agreed, priority lists were still delayed in March in the cases of South Yorkshire, Ayr, Nottingham and Cannock Chase. The Chairman had met with a deputation from South Yorkshire on 1st March, and their proposals for modifying the Committee's classification would be made by them in the light of the explanation given at the meeting, but some months might elapse before they reported. Ayr was leaving it to the workmen's association to suggest modifications. A meeting of Nottingham District Welfare Committee was held on the 12th March. Of the offers made to the Colliery Companies in 17 Districts, 36 replies had come in, of which 15 were acceptances.

With the work in hand, and with a desire that there should be no delay in the preparation of drawings and quantities so that as much progress as possible could be made with the main pithead bath construction programme, in March 1928 the Committee authorised the recruitment of 17 draughtsmen of various grades, 8 quantity surveyors of various grades and the remaining typist to bring the pithead baths technical staff up to the numbers proposed and approved by the Committee in November 1927.[31]

Slow progress continued to be made with the main programme. By April 1928, 110 offers had been made, although only 19 had been accepted. 20 rejections had been received, with 11 of these coming from South Wales where only 2 acceptances had been received out of 30 offers. This unsatisfactory position had been discussed by the Chairman with a deputation from the District Committee. No further progress had been made with the priority lists for South Yorkshire, but 12 preliminary visits had taken place prior to the preparation of sketch plans.

Cdr. Coote visited the pithead baths at Pooley Hall on 10th May 1928 with Dr Collis (member of the Committee), Dr Fisher (Medical Inspector of Mines) and Dr Vernon (Medical Research Council). They were all impressed with the cleanliness of the building, and had the opportunity to meet with some of the miners in the canteen. It was clear that the men saw the bath house as a godsend. They suggested more taps for filling their water bottles, fixed valves on the bath cubicles so as to obtain running water all the time, and more space between the lockers (this would be allowed for in the new designs with double lockers). Cdr. Coote felt that there should be some minor adjustments to the ventilation. The double-tier type lockers were better for drying clothes than the single tier. The self-closing valve was unsatisfactory, which supported the views of the miners. There were no complaints on the grounds of lack of privacy with 2 to 3 men generally using the same cubicle simultaneously.

Difficulties had been encountered at Treorchy with the Council Surveyor over the disposal of effluent, so settling tanks would need to be installed to comply with his requirements at a cost of £450.

By May 1928, a priority list had been agreed with Ayr and the Lothians' list was under consideration by a sub-committee. There were, however, still difficulties with South Yorkshire and Nottinghamshire.

On 15th March 1928, the Joint Secretaries of South Yorkshire District Welfare Committee wrote to the Central Committee to express their intention of withdrawing altogether from the provision of pithead baths by the Miners' Welfare Committee. Lord Chelmsford letter of 26th March, addressed to the Chairman of the District Committee, expressed his exasperation with South Yorkshire's failure to co-operate and to repeat what he had told them three weeks previously; that the Miners' Welfare Committee had the absolute right to decide what type of bath they would erect, and what steps they would take in the construction of the baths.

The South Yorkshire District Committee visited Pooley Hall Baths, which only strengthened their views expressed in their previous letter. In reply to their letter of 19th April, Lord Chelmsford wrote back on 1st May to ask for specific information regarding the features which the District Committee considered unsatisfactory.

On 15th March 1928, Lord Chelmsford wrote to Nottinghamshire District Committee to point out that the District Committee had failed for the last five months to suggest modifications to the priority list already drawn up. The District Committee did not meet until 24th April, after which they suggested that the selection should be primarily based on the willingness of the workmen to accept pithead baths and was considered possible by the colliery company.

Lord Chelmsford replied on 2nd May to say that the Miners' Welfare Committee could not accept the proposal that priority should depend on the two factors suggested by Nottinghamshire. The Central Committee had therefore proceeded with their classification and made offers to the owners of Bestwood, Gedling, Mansfield, Bentinck and Pinxton collieries. However, this decision did not prevent special priority being given to Cinderhill and Bilsthorpe collieries (previously mentioned by Nottinghamshire District Committee but not included in their return dated 21st June 1927), if the District Welfare Committee would confirm the Central Committee's offer of 25% contribution from the District Fund in these cases.

In June 1928, the Committee decided to fix the opening ceremony for Broomside for some day in the week commencing 10th September, but the colliery needed to start work again. In the meantime, it was decided to send a sample of the metal locker seating proposed for Broomside to be tested at

Pooley Hall so that the workmen there could report on it.

By June, 25 preliminary visits had been made to the collieries in the main programme so that sketch plans could be prepared as soon as possible, with a view to the plans and estimates being undertaken as a batch for submission to the next Committee meeting.

The final recommendations of the Lothians District Welfare Committee for their priority list had still not been received. There was no change in South Yorkshire in regard to co-operation, but they had provided their written criticisms of Pooley Hall which listed the space between the lockers, ventilation, number of cubicles, material used for the walls, the concrete floor and supervision by the attendants. A full reply was made addressing all the points raised, and the improvements made in the design of Treorchy and Broomside were explained.[32]

In July, the opening of Broomside was deferred; the Glasgow Iron and Steel Company did not intend to open the colliery until 1st December. The main programme continued to progress, with quantities being prepared for one case which would be ready to go out to tender.

South Yorkshire submitted a letter to the Committee which was considered at the July 1928 meeting. South Yorkshire were offering a grant of £3,380 from the District Fund if the Committee would find the balance (total cost £9,500) from the Baths Fund to build a pithead bath at New Stubbin Colliery. The colliery would provide the site. A blueprint was enclosed with the letter and showed a bath of the simple hall hoisting type which they proposed to adopt as the basis of a scheme to be worked out by the Local Welfare Committee. The Committee were prepared to give priority to this colliery, in view of the contribution from the District Fund even though no priority list had yet been finally settled for South Yorkshire. However, they could not agree to a grant of an unlimited amount to meet the balance, based on the rough plans and estimates submitted. The District was therefore asked to provide detailed working drawings, specifications and bills of quantities before agreement to the proposal could be made.

With detailed maintenance costs available for Pooley Hall, it became possible in September to make estimates for costs of maintenance of pithead baths. For a pithead bath of Pooley Hall's size (908 men) the 'all in' costs were approximately 6.7 pence per week per man accommodated, of which the colliery company met charges estimated at 2.1 pence per week. The estimated costs were thus amply met by the existing subscription of 5d per man per week, without considering the net canteen profits estimated at not less than £65 per annum, which were also available for upkeep purposes. Costings had also been worked out for pithead baths varying in size from 200 to 2,000 men, which showed that estimated costs fell very rapidly from nearly seven pence per head per week in the small installations to less than three pence in the large ones.

With the main programme, reports had been obtained for Southfield (Lanarkshire) and Grassmoor (Derbyshire) as the prospects for both were in doubt. Based on the reports, it was decided to proceed with the original plans. Tenders had been submitted for three of the sixteen schemes (Sackworth, Whitburn and Ravenhead) and the contractors for each were chosen at the September meeting of the Committee.

Pooley Hall had been visited six times since the previous visit in May by various members of staff including Cdr. Coote, Dr Collis, Dr H. M. Vernon, Dr Fisher, Mr Stevenson Taylor and Mr Ripley. All the recommendations made in Cdr. Coote's May report had been adopted by the Management Committee except for those relating to improving the floor drainage and steam leaks, to which they were looking to the contractor to put right. Experiments had been carried out with a new type of shower rose, which was so popular that the Management Committee had asked to have them throughout. Ventilation and drying of clothes in the lockers were examined in quite some detail and suggestions put forward for improvement. 33

At the end of September 1928, South Yorkshire forwarded a plan for the baths at New Stubbin, as requested by the Committee in July 1928. The plan was little more than a sketch, the accompanying specification was incomplete and much too loosely worded, and the sheet of priced items was useless for the purpose of obtaining a tender. The Chairman replied to Mr Clive's letter of 24th September 1928 reiterating the need to have working drawings, specifications and bills of quantities to enable tendering. The plans required further consideration; besides not separating clean from dirty clothes, the spaces allocated for each man had been reduced below the lowest standard of existing installations in South Yorkshire, and there was no provision for lavatory accommodation, first aid room, drinking water or the greasing of boots. The system of ventilation proposed had already been proved to be unsatisfactory.

At the same time as the Chairman wrote to South Yorkshire Welfare Committee about New Stubbin, he also wrote to them separately to point out that it had been seven months since he had met their deputation regarding the Colliery Classification in South Yorkshire, and there was no indication that the District Committee proposed to give any assistance with the list. No offers had been made to any collieries in South Yorkshire so, unless South Yorkshire District Committee forwarded their observations within a month, the Committee intended to proceed with making offers on the basis of their original list of collieries.

At the special request of the Colliery Company at Broomside, who were reopening the pit on 26th November 1928, the pithead baths were opened by the Chairman on Saturday, 24th November 1929 at 2.30pm.

A further 2 tenders in October and 3 in November were considered, and contracts awarded by the Committee at Woodhorn, Grassmoor, Harrington, Chanters and Gibfield Arley. There had been a hold up with the Backworth scheme (passed by the Committee in September) owing to the difficulty in getting the Agent of the Duke of Northumberland to deal with the transfer of the site.

By November 1928, South Yorkshire District Welfare Committee had provided their observations on the priority list and their proposals for revising the classification had been accepted, with the result that 12 offers had been made to collieries in the District. The District Committee had also appointed a sub-committee to collaborate with the Central Committee generally. This then just left the Lothians with no agreed priority list, so they had been given a deadline of 8th December for receipt of their observations on the original classification of their collieries.[34]

The search for suitable sites for the experimental pithead canteens continued in 1928, but seemed to have made very little progress. South Yorkshire District Committee did not think that any colliery would be willing to consider the offer. In Lanark, Auchlochan Colliery, Coalburn was suggested in place of Broomside. In South Wales, Main Colliery had been suggested in view of Penalite being under consideration for an early pithead bath.[35]

The practice of visiting schemes continued in 1928 with the Secretary visiting Durham, Northumberland and Cumberland during the week beginning 7th May 1928. He was accompanied in Durham by Captain O'Kelly and the rest of the time by Mr Parker. Captain O'Kelly and Mr Parker were members of the Advisory Branch. 35 schemes were visited: 20 in Durham, 6 in Northumberland and 9 in Cumberland. These schemes comprised 16 institutes and 28 recreation grounds.

A notable feature in all three Districts was the cordial relationship which existed between the District Welfare Committee and the Central Advisory Branch. The Committee's technical staff were always welcomed. Very few developments in the three Districts took place unless the District Welfare Committee were satisfied that the Advisory Branch had been consulted by the local committee concerned. The District Committees were also particularly careful not to let schemes proceed on a more ambitious scale than money available permitted, so schemes were better finished than those in other districts and there were good examples of the value of progressive development of schemes according to a comprehensive plan.

None of the three Districts had a District Organiser, although Durham was just about to make an appointment. In Cumberland, the success of their schemes, which had cost remarkably little money, had been due very largely to the joint secretaries, Major Scoular and Mr Parker. These two gentlemen had voluntarily (no administration expenses were charged against the Fund in this

District) undertaken many of the duties which an organiser would be expected to perform, and spent a great deal of their time visiting and generally looking after the various schemes.

The Secretary was very impressed with the schemes in Durham, and put them on a par with those in Nottingham.[36]

In July 1928, Cdr. Coote and Mr Parker visited Doncaster Town Institute to investigate and report on the financial situation in which the Institute found itself. Mr Robert Clive, Joint Secretary of the South Yorkshire District Committee had written to the Central Committee on 22nd May 1928 to make them aware of the issue, and it was agreed that Cdr. Coote and Mr Parker would meet with members of the Institute's committee and one of the Trustees on the owner's side on 6th July.

The Institute had been opened in 1924, with five collieries giving their active support with a 1d levy per man being collected by the colliery company concerned. It had been estimated that the scheme would be self-sufficient, but the miners' branches concerned had signified by resolution their willingness to defray any deficit which might arise. This never actually happened. The collieries contributed an ever-decreasing amount annually and had paid nothing by 1928, as apparently they had started to develop local schemes of their own.

In November 1925, the committee were forced to obtain a licence for the sale of intoxicants, despite the Chairman and Secretary of the District Committee, as well as several other members, being teetotallers. The takings from this sale of intoxicants, billiard takings from two tables and the letting of the Hall were the three main sources of income for the Institute in 1928.

Prior to the 1926 Coal Stoppage, the Institute was taking £57.13s a week; 28% of this was clear profit. Their weekly takings had been reduced to £26 per week meaning a loss of £5.10s per week, and they were in a debt of £631.13s 9d.

The Institute Committee had put forward a proposal for structural alterations and additions which would increase the Institute's income. Mr Parker had looked at these and was satisfied that if the alterations could be done for the cost estimated, the general arrangement was as good as it could be expected.

Mr Clive suggested two other alternatives, which were either selling the present building and using the money for another welfare development in Doncaster, or investing the money available for allocation and allotting the income to be used towards maintenance.

At the Central Committee meeting on 13th July 1928, the endowment proposal was ruled out, but it was agreed that Cdr. Coote's report would be sent to the District Committee in the hope that they would be enabled to make a recommendation. Mr Herbert Smith undertook to discuss the matter with the District Committee.

In October 1928, the Committee received Mr Herbert Smith's report recommending the proposed scheme of alterations and additions at an estimated cost of £2,877, subject to modification by the Advisory Branch, but advising that the proposal to pay off the maintenance deficit should be refused. In January 1929, the Committee agreed to an allocation of £2,877.[37]

Following the meeting at Doncaster Town Institute, Cdr. Coote and Mr Parker met with the members of Worksop Institute committee at 5pm. The Local Committee of this scheme wanted to obtain a Stage Play Licence but before they could obtain this, certain regulations of Nottingham County Council had to be complied with. Structural alterations would cost about £2,900 but the District Committee could only agree to recommend a further allocation of £1,200 to this scheme. The Local Committee therefore wanted to raise the balance required with an overdraft at the scheme's bank. The District Committee felt that they could not sanction the overdraft at the bank unless the Central Committee approved.

There were five collieries in the area, and the men were levied for welfare developments and money was being allocated to the Worksop scheme. However, as more schemes developed, there would be less and less money to support the Worksop scheme. Besides the levy money, income was principally obtained from the usage of the Hall, especially when any dramatic entertainment was given. There was no theatre in Worksop. The only other alternative to the proposal was to try to make a profit out of the sale of intoxicants.

As with Doncaster (see above), the Committee decided to send the District Committee Cdr. Coote's report so they could decide.[38]

The Advisory Branch (Building Section) submitted a proposal to the March meeting of the Central Committee that a further Grade II draftsman should be appointed to the Section. Since the appointment of Mr Devlin in December 1927, the work of the Section had again increased as a result of the success of the Recreation Section under Captain O'Kelly. There had been numerous requests for plans for caretakers' houses, pavilions, shelters, open air baths, band stands etc. In addition, the Section was also having to meet the demands of South Wales and Lanarkshire who had definitely decided to use the Advisory Branch from the beginning of 1928, and North Staffordshire District Committee had definitely stated that they wanted all their developments to be supervised by the Advisory Branch. The Central Committee at their March 1928 meeting authorised the appointment of an additional Grade II draughtsman.[39]

Convalescent homes' costs continued to be monitored in 1928. South Yorkshire's home at Scalby and the Lancashire home at Blackpool were included for the first time in the calculations of comparative average cost of upkeep per patient per week. The cost per patient for the older welfare homes varied between £2.10s and £3.6s.5d. Costs for several other convalescent homes of comparable size was obtained and, with the exception of the Convalescent Police Seaside Home at Hove, the cost per patient was lower than the older welfare homes. The difference lay chiefly in the cost per head of staff, so it was difficult to avoid the conclusion that the welfare homes (except South Yorkshire and Cannock Chase) were overstaffed.[40]

In March 1928, the Central Committee considered the Safety in Mines Research Board estimates for 1928/9 which amounted to £57,287 towards which the estimated income from the endowment fund was £12,386 and from the Parliamentary Vote £1,901 leaving £43,000 to be met, if approved, by a direct grant from the Fund, subject to a probable reduction of about £1,500 in respect of savings from 1927/28.

The estimate for 1928/9 was £4,300 more than the previous year and did not include the Board's proposals for capital expenditure at Buxton on an underground roadway which would provide a new gallery for demonstrations to parties of miners and mine officials and for experimental purposes, a dining hall for visitors, canteen and garage. These were to be submitted separately. The estimate did, however, include the honorarium for Professor Dixon (£300 met out of savings 1927/28 and £300 in the estimates 1928/9) who had been directing the research being carried out on wire ropes and timber supports at Imperial College but who was also a member of the Board.

Mr Fudge, Dr Wheeler and Mr Stedman attended on behalf of the Secretary for Mines and the Board to reply to questions.

The Chairman expressed the Committee's concern about the increasing size of the amount being asked for, especially as the Parliamentary grant was falling rather than rising and thought they might fairly ask the Board to keep within a range of £50,000. The grant of £43,000 was allocated after Dr Wheeler had explained the list of increases to the Committee's satisfaction. The honorarium to Dr Dixon was approved by the Committee, after receiving an assurance from Dr Wheeler that there was no objectionable overlap with the work being conducted on wire ropes by the Institute of Mechanical Engineers.

The estimates for the extensions for Buxton was submitted by the Chairman of the Safety in Mines Research Board (Sir Edward Troup) and came to a total of £10,320. The Committee approved the estimate for the roadway on the understanding that its use for experimental purposes would not lead to an application at a later date for another roadway for demonstrations. They also approved the estimate for the canteen building with the request that a charge for all meals was applied.[41]

In November 1928, the Committee received the Second Report of the Miners' Welfare National Scholarship Scheme. A longer period (3½ months against 2 months in 1927) had been given to advertise the second competition and receive applications. The total number of applications that were received for 1928 was 625 of which 213 were from A candidates and 412 from B candidates, of which 85 were girls. 3 A candidates and 21 B candidates had applied for postgraduate scholarships which had become available in 1928 for the first time.

After a succession of careful scrutinies, 24 A and 44 B candidates were selected for personal interview, three of whom were applicants for postgraduate scholarships. This number was more than in 1927, and was larger than the Committee had contemplated.

Eleven A candidates and five B candidates were eventually recommended for awards, one of them being for postgraduate work. Several candidates (4 A and 9 B) who were not recommended for awards were recommended to the Miners' Welfare Committee for special grants.

South Wales and Monmouthshire sent by far the largest number of candidates (42%), both A and B, with Durham following second, a considerable distance behind.[42]

The Committee made several allocations for education in 1928. An allocation of £100 was made to the Forest of Dean Mining School at Cinderford for equipment. £1,364 was allocated to continue the existing scheme of non-vocational adult education in Nottinghamshire and Derbyshire.[43]

A further allocation of £2,500 for equipment and furniture was made to Mansfield Technical College, which had already received £10,200 for buildings and a gymnasium. This allocation was made to cover half of the equipment of the Heat Engines Laboratory and Physics and Chemistry Laboratory. As for furniture, the mine surveying tables would be costly items and mining students would use the laboratory fittings.[44]

It was not until 21st May 1928 that Lord Chelmsford saw Lord Eustace Percy at the Board of Education to discuss the South Wales School of Mines (see above September 1927, page 82). Lord Chelmsford explained that the Miners' Welfare Committee were unwilling to make a grant for maintenance if the Board was not contributing their share. Lord Eustace Percy agreed to getting a special concession made, by which the Local Education Authorities taking over the school would receive a grant from the Board in respect of the past year which would normally have been paid to the owners, but which the latter forfeited by not continuing the school.

Mr Winstanley also inspected the School on 23rd May, and was able to suggest economies which would reduce the cost of maintenance during the school year 1928/9. Letters were also written to the Glamorgan and Monmouthshire Local Education Authorities asking them if they were prepared to take over Treforest and Crumlin respectively on 1st September, provided the rates were relieved of the whole cost of maintenance during the first year. The letters also stated that the Miners' Welfare Committee would be willing to consider giving further assistance during the second year should it be necessary (£7,600 during 1928/9).[45]

Leicestershire Education Authority applied for a grant of £2,000 for an extension to the Coalville Mining Institute which had already received a grant of £4,640. Leicestershire Education Authority had given an undertaking to establish new junior centres and those already opened at Oakthorpe and Ibstock were the best of their kind. Although only £1,500 was available to Leicestershire from the original allocation, £2,000 was recommended with the amount being made up by a supplementary grant from the Reserve.[46]

Although Broomside pithead baths had been opened on 24th November 1928, by January 1929, it was still not be possible to use the baths. There were difficulties with the steam, which contained oil and solid matter. The Colliery Company put in new piping for an isolated boiler so by February 1929, 500 of the possible 560 miners were able to use the baths. The men were highly satisfied and there had been no question of lack of privacy. There were a few cases in which clothes were too wet to dry properly in the lockers. The cleanliness of the building was not so satisfactory, owing to the attendants not being of the right type; they lacked in skills and aptitude.

By March 1929, practically every man employed at Broomside was bathing in the facility. However, the cost of upkeep had been underestimated and this was being investigated. The owners, the Glasgow Iron and Steel Company, had made a claim for reimbursement of expenditure incurred by them in connection with the bath installation of £507.2s.7d. There was doubt about the footpaths outside the building being chargeable, so Mr McCosh was authorised to discuss the claim with the company after which the full payment was recommended by Mr McCosh.

Early results from Broomside showed there was a need for widening the locker passages, conservation of heat in the building required attention and consideration of the provision of special drying accommodation. £350 was authorised by the Committee in May for the installation of one of the special drying rooms which had been requested by Mr Barr, and had been contemplated from the outset. The Committee also authorised the cost incurred in completing the balance of the lockers.

In July 1929, Cdr. Coote was able to report a great improvement in the cleanliness of Broomside, but he was making enquiries into the consumption of coal which was alleged to be nearly 250 tons per month, while the annual consumption at Pooley Hall was only 300 tons.

The baths at Treorchy were opened on 28th February 1929 and there were 800 men using them in the first week. The only problem that arose in the first

Pithead Baths at Treorchy

months was with the Terrazo cubicles, which had failed as a result of frost. The sub-contractor had agreed to replace them in batches of six. The remaining lockers were installed in April.

In May 1929, Cdr. Coote had a discussion with the management committee at Treorchy and took the opportunity to remind the committee of several small matters which required attention. Most of these involved more time than could be spared by the Baths Section architects, and correspondence had not been very successful. (It was suggested that an appointment of a supervisory clerk of works permanently attached to headquarters might overcome the difficulty by seeing that all such matters were promptly dealt with).

Unsatisfactory levels of cleanliness at Treorchy became apparent in June, which was partly due to the lack of understanding of their work by the attendants and partly the lack of entrance gates which would be shortly completed. This was resolved but the usage of the baths remained at 820 men. The reasons given by the men who refused to use the baths were trivial.

In March 1929, a further £1,000 was added to the allocation for Mainsforth to meet the cost of building, furnishings and equipping the canteen. The opening of the baths at Mainsforth was delayed to 18th June 1929 as the work had been delayed by frost. This had to be further delayed to 6th July as the granolithic flooring had to be replaced. The opening ceremony had been highly successful, and over 1,200 men had used the baths the day after the opening.

In June 1929, the repainting of Pooley Hall was approved, the need for which had been to some extent caused by its use for experimental purposes.[47]

The first of the experimental buildings to test the demand for canteen facilities at collieries not provided with pithead baths was completed early in 1929. The experimental canteen at Craghead Colliery, Durham had cost £593.12s.6d. It had been opened by Professor Collis on 17th May. It had been a great success and was not only used by the miners but also members of their families.

Arrangements had been made to proceed with the second experimental canteen at Wain Llwyd in South Wales. However, it was still proving difficult to identify a site in Scotland for the third experimental canteen.[48]

The main programme of pithead baths progressed with 30 schemes going to placement of contracts during 1929. This number did not include the Chislet scheme in Kent, which was being financed out of the District Fund with an additional allocation from the Baths Fund of £1,750. The working drawings had been proceeded with, in the knowledge that there would be an excess which the Colliery Company had undertaken to meet from some other local source.

Alterations to the sketch plans for Blairhall, Fife had been requested by the owners. The scheme accommodated 700 men and the owners had asked for all the floors to be on one level, avoiding steps inside the building, extra space between the lockers, less open cubicles with the provision of facilities for hanging underclothing inside but protected from the spray, as in the Kingshill colliery where the company were erecting their own pithead baths, and modifications of the proposed arrangements of lockers (the upper locker belonged to different man from the one below it). The owners had undertaken to do the extra excavation necessary to construct the floors on one level, so this was approved, but all the other requests were turned down. The space between the lockers was the same as in all the other recent schemes. The substitution of the Kingshill type cubicles would cost £435, so the Committee offered to provide waterproof curtains for half the cubicles at a cost of £30. Allowing one man to have the upper and lower locker would comply with the principle of separating clean from dirty clothes.

In July 1929, Cdr. Coote reminded the Committee that several main programme installations would shortly be completed and subsequently there would be a constant succession of them. He was devoting a very large amount of his time to nursing the experimental baths. The Committee recognised that it was impossible for Cdr. Coote to supervise each scheme, so authority was given to the appointment of an assistant for him.

The Trustees of the Parsonage scheme in Lancashire, which was nearing completion, on learning that accommodation was to be provided for women in the projected scheme at the Maypole Colliery in the same district, had applied in September 1929 for similar accommodation to be assigned to them. There were 70 women employed, and the number was likely to rise to 125 in two years' time. It was impossible to modify the plans to accommodate the women at Parsonage but, as a general principle, it was agreed that, if women were employed, provision should normally be made for them. To overcome the situation at Parsonage, the Central Committee were prepared to consider a grant from the District Fund for the addition of accommodation for women to the present handwashing and lavatory accommodation.

In October 1929, the Trustees of the Smithy Wood (South Yorkshire) scheme asked for the provision of some wash basins on the grounds that certain surface men did not want a complete bath, but would pay the full upkeep contribution if provided with a locker and facilities for washing their face and hands. Cdr. Coote had previously advised against basins because in baths where wash basins already existed, they were either not used (Linton and Ellington), or else gave rise to complaints from other users because of the mess made (Nunnery). It was thought possible to overcome these objections in the scheme suggested by the Trustees of Smithy Wood, so £165 was allocated for the purpose of trying this as an experiment.[49]

The number of allocations for recreational purposes during 1929 was 674, 52 of which were new schemes. These figures brought the total since the beginning of the Fund to 3,784 and 1,111 respectively.

The scheme at Llanbradach was of interest, as the supplemental allocation was made for a model children's playground which was developed under the supervision of the Advisory Branch. An area of 2 ½ acres was made available for this purpose at a cost of £2,400, on the recommendation of the District Committee. The layout incorporated all the most modern ideas about children's playgrounds, and it was hoped that it would serve as an example and incentive to the development of schemes on similar lines elsewhere.

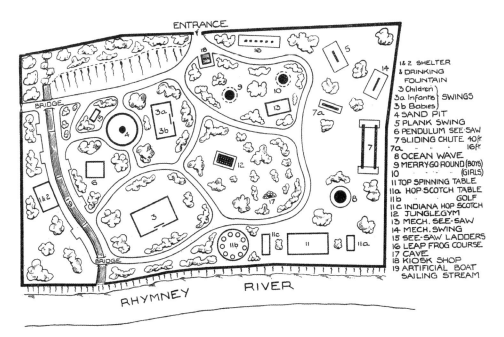

Model children's playground at Llanbradach

There were 4 other schemes of considerable size initiated in 1929: Ashington in Northumberland, Llay in North Wales, Hednesford in Cannock Chase and Kilsyth in Lanark.

£23,000 was allocated for an institute and swimming-bath at Ashington. The institute and the swimming-bath would be separate buildings. The institute would be on two floors and would include a billiards room for six tables, a lecture hall seating 100, a ladies' room, the usual provision for rooms for reading, library, quiet games, committee meetings, office and lavatories and, in addition, a 'super games' room equipped with bias bowls, bull-board, table tennis, trapps, shuffle-board and carpet bowls. The swimming baths would follow the scheme similar to that at Coalville, but would also include the compulsory shower-bath between the changing boxes and the bathing pool proper.

The allocation for the Llay scheme was £20,000 which included the purchase of a site of nearly 10 acres and a two-storey institute. The upper floor would be occupied by a concert hall seating 520 persons, a lecture hall seating 100 persons, a large refreshment room and kitchen and a committee room with six tables, a general room, a smoke room, all supervised from a central control room, and a large reading room with a library leading off it.

The Hednesford scheme was £10,000, allocated for the first two sections of the development of a 16 ½ acre site owned by the Cannock and Rugeley Colliery Company which was held on a 47-year lease. The plans provided for the construction of two bowling greens, eight tennis courts and a putting course on an area covering 3½ acres, a cricket and football area covering about seven acres, a children's playground of three acres and a public area of three acres with bandstand and dancing area.

The allocation for the Kilsyth scheme was £8,000, to develop a recreation ground in an area of 10 acres held on feu. The site was in the middle of the town and it was proposed that the pavilion should be suitable for use as an institute in the winter months.

The number of allocations during the year connected with health of miners was 67 and the number of new schemes was 20 bringing the totals since the inception of the Fund to 379 and 162 respectively.

One new convalescent home was initiated in 1929 by Durham District Committee. Conishead Priory and estate, near Ulverston, Lancashire on the western shore of Morecombe Bay had been purchased for £28,000, and a further £25,000 would need to be spent to provide accommodation for about 170 patients.

The endowment funds were increased at Talygarn, South Wales (by £40,000), Rudyard, North Staffordshire (by £15,000) and Lytham, West Yorkshire (by £10,000). In the latter two cases, the increased endowment was coupled with extensions. The developments at Rudyard cost about £3,200 and were met from the Fund and those at Lytham, estimated to cost about £2,800, were met from accumulated income.

Supplementary allocations were made to the existing endowment funds for the purchase of tickets of admission to convalescent homes in Nottinghamshire (£25,000) and South Derbyshire (£4,000). £40,000 was allocated to South Yorkshire to establish a similar fund.

Hospitals, ambulance services and nursing services received an allocation during 1929 amounting to £26,015, £7,687 and £3,870 respectively.

The grants to hospitals included £2,000 for the increase endowment of the Randolph Wemyss Memorial Hospital, Fife; £7,520 towards the extension of the Montagu Hospital Mexborough in South Yorkshire; £5,700 for the extension of the Rotherham Hospital in South Yorkshire; £5,000 towards the endowment fund of the Harlow Wood Orthopaedic Hospital in Nottinghamshire and £2,000 for the extension of the Paulton Memorial Hospital in Somerset.

The grants for ambulance services included the provision of a challenge shield for Warwick District, an allocation of £2,500 for further development of the work of the St John's Ambulance Association in South Wales, the provision of facilities for classes in the Bristol District, the provision of ambulances at Murton, Shotton and Ryton in Durham, at Cudworth in South Yorkshire and for general service in Somerset.

Durham Miners' Convalescent Home, Conishead Priory

The nursing schemes included the establishment of schemes at Stairfoot in South Yorkshire and at Hartshill in Warwickshire. The Stairfoot scheme involved the erection of a nurses' home with suitable equipment at an estimated cost of £1,020 on a site purchased for £100, the balance being vested in the District Committee as trustees for endowment. The Hartshill scheme consisted wholly of an endowment fund of £1,250.[50]

The estimates of the Safety in Mines Research Board for 1929/30 were considered at the Central Committee meeting in March 1929. The estimate was divided into two parts, the first part dealt with researches already in progress, for which an estimate of £50,000 was given representing a net grant of £36,130 after allowing for the probable endowment income of £12,440 and the probable Treasury grant of £1,430 and the second part dealing with the proposal by Sir Henry Walker for new investigations and publications, for which the estimated expenditure in the full year was £11,500, but for which only £6,000 was applied for in respect for 1929/30.

The Chairman had already had a short discussion with the Secretary for Mines prior to the meeting. Sir Edward Troup (Chairman of the Safety in Mines Research Board) Sir Henry Walker, Professor Wheeler and Mr Stedman had been asked to attend to outline the position and answer any questions.

Following the discussion which followed the withdrawal of the Board members, it was agreed that the Chairman and two members of the Committee should put the Committee's view regarding the proposed new work before the Secretary for Mines. As a matter of principle, the Committee felt that they should not be asked to provide more from the Fund than was necessary to give the Board a total of £50,000 for research purposes and that, if additional expenditure was considered to be essential, it should be met from some other source. On the information they had been given it seemed that much, if not all, of the new work proposed might properly be undertaken by the Mines Department as part of the function of the Inspectorate, but they did not want to be put in the invidious position of having to decide what, if anything, should be dropped.

At the April 1929 meeting of the Central Committee, they again considered the Board's estimates for 1929/30, the previously proposed meeting with the Secretary for Mines having taken place. The Central Committee had invited Mr Faulkner to attend and he urged the Committee not to stand in the way of new researches immediately for the sake of £6,000. The Committee thought that it was unfair to attempt to saddle them with the responsibility of standing in the way. The responsibility lay with the Board who had repeatedly been told that their total expenditure must be brought within the limit of £50,000. The Committee finally decided to inform the Secretary for Mines that they could not provide a larger sum than £36,130 for 1929/30.[51]

During 1929, a sum of £19,801 was provisionally allocated to new schemes for the provision of buildings and equipment for technical mining education and £93,394, already provisionally allocated, was confirmed (ie granted on the approval of schemes in detail). These figures brought the total allocation of grants from the sum of £750,000 set aside for technical mining education to £528,912 of which £456,233 had been confirmed (For further details see Chapter 7 Education).[52]

The sum recommended for education by district welfare committees in 1929 was £6,820 for 61 allocations, compared with £4,226 for 20 allocations in 1928. Over half the sum allocated in 1929 related to various types of non-vocational lecture schemes (12 in total).

There were two grants for provision of equipment at Broomhill in Northumberland (books for the technical library) and Nuneaton in Warwickshire (apparatus and equipment for the use of junior mining classes).

The remaining 47 allocations were special grants for students, of which 32 were made entirely from district funds, a total amount of £1,961.0s.6d as compared with 9 in 1928 totalling £450. 15 special grants were made from the district funds to supplement grants from the general fund, half the cost being found from the general fund and the district funds respectively.

The number of applications for the Miners' Welfare Scholarships in 1929 was 689, an increase of 64 on the figure for 1928. Twelve scholarships were awarded, seven to miners and five to children of miners; of the latter, two were for postgraduate work, one of them in Germany.[53]

The investigation into the excessive coal and water consumption at Broomside pithead baths continued into 1930. The Colliery had run two tests in October 1929 and January 1930, but the loss of condensation was still 50% higher than it should be. The comparative costs for Broomside (1st year) and Pooley Hall (second year) were available in May 1930 and showed higher consumption of coal for steam production at Broomside. There was a suspicion that this was due to the high price charged for coal of low grade. Sir Thomas Hudson Beare and Mr Rayner visited Broomside on 27th August 1930. Here they met with the Colliery Agent and also representatives of the Baths Committee who raised the issue of the charge per week per man, which they had been led to understand would be 4d, but in practice was 6d and this had caused complaints.

The brick pit into which the condensation from the baths was discharged and which had caused extensive leaks was in the process of being replaced with an iron tank. The boiler which supplied the Baths with steam was found to be some considerable distance from the Baths and faults were found in the steam delivery pipes. The quality of the coal was a concern but, since the Colliery

Company used it in all their boilers, this could not be changed but the steam, which was kept on for 24 hours, could be shut off for part of the time and would save fuel.[54]

The Secretary for Mines opened Whitburn Colliery baths near Sunderland on Saturday, 25th January 1930. The design for this scheme had been challenging, as there was no space around the baths so it had to be built on the far side of the main road between Sunderland and South Shields. This necessitated the linking up of the colliery yard and the bath building by means of a bridge over the road, giving direct access at the same time to the railway platform where the majority of the workmen arrived and departed.

At the beginning of 1930, it was possible to map out the main pithead bath programme in many of the districts for the next 15 months, and it was anticipated that it would be possible to put the schemes in hand throughout 1930 at a rate of three a month.[55]

As there had been 68 offers of pithead baths rejected, the Committee in January 1930 requested a breakdown of the reasons given by the colliery owners. Financial difficulties were the most common reason given, followed by probability of the colliery having too short a life and then the company stating that the workmen were against them, but there was no evidence that the men had been properly consulted. It was therefore decided that, in future, all offers would be sent out in duplicate in order that a copy might be handed to the representatives of the workmen concerned.

In February 1930, the Committee considered an appeal made by Mr Robson (joint secretary of the Durham District Committee) on behalf of the Boldon Colliery workmen that the expenditure incurred out of the District Fund on pithead baths since the passage of the Mining Industry Act 1926 should be transferred to the Baths Fund, on the grounds that this was the only pithead bath in Durham erected before the Act. The Boldon workmen had penalised themselves in comparison with the workmen at collieries which were being equipped with baths under the Act. The amount of allocations made to the Boldon Pithead Baths since 1926 had been £4,766. £3,000 of this had to be discounted as it was used to pay off a loan raised for meeting the balance of the original contract costs, but the Committee agreed to an allocation of £1,799 from the Baths Fund as being 'new accommodation'.[56]

Tenders continued to be approved at a rate of approximately three per Committee meeting: Craghead, Blaenavon and Lady Windsor collieries in January; Bannockburn, Cadeby Main and Longwith Collieries in February; Haunchwood, Grimethorpe and Bilsthorpe collieries in March; Ferniegare, Dawdon and Moston collieries in April; Bradford, New Market Silkstone and Pensford collieries in May; Bank, Wharncliffe Silkstone and Sneyd in June;

Frances, Fryston and Baggeridge collieries in July; Sutton Manor, Glapwell and Nine Mile Point collieries in September; Northfield, Linby and North Cleywen collieries in October; Hazlerigg and Dinnington collieries in November. A further three tenders were expected in December which the Chairman was authorised to deal with on the usual lines.[57]

In July 1930, Mr Forshaw, Chief Architect (Baths Section), made a proposal for the appointment of two additional Grade I Draughtsmen, one Junior Draughtsman, and an Engineering Draughtsman. Since January 1930, the staff had produced the tenders at the required rate of three per month, besides submitting 25 new sketch plans without paid overtime which was found necessary in the previous year but, to maintain scheduled progress during the remainder of the financial year, extra staff were required. The work of the Engineering Assistant, Mr Turner, had also increased considerably. The appointment of an Engineering Draughtsman was approved but the other two appointments were deferred to September.[58]

In September 1930, the Central Committee considered a letter from the Trustees of the Llay Main Pithead Baths. The original baths had been limited to 2,000, despite the number employed being 3,320, partly because the owners and the workmen were sure that not more than that number would use the baths, and partly because the amount available for North Wales up to 31st March 1931 did not permit a larger building. The plan for the extension, however, provided for a future increase of 1,500.

The baths had turned out to be more popular than expected, so many men who were paying the weekly subscription for the baths could not have a locker allocated to them. An extension to the installation was required without delay.

The Committee agreed that this should be done, but the Secretary was asked to ascertain first whether any other colliery in the district was particularly anxious for baths to be installed.[59]

Yorkshire Main was the first pithead bath to be fitted with the plenum system for heating lockers. Testing of this new system was undertaken in late October. The results of these tests would determine whether Dawdon, which was under construction, would adopt this system or not.

The test results for Yorkshire Main were reported at the end of November. Using Treorchy as an example of an installation of similar size to Yorkshire Main but heated by direct steam only, the saving from the plenum system was £73 per annum. The other advantages of the plenum system were concentrated steam control, positive ventilation and constant disinfection.[60]

The Secretary for Mines, Mr Shinwell, attended the July meeting at the invitation of the Central Committee to discuss the situation arising out of the correspondence with South Wales District Committee regarding the Bowls and

Billiard competitions. Mr Shinwell was accompanied by Sir Alfred Faulkner, Mr Hurst and Mr Coleman.

On 16th September 1925, Mr Gibson, Joint Secretary of South Wales District Committee, had written to the Secretary personally stating that he had inaugurated a Bowls Competition four months previously and that the final was to be held at Talygarn on 26th September. This was the first the Central Committee had heard of it. Mr Gibson wanted to know whether a grant should be applied for (estimated at £35 for cup and medal) or be regarded as district expenses.

The Secretary replied that it should be a special recommendation. At the end of October 1925, an application was made for £83.13s.6d, of which £34.11s had been spent on refreshments. This was approved but in December, they had found two further items amounting to £26.3s.9d. This was again approved without comment.

On 24th June 1926, the District Committee applied for a grant, estimated at £100, to pay for the railway fares of the teams competing in the competition. Owing to the industrial situation (the stoppage), they had unable to meet their expenses. This was approved, but on the understanding that it applied only during the industrial situation. An estimate of £50 for the final was received in August but the actual account submitted showed expenses of £54.7s.4d of which £12.12s.8d had been spent on refreshments. Lord Chelmsford expressed the opinion that the principle of paying for refreshments out of the Fund was questionable, but approved the rest of the expenses.

In February 1927, a further application for expenses was made for £19.5s.11d of which £16.4s was granted for additional railway fares, and the balance was for inscribing the medals. This was considered by the Central Committee as a further instance of unnecessary expenditure on entertainment, but this application coincided with the 'great row' with the District Committee over the Road Race expenses which the Central Committee chiefly disliked. No comment was made in notifying the allocation to the District Committee.

On 26th September 1927, the District Committee applied for a grant of £31.9s.3d to meet the expenses of their year's final, which had been held at Risca. Of this sum, £4.10s represented belated train fares from the previous year. The cost of refreshments in 1927 were paid for by Risca Urban District Council.

On 9th November 1928, the District Committee applied for a grant of £50.18s.4d for the expenses of the Final at Pontypridd. This sum included £18.19s.4d for refreshments. This grant was approved by the Secretary, who was instructed to inform the District Committee that 'the principle of allocating money for such purposes would be referred to the sub-committee which had been appointed to review the question of grants for purposes of a non-capital nature... pending the decision of the Miners' Welfare Committee as a result of this enquiry, no expenditure should be incurred in respect of next year's competition without express approval of the Committee being obtained in advance'.

In 1929, the Central Committee decided to inform the District Committee that they had always been opposed to these expenses being charged to the Fund, and were not prepared to approve the arrangement any longer. Despite this, Mr Witzel, in the absence of the joint secretaries, sent in an official letter on 16th September stating that the Final had been played at Abercarn and the expenses amounted to £60. The Central Committee reminded the District Committee that they had been consistently warned since the previous year that the expenses would not be met again. The Committee received an official letter stating that they were abandoning the competition in future but the official letter was accompanied by a personal letter to the Secretary stating that the Joint Secretaries were personally liable for £45 and that unless the Miners' Welfare Committee were prepared to make an allocation, they proposed to reimburse themselves by drawing a cheque on the District Expense Account. The personal letter was referred by the Committee to Mr Palk and Mr Mason for their opinions. In the meantime, the Joint Secretaries asked for a meeting on 31st October which was cancelled by Mr Gibson on the morning of the 31st. The interview was eventually held on 29th January 1930. On 14th March 1930, the Secretary received a letter stating that part of the expenses amounting to £34.8s.8d, including the refreshment account, had been settled by payment from the District expenses. On Lord Chelmsford's advice, the Central Committee decided to accept the plea that there had been a misunderstanding as regards the 1929 expenses but made it quite clear that there could be no similar plea in the future. The draft letter to the District Committee was vetted by four members of the Mines Department and Lord Chelmsford.

Between August 1927 and December 1929, a similar situation had arisen with the Billiards Competition that the District Committee had organised.

At the beginning of June 1930, the Central Committee received a letter from the South Wales District Committee requesting a meeting to see whether a satisfactory settlement could be arrived at, so that the unpleasantness which might result if legal proceedings were taken by the Central Committee could be avoided.

Mr Shinwell agreed in principle and was prepared to support the Central Committee in whatever manner might be found necessary. He suggested that the Committee should invite a deputation from South Wales to meet them and see whether the matter could, if possible, be satisfactorily arranged without his personal intervention.

The deputation from South Wales was invited to the September and October meetings, but found it impossible to attend. Mr Gibson subsequently wrote to the Secretary to apologise for their nonattendance. A further invitation was sent for 26th November 1930.

The deputation from the District Committee, composed of Mr B. Nicholas, Mr B. Morrell and Mr Thomas Richards, attended the Committee meeting on 26th November 1930. Mr Gibson was unable to attend. The deputation set out their position that the Central Committee had approved the expenditure in previous years and the great interest the men had in the competitions. Lord Chelmsford explained the legal position and it was pointed out that the District Committee since 1928 had deliberately been carrying on despite the clear decision of the Central Committee. The question was settled by allowing the District to invest a sum of £2,000 as an endowment.[61]

Following the issue of the circular on maintenance grants for non-capital outlay in connection with recreation schemes (MWF 136) at the end of November 1929 (see Chapter 8, Recreation), Fife District Committee sent in two letters; one asking whether the Committee would authorise payment of rates from the District Fund in 1929/30 as formerly and the other observing that the District Committee had already indicated to some Local Committees that grants to the extent of two-thirds of the costs for recovering billiard tables would be recommended and hoping that the Committee would see their way to make grants in these cases. At the January meeting of the Central Committee, it was decided with regard to the first letter that there was no reason for treating Fife differently but, as regards the second letter, they agreed that any promises made by the District Committee prior to the Circular might be honoured.

The Fife Committee wrote back to say that, if no assistance were given with rates, feu-duty and insurance, several of the Institutes would inevitably close. Since 1926, owing to bad trade and unemployment, the institutes had had a very difficult time. Fife had been in communication with the Collector of Rates and had been able to get time granted and legal action postponed. They asked the Central Committee to reconsider. The Committee doubted whether all or any of the schemes fell entirely within the conditions, and asked for further information.

The Fife District Committee replied to the Committee pointing out that that there were a number of cases where some pits had been closed for all or part of the year of rate assessment and seemed to fall under the provision of the circular. In March 1930, the Central Committee were still not satisfied with the information supplied and asked for more.

Fife appointed a small sub-committee to investigate the financial position of individual institutes. They reported that 10 institutes were facing closure unless they received financial assistance. The District Welfare Committee accordingly recommended that the rates, feu-duty and insurance for the 10 named institutes should be paid and they certified that each had been so greatly reduced in numbers of members and in income to be unable to carry on without assistance. The Committee considered that the conditions laid down in the circular had been met and £435.11s.7d was allocated.[62]

Arising out of Circular No 134 (Insurance of Welfare Buildings) issued in October 1929, the Secretary had been asked by Warwick District Committee to visit all Welfare buildings in Warwickshire District, with Mr Parker to report whether the insurance against fire was considered sufficient. 31 schemes were inspected in May 1930, 4 were not insured at all and at least 7 were under insured. The District Committee was putting this in order, but it was doubted whether this matter was receiving equal attention. Coincidently, the Addison Colliery Jubilee Institute at Ryton (Durham) had been destroyed by fire on 18th May 1930. More than £200 worth of books belonging to the Addison Welfare Committee, housed in the Institute, had been destroyed. They were not insured. This was the third welfare building known to have been destroyed in the last 18 months.

Also, in May 1930, the Secretary visited 17 schemes in South Wales District accompanied by Mr Parker and (except for 5 schemes) by Captain O'Kelly. The number of schemes visited on this occasion did not represent a sufficient proportion of the number in the District as a whole to justify a general report, but they included examples which confirmed the previous impressions of schemes in South Wales.

Many of the schemes in South Wales had been initiated on an overly ambitious basis for the size of the supporting community. Difficulties of developing 'the only available sites' was given as an excuse for not spending more on the acquisition of a suitable site from the outset. The Swansea area could have also benefitted from more frequent visits from Mr Mason, the District Organiser.[63]

In July, the Secretary visited 3 schemes in Bristol and 22 in the Somerset District in the company of Mr Parker. They also attended the opening by Lord Chelmsford of the Paulton Hospital (Somerset) extension which consisted of a ward with eight beds and two observation wards.

The only recreational schemes in the Bristol District were the three institutes at Coalpit Heath, Pucklechurch and Bedminister Down. £4,852 had been spent from the Fund on these schemes and, considering their small size, seemed particularly good value for the money.

In Somerset, the recreational schemes consisted of 15 recreation grounds and 12 institutes, the amount allocated for the former had been £11,618 and for the latter £4,782. 12 recreation grounds and 9 institutes were visited. Considering the small amount of money available, the results were very good and testified to the hard work of the Area and Local Committees. All the schemes were well kept, and the small institutes particularly were fine examples of what a few hundred pounds could do when supported by local enthusiasm. All the schemes were self-supporting despite the small membership.[64]

In September 1930, the Secretary visited 15 schemes in the Leicester District in the company of Captain O'Kelly for the first day and Mr Parker on the second day.

The amount allocated for recreation up to 1930 was £41,889 of which £19,000 had gone on the Coalville Baths, £12,212 on nine institutes (two not begun) and £10,677 on ten recreation grounds.

The Secretary had already visited two institutes previously. The five he visited he found to be good value for money, well-kept and well managed, Pegg's Green being the only unsatisfactory one in the two latter respects.

Among nine recreation grounds (Ibstock recreation ground having been visited previously), there was much variation. Four were good and six were poor. Of the £3,238 spent on the poor schemes, £2,140 had been used for the purchase of 35 acres of land, which was unnecessarily expensive and, in two cases, very unsuitable for development except at great expense. It was advised that further assistance should be given to schemes which had proved themselves worthy of it, rather than on a purely per capita basis as it had appeared to have been done in the past.[65]

In March 1930, the Committee had before them the Safety in Mines Research Board's final estimates for 1930/31 which amounted to £51,800 of which it was estimated that £12,443 would be met from the endowment income and £1,458 from the Treasury grant, leaving £36,399 to be found from the Fund in addition to the £1,500 already promised as a contribution to 'safety instruction'.

Mr Fudge, Major Hudspeth and Mr Stedman attended and Major Hudspeth outlined the research being carried out by the Board. With the curtailment of some of the research and some minor economies, they had been able to appoint a Mining Engineer and provide a sum of nearly £4,000 for new work to be organised by him on falls of ground which was the source of far the largest proportion of accidents in mines.

The Committee expressed the view that more work should be undertaken to evolve a reliable gas detector which the Committee asked Mr Fudge to convey back to the Board.[66]

The preliminary estimates for the Safety in Mines Research Board 1931/32, amounting to £56,000, were presented to the Committee in November 1930. The Board was represented by Sir Edward Troup, Dr Wheeler and Mr Stedman.

The preliminary estimates for 1931/32 represented a £4,000 increase on the previous year. The Committee accepted the increased figure of £2,000 for Safety Instruction, but were inclined to stand on their previous limit of £50,000 for the normal research programme. Nearly £4,000 was included in the estimate for work on wire ropes and it was suggested that rope manufacturers might be pressed to contribute some part of this. Professor Wheeler explained that they had already secured an additional £700 (making approximately £1,000 in all) from the Electrical Trades Research Association, which had reduced the provisional estimate.

Dr Wheeler explained that it had become the policy of the Board to give priority to the haulage and falls of ground work and this meant that, if the Committee insisted on their limit of £50,000, the reduction would have to be made in explosive dangers.

The Chairman endeavoured to find out what prospect there was of the Board being satisfied with some other figure, such as £60,000, and suggested that it was the Board's duty to advise how the sum assigned by the Committee should be spent, but not to appeal each year for some higher figure.

It was finally decided to inform the Secretary for Mines that the Committee were prepared to raise their provision for Safety Instruction from £1,500 to £2,000, that they were prepared in due course to receive detailed estimates for the research programme for 1931/32 up to the provisional figure of £54,000 and that, if the life of the Fund was prolonged and they continued to have at their disposal resources similar to those under the present statute, they were prepared in future to raise their limit (excluding the Safety Instruction) from £50,000 to £60,000 to enable the Board to develop progressively the falls of ground and haulage work without prejudice to the reorganisation of the staff they had in view. However, they did expect the Board to refrain from making any proposals for expenditure above the new limit.[67]

In April 1930, a decision was taken to increase the endowment of the National Scholarship Scheme by £10,000 to meet the deficit in 1930/1 of £400. The discrepancy was primarily due the number of scholarships that could be awarded annually with an endowment of £150,000 which had been overestimated when the scheme was designed but only became apparent in 1930 when there had been enough experience to make this clear. The overestimate appeared to have been largely because the estimated costs of the scheme were based mainly on the only comparable scheme existing, that of the Ministry of Agriculture and Fisheries. The Ministry schemes only covered Agriculture degrees, which were offered at universities whose costs were cheaper than the universities to which awards had been made by the Miners' Welfare Scheme. The Ministry scholarships covered only term time while the Miners' Welfare scholarships covered the whole year. Some of the awards were for medical degrees which extended beyond the four years envisaged by the Miners' Welfare scheme.[68]

In May 1930, the successful scholars for the Miners' Welfare National

Scholarship Scheme attended the Committee's meeting. There had been altogether 160 miners' candidates and 460 children of miners' candidates. Overall, those who were successful in 1930 formed the most promising group to whom awards had hitherto been made in any year of the scheme. There were twelve awards made (six A awards and six B awards).[69]

The Committee had become concerned with the number of recommendations that North Wales District Committee had been making for special grants for students from their District Funds, and felt it was necessary to suggest to the District Committee that they should consider limiting these grants in future to cases complying with certain definite conditions; miners or children of miners employed in the mining industry with a definite financial need, a report of a good prospect of being successful in the course, and to have competed for the Miners' Welfare Scholarships unless there was a good reason for the omission. This proposal was considered at the January 1930 meeting of the Committee, and it was decided to send the guidance to North Wales only, so as not to discourage District Committees from recommending special grants.[70]

Birmingham University had first approached the Committee with a proposal for a new mining department in October. The estimated cost of the new building was £30,000 and, if the Miners' Welfare Fund was prepared to find £20,000, the University was prepared to find the balance. The Committee were not convinced that a new department was required and, in February 1930, wrote to ask if there was a possibility of extending the current accommodation. In June 1930, Professor Moss provided the Committee with details of the accommodation provided in the current department and the accommodation in the new building. The present department was considered, until recently, as the most up to date one of any university in the country.

In June 1930, the Committee turned down the scheme on account of the cost. In October 1930, Professor Moss submitted a modified scheme of the extension to the Mining Department at an estimated cost of £9,000. The proposal provided the extra accommodation by modifying the existing building and moving the mineral dressing laboratory to a new building. The University were prepared to provide a sum of £3,000 if the Welfare Committee could find £6,000. The £6,000 was approved at the November meeting of the Committee.[71]

In March 1930, Dudley Education Committee had applied for a grant of £10,000. They proposed to erect a new technical college at a total estimated cost of £136,000 beginning with a part building costing £88,000. This would include a new mining department, and they asked for a contribution from the Miners' Welfare Fund of £10,000. There were only three large collieries in South Staffordshire and Worcester district which would be served by the college. A new department would attract more students but, in relation to the mining population to be served, £10,000 was too great, so a provisional allocation of £6,000 was made.[72]

In September 1930, Cumberland Education Authority applied for a grant to cover the cost of the Miners' portion of the proposed extension of the Workington School and Technical College (Mining Centre including common room estimated cost £7,000). Mr Winstanley had met with the Director, Architect and the Chairman of the Education Committee together with his colleague, Mr Hummel, and Mr Dunn, District Inspector. The Cumberland coalfield was small and scattered, and there was no Advanced Centre accessible from the mining area. When completed, the extended Technical College would function as an Advanced Centre as well as a Senior Centre. An allocation of £8,500 was made. This included the provision for a common room and a 'study room'. Miners came to the classes at Workington from considerable distances, some of them arrived considerably before the time of the classes and some proceeded to the mine for the night shift after the classes.[73]

In November 1930, Fifeshire Education Authority's proposal to improve the accommodation at Fife Mining School, Cowdenbeath was considered by the Committee. The proposal involved the erection of a new building adjoining the site of the current building. The estimated cost of the building and equipment was £23,000. The proposal was likely to be approved by the County Council only if a substantial grant was forthcoming from the Miners' Welfare Fund. Sir Thomas Hudson-Beare recommended that a provisional allocation of £15,000 might be made subject to the detailed proposals of the Authority being approved.

Following a letter from the Board of Education, Durham had reconsidered its scheme for the provision of Mining Centres in its area and submitted a revised scheme in November 1930. The proposals were for senior and advanced centres at Bishop Auckland, Houghton-Le-Spey and Blaydon at a cost of £54,000, £12,000 more than the amount allocated to the Authority by the Welfare Committee in its letter of 19th May 1926 for the purpose of building Mining Centres. Mr Winstanley considered the proposal to be sound, comprehensive and suitable.[74]

1931 was the fifth and final year of the second quinquennium. Mr Shinwell, then Secretary for Mines, on behalf of the Labour Government, was proceeding with his Bill to extend the levy for five years but there was a very grave difference of opinion in the industry about two things; the amount of the levy and its duration. That difference of opinion became acute in the Standing Committee C held on 24th March 1931. The miners took the view that the levy should remain at one penny and the owners thought it should come down to a farthing or perhaps one-eighth of a penny. Mr Shinwell recognised that, in the economic conditions of the industry, there was a case to be examined. Subsequently, Mr

Shinwell announced that he was willing to appoint a committee of inquiry into the question of the issue.

In July 1931, the Mining Industry (Welfare Fund) Act 1931 received Royal Assent and extended the Fund for a further five years. In the same month, Mr Shinwell appointed a Committee of Inquiry consisting of Lord Chelmsford (Chairman), Lord Erskine MP, Mr Gordon McDonald MP, Mr Geoffrey Mander MP, Mr A K McCosh and Mr Alf Smith. The terms of reference were 'To enquire how the objects of Section 20 of the Mining Industry Act 1920 had been met, what remains to be done and whether the scope of the Fund and the existing machinery for it and administration as defined in the Section and as developed in practice are satisfactory for the future and to report on all these matters with particular reference to the question of the amount and the duration of the levy in the future'.

As Chairman of the Inquiry Committee, Lord Chelmsford was not able to continue as the Chairman of the Central Committee, so he was replaced by Lord Noel-Buxton who attended the July meeting of the Committee to formally take over the Chairmanship. Lord Noel-Buxton had been a liberal Member of Parliament for Whitby and Norfolk North. He joined the Labour Party in 1919 and continued as MP for Norfolk North until 1930, when he was raised to the peerage. He served twice as Minister of Agriculture and Fisheries and was a Privy Councillor.[75]

After four years, the Baths Fund was in a significant deficit of £356,248 (deficits of £222,000 from the Royalties Levy, £92,248 from interest and £44,000 from the General Fund) at the beginning of 1931. Instead of the planned £4,000,000 being spent in 10 years, the total amount available would only be £3,109,380 which would have meant a slower rate of bath construction. The Committee decided to make up the deficit on the output levy interest and the General Fund by contributing a further sum of £136,247.14s.11d from the General Fund and to contribute a definite sum of £150,000 from that source in 1931 even if the deficit did not exceed the estimated amount of £122,400.

As to the future, the Committee decided that, if the output levy was extended beyond the end of 1931, to reaffirm the Royal Commission's recommendation that no less that £150,000 per annum should be contributed from the General Fund for Baths.

The company at Broomside had been asked to undertake further modifications to the steam system, based on the advice given by Sir Thomas Hudson Beare and then run further tests. The Company had made alternative proposals, so Mr Rayner had visited Broomside in November where he discovered the Company had closed the steam trap. Sir Thomas Hudson Beare considered this to be unsatisfactory, but it was decided to drop the matter.

In January 1931, Maypole pithead baths (Lancashire) was opened. This installation had a women's section, but no boot cleaning or greasing equipment had been provided in this section, as none had been provided in the women's section at Broomside. As Cdr. Coote thought that women should in future, as a principle, have such equipment, the Committee approved an allocation of £30.

Work on Blaenavon pithead baths had commenced in March 1930, but progress was much slower than expected. The contractor had been warned in November. In December 1930, the scheme was visited again by Mr Rayner and Mr Traylor, who found that little work had been carried out.

At Dinnington Main (South Yorkshire), the workmen had agreed to meet half the cost of substituting an ambulance room for the first aid room, so the Committee agreed to meet the cost of the other half, which added a further £350 to the cost of the installation.

The workmen were still pressing for the space in front of the building at Dinnington to be made suitable for accommodating buses. They had submitted a specification and estimate of £193. In the circumstances, the Committee agreed to provide the sum if the workmen undertook to get the work done satisfactorily.[76]

The decision on the extension for Llay Main (North Wales) had been delayed from the Committee's November 1930 meeting pending the reply from the District Committee. The District Committee wanted to see Llay Main done first and extended in 1931 if the Committee could see their way to include Hafod in the programme for 1932. The Llay Main extension would take up the estimated share of the District for 1931 and 1932, but Hafod could be undertaken in 1932 by the Committee temporarily financing Hafod from other balances on the Baths Fund.[77]

The openings of the Baths at Moston, Woolmer, Wearmouth and Auchengeich collieries were reported at the March meeting of the Committee. The first three of these were used to over 90% capacity in the first week.

Maypole had opened at the end of January, with accommodation for 1,512 men and 36 women as agreed at the preliminary investigation in June 1929. The numbers employed had risen to 1,737 men and 39 women and were expected to increase to 2,000 men and 42 women and the Trustees had applied for an immediate extension as they had a waiting list of 60. All the workmen contributed to the upkeep levy, whether they could be accommodated or not. The Committee approved an extension for 378 men at an estimated cost of £2,900 and £75 for the addition of a storeroom which could be met from the savings on the current contract.

The number employed at Cannop, which had opened in December 1930, had also increased from 960 to 1,050 men and the Trustees had asked for additional lockers and cubicles because the winding rate had increased. A plan was selected providing 48 pairs of lockers and 12 cubicles and an allocation of £1,500 was made to meet the cost of these.

Cdr. Coote and the Secretary had met with the Management Committee at Treorchy to discuss certain matters with which the Treorchy Committee felt dissatisfied. The Central Committee subsequently decided to renovate the cubicles, give the condensing tank and pipes a coat of special paint, make good the damp-proofing of the walls and to provide two new water coolers, but not to do anything about the accommodation for overcoats, water connections, electric wiring and decorations.[78]

Devon had been opened on 11th February, but the number of men employed had risen from 408 to 519 by April and was expected to rise to 650 shortly. There was a waiting list of 110. An allocation of £2,000 was approved to add 208 lockers and 11 cubicles.

A water treatment plant had had to be installed at Pensford at an estimated cost of £250, but it was expected that this would be covered by the contract. At Britannia, arrangements to discharge the bath waste into the sewers of the Rhymney Valley Sewage Board had had to be switched to the sewers of the Bedwellty Urban Council in the High Street at Pengam at an extra cost of approximately £350.

Lothians District Committee applied for expenses amounting to £57.5s.7d incurred by the Shotts Iron Company Ltd. in their appeal against assessment at Roshin Pithead Baths. They had successfully appealed against the Rates Assessor's figure of £100 which had been reduced to £19.2s.6d by the Valuation Appeal Court. These expenses were paid by the Baths Fund, as the decision would be of value in pursuing other appeals.[79]

Cdr. Coote reported to the Committee on the 5 schemes which had been opened in May 1931: Rose Heyworth (South Wales), Badderley (Warwick), Newmarket Silkstone (West Yorkshire), Bradford (Lancashire) and Viewpark (Lanark).

In May 1931, Lanark District Committee made a similar application to Lothians District Committee for reimbursement of legal fees amounting to £13.9s.6d in connection with their rate assessments at Fortissat and Southfields.

Upkeep costs for the first year for Ravenhead Colliery (Lancashire), Whitburn (Durham) and the second year at Broomside were reported at the May Committee meeting. Broomside had spent a sum of £108.8s.9d out of the revenue on improvements to the approach to the site in the expectation that they would be refunded the amount. After a report on the subject by Cdr. Coote, the Committee decided to meet the cost. It was noted that the water and coal consumption at Broomside had also decreased.[80]

In June 1931, the Committee considered an application for a laundry, repair shop, store house and cycle accommodation for Florence (Staffordshire) which had been opened in April 1930. In the ordinary way, the District would be asked to recommend a grant from the District Fund but the District had already met half the cost of each installation and made available £70,000 in the last five years, so the Committee decided that the District Committee, if they approved the proposal, might reasonably expect the addition to be provided from what they had already contributed.

An additional £450 was allocated to Blaenavon Pithead Baths towards the cost of laying the water main from the Bedwellty Council Storage to the Baths. The Urban Council had hoped to obtain a grant from either the Ministry of Health or the Unemployment Grants Committee, but their application had been unfavourably received.[81]

The openings of pithead baths at Wharnscliffe, Silkstone, Horden, Bannockburn and Bilsthorpe were reported at the July meeting of the Committee.

Loganlea pithead bath had been opened in May 1930 with accommodation for 504. The numbers at the pit had increased to 629 and there was a long waiting list. £975 was allocated to address this problem by adding 120 pairs of lockers.

In July 1931, Mr Forshaw, Chief Architect, presented a report in which he expressed his fear that the pithead baths building programme would fall short of the planned number by two for a second year. Each year the loss of one scheme could be attributed to the withdrawal of a colliery after the work on the plans for it were well in advance: Ouston in 1930 and St Helens was probably a similar case for 1931.

The loss of the second scheme each year was a result of the disorganisation forced on the Building Section by having to wait for essential information from Colliery Companies, local authorities, water companies etc. There was additionally the increase in extensions and additions outside the main programme which would further impact on the main programme. To meet the increase in work, the Committee agreed to an increase in provision of temporary staff on the quantity surveyor side, and advised Mr Forshaw to keep the architectural side under review and to report again if necessary.[82]

By the September meeting of the Committee, a further four baths had been opened at Bilsthorpe, Craghead, Hauchwood and Langwith. Bilsthorpe also had a canteen which was serving as many as 340 men at a time.[83]

The tender for the erection of the women's baths at Parsonage Colliery (Lancashire), which had already been provided with men's baths, was approved at the September 1931 meeting. The plans had been based on the provision made at Maypole Colliery which was owned by the same company. The colliery company then asked for the scheme to be reconsidered, partly as they anticipated employing more women and partly because they had learnt quite a lot about women's requirements from their experience at Maypole.

Mr Rayner, Mr Kemp, and Cdr. Coote met the Company's General Manager, Agent and Colliery Manager on 14th October. A three hour discussion produced valuable information that the Baths Building Branch had been trying to get ever since Maypole was completed. As the women entered the building at the same time, a greater allowance for cubicles, wash basins and space for dressing and undressing between lockers was required. A rest room was also required. It was therefore proposed to provide one cubicle for every six women, and enough hand-washing space for thirty. It was felt that a central seat between lockers would meet the women's requirements. If these proposals were adopted by the Committee, the same standard would have to be adopted in any future installations for women.

A further report was made to the Committee by Mr Forshaw in November 1931 on the need for an increase in Architectural Staff, to prevent the work of the main construction programme falling behind. This was the third time he had raised the problem. In July 1931, he had outlined the difficulties that were being encountered and, since then, another large extension (Wearmouth) had been authorised and the women's accommodation at Parsonage had had to be redesigned. He could foresee that the number of tenders submitted would have to fall as the Quantity Surveyors were approaching breaking point. The size of the present staff did not permit any margin for undertaking increasing numbers of extensions and ancillary accommodation being dealt with and the constant pressure of work was compromising the opportunity to improve the design of buildings and equipment. He recommended the recruitment of 3 additional Architectural Draughtsmen, one of each grade and one additional Mechanical Draughtsman Grade I.[84]

In January 1931, the Central Committee had again under consideration the legal charges incurred by South Wales District Welfare Committee. In 1926, with the approval of the Central Committee, South Wales had instructed Messrs Morgan, Bruce and Nicholas and Messrs Kensoles and Prosser and Co., Joint Solicitors to examine the titles of the properties in the South Wales District in order to verify that trusts had been set up appropriately in order to protect the monies that had been allocated from the Miners' Welfare Fund.

An examination of the titles revealed that not only had no uniform method been adopted in establishing the various associations but also, in a very large number of cases, no trusts as to users were declared at all, that in a very few cases was any provision made to ensure that the monies allocated from the Fund were to be used for the purposes declared in the Mining Industry Act 1920, that Trusts of a Charitable nature did not comply with the provision of the Mortmain Charitable Uses Act 1888 rendering the whole title void and that, in some cases, associations had been registered under the Friendly Society Act as Working Men's Clubs. In all, over 200 schemes had to be dealt with.

At the April 1929 meeting of the Central Committee, a letter was read from the District Committee furnishing estimated figures of liability in respect of the Joint Solicitors' charges up to 31st March 1929. These figures caused the Committee much concern and they expressed a hope that Mr Naish (Mines Department Accountant) would be able to find an opportunity of examining the position in detail when he was in Cardiff.

Mr Naish met the Joint Solicitors on 28th May 1929, and, after a general discussion, the Joint Solicitors agreed that they would not press for the full scale of fees but would grant an abatement. At that date, the work was so far from completion that it was impossible to estimate the likely total expenditure. Further meetings were held with the Joint Solicitors in Cardiff on 19th September 1929, 24th January, and 20th June 1930 when Mr Naish was accompanied by Mr Witzel, representing the District Welfare Committee. However, matters were still not sufficiently advanced to enable a settlement to be negotiated.

A complete statement of costs, including an estimate to cover outstanding matters, was dispatched to Mr Witzel under cover of a letter dated 13th September 1930. A total of £5,364.12s.9d was quoted to cover completed and uncompleted matters.

Advice was taken by Mr Naish from the Solicitors' Department of the Board of Trade who advised that an ad hoc arrangement would be more likely to give a more satisfactory settlement from the Central Committee's point of view.

As Mr Naish was not satisfied with the offer of £315 rebate, on 7th November 1930, accompanied by Mr Witzel in Cardiff, Mr Naish met Mr Hall of Messrs Morgan, Bruce and Nicholas and Mr Kenshole of Messrs Kenshole, Prosser, and Company. After a protracted discussion, Mr Naish managed to reduce the claims to £4,820 which was formally approved by the District Committee on 12th November 1930 and forwarded to the Central Committee for endorsement.[85]

The Secretary visited North Staffordshire in September 1931 to inspect the recreational schemes which had received grants from the District Fund. There were only seven schemes for which £10,636 had been allocated, representing only ¼% of the total allocations from the Fund for recreation while the number of miners in the District was about 2½% of the whole country. Most of the District money had been devoted to the Convalescent Home at Rudyard and the provision of pithead baths but there was still a balance of £35,000.

Except for small institutes erected recently at Leycett and Fegg Hayes, all the schemes were cricket clubs of longstanding at Silverdale, Scott Hay, Bignall End, Chell and Norton. Pavilion-institutes had been provided at Scott Hay and Bignall End (which also had a bowling green) and tennis courts at Silverdale.

Most of the work had been done under the supervision of the Advisory Branch. The schemes were well supported, and there was evidence of considerable voluntary effort. However, no provision had been made for children, and none of the institutes had tried to secure a circulating library service from the Local Authorities.

A great many of the miners in this District lived in the built-up areas of the 'Five Towns' where it was difficult to see what could be done apart from the convalescent facilities and pithead baths, but there were still places suitable for recreation grounds and institutes in the District.[86]

At the February 1931 meeting of the Committee, applications for the replacement of one ambulance in Northumberland and two in Durham were under consideration. Two had been purchased in 1924 and one in 1923. The decision on these applications was deferred while the Secretary made enquiries.

In April, the Secretary submitted tables summarising the number, cost, and date of purchase of ambulances provided by the Fund. Four vehicles had already been replaced prior to the three replacements under consideration. As to the existing depreciation arrangements, adequate arrangements existed only in the five Scottish schemes, South Derbyshire (endowment) and in Brodsworth in South Yorkshire. It was agreed that the matter required further investigation and Professor Collis and the Secretary agreed to do this. Meanwhile, the three applications were approved but the District Committees were informed that they must not submit any more applications for replacements pending the completion of the enquiry.

In July 1931, Professor Collis submitted a summary of the information collected since the April meeting (see Chapter 9 for further details) regarding Welfare Ambulances. He had concluded that ambulances provided for individual collieries were likely to be uneconomic but centralised schemes, as in South Wales, Somerset and South Derby, should be encouraged. A centralised scheme should be provided with a sufficient endowment to meet the greater part of the replacement cost or allocations for complete overhauls at the end of five years and for replacements after ten years. It was agreed that the matter should be referred to the Inquiry Committee under the Chairmanship of Lord Chelmsford. It was also suggested that the advantages of a centralised scheme would be summarised and circulated to District Committees with a view to discussion at the Annual Conference in November 1931.

A full discussion of the issue was held at the Annual Conference and Districts were asked to submit any suggestions they might have on Welfare Ambulances as the Inquiry Committee would be laying down lines of conduct for the future.[87]

The final estimates of the Safety in Mines Research Board for 1931/32 were presented at the March 1931 meeting of the Central Committee. Mr Woodburn and Mr Fowler attended on behalf of the Board and were asked to explain the increase of £484 on the work on Falls of Ground being carried out by Mr Hudspeth, the work at Imperial College and the work on Wire Ropes.

The Committee approved the estimates of a net total of £54,667 of which £14,133 would be met from endowment income and the Treasury grant and allocated a sum of £40,550 to cover the balance including a special grant of £2,000 to meet the cost of Safety Instruction.[88]

South Yorkshire and West Yorkshire District Committees each applied for funding for Safety-First Badges in July 1931. The Districts were recommending that the compulsory subjects of the first year of the Junior Course (for boys who were entering the pits for the first time) should include a course of Instruction in Safety Principles to be held for 1½ hours each week during the winter session. In coming to this decision, they were largely influenced by the fact that the proportion of accidents to boys was extremely high in the first year of their work. A badge would be provided for mining students who completed the course in Safety Principles satisfactorily during the first year of their employment by passing a test having attended not less than two-thirds of the possible attendances. The applications by South Yorkshire (£36) and West Yorkshire (£24) for a grant from the Miners' Welfare Fund would cover the cost of 2000 badges, which would more than cover the number qualifying in the first year. Each badge would be enamelled, and the holder's name engraved on its back.[89]

In January 1931, the Committee considered an application from Sheffield University Mining Department for £11,210. The Committee had already made an allocation of £8,000 for the new mining department on condition that a like sum would be raised locally (£9,942 achieved). The original estimates for the total cost of the site, building, fittings and equipment was £26,000 but the only available site was found to have a layer of made ground at the surface, which necessitated the foundations being deepened; this involved an additional expenditure of £2,745. The total cost was £29,152, towards which the University then had £17,942 and were asking for an allocation for the balance. Due to the depressed state of the Mining Industry, the University could not ask for further assistance from the local Owners; the local Coal Trades Association had contributed £35,827 in the last 8 years for the upkeep of the departments of Mining and Fuel Technology, and would largely provide for the maintenance of the new department when built. The application was supported by Mr Winstanley, the Committee's Education Assessor for England and Wales.

Staffordshire Education Committee also made an application for a grant in January 1931. This was to enable them to provide a new senior mining course centre at Knutton to serve the area around Silverdale, Chesterton, Audley,

Halmerend, Leycett and Madeley. Senior classes had already been provided at Silverend for the last four years during which time the student numbers had increased, but the classes were held in an old-fashioned elementary school and only in the evening. It was therefore proposed to build a small institute beside a new senior school which was being built at Knutton. The school would be available for the mining students in the evening and day classes could be held in the institute. The freehold of the land on which the institute would stand had been purchased and the estimated cost of the building was £5,300 and of the furniture and equipment £750. The application was supported by Mr Winstanley and provisionally approved by the Committee.[90]

An application for a new mining department at Nottingham University College had come before the Central Committee at the beginning of 1931. The mining department was still in the city with the main university building situated over 4 miles away. The College Authorities had made very expensive proposals which, in the opinion of Mr Winstanley, were considerably in excess of the most optimistic forecasts of the probable demand for full-time mining courses. The total area of the proposed building was double the total area of the new mining department at Leeds University, and had an estimated cost of £51,800 to £53,750, plus £5,000 for internal furnishings.

Any assistance given by the Fund would have to be regarded as for the provision of a new advanced mining education centre, not for a new university centre due to the proximity of Sheffield and Birmingham. The placing of the new department close to the main buildings of the College would more conveniently serve the whole and part-time students, but disadvantage evening students unless rapid and cheap transport was provided.

Mr Winstanley and Mr Anderson met Professor Macmillan in Nottingham on 9th February, and it was agreed that new sketch plans showing the minimum requirements for accommodation at the proposed new centre for advanced mining studies should be submitted to the Miners' Welfare Committee.

The Committee then gave further consideration to the proposals of the College Authorities and came to the conclusion that a senior and advanced course mining centre in the city of Nottingham would meet the needs of the part-time and evening students (who far outnumbered the whole time) much better than a centre at Highfields would. They recognised that the accommodation at Shakespeare Street (the site they then occupied) was not altogether satisfactory, but would be prepared to consider a grant towards the cost of its improvement.

On the instruction of the Central Committee given in March 1931, Mr Anderson and Mr Winstanley had a discussion with Principal Stewart of Nottingham University College regarding the proposed new mining department. They found that the total number of students for 1930–31 was only 70 and had been steadily declining, so the present accommodation, while not altogether suitable, made it difficult to justify a grant from the Miners' Welfare Fund large enough to enable the college to proceed with a new building. Advice was given to Mr Stewart as to how he might increase student numbers to improve the likelihood of their application being successful. Mr Stewart agreed to follow Mr Anderson's and Mr Winstanley's advice regarding numbers, and said he would recommend the withdrawal of the present application to his Advisory Committee until they had a stronger case.[91]

The Glamorgan Education Authority's proposal to improve and extend the Treforest School of Mining, which was given over to them by the former owners in 1929, was considered in March 1931. The Miners' Welfare Committee had already paid the cost of maintenance for one year following the transfer and, at the same time, had informed the Education Authority that they were prepared to consider making an allocation for extensions and improvements to the school and for equipment and were invited to submit their proposals. The extensions were estimated to cost £47,000, and with equipment and furniture, the proposal came to £57,721.

Mr Winstanley found the plans satisfactory, and the extensions would enable Treforest to rank as fully-equipped mining college, capable of dealing with all aspects of mining education to the highest level. He suggested that the Education Authority should be informed that while the Miners' Welfare Committee were prepared to make an allocation of £20,000 towards the cost of their proposals, this sum would be substantially increased if they could come to an arrangement with the University of Wales, in the same way as Manchester College of Technology provided the faculty of technology for the University of Manchester.

In May 1931, the Committee agreed that they were prepared to make a grant up to £47,000.

A meeting of representatives of the Education Authority and Cardiff University College discussed their proposal and appointed a sub-committee on which Mr A. M. Anderson (Assistant Secretary) represented the Miners' Welfare Committee. The main proposals of the sub-committee were as follows:

1. Students at the University College taking degrees in mining would spend two years studying pure science at the college, and two years studying science at Treforest, the latter to include a period of work in a mine.
2. The present staff at Treforest would be accepted as suitable, but a Professor of Mining would be appointed by the College who would be head of the department of the mining school and would control the work of the mining students both at the College and mining school, and the non-university mining work at the school.

3. The College would pay the salary of the Professor, and the Education Authority would be responsible for the accommodation.

These proposals met with Mr Winstanley's approval. The amount of the allocation from the Fund was then dependen t on the approval of the Glamorgan County Council and the University of Wales and the final estimate.[92]

Proposals for the mining department at the proposed new Doncaster Technical School had been considered in February 1931, and Mr Winstanley had been asked to investigate whether the Committee were justified in increasing their provisional allocation of £3,500. Mr Winstanley discussed the matter with Doncaster Education Authority. Subsequently, a letter was received from Doncaster Education Authority asking if the Committee's allocation might be increased as the estimated proportion of the new building (total cost £41,500) to be spent on the mining department was £18,000 (previously £17,000). In the light of this, Mr Winstanley recommended a further grant of £10,000, making £13,500 in all, which brought Doncaster into line with allocations already made to other county boroughs in the area.

In November 1931, the Central Committee was made aware by Doncaster Education Committee that an old river, enclosed in a culvert, had been found on the ground and that the additional work required had increased the original anticipated expenditure by £2,521. It was agreed to increase the allocation by that amount as this new allocation would still not bring it up to the estimated cost of the mining part of School.[93]

In October 1931, the Committee was asked by the Secretary for Mines to consider a certain percentage reduction in their staff salaries which had recently been imposed by the Treasury on Civil Servants in receipt of inclusive salaries.

The Country had recently come off the gold standard which was likely to constitute a cut in money values of the salaries, many of which appeared to the Chairman to be already low. The staff also had no security of tenure or pension rights.

For staff employed by the Miners' Welfare Committee at Headquarters and those employed by the District Welfare Committees whose salaries were paid out of the Fund, any cut in salary would accrue not to the Exchequer but the Miners' Welfare Fund. After a long discussion, the meeting passed two resolutions, as they were aware that the first resolution would meet with strong departmental and ministerial pressure.

Resolution 1. 'That in view of the conditions under which their staff are employed, the Miners' Welfare Committee cannot see their way to making any reduction in the present rates of pay'.

Resolution 2. 'That the Miners' Welfare Committee offer to assist the Exchequer by paying in future the cost of the salaries, expenses and accommodation of those members of the Mines Department staff who are directly occupied on secretarial work of the Fund and whose services are at present provided at the expense of the State'.

The Committee then invited Sir Edward Troup to hear the result of the meeting, as the Mines Department had proposed similar cuts to be applied to the Research Board staff. The Committee decided that Resolution 2 would apply to the secretarial staff of the Board.[94]

While the Miners' Welfare Fund finished 1931 with the certainty of an extension for a further 5 years, the Fund's future income was still under consideration by the Inquiry Committee.

FOUR

THE COMMITTEE BECOMES THE COMMISSION
1932–1939

1932 was a year of uncertainty for the Committee, as they waited for the publication of the Inquiry Committee under the Chairmanship of Lord Chelmsford, which completed its report in December but was not published until the end of January 1933.

After the Inquiry Committee had been set up in July 1931, the Committee took the view that 'It would be wise both for ourselves and for the district welfare committees not to become too deeply committed as regards the application of future revenue, lest some modification of the rate of the levy or in the purposes on which it may be spent be recommended and adopted by the Government before the expiration of the period recently enacted'. In view of the uncertainty as to the future of the Miners' Welfare Fund, the Committee decided to make no more allocations for new schemes in 1932, except for schemes or self-contained parts, the completion of which was not dependent upon further allocations in the future.

The Committee in 1932 remained unaltered from the previous year, except for the replacement of Mr A. J. Cook, who had died in 1931, by Mr Peter Lee and, on the promotion of Mr Ravenshear to other duties in the Mines Department, Mr Stedman was appointed as Secretary to the Committee on 3rd June 1932.

There was a further reduction in 1932 in the amount paid into the Fund from the output levy; £795,236 compared with £998,748 in 1931 and £1,038,041 in 1930. There was also a reduction in the receipts from the royalties levy; £204,000 compared with £220,000 in 1931 and £217,000 in 1930.[1]

Despite the Committee expressing in 1931, their strong disapproval of Local and District Committees making commitments without approval having been obtained, the practice had not ceased in 1932. In 1932, the Committee did withhold a grant in such circumstances and, if further instances recurred, the Committee felt bound to make a rule that no grants would be made from the Fund for work already carried out whether paid for or not.

The number of allocations for recreational purposes made in 1932 was 565, bringing the number of allocations since the Fund was established to a total of 5,657. The number of allocations for new schemes was 40 and altogether 1,289 different schemes had received allocations.

The largest allocations made during 1932 for new schemes were £4,600 for a recreation ground at Snydale (West Yorkshire), £4,500 for the Workmen's Library and Institute at Cymmer, Porth (South Wales), £4,000 for Tylorstown Workmen's Hall and Institute (South Wales) and £3,381 for Hamersterley Recreation Ground (Durham). The Snydale allocation was for purchasing seven acres of land and laying it out as a recreation ground, including football and cricket grounds, three tennis courts, a bowling green, a pavilion and a children's playground. The grant for Cymmer was for the alteration and extension of an institute erected in 1893, and that for Tylorstown, for a new hall and institute to be erected on a site purchased for £2,080. The total cost of the latter scheme was estimated at £11,000 of which the Local Committee had already raised about £3,400. The Hamersterley Recreation Ground would cost about £6,200 to complete and was on a site of 6½ acres, about half of which was purchased for £25 and the remainder presented by the colliery company. The allocation being made would provide for a bowling green, four hard tennis courts, a pavilion and a children's playground.

The largest of the supplementary allocations was £8,000 for Thoresby Institute and Recreation Ground, £7,050 for Clipstone Institute and Recreation Ground, £5,886 for Ollerton Institute and Recreation Ground (all in Nottinghamshire) and £6,000 for Ifton Institute and Recreation Ground (North Wales). The Thoresby allocation was to provide an institute and to add a cricket and football field to the recreation ground, that for Clipstone was for the provision of a club and institute in addition to the existing recreation ground and that for Ollerton was to extend the existing institute, to repay part of a loan made by the colliery company in respect of its original erection and to add various features to the recreation ground. The allocation for Ifton was to complete the institute, for which a grant of £5,000 had already been made, and to provide a recreation ground.

An allocation of £5,000 was made to the South Wales Federation of Boys' Clubs for the provision of club buildings. The same amount was granted in 1931 from which four clubs had been provided.

Several allocations were made for several purposes new to the Fund. One of these was an allocation of £750 from the South Wales District Fund towards the building of a conference and holiday centre at Cold Knap. The centre was being provided by the Welsh National Council of Young Men's Christian Association at a total cost of £5,000, and was intended to serve as a meeting place for workmen's institute conferences, or for welfare, social or other organisations that needed to bring workers together for longer or shorter periods during the year. It was estimated that 73% of the persons attending these meetings would belong to the mining community. In addition, the centre would be used to provide workers' families with holiday accommodation at a cheap rate and 25–30% of the available holiday places would be allocated to members of the mining community of South Wales.

Another new type of scheme was for two institutes, for which £1,400 was allocated from the Durham District Fund for the use of the residents in the Aged Miners' Homes at Shincliffe and Houghall which were old colliery villages occupied solely by aged miners, who were many miles from any institute of any description.[2]

During 1932, 68 allocations, of which 15 were new schemes, were made in connection with the health of miners bringing the total of such allocations to 598. The total amount allocated was £448,814 which was four times as much as the amount allocated in 1931.

Further sums were added to endowment funds; £60,000 to the Blackpool home (Lancashire and Cheshire District), £60,000 for the Conishead home (Durham), £40,000 for the home at Skegness (Derbyshire), £15,000 for Horton Lodge (North Staffordshire) and £13,000 for the two South Yorkshire homes at Scalby and Rhyl. The Blackpool and South Yorkshire allocations and part of that for Horton Lodge home were required to compensate for the loss of income owing to the conversion of five per cent war stock.

Additions were also made to the endowments of the South Yorkshire Convalescent Treatment Fund (£57,500), the Nottingham Convalescent Home Fund (£50,000) and to Waterloo Main Convalescent Fund in West Yorkshire (£650). The last two Funds were for the purchase of tickets for places in convalescent homes not provided by the Welfare Fund. The South Yorkshire Fund was used partly for this purpose, and partly to provide convalescent treatment in the districts' homes at Scalby and Rhyl. £10,000 was allocated for the endowment of a new convalescent treatment fund established in Leicestershire.

Allocations were also made for improvements; £13,000 from Durham District for the improvement of Conishead convalescent home and £1,948 for improvements at the two Ayrshire convalescent homes at Kirkmichael and Troon.

The largest allocations for hospital treatment were made to Mexborough (Montagu) Hospital (South Yorkshire) for a miners' hostel and an endowment (£10,764) and to Mansfield Hospital in Nottingham District for a new Xray department, a new operating theatre, new casualty ward and outpatient department (£10,000).

Allocations were made from South Wales District Fund to six hospitals (total £8,100). In South Yorkshire, two allocations were made for the Barnsley (Beckett) Hospital, one of £548 to complete the new casualty ward and outpatient department, for which £22,858 had previously been granted, and one of £3,204 for the endowment of the department.

One allocation of £2,000 was made in 1932 for a new ambulance at Elsecar (South Yorkshire), this included £1,300 for endowment. The usual annual grant (£2,000) was made in South Wales to the Welsh Priory of the St John Ambulance Association for providing new ambulances and reconditioning old ones. £4,000 was allocated to complete the endowment of the South Derbyshire ambulance scheme, for which £16,000 had already been granted; this endowment would cover the cost of depreciation and replacement of two ambulances.

The endowment of the Nottinghamshire Special Treatment after Colliery Accidents Fund was increased in 1932 from £20,000 to £29,000 to make the income sufficient to meet current expenditure without supplemental grants for that purpose. Two allocations were made for the continuation of the scheme for providing Special Treatment for Accidents or Illness in the Forest of Dean and £3,000 was added to the endowment in the same district of the trust fund which provided both for assistance to students and also to cases of illness or accident.

Six allocations were made during the year for nursing services, the largest being for £1,000 to the Whitley Nursing Association in Warwickshire for a house for two nurses.

Proposals for making allocations for providing homes for aged miners were first made in 1922 but the Committee were advised that this was not a permissible purpose under Section 20 of the Mining Industry Act 1920. When the question was again raised with the Secretary for Mines in 1929, he decided that he would not veto allocations for this purpose if it was the wish of the Committee and both sides of the industry in the districts concerned agreed that money should be expended in this way. Following this decision, allocations for aged miners' homes were made in 1932 from the Northumberland District Fund (£25,000) and from the Durham District Fund (£7,360) to the Northumberland and Durham Aged Miners' Homes Association, respectively. The Northumberland allocation of £25,000 and £5,000 from the Durham Fund were for building new homes while the remaining Durham allocation was for the endowment of homes provided by the Association.[3]

During 1932, £476,849 from the Baths Fund and £24,466 from the Districts Fund was allocated for new pithead baths, £6,504 for extensions, £1,102 for minor additions or alterations to complete schemes and £23,876 for the Committee's architects, quantity surveyors and engineers for all the installations in hand and for the general incidental expenses of the work.

31 allocations from the Baths Fund were made for new bath installations in 1932. Part of the cost of those at Stafford and Betteshanger were met from the North Staffordshire and Kent Districts Funds, respectively. The installation at Whitehill was wholly provided from the Ayrshire District Fund. The 31 baths

could provide accommodation for 42,336 men and 96 women with an average of 1,323 men per installation.

Additional facilities were provided at some schemes out of the District Funds and included 11 canteens at Manor Powis, Kinneil and Polmaise Nos 3 and 4 in Lanarkshire, Hatfield Main, Dinnington Main and Manton in South Yorkshire, Silksworth in Durham, Old Roundwood in West Yorkshire, Sherwood in Nottingham and Hall End in Warwickshire, 2 cycle stores at Boldon in Durham and Coalpit Heath in Bristol, a laundry to wash men's clothes and towels and a swimming pool at Sherwood.

£1,150 was allocated for a drying house at Hartley Bank Colliery (West Yorkshire) for the workmen's clothes. This colliery would have had to wait some years to get a full bath installation. The scheme was designed by a local architect, with the assistance of the Committee's staff, and provided hangers (instead of lockers) for the clothes of about 500 men and a few washing basins.

Two allocations were made from the Kent District Fund to make the final payment (£1,059) in respect of a loan from the colliery company towards the cost of the baths at Chislet provided in 1924, and £1,000 to repay the loan advancement of the owners of Tilmanstone colliery for constructing a subway between the pithead bathhouse and the lamp-room. The subway ran under a public road which crossed the line of travel from and to the bathhouse.

By the end of 1932, 136 installations accommodating 108,216 men and 302 women had been built or were in the process of erection since the Mining Industry Act 1926. 14 installations for 15,116 men were built prior to the 1926 Act at the cost of the District Funds. A further 11 installations had been provided by colliery companies, accommodating 4,592 men, and 5 jointly by the colliery companies and the District Funds for 3,814 men.

Developments and improvements in design continued to be made. The most important during 1932 was the general adoption of the three-sided cubicle fully screened with a curtain. This new design was easier to clean and was cheaper to provide. The other improvements included the use of black glazed tiles and black cement in the pit entrance hall, and a new form of roof with a flat ceiling of fireproof material enclosing the steelwork which would minimise cleaning and painting of the locker rooms.

During 1932, the Committee received income and expenditure accounts for 60 baths, together with information on the number of men using them and the quantities of fuel, water and electricity consumed. There was conclusive evidence of the success and popularity of the great majority of baths. However, owing to the difficulties throughout the industry, the number of men employed at some collieries was less than could be accommodated in the baths.[4]

The estimates of the Safety in Mines Research Board for 1932/3 amounted to £57,889. After allowing for the estimated endowment income of £12,414 and the estimated Treasury grant of £1,775, £43,700 was allocated from the General Fund with an additional sum of £3,050 for Safety Instruction. The estimate included £11,043 for research into falls of ground, £5,380 on explosives of coal dust or firedamp and £5,455 for research into spontaneous combustion. The estimate for health research was £1,700.

The work on safety instruction had been developing and a notable feature of the year's work was the production of further cinema films taken underground which had aroused much interest.

An allocation of £1,500 was also made during the year at the invitation of the Secretary for Mines, with the support of the Safety in Mines Research Board, to meet the cost of a trial under working conditions of the Ringrose automatic fire damp detector. This detector had been improved after laboratory experiments and had been tested at a Yorkshire colliery on a small scale under the Safety in Mines Research Board, with reasonably consistent and reliable results. With the aid of the grant, it was being tested at three collieries; one in Lancashire , one in Yorkshire, and one in South Wales, in order not only to ascertain its reliability when used every day in working numbers under normal pit conditions but also to obtain information regarding its maintenance in the lamp-room and the general effect of its use underground. The conduct of the trial at each pit was in the hands of a committee consisting of representatives of the workmen and officials as well as the owners, management and Mines Inspectorate. The Safety in Mines Research Board was assisting these committees by making such special tests of the detectors under trial as might be thought necessary from time to time.[5]

The number of allocations made for education from the District Funds in 1932 was 127 amounting to £12,565. £250 from the Nottingham District Fund paid for travelling expenses of students attending advanced mining classes at Nottingham University College. £250 funded the continuation of North Staffordshire vocational and non-vocational education scheme. £100 from the West Yorkshire District Fund provided for books from the mining library at Castleford and District Mining Technical College. £50 funded the scheme for safety badges in Nottinghamshire. Small allocations were made in 1931 for similar safety badge schemes in the two Yorkshire Districts.

As in former years, District Committees were invited to recommend allocations from their District Fund of half of all special grants made by the Committee on the recommendation of the Miners' Welfare National Scholarship Scheme. Very many of the District Committees approached agreed except Ayrshire and Lancashire and Cheshire. There were 18 such grants made, six to mine workers and 12 to children of mine workers and the half share amounted to £360.

Six allocations were made for the continuation of existing schemes for non-vocational education in Nottinghamshire (£1,600), Derbyshire (£1,600), South Yorkshire (£1,068), West Yorkshire (£712), North Staffordshire (£100) and the Forest of Dean (£80).

Grants were made from South Yorkshire and Derbyshire District Funds for the Young Men's Christian Association Farm Training Scheme. The object of this scheme was to train unemployed boys aged from 14 to 17 in farm work lasting three months and, at the end of this time, the boys were found openings as farm learners, receiving the rate of pay determined by the National Wages Board. The boys had to be unemployed mineworkers or sons of mineworkers.

Forty-one allocations, amounting to £21,791, were made from the General Fund for educational purposes during 1932. The total allocated from the sum of £750,000 set aside for mining education buildings and equipment stood at £689,418 in 1932 (for more details see Chapter 7).

The number of applications in 1932 for scholarships under the Miners' Welfare National Scholarship Scheme was 723, an increase of 51% on the figure for 1931. Nineteen scholarships were awarded, seven to miners and twelve to miners' children, two of the latter being girls. Eleven scholars completed their scholarships in 1932, three of them obtaining first-class honours, four second-class honours and one third-class honours and two ordinary degrees. The other scholar, who was a medical student, failed to complete her qualification in 1932 but hoped to do so in 1933. Two of the scholars who obtained first class honours were granted extensions of their scholarships to enable them to undertake post-graduate work.[6]

1933 was a difficult year for the Fund. At the end of January, the Report of the Departmental Committee of Inquiry (1931) was published with its recommendations for an alteration of the amount of the output levy, for discontinuation of the distinction between the General and District Funds and for the appointment of local organisers by the Central Committee. These recommendations evoked a great deal of controversy on which the Committee refrained from making any comment as the Committee regarded itself as the impartial administrator of the Fund as constituted and regulated by Parliament.

On 5th April 1933, the Secretary for Mines announced in the House of Commons that the Government had decided to introduce legislation to reduce the amount of the output levy from 1d to ½d per ton and to extend the duration of the Fund for a period of 20 years. The Bill was introduced into the House of Commons on 21st December 1933.

Under the existing law, the levy in respect of the 1932 output was payable (before 31st March) on the 1d basis but the Secretary for Mines announced that the Government would consider, in connection with the amending Bill, how far practical effect could be given to a recommendation of the Inquiry Committee that the reduction to ½ d per ton could commence with the levy for the 1932 output. The Secretary for Mines had suggested that the 1932 paid at 1d per ton should cover two years. In consequence, the contribution paid into the Fund in 1933 amounted to £427,211 from the 1932 levy (49.1% of the sums due at the rate of 1d per ton).

The Committee having expected in January 1933 that the year's revenue would amount to about £869,500, received notice in April of the intended reduction to about £434,750. Some of the District Committees had already made plans for the allocation of the District Funds, and the annual grant for research and the supplement to the Baths Fund, had already been made.

The preliminaries for a bath installation took from 12 to 18 months, so by April 1933, arrangements for all projects involved in the 1933 bath building programme were well underway. Although it was calculated that the revenue of the Baths Fund in 1933 would probably be £276,000, this was £116,000 short of the figure recommended by the Inquiry Committee of £392,000 for the annual expenditure on pithead baths.

To meet this situation, the Committee took the decision to assist the Baths Fund from the District Fund rather than reduce the rate of building of the baths.[7]

Thirty-six baths accommodating 46,912 men were opened in 1933. 33 new baths and 3 extensions were under construction during 1933, of which 9 had been either under construction or allocated a grant before 1933. The delays in starting were due to a variety of reasons, the primary being a difference with the landlords regarding the terms of the site deeds. Two schemes were held up for revision of the plans after working drawings had been completed, as the colliery owners had altered their policy for future working of the colliery which made it desirable to reduce the accommodation.

The usage of the baths, based on returns from 80 installations, was 87% with most of the men paying between 3d and 6d weekly contribution towards maintenance costs. 66 of the 80 installations not only showed a surplus of revenue over-running expenses but had succeeded in setting aside a reserve at the rate of 1% of the capital value of the installation. Deficits in the other fourteen were almost always explained by the reduction in the number of bathers, owing to bad trade, below that for which the baths had been built and it being impossible to reduce the upkeep costs of the baths proportionately. The Committee commended the colliery owners who made contributions to the upkeep of 68 of the 80 installations.[8]

As large baths were more economical to build based on average cost per person, small collieries with under 250 men tended to be ignored, with only

3 installations having been constructed between 1927 and 1932. In 1933, the Committee took the decision to look afresh at installations at small collieries by building a modified installation for 120 at Toftshaw Moor Colliery, West Yorkshire. Several economies were introduced, including dispensing with cubicles and placing the showers together in one room. The tender for this building came out at £19.3s per head, a figure which would have been reduced to £16.6s per head if the colliery could have supplied the steam. An installation for 120 men, built on a normal plan and equipped accordingly to the standard scale would have cost £24.3s per head.

11 canteens were built using grants from the District Funds in 1933 bringing the total to 66 at bath installations built by the Welfare Committee. Almost all canteens, for which accounts had been received, made an annual profit of £77.

At Craghead Colliery, Durham, the Baths Committee had arranged, early in 1933, for a cobbler to be accommodated in a corner of the bath's fuel store. The 'shop' was so successful that the Committee provided more suitable accommodation, the cost of which was met from their surplus revenue.

In 1933, five grants from the District Funds were made for cycle stores, three in connection with the bath installations at Woolmer (Lothians), Westoe (Durham) and Dodsworth (South Yorkshire), and two for collieries where there were no baths (Crigglestone, West Yorkshire, and Britain, Derbyshire). A grant of £620 was made from the District Fund to provide a covered way from the baths at Baggeridge Colliery, South Staffordshire, total cost £920 of which £300 was provided by the Colliery Owners and the Baths Committee equally.[9]

During 1933, the grants from the District Funds for recreation purposes amounted to £284,868 as compared with £311,047 in 1932. The total grants for recreation had reached £4,810,174.

The report of the Chelmsford Inquiry Committee had expressed the view that the first consideration in the matter of outdoor recreation should be given to children. The amount allocated for children's playgrounds in 1933 only amounted to £12,241, about 4.3% of the total sum allocated for recreational purposes. The grants made for children's playgrounds in 1933 were for 30 new playgrounds, amounting to £10,041 and to 19 existing playgrounds amounting to £2,200. Of these 49 playgrounds, 18 were or would be maintained by the Local Authority. Only 12 Districts applied for grants for children's playgrounds.

Three grants for boys' clubs were made in 1933, upon the recommendation of the West Yorkshire Committee, the first to be made outside South Wales. Two of the grants amounting to £350 were for a new club at Pontefract under the auspices of the Yorkshire Branch of the National Association of the Boys Clubs. The other grant of £150 was made towards a gymnasium at the Boys' Club at Wakefield. A grant of £2,500 was made to the South Wales Federation of

Boys' Clubs for a club building and £1,935 for furniture, games and gymnasium equipment at 12 different clubs, 8 of which had not previously had any grant for this purpose.

The camp at St Athans, in South Wales, continued to be the only permanent camp established by means of the Miners' Welfare Fund. It was also the only miners' welfare recreation scheme whose maintenance was regularly provided by means of annual grants from the Fund amounting to a total of £5,049 in 1933.

A total of £56,803 was made in grants for the provision of 20 new miners' welfare institutes and halls in addition to £22,061 to supplement earlier grants for 17 other institutes and halls. £13,200 was allocated for an institute at Lochore in Fifeshire, comprising a hall for about 450 people, the usual institute accommodation and a caretaker's quarters. £12,500 provided a similar institute at Bow Hill in Fifeshire. Both institutes replaced old buildings rented from colliery owners.

South Wales allocated the largest total (£36,798) for institutes and halls including £5,750 for a new institute at Trehafod, £5,000 towards the cost of a hall at Ffaldau for which the local committee had themselves contributed £3,000, £3,750 for the acquisition and extension of an institute of the Tonypandy Public Library erected in 1897 and £2,370 and £1,154 respectively for the provision of new village halls at Wyllie and Forge Side. Sums amounting to £18,766 were granted to supplement grants previously made for 11 new institutes and halls.

Three grants were made during 1933 for new swimming baths. A local committee at Six Bells, in South Wales District, had constructed a swimming bath to which a grant of £750 was made to provide dressing cubicles, the usual offices, water supply, drainage, fencing and a pavilion. A grant of £250 was made for a bath at Seven Sisters in the same District, which the Local Committee had also constructed themselves, to provide dressing boxes and cloakroom accommodation. A grant of £1,200 was made for a bathing and paddling pool at the South Kirby recreation ground in West Yorkshire which was owned by the Parish Council.

Allocations amounting to £34,837 for 17 new recreation grounds, excluding grants for children's playgrounds, were made during 1933. The largest grant was for £10,000 for a new ground at Chopwell in Durham, including a children's playground costing £1,030, on a site of 16 acres purchased with a previous grant. It was proposed to provide cricket and football grounds, six tennis courts, two bowling greens, quoit pitches and a park area. The second largest grant of £6,069 was also in Durham and was for a new ground at Heworth. The grant was to cover the cost of 2 ¾ acres of land, a hall and sports pavilion and six tennis courts. The Fifeshire allocation of £5,266 was for a new recreation ground at Townhill on a site of 8½ acres owned by the Dunfermline Town Council which was mainly occupied by an old pit heap. This scheme would include a pavilion, cricket and football grounds and tennis courts. The West Yorkshire grant of £2,000 was for a new recreation ground of 5½ acres at Upton Colliery with a bowling green and children's playground (costing £550). Further developments were contemplated for the future.

Three grants were made for the purposes that had not previously had any recommendations. A grant of £222 was made from the South Wales District Fund, mainly to construct a rifle range behind the hall at Brynn. Again in South Wales, a grant of £149 was made for a shelter at Sirhowy Angling Society's fish ponds at Ysbugorwyn, and £75 to the Tredegar Angling Society for the construction of a fish-trap at a reservoir in order to prevent loss of fish during times of flooding. 90% of the members of both Societies were connected with the mining industry.[10]

In 1933, £145,962 was allocated under the heading of Health bringing the total since the Fund came into being to £3,205,704.

£36,070 was allocated to Convalescent Homes and Funds. A further £20,000 was allocated to the endowment fund for the Lancashire District Home at Blackpool. £7,750 was allocated to increase the endowments of five local convalescent home tickets in West Yorkshire and £1,005 for a new local fund in South Yorkshire primarily for defraying the expenses of members travelling to and from convalescent homes. A further grant of £6,358 was made for the improvement of the Durham home, the grant of £13,000 made in 1932 having proved insufficient.

Grants were made to 28 different hospitals in 1933 amounting to £70,221. The three largest grants in 1933 were from the South Yorkshire District for £25,000 to Sheffield Royal Hospital towards the cost of an X-ray department, massage department, laboratories and operating theatre; £9,500 to Doncaster Infirmary towards the cost of a casualty ward, dispensary and electrical department and £6,638 to the Mexborough (Montagu) Hospital towards the cost of two medical wards, a children's ward, an outpatients' and pathological department.

Grants totalling £6,775 were made from the South Wales District Fund to 7 hospitals for capital expenditure: Tredegar Park Cottage Hospital, Maesteg Hospital, Treherbert Cottage Hospital, Porth and District Hospital, Abertillery and District Hospital, Blaina and District Hospital and Oakdale Cottage Hospital. In Durham, £4,482 was granted to three hospitals: Holmside and South Moor Cottage Hospital, Durham County Hospital and Whickham and District War Memorial Cottage Hospital. In West Yorkshire, £2,438 was allocated towards the building extension fund at Pontefract General Infirmary. From the Derbyshire District Fund, £4,450 was granted to 7 hospitals: Chesterfield and Derbyshire Royal Hospital, Ilkeston General Hospital, Sheffield Royal Infirmary,

Ripley Hospital, Heanor, Derbyshire Royal Infirmary and Nottingham General Hospital.

A new endowment fund was established with a grant of £6,000 from the Somerset District Fund for a contributory scheme for the provision of special hospital treatment, payment of travelling expenses of patients and, if funds permitted, the provision for convalescent treatment.

The Chelmsford Inquiry Committee had commented adversely upon the provision of 'Welfare Fund' ambulances for isolated localities, without any arrangement for co-operation or co-ordination over a wider area; it recommended that in future 'grants for ambulances should only be made in such a way that it will fit in with a co-ordinated district scheme and on condition that they co-operate with other ambulances in the neighbourhood'. The Committee was entirely in agreement with this recommendation, but they had no authority to prepare or enforce any co-ordinated district schemes linked with other ambulance services. This problem required consideration, in the first instance, by the Minister of Health. Meanwhile, new grants would be conditional on the ambulance receiving the grant taking its proper place in any co-ordinated scheme being approved by the Committee for the district concerned.

On the other hand, the Committee did not agree with the recommendation of the Inquiry against grants for replacements and inferentially, against grants for endowments.

The total grants made from the Welfare Fund for ambulance services up to the end of 1933 was £116,733. Those made during 1933 amounted to £12,717. Three grants were made for endowments and six for new ambulances where there was no risk of overlapping other welfare ambulances. In South Wales, the usual grant to St John Ambulance Association was made but the amount, £1,000, was smaller than in the past.

Grants in 1933 for 13 nursing services to the value £6,905 were made bringing the total grants from the Fund to £60,782.

The largest grant of the year was £2,000 from the Lothians District Fund for a nurses' cottage at Rosewell with a garage and a small motor car. The South Yorkshire Fund made 4 grants for endowments amounting to £1,070 and £300 to provide a house at Dodsworth. In West Yorkshire, three endowment grants were made amounting to £2,700. In Northumberland, a grant of £300 was made towards the cost of a building at Scremerston Colliery, to be used jointly as the colliery ambulance room and as the centre for the District Nursing Association and for first aid and ambulance classes. The Colliery Owners were helping materially towards the cost of the building and equipment and would assist in maintenance.

£13,840 was granted in 1933 to the Durham Aged Miners' Association for endowments varying from £513 to £4,438 for homes at nine different places.[11]

The total amount allocated during 1933 for educational purposes was £33,008 of which £25,740 was from the General Fund and £7,268 from the District Funds. From the sum of £750,000 which had been reserved from the General Fund for expenditure on mining education buildings and equipment, the amount granted by 1933 was £714,188. The Chelmsford Inquiry Committee, on the strength of the evidence given by the Board of Education and the Scottish Education Department as to what further expenditure was required to complete the provision for mining education (excluding universities), had recommended a sum of £36,000. When considering this recommendation, the Committee formed the opinion that £790,000 should be ample so £40,000 was added to the previously reserved sum.

The number of applicants for scholarships in 1933 under the Miners' Welfare National Scholarship Scheme was 652. Eleven scholarships were awarded, three to mineworkers and eight to children of mineworkers, one of the latter being a girl. Fourteen scholars completed their scholarships during the year. Five of them obtained first-class, six second-class and one third-class honours degrees. One did not complete his degree course but hoped to do so in 1934. The remaining scholar, who was doing postgraduate work, obtained an MSc degree from Birmingham University in mechanical engineering and had then obtained an appointment (in open competition) as a research worker employed by the Safety in Mines Research Board.

The Chelmsford Inquiry Committee recommended that £75,000 should be used to endow a scheme for the provision of scholarships for part-time day courses in advanced mining and that a fund should be endowed to make permanent provision for the grants to students that had been directly provided from grants from the General Fund and District Funds.[12]

The estimates of the Safety in Mines Research Board for 1933-34 amounted to £57,868 and £3,960 for safety instruction work. The estimates included a sum of £11,050 for research into falls of ground, £8,245 for research on explosions of coal dust and firedamp, £5,477 for research on explosives and £2,966 for research on wire ropes. The estimate for health research was £1,700. Provision was made for the addition of another investigator to the small staff engaged in investigations into causes of haulage accidents. The estimated income of the Board for 1933/34 from the Endowment Fund was £12,416, the contribution from the Exchequer had been fixed at £1,750 and an unspent balance from the previous grants amounting to £1,573 was available so the net sum required from the Fund for 1933/34 was £42,129 for research and £3,960 for safety instruction, total £46,089.

In making a grant of that amount, the Board was informed that, in view of the Government's declared intention to reduce the amount of the output welfare levy for the future, the Committee could give no assurance that in succeeding years that the grant might not be reduced. This was not an opportune time for the Board to add to their commitments. The Board, under these circumstances, reduced the estimate for safety instruction work to £3,171.[13]

Lord Noel-Buxton resigned the Chairmanship of the Committee in June 1934 and was succeeded in August 1934 by Sir Frederick Sykes. Mr Peter Lee, one of the representatives of the Committee nominated by the MFGB, resigned in September and was succeeded by Mr W. Lawther. Mr G. H. Winstanley, the Assessor appointed by the Board of Education was replaced in September by Mr E. G. Savage. Mr A. M. Anderson, Assistant Secretary to the Committee, was replaced by Mr T. A. Bennett MBE, formerly Mines Department Accountant for the Miners' Welfare Fund.

On 28th March 1934, the Royal Assent was given to the Mining Industry (Welfare Fund) Act which made two radical changes to the Welfare Fund. In the first place, the Act reduced the amount of the welfare levy on the output of coal from 1d to ½d per ton commencing with the year 1932 and required the Committee to make the following appropriations in 1934 and succeeding years from the proceeds of the levy before crediting the four-fifths due to the District Funds.

a) such sum as will, together with the proceeds of the royalties welfare levy each year, amount to £375,000, which was to be applied to pithead baths; and

b) £20,000 which was to be applied to research into methods of improving the health and safety of workers in or about coal mines.

In 1934, the total receipts of the output levy were £416,767, of which £214,091 was appropriated to the Districts and General Funds. Four fifths of this amount, £171,273 was credited to the Districts Fund. To this was added £38,823 for interest earned by the balances standing to the credit of some Districts, making the total sum available for the Districts Fund in 1934 £210,096, which was only 31% of the sum available in 1932 (£674,944), the last year of the 1d levy.

The Committee felt that the policy to be followed in the administration of the Fund needed to be reconsidered in relation to the changes made by the Act to the amount and the period of the levy for a further 18 years after 1934.

The Chairman recommended a survey of the mining communities and the extent to which their needs had been met from the Welfare Fund, or from other resources, for indoor and outdoor recreation and leisure occupation, generally paying particular attention to the needs of isolated communities; especially

Mr T. A. Bennett, MBE, with his wife and mother

those dependent upon small collieries and the needs of impecunious schemes for revenue-producing facilities.

Difficulties in some places of maintaining welfare schemes had been an ongoing problem for the Committee. With the welfare levy having been changed from a temporary levy to one of long duration, the Committee had the power and the duty to endeavour to ensure the permanence of the welfare schemes. The most promising and economical course of action for ensuring, not only the financial success but the further development of all welfare schemes was to maintain regular and frequent contact with the management committees of the local schemes.

Realising that many District Committees did not have the staff to maintain regular and frequent contact with the management committees of their local schemes, the Committee formed a Districts Branch of the central staff, selected and trained for these duties under the charge of Mr R. Whitfield Parker. Its services were available in any district where requested. When in a district, the Branch acted according to the direction of and in close co-operation with the District Committee, but at the same time, was able to represent the Committee's policy and rules. The Architect's Branch, which built the pithead baths and canteens etc. under the charge of Mr J. H. Forshaw, took over the functions of the former Advisory Branch in providing architect's services for institutes, pavilions and other buildings. Cdr. B. T. Coote, the Committee's Welfare Advisor, would devote his whole time to advancing the Committee's aim of encouraging amongst the mining communities a fuller understanding of the objectives and ideals of welfare work.[14]

Although £162,600 was granted from District Funds to recreation schemes, the amount was naturally smaller than in 1933 when it was £284,868. £28,684 was allocated for 20 new recreation grounds and £55,762 for additions and improvements to grounds that had already been started. Of the total amount of £84,446, £14,383 was spent on children's playgrounds, thus increasing the percentage spent on recreational schemes for children from 4.3% in 1933 to 8.8%. 15 new playgrounds for children and young people and 20 existing schemes received grants. Bolsover children's playground received £2,000 from Derbyshire District Fund. £1,600 was granted for a children's playground and football pitch at Coalsnaughton, Fife which, once constructed, would be maintained by the local authority. Lanarkshire made four grants of £180 for assisting local authorities in making four children's playgrounds.

In South Yorkshire, the principal grants were £1,000 and £580 for new playgrounds at Rotherham and Maltby respectively and £950 for improvements at Carcroft. In West Yorkshire, there was a grant of £1,705 for a playground at Rothwell.

Bowls and tennis received most attention in 1934, bowls being the object of grants in 30 schemes in 12 Districts and tennis in 30 schemes in 9 Districts.

Cricket received grants in 30 schemes in 6 Districts but principally in Yorkshire (South and West), Durham and Northumberland and football in 17 schemes in 8 Districts. Grants were made for constructing two golf courses as part of miners' welfare schemes: £1,000 for a 9-hole course at Backworth, Northumberland and £650 for a 9-hole pitching and putting course at Bolsover, Derbyshire.

£68,537 in grants were made in 1934 for institutes, halls and places of indoor recreation. The total included £15,780 for nine new schemes and £52,757 for 170 supplemental grants to schemes previously supported by the Fund.

The small institute at Nelson in South Wales received its first grant for the repayment of its mortgage of £2,000, and £184 for repairs and renovation.

In Lanarkshire, £1,020 was granted as a new scheme to Blackburn Baillie Institute for payment of debts and for repairs and renovations. Another grant was made to the new institute at Strathaven for £650 made towards the cost of adapting and equipping a disused school loaned by the County Council, the total cost of the alterations and equipment estimated at £1,943, the balance being raised locally. The institute was intended to cater especially for the unemployed, with a practical instruction room and gymnasium in addition to a small hall and the usual institute accommodation.

Two grants for new schemes in Northumberland included £3,750, as part of a composite grant of £12,415, to purchase Backworth Hall and grounds (£8,000) and to develop the grounds of 85 acres for recreation purposes (£4,415). It was proposed that the Hall, a stone-built mansion erected in 1770, should be used as an institute. The other grant was for the purchase of Ellington and Lynemouth Institute from the Ashington Colliery Company, by whom it had been erected in 1927. The total cost, including redecoration, was £10,646, towards which a grant of £7,259 was made in 1934.

A further £2,000 was granted for Boys' Clubs to the South Wales Federation of Boys' Clubs for the provision of buildings in colliery towns. This brought the total of the grants to this organisation up to £14,562.

Two boys clubs under the auspices of the Yorkshire Branch of the National Association of Boys' Clubs received grants: £250 from the South Yorkshire District Fund for the Club at Barnsley towards the £850 required for providing a gymnasium, workshop, shower baths, lavatories and lockers and £400 from West Yorkshire District Fund to provide a room for handicrafts, a library, shower baths, lavatories and central heating at Castleford Town Boys' Club.

The annual grant for running expenses to the boys camp at St Athans in South Wales had to be reduced to £3,000 in 1934 from £4,754 in 1933.

A total of £1,478 was granted for swimming pools. Of this total, £478 was for improvements of indoor pools, the chief grants being £246 from the Derbyshire District Fund for foot baths and lavatories at the swimming bath at the Claycross and Danesmoor Welfare Scheme. £1,000 was granted for outdoor pools, of which £800 was for a filtration plant at the swimming pool at the Blaenavon Welfare Scheme.

A grant of £511 was made from the Lothians District Fund to meet the cost of new instruments for the Newtongrange Lothian Silver Band, which was closely associated with the local welfare scheme.[15]

In the course of the Committee's investigation of certain recommendations for recreation grants received from the Fifeshire District Committee in November 1933 and January 1934, it appeared that the systems in place in this district with regard to making recommendations, keeping accounts, making applications for payments and other matters were not satisfactory. At the Secretary's request, Mr Bennett, the Mines Department Accountant for the Miners' Welfare Fund, visited the District Committee's office on 27th and 28th March. An interim report was made by Mr Bennett on 9th April 1934, as a result of which the District Committee were asked to support all future applications for payment of allocations already made by architect's certificates or accounts rendered, and to refrain from submitting fresh recommendations pending the conclusion of the accountant's examination.

Mr Bennett's full report was received on 29th August, having been delayed owing partly to the necessity for awaiting further information from the District Committee, and partly to other demands on Mr Bennett's time. His report revealed a whole catalogue of the District's failures to follow guidelines set out by the Central Committee for the allocation of District Funds.

The books showed that at 31st March 1934, expenditure had been incurred and paid by the District Committee amounting to £2,229.4s.1d in respect of 25 different schemes, without the approval of the Central Committee for the allocation of money from the District Fund to meet the expenditure. Some of the items included in the above amount were for purposes which did not ordinarily receive sanction from the Central Committee.

It appeared that on some allocations that had been made by the Central Committee and remitted to the District Committee, balances which were not required for the purposes for which the allocations were made remained unspent. The District was requested to refund these unspent balances and to only request payments to meet accounts actually due, and the requests to be supported by architect's certificates or accounts rendered.

To meet the expenditure of £2,229.4s.1d, the District Committee had used money obtained for other specified schemes, upon the certificates signed by the Joint Secretaries and the Clerk, stating that the money was required for immediate expenditure upon schemes specified and undertaken to apply it solely for these schemes. Such action appeared to reflect gravely upon those who signed the certificates. The District was asked what assurances could be given to restore confidence in the certificates.

The information supplied on behalf of the District Committee in support of the recommendations in certain cases did not disclose the fact that the expenditure had already been incurred and, indeed, implied that the opposite was the case.

The Annual Return of expenditure and unspent balance had failed to disclose the whole position. Mr Bennett's suggestion that the District Committee should employ professional auditors was one with which the Central Committee concurred.

The Secretary wrote to the District Committee on 6th September, inviting comments on Mr Bennett's findings. The District Committee replied on 2nd October, accepting all the suggestions made in the Secretary's letter.[16]

In accordance with the requirements of the Mining Industry (Welfare Fund) Act 1934, the Baths Fund received £375,000 in 1934, stabilising its revenue which had fallen to £277,215 in 1933. The total allocation from the Miners' Welfare Fund up to the end of 1934 for pithead baths was £3,360,278 and for other welfare purposes £94,185, making a grand total of £3,454,463 of which the Central Committee's architectural staff were responsible for constructional work in respect of £3,293,784.

In 1934, 27 baths were completed, providing accommodation for 35,702 men and 56 women bringing the total up to 154 baths for 200,674 men and 262 women. In addition, there were 32 installations accommodating 24,643 men which had been built by colliery companies or colliery welfare committees mostly before the Fund assumed this function.

The usage of the baths based on returns from 112 installations had risen to 89% with 87.5% of men contributing from 3d to 6d per week. Only 20 out of the 112 were showing a deficit balance after paying the actual cost of maintenance, repairs and renewals.

The experimental installation at the small colliery at Toftshaw with accommodation for 120, (subsequently increased to 126) was opened in April 1934, and had proved a great success. Each man had been provided with separate clean and pit clothes lockers as usual, but the cubicles had been abolished and replaced by 15 showers in a single bathing room. The baths were operated by one attendant working for three short periods daily, the work having been reduced by not only the lack of cubicles to clean but also by fitting a boiler with an automatic self-stoking appliance which had been added to the final cost of £19.4s per head.

The cost per head for the smaller collieries was substantially higher than for the larger baths, so further economies needed to be found. Cheaper materials would lead to increased costs in upkeep. One suggestion was the replacement of lockers with open hooks or racks for hanging pit clothes, while retaining lockers for home clothes.

The Act of 1934 empowered the Committee to provide out of the £375,000 a year from the Baths Fund such accommodation that the Committee thought conveniently and properly combined with pithead baths. Under this power, the Committee decided to provide bath installations with canteens at the cost of the Baths Fund. However, the Fund could not take over the responsibility of the canteens at installations provided from allocations before 1934. These canteens would continue to be the responsibility of the District Funds.

The sums allocated from the District Funds for canteens at baths provided before 1934 amounted to £63,517 for 67 canteens. In addition, two canteens were provided out of allocations for baths from the Northumberland District Fund, and two experimental canteens were built independently of the baths out of grants amounting to £1,623 from the General Fund.

During 1934, grants for canteens were made from the Baths Fund for 16 new bath installations at a total cost of £15,446. Of the 35 canteens for which accounts were available in 1934, all but four showed a profit on the year's working. The service of canteens was, in some instances, extended to include the sale of tools, boots and other articles of clothing.

Cycle stores had been provided out of District Funds at 37 collieries, at a total cost of £13,561, of which £1,507 was allocated in 1934 for five new stores and one extension.[17]

In 1934, the allocations for health purposes amounted to £88,818, 30% of the total allocations for the year.

Four-fifths of the money devoted to health purposes was for convalescent homes and Funds amounting to £2,593,686, of which £73,106 was allocated in 1934.

£6,000 was allocated from the Lanarkshire District Fund in 1934 to extend the National Convalescent Home for Miners at Saltcoats to provide accommodation for 24 additional patients making a total of 34.

Grants amounting to £4,235 were made to the Durham Home at Conishead Priory, Ulverston, Lancashire to increase the endowment fund and to provide a bowling green, fire escapes and refrigeration plant.

A grant of £2,850 from the South Yorkshire District Fund was made to increase the accommodation at the Home at Scalby near Scarborough from 39 to 48 patients, and to adapt a cottage at the home at Rhyl, North Wales, to provide accommodation for 8 patients.

The allocation of £2,050 from Derbyshire District Fund was for improvements to the women's accommodation at the home at Skegness, which had beds for 30 women and 120 men. In Ayrshire, two grants were made: £224 for reconditioning the lodge for the use of the gardener at Kirkmichael House and £219 for road charges at the Troon home.

The total sum allocated for tickets of admission to other homes or to endowment funds for this purpose was £600,344, of which £56,950 was allocated in 1934.

South Yorkshire had an endowment fund for the District generally which amounted to £282,500 by 1934. The income from the endowment fund was used to maintain the two convalescent homes at Scalby and Rhyl as well as purchase tickets for admission to other homes. The income from West Yorkshire's endowment fund of £42,000 was used wholly for tickets for admission to homes other than the District Miners' Home at Lytham. The largest allocation in 1934 was £50,000 for endowing a Ticket Fund for Northumberland which had no miners' home or previous provision from the Welfare Fund for convalescents.

By 1934, £379,564 had been allocated to hospitals, of which allocations amounting to £5,598 were made in 1934. £1,900 from Nottinghamshire District Fund was granted to Harlow Wood Orthopaedic Hospital, additional to the £5,000 allocated in 1932 towards a new ward costing £14,000. £1,012 was allocated in South Yorkshire to modernise the operating theatre at the Warde-Aldam Cottage Hospital, South Elmshall. £1,000 was allocated in South Staffordshire to endow a bed at the Guest Hospital. Two grants, amounting to £636, were made in South Wales to Tredegar Park Cottage Hospital (£415 supplemental to £3,750 in 1932 and 1933) and Porth and District Hospital (£221). £550 (supplemental to £10,000 in 1932) was allocated in Derbyshire to equip a new X-ray Department of the Mansfield and District Hospital from the District Fund.

The allocations for ambulance services amounted to £120,927 of which a total of £4,257 was made in 1934. The allocations in 1934 included 4 new ambulances at Sacriston, County Durham, Whitechapel in Northumberland, Wentworth Silkstone in South Yorkshire and Rosehall, Lanarkshire. In all the cases, the grants were made subject to the area served by the ambulance being adjusted, if necessary, to take its proper place in any co-ordination scheme.

Grants for special medical treatment and appliances amounted to £86,519 of which £707 were made in 1934: £295 to continue the provision of spinal treatment and convalescent facilities in the Forest of Dean, £262 in Durham for the four invalid tricycles and £150 to supplement the endowment fund and provide spectacles for miners suffering from nystagmus after accidents and for miners' children in South Derbyshire.

9 nursing services received grants in 1934 to the value of £5,150 bringing the total allocated from the Welfare Fund for this purpose to £65,558. £3,000 was allocated in West Yorkshire to create an endowment, the income from which would be used to assist Nursing Associations working in the Castleford area. The £1,225 allocated in South Yorkshire included £500 towards the cost of erecting and equipping a nurses' home at Swinton at an estimated cost of £1,000, the balance being raised locally. The grant of £775 in Northumberland was to provide a Nurses' Home at Choppington, on a site given by the colliery company.[18]

By the end of 1934, £773,420 out of the £790,000 had been allocated for buildings and equipment for mining education. In addition, £20,790 had been granted for similar purposes from the Districts Fund.

During 1934, a total of £60,234 of grants were made from the General Fund for mining education and £50 from the Warwickshire District Fund.

The grant of £42,000 for the Treforest School of Mining was the largest made from the Miners' Welfare Fund for any mining education institution. The School had been instituted in 1913 by a body of colliery owners. In 1927, it was offered as a gift to Glamorgan Education Authority. A grant was applied for by the Authority in 1931 but the amount was larger than the Committee felt able to make for an advanced centre. The Committee had considered making a grant to the Cardiff University College as well, so discussions were initiated in 1931 for a joint scheme between the University and the School. These discussions were brought to a successful conclusion in 1934 and £42,000 was granted to fit the Treforest School to serve the dual purpose of the University Mining Department and the county advanced centre. For the new degree course in mining, two years would be spent in the laboratories at Cardiff University College, then two years at Treforest.

Sunderland Technical College received a grant of £7,527 towards the cost of two laboratories, three classrooms and mine surveying, lamp-testing and staff rooms.

The grant of £5,000 to the Heriot Watt College, Edinburgh, was to help towards the cost of a considerable scheme of extensions at the College.

The number of applicants for the Miners' Welfare National Scholarship Scheme was 692 in 1934, and fifteen scholarships were awarded; seven to mineworkers and eight to children of mineworkers. Twenty-one scholars completed their degrees in 1934, including three doing research work. One of the latter was Mr D Phillips, originally a mineworker, who had completed his PhD at Cambridge and was employed as a research worker by the Safety in Mines Research Board in their researches into 'Falls of Ground' (see Chapter 6). Of the other eighteen scholars, three failed in one subject but were likely to complete their degrees successfully by retaking their examinations in 1935.

In 1934, twenty-four grants were made to students recommended by the Selection Committee of the Miners' Welfare National Scholarship Scheme. In previous years, the grants had been jointly funded from the District Funds and the General Fund but, following the Welfare Fund Act 1934, the Committee decided to find the twenty-four grants from the General Fund, totalling £995.

As the awards of these special grants had proved such a valuable supplement to the National Scholarship Scheme, the Committee made a permanent provision for them by devoting a sum of £25,000 from the General Fund to form an endowment fund, providing an income of about £875 for the awards.

The Committee made a grant of £75,000 from the General Fund for the Scholarship Scheme for Part-time Students of Mining which had been worked out for the Board of Education and the Scottish Education Department, following proposals made in 1931 for such a scheme by Mr Winstanley (see Chapter 7). Detailed regulations had yet to be prepared, but it was hoped to be able to award about thirty scholarships each year, tenable for four years on an average of £20 a year which should be sufficient to cover the cost of fees, books, instruments and travelling expenses and perhaps, to provide some small amount to compensate for loss of wages. The Committee hoped that the establishment of these scholarships would not only enable students to take advantage of existing part-time day courses but also encourage local education authorities to provide fresh courses for this purpose.

Grants made for non-vocational lectures in 1934 amounted to £1,967, £1,645 from the District Funds and £322 from the General Fund. £1,112 of this total was granted to the scheme organised in Yorkshire by Miners' Lectures Joint Committee (Yorkshire) of the Workers' Educational Association. Because of the reduction of the Welfare Levy, the scheme in Nottinghamshire and Derbyshire organised by the Adult Education Department of the Nottingham University College which had recently been granted £4,000 a year, received no grant at all.

Prior to 1934, grants for safety instruction of colliery boys had been made in Northumberland, Durham, South and West Yorkshire, Nottinghamshire and Derbyshire. During 1934, grants were made in North Wales (£225), Lancashire (£207), Durham (£160), South Yorkshire (£150) and West Yorkshire (£100). The two Yorkshire grants were to cover the succeeding five years.

Mr Winstanley, in consultation with Mr Fudge, Mines Department, and the Secretary also undertook a review of this scheme which was presented to the Committee in March 1934 (see Chapter 7, Education).

For the future, Mr Winstanley suggested that the work would be better co-ordinated, and its importance more effectively recognised as what ought soon to become a national movement, if grants in aid were in future made from the General Fund instead of the District Funds.

At the March meeting, the Committee agreed in principle that the cost of the safety badges would in future be met from the General Fund, but reserved their decision on other expenditure pending submission of information as to the reasons for dealing with them centrally rather than in the districts.

In April 1934, the Committee were in receipt of a memorandum from Mr Fudge and the Chairman had received a personal letter from the Secretary for Mines expressing his firm conviction of the great value of this work. Mr Fudge's memorandum pointed out that the total sum involved was small (not more than £350 a year perhaps rising to £500). With district funds depleted, some Districts might refuse to help at all, as had recently happened in Lancashire. The cost of presentation of the badges would vary. Those districts near Buxton could send parties of boys there, and the cost would be met by the Safety in Mines

Research Board out of their grant for Safety Instruction made by the Welfare Committee from the General Fund. Other Districts would not be able to take advantage of these facilities.

It was noted that the influence of the Welfare Committee, at this experimental stage of development, could be an important factor for good, and this influence could be built up if the Committee showed its interest and gave financial support to the very limited extent that was needed, as the great bulk of the cost continued to fall on the Local Education Authorities.

At its April meeting, the Committee took the decision to make a grant for the safety badges from the General Fund, and to ask Mr Forshaw to submit designs for a national badge. This decision was not supported by either Mr Winstanley or Mr Mallinson in the Mines Department, and the Committee was asked to revise their decision. At the May meeting, the matter was discussed but was deferred to the June meeting, as some members of the Committee who had taken part in the previous discussion were absent. The decision made at the June 1934 meeting was that the provision of badges should continue without alteration, with grants being made from the District Funds upon the recommendations of the District Committees to provide District badges.[19]

The Safety in Mines Research Board's estimates for 1934/35 amounted to £58,438 for Research and £3,155 for Safety Instruction. £12,416 was available from the Endowment Fund, £1,750 from the Exchequer and £3,217 from savings on previous grants leaving the Committee to make a grant of £44,210 from the General Fund. The grant of £44,210 included the £20,000 to be appropriated for research under the Act of 1934.

A sum of £11,259 was included in the estimates for research into falls of ground and £3,400 for research into haulage accidents, £8,319 for research on explosions of coal dust or firedamp, £5,487 for research into the safe use of explosives, £2,751 for research on wire ropes, £2,210 for health research, £2,140 for electrical researches and £2,052 for research into spontaneous combustion. The remaining expenditure was for the maintenance of the Research Stations at Buxton and Sheffield and for the general work of the Research Board.[20]

The 1934 Act gave effect to the inclusion within the Fund of 'persons who had ceased to be employed as such workers by reason of age or disability'. The case of aged miners' homes was thus met by this inclusion. Up to the end of 1934, £53,963 had been allocated for aged miners' homes from the District Funds of Durham, Northumberland and West Yorkshire. In 1934, grants amounting to £5,463 were made to the Durham Aged Miners' Home Association for the endowment of houses occupied by three specified collieries, Littleburn, Byermoor and Bearpark. The grant in West Yorkshire was for building four cottages for aged miners at Stanley, the management and control of the property being vested in a local committee representative of the mine owners and workers.[21]

In January 1935, the Committee were made aware of how the duties of the Committee's staff had been distributed after the decision taken by the Committee to re-organise the central staff at their meeting on 20th November 1934 and reported in the thirteenth Annual Report of the Welfare Fund (see pages 137–138). The general principles laid down by the Committee were that the staff would be organised on the basis of a central secretariat and three executive branches and that the Secretary would be the controlling head of the whole staff and would be directly responsible to the Committee.

The Secretarial Branch would be in the charge of the Assistant Secretary, Mr Bennet, and would be responsible for preparing the Committee's financial programme and estimates and generally to act as controller of finance for the District Funds, General Fund and the Baths Fund.

The Welfare Adviser's Branch, under the charge of Cdr. Coote, would continue to advance welfare ideals both within the Districts and the pithead baths.

The Architects' Branch, headed by Mr Forshaw, would provide architects, engineers and quantity surveyors for pithead baths construction, and a similar function for recreation schemes. This Branch would also assist the Districts Branch in the compilation of district surveys and the preparation of the District 5-year plans.

The Districts Branch, with Mr Parker as District Adviser and Capt. O'Kelly as Technical Officer for outdoor recreation, was to act as liaison with the District Committees to secure closer understanding and co-operation with them and to assist them in the management of their schemes and preparation of new schemes.

The Secretary presented recommendations to the Committee for additional staff to give effect to the new departures in policy. A sub-committee comprising the Chairman, Mr J. T. Brown, Sir Arthur Lowes Dickinson and Mr Herbert Smith, was appointed to consider these recommendations. The sub-committee met on 23rd January and agreed that an increase in the secretarial and clerical staff was necessary, and recommended the appointment of three clerks. On the technical side, the sub-committee recommended a draughtsman to assist Mr Forshaw, so as to enable him to devote his time more fully to supervision and important structural problems, but this appointment was to be reviewed in a year's time.[22]

The sub-committee on 23rd January 1935 also met a deputation led by Mr F. Llewellyn Jacob, Chairman of the South Wales District Committee, to discuss the circumstances in which recommendations for grants from the District Fund were dealt with, particularly those cases where the recommendations had either been refused or deferred by the Central Committee.

The District Committee had submitted a memorandum which dealt with a number of difficulties with which they were faced in recommending allocations. These included the effect of the fall of coal output in the District reducing the rate of the levy and the appropriation for Baths and Research. Many of the schemes were in distressed areas and had debts and, in some cases, were threatened with foreclosure. The District had lost 44,700 mining jobs since 1929, which had resulted in loss of income of schemes.

The District Committee had taken action to deal with the problems, but South Wales had special difficulties and asked the Committee to relax its rules which it said, although sound in normal times, were too rigid under existing conditions particularly regarding maintenance.

The District Committee were asked to provide a five-year plan, and procedures for the investigation of schemes. This information was provided by the District Committee just in time for the February meeting of the Committee. The Committee decided to defer the consideration of the matter until they had had time to examine the information but some of the recommendations which had previously been refused or deferred were dealt with. The statement of procedures the District Committee proposed to follow when making recommendations to the Central Committee and their proposals for utilising the District Fund during the next five years were discussed at the March 1935 meeting of the Committee.[23]

In February 1935, Sir Arthur Lowes Dickinson, who had been a member of the Committee for nine and half years, died. Professor Patrick Abercrombie, who had wide experience in architecture and town planning, took his place.

Financially, the amounts of revenue were slightly increased in 1935 with £736,588 being received in comparison to £660,982 in 1934. The receipts of the Fund during the 15 ½ years since its institution stood at £15,247,118.

Of the grants made in 1935, £393,066, half of the total, was for pithead baths and other forms of pit welfare, £178,135 (24.2% of the total) was for recreation, and £72,835 (9.9%) for health.

The Welfare Fund had embarked upon a new stage, with less money but a large measure of permanence. With less money, there had to be greater care in ensuring that grants were only made where there was a real need, and where good value was obtained for that money. Besides taking steps to avoid wasting money in duplication and overlapping, the Committee looked to more co-ordination with social service organisations and the National Playing Field Association, and particularly with local government authorities when grants were allocated for recreation.

The Committee looked to adopt a long-term policy designed to help the local welfare schemes make themselves permanent, to carry on efficiently at the lowest cost to their members, and to cater for more of the mining community.

This policy required more constructive methods to be applied to making grants, and the employment of District Organisers was seen as the way forward in maintaining and supporting local welfare schemes.

District Organisers were paid by the Central Committee but were placed at the disposal of the District Committees to carry out their directions. Their employment in every District was advocated in 1934 and ten were promptly appointed in response to requests from several Districts. The success of these appointments encouraged the Committee to discuss further appointments with District Committees.

The Districts Branch also played its part in assisting maintenance problems in the case of recreation grounds. At the invitation of District Committees, six meetings of groundsmen were held in 1935, in four districts, for instructional purposes. 200 groundsmen attended to discuss and receive advice on bowling greens, following which a pamphlet was produced which was issued to the groundsmen for future reference. The Districts Branch, following the meetings, were asked to visit more than 100 greens to give advice.

In 1935, children's playgrounds, bowling greens and hard tennis courts headed the list of grants for recreation amounting to a total of £40,708. Grants amounting to £15,850 were made for pavilions.

An unusual scheme in 1935 involved the partial restoration of Backworth Hall, Northumberland and its conversion into a miners' welfare centre, with extensive recreation facilities including a nine-hole golf course in the grounds at a total cost of £17,415.

Grants amounting to £10,249 were made for 4 new institutes and 1 new hall and £563 for 3 institutes which had not previously been assisted from the Fund. £4,331 was granted for non-capital expenditure at 74 schemes. Of this sum, £2,690 was granted in special circumstances for decorations and £1,641 for other maintenance charges including £672 towards feu duty, rates and insurance of 26 schemes in Fife District and £772 towards the obligations of the Trustees and Management Committee upon winding up the institute at Esh, Durham as a result of the closure of the neighbouring colliery. The Fife District Committee claimed that there were exceptional conditions to justify maintenance grants recommended by them but hoped that the need would disappear with the newly appointed District Organiser.

By 1935, Kent District Welfare Committee had only spent £6,782 on recreation schemes, having given priority to the provision of pithead baths (see page 79). Recreation facilities were provided by the local authorities in places such as Deal but they did not meet the miners' needs. Moreover, owing to recent housing developments around the collieries, about 4,500 miners out of a total of 7,500 now lived near the collieries.

Backworth Hall

In 1935, the total credits of the District Fund amounted to £930. With £1,143 repayable to the Baths Fund under existing arrangements, only £787 would be available for recreation.

In these circumstances, the District Committee asked for further payments from the District Fund to the Baths Fund to be eased as much as possible. This application was refused by the Central Committee in June, as the District Committee in their application had not considered the recommendations of the Districts Branch as to the most urgent welfare needs of the District.

The application was renewed and pressed strongly when the Chairman visited Kent. Kent did have, as far as miners' welfare was concerned, difficulties and problems which hardly affected other districts. It was therefore suggested that the repayments to the Baths Fund might be spread over the next 5 ½ years, conditional upon the District Committee adopting a five-year programme approved by the Districts Branch, which gave preference to schemes for miners willing to make some contribution themselves. This would give about £9,883 for use on district welfare schemes during the 5 ½ years to 31st March 1941, of which £2,910 instead of £1,767 would be available at once or the following year, £4,360 instead of £2,567.

By the end of 1935, 194 pithead baths had been built or were under construction, accommodating 258,984 men and 538 women, and seventeen more for 20,966 men and 54 women had been planned and the money allocated from the Miners' Welfare Baths Fund. This total was brought up to 244 baths by the other 33 installations not built using money from the Baths Fund.

As there was a large unsatisfied demand, the Committee took steps to increase the number of baths to be built in the next two years by regulating the Committee's commitments in relation to cash balance, instead of the balance of credits over allocation. The Committee proposed that a number of installations under preparation should be somewhat in excess of the money available, so that there would always be a scheme ready for building as soon as the state of the Fund permitted the placing of the contract. If local difficulties were experienced at one scheme, its place would be taken by another so as not to delay the building programme, pending the resolution of the difficulties.

The urgency of the demand for baths had induced several District Committees (North Staffordshire, Lancashire, Ayr, Kent, South Yorkshire, West Yorkshire, Durham and Warwick) to recommend that the Committee should use their District Funds to supplement the Baths Fund. Up to the end of 1935, £423,096 had been allocated from the District Funds for baths.

In 1935, the usage of the baths based on returns from 114 installations had increased to 90%, and in 89% of the baths, the men's weekly subscription was 6d or less. Only 15 installations out of 114 showed a debit balance after charging the actual cost of repairs and renewals.

In 1935, following the success of the installation at Toftshaw Moor Colliery, a start had been made on building an installation for 200 men at Grange Ash Colliery, West Yorkshire on similar lines and arrangements for small installations in several other districts were being planned so as to extend the experiment further.

The Committee continued to encourage colliery owners to make general improvements at the pithead when installing pithead baths. Recent examples included the Rising Sun Colliery, Northumberland and Manvers Main and Silverwood Collieries, South Yorkshire.

Under the same influence, the Fife Coal Company requested assistance in laying out their new Comrie Colliery near the village of Oakley. In collaboration with the Company's officials, the Architects' Branch prepared sketch plans for the lay-out and buildings and the work would be carried through by the Company's architect.

By the end of 1935, £139,692 had been allocated for pithead welfare excluding pithead baths. Of this sum, £109,952 had been allocated from District Funds.

Before 1934, pithead canteens had been provided out of the District Funds but only if recommended by the District Committee. At baths provided in 1934 and 1935, 28 canteens had been included, wherever they were required, at the cost of the Baths Fund by virtue of the Welfare Fund Act 1934.

Cycle stores had been provided out of District Funds at 77 collieries with grants amounting to £27,206. Half of this total was granted in 1935, £13,049 for 38 new stores.

When cycle stores were built as an adjunct to a bath installation, a blank wall of the building was utilised. However, if the number of cycles to be stored was more than 200, a store separate from the bath building was more economical. In exposed positions, sheds with enclosures had to be used adding approximately 3s per cycle to the cost of the store.

In 1935, the allocations for health purposes amounted to £72,835. Of this amount, £34,926 was made in grants to convalescent homes and their funds. £20,485 was granted in Ayrshire: £10,485 for increasing the accommodation and making other improvements at Troon and £10,000 was added to the endowment of the home. In Durham, £7,326 was added to the endowment of the home at Ulverston increasing the total allocated for the endowment to £309,764 and £5,764 was granted for additions, alterations and equipment.

The total sum allocated in 1935 for convalescent home tickets was £24,210 of which £24,000 was allocated to South Yorkshire's endowment fund bringing this to a total of £306,500. The income from this fund was used to maintain the convalescent homes at Scalby and Rhyl.

£3,444 was granted to hospitals in 1935 and only £1,816 to ambulance services, most of which went to assist the St John Ambulance Association in South Wales. In South Derbyshire, a co-ordinated scheme of ambulances had been established in the interest of economy and efficiency of the service as well as cost. The Committee hoped that the other districts where ambulances had been provided by the Welfare Fund would carefully consider a similar scheme of co-ordination.

Schemes for providing miners and their dependents with special medical treatment and appliances amounted to £7,516 in 1935. Grants for nursing services amounted to £923. 24

A deputation from Lancashire District Committee had attended the February meeting of the Committee in support of a recommendation that 30% of the District Fund (about £55,000) should be appropriated for certain health purposes. This recommendation was approved subject to certain minor alterations, and £45,000 was allocated for a Trust Fund of which the income was to be applied for approved purposes and £500 for the disbursement for approved purposes.

After the Trust Deed had been drafted and examined by the Committee's legal advisers, the Committee received a letter from the District Committee dated 15th May 1935, stating that the District Committee had decided to abandon the proposal preferring that the money should remain in an open Fund and that District Committee itself should deal with the applications as the income from the Trust Fund would not be sufficient to meet the purposes for which it was intended.

The Secretary wrote back to say that the letter would be considered at the

Committee meeting on 18th June, but the Central Committee had not hitherto placed a sum as large as £55,000 in the hands of a District Committee for distribution to individuals or amongst such a variety of purposes. The District Committee were asked to provide full information as to the number, amount and urgency of the requirements for assistance in each of the categories, distinguishing between capital and non-capital expenditure. They were also reminded that they were yet to provide the monthly list of grants made from the allocation of £500 or the regulations governing the making of grants out of this money.

On 27th May, the District Committee replied that they had not anticipated that the full amount of £55,000 should be transferred to them, but contemplated applying for grants from this Fund as required for health purposes, the supply of surgical appliances and railway fares of men visiting convalescent homes and other institutions for treatment.

At their June meeting, the Committee took the decision that the Assistant Secretary should consult the District Secretaries regarding the details of the procedure of the District Committee for dealing with Health Purposes and Local Schemes.

The District Committee were found to have clear procedures to be followed in dealing with grants, but it appeared that, although the District Committee had advised Area Committees that no commitments should be entered into until the grant had been approved by the Central Committee, one or two instances had occurred where this had not happened, apparently owing to a misunderstanding.

The District Committee had received applications for payments to hospitals and subscriptions to Nursing Services aggregating to about £14,000. A sub-committee had been appointed to survey the needs of the District and when completed, the District Committee proposed to consult the Central Committee with a view to obtaining the advice of the Ministry of Health.

The District Committee's procedures for grants for convalescent treatment for miners, miners' wives and females employed in the industry, institutional and spa treatment and provision of surgical appliances were satisfactory, but the Assistant Secretary advised that specific rules and regulations governing the conditions for grants should be drawn up and issued to Area Committees.

Some of the grants for surgical appliances, particularly repairs, amounted to only a few shillings, so it was suggested that the District Committee should consider limiting payments to an initial outlay and excluding grants for small sums under 10/-.

The decision by the District to make grants for health purposes and local schemes had created a considerable additional amount of work, so an increase in office staff and remodelling of the accounting system was recommended to meet the requirements of the District.

The District Committee had submitted a recommendation for a grant of £4,000 at the June meeting of the Central Committee, to be used in making direct payments from the District Fund for health purposes and local schemes (excepting hospital and nursing services), a grant of £500 for similar purposes having been approved by the Central Committee at the February meeting.

In view of the urgent request of the District Committee to meet the outstanding commitments, the Chairman had approved a provisional sum of £500. Following the Assistant Secretary's discussion with the Joint Secretaries, it was apparent that the whole of the £4,000 would be needed in addition to the £500, making £4,500 to meet the likely expenditure for 1935.[25]

Out of the £790,000 earmarked out of the General Fund for building and equipment for mining instruction, only £15,282 remained in 1935. Grants amounting to only £1,680 were made in 1935.

The Secretary for Mines opened the Fife Mining School at Cowdenbeath in March 1935. Also completed during the year were two new Senior Course Mining Centres at Tredegar, South Wales, and Hemsworth, West Yorkshire, and two extensions at Channock Chase Mining College and Heanor Mining and Technical School, Derbyshire.

The number of applicants for the Miners' Welfare National Scholarship scheme was 643. 81% were children of mineworkers and 18 scholarships were awarded (five 'A' candidates and thirteen 'B'). Of the unsuccessful candidates,

Fife Mining School, Cowdenbeath

19 were recommended for the Miners' Welfare Exhibitions provided from the Miners' Welfare Fund.

Thirteen scholars completed their scholarships in 1935, including two who were doing research work. All of the other eleven obtained degrees, four obtaining first class honours.

In addition to the scholarships and exhibitions schemes, 56 new students were recommended by District Committees to receive grants from the District Funds. There were already 58 students in receipt of grants bringing the total value of the special grants to £3,311. The object of the grant was not necessarily to enable the student to take a university degree course but often it was for much less advanced work and not infrequently for training for an occupation though seldom mining.

In 1935, the scheme of non-vocational lectures organised in Yorkshire by the Miners' Lectures Joint Committee (Yorkshire) of the Workers' Educational Association was granted £1,112 as in 1934, four-fifths from the two Yorkshire Districts Fund and one-fifth from the General Fund. In order to keep the scheme of non-vocational lectures organised by the Adult Education Department of Nottingham University College going, as a temporary measure while more permanent arrangements were being put in place, the Committee agreed to contribute £1,000 for three years. In addition, the two Districts, Nottinghamshire and Derbyshire, would contribute £500 each from their District Funds making £2,000 a year. £1,200 was additionally granted from Nottinghamshire District Fund and £300 from the General Fund as arrears for the grant that had not been received by the scheme in 1934.[26]

In February 1935, the Safety in Mines Research Board submitted their estimated expenditure for the year 1935/36 amounting to a total of £61,867. Towards this, £12,416 was available from the Endowment Fund, £1,750 from the Exchequer, £2,334 from savings on previous grants and the Committee made a grant of £45,367 from the General Fund.

£11,556 was included in the estimates for research into falls of ground and £3,630 for research into haulage accidents, £7,783 for research into explosions of coal dust or firedamp, £2,648 for research on wire ropes, £2,324 for electrical research, £2,048 for research on spontaneous combustion and £3,160 for safety instruction. The remaining expenditure was for maintenance of the Research Stations at Buxton and Sheffield and for general work of the Research Board.

As the grant made by the Committee in 1935 to the Board was 11% of the output levy (½ d per ton instead of 1d prior to 1934), the Committee informed the Board in May 1935 that they might have difficulty in maintaining grants in the future. They asked the Board to consider whether their demands on the Welfare Fund could not be reduced. Although the Board had appointed a sub-committee to review their research programmes to see if reductions in annual expenditure could be identified, no substantial reductions could be identified for the next five years but the Board undertook to reconsider the whole question in 1940.

The Committee had suggested that manufacturers should be asked to contribute towards some of the research; the Board replied that they had not overlooked this, but they attached great importance to preserving proper control of their work and publications of its results.

The Committee were proceeding to press the Research Board to explore further the possibilities of securing contributions from other interests, and were in the course of discussing the question of stabilising the Committee's grant for research for five years with them, when the government announced the appointment of the Royal Commission on Safety in Mines under the Chairmanship of Lord Rockley.

In November 1935, the Committee was informed by the Secretary for Mines that the inquiries and findings of the Commission would affect the planning and perspective of the Board's work. The Committee decided not to press the matter further.[27]

The membership of the Committee in 1936 remained unchanged except for the appointment in August of Mr Joseph Jones, President of the Mineworkers' Federation of Great Britain in place of Mr Ebby Edwards.

The total receipt of the Fund in 1936 was £729,225, including sums amounting to £81,875 derived from investments representing balances of the Welfare Fund awaiting disbursement and from profits on investments realised. £375,000 (51.4%) of this total amount was allocated to the Baths Fund, £263,556 (36.2%) to the Districts Fund and £90,669 (12.4%) to the General Fund.

With the demand for pithead baths far exceeding the available resources, at the beginning of 1936 the Central Committee looked at the problem anew with the result that, by modification of a financial method rendered practicable by the Welfare Fund Act of 1934, they decided to make a substantial increase in the number of new installations to be started in 1937 and 1938.

The financial rearrangement upon which this acceleration was based could be explained as follows. The total sum required for an installation had previously been allocated on the date when the building contractor's tender was approved by the committee, but the money was paid over to the contractor by instalments during the progress of the work, and the final payment was not made until some months after the building was completed; perhaps two years or more after the allocation was made. Consequently, there had been a difference of more than £500,000 between the total actually paid out, this difference representing the sums required to meet contract commitments.

With the Act of 1934 having extended the period of the Fund to twenty years instead of five, the Central Committee decided that it had become less important on financial grounds to limit the allocations for the baths strictly according to the sum standing to the credit of the Baths Fund for the time being. The central Committee therefore felt that they would be justified in reducing the working balance of more than £500,000 by making allocations during 1937 and 1938 at the rate of £250,000 a year more than the statutory figure of £375,000 a year, at a total of £625,000 a year.

The first step was to get the additional staff. The appointments were made in February and March, and by June or July, the new men were able to take their places in the work of the expanded programme.

By the end of 1936, negotiations had commenced for 76 installations, accounting for £1,200,000 of the £1,250,000 programme at which the Committee aimed for in the two-year period 1937/8. This was in addition to the 51 installations (costing £947,000 provided out of the receipts of the Welfare Fund prior to 31st December 1936) which were already in the course of construction or for which tenders had already been obtained. The baths under construction, or in the course of being designed or negotiated for at the end of 1936, numbered 127 at an estimated cost of two million pounds.

Before undertaking to provide baths at any colliery, the Central Committee made it their business, with the co-operation of the colliery owners to ensure that the workmen would not have to pay more than a reasonable amount as their weekly subscription for using the baths, the amount being determined according to the cost of operating the baths and the extent to which the colliery owners were willing to assist.

The maintenance problem was discussed at the first visit of the Architects' Branch to the colliery. Next a sketch plan and approximate estimate was made to see whether a building with the required accommodation could be built on the site offered. The colliery company and the workmen were given an early opportunity to examine the scheme and either approve it or suggest alterations. In 1936, nine of the 49 new installations which passed this stage underwent alterations, with the sketch plan having to be redone up to four times.

The site then had to be acquired for the trustees of the future baths. These negotiations had to be undertaken by the colliery company before the Central Committee could commit itself to any expenditure. This legal work frequently caused delays. Arrangements for services (drainage, water and electricity) to be provided to the baths were another source of delay as well as collieries deciding to alter the workings of the colliery when working drawings had already been prepared.

Disappointment was expressed at the Annual Conference of District

Committees in November 1936 that the increased rate of expenditure could not be continued after 1938, and a report of the discussion was placed before the Secretary for Mines.

Early in March 1937, the Secretary for Mines intimated that, while he could not anticipate any decision that Parliament might ultimately reach in this matter, he was satisfied that this accelerated programme which the Committee had in mind for the next two years was in every way desirable. He had concluded that he was justified in authorising the Committee to base their programme on the assumption that they would have £625,000 a year at their disposal, up to and including the year 1944.

By the end of 1936, the revival of trade, the rehousing projects and the measures taken for rearmament had already affected conditions in the building trade, and had impeded progress on the pithead bath programme owing to difficulties in securing skilled labour, materials and fittings. Sixteen new installations and three extensions were completed during 1936, and 41 new installations and five extensions were in the course of construction at the end of the year. In addition, tenders had been obtained and the money allocated for ten installations and sketch plans and estimates of costs had been prepared for 45 installations and four extensions.

The average cost per person of all installations in 1936 rose to £12.16s compared with £12.4s.4d in 1935 as a result of the increased wages and cost of equipment. The demand for skilled labour and materials also made it impossible to forecast costs with any accuracy. The majority of baths were also in isolated places, with contractors finding it necessary to offer special wages to secure labour.

To contend with these problems, the central staff purchased standard fittings and equipment in bulk by competitive tendering and by contracts covering suitable periods, which enabled manufacturers to reserve supplies of material to stabilise the labour requirements.

The cost of installations where women were employed was significantly higher at £40 and sometimes as high as £50 per head. This was due to the low numbers of women employed, and the fact that separate accommodation and full facilities were required for those women.

The construction of small installations continued in 1936, with sixteen schemes for 400 men or less having been built or in the course of preparation at the end of 1936. The small installation at Grange Ash Colliery, West Yorkshire, was opened in August 1936, having been started in 1935 (see page 152 above). At the small installations under construction, buffet canteens were included, being incorporated with the attendant's room in order to reduce labour and running costs.

At a very small colliery, employing 24 men and remotely situated at Brora in the Highlands of Scotland, baths were badly needed in consequence of the exceptional working conditions. Due to its remote position, the men had never benefitted from the Welfare Fund. The plan provided for a 'clean' and dirty area, a bath room with three open showers between the changing room, a lavatory, small cupboard for the attendant and a calorifier space adjacent to the pit locker room for drying very wet pit clothes. Steam was available from the colliery boilers, water from the river bounding the colliery yard. Bricks were manufactured on the spot.

The Committee continued to work with colliery companies to improve the layout and design of colliery surface buildings. At the invitation of Messrs Bestwood Coal and Iron Co Ltd, Nottingham, the Architects' Branch had collaborated with the Company's architect in his proposals for the surface lay-out of the new Calverton Colliery. In conjunction with the pithead baths schemes at Wheldale Colliery and Maltby Main Colliery, new lamp-rooms and covered ways from the shaft to the baths had been planned for the owners.

When a baths installation was ready for use, the Central Committee handed it over to the Trustees and arranged for it to be run by a colliery committee, comprising representatives of employers and employed in equal numbers with the Trustees acting as members ex officio. A few regulations were prescribed in the Central Committee's Trust Deed but upon all management questions, the Baths Committee had full discretion as well as responsibility. Their first two or three meetings, however, were attended by the Central Committee's Staff to give the Baths Management Committee the benefit of advice based upon the experience of the existing installations.

If problems arose, the Baths Management Committee were able to call upon the Central Staff for help and advice. Amongst the more general problems which had engaged the Central Committee during 1936 was the question of unemployment insurance for baths attendants, and the assessment of baths for local rating purposes. The Central Committee were able, through representation to the Ministry of Labour, to have the baths and canteen attendants included in the National Unemployment Insurance Scheme from 2nd March 1936.[28]

The ramping up of the Baths programme, and the attention to detail both before and after baths were built and handed over, had an impact on administrative costs. For the financial year ending 31st March 1936, the administrative cost of the Welfare Fund came to £40,184, of which £24,225 was attributed to the Baths Fund. The estimates for administrative expenses for 1936/37 presented to the March 1936 meeting of the Central Committee came to £51,606 with £28,427 being allocated to the Baths Fund.

This increase in administrative costs was not well-received, either by the

Small Colliery at Brora

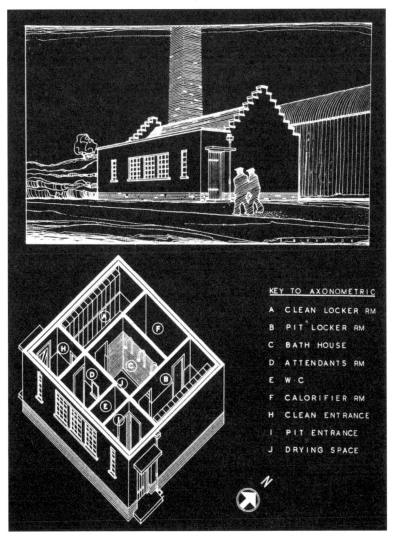

KEY TO AXONOMETRIC

A CLEAN LOCKER RM

B PIT LOCKER RM

C BATH HOUSE

D ATTENDANTS RM

E W.C

F CALORIFIER RM

H CLEAN ENTRANCE

I PIT ENTRANCE

J DRYING SPACE

Plan for pithead baths at Brora

Joint Consultative Committee of the Mining Association and Mineworkers or the District Committees. At the April meeting of the Central Committee, it was reported that Mr Ebby Edwards had felt compelled to resign because, as Secretary of the Joint Consultative Committee, he had been instructed by that body to write to the Secretary for Mines criticising the Central Welfare Committee. Mr J. T. Brown and Dr W. Hargreaves, both members of the Committee and the Mining Association, were also considering resignation because it appeared that they did not represent the views of their Association. The criticism certainly did not come from the Mineworkers' Federation. It was suspected that it came from South Wales, which had from the start pressed for complete autonomy.

By September 1936, the Central Committee was being criticised over the administration costs in the press by two or three Secretaries of District Committees, particularly in the South Wales Press. It was decided that the Secretary should not reply officially. A request by Nottinghamshire District Committee for the Chairman of the Central Committee to receive a deputation to present their views of the cost of administration was turned down, on the basis that the Joint Consultative Committee of the Coal Industry had assumed the task of presenting the criticism.

The expenses of the central administration were an agenda item at the 14th Conference of District Miners' Welfare Committees held on 17th November 1936, and had been proposed by Derbyshire District Committee. District Committees felt aggrieved that the amount of money available to the District Funds had been reduced by approximately 75% since 1934. A statement of the facts regarding administrative expenditure was circulated at the Conference.

Of the £40,184 up to 31st March 1936 designated as administrative expenses, £24,225 was the payment of the architects, quantity surveyors and other technical staff and the usual incidentals of construction work connected with pithead baths. In ordinary accounting practice, this expenditure would have been included as part of the cost of building. The cost of the technical staff employed in connection with recreational schemes was £3,200. Therefore, altogether £27,425 of the £40,184 was for construction work and not administrative expenses in the ordinary sense of the term.[29]

A notable development during 1936 in the field of recreation and social welfare was the growth of the movement to raise the standard of physical fitness and physical development of the nation. The movement had received a stimulus in 1935 from King George V's Jubilee message and the dedication of the Jubilee Trust 'to advance the physical, mental and spiritual welfare of the younger generation by the encouragement' amongst other things 'of physical exercise, training and self-discipline'. In June 1936, the King George V Memorial Fund was launched, with the provision of playing fields as one of its objects.

At about the same time, Local Government Authorities had been urged by the Board of Education to use their power more freely to provide recreation grounds out of public money so the Committee was seeking their co-operation with both outlay and upkeep with future Miners' Welfare Schemes. The National Playing Fields Association had assisted a few miners' welfare schemes. The Committee had also linked up with the newly formed Central Council of Recreative Physical Training.

A total of £167,488 was allocated in 1936 for recreation and social welfare of which £41,372 was for new schemes. £87,530 was granted for a total of 349 recreation grounds schemes. Again, the chief expenditure was for children's playgrounds, bowls and tennis courts. Of the 51 grants for children's playgrounds, 22 were for new schemes.

Of the larger outdoor recreational developments that had been in preparation or under construction during 1936, some had notable features. Coalsnaughton Recreation Scheme, comprising 4 acres, was developed at a cost of £1,800, £1,600 being from a grant by the District Fund and the remaining £200 being contributed by the National Playing Fields Association and the Carnegie United Kingdom Trust. On completion, this scheme was handed over to the Hillsfoots District Council for maintenance.

In South Wales, an interesting children's playground was under construction at Ynysmeudwy, in which an old people's garden and shelter were to be incorporated. The site was fairly steep, and the layout had not been easy.

The money for the new Community Centre at Kells, Whitehaven, was being provided by the Special Areas Commissioners through the National Council of Social Service.

£71,486 was granted for institutes, halls and places of indoor recreation. Two grants to existing institutes were for the dismantling, removal and re-erection in other villages of buildings which had fallen into disuse as a result of the closing down of collieries and the demolition of dwelling houses.

£52,175 of the £71,486 was spent on equipping and reconditioning buildings which had previously been provided or assisted from the Fund.

£5,807 was allocated to other recreational purposes of which £3,287 was granted to St Athans Camp in South Wales and £2,000 to the South Wales Federation of Boys' Clubs. The Federation, which had 54 affiliated clubs, had received a total of £18,561 from the Miners' Welfare Fund.[30]

Cdr. Coote wrote to the Committee on 7th February 1936, informing them that he had received and proposed to accept an offer of another post even though it entailed considerable financial loss. He felt that the Miners' Welfare Fund no longer needed the services of a pioneer, whereas there would be scope for pioneering work in the new post offered to him. He asked for a gratuity because his future salary would be insufficient to cover the yearly premium of £54 payable until the age of 65 under his life insurance policy taken out upon his appointment under the Committee.

The Committee decided to propose to Cdr. Coote that they should continue to employ him as a consultant, to advise upon special questions as necessary, and pay him a yearly retaining fee equal to the amount of the premiums under the life insurance policy. Cdr. Coote accepted the Committee's proposal and asked for his period of notice to expire on 31st August.[31]

Expenditure on health purposes in 1936 was £84,259, or 8.8% of all expenditure from the Fund during 1936.

The extension to the Troon Convalescent Home (for women) in Ayrshire opened in July 1936. £10,485 had been spent on the recent extension which had increased the number of beds from 30 to 48 besides improving the accommodation and the convenience of the building in other respects.

Grants for hospitals in 1936 totalled £33,789, of which ambulance services amounted to £8,130, special medical treatment and appliances £6,889 and nursing services £4,020. In Warwickshire, where district nursing services had been the object of numerous grants from the District Fund, the District Committee had asked the District Organiser to survey the mining communities in relation to the provision of nursing services. The report and recommendations, which had received the approval of the Ministry of Health, had proved of valuable assistance to the District Committee in making further

Troon Convalescent Home

grants. The survey had also resulted in establishing closer co-operation with other local bodies providing nursing services.

With the building and equipment programme for mining education nearly complete. Only £5,766 was allocated in 1936 for this purpose, £4,956 from the General Fund amongst six centres and £810 from the Districts Fund. However, there were several schemes which had been completed.

Preston Lodge Mining School, East Lothian, which had been provided from a grant of £5,000 from the Welfare Fund, was opened in December 1936 by Sir Thomas Hudson Beare, Regus Professor of Engineering and Dean of the Faculty of Science, Edinburgh, and Assessor to the Central Committee. The new School was badly needed as the mining classes had been carried out at a secondary school where there was no room for equipment.

Dudley and Staffordshire Technical College was opened by The Right Honourable Oliver Stanley, PC, MC, MP, President of the Board of Education, in March 1936. Costing £110,000, towards which grants had been made from the Welfare fund to a total of £7,540, the college filled the need for an advanced centre for technical education in these districts. The mining department included rooms for mining science, surveying, gas-testing and lectures and would provide facilities for the training of candidates for First-Class and Second-Class Certificates of Competency, Surveyor's Certificate and Firemen's Certificate.

Preston Lodge Mining School, East Lothian

Extensions to the Quaker's Yard Mining and Technical Institute, Merthyr Tydfil, were opened in May 1936 by Alderman Lewis Jones JP, Mayor of Merthyr Tydfil. The extensions comprised an engineering laboratory, woodwork room, classrooms, shower baths and students' common room which would be used by the mining students. The Welfare Fund had made a grant of £3,840 towards the cost of the extensions.

The number of applicants for the Miners' Welfare National Scholarship Scheme in 1936 was 497. Fifteen scholarships were awarded, of which seven were for mineworkers and eight were for children of mineworkers. Thirteen scholars completed their scholarships in 1936, including one doing research.

The Miners' Welfare National Students' Exhibition Scheme was established in 1936 by means of an endowment grant of £25,000 from the General Fund, the money (about £880 per annum) providing exhibitions for meritorious but unsuccessful candidates for the Mines' Welfare Scholarships. The number of exhibitions awarded in 1936 was 19, of which 2 were mineworkers and 17 children of mineworkers.

During 1936, special grants to students for subjects other than mining were made to 63 students for the first time, and to 54 who had already received grants. New grants for students of mining numbered 9 and there were two grants to students who had already received grants.

The number of districts that had adopted safety instruction for pit boys in safety principles had grown to thirteen in 1936. Four of these districts, Fifeshire, Lothians, Ayrshire and South Wales, made grants for the first time in 1936.

The Safety in Mines Research Board's estimates for 1936/7 amounted to £60,548. Towards this, £12,416 was available from the income of the Endowment Fund, £1,750 from the Exchequer, £1,186 from the unused balance of the previous grants and the Committee granted £44,996.

The estimates included £18,096 for researches into dust and firedamp explosions, safety lamps, spontaneous combustion and safe use of explosives and electrical apparatus in coal mines. Estimates for research into falls of ground (£10,985) and haulage accidents (£4,050) covered researches being carried out by District Research Committees as well as directly under the Board.[32]

The total estimated receipt of the Fund in 1937 was £723,800 including £60,000 derived from investments. £375,000 of this total sum was allocated to the Baths Fund, £261,040 to the District Funds and £87,760 to the General Fund.[33]

There were continued delays in 1937 in building contracts for pithead baths, due to shortages of skilled labour and delays in delivery of materials by manufacturers and merchants. Although shortage of labour had recovered in the autumn, the improvement had been effectively cancelled out by the winter conditions and delays due to non-delivery of materials showed no sign of improvement.

During the period 1st December 1936 to 31st January 1937, 23 members of the Architects' Branch were absent owing to sickness due chiefly to the influenza epidemic. This represented a total of 838 hours lost.

On a brighter note, the Miners' Welfare Committee had been invited to submit drawings and photographs of completed buildings representative of the work carried out by the Committee's architects for an exhibition of British Architecture at the Royal Academy, being held from January to March 1937. The purpose of the exhibition was to present good examples of British Architecture of the early twentieth century up to 1937.

Interest in the Architects' Branch's work was also shown by the British Aluminium Company Ltd., who were considering providing bathing and clothes storage arrangements for their employees. A visit to three installations in Lanarkshire was arranged for two representatives in January 1937. Dr Adams, the architect and town planning consultant who was advising the Coronation Planting Committee, was referred to the Architects' Branch, who proposed to assist by loaning examples of the Committee's work in connection with outdoor schemes.

The Committee consulted the District Committees in January 1937 to ensure that their list of applications for baths included all those made to District Committees. This confirmed that there were 217 to be provided in or after 1937 out of the Baths Fund at an estimated cost of £2,845,453 plus technical expenses. At the rate of £625,000, this sum represented about 4½ years with 45 or 46 schemes a year. There were already 77 schemes in preparation in February 1937 but there were 73 outstanding applications which were more than 3 years old. A systematic attempt to dispose of these applications in the programme for 1939 and 1940 would involve not only departing from the basis of apportionment among the Districts but also asking District Committees in some instances to alter their priority lists.

At the January 1937 meeting of the Committee, the Chairman asked whether the Architectural staff were adequate to deal with the programme for 1937 and 1938. Mr Forshaw undertook a careful examination, and suggested that it would be advisable to make adjustments to the organisation of the technical staff and to set aside a 'provisional sum' for additional assistance.

The Estimates Sub-Committee examined Mr Forshaw's proposals at their meeting on 16th February. The Sub-Committee approved the proposal to transfer the Recreation Grounds construction and maintenance work from the Districts Branch to the Architects' Branch, but they deferred the proposal for 'provisional sums' for special temporary assistance when required. The

Sub-Committee, however, approved two new posts of Architect from the 1st April. Two Senior Architectural Assistants were to be promoted to these posts and appointments were to be made to fill the consequential vacancies. Three Architects were to receive bonuses of £40 in 1938 and 1939 and three were to receive £30 bonus the next year. Two posts of Quantity Surveyors' Assistants Grade I were to be established in place of one Quantity Surveyor and one Grade II, and two members of staff to be appointed to these posts.

The Recreation Section was transferred to the Architects' Branch of 1st April 1937.[34]

In 1937, the Government were in active preparation of precautionary measures which would be necessary in time of war, for safeguarding the civil population against the effects of air attacks. One of the most vital of the precautionary measures was the organisation of facilities for dealing with poison gas victims of air raids, particularly victims of mustard gas. The main treatment for these victims was to remove all their clothes and to wash them in hot water as quickly as possible. It was probable that existing buildings would be used, and pithead baths were particularly suitable.

The Home Office Air Raids Precaution Department had approached the Miners' Welfare Committee, and, in March 1937, the Committee shared the discussions they had had with the Department for Mines and the District Committees.[35]

In May 1937, the Committee considered the design for the installation at Alexandra and Batock Colliery, Lancashire. The sketch plan illustrated a form of construction which was considered suitable for buildings that were not required to last permanently. The construction used concrete foundations, floors and plinths, asbestos sheet walling with light steel stanchions, and a timber framed roof covered with felt.

Building costs were again causing concern in May 1937, with tenders in excess of the estimates approved by the Committee. This was particularly acute in connection with engineering works costing twice those of the previous year. There continued to be problems with obtaining skilled labour and materials.

By July 1937, ten installations and two extensions had been completed and put into use. It was estimated that an additional twenty-one installations would be completed by 31st December 1937. However, there were delays on twenty-five contracts which were in progress. Steel delivery delays accounted for many of these, as well as a lack of brick layers. There had been an underground fire under one site, leading to a month's delay while it was awaiting reinforcement.[36]

At the preliminary investigation held at Wolstanton Colliery (North Staffordshire) on 20th May 1937, the Management had asked that the projected pithead baths should accommodate both their coal and ironstone miners. The colliery was unique in the country where ancillary mineral formed so large a part of the total activities. At the June 1937 Committee meeting, the matter was deferred while advice was sought from the Inland Revenue Authorities, who confirmed in July that the Royalties Welfare Levy was paid on the ironstone output of the colliery.

In January 1929, at the preliminary investigation for pithead baths at Dinnington Main (South Yorkshire), the Company was told that provision for ancillary workers (coke oven and brickyard hands) could not be made at the cost of the Welfare Fund and the installation was designed to accommodate 3,024 men. While the baths were under construction, the number of men employed fell dramatically and stood at 1,590 by September 1931, of which 100 were coke oven and brickyard hands. 1,440 pairs of lockers were provided at the opening in June 1932 and subsequently a further 216. An application for a further 288 pairs of lockers was considered at the June 1937 meeting. Similar applications had previously been received from Shotten and Monckton Main No 1 and 2 where the companies concerned had been told that they would have to pay for the accommodation of their coke oven and brickyard workers. Mr Herbert Smith and Mr Parker were asked to investigate the problem at Dinnington. They found that the coke oven, by-product workers and wagon repairers were employed on the colliery premises and could be included as surface workers. They were also members of the Yorkshire Miners' Association. The representatives of the colliery agreed to withdraw the application for locker accommodation for the cottage men and brickyard workers, but asked for the provision of lockers for a further 288 men.[37]

On 16th July 1937, members of the Committee (Sir Federick Sykes, Professor Collis, Professor Abercrombie, Mr W. Lawther, Mr Herbert Smith, Dr Quine and Sir Thomas Hudson Beare) toured four pithead baths in Nottinghamshire, South and West Yorkshire. They were accompanied by the Secretary, Assistant Secretary and members of the Architects' and Districts Branches.

The party was able to see the baths in use by the largest shift at Grange Ash (West Yorkshire) but the visits to Bentinck Colliery (Nottinghamshire), Manvers Main (South Yorkshire) and Rothwell Haigh (Fanny) Colliery did not coincide with this time. The visit to Rothwell Haigh (Fanny) Colliery was combined with a visit to Rothwell Park Recreation Ground.

The good effect of planting at Bentinck and Manvers Main was observed. For several years, the sum of £20 in the building contracts for baths was included for surface planting.

The party were generally pleased with the 4 pithead baths they visited, although Rothwell Haigh did need some maintenance. The policy of gradual introduction of open showers had been the right one to follow.

The party had the opportunity to hear about the success of Rothwell Park

Recreation Ground from the local committee, and afterwards to visit the grounds. The local authority was developing the adjacent land on the east side of the park.[38]

By September 1937, there had been setbacks to the flow of work in the preparation of schemes for pithead baths for tender. The more serious reasons were delays due to changed conditions, inability to obtain extra surveyors for which approval had been given, abnormal cases of prolonged sickness in the case of two senior draughtsmen, and resignations in the junior grades for which replacements were not easily found.

Despite the setbacks, twenty one installations and five extensions had been completed by 31st December 1937. There were also 70 installations and five extensions under construction and 82 schemes and one extension in preparation at the end of 1937.[39]

Although not every District had a District Organiser, in the Districts where they were employed, they were making a difference to the way local recreational schemes were managed. In Fife and Clackmannan District, their District Organiser, Mr Herd, had visited an institute in the District that had a bad reputation. He found that 50 people were playing cards for money. He discussed the situation with the Secretary and the Committee members present and they agreed that the cards should be collected immediately. Mr Herd spoke very strongly about gambling within institute premises. On examining the finance books for the previous months, he found that a certain income had been derived from gambling games. Because of the no-gambling rule, the institute's Committee had subsequently provided various indoor games which proved so popular that an additional caretaker had to be employed as billiards room attendant upstairs.[40]

The District Organiser in Northumberland had been asked to prepare a report on the condition of bowling greens by the District Welfare Committee. His main criticism was that the deterioration of the bowling greens (and other parts of the recreation grounds) was due to the poor type of groundsmen so the District Committee had issued instructions to local committee that, in future, no groundsman was to be appointed without prior consultation with the District Organiser.

In Kent, close co-operation was being maintained with the National Playing Fields Association through the District Organiser. The first result had been the Association's expressed willingness to provide a children's playground at Eythorne, in conjunction with the Tilmanstone Miners' Welfare Scheme. The Central Council of Recreational Physical Training were also arranging a play leadership demonstration at Chislet on the children's playground being constructed as part of the Recreation scheme. The District Organiser had also arranged for the local authorities to contribute to the wages of a superintendent for the playground.

The question of overlapping of Miners' Welfare Schemes by National Council of Social Service huts in South Wales had been discussed with representatives of the South Wales District Welfare Committee. It was evident, despite the National Council's assurances that proper co-operation was not maintained, and huts had been erected in proximity to Miners' Welfare Schemes. A further meeting had therefore been arranged with the Ministry of Labour and the National Council to ensure that use would be made of Miners' Welfare Schemes in conjunction with the National Council's activities.[41]

A meeting subsequently took place at the Mines Department on 16th March between the National Council of Social Service (Mr Sholton Jack, Secretary; Sir Percy Watkins, South Wales Representative; and Mr Adams, Northern Area representative), the Ministry of Labour (Mr Somervell and Mr Allen), the Mines Department (Mr Nott-Bower) and the Miners' Welfare Committee (Mr Stedman and Mr Parker). A full discussion took place with a view to making arrangements for better co-operation in Mining Districts in the future especially in South Wales. Subsequently, through the services of the Central Staff, a Joint Committee of the South Wales Miners' Welfare Committee and the South Wales branch of the National Council of Social Service was formed.

On 1st and 2nd April 1937, at the request of the Ocean Coal Company Welfare Supervisor, the nine pithead baths at the Company's collieries were visited by the Districts Branch to prepare reports on the standard of maintenance of each installation for the Company and the Baths Committees.[42]

In May 1937, it was reported that the Districts Branch had had under consideration the question of approaching water companies in order to obtain reduced charges. At a recent meeting with Management Committees, it was suggested to them that they should, through any local councillor on their Committees, take steps in this direction. Precedent had already been set in three cases.

The General Manager of the Edinburgh Collieries Company had approached the East Lothians Water Board, and the District Organiser in Fifeshire, helped by the owners and miners, had almost completed negotiating with the Fifeshire Water Board. In both cases it was confidently expected that a free allowance of ten gallons per man per day would be the outcome. The Wemyss Water Trust in East Fifeshire was already supplying free water up to 7 gallons per man per day to the Michael and Lochhead Pithead Baths.

Further approaches were made to Water Companies on the North-East coast. The Central Committee's desire to obtain advantageous terms for pithead baths was put before the officials of the Companies concerned. Strong opposition was met, as it was firmly believed that any reduction in charges for water would benefit the coal owners. The correct situation was explained.[43]

The Districts Branch also sought to reduce the cost of steam, coal and electricity at pithead baths. The Head of the Branch met representatives of Messrs Forster Raw and Company who managed a considerable number of collieries in Durham and Northumberland. The Head of the Branch managed to agree a standard cost for all their pithead baths for electricity, coal and water.[44]

On 20th April, a deputation from Nottinghamshire District Committee met representatives from the Central Committee to discuss loans from colliery companies, and the rule against grants for the provision or improvement of facilities for sale of alcoholic drinks.

It had been the custom in the District for Colliery Companies to finance schemes where the allocations from the District Fund were not immediately available, and to make refunds as and when the credits of the Fund were sufficient. However, the rules of the Central Committee permitted grants for repayment of Colliery Companies' loans, but the Committee were unable to guarantee repayment in respect of such loans as they had no power to enter into any agreement intended to bind the Committee or their successors to allocate money which might be in the Fund at some future date. Repayment would have to be regarded being on the footing of a 'gentleman's agreement'.

A scheme at Welbeck had been submitted to the District Committee and the Colliery Company was prepared to advance the £4,000 required, in order that the scheme could be put in hand. The District Fund, however, had an unallocated balance at the end of March 1936 of over £10,000, with a further £11,000 still to be credited in respect of the levy on the 1936 output. The District Committee still had not submitted their five-year plan for the utilisation of their District Fund, which would assist the Committee in determining whether the District's resources were insufficient to meet the needs of the District.

Nottinghamshire were under the misunderstanding that they needed to supply exact costings, while only approximate figures were acceptable. They therefore felt sure that they could meet the requirements of the Committee for their five-year plan and were satisfied that allocations would be made in approved cases to repay loans as money became available. Their five-year plan (1937–41) was submitted for consideration in May 1938.

The meeting then went on to consider the new proposed Institute at Blidworth, which would replace the current Miners' Welfare Scheme which comprised an army hut converted into a fully licenced Institute with a recreation ground. This was the only social amenity for the four to five thousand people living in the community. A grant of £2,000 had been recommended in September 1936 by the District Committee, subject to a loan from Newstead Colliery

Company Limited of £7,000, repayable in four annual instalments, which had been deferred by the Central Committee to enable the District Committee to consider, as an alternative, the provision of an unlicensed institute.

Staff of the Central Committee were aware that all institutes in Nottinghamshire were licenced and they should have known that Blidworth would not be an exception, but it wasn't until November 1936, when the formal recommendation had been made, that the District Committee was informed that the Central Committee would not make a grant because of the provision of the sale of intoxicants. This was considered to be very unfair to the workmen.

The rule of the Central Committee which had been made following the recommendations of the Chelmsford Inquiry Committee, did not prohibit the sale of intoxicants but prevented the expenditure of Miners' Welfare Fund money on providing such facilities for the sale of intoxicants.

After a full discussion, it was agreed that Nottinghamshire District Committee should reconsider submitting an application for a grant, excluding the cost of the bar, and the Central Committee would consult the Board of Trade Solicitor as to whether the Committee was empowered by law to regulate grants for the purpose of providing or improving facilities for the sale of alcoholic drinks.

A further joint meeting with Nottinghamshire and Derbyshire District Committee was held on 15th July 1937 at Victoria Station Hotel, Nottingham, to deal with the position that had arisen, particularly concerning the two districts, following the opinion of the Board of Trade Solicitor on the Committee's rule, made in 1933, not to approve any further grants for the provision or improvement of facilities for the sale of alcoholic drinks.

In the opinion of the solicitor, this rule required the approval of the Secretary for Mines to establish its validity. This opinion had been considered by the Central Committee in May and June, and it had been decided to discuss the matter further with the two District Committees.

Following the meeting with the two Districts, at the July meeting of the Central Committee, they decided that they would in future be prepared to consider recommendations from District Committees for exceptions in special circumstances to the rule against making grants from the Welfare Fund for providing or improving facilities for the sale of intoxicants, but that it would be necessary for every case to be investigated and reported upon by the District Branch.

The Committee reconsidered the recommendations of the Derbyshire Committee for grants of £94.1s for a cash register at Heanor and £711.13s.6d for alterations to Somercotes and Riddings, of which sum, about half related to alterations to provide a bar, billiards and smoke room.

The Committee further agreed to allow the cost of the bar at Blidworth Institute to be included in the future instalments of a grant to be recommended in respect of the provision of this Institute.[45]

In July 1937, the Committee considered the replies to the questionnaire on the co-ordination of the Miners' Welfare Ambulances in Durham and Northumberland. No replies had been obtained from Northumberland District Committee on their schemes, as they considered that they had answered these when they jointly met Sir Frederick Sykes with Durham District Committee in June 1936 in Newcastle.

In respect of the 29 ambulance schemes in Durham, there were considerable practical difficulties operating against achieving any systematic co-ordination of these ambulances, so the Committee decided not to press the question further.

When considering further grants for ambulances, the Committee agreed to consider recommendations for new schemes, subject to the Trust Deeds including the usual provision for co-ordination since it was likely that this would receive consideration on a county, regional or national basis by other Government Authorities. In October 1937, the Public Health Act 1936 would come into force, giving local government authorities the power to provide ambulances.[46]

By 1937, the balance available for allocation for mining education buildings and equipment was only £35,413.

Nottinghamshire Education Committee had applied for a grant of £1,323.16s,6d to provide equipment for the Mining department at Worksop Technical College which had opened in 1930, costing about £31,000 of which the Miners' Welfare Fund had contributed £9,800 towards the building and £4,000 towards the erection and finishing of the gymnasium. The Authority were planning an extension, but there was an urgent need for equipment for advanced mining instruction. After amendments, the cost was reduced to £939 and a grant of £313 was approved to reflect the line taken elsewhere of contributing one third of the total.

In 1927, the Miners' Welfare Committee had increased their grant towards the extension of Manchester College of Technology on the understanding that at least £10,000 towards the cost of improving facilities for mining education would be provided from other sources. The increased demand for mining courses did not materialise so, based on the 1935/6 figures, Mr Savage, the Committee's assessor for Education in England and Wales, recommended that the provisional allocation of £10,000 should only be confirmed to the extent of £1,500 only, a reduction of £8,500.[47]

The estimates for the Safety in Mines Research Board1937/8 were presented at the January 1937 meeting of the Central Committee. The total was £57,100 of which £12,416 would be contributed from the Endowment Fund and £1,750 from the Exchequer, leaving the Committee to find £42,944. A further sum of £3,225 would be required for Safety Instruction.

With the estimates, the Board had made provision for spending £1,000 during the year on research, in co-operation with the Medical Research Council and other bodies, into silicosis and kindred diseases among coal miners.

Since 1st June 1931, Medical Boards, under the Workmen's Compensation Acts, commenced certification of cases of silicosis in coal mines, and up to 31st May 1936, more than 1,100 certificates of silicosis had been issued by the Boards. There were also many other cases among coal miners where death or disability had been caused by forms of lung trouble, which though not regarded as silicosis was probably due, at least in part, to the nature of the employment. Nearly 90% of the certificates referred to cases which had occurred in South Wales for which there was no satisfactory explanation.

There was urgent need for further work on the diagnosis and prevention of this group of diseases. These problems were so difficult and obscure as to require scientific teamwork on a large scale in which medical, mining, geological and other experts would each play their part. The investigation was still under discussion, but the Safety in Mines Research Board considered that £1,000 would be sufficient for 1937–38 but a further sum would be required for the next financial year.[48]

The Miners' Welfare Committee were asked by the Royal Commission on Safety in Coal Mines 'to provide for their information a statement of its future policy' regarding subsidising research out of the Welfare Fund. A paper was prepared setting out the history of the funding of the Safety in Mines Research Board and the impact of the reduction of the Output Levy and the money accruing to the General Fund from which the Board obtained its annual grants. This paper was considered at the March 1937 meeting of the Central Committee.

The question of stabilising the annual grant for research for a period was, at the Welfare Committee's request, examined by Mr Fudge, Head of the Health and Safety Division of the Mines Department, in consultation with the Secretaries of the Central Committee and the Safety in Mines Research Board. Mr Fudge's proposal was that for a period of five financial years, the annual grant from the Welfare Fund should be stabilised at £44,000, including the statutory £20,000. This sum would be a maximum covering safety instruction and all other purposes. This proposal was based on the assumption that the Board would be allowed to keep as a reserve any savings they could effect to moneys already at their disposal and to add or spend from that reserve, at their discretion, during the stabilisation period.

The Welfare Committee would be prepared to accept as a basis of their future policy, Mr Fudge's recommendation, if they could be assured that an adequate share, say half, of the sum required for the researches would be forthcoming from manufacturing interests and the Exchequer.[49]

The total estimated receipts for the Miners' Welfare Fund in 1938 was £744,000 of which £275,200 was appropriated to the Districts Fund, £93,800 to the General Fund and £375,000 to the Baths Fund.[50]

In 1938, the Pithead Baths programme continued to be beset with delays, but 53 schemes were completed. This number did, however, include seventeen schemes which had been carried forward from 1937. Twenty schemes from 1938 had to be carried into 1939.

Although shortages of labour and materials were less acutely felt in 1938 than 1937, the uncertainty about the imminence of war and fluctuations had occurred creating difficulties and delays. While competitive tendering had generally received the keenest price, the lowest tenders were sometimes submitted by contractors whose organisation and resources were not likely to give the quickest progress of the execution of the work. Abnormal weather had also played its part, particularly on isolated schemes and unforeseen difficulties with sites and prolonged negotiations with Local Authorities.[51]

Following on from the Committee's tour of the pithead baths in Nottinghamshire, and South and West Yorkshire on 16th July 1937 (see page 168), Mr Forshaw put forward a number of proposals to improve future pithead baths which the Committee considered at their meeting on 18th January 1938.

To encourage better layout and planting of the site, it was suggested that the allowance should be increased from £20 to £40, where it was justified by the size of the scheme or there was an opportunity for planting.

Paint would be used instead of distemper. Alternative means of storing boots in the locker rooms to avoid pilfering and deterioration of the leather by exposure to heat would be explored by the architectural staff with a view to practical trials. The list of equipment and fittings in the First Aid room would be reviewed by Dr Quine in discussion with Dr Fisher. Vacuum cleaners were being installed experimentally (two central and four portable) and the report on the experience of these would inform their future use in pithead baths.[52]

The staff sub-committee also had a meeting on 18th January 1938, and considered Mr Forshaw's memorandum in which he had reviewed the staffing of his Branch in the light of the experience in 1937, and submitted proposals for adding to the staff and improving salaries and recommending that the Quantity Surveyors should in future be separated from the Architects' Branch. After discussing the latter with Mr Forshaw and Mr Rayner, the sub-committee decided it could not accept this recommendation.

Mr Forshaw's proposals on salaries and duties of the senior ranks were discussed with Mr Forshaw and later with Mr Kemp, Assistant Chief Architect.

The Committee approved of the duties, but did not feel able to accept Mr Forshaw's salary proposals in full; they requested that the Mines Department, in consultation with Mr Stedman, submit alternative proposals. No decision was taken on the proposal for additional staff.[53]

In May 1938, the Empire Exhibition was opened by King George VI and the Queen. This was a large-scale international trade fair held in Bellahouston Park in Glasgow. The Committee's architectural staff been involved in two exhibits. Sketch plans for a model mine had been produced by the staff at the request of the Mining Association Committee. The Miners' Welfare exhibit was a model of the recreational facilities being provided at Hamstead, South Staffordshire. [54]

With the District Committees settling the priority lists for the provision of pithead baths rather than the Central Committee as in the early days of the pithead bath programme, the Committee asked the Secretary, in March 1938, to review the ruling, circulated to District Committees in October 1926, that preference would be given to collieries where owners were prepared to contribute to the cost of building the baths.

In May 1938, West Yorkshire District Committee had written to the Central Committee in regard to the case of the Allerton Bywater Colliery, to say that they were opposed to the procedure of allowing a colliery to purchase priority for the provision of a pithead baths installation by the contribution of 10% of the capital cost. The Central Committee decided at their June 1938 meeting that the rule could no longer be justified and a letter, dated 14th June 1938, stating that the rule had been rescinded was sent by the Secretary to all District Committees.[55]

In November 1938, the Committee received the report on the six vacuum cleaners (four portable plants and two central plants) installed in six new pithead baths. One portable plant and one central plant were still being installed.

At the time that the experiment was authorised in June 1937, there were 22 installations using vacuum cleaners purchased out of their own funds, and reports in every case showed that a vacuum cleaner provided a satisfactory and efficient method of cleaning. The number of installations equipped with vacuum cleaners had increased by November 1938 to 33, including the four used for the experiment. Superintendents and baths committees were definite in their opinion that vacuum cleaners were an asset. They were used at least once a week, chiefly for cleaning the tops of the lockers, the ducting, roof members and pipes but not generally for floors.

The results of the experiment showed that vacuum plants kept surface finishes clean and preserved, inaccessible parts of the building could be reached, and it avoided the re-deposit of dust which resulted from the alternative method of dry sweeping.

The results supported the provision of portable plants for single-storey baths, and central plants for those with two or more storeys, as part of the standard equipment of all schemes for which the building contract had not yet been placed.[56]

At the end of December 1937, the Central Committee issued a circular to all District Committees in England and Wales on the Physical Training and Recreation Act 1937, which provided for the development of facilities for, and the encouragement of physical training and recreation and facilitated the establishment of centres for social activities. The circular had an enclosed copy of a pamphlet entitled 'National Fitness, The First Step' which had been issued by the National Council for Physical Training and Recreation for England and Wales.

Locally, the advancement of the movement for physical training and recreation would be in the hands of the Area Committees, twenty two in England and Wales and five in Scotland. Some of the purposes of the Miners' Welfare Fund and some of the facilities provided or contemplated at Miners' Welfare schemes came within the scope of the Area Committees so the Central Committee were suggesting that the District Committees make themselves known to the Area Committees, so that the interests of the Miners' Welfare Fund interests could be represented on the sub-committees covering their Coal Districts.[57]

Progress was being made with appointing Central Committee District Organisers. On 1st January 1938, Mr P. Callimore took up his appointment as District Organiser for West Yorkshire. On 14th January 1938, the Chairman accompanied by Mr Llewellyn Jacob, the Secretary and the Head of the Districts Branch met with South Wales District Committee to discuss the appointment of the successor to Mr C. S. Mason, who had resigned as from 1st February.

At the meeting on 1st February, it was agreed that two District Organisers should be appointed, each to have charge of half the South Wales District. They would be appointed to the staff of the Districts Branch of the Central Committee, and their salaries and expenses would be charged to the General Fund. The Central Committee would select the shortlist but the District Committee with the assistance of Mr Stedman and Mr Parker would select the candidates, interview them and nominate two for appointment.

Mr Daniels and Mr Jones were appointed the new District Organisers for South Wales, and they reported to Headquarters on 11th April. After a course of instruction, including visits to Organisers in other districts, they would take up duties in the areas assigned to them.[58]

At the May 1937 meeting, the Miners' Welfare Committee had considered the question of summer camps for pit boys, and had decided that the subject should be investigated. Discussions had taken place with Captain Paterson

(Duke of York's Camp), Captain Glynn Jones (St Athans Camp), the Camps Committee of the Central Council of Recreative Physical Training, the National Association of Boys Clubs and Sir Robert Burrows.

These discussions had led to the conclusion that the value of boys' camps was not likely to be considered unless they were instituted as part of a broader movement for the welfare of boys, working chiefly through boys' clubs.

Little had been done for boys (or girls) between 14 and 18 years of age, except in South Wales where many successful boys' clubs and popular boys' camps had been organised through the initiative and energy of an able leader - Captain Glynn Jones.

There had been almost universal neglect of this branch of welfare work during the 17 years since the Welfare Fund had been instituted so there was a need for the Central Committee to take the initiative in most Districts in getting the movement started and launching it.

North Wales, Warwickshire and Lancashire were suggested as districts where it might be possible to start the schemes and they all had an interest in this area of welfare. A leader, with the support of the respective District Miners' Welfare Committee, would be appointed to stimulate interest amongst boys, colliery officials and other prominent people in the most favourable localities. This would lead to the establishment of a pioneer boys club and a summer camp for boys. The club would be established in premises belonging to a Miners' Welfare scheme. A sub-committee of the District Committee would be formed to sponsor the boys' clubs in the District. Maintenance expenses of the club and camp would be defrayed from subscriptions of the boys and from funds raised by the leader of the boys locally.

During the first three years while the scheme in each district was being launched, it would be necessary to make a grant from the General Fund (£2,000), on condition that contributions were also available from the District Fund (£1,000) and the National Association of Boys' Clubs (£300) for each scheme.[59]

By October 1938, the Warwickshire District Committee had accepted the Central Committee's offer of assistance towards a scheme for furtherance of Boys' Club activities in the District. It was expected that Trustees would be appointed to administer the pooled grants from the General Fund, District Fund and the National Association of Boys' Clubs.

The other districts that had been approached, North Wales and Lancashire, had not responded as enthusiastically and consideration was being given to transferring the offer to other districts.[57]

The duties of District Organisers in connection with Pithead Baths had been discussed at the Seventh District Organisers' Conference held on 28th September 1937. It was agreed that the Head of the Districts Branch, in consultation with

Mr Forshaw would draft a memorandum on the subject for early discussion. At that time, District Organisers were visiting pithead baths when the opportunity occurred, but no definite line regarding advice was being given.

The standard of cleanliness and the general organisation of maintenance at many pithead baths were not as good as they should be. Many Management Committees, lacking experience beyond their own installation, did not realise how an installation should be kept. This unsatisfactory position was largely due to the methods of appointing the baths' staff.

In the case of new baths, these matters had received special notice in the advice given to the Management Committees by the Districts Branch prior to the opening and definite improvements had resulted. Once the baths had opened, however, the services of the District Branch normally ceased, but many Management Committees had expressed a wish to maintain contact with the Branch for assistance. It was therefore proposed that the District Organisers should add this work to their duties. They had attended the pre-opening meetings with the Management Committees and were usually already known to some of the members of the Management Committee and they were also members of other welfare schemes.

The District Organiser would be able to liaise between the Central Staff and the Management Committee and would be able to give assistance with staffing, baths' maintenance, both internally and externally, canteen management, finance and legal matters.[60]

In March 1938, Mr Parker, Head of the Districts Branch, put forward proposals for taking steps in 1938/9 towards achieving the ultimate object of the Central Committee that every Welfare District should have the services of a District Organiser whose appointment had been made by the Central Committee. Fifteen Districts already had District Organisers appointed by the Central Committee. Five Districts still appointed their own Organisers and five had no Organisers.

For those districts without Organisers, Lothians would be a difficult problem owing to the waywardness of the Coal Owners' Secretary. However, in the event of the agreement of the District Committee, this District, Fife and Ayrshire could be served by the District Organiser already working in Fife.

In Lancashire, most of the welfare schemes were Pithead Welfare so it was suggested that the recently appointed District Organiser in West Yorkshire could take this work once he had settled into his duties in his own district first.

A joint appointment of a District Organiser for Derbyshire and Nottinghamshire was suggested. Derbyshire had a part-time supervisor who was very well thought of by the District Committee, but whose duties seldom went beyond investigating grants.

In South Derbyshire, practically all the Recreation Schemes had been handed over to the local authority, but the assistance of a District Organiser would be useful, and the district could be conveniently served by the Organiser for the West Midland Group.

The West Midland Group would in future include North Staffordshire, Cannock Chase, South Staffordshire, North Wales and South Derbyshire. It currently included Warwick and Leicester but excluded South Derbyshire. The current configuration made it impossible for one man to adequately discharge the duties. The South Midland Group had been created to include Warwick, Leicester and the Forest of Dean and would have a new Organiser from 1st July 1938.

Lanark and Durham had their own District Organisers, and it was not proposed to change this unless the posts were vacated by the present holders. However, in South Yorkshire, it was proposed to hold a joint meeting with the District Committee to discuss arrangements for the Central Committee to take over the District Committee's Organiser. This meeting took place on 6th November 1938.[61]

In May 1938, the Chairman, accompanied by the Secretary, Chief Architect and the Head of the Districts Branch, visited schemes in Fife and the Lothians. The Chairman met the Lothians District Committee in Edinburgh during the tour and discussed the proposal that a District Organiser should be appointed in their District. The District Committee having agreed to the appointment of a District Organiser for their District, the Head of the Districts Branch met the Joint Secretaries on 30th June to agree the procedure for making the appointment. Mr Syme was appointed after interviews had taken place on 5th August, and he reported to Headquarters on 5th September.[62]

Two discussions with the local architects (Messrs Naylor and Widdows), including a visit to the site of the proposed holiday camp for Derbyshire Miners at Skegness, had taken place since the April meeting of the Central Committee. The main lines of the camp layout had been agreed and the detail and planning of the various units had been discussed with the local architects. Professor Abercrombie had examined the proposals. The revised layout plan was then considered at the May meeting of the Central Committee. The final sketch plan was approved by the District Committee, who proposed to recommend a grant on the local architect's estimate and to proceed with construction as soon as the legal position had been agreed.

On 17th August, Mr Rayner and Mr Saise met Mr Widdows and members of the District Committee to inspect a sample chalet which had been erected by the Contractor who would carry out the camp. A complete chalet block had been erected and were far superior to those in the latest types of holiday camps.

As further evidence of interest in holiday camps, Mr Drummond of the

Ashington Coal Company in Northumberland had applied on behalf of the District Committee in September 1938, for the advice of the Central Committee staff in establishing a holiday camp on the North East Coast.

In November, interest had further increased in the proposals for holidays with pay. The Architects' Branch was keeping in touch with new developments, especially with planning and construction. Visits had been made to the Civil Service Camp (500 persons) at Corton near Lowestoft, and to the new camp known as Rogerson Hall (360 persons) established in the same neighbourhood by the Workers' Travel Association Limited which had been opened in September 1938.[63]

On 24th June 1938, the Inter-Departmental Committee on the Rehabilitation of Persons injured by Accidents wrote to the Central Committee. The Committee had issued an Interim Report in May 1937, recommending the treatment of fractures at hospitals should be organised in accordance with a scheme outlined in the Interim Report. The Committee had taken as its starting point the principles of the organisation and methods of treatment of fractures which were laid down in the Report by the British Medical Association in 1935. It recommended the concentration of cases in one department under a single control, continuity of treatment and supervision by the department until rehabilitation, i.e. restoration of working capacity, had been effected to the fullest possible extent and a system of records of cases which would permit the history of each case to be followed from start to finish and the final results ascertained.

The aim was to cover the country with a network of 'fracture services', which for the most part needed to be attached to existing hospitals.

The number of fracture cases treated annually in hospital was well over 200,000, of which not more than 50,000 were treated in departments organised according to these principles.

The subject of fracture clinics had aroused much interest already in several colliery areas. Dr Fisher spoke in favour of the establishment of such clinics in colliery centres when he gave evidence before the Royal Commission on Safety in Coal Mines.

The Inter-Departmental Committee, whose Medical Secretary was Dr Quine, medical assessor to the Central Committee, were drafting its second report in which arrangements for the organisation of Fracture Departments or Clinics would be considered in greater detail. The Committee wished to mention the Miners' Welfare Committee in the text and sent a draft passage which the Committee considered at their July 1938 meeting.[64]

Also at the July meeting, the Committee were asked by Mr Lawther to consider whether small local clinics for the treatment of miners suffering from rheumatism would be a suitable purpose for grants from the Miners' Welfare Fund, and, if so, whether any advice as to accommodation, equipment and cost could be obtained.

The Committee sought advice from Dr Fisher, HM Medical Inspector of Mines, and Dr Quine, which was considered in November 1938. Reliable figures on the incidence of rheumatism and other conditions among miners was not obtainable, as these maladies did not come under the Workmen's Compensation Acts. Medical knowledge about rheumatism was very incomplete. Treatment usually involved heat and massage.

The Empire Rheumatism Council were willing to prepare a model scheme for the establishment and operation of a small local clinic but no recommendation for a grant for this purpose had so far been received from District Committees.[65]

The estimates of the Safety in Mines Research Board for 1938/9 were considered at the January 1938 meeting of the Committee. The Board were applying for a grant of £47,233 from the General Fund against their total estimated expenditure in 1938/9 of £61,399, including £3,375 for safety instruction. These estimates showed an increase of £1,064 (£914 research, £150 safety instruction) on the previous year but they were within the limit of £63,000 recognised by the Miners' Welfare Committee pending the Report of the Royal Commission.

The investigation into pulmonary diseases among coal miners in co-operation with the Medical Research Council and other bodies had not commenced until December 1937, so only half of £1,000 allocated had been spent by the end of the year, but the work was expected to proceed and provision had been made in the 1938/9 estimates for £1,000 towards the cost.

The increase in the estimates for research of £914 was mainly due to staff costs. There had, however, been additional costs incurred during the year. The Committee had approved an expenditure of £1,300 for a new research laboratory at Buxton, but before the end of the year, it would be necessary to rebuild the Pulveriser House (a light building which had lasted since 1925, but was so dilapidated that motors and coal dust had to be protected in wet weather). A lathe purchased in 1922, which was no longer serviceable, would need to be replaced. A new utility van would be required to replace the existing van, which had run for over 60,000 miles. These four items amounted to about £2,050 and were not included in the estimates.

It would appear that the Committee were not happy with the Board's estimates (there are no minutes of meetings for 1938) as a Joint Sub-Committee was set up to discuss the Board's research work programmes with reference to the extent to which they dealt with the problems that might have a bearing upon other questions beside that of the personal safety and health of the miner.

This meeting took place on 15th February 1938, where representatives from the Central Committee and the Safety in Mines Research Board were present.

While the Committee had no wish to reduce the grant for research, they were not satisfied that the expenditure was entirely restricted to work on problems relating to the personal safety and health of the miner. Where researches had an economic value, the Committee considered that Industry and other bodies benefitted from the results of researches into explosives, wire ropes, haulage and lighting.

The Committee had a duty to make quite sure that the grants from the Fund were spent on researches which were clearly directed towards the personal safety and health of the miner. It was suggested that it might help to have a joint discussion each year when the estimates were submitted to leave no doubt as to the directions of the researches.[66]

With the annexing of Sudetenland in Czechoslovakia by Germany at the beginning of October 1938, it became necessary for the Committee to consider what measures should be taken immediately regarding the conduct of the work of the Miners' Welfare Fund if war broke out. It might be impossible to hold a Committee meeting, so a draft circular to District Committees was required which could be reviewed periodically so that it could be issued after the outbreak of war, after final approval by the Chairman.

In the event of war, the Districts would not make any further recommendations, or enter into any new contracts, but work already commenced should continue. It was envisaged that the Central Committee would be temporarily moved.[67]

1939 was an extraordinary year for the Miners' Welfare Fund. The Royal Commission on Safety in Coal Mines was published on 20th December 1938, the Mining Industry (Welfare Fund) Act 1939 was given Royal Assent on 27th March 1939, and war was declared on 3rd September 1939.

The Royal Commission on Safety in Coal Mines had looked very closely into research. The Commission acknowledged the great value of the results achieved, but there was still much to be done to make working conditions safer and healthier; the Commission questioned whether the work of research, as a whole, was as efficiently organised as it might be. There was not, at that time, a sufficiently effective system of central co-ordination.

The essential function of co-ordination was seen as providing a clearing house through which a general knowledge of what was going on was collected and its result disseminated. This was more likely to be achieved through a representative committee set up by the Mines Department than through any central body which could be set up directly by the Coal Industry itself. The Secretary for Mines needed to be largely guided by the results of research in exercising his power to make new regulations, and the control of research would therefore seem to be essential to the administrative function of the Mines Department. There would be a distinct advantage if the executive side of the research work were under the direct administrative control of the Secretary for Mines. The whole research organisation would then be an integral part of the Department with arrangements for interchange and close co-operation between its staff, the staff of the Department's Testing Stations and the Inspectorate.

The central Research Board would continue on the same lines as before, but it would be a consultative and advisory, instead of a mainly administrative, body. The responsibility for organising and directing in detail any research that might be decided upon would continue to rest with the scientific and technical heads of research organisations.

The Mines Department and the Research Board would provide, so far as it was practicable, for co-operation and co-ordination between all organisations engaged in research concerning safety and health in mines, for testing the results of research under working conditions and for making them effective in industry.

Representatives of the Committee and the Safety in Mines Research Board met on 10th January 1939 in the Joint Sub-Committee to consider the Board's estimates for 1939/40, in accordance with the arrangements agreed between the Committee and the Board in February 1938.

Although the recommendations of the Royal Commission were available, no guidance had been issued by the Mines Department, so the estimates were considered as they had been in previous years.

The original estimates amounted to £64,243 (£59,120 for research, £3,393 for Safety Instruction and £1,730 for supplementary estimate). The Committee were willing to make a grant to cover the expenditure of the Board up to the limit of £63,000. As to the balance of £1,243, the Committee suggested that this might be met out of the potential savings during the current financial year.

At the November 1939 meeting, the Commission at its first meeting, considered a letter sent by Mr Fudge, Mines Department, on behalf of the Safety in Mines Research Board, setting out their estimates for 1940/41. At a special meeting of the Board held on 28th September 1939, it had been decided unanimously that it ought to continue to work during the War so far as circumstances permitted.

The Board realised that its previous programme of work would necessarily have to be varied from time to time to deal with safety problems created by the War itself such as increased use of steel and concrete to substitute for pit timbers, changes in the constitution of mining explosives and ARP Regulations regarding lighting.

Apart from the safety problems of the Coal Industry, the Board's advice might be sought on other problems connected with the conduct of war. There had already been two requests for help from the Air Force.

With the uncertainty as to the future of the Board's work and the difficulties created by the death of Dr Wheeler, the Board's Director of Research, on 28th October 1939, the Board asked the Committee to dispense with the detailed estimates for 1940/41 and to grant a lump sum of £63,000. The war had unavoidably held up the Board's plans for development. Mr Fudge felt that it would be a wise thing if the Board were permitted to set aside a reserve of any savings made from the grant of £63,000, out of which at least the cost of development work could be met.[68]

In January 1939, the Committee were made aware that the Mining Industry (Welfare Fund) Bill had been considered at a meeting of the Joint Consultative Committee of the Mining Industry, who had made representation to the Secretary for Mines to amend the Bill so that the increase of the output levy from ½d to 1d was deferred until the 1939 output. They had at the same time proposed that the new levy should be payable quarterly instead of yearly as hitherto. Both sides of the Industry were agreed that a retrospective levy would cause financial difficulties as no provision for an additional levy had been made in the wages agreements for 1938.

If the additional ½d per ton was deferred until the 1939 output, no more contracts for baths could be placed until 1940. In addition, £72,000 would have to be found from the General or Districts Fund in addition to the normal receipts of the Baths Fund to meet liabilities on contracts already placed.

By March 1939, an alternative to dislocating the pithead baths' building programme for 1939 had been conceived. A Baths Deficiency Reserve would be created using £325,000 (the cost of the 19 contracts not yet committed to in 1939) from the General Fund, to be reimbursed from the Baths Fund when excess credits became available at the end of 1940. The necessary financial procedure would have to be arranged by the Mines Department. In 1940, the Baths Fund credits for the year would amount to about £840,000 while the overallocation on 31st December 1939 would only be about £565,400.[69]

At the March 1939 meeting of the Committee, the Administration and Building Expenses of the Central Committee for 1939/40 were considered, without the Committee's Assessors and Staff being present. An estimate of £51,273 for the Architects' Branch, an increase of £4,306 of which £1,743 was due to new proposals put forward by Mr Forshaw, had been submitted.

During the considerable discussion regarding the architectural work, several members of the Committee said that they had heard criticism in the Districts alleging extravagance and unnecessary travelling. There appeared to be a tendency to undertake architectural work which might well be carried out by the colliery staff. The Committee therefore decided that the Architects' Branch should not in future undertake any work at collieries unless it was directly associated with baths installations.

The Committee decided to approve the estimates for the Architects' Branch but not Mr Forshaw's new proposals. It was also agreed that the criticisms of the Branch should be examined at the next meeting.

In April 1939, the criticism of unnecessary travelling was refuted. Initially, the visits had been seen as unnecessary but it was lately realised that it was in the best interest of the welfare in the District that they should take advantage of the wide experience and special knowledge of the Central Committee's staff.

As to buildings, the pithead baths were seen to be too elaborate and consequentially high cost. This assumption seemed to have arisen out of the belief that good design was expensive and economy in building was necessarily associated with ugliness. It was not appreciated that in planning Miners' Welfare buildings, special regard had to be paid to the question of maintenance costs. Any saving on capital cost would result in a disproportionate increase in maintenance costs.

The Committee felt that there was a need in the districts for education in the economics of pithead baths building and maintenance. As to building expenses, the Committee agreed that Mr Forshaw should submit a memorandum on the advantages and disadvantages (with financial effects) of centralisation and decentralisation of supervision of Miners' Welfare building work.[70]

During the debate in the House of Commons on the Mining Industry (Welfare Fund) Bill, it was suggested that there should be uniformity regarding the workmen's subscriptions and the colliery company's contribution towards maintenance. A similar opinion had been expressed by Mr Reed of the Fife Coal Co and Chairman of the Fife and Clackmannan District Committee at the Annual Conference of District Representatives in November 1938. At the Committee's April meeting, a decision was taken to consult the Mining Association and the Mineworkers' Federation with a view to the question being considered by the District Committees and the Joint Consultative Committee of the Mining Industry.

A draft memorandum had been submitted to the Mining Association. The Central Committee of the Mining Association had replied that they had no power under their constitution to take any action to suggest that colliery companies should contribute to the upkeep of pithead baths. It was therefore agreed by the Committee at their July meeting that the Secretary would redraft paragraph 10 of form B3 Provision of Pithead Baths out of the Miners' Welfare Fund, to ask colliery owners to ensure that men's subscriptions did not exceed 6d per week.[71]

THE MINERS' WELFARE FUND 1921–1952

By January 1939, the Committee had received the information on rheumatism clinics from the Empire Rheumatism Council that they had requested after their meeting in July 1938. They had also received an application from Durham District to set up a clinic at Horden Baths, the costs to be defrayed out of the Baths Fund.

The Committee did not feel that they would be justified in opening the resources of the Baths Fund to applications for rheumatism clinics, but they were not unsympathetic to the proposal to institute a rheumatism clinic at Horden as a new experiment. The Committee might be prepared to consider supplementing a grant from the District Fund by a proportionate grant from the General Fund.

If the District did not object in principle to recommend a grant, the next step would be to seek the advice of the Empire Rheumatism Council by arranging a meeting at Horden, where the local Baths and Welfare Committees and representatives of the District Committee, Central Committee and the Empire Rheumatism Council could discuss the proposal.

In April 1939, the Committee had sketch plans prepared, in consultation with the Empire Rheumatism Council, for two alternative schemes. The first was for clinics at Horden, Blackhale and Shotton Collieries, and the second was for Horden Colliery only. The estimated cost for the first scheme was £3,400 with annual maintenance costs amounting to £2,550. The second scheme had an estimated setup cost of £2,400 and annual maintenance costs of £1,635.

The Committee agreed to make a grant from the General Fund for half the capital cost of either scheme, subject to the District Committee recommending a grant to the other half from the District Fund and the future maintenance being guaranteed by the Local Miners' Welfare Committee.[72]

A proposed procedure for grants for Construction Work (Buildings and Grounds) had been produced by the central staff with the object of instituting a uniform course of action for all Districts for the Committee to consider at their January 1939 meeting. The procedure detailed the process from a local committee initiating proposals to the final payment of the contract work when the scheme had been finished. This procedure had already been adopted by the South Wales District Committee.

The Committee approved the procedure in principle and suggested that it should be put before other District Committees by the Districts Branch with a view to its institution eventually in all Districts.[73]

The funding of cycle stores and pithead canteens had again been raised. At the Annual Conference of District Representatives in November 1938, Fife had proposed that the cost should come out of the Baths Fund. The proposal had previously been made in 1934 by Nottinghamshire and Derbyshire and rejected by the Central Committee. In 1939, only 96 out of 290 installations had cycle stores. Equipping those without would be an additional cost to the Baths Fund, estimated at £16,000 to £17,000, the equivalent cost of baths for 1,000 men.[74]

In February 1939, South Wales District Committee wrote to the Central Committee asking for the 1934 limitation on providing canteens at pithead baths to be withdrawn. The rule of drawing the line at the 1st January 1934 followed the passing of the Welfare Fund Act 1934, which empowered the committee to provide canteens from the Baths Fund. The Mining Industry (Welfare Fund) Act 1939, while providing additional funds to increase the provision of pithead baths at collieries without baths, made no specific reference to canteens.

The question of providing canteens at pithead baths built prior to 1934 had been discussed at two Annual Conferences, the last being in 1937 when it received the support of only one District. The District Committees had been informed in a circular dated 3rd February 1938 that the Central Committee were unable to agree to provide these canteens while the money available was insufficient to meet the demands for Baths. Eighty-seven canteens, costing £85,000, had been provided out of District Funds or from other sources up to 31st December 1938. There were over 100 of the older schemes (pre 1934) still without canteens and to provide them would cost about £115,000. The contingent liability to the Baths Fund would therefore have amounted to approximately £200,000, representing the cost of about 15 baths installations.

With the pressing need for pithead baths, the Committee wrote to the South Wales District Committee informing them that they could not alter the rule on pithead canteens.[75]

The Secretary and Mr Forshaw had prepared memoranda on Pithead Baths at Small Collieries for the June 1939 Committee meeting as modifications of the normal type of installation would have to be made to avoid prohibitive costs. Mr Forshaw had already produced a memorandum on the design, construction and cost of small baths for the May 1939 meeting.

In June 1939, the Committee had become aware of the Coal Commission's intention to reduce the number of undertakings, implying that many small collieries would be closed. To provide baths at small collieries was a waste of money unless definite guarantees as to their life was forthcoming. The Committee therefore decided that the time was not opportune to proceed with a programme for providing installations for small collieries, but they did agree that collieries would be classified as small if they employed up to 300 men.[76]

The June 1939 meeting of the Committee started without the Assessors or the Staff present as the Committee wanted to discuss staffing issues.

Mr Forshaw had been appointed Deputy Chief Architect to the London County Council and the Committee needed to discuss the process for his replacement and they eventually decided that the post should be advertised.

Clause 2 of the Mining Industry (Welfare Fund) Act 1939 provided for the incorporation of a Miners' Commission to take over the powers and duties of the existing Miners' Welfare Committee which was not a body corporate. The Committee discussed their reconstitution as a Commission at the meeting and considered the positions of their Secretary and Assistant Secretary in the light of this development and the expansion of work. Their views were then conveyed by the Chairman in a letter to the Secretary for Mines.

Also at this June meeting, the Committee confirmed the Chairman's approval of the earmarking of four members of staff (Messrs Parker, O'Kelly, R. L. Hills and Bettington) for other work under the Mines Department in the event of an emergency.[77]

This was not the first time in 1939 that the Committee had discussed staff-related issues that would arise if war was declared. In January 1939, the Committee received the Mines Department's proposal to appoint the Chief Districts Officer (Mr Parker) to be a Coal Export Officer under the wartime emergency organisation. The Committee could not refuse, but hoped that the Department would realise that the need for Miners' Welfare schemes of all kinds would certainly increase during wartime, and would consider the matter before arranging further depletion of staff.

Mr G. H. Pryor from the Mines Department attended the March 1939 Committee meeting, to discuss the policy of the government of making arrangements for removing out of central London in peacetime any government office or part of it which could conduct its business elsewhere, so as to relieve the problem of evacuation if this was necessary in wartime.

The Committee expressed the view that upon the outbreak of war, it would be desirable , if possible, to complete pithead baths which were actually under construction, but other constructional work would probably have to stop and the staff concerned released to other employment. Staff working in the Districts would need to be retained to support welfare work in the coal fields.

In May 1939, a circular letter to District Committees was issued giving information in regard to the use of private premises including miners' welfare institutes and pithead baths for air raid precaution purposes, and advising them as to the appropriate action to be taken in Miners' Welfare interests.

The Committee, also in May 1939, considered other Air Raid precautions relating to requirements of lights at pithead baths, institutes and other welfare buildings, camouflage of pithead baths, use of air raid shelters and protection of baths against blast splinters and bombs.

For pithead baths completed after 1st May 1939, compliance with the requirements would be arranged by the Committee at the cost of the Baths

Fund. For pithead baths completed before 1st May 1939, compliance would be arranged by the Management Committee. Applications for grants from the Baths Fund towards the cost would be considered on their merits.

In June 1939, the Committee decided to issue a circular to the Management Committees of all pithead baths completed before 1st January 1939 informing them of the necessity for making arrangements for obscuring lights from baths in the event of war under the Civil Defence Bill. Enclosed with the circular was a pamphlet issued by the Air Raid Precautions Department entitled 'War Time Lighting for Industrial and Commercial Premises'. Provided the Miners' Welfare Committee were satisfied that the measures proposed were effective and economical, they would make grants from the Miners' Welfare Fund to reimburse the Baths Committees for half the sum expended by them upon these measures.

At the Baths completed after 1st January 1939, the necessary measure would be taken by the Architects' Branch under the building contracts, the baths' allocation being adjusted to cover the whole cost.

The position of the Miners' Welfare Committee's staff in wartime was also considered in May 1939 as it was possible that, in the event of war, the activities of the Miners' Welfare Committee might be considerably curtailed. It was agreed that those with not less than eighteen months' service who had joined H. M. Forces, gained whole-time service with the civil defence forces, or accepted whole-time civil employment in a government department, would have their salaries guaranteed; there would also be an undertaking, so far as it was within their power to do so, of the reinstatement of such staff at the conclusion of hostilities on terms not less favourable than those at the time of their release. 78

In April 1939, the Committee needed to take decisions so that the Miners' National Mining Education Scholarship for part-time courses could be awarded in 1939.

The Committee were required to appoint assessors to moderate the examination papers of the different institutions that set the examinations, and to scrutinise the examination scripts of the candidates. Approximately thirty new scholarships would be available for award each year.

One assessor would probably be sufficient, and Mr Savage put forward the names of Mr I. C. F. Statham, Professor of Mining, University of Sheffield and Mr F. S. Atkinson, Professor of Mining, University of Leeds. The fees payable to the assessor were estimated not to exceed £80 a year for England and Wales and Scotland.

The Committee also approved the institutions at which scholarships were tenable. Applications had been received from four institutions in Scotland, ten in England and three in Wales, comprising practically all the mining centres which provided part-time day mining classes.

Professor Statham was chosen as the assessor, and his report and recommendation for 32 scholarships were considered at the September meeting of the Committee.

By November 1939, twenty-five of the scholars had entered the courses for which the awards were made. In 7 cases where the awards had not been taken up, four of the students had joined H. M. Forces, two were now ineligible in view of altered circumstances, and one did not need assistance.

The Commission decided to recommend that the Trustees suspend the awards in the case of the four students who had joined H. M. Forces, with a view to restoration in due course. A meeting had been arranged between the Assessor and Messrs Savage and Bennett to consider the suggestion which had been made at the October meeting to extend the scope of the scheme to mine surveying and electrical engineering. The Mines Department would shortly submit their views on this matter.[79]

In July 1939, the Committee considered the delay that was taking place in proceeding with the proposal for a new mining department at Cardiff University College owing to Glamorgan Education Authority hesitating in releasing the College from the arrangement for locating the new mining department at Treforest. The Committee were informed that the Authority had arranged to discuss the matter on 28th July 1939.

Although, originally it was hoped to establish the new mining department at Cardiff University College, the decision was taken in 1934 to locate it at Treforest and a grant of £42,000 was approved and in 1936 the Board of Education approved the sketch plans. Owing to Glamorgan Education Authority's financial difficulties due to the adverse economic conditions, there had been some delay in pushing forward the scheme.

By 1938, circumstances had changed and the Monmouthshire and South Wales Coal Owners' Association had given an understanding to contribute £5,000 a year to the University for seven years (which they had stated that they were prepared to extend to twenty-one years) provided the new mining department was established at Cardiff University. It was therefore proposed that the Committee should give approval to two separate schemes: a new mining department at Cardiff University College and an extension of Treforest School of Mines for an advanced centre for mining instruction amounting to a total of £50,000.

At the meeting on 18th July attended by a deputation from Glamorgan Education Authority (Sir William Jenkins and Mr F. E. Rees, Director of Education) and representatives of the Miners' Welfare Committee (Mr Stedman, Mr Bennett, Mr Wynn Wheldon, Welsh Department of the Board of Education, and Mr Savage, Assessor to the Committee), it emerged that the main grievance of the Authority was the procedure for the selection of students for the university course which was solely under the control of the University Authorities.

Mr Stedman concluded the meeting by pointing out that the Committee were unlikely to alter their approval of the schemes for the University and Treforest, but he suggested that the Authority should submit their points about the selection of students for Cardiff University.[80]

When the Committee met on 19th September 1939, the country was at war and they needed to consider the special measures that were required. As a matter of general policy, every effort would be made to carry on all the work of the Miners' Welfare Fund with as little dislocation as possible.

The Committee were determined to proceed with the pithead baths programme without reduction, if possible. The Committee wanted to secure some measure of priority for building baths. Mr Pryor from the Mines Department was present at the meeting and thought that the Mines Department would support this. At that time builders were unable to submit satisfactory tenders so new contracts were being deferred pending clarification of future building conditions.

The same considerations prevented the commencement of big contracts for Districts Fund work, but the Committee decided to authorise new contracts up to the value of £750 if builders gave assurances to complete and if the District Committee were prepared to recommend an increase of the allocation, if necessary, to meet any increase in cost.

Baths and Districts Fund works under construction under the Architects' Branch would proceed to completion if possible. Allowances would be made for increases in the cost of labour and materials due to war conditions.

Further letters would be sent out to District Committees about the need for continuing the use of Miners' Welfare schemes (including pithead baths) in wartime and about the requisitioning of schemes by military and civil authorities.

£1,200 was allocated from the Baths Fund for camouflaging pithead baths which were conspicuous by position and colour, the whole cost to be defrayed from the Baths Fund.

In the existing conditions, it was considered inappropriate to proceed with the appointment of Mr Forshaw's position. For the time being, Messrs Rayner and Kemp would continue in charge of the Quantity Surveyors' Section and the Architects' Section respectively, on a parity as regarding responsibility and scale of salary.

The decision taken by the Committee at their June meeting regarding staff released for war service not suffering loss of pay when called up would, with the outbreak of war, apply to all staff on military service, or war work approved by the Committee.

With regards to the evacuation, the Committee preferred to arrange for office premises to be available for their use near London, in the event of it becoming impossible for the administration to remain at its present offices.

Finally, the Committee decided to make representation to the Secretary for Mines that the appointment of the Miners' Welfare Commission under the Act passed in March 1939 should be made without delay.

In October 1939, the Secretary reported that negotiations were in progress for a house at Ashstead, Surrey. That locality had been selected as being the least inconvenient to the majority of the staff, but there would be extra expenses for billeting or travelling. The Committee meetings would continue to be held in London at Romney House, if possible.

The Mines Department had informed the Chairman that the appointment of the Commission would be made during the next few weeks. Lord Aberdare and Professor Abercrombie had tendered provisional resignations, but they agreed to withdraw them.

The Board of Trade by Minute of Appointment, dated 21st November 1939, had appointed the members of the Miners' Welfare Committee and Mr W J Drummond, a member of the Mining Association of Great Britain, to be members of the Miners' Welfare Commission for a period not exceeding one year from that date, and by the Miners' Welfare Commission (Commencement) Order, 1939, to be the date from which all powers, duties, property and liabilities of the Miners' Welfare Committee should be transferred to the Commission.

Major-General, The Rt Hon Sir Frederick Sykes MP was appointed as Chairman of the Commission, and Mr A. D. Stedman and Mr T. A. Bennett were appointed as Secretary and Assistant Secretary respectively of the Commission. All the staff employed by the Mines Department on behalf of the Miners' Welfare Committee were transferred to the Commission.

The change from a Committee to a Commission did not involve any alteration in the principles of the administration of the Fund or in the part played by the District Committees, but, in details, the conduct of the administration would be facilitated. The change was made in order that the body responsible for allocating the Welfare Fund might be enabled to enter into and enforce agreements and contracts, and to take legal action, as a body, the absence of these powers having been found to cause hindrances in the administration of the Fund, particularly in the arrangements for building pithead baths and other welfare facilities. The constitution of the Miners' Welfare Commission would also strengthen the administration and responsibilities of the District Miners' Welfare Committees.

During the 19 years of the Welfare Committee, a total of £18,802,285 was received and £18,655,120 grants were made, and £17,617,047 grants paid.

The receipts of the General Fund for the nineteen years had been £2,990,994.

Grants amounting to £2,394,443 had been made, chiefly for research (£1,073,528), education (£1,014,979) and administration expenses (£202,941).

The total of the grants allocated from the Districts Fund for the nineteen years was £10,575,989, of which £10,366,275 had been paid out. Of the total allocated, 55% was for recreational schemes, 34% for health schemes and the remaining 11% was spent half on pithead baths and the other half on other pithead welfare (chiefly canteens and cycle stores), educational purposes, aged miners' homes and administration expenses of the District Committees.

At the end of 1939, pithead baths had been provided at 345 collieries for 430,228 persons, including 38 installations under construction. The total outlay involved was £6,108,222, of which the Baths Fund had provided £5,680,688 and £423,534 was from the Districts Fund.

£5,763,900, 31% of the Welfare Fund had been granted for providing or improving schemes for recreation and amusement. Over half of the total had come from the Districts Fund (54%). The proportion of the Welfare Fund which had been allocated for recreational purposes was equivalent to nearly £2 per head of the mining population (estimated at three million persons) and during the nineteen years of the Fund, the annual sum had averaged £303,000. No other organisation for the provision of recreation facilities in the country had been able to make such generous provision.

The sums allocated from the Welfare Fund to health schemes assisting the sick and injured amounted to £3,629, 404 (19.4% of the whole Fund). More than three-quarters of the total had been allocated for the establishment of 15 convalescent homes.

Grants totalling £734,211 from the General Fund and £23,950 from the Districts Fund had be made towards the costs of buildings and equipment for senior, advanced and university mining courses. The grants from the General Fund covered seventy-five senior or advanced centres and projected centres and eight universities.

During the thirteen years of the Miners' National Scholarship Scheme, 183 scholarships were awarded, of which 24 were for the study of mining and 159 for other subjects. During the four years of the Miners' Welfare National Student Exhibition Scheme, 48 exhibitions had been awarded, of which one was for mining. In addition to these, 882 students were assisted in various educational courses at universities, training colleges, technical schools and other educational institutions.[81]

FIVE

THE WAR YEARS
1940–1945

The Chairman of the Commission had predicted at the end of his foreword to the Miners' Welfare Fund Annual Report 1939 that the war would present difficulties in the Commission's work but, with everyone pulling together, the results for which the Commission was working would show no deterioration. The successes of the Commission during the war years were, undoubtably, brought about by the personal efforts of the staff, both centrally and at district level, whose adaptability succeeded in meeting the innumerable and inevitable difficulties.

The Miners' Welfare Commission's staff saw many changes due to the war and some to other causes. A large number of architectural staff were released in 1940, as a result of the reduction of constructional work due to the severe restrictions on labour and materials. The staff who were retained found themselves, a year later, faced with a large and urgent programme of colliery canteen building, followed in less than two years by a no less urgent programme of miners' rehabilitation centres. These programmes and the problems arising from wartime restrictions upon Miners' Welfare Schemes in other directions made very heavy demands upon the non-technical as well as the technical staff of the Commission reduced, as they continuously were, by the flow of the younger men and women into H. M. Forces.

When France surrendered in June 1940, the Commission decided that the time had arrived to move its office outside the London target area, so in July the office was transferred to premises in Ashstead, which had been leased in October 1939 (see Chapter 4, page 194). When the Battle of Britain began in August 1940, with the recurring aerial bombardments causing serious loss of working time and detriment to the health amongst the workers remaining in London, the Commission's decision was fully justified. Romney House, the Commission's former office, suffered a direct hit, besides other additional damage.

Many of the staff found Ashstead too far to travel to daily, so they had to be billeted locally. Many of the Architects' Department had to be relocated a second time in the Autumn of 1941, as it became necessary to decentralise the canteen construction work by setting up branch offices in the coalfields and posting London technical staff there.

From January 1940, owing to travel difficulties and the heavy engagements of the members, the Commission was forced to alter its practice of holding meetings each month and to miss alternate months unless required by urgent business.

There were changes in the Commission's membership. Mr Andrew Clarke died in February 1940. He had replaced Mr Herbert Smith, who had died in 1938. Mr Clarke's place was taken by Mr W. E. Jones in June 1940. Sir Thomas Hudson Beare died in June 1940, and he was replaced by Mr J. Lambie in September 1940. Mr E. G. Savage was appointed Chief Education Officer to the London County Council, and was replaced by Mr W. Elliot.[1]

In 1940, the receipt of the Miners' Welfare Fund amounted to a total of £1,175,811, with the Output Levy amounting to £960,547, the Royalties Levy to £170,000 and income from investment to £45,264. £235,659 was apportioned to the District Fund, £84,975 to the General Fund and £855,177 to the Baths Fund.[2]

During the first three months of 1940, the Commission was able to place contracts for new pithead baths amounting to £201,000 (a yearly rate of £804,000). However, in January 1940 it was not possible to forecast developments regarding supplies and there was some indication of the probable further loss of staff during 1940. The Royal Proclamation, signed on 1st January 1940, rendered liable for military service all men, who on that date, were over 19 or under 28. Seventeen of the Architects, Engineering and Recreation schemes were affected. In addition, three men were members of the Royal Naval Volunteer Special Reserve and were liable to be called up. The Quantity Surveyors were not so seriously affected, as their occupation was still a reserved one.

The severe winter weather had brought the building industry to a standstill for rather longer than usual and the baths contracts had suffered so, by February 1940, eight baths that should have opened in January and February had been postponed to March and April. There were delays in obtaining materials and economies were being used to conserve materials such as timber used for shuttering for concrete work.[3]

The possible liability of pithead baths' attendants for military service had prompted the Secretary and a representative of the Mines Department to appear before the War Cabinet Sub-Committee on the Schedule of Reserved Occupation, in support of an application made on behalf of the Commission for the reservation of pithead attendants at the age of 25. At the April meeting of the Commission, it was reported that the Sub-Committee had agreed to include them at the age of 35 when the time came for men of that age to be registered. In the case of superintendents aged 27 or more, however, temporary postponement of calling up would be arranged where necessary. However, for canteen attendants, the Commission had to advise Baths Management Committees to consider the employment of women instead.[4]

By May 1940, new methods of construction were being applied to plans for new schemes for pithead baths designed to effect economies in the use of steel and timber. Since July 1939, the Works and Building Priority Sub-Committee (Ministry of Labour) had several times called for estimates for the Commission's forward programme of expenditure up to December 1941, and the requirements for timber, steel, cement, bricks and labour needed for actual consumption of the building programme for various periods ranging from six to nine months in advance. The position in May 1940 was that the allocation for timber and steel already made would complete the installations due for opening in 1940, and would maintain progress on others under construction. However, the future was obscure.

In June 1940, the Chairman had a discussion with the Secretary for Mines regarding the policy to be followed by the Commission on pithead bath construction in the current circumstances. (France had surrendered, and the Western front had collapsed, and materials and labour were needed for immediate military or economic war objectives). As a result of the discussion, it was suggested that work under construction should be completed so far as supplies of labour and materials available would permit. No new construction should be commenced.

On 1st July 1940, the following instructions were issued which applied to all construction work paid for out of the Welfare Fund, whether for pithead baths, institutes or other purposes:

a) No new contracts were to be placed, until further notice, except for essential repairs or work necessary to maintain the proper use of existing accommodation or facilities, and even in these cases, it was necessary before the work was commenced to have an assurance from the contractor that sufficient labour and materials were available for it to be completed.

b) Buildings upon which construction was well advanced were to be completed if labour was available and if the requisite supplies of materials had been delivered to the site, or were in merchants' or manufacturers' hands.

c) For buildings which had not reached an advanced stage of construction, no assistance was obtainable from the Civil Building Control towards obtaining labour or materials. Contractors were to carry the work to a stage at which it could safely be left until circumstances permitted the completion of the contract, but they were not to be pressed to carry the work further than this.

Subsequent experience proved this decision was fully justified. The delays and difficulties which prevented the Commission from completing more than 13 of the current contracts (eleven new baths and two extensions) during the first six months of 1940 increased. Of the 44 contracts (39 new baths and five extensions) under construction on 1st July, it was only possible during the remaining six months of 1940 to complete eight contracts and to advance five to a suitable stage for suspending the work. The other 30 contracts were not disposed of until April 1942 when fourteen had been completed (the contracts having averaged twice the normal time) and sixteen had been suspended.

As soon as it became evident that the building of pithead baths would be suspended indefinitely, the Commission made no delay in releasing as many of its technical staff to the Forces and other work. By November 1940, the Architects' Section, with an authorised establishment of 68 had been reduced to 25. Mr Rayner, Chief Quantity Surveyor, had also been released for three months to assist Sir Warren Fisher, the London Commissioner for War Debris Survey and Disposal. Mr Bowra was appointed as acting Chief Quantity Surveyor in his absence.[5]

As early as November 1940, the Committee were looking towards a post war building programme for pithead baths, as the Baths Fund would have a large credit balance (about £1,810,000 by the end of 1942). The Commission needed to have more reliable data than that available to draw up a post-war programme for the completion of the task of providing pithead baths within a given period of time. The hiatus in building was an opportunity to obtain this data and a survey of collieries remaining to be provided with baths was recommended. Giving regard to the available staff, it was agreed that an experimental survey should be undertaken in a district containing a variety of types and sizes of collieries employing more than 50 men and that the inclusion of other districts should be considered later in the light of the results.[6]

When grants from a District Fund were made for cycle stores, cloakrooms and canteens on land occupied by a colliery company , the usual requirement for the site to be transferred to welfare trustees was waived (unless trustees were already in office as pithead baths had been built), and it was accepted that the District Committee's recommendation was a sufficient assurance that the colliery receiving the grant had a reasonable expectation of life.

In eight cases in Lancashire, however, the life of the colliery after expenditure of the grant had been too short to justify the expenditure. In the cases of Westhoughton and Garswood, where £500 had been granted to each colliery, the District Committee had asked, upon the closure of the colliery, if the Commission would be prepared to dispose of the buildings. As the form of agreement did not give the Miners' Welfare Commission any legal standing, the Commission could not take any action itself.

The existing practice was reviewed by the Board of Trade Solicitor and a revised form of Agreement (Form PHB.29 and 29A) was approved for use, where grants were made either for removable structures, or for a total sum not amounting to £500 at any colliery.

The Commission also decided that a conveyance or a long lease and trust deed was required where total grants exceeded £500 at any colliery, and were for structures which were not removable so as to secure a legal title which would enable the property to be realised for the benefit of the Welfare Fund, in case of failure of the scheme. Cases in this category would then be placed upon the same footing as Miners' Welfare schemes for baths, institutes and recreation grounds.[7]

In September 1938, South Derbyshire District Committee were asked to carry out a district survey by the Miners' Welfare Committee as the recommendations for grants seemed to be one sided. About 78% of grants had been for health purposes: hospitals, convalescent homes, medical and surgical treatment and ambulances. It seemed doubtful whether the other purposes for which the Fund was established were being sufficiently served by the remaining 22% of the District Fund, which included only 9% for recreation, 8% for pit welfare and 2% for education, with 3% for administration. In all other Districts together, 55% had gone to recreation and only 34% to health purposes.

This question was raised in 1938, in connection with a proposal of the District Committee to grant £10,000 to the Burton-on-Trent Infirmary, payable in ten annual instalments of £1,000, representing approximately 60% of the annual income of the District Fund. The Committee had asked the District Committee to have a district survey carried out by the Central Committee's District Organisers and to reconsider the question of recommending further instalments in the light of the needs of the District as shown by the survey report. A second grant of £1,000 was approved in August 1939 pending the consideration of the survey report.

Also in 1938, the District Committee were asked in connection with the maintenance grant of £143.18s.9d for the District Ambulance Scheme, to consider making a small charge for the use of the ambulance, so as to avoid the need for such maintenance grants. Consideration of a recommendation for a further grant of £1,000 for the endowment of the scheme was deferred pending the discussion of the District survey.

By January 1940, the survey had been completed by the District Branch and presented to the District Committee, and copies had been circulated to each member of the Commission together with a copy of the District's observations. As the District Committee had turned down all the suggestions put forward in the survey report, it was agreed that the District Committee should be invited to meet representatives of the Commission to discuss the recommendations of the survey report.

Representatives of the Commission met with the deputation from South Derbyshire on the afternoon of 19th March 1940 at the Royal Empire Society, Northumberland Avenue, London, and discussed the recommendations contained in the report prepared by the District Organisers, Mr Atkinson and Mr Skinner. After an exchange of views at the meeting between the Commission and the deputation, agreement was reached on a number of issues.

South Derbyshire was the only remaining district which had no District Organiser, and they were pressed to accept the appointment of one. Mr Skinner, who had been one of the District Organisers who had undertaken the survey, and who was the District Organiser for Leicestershire and Warwickshire, could be assigned to South Derbyshire also. (This would appear to have taken place, as in September 1940 it was reported that a movement had been started in South Derbyshire to establish four boys' clubs in mining communities, largely due to the initiative of the District Organiser).

The grant of £1,000 was approved for the Burton Hospital in respect of the year 1940, but with the proviso that the total grant should be limited to £5,000 and the grant of £1,000 was approved for South Derbyshire District Ambulance scheme; it was also subject to the condition that no further grants were recommended for endowment for the maintenance of the scheme, including replacements of ambulances.

It was essential that the District Committee should tackle the problem of future planning of District Funds with greater emphasis on recreation and institute schemes.[8]

Although there had been only a few cases of war damage to baths and institutes, in September 1940 the Commission decided to look again at their decision taken in November 1939 to 'adopt the principle that the cost of restoration of loss or damage to Miners' Welfare property (Baths, Institutes etc) as a result of war operations should fall to the Miners' Welfare Fund subject to the resources (of the Fund) available and to any compensation which might be received from the Government after the war'.

It had become known that, in the case of essential buildings or land damaged by war, the Government was prepared to make loans (subject to interest) to the owners of such properties, if the latter was unable to carry out the work of restoration or reinstatement without financial assistance. To obtain loans for Miners' Welfare premises, it would have been necessary to secure a declaration from the appropriate government department classifying the property as essential buildings. The government had also recently decided to reconsider its decision against a war damage insurance scheme, but it seemed unlikely that the need for assistance from the Welfare Fund would be entirely removed.

The Commission decided that it should stand, and that Trustees of the

Miner's Welfare Schemes should not apply for loans for restoration of war damage but should enter any future Government insurance scheme, the premium being refunded from the Welfare Fund and the Commission's staff would explore the possibility of effecting the insurance on the Trustees' behalf as 'block' transaction.

Two circular letters on the procedure for dealing with cases of war damage were circulated; one to the Management Committees of the Miners' Welfare Schemes who would obtain grants from District Funds and one to the Pithead Baths Committees who would obtain grants from the Baths Fund.[9]

In September 1940, the Commission also considered a paper outlining suggestions for the future aims of Miners' Welfare and the preparatory work to be done pending the end of hostilities. The Commission felt that the importance and scope of the subject demanded that it should receive consideration again at a subsequent meeting, but it was agreed that preparatory investigations in the form of District surveys and surveys of all collieries without baths should proceed.[10]

On 29th November 1939, Professor Statham (Assessor to the Miners' Welfare National Part-time Day Advanced Mining Education Scholarship Scheme), Mr Savage, Mr Hummel (Board of Education Inspector) and the Commission's Assistant Secretary met at Sheffield University to discuss Professor Statham's suggestion of the possibility of introducing a uniform examination and setting up selection panels for the purpose of the scheme. The opportunity was also taken to discuss other matters including the suggestion that the scheme should be extended to include mine surveying and electrical engineering and the question of the universal adoption of a four-year advanced course in mining for which the scholarship was tenable.

The report of the meeting was considered by the Commission at their meeting in January 1940. At this meeting, the Assistant Secretary confirmed that all institutions in England and Wales at which the scholarships were tenable had agreed to conform to a four-year advanced mining course. As to Scotland, it was hoped to arrange a meeting between Sir Thomas Hudson Beare, the Assistant Secretary and representatives of the Scottish Education Authorities concerned at the end of January with a view to an agreement for securing applications from Scotland for the 1940 competition.

The Commission agreed that action should be taken to institute a uniform examination commencing in 1941 and that draft examination papers should be submitted for approval by the Assessor in respect of the 1940 competition. Enquiries were to be made with a view to submitting proposals for instituting local selection panels. The question of extending the Scheme to include surveying and electrical engineering courses would be further considered in receipt of the Mines Department's observations by Mr Fudge.[11]

In March 1940, the Commission yet again considered the proposed new mining department at Cardiff University College and Treforest School of Mining. The Commission were in receipt of a reply from Glamorgan Education Authority to the Commission's letter of 21st September 1939, urging the authority to do three things which appeared to be necessary for progress to be made in connection with the proposal that a new mining department at Cardiff University College, and the new advanced centre of mining at Treforest, should be located at Cardiff and Treforest respectively instead of one unit at Treforest as originally proposed, namely:

i) to release the University College from the Agreement of 1933 (for the location of the University mining department at the Treforest School of Mines)
ii) to state their view regarding the selection of student entrants to the proposed new mining department of the College and to suggest conditions to protect the interests of Treforest in securing such entrants; and
iii) to accept the offer of a grant of £18,000 for Treforest.

The authority had replied that they saw no reason for abrogating the Agreement with Cardiff University College. Apparently, the authority had delayed replying while engaged in trying to enlist the support of the South Wales Miners' Federation for the original Treforest scheme. The Federation, however, had intimated to the Commission that its Executive Council had unanimously decided to favour the Cardiff scheme.

The negative attitude of the authority had therefore left the position very much as it had been in 1936, when the Commission decided in favour of locating the university department at Cardiff following the offer of the South Wales coal owners to contribute £5,000 a year towards maintenance of the new department if located at Cardiff, coupled with financial support of a comprehensive mining degree scholarship scheme.

The prospects of providing a new department of mining at Cardiff University College in the near future appeared to the Commission to be doubtful, particularly in view of the declared view of the college that it would be unwilling to proceed with the proposal unless the Glamorgan Authority agreed to release the college from the agreement of 1933. In addition, the restriction on building operations as a result of war conditions would make it difficult to proceed at that time even if there was no other question at issue. In these circumstances, the Commission decided to ask the South Wales Coal Owners' Association whether, notwithstanding the postponement of the scheme until after the war, they would be prepared to adhere to their offer to contribute the sum of £5,000 a year towards the maintenance of a new mining department at Cardiff, and to give an assurance that this payment would be made, all things being equal, for a period of 21 years.[12]

The Commission in March 1940 made a grant of £48,834 in respect of the estimated expenditure of the Safety in Mines Research Board in the year 1940/41. Any savings in that year and in 1939/40 were to be set aside as a reserve towards the cost of carrying out the Board's plans for developments which had been held up by the war. The approval of the Commission was given upon the condition that the researches upon which the contribution from the Miners' Welfare Fund was expended, would be concerned solely with welfare problems.

The war had necessitated important changes in the Board's research programme relating to 'Falls of Ground'. With the need for a large reduction during the war in the use of imported timber for mine supports, there was great activity throughout the coal mining industry in the development of the use of home-grown timber and substitutes for timber, such as steel and reinforced concrete. The Board's activities were chiefly directed towards ensuring the safety and strength of these substitutes were adequate, to co-operate with Colliery managements in the solution of the technical problems of their application and, generally to make widely known the important bearings of the Board's work and its results on the safety aspects of those problems.

Reinforced concrete was being studied by the Board's staff at the Royal School of Mines, London, and a series of articles covering matters such as 'packing', 'chocks', 'steel props', 'concrete props' etc. had been published in the Technical Press. These would be followed up by a series of pamphlets covering the same ground.

The special wartime work on mine supports was being carried out in close association with the Mines Inspectorate and with the Director of Mining Supplies, whose staff (paid by the Mines Department) included Professor Hogan and several of the District Investigators who formerly worked on the problems of roof supports.[13]

In November 1940, the Commission needed to address the problems arising out of the unemployment amongst miners which had recently increased in some areas, notably in Durham and South Wales. The problem had already been discussed by the Chief Districts Officer, Mr Whitfield Parker, with representatives of the South Wales District Committee and by the Deputy Chief Districts Officer with representatives of the Durham District Committee.

The Chief Districts Officer had arranged to hold meetings with representatives of the Miners' Welfare Schemes in South Wales to discuss what steps should be taken by the Management Committees to deal with the problems. His proposals for dealing with the problems would, as far as possible, avoid the need for maintenance grants by ensuring that schemes catering for the unemployed continued to be self-supporting.

The Chief Districts Officer subsequently met the South Wales District Committee and Joint Secretaries on several occasions to advise on formulating a scheme to meet this serious problem. The District Committee, in a letter dated 19th December 1940, stated that they had appointed a subcommittee to prepare recommendations to be submitted to the full Joint Committee and subsequently to a conference of representatives of the Welfare Schemes.

In Durham, the number of miners who had lost employment since 1st June 1940 was 20,451 (equivalent to 19% of the total employed in June). On the assumption that the men formerly paid 2d each week for the local welfare schemes, the total loss of revenue from this source amounted to about £8,800 a year. Additionally, Durham's District Organiser, Mr Graham, was on indefinite sick leave.

Durham District Committee had proposed that maintenance grants to schemes affected by unemployment should be made from the General Fund and not out of the District Fund. The District Committee had pointed out that Durham and South Wales would suffer a large decrease in Welfare Fund receipts.

The Commission decided to consult the Mines Department regarding the possibility of pooling a portion of the Districts Fund, for the purpose of assisting districts abnormally affected by war or national conditions.

The Commission agreed to accept recommendations from the Durham District Committee for maintenance grants in necessitous cases, subject to the application of the conditions laid down in the circular letter of 26th November 1929 as these conditions did not appear to be inappropriate to the current circumstances. However, all the grants would be charged to the District Fund and not the General Fund.

Realising the seriousness of the situation in Durham, the Commission decided to offer to provide the District Committee with a substitute for Mr Graham during his absence.[14]

In 1941, the total receipts of the Miners' Welfare Fund were slightly reduced to £1,064,379, with the Output Levy amounting to £871,676, the Royalties Levy to £152,000 and interest from investments to £40,703. In consequence only £182,094 was allocated to the Districts Fund, £69,336 to the General Fund and £812,949 to the Baths Fund.[15]

At the beginning of 1941, seventeen pithead baths and three extensions remained to be completed, and ten baths and one extension remained to be closed down at stages short of completion.

Progress in completing or bringing baths to stages short of completion was slow. Although shortages of labour and difficulty in obtaining supplies of materials and fittings were the chief causes for delays, severe winter weather conditions had, in certain districts, caused complete cessation of all building work for several weeks.

Work on the baths at Denaby Main had been stopped at the carcase stage in February, as the building had been requisitioned by the Ministry of Supply for a firm of machine tool manufacturers who were engaged on war production. Messrs Edgar Allen and Co. Ltd. took over the baths on 5th May

The Ministry of Supply had, on behalf of the Directors of Gauges, Jigs and Tools, enquired in May 1941 if any further buildings were available. Hapton Valley pithead baths (Lancashire) had been completed to carcase stage, and a further five baths schemes were nearing carcase completion.

The terms of agreement between the Commission and the Ministry of Supply for the use of baths were agreed at the May meeting of the Commission.

Towards the end of March 1941, the Chief Architect of the Ministry of Works and Buildings made a verbal request for the loan of some of the Commission's architects, including the Acting Chief Architect, to assist on an urgent programme of new buildings closely connected with the war effort. It was decided to loan Mr Parry and Mr Duddington at once. At the May meeting of the Commission, it was deemed essential that the Acting Chief Architect should be retained. The architectural staff had been reduced from 67 to 23 but it might be possible, in due course, to release two or three more. The principle of retaining a nucleus staff on which to reconstruct the organisation after the war and which, meanwhile, would undertake the war-time work of the Architects Section, needed to be adhered to. This wartime work included the completing and closing down short of completion of buildings already under construction, work essential for the proper maintenance of existing facilities and giving advice on structural maintenance problems, repair of air-raid damage to Miners' Welfare buildings and grounds, and making preparations for resuming the building programme as soon as conditions or circumstances would permit.

By July 1941, of the 38 baths and five extensions that were under construction when the Commission decided to suspend the building programme in July 1940, thirteen baths and two extensions remained to be completed or stopped short of completion. Except for Comrie (Fife), it was hoped to complete the rest by September. It had been exceptionally difficult to obtain labour for Comrie, and it was suggested that work might be suspended when the building had been made wind and watertight.

An application for pithead baths at Berry Hill Colliery (North Staffordshire) had been received. The Commission had received a report from the District Organiser at their May meeting which had indicated that 'it was virtually impossible to keep men at the Colliery in face of the fact that most of the Collieries in North Staffordshire district were equipped with Baths and that the Company were contemplating making some kind of provisional arrangement for bathing pending the erection of a pithead bath'.

The Colliery Company, supported by the North Staffordshire Colliery Owners' Association, had put their views in writing to the Mines Department and to the Commission at the end of June and beginning of July, respectively. Tenders for the Baths at Berry Hill had been received in May 1940, but were not submitted for approval following the Commission's decision to suspend the pithead baths programme temporarily.

Mr Kemp, Acting Chief Architect, had contacted the Contractors and the Ministry of Works and Buildings. The Contractors were still wishing to carry out the work, but costs had increased by about 20%. The Ministry of Works and Buildings were prepared to consider the release of controlled, materials. Mr Kemp, on this basis, recommended a modified scheme to conform with the requirements of building control but which could be completed after the war. The modified scheme would probably take about nine months to build.

In July 1941, the Ministry of Works and Buildings asked for a loan of a senior architect and any architectural assistants who could be spared. Mr Dempster, senior architect, and Mr Thomas, architectural assistant, were lent reducing the Staff of the Architects' Branch to twenty one. The staff of Clerks of Works were reduced to ten and would be paired in five groups to prepare for the reorganisation of the staff based on five architects groups for the post-war programme.

By October 1941, there was still one installation to be completed, six to be stopped short of completion and one extension to be completed. However, building had commenced at Berry Hill Colliery Baths on 20th September 1941.

Pressing applications had been received for three pithead baths and an extension to an existing installation. The applications were referred to the Mines Department who, in view of the extent of labour and materials needed for the canteen programme, had decided not to sponsor these applications.

At the end of their meeting in October, the Commission reviewed the position regarding filling the post of Chief Architect, which had been vacant since 30th June 1939. The Commission took the view that the service of the Architects' Branch, which had entered a spell of renewed activity with the demand for colliery canteens, would be prejudiced if the filling of the post were further deferred. On the other hand, the members of the Commission were unanimous in expressing full satisfaction with the services of Mr Kemp. The Commission accordingly decided that Mr Kemp should be appointed Chief Architect.[16]

In January 1941, Mr Whitfield Parker reported to the Commission on the progress with the Miners' Welfare Scheme in Warwickshire, Nottinghamshire, South Derbyshire and West Yorkshire and asked the Commission to extend the scope of its decision to make experimental grants from the General Fund for boys' clubs schemes, in order that two more districts, Forest of Dean and Fife, might be considered for grants.

On 7th May 1941, Mr Lambie and Mr Whitfield Parker had met with representatives of the Scottish Education Department, in connection with the responsibility for providing financial assistance to Miners' Welfare Youth Schemes in Scotland. As a result of the meeting, it was understood that, as in England and Wales, Local Education Authorities in Scotland would provide assistance towards the cost of Youth Schemes (with a 50% grant from the Scottish Education Department in respect of such expenditure) and that the Department might make direct grants for other approved expenditure not aided by the Local Authority. As regards grants from the Fund, for Miners' Welfare Youth Schemes in Scotland, the Commission confirmed that, as in England and Wales, grants would normally be considered on the basis of 50% expenditure including the leaders' salaries and expenses, limited to a period not exceeding three years. The Heathcote Boys' Club (South Derbyshire) was opened on 3rd May. In Nottinghamshire, Flights of Air Training Corps had been formed in connection with the Clubs, but the District Miners' Welfare Youth Council were ensuring that these Flights did not interfere with the normal boys' clubs' activities. The report by Mr Jefferies, District Organiser for Warwickshire, on the activities of the Warwickshire Boys' Club over the Easter holidays, which included a day of sports activities and a visit to Birch Coppice Colliery, was passed onto the Mines Department resulting in a letter from the Secretary for Mines personally supporting the work.[17]

Early in 1941, there was a widespread expression of opinion that the standard civilian rations provided insufficient food to maintain heavy workers, particularly miners, in full strength so that coal production would not suffer. In March 1941, the Secretary for Mines (Mr Grenfell) approached the Minister of Food (Lord Woolton) to give miners larger rations at home. The Minister of Food was unable to accede to this request. The Government, with the agreement of the Trades Union Congress, having adopted a general policy that, so far as possible, additional food should be provided for industrial workers not by differential rations at home but by making provision for them (in the words of Mr Bevin, the Minister of Labour) 'to feed on the job' at work canteens. Pending the general provision of such canteens, certain classes of workers (including underground workers at mines) were to have, at home, a supplementary ration of 8oz of cheese per week.

In these circumstances, the Secretary for Mines asked the Commission to assist in getting canteens set up at collieries which had none, and the Minister of Food offered a supply of ready-made soup for issue at the then existing canteens, and agreed to allow meals to be prepared in the canteens.

The Commission, while agreeing to assist the two ministries in these projects, had doubts about their value and at once expressed the view that a more satisfactory course would be to arrange for extra supplies for miners to be obtainable at their homes, a view that the Commission repeated from time to time.

While the discussion between the two Ministries were still in progress, the Commission, on 8th May 1941, addressed a letter to District Miners' Welfare Committees advising that existing canteens should be registered with the Ministry of Food as catering establishments, inviting the co-operation of the District Committees in getting canteens established at collieries that had none, and offering to make grants from the Miners' Welfare Fund (Districts Fund) towards the cost of any necessary equipment and utensils (not buildings), up to such amounts as might be recommended by the District Committees, colliery companies being expected to provide accommodation in the absence of an existing canteen.

A few days later, the Essential Work (Coalmining Industry) Order 1941 was made by the Ministry of Labour and National Service, requiring, amongst other things, satisfactory provision to be made at collieries for the welfare of persons employed, which included the provision of a canteen wherever required; the Secretary for Mines issued an appeal to colliery companies to set up canteens as a means of increasing the output of coal, which was urgently needed.

Some District Committees responded well to the Commission's call to action, but many had little experience to guide them in recommending grants from their District Funds, and small balances to draw upon. Miners were slow to show any desire to have canteens, except in a few Districts, and most colliery companies awaited evidence of adequate demand before entering upon a catering service, an activity with which they were unfamiliar.

The pre-war canteen had not been intended to provide full meals, the table and seating accommodation had been limited and the trade in 1940, on average, had been slightly less than 1s a week per person employed at the collieries. Although, as explained in the Commission's circular of 8th May 1941, it was permissible for all these 250 canteens to take immediate advantage of extra rations by registering as catering establishments and to use them for sandwiches, meat pies, sausage rolls, cakes etc. until accommodation for hot meals could be made available, only 120 canteens altogether out the 250 and the others newly set up, had registered by 22nd July 1941.

Reviewing the situation at their meeting on 22nd July 1941, the Commission concluded that, if the setting up of canteens was to proceed in all Districts as quickly as possible, further measures were required. It was therefore decided that, in addition to grants from the District Funds for equipment, grants would be made from the Baths Fund, subject to statutory authority being obtained, in order to defray the initial capital expenditure on buildings and that the colliery companies should be encouraged and assisted by all other means short of relieving them of the responsibility for establishing canteens.

Statutory authority was forthcoming when Defence Regulation (No 60BA) was established in October 1941, empowering the Commission during the emergency to apply to the Baths Fund for any of the purposes of the Miners' Welfare Fund. The Commission was further empowered by the Mines and Quarries (Canteen) Order made by the Secretary for Mines in November 1941, to direct the owner of any colliery to make arrangements for the establishment and maintenance of a canteen.

It soon became evident that the dual system of grants from the Districts Fund and the Baths Fund was not conducive to speed and effectiveness, so a special meeting of the Commission was held on 13th August 1941 when the Commission decided that the Baths Fund must relieve the Districts Fund of responsibility for equipment and must defray the whole of the initial capital outlay. This did not apply to expenditure on ancillary accommodation for handwashing, changing clothes etc., which were provided by grants from the Districts Fund recommended by the District Committees.

In accordance with its traditional policy, the Commission laid down that grants would not be made towards any costs of operation or maintenance. Once provided, canteens had to be self-supporting.

These decisions involved the Commission in a large measure of supervision over all proposals for canteens; the type of service, the type and plan of the building and the equipment, new duties for which qualified staff had to be obtained and existing staff retrained. Standardisation of design, construction and equipment was essential, although the standards necessarily fell short of the Commission's pre-war practice. Conditions for grants, notes for the guidance of companies, notes for architects on standard canteens, type plans, constructional details in conformity with the war-time building regulations and standard lists of equipment, were prepared with all speed and were issued to owners on 6th September 1941. The circular letter (MWC 56) pointed out that the Commission could not relieve them of the duty of providing canteens, but only undertook to make grants to reimburse them for 'approved' capital expenditure and said that the type of service provided should be that for which a demand was manifested by the workmen.

To avoid legal delays, the canteens were to be built on land owned or leased by the colliery owners and the utilisation of the building and its management for the purposes of a canteen were safeguarded and regulated by the provisions of a formal Agreement between the colliery owners and the Commission, instead of by a trust deed as was normal practice.

The circular letter was followed up by the Commission's staff who convened group meetings of representatives of the owners and workmen of all collieries to urge them to take immediate steps to institute canteens, giving them full information on how to go about it. Visits were then made by the District Officers to individual collieries to discuss the choice of service, and the best means of providing for local requirements.

After these meetings, colliery owners, with the help of a memorandum issued by the Commission, instructed their own architects to prepare plans and details. These were then examined by the Commission's architects, who were required to satisfy themselves that the proposals were acceptable as regard to type of service, scale of accommodation, economy of building labour and materials, compliance with wartime building regulations and economy of expenditure. When the Commission's architects had approved plans and details, they authorised companies to proceed and took steps to obtain release of labour and materials.

Where a wartime canteen was to be added to pithead baths, or was to be developed by extending an existing baths canteen, the colliery company, though retaining responsibility for initiating the proposal, was relieved of responsibility for planning, constructing and equipping the canteen, this work was undertaken by the Commission's architects (or by a firm of local architects appointed by the Commission) acting on behalf of the trustees of the baths.

As to equipment, detailed schedules for various sizes of canteens were prepared in consultation with the Ministry of Food. These schedules were based on minimum standards in view of the temporary nature and urgency of the project, and the need for economy in labour and materials.

The urgency of the war-time canteen programme made very heavy demands upon the Commission's staff who, with reduced numbers, were struggling with their regular work of temporarily winding up the baths building programme and the numerous day-to-day problems arising out of war conditions. So in September 1941, technical staff (grouped in 5 divisions, each in charge of an architect) were drafted to coalfields and powers were delegated to them and to District Miners' Welfare Officers (at that time numbering only 13) who were to report to the District Committees and to receive general directions from the Commission.[18]

To cope with the additional work involved, the number of the Commission's technical staff needed to increase. The first step in this direction was taken by securing, between August and October 1941, the return of five architects who were on loan to other departments. With the return of these officers, the total strength of the Architects' Branch was increased from sixteen to twenty one. It was anticipated that a further increase in staff would be required, so in October 1941 the Commission gave authority to any increase to the staff of the Architects' Branch that might become necessary to deal with canteen work.

In May 1941, the Commission became concerned about the arrangements for the distribution of additional food for miners, in particular the soup which had been arranged by the Mines Department with the Ministry of Food. Staff had spent much time in working out plans for the distribution of soup, which the Ministry of Food could not guarantee to supply. Supplies of food were restricted in mining areas, when extra supplies were available in adjoining areas through the British Restaurants set up in conjunction with the Ministry of Food.

The Commission thought that the action of the Ministry of Food had had an unsettling effect on the mining community to the detriment of their work, and that it appeared to show a lack of appreciation of the peculiar conditions of the mining industry and of the important parts miners were playing in the war effort. It was agreed that the Chairman and Mr Lawther would seek a meeting with Lord Woolton, Minister of Food.

Subsequent to the Commission's meeting on 20th May, The Chairman, Mr Lawther and the Secretary, in company with the Secretary for Mines, met Lord Woolton and Sir Henry French. Lord Woolton would not agree to the additional meat ration being available through normal retail channels. Concessions were made that the full meat ration of one penny per main meal per day to registered canteens would apply to the colliery canteens, irrespective of whether the meal was consumed in the canteen, premises or underground. A further concession was made that food could be prepared by a catering establishment for distribution at colliery canteens.

Lord Woolton agreed that officials of the Ministry of Food should co-operate with the Commission's staff in the establishment of canteens, and in securing priority for the necessary canteen equipment. As a consequence of this co-operation, District Organisers were greatly assisted in their work by the Ministry of Food Catering Officers in securing priority for canteen equipment.

One of the earliest and most successful schemes for giving miners extra food at their place of work was the North Staffordshire Miners' Food Preparation Centre. Nearly all the collieries in that District already had snack canteens and there was no demand for full meals, so it was decided in July 1941 to provide sandwich meals, made and packed at a central depot. The scheme was worked out by the District Officer under direction of the District Miners' Welfare Committee.

A disused school at Cobridge in Stoke-on-Trent was leased by the Colliery

Owners' Association and handed over to the District Miners' Welfare Committee, to be managed by a sub-committee. When the building had been adapted and equipped at the end of September 1941, it was put into operation under a contract with a catering firm. The cost of adapting the building and providing the equipment amounted to £8,948 up to the end of 1945, and was defrayed by grants from the Welfare Fund.

Meals consisted of two sandwiches, one meat and one of bacon, or occasionally cheese or jam, for which the miners paid 5d, though the cost to the colliery was slightly more than that. The centre served the whole of the North Staffordshire coalfield, with 21,000 miners and nearly 50,000 meals a week were supplied to 22 collieries. The Centre was able to supply weekly a liberal slice of fruit cake made with fruit of pre-war quantities, thanks to the centre's generous entitlement of ration points.[19]

Arising out of a parliamentary debate held on 2nd October 1941, where members showed great interest in the miners' food situation, a member, Mr David Robertson, secured the support of the President of the Board of Trade (Sir Andrew Duncan) for a scheme enabling miners to have hot meals underground, which he had already instituted experimentally with some measure of success at New Battle (Easthouses) Colliery in the Lothians. The meals were prepared on the surface and taken underground in insulated containers, which could keep them hot for a sufficient time. The container was a quart size Thermos jar fitted with a metal dish for pudding. The containers each held a complete meal for one person and were carried underground by the miners themselves.

On 26th November 1941, the Commission visited Newbattle (Easthouses) Colliery in the morning and held their meeting at the North British Station Hotel, Edinburgh, in the afternoon. Members of the Commission were able to descend into the mine and see the hot meals, which had been prepared on the surface in the kitchen canteen, consumed by the workers. The containers, which had been prepared by Thermos Ltd., were demonstrated by Mr D. Robertson MP.

As 70% of the underground workers at Easthouses Colliery were taking hot meals, the Commission, at their meeting in the afternoon, took the decision to defray the expenditure involved in carrying out four more trials of the system at other collieries, with varying conditions, on the understanding that Mr Robertson would keep the Commission informed of the arrangements and progress.

By the end of December 1941, canteens had been registered as catering establishments at 650 collieries (employing 77% of all miners) out of a total of about 1,030 collieries with more than 50 work people each. Most of the canteens were providing only sandwiches or snacks with only 40 providing full meals. [20]

At its January 1941 meeting, the Commission had decided to ask the Secretary for Mines to consider seeking an amendment of the War Damages Bill so as to provide full relief from liability for contribution under the compulsory scheme for buildings and immovable property when any property met the following conditions:

a) the property had been provided wholly or mainly by means of grants from the Miners' Welfare Fund; and
b) the property was either held for charitable purposes (without limitation of purpose as currently provided under the Bill) or registered under the Friendly Society Acts; and
c) the present conditions of the Bill as to the property being held and occupied for charitable purposes.

The Secretary for Mines had replied that the Treasury would be unwilling to grant such relief but he was prepared, with the concurrence of the Treasury, to acquiesce in the Commission bearing as a capital charge such contributions and premiums as might be payable in respect of the Miners' Welfare Schemes.

Parliament made no fundamental change to those sections of the Bill which affected Miners' Welfare Property. The cost of insurance under the two compulsory schemes up to 30th September 1941, would have probably amounted to about £81,000, being £32,800 for buildings and immovable property and £48,200 for moveable property, the contribution in respect of buildings and immovable property being payable over a period of 5 years. The principle of making grants from the Districts Fund to cover the contribution had already been accepted by the District Committees.

In March 1941, the Commission decided that grants would be made from the Districts Fund and the Baths Fund (in respect of districts and baths schemes as the case might be) to cover the contribution or premium in respect of the compulsory insurance of Miners' Welfare property, both immovable and removable. Approval of such grants would be made subject to the trustees and management committees entering into an agreement with the Commission to obtain its approval before expending any monies received in respect of compensation for war damage. If necessary, grants would be made for the restoration of war damage, by way of temporary advances, pending compensation being paid by the Government, these grants also being subject to trustees and management committees entering into an agreement with the Commission to repay grants when compensation was received.

The War Damage Act received Royal Assent on 26th March 1941. On 6th May 1941, a circular letter was issued to District Committees and all Miners' Welfare Schemes regarding the operation of the War Damage Act 1941, and the conditions on which grants would be made for the District Funds and Baths Fund for contributions payable under the Act and for advances for restoration of Miners' Welfare property pending compensation being received from the War Damage Commission.[21]

In November 1940, the Safety in Mines Research Board had asked the Commission for advice on the provision of clothes drying, washing and canteen accommodation for their manual staff at Buxton Research Station, and they also asked for a report on the condition of the block. The matter was referred to the Chairman, who agreed that the Architects' Branch should assist the Board with technical advice. Mr Dudding's report drew attention to the serious dilapidations which existed and included recommendations and an approximate estimate of the cost of repairs. After considering the report, the Board decided that they must consider their future policy on the buildings and requested the Commission's Architects should again visit Buxton to undertake a preliminary survey, and report upon the other buildings and also that they should attend the Governing Committee's meeting at Buxton on 26th February 1941 to help and guide them in their discussions.

The Acting Chief Architect attended the meeting with Mr Dudding. The Board would be acting on the basis of their reports, which included the recommendation that £2,200 was expended on the essential improvements and repairs to the existing buildings. The Board's Governing Committee had also asked for architectural and legal assistance of the staff of the Miners' Welfare Commission with a scheme for new buildings and purchase or renewal of the lease of the station.

In March 1941, the Commission approved a grant of £48,000 towards the estimated expenditure of the Safety in Mines Research Board for the year 1941/42. As in the case of the previous two years, any savings in that year would be set aside as a reserve towards the cost of carrying out developments held up by the war. The approval of the Commission was given upon the conditions attached to the grant in 1940/41. The Board would continue to require payment of an appropriate sum for assistance afforded to other government departments or bodies, and a detailed statement needed to be submitted at the end of the financial year. The Board was expected to obtain the Commission's approval for any expenditure from the reserve fund.[22]

A meeting had been held on 15th January 1941 at Sheffield University to draw up a scheme for introducing a uniform examination for the National Welfare Advanced Mining Part-time Scholarship Scheme and setting up selection panels as already approved by the Commission in principle. Those present at the meeting were Professor Statham (Assessor to the Scheme), Mr Elliot, Mr Hummel, Mr Lambie and the Assistant Secretary.

It was hoped that the proposed arrangements could be put into operation in 1941, and should remove the difficulties experienced by the Assessor in his task of assessing the examination papers submitted by the various examining bodies.[23]

1942 saw the Coalition Government assume full control of the coal industry, and to organise it as a national service under Command Paper 6364 on Coal. This step was taken to secure an increase in the output of coal and to maintain it at an adequate level. The essential factor in this was manpower.

After the Allied defeat in France, there was loss of manpower in the industry and this had continued unchecked until the summer of 1941, when the recruitment of miners to the Forces and other industries was stopped under the Essential Works (Coal Mines Industry) Order but, in spite of this, there was continued wastage of manpower, estimated at about 25,000 per annum.

In 1941, 33,000 ex-miners were returned to the mines from other industries and an estimated 11,500 would return from the Forces in 1942. Two further steps had been taken by the government to close the gap between those entering and leaving the industry. Firstly, coal mining had been put in the priority industries to which de-reserved men could choose to go if they pleased, rather than go into the armed forces. The Forster Committee had been appointed in 1942 to try to attract juveniles into the industry.

There would be a Minister of Fuel, Light and Power with powers adequate to assure full and effective control, and there would be a National Coal Board to advise the Minister. The Mines Department would be absorbed into the new Ministry.

Major Gwilym Lloyd George, the son of David Lloyd George, was appointed as Minister of Fuel, Light and Power on 11th June 1942.[24]

In 1942, the total receipts of the Miners' Welfare Fund were £1,059,514 of which £879,150 came from the Output Levy, £124,000 from the Royalties Levy and £56,364 from investments. £822,931 was allocated to the Baths Fund, £173,067 to the Districts Fund and £63,516 to the General Fund.[25]

By January 1942, Mr Robertson had experimented with hot meals underground at Chisnall Hall (Lancashire), Haigh (South Yorkshire) and Victoria (North Staffordshire). Approaches had been made to Pemberton (Lancashire) and Blidsworth (Nottinghamshire) and men at the latter colliery had refused the offer of an experimental installation. As Mr Robertson was acting independently, information was not complete but reports reaching the Commission indicated that the percentage of workers participating in the underground meals were not favourable. At Easterhouses (Lothians), an extension of the experiment had been arranged at Lingerwood and Lady Victoria, part of the Newbattle group, served from the Easterhouses' canteen.

No approach had been made by the Commission to the District Welfare Committees to ascertain their views on the experiment, but seven Districts had informed the Commission that they were not in favour.

The experiments lasted for various periods from two to six weeks. Meals were provided free for a few days after which the charge was 8d per meal, payable weekly in advance. The price was less than the cost and resulted in trading losses of £951 (excluding the pay of the officers and sergeant cooks of the Army Catering Corps loaned for the experiment), which losses were not accepted as a charge against the Miners' Welfare Fund. The net cost falling to the Miners' Welfare Fund in respect to these experiments amounted to £4,485.

Despite the cheapness of the meals, very few of the underground miners took them; only 4% at Haigh,10% at Biddolph (North Staffordshire), 8% at Lingerwood and 13% at Lady Victoria.

By April 1942, the cooking equipment used in Mr Robertson's underground experiments had been disposed of. The National Physical Laboratory were studying the question of an improved container.[26]

The Commission again considered the question of the provision of handwashing and sanitary accommodation at canteens where there were no pithead baths in April 1942. In November 1941, the Commission had considered letters from West Yorkshire District Committee and Wigan Coal Company urging that canteens should be provided with handwashing and sanitary conveniences where there were no pithead baths. In November 1941, the Commission had decided that for collieries without pithead baths, where washing accommodation was asked for, it might be included in the plans with a view to building it when labour and materials were available. In April 1942, the Commission again refused, as it had in November 1941, to provide the accommodation out of the Baths Fund but made it permissible (under conditions) as a charge on the District Fund. The Commission needed to be reassured by the District Committee that the accommodation was essential and suitable arrangements had been made for the provision of soap and towels.[27]

By 18th April 1942, 742 canteens had been established, and the number of full-meal canteens in operation and in preparation had risen to 411. By June 1942, the demand for canteens was growing, with 89% of miners employed enjoying a food service.

Early in May, the labour force allocated was inadequate to meet the requirements for the canteen building programme. There were also requirements for Shireoaks pithead baths and the handwashing accommodation in connection with canteens. The Ministry of Works and Planning was approached on 15th May, who forecasted an early change to the system of allocation of the labour force and a reduction of the amount available. The question was considered by the Ministerial Building Directorate on 12th June and then referred to the new Ministry of Fuel and Power for a definite decision.

On 24th June 1942, the Ministry of Fuel and Power held a meeting to consider the future of the Commission's canteen programme. Considering the drastic cuts which had been applied to all building, the colliery canteen programme had suffered comparatively lightly with the predicted peak of the building being reached in December 1942 rather than September.

By October 1942, 77 contracts had been completed and 75 new contracts had been authorised. A large proportion of the contracts under construction had had to be commenced without a priority symbol as the Ministry of Works and Planning had temporarily suspended the issue of certificates. However, the Building Directorate did reach an agreement on the priority of colliery canteens and the issue of priority certificates had commenced again but the labour position was likely to remain very difficult.

The Commission also approved a request, sponsored by Lancashire District Committee and the Regional Labour Director, for the provision of bathing accommodation in an existing building at Huncoat Colliery using disused fittings from another installation. There was extreme wetness in all the workings in the pit and a need for bathing accommodation.

By December 1942, 831 canteens were in operation and the building work in hand covered all known demands for new canteens and extensions. It was estimated that by August 1943, the demand for canteens would have been substantially satisfied, and the estimated cost (£1,310,000) of the canteen programme would not be greatly exceeded.[28]

As one measure to check wastage of labour in the coal industry, a Mines Medical Service was to be established to co-ordinate and, where necessary, supplement the facilities available for medical treatment of miners, and to deal with applications for release from the industry on medical grounds.

The proposal to set up a Mines Medical Service was referred to a Committee under the Chairmanship of Mr Tom Smith, Parliamentary Secretary of the Ministry of Fuel and Power. The subsequent report, in September 1942, recommended amongst other things that, in so far as the existing hospital services failed to meet the particular need of coal miners for rehabilitation treatment, immediate and energetic action should be taken by the Miners' Welfare Commission to provide them with special rehabilitation centres. The Ministry of Fuel and Power adopted the report and invited the Commission to implement this recommendation.

In its widest sense, rehabilitation covers the whole range of medical and social services, from the time of the onset of the individual's disability to the point at which they are restored to normal activity (or the nearest possible approach to it). Besides treating the actual injury, rehabilitation aims to restore general muscle tone, full function of the body and limbs, general health, strength and self-confidence, and then resettling the individual in industry in their own old occupation, or retraining and settling them in some other occupation more suited to physical capacity, if altered. Rehabilitation aims at complete recovery, in respect of the psychological as well as the physical disability, and it is complete only when the patient knows for themself that their ability has been restored.

For surgical treatment, it was most important that fracture cases should go to a specialised fracture department, staffed by a single team under a surgeon-in-charge, as recommended by reports in 1937 and 1939 of the Delevingne Committee of the Home Office, Ministry of Health and Scottish Office.

Certain selected hospitals were provided with specialised fracture departments under the Emergency Medical Scheme arranged by the Ministry of Health. Although this scheme, when first designed, was intended mainly to cope with air-raid needs and to help armed services; in 1941 it was made available for fracture accidents among workers in war industries including mining.

The Miners' Welfare Commission had in 1938 suggested to District Welfare Committees that, if at any time they were considering recommending a grant to a hospital, they should ask the hospital, in suitable cases, to organise a fracture service on the lines recommended by the Delevingne Committee. Grants for fracture or orthopaedic departments had been made to hospitals in South Yorkshire, South Derbyshire, Cumberland and South Wales.

In April 1942, the Commission confirmed, in principle, its decision taken in January 1942 to establish separate rehabilitation centres for miners with the aid of 50% of the District Funds. In January 1942, the Commission had given approval, in principle, to the sale of the Nottinghamshire Miners' Welfare Convalescent Home at Mansfield to the Midland Owners' Mutual Company Ltd for a miners' rehabilitation centre and an allocation of £10,000 out of the Durham District Fund was approved towards the capital cost of £20,000 of establishing a miners' rehabilitation centre in Durham.

In April 1942, the Commission approved the recommendation from South Wales District Committee for a grant of £50,000 for providing a rehabilitation centre for miners in South Wales. They also decided to inform the District Committee that no objection, in principle, would be raised by the Commission if the Trustees of Talygarn decided that the interests of their convalescent home trusts would be best served in selling Talygarn to other Trustees for the use as a rehabilitation centre.

In August 1942, the Commission appointed a medical sub-committee for rehabilitation centres to examine the whole problem of providing rehabilitation services particularly in relation to the South Wales scheme and Mansfield. The

Commission asked Professor Collis and Dr Fisher, Medical Inspector of Mines, to be members of the sub-committee, and they were joined by Mr Llewellin Jacob, Mr Browne and Mr Drummond, all members of the Commission.

At its October 1942 meeting, the Committee viewed the film entitled 'Life Begins Again', which had been produced under the auspices of the Ministry of Information and dealt with the work of rehabilitation including the Miners' Rehabilitation Centre, Mansfield.

The meeting was attended by Mr Tom Smith, and the Chairman reported that a letter had been received from the Minister of Fuel and Power giving an assurance that, if the Commission undertook the responsibility for the rehabilitation of miners, the Miners' Welfare Fund would be appropriately augmented by legislative action, if and when the Government were satisfied that such augmentation would be necessary to cover the expenditure involved.

With the assurance from the government, and adopting the recommendations of its Medical Sub-Committee's interim report, the Commission decided to undertake responsibility for securing the establishment of a national scheme for rehabilitation treatment for all workers in or about coal mines who might require such treatment, whether they were injured at work or at home. This policy would be put into effect by arrangement based on several principles. The centre would be provided and equipped by the Commission out of the central funds of the Miners' Welfare Fund. Each centre would be held by the Commission as Trustee under a trust deed providing for management by a District Miners' Rehabilitation Committee appointed by the Commission. No charge for treatment was to be made to patients from whose wages a weekly deduction was made for hospital maintenance, but the balance of the cost of maintaining the centre and reimbursing the patients their out-of-pocket expenses for travelling to be defrayed from the central funds of the Miners' Welfare Fund. The Surgeon-in-Charge of each centre was to be appointed by the Commission, the Management Committee being represented on the interviewing committee. Appointments of other medical, treatment staff and ancillary staff was to be made by the Management Committee, subject to the prior approval of the Commission in each instance.

The services of a consulting orthopaedic surgeon of high standing would be needed to advise the Commission in the provision and conduct of the rehabilitation centres.

In December 1942, the Commission considered the second report of the Medical Sub-Committee on Miners' Rehabilitation Treatment, which set out detailed proposals as to how the Commission could add rehabilitation to its many other activities.

In Lancashire and Cheshire, a new centre would be established to meet the needs of the District. The Northern Employers' Indemnity Company, who for two years had been conducting a rehabilitation clinic at Wigan for miners as outpatients, would be reimbursed by the Commission for any further rent unavoidably payable by them if and when the work of their centre, the lease of which had two years to run, was transferred to the Commission's centre. Any of their equipment that could be used at the latter centre would be purchased.

In Northumberland and Durham, it might be necessary to ask the War Office to release the premises in their occupation for the required treatment centres.

In Scotland, the Gleneagles rehabilitation centre would be ready for treating patients early in January 1943. The Department of Health for Scotland had enquired as to whether grants for assistance for travelling expenses of patients and provision of entertainment at the centre would be available and the Commission agreed to both travelling expenses and grants for entertainment on approved estimates for general application to rehabilitation centres.

In Nottinghamshire, the Commission approved the purchase of Berry Hill Hall and grounds from the Trustees of the Mansfield and District Convalescent Home. The Commission would take over and operate the centre from 1st January 1943, and retain the services of Mr Nicoll (Medical Officer) and the treatment staff.

In Warwickshire, the Commission adopted the proposal that Warwickshire Miners' Welfare Home at Higham Grange, which was capable of accommodating 50 patients, should be acquired by the Commission for adaptation as a rehabilitation centre to serve the five districts of Warwickshire, South Derbyshire, Cannock Chase, South Staffordshire and Leicestershire.

The South Wales and Monmouthshire District Committee had agreed in principle to the proposed sale of Talygarn Convalescent Home to the Commission. Discussions were proceeding with the Ministry of Health for the proposed centre at Talygarn to be supervised by an orthopaedic surgeon appointed by the Ministry for their new EMS Hospital at Morriston.

The Commission adopted the recommendation of the Medical Sub-Committee to appoint Mr R. Watson-Jones (Consultant of the RAF and Hon Orthopaedic Surgeon of the Royal Infirmary, Liverpool) to act as consultant to the Commission and expressed its appreciation of his offer to act in an honorary capacity during the war. They also decided that a suitable medical officer should be appointed to the staff of the Commission to assist Mr Watson-Jones in this work.

The estimate of the capital cost of establishing fifteen centres was £450,000 and the annual maintenance cost was £120,000 with an additional £20,000 if an allowance of 35/- per week were made to patients not in receipt of compensation.

At their December 1942 meeting, the Commission agreed that the financial arrangements in connection with the establishment of miners' welfare rehabilitation centres should be discussed with the Ministry of Fuel and Power. However, relying on the promise of the Ministry of Fuel and Power to augment the Welfare Fund appropriately (if and when necessary) to cover the expenditure, the Commission approved an initial allocation from the Baths Fund for expenditure on the provision of rehabilitation centres for miners.[29]

Under the National Miners' Welfare Scholarship and Exhibition Schemes, twelve new scholarships and eleven exhibitions had been recommended for award in 1942.

Nominations for appointments to the Advisory Committee under the uniform examination scheme for the Part-Time Day Advanced Mining Scholarships had been made by eight regional examining bodies and kindred organisations in England, Scotland and Wales. The nominations had been considered by Mr Elliot regarding England and Wales, and Mr Lambie for Scotland. As it had been decided that four members instead of two originally proposed to represent organisations in England, the six persons appointed members of the Advisory Committee were Mr T. Bryson, Mr G. Fletcher, Mr R. L. Hay and Mr F. Oxley for England; Mr R. James for Wales and Mr R. McAdam for Scotland.[30]

In 1943, the total receipts of the Miners' Welfare Fund were £1,002,454 of which £829,647 came from the Output Levy, £100,000 from the Royalties Levy and £72,807 from Investments. £149,460 was appropriated to the Districts Fund, £63,180 to the General Fund and £789,814 to the Pithead Baths Fund. [31]

By the end of January 1943, £1,468,335 had been allocated for canteens which included £170,744 for pre-September 1941 canteens, £6,000 for the underground feeding experiment and £324,856 for equipment. There continued to be shortages of labour.

At the beginning of January 1943, 188 canteens were serving full meals, but only 29% of the canteen customers were taking full meals due to the lack of variety of food served.

By April 1943, the labour position with the colliery canteens had slightly eased. The Chief Mining Supplies Officer had made arrangements with the Ministry of Works to raise the labour ceiling from 1,200 to 1,400 for canteens and rehabilitation centres.

182 contracts were in progress in June 1943 with 56 canteens or enlargements in hand, leaving 268 jobs outstanding, the majority of which would be completed by October subject to the labour force being maintained. However, during June, the Ministry of Fuel and Power indicated that they would be required to suspend the canteen building programme except for more urgent cases, but after representations had been made to them on the Commission's behalf, they decided to adhere to the programme in hand. The labour force, which had been reduced to 800 was sufficient for all known requirements.

Although 876 canteens were in operation in October 1943, 139 contracts under construction and 89 schemes in preparation, it was anticipated that the 228 outstanding schemes would not be completed until the end of 1944. It was also anticipated that North Staffordshire and South Wales would be making new applications for enlargements of existing canteens.

Progress was made throughout the year on the building of the modified baths at Shireoaks, Huncoat, Dullatur and Ayr 9 and 10.

An application had been made for a pithead bath at Rankin (Lanarkshire) by the colliery company, which had been supported by the District Committee and the Ministry of Fuel and Power, on the grounds that it was urgently required and that a suitable building and redundant fittings were available. Approval was given by the Commission, subject to the colliery company providing the building free of charge and finding the necessary building labour, the cost of which would be defrayed from the Miners' Welfare Fund on the basis of the recognised trade rates.[32]

The War Office had refused to release 'The Hermitage' in Chester-Le-Street from military occupation in order that it might be acquired as a rehabilitation treatment centre for Durham miners despite the premises not being fully used. Therefore, in February 1943, the Chairman undertook to approach the Secretary for War personally with a view to securing the release of the premises.

The Director of the Midland Colliery Owners' Mutual Indemnity Company had suggested that a tablet should be fixed in Berry Hill Hall to commemorate the establishment there, on 19th April 1940, of the first miners' residential rehabilitation centre by the Indemnity Company, in association with the Butterley Company and Bolsover Colliery Company, and a recognition of the services rendered in connection with the centre by Mr Guy de G. Warren as General Manager and Mr E. A. Nicoll as Medical Officer. In January 1943, the Commission agreed to this suggestion subject to the agreement of the Management Committee.

By February 1943, South Derbyshire, Leicestershire, Warwickshire, South Staffordshire and Cannock Chase District Committees had agreed a joint scheme and Warwickshire District Committee had offered Higham Grange to the Commission for a rehabilitation centre. The Chief Architect's report indicated that the property would require substantial additions to fit it for a rehabilitation centre, which would take at least nine months. In these circumstances, as the centre needed to be brought into use as quickly as possible, Mr Watson-Jones suggested that improvised accommodation should be made available whilst the building work was in progress.

In North Staffordshire, the Coal Owners' Indemnity Company had purchased Betley Court, near Stoke, which was being adapted by the Ministry of Health as a rehabilitation centre for the Stoke Infirmary, at which all the injured miners in North Staffordshire were treated. The District Committee were satisfied with what was being done, and thought that no advantage would be gained by the Commission providing a centre.

The Commission had accepted the Board of Management's offer to sell Talygarn including the freehold estate, buildings, furnishings, fittings and equipment for the sum of £50,000, subject to the Ministry of Fuel and Power's agreement.

The Commission confirmed the appointments of members of Management Committees for the period of three years from 17th December 1942 for Berry Hill Hall at their meeting in February 1943. They also considered the Model Regulations for the management of rehabilitation centres which were subsequently submitted to the Joint Standing Consultative Committee of the Mining Association of Great Britain and the Mineworkers' Federation of Great Britain for their comments.

The recruitment of medical officers for each centre was discussed and Mr Watson-Jones indicated that it would be better to combine the post at the centre with an EMS post under the Ministry of Health.

At their February meeting, the Commission agreed to Mr Watson-Jones' post being designated as Director of Rehabilitation and that a Rehabilitation Advisory Committee, comprising Dr Fisher and medical men experienced in rehabilitation, with Mr Watson-Jones as Chairman, should be appointed. They also agreed to the suggestion made by Mr Watson-Jones that there should be periodical conferences of medical officers of the centres, at which their experience could be pooled and information exchanged.

It was reported at the Commission's April meeting that the Secretary of State for Scotland had appointed a Consultative Committee under the chairmanship of Sir Robert Bruce to ensure that the fitness centre at Gleneagles Hospital was used to its fullest advantage by the mining industry in Scotland and that patients treated at the centre were assisted in re-employment.

South Yorkshire District Committee, in consultation with the Regional Hospital Officer of the Ministry of Health, had made arrangements for rehabilitation treatment to be given at three hospital centres: Wakefield (Pinderfields), Sheffield (Woofinden) and Doncaster (Infirmary) to serve as a temporary scheme pending the establishment of a residential centre for miners.

In West Yorkshire, the District Committee had made, in consultation with the Regional Hospital Officer of the Ministry of Health, arrangements for rehabilitation treatment to be given to miners at Wakefield (Pinderfields).

In April 1943, the Commission decided to accept the offer made by the Trustees of the Warwickshire Miners' Welfare Convalescent Home to sell Higham Grange including the freehold for £13,500 plus a sum for the furniture, fittings and equipment.

The Commission officially appointed the members of the Management Committee of the Monmouthshire and South Wales Rehabilitation Centre for a period of three years from 23rd February 1943 (the date of the first meeting of the Committee) at their April 1943 meeting. The Commission also confirmed that miners of the Forest of Dean should be entitled to use of this centre.

The Rehabilitation Advisory Committee had held their first meeting on 7th April 1943. Mr Watson-Jones (Chairman) and Dr Fisher had been joined on the Committee by Mr Alexander Miller, Mr E. A. Nicoll, Mr L. Smillie and Mr C. S. Walker. The Commission asked the Committee to prepare a memorandum covering the scheme of rehabilitation treatment of miners, for issue to the Mining Association of Great Britain and to the Mineworkers' Federation of Great Britain.

At the June 1943 meeting of the Commission, it was reported that Hartford Hall and adjoining land had been purchased for £8,000 to provide a rehabilitation centre for Northumberland. Alterations and additions to adapt the premises would take several months so the target date for opening needed to be postponed to October. It had been suggested to the Royal Victoria Infirmary, Newcastle, following a meeting between the Commission's Medical Advisory Sub-Committee and representatives of the Northumberland and Durham District Miners' Welfare Committees, that the Commission should be allowed the service of two surgeons, working under the supervision of Mr Gordon Irwin, to conduct the rehabilitation treatment of the Northumberland and Durham centres respectively.

In Durham, the Hermitage, Chester-Le-Street, had been purchased together with 184½ acres of land for £18,000. The Commission approved an allocation of £15,000 for the conversion of the premises. The work would take three months to carry out so the target date for opening was October.

In Lancashire and Cheshire, the District Committee had recommended that Oakmere Hall and grounds should be acquired for a rehabilitation centre and this recommendation was adopted by the Commission at its June meeting.

Professor Collis and the Secretary had met with the Cumberland District Committee to ask them to make proposals in conjuction with the Whitehaven Hospital to bring the coal mining industry into closer contact with the rehabilitation centre, and to ensure that fracture cases were sent to Whitehaven Hospital for treatment.

The draft explanatory notes for issue to the mining industry, prepared by the Rehabilitation Advisory Committee, were considered by the Commission at their June meeting. Under the paragraph headed 'Welfare and Re-employment of Patients', a return to work after leaving the Rehabilitation Centre was envisaged. The ease of mind created by an assurance of re-employment on completion of treatment was a most important requisite for rehabilitation. The surgeons attached such value to the psychological effects induced by this consideration that the Commission decided to bring it to the notice of the Joint Standing Consultative Committee and to invite the Committee to consider whether they could give assistance in this direction.

By October 1943, the Northumberland and Durham Rehabilitation Committees were proceeding with appointments of staff for their respective rehabilitation centres. Cumberland had suggested the purchase of the Glenholme Nursing Home as a rehabilitation centre and hostel for Cumberland miners and other patients. As the accommodation needed to meet the needs of miners of Cumberland was only six beds, the Commission decided to further examine this proposal.

In Nottinghamshire, the Rehabilitation Committee, at their meeting on 11th August had agreed to the proposal of the Commission that Derbyshire miners should be admitted to Berry Hill Hall and that representatives from Derbyshire District Miners' Welfare Committee should be added to the present Rehabilitation Committee.

Representatives of the Commission and a sub-committee of Kent District Committee had met on 8th October 1943 to discuss the rehabilitation scheme for Kent. Hospital treatment would be concentrated at Canterbury Hospital which would pass onto Orpington EMS orthopaedic hospital those cases which would seem to require rehabilitation treatment as inpatients. For other cases, rehabilitation treatment would be provided at a special clinic for miners to be established by the Commission.

By December 1943, the provision of miners' rehabilitation treatment so far covered 60% of the men employed in the industry and facilities were in the course of being provided for a further 34% of men, leaving just 6% in respect of whom provision was under consideration.

The Whitehaven and West Cumberland Hospital had submitted a proposal to purchase the Glenholme Nursing Home for use as a rehabilitation centre for Cumberland, and a hostel for miners and other patients. The Commission had approved the proposal and agreed to assist with a grant of 50% of the cost of purchase, adaptation and equipment up to the amount of £3,000 subject to several conditions which included six beds being reserved for miners.

By December 1943, South Yorkshire District Committee had made arrangements for injured mine workers in the Sheffield and Doncaster areas to receive treatment at the Woofinden Home and Wharncliffe EMS Hospital, Sheffield and the Doncaster Infirmary respectively.

Mr Watson-Jones made the Commission aware in December 1943, that he was unable to devote as much time as then seemed to be required for the direction and supervision of the Commission's Rehabilitation Centres. The Commission referred the matter to a sub-committee comprising the Chairman, Professor Collis, Mr Fudge and the Secretary to make suitable arrangements.[33]

Although the Commission had set up a sub-committee consisting of Professor Collis, Mr Drummond and Mr Horner to examine the Future Programme of the Miners' Welfare Fund as early as October 1942, it proved impossible to complete the necessary preparatory work to enable the sub-committee to commence its meetings in 1942 due to the preoccupation with the establishment of the Miners' Rehabilitation Centres.

At the April 1943 meeting of the Commission, it was agreed that arrangements should be made by the Chairman and the Future Programme Sub-Committee to meet the Minister of Fuel and Power to discuss the Pithead Baths Fund, functions of the Ministry and the Commission in relation to welfare matters, safety research, health research, colliery clinics, the Forster Report on the recruitment of Juveniles and war-time building.

The meeting with the Minister of Fuel and Power was held on 27th May 1943, and a number of points emerged. The question of to what extent the Commission's expenditure on miners' rehabilitation centres would be recouped was under consideration by the Minister, and Mr Fudge promised to confirm the result to the Commission in the near future.

The Minister agreed that safety research should cease to be a function of the Commission. The Commission therefore agreed that it would surrender any claim for repayment in respect to the grants made from the Miners' Welfare Fund for the assets of the Research Board, in particular the Endowment Fund and the premises of the Research Stations.

Mr Fudge would look into wording a definition of the respective functions of the Ministry and of the Commission in relation to Welfare matters, with a view to submitting a paper for consideration by the Commission at its next meeting.

The question of building improvised pithead baths during the war was also discussed at the request of the Ministry of Fuel and Power at the Commission's meeting in June 1943. The Ministry had raised the question of whether, as standard pithead baths could not be provided during wartime, it would be possible to provide 'the bare minimum necessities for washing and for clothes drying in temporary huts or shelters, in much the same way as was already done at Army and RAF camps up and down the country'. A memorandum on the subject had been prepared by the Secretary and the Chief Architect, and the conclusions reached in the memorandum were adopted by the Commission.

At their August meeting, the Commisson considered a letter dated 27th July 1943 from the Ministry of Fuel and Power, containing a note of the decision reached by the Minister regarding the matters that were left outstanding at their meeting with representatives of the Commission on 27th May. After considerable discussion, the Commission sought an interview with the Minister but was asked to submit its representations in writing. The Commission sent these on 6th September.

The Minister had felt that there was not sufficient justification for asking parliament for legislation to reverse its earlier decision that the Output Levy should drop to ½ d per ton at the end of 1943. The Commission pointed out that the question before parliament in 1939 was a proposal to increase and not drop the Levy for a period of five years. This was before the demand for baths had reached its current strength.

Even before the five years was over, other welfare issues had come to the fore, such as rehabilitation centres and war-time canteens, which were being provided from the Baths Fund at the request of the Minister and his predecessor. While the receipts from the additional ½ d Levy imposed by Statute in 1939 for five years for the purpose of accelerating pithead baths was estimated at £2,254,000, £1,943,711 of the Baths Fund money had already been used for rehabilitation centres and canteens and the expenditure on them would have risen to £2,541,000 by the end of 1944. Thereafter, the cost of maintaining the rehabilitation centres, estimated at £120,000 a year (equivalent to two-thirds of the total Districts Fund), would have to be provided from some other source because the authority for using the Baths Fund under Defence Regulation 60BA would lapse at the end of the war.

The Commission understood that in asking it to provide rehabilitation centres, the Minister would promise to take appropriate steps immediately to ensure that the Commission had sufficient income to finance the centres and would not leave it to some indefinite date in the future. The system of asking parliament to vote monies as and when required was not convenient in dealing with the Miners' Welfare Fund.

Turning to the Nation Building Programme, the Commission appreciated that building control was likely to continue for a time after the cessation of hostilities but, at the request of the Ministry of Works, it had submitted a post-war building programme which covered a ten-year period commencing upon the cessation of hostilities, and were hopeful that its programme would be included in the National Building Programme. The Commission's claim to a high degree of priority for building baths after the war was justified, on the evidence of widespread demand amongst the miners and colliery owners for pithead baths. The Forster Committee had recommended that 'a very strong priority' should be given to pithead baths in relation to recruitment of youths. If the building programme was to be completed in a limited period, preparatory work needed to be undertaken immediately, and this necessitated immediate decisions as to the length of the building period and the amount of financial provision.

The total cost of providing baths at all unequipped collieries was estimated, at post-war prices, to be about £9,250,000. The Minister's letter of 27th July stated that 'the reduced levy of ½ d per ton will keep the Commission's resources at a level sufficient to meet its current and prospective expenditure for some years to come'.

The Commission estimated, on the basis set out by the Minister, that the Baths Fund would be in significant deficit by 1947 and this would continue at £1,924,000 for 1948 and £1,045,000 for each subsequent year. It was therefore essential that an early decision should be taken, after consultation with the Industry, as to the period of the building programme and the means of funding over that period.

Mr Fudge attended the October meeting of the Commission to convey the views of the Minister of Fuel and Power, on the representations made by the Commission in its letter of 6th September 1943.

The Minister was not convinced that the maintenance of the levy at 1d per ton was a matter of necessity, nevertheless, if the amount of the levy was the only the issue, the Minister would be prepared to ask the Cabinet for authority to introduce into the House of Commons a short Bill continuing the levy at 1d per ton until 1951, when the output levy was due to terminate; the Minister did not feel able to propose legislation to his colleagues if other issues were added which would cause controversy, such as the power to make compulsory deductions from workmen's wages for subscriptions for the maintenance of pithead baths, the release of the Commission from the obligation to provide funds to finance safety in mines research, or any matter concerning the reconstitution of the administration of the Fund which the Commission might be considering.

However, the continuance of the 1d levy could be disassociated from all other questions, and if the Minister could be assured that he could rely upon agreement, both inside and outside parliament, to defer legislation on these issues for the time being, then he would ask the Cabinet for authority to introduce a single-clause Bill for the sole purpose of continuing the levy at 1d until 1951.

The Commission agreed that this would meet the essential need for a firm basis for its post-war baths-building programme, and that they would not ask for any other issues to be dealt with at the same time.

The Mining Industry (Welfare Fund) Bill to continue the output levy at the rate of 1d per ton until 1951 had its second reading in the House of Lords on 7th December 1943, and was given Royal Assent on 16th December 1943.[34]

The estimates for the Safety in Mines Research Board for 1943/44 were considered at the Commission's April 1943 meeting. They approved a sum of

£33,800, which represented half of the estimated receipt of the General Fund in 1943. There were other calls upon the other half of the General Fund, so the Commission was prevented from giving the Board a larger grant. The Commission also approved the proposal of the Board to purchase the site of the Buxton Research Station at a cost of £4,000, which was defrayed from the Board's Reserve Fund.[35]

The total receipts of the Miners' Welfare Fund in 1944 dropped to £931,528, with the Output Levy falling to £771,565 due to the reduced output of coal, the Royalties Levy to £89,000 as a result of the drop in coal output, and the rise in income tax and £70,963 from investments. £11,149 was allocated to the Districts Fund, £59,112 to the General Fund and £761,267 to the Baths Fund.[36]

By February 1944, there were 881 canteens in operation of which 441 were serving full meals. The number of canteens in operation was 12 less than that reported in December 1943 as 12 collieries with canteens had closed.

Although the TUC had been persuaded to support the miners' demand for extra rations at home, the Ministry of Food had maintained their refusal to accede to this demand. They had suggested that the miners would take greater advantage of the colliery canteen if the meals were prepared, cooked and served better, and if the canteens drew the full quantities of rationed food to which they were entitled.

Of the four modified baths installations under construction, only the two in Lanarkshire (Rankin and Dullatur) were expected to be completed for use at the end of February. Shireoaks (South Yorkshire) and Ayr 9 and 10 were still awaiting deliveries.

By the end of October 1944, 904 canteens were in operation, of which 510 were serving full meals. Measures to improve services were being actively pursued. Canteen Management Committees were benefitting from the efforts of the Wartime Advisers of Food, a number of whom had been recruited specifically to assist colliery canteens.[37]

The establishment of rehabilitation services for miners continued to occupy a considerable amount of the Commission's time. By February 1944, 67% of the men employed in the industry had been covered by the facilities provided and provision for a further 27% was in hand, leaving 6% in respect of whom provision was under consideration.

Lanarkshire had asked for assistance in establishing an outpatient clinic accessible to the Lanarkshire district as a whole, which had been recommended by the Rehabilitation Committee. The Commission did not usually undertake to provide outpatient clinics but the hospitals for miners' accident cases were in Glasgow, making daily attendance at outpatient clinics impractical. There was, however a clinic, run by the Lanarkshire Orthopaedic Association, at

Motherwell attended by Mr Alexander Miller, Surgeon at Glasgow Infirmary, a member of the Rehabilitation Advisory Committee. It was also served by a Sister who also treated patients at three outlying clinics. The existing clinic had been so successful an experiment that it was pleaded that it merited expansion and development on a larger scale. Subject to the District Welfare Committee's recommendation and costings, the Commission, at their February meeting, were prepared to support the proposal.

In February 1944, the acquisition by the Commission was agreed for Hartford Hall (Northumberland), The Hermitage (Durham) and Oakmere Hall (Lancashire), and the Commission confirmed the costs of adaptions of each of the properties.

Hartford Hall was formally opened by the Chairman, supported by Mr Drummond and Mr Lawther, on 6th June. The Hermitage was opened by the Chairman on 24th June 1944 and Oakmere Hall was opened on 28th October 1944 by the Chairman.

Mr Watson-Jones recommended that the scope of the Rehabilitation Advisory Committee should be extended to embrace branches of medicine which had a bearing on rehabilitation, and strengthen co-ordination with the general health services. He recommended inviting Mr Fairbank, Mr Holdsworth, Dr Donald Hunter, Professor Platt, Professor Ryle and Sir Robert Stanton Woods to join the Committee. Only Professor Ryle was unable to accept this invitation.

As Mr Watson-Jones had found that the medical work of the miners' rehabilitation centres had proved to be greater than he could undertake himself, he called for the appointment of a part-time executive officer and suggested that Mr Nicoll should be invited to accept the appointment. He also asked the Commission to discontinue his own title of Director of Rehabilitation. Both these proposals were approved by the Commission.

By June 1944, Mr E. A. Nicoll had accepted the position of Consulting Surgeon to the Commission's Rehabilitation Medical Committee. He had obtained relief from some of his work at the Mansfield Hospital, so that his duties would not make any substantial difference to his work for Berry Hill Hall where he would continue to be the Surgeon-in-Charge. The need, however, remained at Berry Hill Hall for an Assistant Surgeon when the beds were increased to 60.

Arrangements were to be made for Mr Nicoll to visit all the Commission's Centres. However, the invasion requirements had 'frozen' the movement of certain surgeons, including Mr Nicoll.

By April 1944, the Lanarkshire Orthopaedic Association and the Lanarkshire District Committee had accepted the Commission's conditions for establishing an outpatient rehabilitation centre at Uddingston Miners' Welfare Institute, and the Commission had confirmed the appointment to the Management Committee.

Representatives of the Commission, South Yorkshire District Committee, the Ministry of Health and the surgeons concerned had met on 14th March 1944 to discuss the provision of rehabilitation for miners in the Barnsley area, and had recommended the upgrading of the Becket Hospital to a Fracture 'A' department and to establish a miners' rehabilitation centre in the area. This had been approved by the Rehabilitation Advisory Committee.

Gleneagles Fitness Centre had 200 beds reserved for miners but, by June 1944, it was clear that these had not been fully used. The Department of Health for Scotland had accordingly made a proposal that some of the beds should be made available to civilians other than miners. The Gleneagles' Consultative Committee decided that 60 beds might be used for other types of patients.

A new proposal was put forward to Kent District Committee in June that, instead of obtaining suitable premises for a rehabilitation clinic, a rehabilitation centre should be established in hospital huts at the Kent and Canterbury Hospital, Canterbury, as part of the hospital service. The Ministry of Health were willing to provide huts and all necessary equipment.

The Kent District Committee had declined to accept the scheme for Kent miners to receive rehabilitation treatment in the new department being provided by the Ministry of Health at the Kent and Canterbury Hospital. However, after discussion with the Commission's Secretary, The District Committee agreed to appoint a Sub-Committee to discuss the proposal further on 29th November 1944 with the representatives of the Hospital and the Commission.

As an interim arrangement, a number of the District Officers (known as District Organisers prior to October 1942) had been acting as Secretaries of the Commission's Rehabilitation Centres. A meeting of these Officers was held at Ashley Court on 31st May 1944 to discuss the duties of the District Officers in connection with the rehabilitation centres, and the need to place as much work as possible upon the staff of the Centre in order that the District Officers might continue to devote the necessary attention to their normal work.[38]

In September and October 1944, the Committee revised the draft report of the Future Programme Sub-Committee entitled 'The Miners' Welfare Fund Looks Forward'.

The Sub-Committee, under the Chairmanship of Professor Collis, had held twelve meetings during which they had examined all the objects covered by the Welfare Fund and submitted a series of interim reports which formed the basis of this draft Report.

The standards of coal production and national taxation had resulted in greatly reduced receipts from both the Output and Royalties levies, and the decrease had made itself felt most seriously in the General and Districts Funds. Quite apart from the effect of post-war restriction on building works and supplies of equipment, new constructions on any considerable scale would be impracticable (except pithead baths) because the available funds from the receipts would not be available.

It was therefore incumbent on the Commission to make recommendations for the Future Programme of the Welfare Fund, on which both the Mining Association of Great Britain and the Mineworkers' Federation of Great Britain could comment so that there might be the largest possible general agreement upon the terms of the final report, which would govern all future policy and practice in the administration of the Fund.

Pithead baths were the most urgent of all purposes for the Welfare Fund. The provision of adequate welfare facilities at the pithead would not only influence the miner's opinion of his working environment, but his general social status and outlook and the attitude of boys towards entering the industry. Conversely, the great improvement in the social conditions of the nation would be expected to stimulate demand for a higher standard of welfare provision at the pithead. It was therefore recommended that the provision of pithead baths should be completed within the shortest possible period, and in any case, within a maximum of ten years after the resumption of building was authorised. The Baths Fund would be shared between Districts in proportion to the amount of the output levy received from each. The order of priority for the provision of pithead baths at collieries in each District would be recommended by the District Committees.

Canteens would continue to be provided, at the cost of the Baths Fund, at new installations wherever required; the existing wartime canteens would not be replaced unless quite unsuitable for requirement. When a permanent trend of demand became clear, the wartime canteens should be brought up to peacetime standards or replaced, if necessary, at the cost of the Baths Fund. Canteen Agreements with the colliery companies could not be terminated until four years after the war or if a baths installation with a new canteen was built or the Canteen Committee and the Commission agreed that the old canteen was no longer required.

With the proposal to provide cycle stores out of the Baths Fund, it was recommended that, whenever new baths installations were provided, any canteen, cycle store or any other scheme already provided at the same colliery from the Welfare Fund, should be amalgamated with the baths under a single Trust Fund and Management Committee.

A large part of the Districts Fund had been devoted to Institutes and Recreation grounds. Up to the end of 1943, this totalled £5,918,507 (54% of the Districts Fund) which had been allocated according to recommendations made by the Districts upon applications emanating from the local committees and there had been no concerted plan. Recreation grounds and children's playgrounds were recognised as belonging to the remit of Local Authorities rather than the Welfare Fund.

Many of the institutes were looked upon as men's clubs but, if they were to fulfil their proper function in providing wider membership, full provision would need to be made for the social, recreational and cultural life of all ages and for both sexes, jointly and separately. The advance of education and the raising of the standards of life in other directions had combined to create a demand for a much-varied use of leisure time.

In future, the Welfare Fund would cease to make grants for new recreation grounds or children's playgrounds but allocations from District Funds would continue for improvements or extensions to existing schemes.

Local Education Authorities and the Ministry of Education had statutory duties under the Education Act, 1944, to encourage cultural activities so close co-operation with the Local Education Authorities was recommended to widen the scope of the activities in the Institutes and to enable the local committees to take specific measures to provide both indoor and outdoor activities for women's groups, who had not been universally catered for adequately.

Few institutes catered specially for young people of the age of 18–25, apart from occasional dances. Little attempt had been made to provide accommodation or organise activities for young people of both sexes, or even provide them with a café. This point had been stressed in the Report (1943) on the 18-plus Age Group Enquiry prepared for the Trustees of the Carnegie United Kingdom Trust. It was therefore recommended that, in consultation with Local Education Authorities, facilities, including a café, should be provided for this age group.

District Committees in 11 Districts had fostered the development of boys' clubs for the 14-18 age group or had taken preparatory steps to do so; in one District, a parallel movement of organising clubs had progressed satisfactorily. In South Wales, the movement had been in progress for many years under the South Wales Federation of Boys' Clubs but, in most cases, these clubs (160 in number) had no direct connection with the Miners' Welfare schemes.

In other Districts, developments had been effected through the District Miners' Welfare Youth Councils. Representation of the Local Authorities and the Voluntary Youth Associations had been included in the membership of the Miners' Welfare Youth Councils and, in this way, co-ordination with their activities and equitable financial responsibility had been possible.

The Report (July, 1942) of the Forster Committee on the Recruitment of Juveniles in the Coal Industry said 'we command for consideration the further development of boys' clubs with attendant cultural pursuits in coal mining districts', thus emphasising the complementary function of the boys' clubs to the colliery training centres.

District Committees were to be encouraged to promote or extend the formation of boys', girls' and youth clubs in co-operation with the County Youth Committees of the Local Authorities and the County Association of Boys' Clubs and Girls' Clubs.

It was recommended that every District Committee should formulate a tentative plan for linking and federating all recreation schemes, in both small mining villages and the more densely populated coal districts in order to stimulate additional activities based on the available information and local knowledge of the District Committee. The plan would be prepared with the help of the District Miners' Welfare Officer and implemented with the approval of the Commission on an 'appointed day'.

Subsequently, a long-term plan would be produced, in consultation with the Local Education Authority, with a view to regulating and controlling future development of recreation. A detailed survey would be made by the District Officer of all existing schemes for recreation and leisure time occupation and of industrial and housing developments, and the report would be submitted to the Area Committees for their recommendations. No grants would be made from the District Funds for any purposes for two years from the 'appointed day', so as to allow the completion of the survey and long-term plan, excepting grants required to maintain existing facilities or to assist the provision of leadership to expand activities and broaden membership of the local recreation schemes.

Good housing was a pre-requisite for achieving the objective of the Welfare Fund to ensure satisfactory 'social well-being and condition of living' for mineworkers, although the law did not allow the use of the Welfare Fund for housing. The Report (July 1942) of the Forster Committee had drawn attention to the need for improved housing conditions in certain mining districts, which was of prior importance to the provision of leisure-time social amenities. This underlined the Commission's recommendation to include an assessment of housing needs in the proposed surveys to be carried out by District Committees so that they could ensure that Local Authorities' housing proposals would meet these needs.

The existing administrative and executive machinery of the Districts had been evolved in haste and inexperience at a time when the Welfare Fund was only a five-year experiment, and before the current structure of the local Miners' Welfare Schemes, with their management committees, chairmen and secretaries, had come into existence. It was, therefore, an opportune time to review this machinery in the light of the 24 years' experience which was available for guidance.

On 20th October 1921, the Secretary for the Mines, with the agreement of the Miners' Welfare Committee, had invited coal owners and colliery workers to set up special ad hoc committees in each district to whom the Central Committee could refer all local applications for grants from the Fund for consideration and report (see Chapter 2, p29). The District Committees appointed in response to this invitation had continued to exist, although, originally only intended as a temporary expedient pending the formation of District Committees constituted according to Regulations made under the Mining Industry Act, 1920.

Consequently, there had been no definition of the duties of the District Committees. Duties had gradually been tacitly assumed by District Committees or delegated voluntarily by the Commission without ever being listed in writing, and this had caused confusion in thought and action which needed to be removed.

The members of the District Committees were usually appointed by the District Associations of Mine Owners and Mine Workers but, as there was no constitution, there were no uniform recognised standards such as numbers of representatives, both sides being equal, number, mode of election and length of appointment for representatives.

It was proposed that District Committees should receive formal appointments by the Miners' Welfare Commission and should be composed of two representatives (one representing the mine owners and one the mine workers) nominated by each Area Committee (or Local Committee) in the District, two or three representatives nominated both by the District Mine Owners' Association and the District Mineworkers' Association, two co-opted women members who were actively associated with the local Miners' Welfare Schemes and a co-opted member who was actively associated with organised activities of youth (under 25) in the District. Members would be appointed for three years. The duties of the District Committees would be defined in writing.

It was suggested that the Area Committees should be set up to give assistance and co-ordinate the activities of groups of Welfare schemes, and to assist the District Committees in preparing and carrying out the District Welfare plans.

Twenty District Committees had Joint Secretaries (the Secretary of the District Coal Owners' Association and an official of the District Mineworkers' Association) and five had only one Secretary who was the Secretary of the Coal Owners' Association. In all but two Districts, the Committees' secretarial and office work was done in the offices of the Coal Owners' Association, for a charge. It was therefore recommended that each District Committee (or groups of District Committees in the case of small districts), while continuing, so far as possible, to employ the same staff, should have a District office which should not be situated in the premises of either the District Coal Owners' Association or the District Mineworkers' Association, and that all the welfare business should be conducted in the same premises.

With the White Paper on the National Health Service issued in February 1944, it was already suspected that the Miners' Welfare Fund would have a smaller field of activity in health.

Seventeen convalescent homes had been established, although three had been recently converted into rehabilitation centres. In 1944, two were temporarily under requisition for war purposes, leaving twelve in operation. In common with most convalescent homes of pre-war days, little, if any medical or nursing attention was given to the patients. Under the National Health Service, it would be the duty of Local Health Authorities to secure the provision of convalescent treatment and they would want existing convalescent homes to give positive treatment.

It was suggested that Management Committees of Miners' Welfare Convalescent Homes should consider whether greater value might be obtained from the homes by transforming them into places for specific recuperative treatment under medical supervision, and whether reciprocal arrangements amongst themselves for admitting patients from other Districts might better suit individual patients.

As the National Health Service was expected to provide for the establishment of adequate and co-ordinated ambulance services for the whole population and adequate nursing services would become a statutory responsibility of Local Health Authorities, no more grants were to be made from the Miners' Welfare Fund for either ambulances or nursing services.

Grants for special medical treatment had been made in seventeen Districts to 53 schemes. The greater part of the grants had been to eight health treatment schemes in six Districts, which mainly covered convalescent and hospital treatment. The remainder of the grants had been for the provision of artificial limbs, medical and surgical appliances, splinterless glasses, invalid chairs and (in South Wales) workshops for blind persons.

Statutory provision had been made for artificial limbs and other surgical appliances through National Health Insurance or by Public Assistance, but these resources had not sufficed. It therefore remained to be seen if the National Health Service would provide all that was necessary, or if there would still be a need for the Welfare Fund to continue its assistance.

Under the heading of special medical treatment for miners, the problems of providing treatment for pneumoconiosis, nystagmus and rheumatism were still being explored.

Methods of treating pneumoconiosis (fibrosis of the lungs due to dust including the condition known as dust reticulation) had been studied by the Ministry of Fuel and Power. The report (published August 1944) recommended the early establishment of a Treatment and Rehabilitation Centre equipped with facilities for clinical study and research, attached to a special unit in an existing hospital.

During the war there had been an increase in the incidence of miners' nystagmus, which could not be correlated with any marked change in the standard of lighting which had previously been seen as the fundamental cause of the disease. Research on this condition had previously been carried out by the Medical Research Council, but the Nuffield Laboratory of Ophthalmology at Oxford were considering undertaking research into this condition. Research work of this kind was no longer considered to be a function of the Welfare Fund.

The Ministry of Health had been planning a national rheumatism scheme prior to the establishment of the National Health Service. However, it remained to be seen if this scheme would adequately meet the requirements of the mineworkers, so grants might need to be made from the Welfare Fund to provide District teatment centres for inpatients, with peripheral clinics for outpatients.

Since the end of 1942, six rehabilitation centres (with one more in preparation), together with special arrangements for rehabilitation treatment for miners at eight hospitals, and supplemented by the facilities provided by the Emergency Medical Service, had been provided out of the Pithead Baths Fund under the authority of Defence Regulation 60B. This provision had met the more urgent requirements of the mining industry at the time, but it was expected that the centres would, in due course, take their place in the National Health Service and receive maintenance grants from public funds.

The Education Act 1944, which had received Royal Assent on 3rd August 1944, 'involved the reconstruction of the public system of education'. Under this Act, the previous power of a Local Education Authority to supply higher education or aid the supply of such education was converted into a duty to provide adequate facilities for further education which included vocational, technical, commercial and art education, and also cultural training and recreational activities. The Authority would be required to submit a scheme which, when approved by the Ministry of Education, would be put into effect in stages as the Minister determined.

There were, therefore, no further grants, excepting those already promised, to be made for building and equipment for mining schools, which had become the duty of the Local Education Authorities.

The Report of the Forster Committee on Recruitment of Juveniles in the Coal Mining Industry (July 1944) recommended that juvenile entrants should undergo eight weeks' general instruction at suitable centres, at collieries or at mining schools, together with practical demonstrations in a non-productive underground training gallery, followed by another eight weeks' practical work in the actual production unit reserved for training purposes. This recommendation, in common with most of those in the report, involved long-term schemes, mainly for post-war application.

Since the Report was issued, discussions had been ongoing between all the mining and educational bodies concerned, but no decisions had been made by the government so it was recommended that the Miners' Welfare Fund made no further grants for colliery training schemes for boys.

The Miners' Welfare National Scholarship Scheme, the National Students' Exhibition Scheme and the Miners' Welfare National Part-time Day Advanced Mining Scholarship Scheme would remain in their present forms. However, when the Royal Commission on Safety in Coal Mines was implemented, a review of the Miners' Part-time Day Advanced Mining Scholarship Scheme would be needed regarding the reconstitution of the Board of Mining Examinations and the statutory certification of mine managers, under-managers and mine surveyors.

It was expected that safety instruction for mining boys would be incorporated on a compulsory footing in the curriculum of the training schemes for juvenile entrants, so the need for providing badges and certificates from the Welfare Fund would disappear.

There had been a growing recognition of the duties of the State towards research, with the result that the government had recently undertaken to relieve the Welfare Fund of any future obligation under this heading, on the understanding that the statutory requirement of a grant of £20,000 from the Fund would be continued until a suitable opportunity occurred for legislation for its repeal. The income of the endowment fund would be included in the Parliamentary Vote of the Ministry of Fuel and Power. 39

1945 was a year of great uncertainty for the Welfare Commission. At the end of 1944, the Commission had produced its report 'Miners' Welfare looks forward' setting out its proposals for the future, but this report had to be considered by the coal industry and the District Miners' Welfare Committees. The end of the war would not only bring to a conclusion the special arrangements for the funding of the wartime canteens and rehabilitation centres out of the Baths Fund under Defence Regulation (No. 60BA), but also a change in government, in July 1945.

The receipts of the Miners' Welfare Fund saw a further fall in 1945. The Fund received a total of £930,854, of which £758,633 came from the Output Levy, £102,000 from the Royalties Levy and £70,221 from Investments. £116,354 was allocated to the Districts Fund, £54,266 to the General Fund and £760,234 to the Pithead Baths Fund.[40]

In July 1944, the Minister of Fuel and Power , in consultation with the Chairman of the Commission, had decided to ask the government to agree to some relaxation of the bar on building pithead baths and to suggest that building should be resumed to the extent of about 12 installations during

1945. The government agreed, but there was some delay in giving permission to proceed due to the demand made on the building trade by the V-bomb damage.

In February 1945, the Commission received a qualified agreement from the Ministries of Works and Labour for the requisite supplies of labour and materials to resume the building of pithead baths. The Ministry of Fuel and Power's allocation would cover the requirements of labour and materials for the first six months of 1945. Allocations for the second half of the year had not been made, but the Chief Architect felt that a programme could proceed without suspension, at a somewhat restricted rate.

It was decided to proceed with the work to complete thirteen baths and one extension, where construction had been commenced before the building programme was stopped. Denaby Main would have to be excluded until it was released by the Ministry of Supply. Ravensworth (Betty and Ann) no longer required extending, and Ouston 'E' had closed.

Subject to priority being confirmed by the District Committees and the expectation of the life of the collieries being verified, preparatory work would be resumed for twenty baths and three extensions, which had reached an advanced stage when building was suspended so that building could restart during 1946 and 1947. It seemed unlikely that during 1946 and 1947, the Commission would be allowed to build a greater number, but the Commission's staff would be occupied with the large amount of preliminary work required to commence the post-war programme, aiming to provide the pithead baths for all unequipped collieries during the succeeding seven years.

In connection with the full programme for building baths, it was proposed to form a Planning Section of the Architects' Department. Staff who had been dispersed in the coalfields for wartime canteens would be brought back, and additional accommodation would be required. Enquiries had so far failed to find offices in London adequate for the whole of the Commission staff.

In March 1945, the building programme for 1945 and 1946 was approved subject to New Moor (Northumberland) being included at the same time as Ashington (planned for 1946) because of the interchange of miners between the two collieries under the cavilling system.

Fife District Committee had written to the Commission recommending that temporary or prefabricated buildings could be provided at the smaller collieries, and that priority should be given to small collieries of comparatively short life. The Commission were sympathetic to the District Committee's desire to make special arrangements to meet the case of small collieries, and decided that the whole problem should be studied by the Architects' Branch, and approved a proposal for a supplementary survey of collieries employing less than 50 men (omitted from the now completed main survey) for the purpose of studying the problem and submitting proposals.

As District Committees were recommending the order of priority for baths building in their districts, Fife District Committee would be able to give priority to short-life collieries, large or small, if they so desired.

With the end of the war in Europe in May 1945, the Commission were becoming very concerned about the position when Regulation 60BA lapsed, and with it the power to use the Baths Fund monies for canteens not combined with baths. In February 1945, the Commission had received a reply to their letter to the Minister of Fuel and Power enquiring whether work on the provision of wartime colliery canteens could be reduced. The Minister had replied that interruption of the canteen building programme should be avoided, on the understanding that the position would be reviewed if the baths programme seemed likely to be prejudiced. He had, however, gone on to suggest that the post-war baths programme which the Commission contemplated was 'ambitious' and 'highly speculative'.

The Chairman had written back to the Minister on 19th February 1945, expressing the Commission's anxiety over the Minister's suggestion about the post-war baths programme. The Minister replied on 30th March that funds had already and definitely been assured for pithead baths, and would be ample to meet the expenditure for several years to come, and that firm assurances had more than once been given to the effect that the provision of pithead baths must be made complete, but that it must be made clear that there was no possibility of the monies expended by the Commission on canteens being refunded.

A letter inviting District Committees to revise and complete their priority lists of collieries requiring baths was sent out in July 1945.

The Chief Architect submitted the results of the preliminary survey of all collieries not equipped with baths. 509 collieries, costing £8,628,000 were required. This number excluded collieries of less than ten years life, and collieries employing 80 or less. A yet unknown number of extensions would be required, plus replacement of about twelve old installations. The 509 collieries had been classified as to their length of life and as to availability of site and services. 62 (12%) of the collieries had a life of less than fifteen years. During the early years of the building programme, consideration might be given to those Districts with a high number of collieries with a life of less than fifteen years to having a larger share of installations, than they would if the sharing in proportion to the output levy receipts were strictly adhered to as in the past. This would, however, ensure that collieries that had less than fifteen years would have their installations before the cut-off of a life of less than ten years.

The Chief Architect had reviewed the methods and procedures for building pithead baths to ensure that maximum speed and efficiency could be achieved throughout the preparatory and contract stages once the main pithead baths building programme commenced. It was hoped that the changes relating to the construction and equipment approved by the Commission at its May 1945 meeting could be tested at some of the installations to be completed under the 'limited' programme.

In September 1945, the Chief Architect presented his memorandum on pithead baths at small collieries (more than 50 men) and at collieries of comparatively short life (fifteen years or less) following the request of the Committee in March 1945 to look into this problem.

The Commission agreed that baths of a secondary standard would only be provided at collieries where it was quite definite that the life could not be more than fifteen years. The chief departures from the standard being the provision of only one locker per man, and the use of semi-permanent construction (Lighter or cheaper types of foundations, walls, roofs, fittings and finishes).

At collieries with a life of more than fifteen years and employing 51–250 men, the provision of two lockers per man would be continued, but economies in capital cost would be secured by adopting the maximum degree of standardisation of planning and construction, and in the use of materials and labour most readily available locally from time to time.

The Chief Architect would submit a further memorandum on the problem of making special arrangements to meet the case of collieries employing 50 men or fewer.

The Ministry of Fuel and Power had agreed, by October 1945, to allocate sufficient labour to enable the Commission to proceed with the erection of thirty installations in 1946, instead of the fourteen hitherto approved. The Ministry had also agreed that the Commission could prepare labour estimates for completing the baths building programme in seven years from 1st January 1946, instead of ten years from the general resumption of building.

The Secretary submitted a memorandum to the October 1945 meeting of the Commission setting out the number of installation tenders and estimated cost per contract for the seven years of the building programme 1946/52. The Commission approved the proposal, but it also had to be submitted to the Minister; both because the cost would exceed the estimated receipts of the Baths Fund, and because the Minister had expressed the view that the responsibility for providing pithead baths should (as and when possible) be taken over by the National Coal Board.

Although the letters regarding the District Priority lists for pithead baths, approved by the July 1945 meeting of the Commission, had been sent out by the middle of September, only four districts had returned their priority lists by November 1945.

Although the Chief Architect had identified seventeen further collieries to complete the suggested programme of thirty installations for 1946, the Chief Architect was of the opinion that there was no possibility of placing contracts for the new baths without suitable office accommodation and additional staff. 41

By the end of 1945, 912 canteens had been set up by grants from the Welfare Fund including five central food depots. A further thirteen canteens were under construction. The number of canteens serving full meals had risen to 71%. On the other hand, 39 canteens and depots serving 60 collieries had closed owing to lack of support.[42]

At the May 1945 meeting, the Commission had decided to ask the Minister of Fuel and Power (Major Lloyd George) to meet them for a general discussion on rehabilitation, canteens, the baths building programme and research arising out of the end of the European war. The meeting was not held because, the Minister deferred it until after the General Election.

The Chairman wrote in September to Mr Shinwell (now Minister for Fuel and Power in the new Labour government) renewing the request, as it appeared desirable to make early contact with the new Minister so as to ascertain how the Commission's work might be affected by the new government's policy.

At their September meeting, the Commission considered the agenda, submitted by the Secretary, which listed the issues on which the Commission needed clarification. The Commission thought it might be a little premature to ask the Minister to deal with the effect of nationalisation of the coal industry upon the Miners' Welfare Fund, but the Commission needed to ask him for guidance as to how far ahead the Commission might plan its programme for the provision of pithead baths and canteens and to secure necessary office accommodation in London.

However, they did need to know how quickly they would be enabled to carry out the pithead baths building programme, whether the obligation of the colliery companies under the Canteen Order 1941 to provide canteens at mines under Defence Regulation 60BA would continue until nationalisation, whether the financial provision for rehabilitation was to continue to come from the Baths Fund, and if the future provision for research would be forthcoming from another source other than the Miners' Welfare Fund.

The Chairman met the Minister of Fuel and Power on 2nd October 1945. The future of the Commission and its work were now dependent upon the development of the Government's coal policy, and the Minister's proposals included the National Coal Board taking the place of the present coal owners. The Commission should carry on subject to increased powers of supervision of the Minister. The Commission would act as agent for the National Coal Board pending final redistribution of responsibilities for welfare work for a period of time which the Minister was unable to specify. During this period, it might be necessary to have a different method of providing funds for the Commission.

In the Minister's view, welfare work for miners wanted completely recasting. Pithead baths were the function of a good employer, and many welfare schemes should be the obligation of the Local Authority, leaving to welfare work proper, convalescent homes, rehabilitation and rest centres, etc.

The Minister then reminded Sir Frederick Sykes that, in November 1946, he would have to appoint or reappoint the three independent members of the Commission. He felt that this was an opportunity for appointing a woman member, and he asked Sir Frederick how he thought that room might be made for one. Sir Frederick said that he himself was quite ready to retire when the Commission was reorganised.

The Minister then raised the question of the Commission's idea of taking premises in Mayfair, which he was strongly opposed and would not approve. The Chairman pointed out that the Ministry of Works and the Ministry of Fuel and Power had failed to find accommodation in the past two years, and it was essential for the baths programme that suitable central accommodation was found.

The question of the £20,000 contribution to research ought to go on for the time being, pending settlement of the reorganisation of the coal industry.

The Commission considered the report of the meeting with the Minister of Fuel and Power at their October meeting. While the Commission were happy to continue with their present duties, they required guidance from the Minister upon a few matters which were giving rise to uncertainty and required discussion. It was agreed that the Secretary would prepare a memorandum for submission in writing to the Minister, after approval of the members of the Commission. Meanwhile, the Chairman undertook to ask the Minister for a meeting in the afternoon of 19th or 20th November.

The memorandum was again considered at the end of the November 1945 meeting, after the Commission staff had withdrawn. The revised memorandum was discussed by the Commission in anticipation of the meeting with the Minister in the afternoon. Alterations were made and it was decided that a revised copy should be substituted for that already sent to the Minister.[43]

Six residential rehabilitation centres (Berry Hill Hall, North Midlands; Talygarn, South Wales: Higham Grange, South Midlands; Hartford Hall, Northumberland; The Hermitage, Durham and Oakmere Hall, Lancashire); were in operation at the beginning of 1945 and Mr Nicoll, in his capacity of Consulting Surgeon, had visited Higham Grange, Hartford Hall and the Hermitage at the end of 1944.

Most of the centres were experiencing problems. Berry Hill Hall was only able to achieve 61.3% utilisation rate, owing to shortage of treatment staff, but an additional physiotherapist was commencing duties on 1st January 1945. Higham Grange was having difficulty in obtaining co-operation from the local hospitals with specialist staff. The Sunderland Royal Infirmary, which served 35% of the coalfield, was not sending patients to the Hermitage but the Royal Victoria Infirmary were transferring patients prematurely. The utilisation of Oakmere Hall was being intentionally kept low pending the appointment of the Surgeon-in-Charge.

In Lanarkshire, the Uddingston Miners' Institute was still occupied by the Ministry of Labour, but adaptation of the Institute was in progress and it was hoped to commence some rehabilitation in the portion of the building not occupied by the Ministry, who were not expected to vacate the premises before the end of May 1945.

At Berry Hill Hall, Discharge Conferences had been introduced by March 1945 as an experiment. These were attended by industrial medical officers from the colliery companies, District Officers from the Miners' Welfare Commission, a representative of either the Nottinghamshire or Derbyshire Miners' Union, the Regional Medical Officer of the Ministry of Fuel and Power, a representative of the Ministry of Labour specially concerned with retraining, and the patient's captain.

Each case due for discharge within the next two weeks was seen and the surgeon outlined the history and progress, assessed the end-result and put forward a plan of reinstatement (or retraining) which was then discussed with the patient. This served as a basis for discussion, and might be altered or modified, but in the end, some definite plan was agreed on all round the table and left for the District Officers to implement. Careful contact was kept with each case after discharge and, if the plan was not working out as anticipated, the patient was brought back, and the conference confronted with its own failure. These conferences were strongly supported by the men.

A delegation from Cumberland attended at the Ministry of Fuel and Power on 26th April 1945 to draw attention to the delay in providing at Whitehaven Hospital facilities for rehabilitation as effective as those at the Commission's centres for miners in the major coalfields. Members of the Commission's staff attended and explained that the provision of facilities at hospitals were primarily the concern of the Ministry of Health. The delay had been due to the failure of the hospital to develop and pursue a scheme which did not involve more building work than could be sanctioned by the Ministry. Afterwards, the Commission's staff saw the Ministry of Health and arrangements were made for the Executive Committee of the Miners' Rehabilitation Medical Committee to visit Whitehaven on 28th May together with Dr Balme, Director of Rehabilitation of the Ministry of Health, in order to examine the problem afresh and agree with the hospital, if possible, upon an immediate solution.

At the meeting on 28th May, it was agreed that the Ministry of Health's offer to provide two army huts, free of charge, for erection at the Whitehaven and West Cumberland Hospital, should be used to provide a gymnasium, treatment block and dormitory for nine beds.

In November 1945, the Commission received a deputation from the Cumberland District Miners' Welfare Committee regarding rehabilitation for Cumberland miners. One of the army huts was still being used by a nursery, and was unlikely to be available for several months. Apparently, this difficulty had only just come to light.

The deputation expressed the view that the Cumberland miners had not yet received adequate rehabilitation facilities of the type which they were entitled to expect.

At their April meeting, the Executive Committee of the Miners' Rehabilitation Medical Committee agreed that Yorkshire was too large an area to be served by one centre. Firbeck Hall, if possible, should be acquired to provide a centre for the Doncaster area. The Woofindin Home should be supported as a centre for the Sheffield area and a new centre should be provided for the Barnsley area, preferably somewhere between Wakefield and Barnsley. However, on hearing that the Ministry of Health representatives on the Standing Rehabilitation and Resettlement Committee had reported that there was no prospect of Pinderfields being closed as a rehabilitation centre for some time after the war,

16th century Firbeck Hall in 1935

the Committee agreed that miners from the Leeds area could appropriately continue to go to Pinderfields (Wakefield).

On 14th August 1945, a meeting was held in Sheffield, attended by representatives of the District Welfare Committees for South Yorkshire and West Yorkshire, the Royal Sheffield Infirmary and Hospital, the Ministry of Health and the Miners' Welfare Commission to discuss rehabilitation in Yorkshire in general and in particular the proposal to acquire Firbeck Hall.

It was agreed that the purchase of Firbeck Hall should be completed and arrangements made to equip it as a rehabilitation centre. Consideration of developing further facilities in South Yorkshire should be deferred until experience had been gained of Firbeck Hall in operation. Pinderfields would continue to serve the West Yorkshire coalfield until the need for a permanent centre became more urgent.

In May 1945, the Commission approved a grant of £800 from the Baths Fund to the Kent and Canterbury Hospital towards the capital cost of £1,800 for the rehabilitation department attached to the hospital, with the agreement of the Kent District Miners' Welfare Committee.

Subsequent investigation of the new rehabilitation department at the Canterbury Hospital revealed that only 10 miners had received active rehabilitation treatment during the period July to September 1945. A meeting of the District Welfare Committee's Rehabilitation Sub-Committee was therefore called for 25th October at Canterbury to discuss this matter. It was concluded that publicity featuring the facilities was needed among the surgeons and doctors in the area.

In June 1945, the Miners' Rehabilitation Medical Committee discussed the conflict between the continuity of treatment by an individual surgeon and segregation of miners during the rehabilitation stage at the centre. This problem was particularly acute in the West Midlands where there were 16 hospitals catering for 51,000 miners, and in South Wales where there was a great variety in the quality of treatment provided, although some of the smaller hospitals transferred certain cases to larger hospitals. *The Lancet*, dated 12th May 1945, had stressed the advisability of surgeons who governed primary treatment continuing as one of the team in controlling rehabilitation.

It was suggested that a surgeon could be appointed as either an 'Associate Surgeon' or a 'Visiting Surgeon' depending on the proportion of patients who had received primary treatment under his control. If a substantial proportion of the patients were under his control at the primary stage, he should be on the salaried staff as a 'Visiting Surgeon'. If the proportion was small, he should hold the honorary position of 'Associate Surgeon'.

At the end of June 1945, the Commission received a letter from the Ministry of Health in reply to the Commission's letter dated 23rd May 1945, enquiring as to the position of the Miners' Rehabilitation Centres under the future National Health Service. It was anticipated that rehabilitation centres would form part of the proposed comprehensive health services, but it was desirable that patients other than miners would be admitted. As to the maintenance of the centres and the date of any prospective change, this was not entirely clear, but the rehabilitation centres might play their part as independent institutions receiving payments in accordance with the principles laid down in the White Paper on a National Health service on page 23, which referred to voluntary hospitals, and seemed to envisage the end of the voluntary movement.

The question of re-employment of rehabilitated miners in the mining industry was placed on the agenda of a conference of the Regional Labour Directors of the Ministry of Fuel and Power, held on 12th April 1945. Unfortunately, the discussion was not brought to a conclusion.

Subsequently, on 15th May, the Executive Committee of the Miners' Rehabilitation Medical Committee, accompanied by Professor Collis, Mr Steadman, Mr R. Whitfield Parker and Mr Freston met certain officers of the Ministry of Fuel and Power to discuss this question.

The Rehabilitation Committee set up by the Commission to manage its rehabilitation centres had acted on the assumption that it was most important, in the interest of the manpower situation that existed in the mining industry in 1942, to resettle as many ex-patients of the centres as possible. Three categories, relating to possible re-employment in the mining industry, had been identified: pre-accident work (A), temporary light work at the colliery (B) and permanent light work at the colliery (C). Each miner was placed in the relevant group by the Surgeons-in-Charge of centres at discharge.

In practice, little difficulty had been experienced in placing men in Category A and, until recently, not much trouble in respect of men in Category B, but men in Category C had never been easy to place and it was becoming increasingly difficult to do so.

In discussion with Mr Hicken, Regional Labour Director at Nottingham, it came to light that in his Region the manpower situation in the coal mining industry had radically altered since the summer of 1942 and there was no longer a shortage of unskilled labour for haulage or surface work.

This situation was confirmed at the meeting on 15th May, when it was suggested that the manpower position in the mining industry was such that the Commission should consider the problem of re-employment and resettlement of rehabilitated miners solely from the view of what was the best interests of the rehabilitated miner.

Following the meeting, the Commission wrote to the Ministry on 25th May asking for confirmation of the Ministry's view, so that the Commission could take a slightly different approach during the rehabilitation treatment.

The Ministry confirmed this view in their reply and admitted that in certain coalfields in which rationalisation was in progress, there was a growing problem of redundancy which could not be met by the transfer of men to underground work because of age or physical condition and, as a result of the Reid Committee, this trend would continue.

The Miners' Rehabilitation Medical Committee held a meeting to consider re-employment and resettlement. It was agreed that closer attention needed to be paid to the whole question of getting men resettled in the community and the causes of delay in men getting back to work needed investigation. To facilitate this, all centres required either a whole-time social worker or a person whose primary duties was to follow up all discharged men.

In October 1945, the Miners' Rehabilitation Medical Committee looked at the issue again having received comments from the Miners' Welfare Commission, and a report from the Lanarkshire Social Worker. There was general agreement that it was impossible to exaggerate the importance of the work of a social worker at the stage of rehabilitation. The function of a medico-social worker and a link between surgeon, patients and industry was incalculable.

The medico-social worker could provide the surgeon with information on the home conditions and social background of the patient, obtain information of possibilities of employment either in the coal industry or in other industries, and information on existing training schemes. The medico-social worker would provide a contact with the surgeon, would be able to provide a guide to social legislation, act as an intermediary between the worker and industry, the Ministry of Labour and State, and voluntary agencies which could help in time of difficulty.

The Medical Committee also appointed a Committee (Mr Freston, Mr E. A. Nicoll and Mr Whitfield Parker) to enquire into the problem as it affected individual centres and to report back to the Committee.

By October 1945, the utilisation rate of the Hermitage (Durham) had reached a level that the Surgeon-in-Charge had warned that an extension of accommodation would be necessary. At the October meeting of the Medical Committee, a second centre for Durham had been recommended, preferably purpose-built to serve Sunderland Royal Infirmary, West Hartlepool Hospital and Monkwearmouth and Southwick Hospital.

In October 1945, the Consulting Surgeon visited Fife. Gleneagles was to be relinquished in the near future, but plans were in preparation for a new residential centre to serve the whole of Scotland. To inform the Medical Committee, a letter was addressed to the Scottish Department of Health asking for information as to their plans and their views on the problem of rehabilitation as it affected injured miners.[44]

At their May 1945 meeting, the Commission approved the statutory grant from the General Fund of £20,000 for the Safety in Mines Research Board for 1945/46. The estimated expenditure of the Board for 1945/46 was £77,764 and the balance would be made up from the Endowment Fund (£10,650) and H. M. Exchequer (£46,764).

The Commission also received a statement on the progress of researches carried out during 1944 by the Safety in Mines Research Board. A great deal of war work, of a kind for which the Board's staff and stations were considered pre-eminently suitable, had continued to be done for the fighting services through the Ministry of Supply on a basis of full repayment of costs.

The search for the best type of stone dust for preventing explosions had continued. Laboratory tests had been made on the strength of home-grown woods to determine their suitability as mine supports. Work had continued on the Falls of Ground researches, particularly on roof control and the influences of strata control on gas emissions. The investigation of man-riding haulage practice in the Lancashire coalfield had been completed and a report prepared. Although the work on spontaneous combustion of coal had been suspended in 1939, two features of mine fires in 1944 had called for the resumption of this work.[45]

Ninety-five candidates sat the examination for the Miners' Welfare National Part-time Advanced Mining Scholarship scheme in 1945. Of the twenty six approved institutions at which the scholarships were tenable, eighteen took part in the examination. The Assessors recommended 46 scholarships for awards including four placed on a special reserve list. This was eleven more than the previous year.[46]

By the end of December, the Commission still had not received a reply to the questions put by them to the Minister of Fuel and Power at the meeting held on 13th November. A year of uncertainty had ended as it had begun.

SIX

SAFETY IN MINES RESEARCH BOARD

In 1920 the responsibility for the Eskmeals testing station in Cumberland passed to the Mines Department. It had originally been built by the Home Office in 1911–12 to carry out experiments under the direction of the Explosions in Mines Committee.

In July 1921, the Secretary for Mines appointed a Board to conduct and co-ordinate research into the causes of mining dangers and the means of preventing them. Initially this was called the Mining Dangers Research Board. In May 1922, its name was changed to the Safety in Mines Research Board.

In January 1922, Mr Gowers, Under-Secretary for Mines, and Mr Foley, Chairman of the Mining Dangers Research Board, attended the Miners' Welfare Fund Central Committee meeting to discuss the memorandum by the mines department on the Experimental Station at Eskmeals. The Mines Department were satisfied that the Experimental Station needed to be moved, but it was impossible to get this done at the expense of the State. There was a definite provision in the Mining Act of 1920 for part of the Fund to be devoted to research, so it was suggested that the Fund might agree in principle to find the money for the capital cost together with a certain amount towards the upkeep. As to whether the Committee had a say in the decision on the new site, they could either leave it to the Mining Dangers Research Board altogether or they could simply agree in principle to the scheme and ask to have the proposed new site submitted to them first for their approval.

The Committee agreed in principle to the transfer of the station, and to guarantee the capital cost of the transference. The final recommendation of the site was to be submitted to the Committee for approval. Mr Foley also agreed to let the Committee have a general overview of research work prepared for their information.[1]

The Safety in Mines Research Board was an expert body which included a member drawn from the coal mine owners and the Chief Inspector of Mines. They were able to invite members of other Advisory Committees to attend meetings to inform their decisions. In the case of the Board's discussion on the transfer of Eskmeals, the Secretary for Mines, in July 1922, proposed that that they should ask the Advisory Committee of the Coal Mining Industry to nominate four members to consult with the Board, namely one representative of the owners; one of the miners; a mining engineer and a colliery manager. These representatives were invited to the Board's special meeting in November 1922. Three members of the Coal Advisory Committee (Colonel Blackett, Sir George Seilby and Mr Frank Hodges) were unable to attend but Dr J. S. Haldane, Mr W. Hargraves and Captain F. Muschamp attended. After a full discussion, it was decided to continue at Eskmeals and with the small-scale work on the same lines until there was greater knowledge of the research work to be done. In the interim, the Board should ask the Welfare Committee to release the allocation of £500,000 (see below).

From the inception of the Board, sub-committees were set up to oversee specific areas of research. The Mining Illumination and Safety Lamp Committee, the Explosive Research Committee and the Inventions Committee were the first to be set up by the Board.[2]

Allocations from the General Fund of the Miners' Welfare Fund for research purposes were normally administered, through the Secretary for Mines, by the Board. These allocations could be divided into two groups; allocations for the purpose of defraying the cost of the work carried out by the Board by their own staff and under direct supervision of a special ad hoc committee, and allocations for the payment of grants to independent investigators or research bodies. Conditions applicable to each grant and designed to safeguard the Fund had been drawn up by the Board in 1922 and approved by the Central Committee of the Fund.[3]

As a general principle, the research work could only be financed from the Fund as long as it dealt with questions relating to the safety and health of workers in coal mines. Assistance could not be given towards enquiries of a purely economic nature.

The Committee's allocations to the Board were limited in 1921 and 1922 due to the magnitude and complexity of the preliminary investigations which the Committee had found necessary before making any allocations. The Committee made a few allocations during this period. In June 1921, the Board recommended a scheme for a new research station and a provisional allocation of £500,000 from the General Fund was made for this purpose. The proposal was subsequently withdrawn, but the Committee continued to earmark the £500,000 for research during the statutory five-year period of the Fund.[4]

Two large allocations were made in 1922. The first was made to the Explosives in Mines Research Committee, which had been appointed jointly by the Safety in Mines Research Board and the Chemistry Co-ordinating Research Board of the Department of Scientific and Industrial Research. The 'gallery' test to which explosives were submitted in this country before they were placed on the official list of 'Permitted Explosives' had resulted in the introduction of explosives of a special type, which under most conditions afforded a very considerable degree of safety if properly used. There was, however, no precise knowledge of the characteristics of an explosive which caused its explosion to ignite inflammable mixtures of firedamp and air and of coal dust and air, or the characteristics of these mixtures which caused them to be ignited in this way. £10,000 was allocated to the Explosives in Mines Research Committee for twelve months to undertake research which might lead to improved types of coal mining explosives and to improve methods of testing.

The second allocation of £12,000 was made to the Safety in Mines Research Board to proceed with certain research work regarding safety lamps and coal dust, pending the development of the Board's plans for a complete research organisation for the coal mining industry.

Three smaller allocations were made to defray the costs of research into atmospheric conditions in deep mines and spontaneous combustion of coal. 5

By 1923, the Board had established a programme of research under the supervision of Dr Wheeler, Professor of Fuel and Technology at Sheffield University and a Board member. They had also agreed with the Central Committee that, instead of making separate applications for pieces of research, they would provide estimates for financial years from 1st April to 31st March.[6]

Research was broadly divided into safety research and health research and expenditure on safety research was further divided into capital and maintenance.

In 1923, under safety research, £22,000 was allocated as capital expenditure on various articles of equipment required for experimental work at the small-scale research station at Sheffield. However, most of this equipment would be available for transfer to the new site of a large-scale research station when it had been selected.

Maintenance expenditure was allocated for new and ongoing research carried out by the Safety in Mines Research Board, either by their own staff or under the supervision of special ad hoc committees. This research fell under ten broad headings:

Coal dust explosions
Firedamp explosions
Support of underground workings
Spontaneous combustion of coal
Electricity in mines
Mining explosives and shot-firing appliances
Safety lamps (flame and electric)
Wire ropes

Shaft safety appliances

Examination of safety inventions

For the financial year ending 31st March 1923, £18,050 was allocated for this research but only £3,221.19s.7d was spent, the balance being surrendered to the Miners' Welfare Fund at the end of the year. For the subsequent year ending 31st March 1924, the Committee allocated £16,500.[7]

In 1923, the incidence of loss of life and injury from falls of roof and side had become so heavy that the Board appointed a Committee on the Support of Workings in Mines. The Committee had carried out careful investigations in the South Wales coalfields and was extending its enquiries to other fields.

Health research was carried out through the Health Advisory Committee of the Department for Mines and the Medical Research Council into the effect of mine dust on health, miners' nystagmus, beat hand, beat knee and beat elbow. The last three were a form of subcutaneous cellulitis affecting the hand, elbow and knee which caused pain and disability in affected miners and were compensatable in Great Britain.

The Research Board had also entered a full scheme of co-operation into safety in mines with the United States of America's Bureau of Mines. Representatives of the Research Board and the Mines Inspectorate had visited the United States and a representative of the Bureau of Mines had visited the UK. Definite arrangements had been made for the exchange of staff and for co-ordination of work to avoid unnecessary duplication.[8]

The Board had continued at Eskmeals Experimental Station temporarily in 1923 while they gained further experience in explosive experiments. However, the Board were not satisfied that Eskmeals was a suitable site for its other researches even temporarily, and it submitted proposals for the development of these in temporary premises at Sheffield, well situated near important coalfields and close to the University of Sheffield. The premises served for small-scale work, but the Board were hoping for better accommodation.

By 1924, with a further year's experience, the importance of locating the bulk of the work at or near a centre of scientific learning had been confirmed. However, the results of the year's large-scale explosive experiments had made it clear that there was no prospect for some years of reducing the scale of this work which needed to be conducted at an isolated spot.

Eskmeals was considered unsuitable for the large-scale work for several reasons. Communication with Sheffield and the other university towns which might form a suitable home for laboratory work was poor. This would create difficulties in supervision and co-ordination of work. Eskmeals was remote from more important coalfields and was not an economical station to work.

There was little accommodation for staff, an almost complete lack of social amenities, and no facilities for research workers to study and keep in touch with current scientific work.

The Board had found a site at Buxton which satisfied practically all the conditions required for a station for large-scale experiments, including a perfectly level position for the four-foot explosion tube up to a length of 2,000 feet. The Board did not propose to transfer the whole of the small-scale work to the new station, but plenty of space was available for any work which the Board might do there. The Board submitted an estimate of £30,000 to establish the proposed new Experimental Station at Buxton to the Secretary for Mines in March 1924. The estimate was approved by the Central Miners' Welfare Committee at a special meeting at the end of March 1924.[9]

In May 1924, the Board appointed a Committee to act on its behalf, in the event of any question arising in connection with the arrangement of the station which required the decision of the Board. The Committee was chaired by Sir Edward Troup and included four members of the Board and representatives of the Mines Department.

The Board hoped to lease the site at Buxton for twenty one years, with an option to terminate the lease at the end of each period of seven years. The Eskmeals lease needed to be terminated by 30th June 1925, otherwise it would continue for a further seven years.

By September 1924, the Mines Department had expressed a wish to purchase the Buxton site, but this was resisted by the Duke of Devonshire's agent who wanted to offer the site for lease for £170 a year. By October 1924, this offer had been withdrawn by the Duke's agent. However, by January 1925, arrangements had been made with the farmer concerned to give the Board immediate possession of the land required for building, and the architects had been instructed to proceed with plans and estimates of cost.[10]

During 1924, the Miners' Welfare Committee allocated a further £1,000 for the period ending 31st March 1924 for additional equipment at the small scale research station at Sheffield, making a total of £23,000 for capital expenditure of which £8,407.13s.3d was still unspent at 31st March 1924, £4,600 having been kept for a new explosive tube. Two allocations were made for 1924/25 for capital expenditure: £30,000 for transferring the Eskmeals research station and £250 for preliminary expenses for the plans and estimates for the proposed new buildings at Sheffield.

£31,391.10s.7d (£45,000 minus £14,648.9s.5d of unexpended balances of allocations 1923/24) was allocated to 1924/25 to continue with the research programme of the Board. Except for 2 investigations, the allocations were due to expire on the 31st March 1924. The annual estimate covered the research work being conducted directly by the Board, the Explosives in Mines Research Committee, independent investigators, the Deep and Hot Mines Committee and the Medical Research Council.[11]

The Board appointed a committee in November 1924 to consider the accommodation to be provided in the new building at Sheffield and they had met on 28th November. Their proposals were formally submitted to the Secretary for Mines and an allocation of a nominal sum of £250 for contingent preliminary expenses was obtained from the Miners' Welfare Committee. Subsequently, the Fuel Research Board asked whether it would be possible for the Board to provide accommodation for their Sheffield staff.

The Board's Committee met the Vice-Chancellor and Registrar of the University and the Architect on 13th January 1925, and discussed with them the terms of the lease of the site, the character and accommodation of the new building, and the problem of clearing the site which was currently occupied by small dwelling-houses and shops.

In 1925, £45,617 was allocated for researches conducted by the Safety in Mines Research Board and its Sub-Committees, including the Explosives in Mines Research Committee. Most of these researches were a continuation of work in progress. Research into electrical shot-firing apparatus was terminated during 1925, but wireless communication in mines had been included for the first time in electrical researches. The design of a device for trapping dust generated by rock drills and the winning of coal without explosives was a new area of research included in researches into mechanical appliances. Research on overwind prevention appliances and winding speed controllers carried out by Professor Ritson, assisted by Mr W. L. Grassham at Leeds University was completed in 1925.[12]

In January 1926, the Board was given an assurance by Sheffield University that they would be able to clear the tenants from the houses on the site for the new building for the new Sheffield station.

The Building Committee had revisited the plans and recommended a building on four floors at a cost of £27,000 including equipment. The plans provided accommodation for the Fuel Research Board's survey of the seams in the Yorkshire Coalfield. The Fuel Research Board would only temporarily occupy the building pending the expansion of the Board's requirements but, during their occupancy, they would contribute a proportionate annual contribution towards the interest on the capital, the ground rent and the cost of the maintenance of the building.

The accommodation to be provided had been cut down to the minimum in order to reduce the cost, with the result that staff might be a little cramped and it might be necessary for one or two of them to work in the university.

A memorandum was prepared for the Secretary for Mines so that he could submit the request from the Board for the allocation for the Sheffield station to the Miners' Welfare Committee.[12]

The allocation of the £500,000 earmarked for research during the first quinquennium was completed in 1926. The Board had research centres for both large and small-scale experiments at Harpur Hill, Buxton and Sheffield respectively, and an endowment fund of £253,405.3s.8d to support the research work of the Board in the future years. For the financial year 1926–27, the Board was allocated a total of £51,500. This allocation supported work already in progress by the Board or other bodies or individuals. Research being carried out by Mr A. G. Gulliford, a colliery lamp man under the supervision of Dr Wheeler, on the construction of a firedamp detector and estimator for electric safety-lamps, was completed in 1926. Dr H. M. Vernon of the Industrial Fatigue Research Board started his research work in 1926 into the effect of pithead baths on health and absenteeism for the Medical Research Council. The Board published papers on researches from time to time as results became available. Twenty-nine such papers had been published by 31st December 1926. [13]

In March 1927, the Board's estimates for 1927/8 were considered by the Miners' Welfare Committee. The total was £53,562 of which income from the Endowment Fund provided £12,725, the research proportion of the Parliamentary vote amounted to £2,137 and the Miners' Welfare Committee allocated £38,700. The estimates were for work already in progress. A further 3 research papers which had been published in 1927 were reported to the Committee, one of which was a report of the Support of Workings in Mines Committee on 'The Support of Underground Workings in the East Midland Coalfield (Yorkshire, Derbyshire excluding South Derbyshire and Nottinghamshire)'.[14]

In June 1927, the Board held its meeting on 13th at the Buxton Hydro Hotel, as Lord Chelmsford had agreed to open Buxton Research Station the next day.

The main item for discussion was the dissemination of the results of researches undertaken by the Board. The Miners' Welfare Committee had expressed a desire that the Board should consider the question of securing wider distribution of the results of its researches. Mr G. H. Winstanley, one of the Committee's Assessors for Education, had produced suggestions as how this could be achieved for the Board's consideration.

There was common ground over the desirability of lectures and demonstrations for explaining the Board's researches at Miners' Welfare Institutes as well as mining schools. Mr Winstanley considered that these lectures should be given by the ordinary teachers of mining, but Dr Wheeler preferred the appointment of special lecturers and demonstrators to deliver, in co-operation with the teachers of mining, two or three lectures carefully prepared for them.

Mr Winstanley had also made two suggestions regarding the Board's publications: the issue of 'popular' explanations of the Board's publications and a wider free distribution of them. The Board supported the first suggestion but considered that this kind of work would require specially qualified authors.

The Board already published the Board's papers (scientific articles and reports) at a low price in the expectation that copies would be bought by teachers of mining. The issue of a new paper was always widely announced in the press and the Board decided that, in future, Local Education Authorities would be notified so that the authority could provide its teachers and each Professor of Mining with copies.

The Board also agreed to send a copy of their Annual Report to each Miners' Welfare Institute with a letter, drawing attention to the list of publications and asking them to indicate any copies which the Institute would like to have for its members.

They also agreed to prepare a precis of each new paper and to circulate the precis to the Welfare Institutes, telling them that they would be given a copy of the paper if they applied. Dr Wheeler also undertook to make a precis for each of the past papers for the same purpose.

Dr Wheeler, Sir Edward Troup (Chairman of the Board), Mr Winstanley, Mr Foley, Mr Ravenshear and Mr Stedman subsequently met on 24th June 1927 to discuss the two topics.

It was agreed that lectures should be held for miners who did not attend courses of instruction provided by the Local Education Authorities. Dr Wheeler undertook to prepare two or three outline illustrated lectures on subjects such as coal and flameproof electrical apparatus. The selection of titles needed to be centred on the miner rather than the mine.

An attempt would be made to obtain lecturers from amongst the Local Authorities' organisers or teachers of mining education. 10 or 12 suitable candidates would be required, and this would be raised during the Conference of Mining Education Organisers at Buxton in July 1927. The selected lecturers would attend the Board's laboratories at Sheffield for a weekend for instruction by Dr Wheeler.

Lectures would be started at one or two places widely separated as an experiment. The lectures would be given at Welfare Institutes. Arrangements for the lectures would be made by the County Organiser of Mining Education but reliance for securing an audience would be placed chiefly on the mine manager and the Institute committee.

As to the wider dissemination of the Board's Papers, Dr Wheeler had already started on the preparation of a 'popular' explanation of these.[15]

During 1927 several demonstrations of coal dust had been given at Buxton to parties of miners and mining engineers. They had been greatly appreciated and many applications had been made for similar demonstrations the next year. 16

Dr Wheeler had periodically been in touch with M. Audibert, Director of the Station d'Essais, France, concerning their common research work related to coal dust and explosives. In July 1927, the Board gave Dr Wheeler permission to talk over officially with M. Audibert definite proposals for co-operation which would probably not involve interchange of personnel except for short periods. M. Audibert subsequently visited Buxton Research Station in September 1927.[17]

Following Dr Wheeler's and Mr Hay's visit to America in November and December 1927, in January 1928, the Board considered Dr Wheeler's proposals for co-operative research between the Board and the Bureau of Mining in the USA. Co-operation had already led to the Americans greatly improving British rescue apparatus, especially portable breathing apparatus and latterly gas masks. American research into explosives had been a valuable check against the ones carried out by the Board. The Americans had exhaustively studied the release of stone dust barriers to stop a coal dust explosion, and their electrical research was increasing so that the Board could leave this work to them. Dr Wheeler therefore proposed that a new programme on falls of ground for study by the Board and the Bureau of Mines should be included in the new programme. This would be an investigation into the methods and application for testing the soundness of roofs.[18]

In March 1928, the Central Committee agreed to a grant of £43,000 for 1928/9 which was £4,300 more than the previous year. There were several developments which had led to this increase.

There had been an extension to the researches at Buxton on the firing of explosives, involving an increase of £800.

£400 had been set aside in response to the request already received for several coal dust explosion demonstrations for miners. These demonstrations were in great demand and served the purpose of informing the mining community of the results of the Board's work, and of assisting the research staff through contact with those working underground.

A provisional sum of £500 had been included in the estimates for the expenses of lectures and conferences and the provision of models and lantern slides. A first batch of 'simple language' summaries of the Board's publications were to be issued.

The Board proposed to extend the researches for the improvement of rescue apparatus to be undertaken under Professor Ritson at Leeds University at a cost of £1,500.

Progress with wire researches had necessitated an additional expenditure of £800.

Research on mine ventilation in co-operation with the Midland Institute of Mining Engineers had been arranged, but this was not expected to involve any substantial cost to the Board.

Otherwise, the scope of the work to be undertaken in 1928/9 remained the same as the previous year. Several of the investigations were complete, as far as was necessary, but many others were waiting for investigators to become available.[19]

In May 1928, the Board received the outcome of their application to the Miners' Welfare Committee for a tunnel and new buildings at Buxton Research Station. The estimates had been accepted by the Committee in April 1928 in principle, subject to more precise estimates.

The Board had noted the minutes of the Welfare Committee which stated:

'The Chairman repeated the warning he had given at the previous meeting and hoped the Board would make a serious attempt to keep next year's expenditure within a gross limit of £50,000. The whole discussion had shown how increasingly apprehensive the Committee felt at the growth of the Board's expenditure. They would be most unwilling to reject any reasonable proposal, but their financial position might compel them to if the expenditure continued to rise.'

The Board's work was gradually changing in character, laboratory work giving place to large-scale tests which would generally increase the cost. However, the Board agreed that they had to make a serious attempt to keep the next year's expenditure within a gross limit of £50,000.[20]

In October 1928, the Board had been notified that the French Government had accepted the proposal of co-operation between the French Mines Department and the Board. The Foreign Office had been asked to notify the US Government of this and to suggest that they should complete the circle by making a similar arrangement with France. The USA were also being informed that Britain intended approaching Germany and Belgium with a similar object.

On 11th October 1928, the Prime Minister opened the Sheffield Research Station.[21]

Early in October 1928, a 100-foot length of the 4-foot gallery at Buxton Research Station had been blown up during an experiment on the ignition of top hard coal dust. Dr Wheeler was reluctant to continue experiments in the 4-foot gallery until it had been strengthened. By November, it was realised that until the tunnel was driven, it was impossible to estimate the cost of the lining. The total cost of the tunnel would be £7,320, which would not be covered by the grant already made by the Welfare Committee.

The Miners' Welfare Committee's Maintenance Sub-Committee, on 18th December 1928, considered the Board's memorandum acquainting them that the estimated cost (£5,320) of the mine [N.B. mine and tunnel are used in the minutes interchangeably for what appears to be the same facility] would be exceeded on account of the necessity for more lining. The Sub-Committee referred this on to the full Committee while allowing the contract work to continue.

The Board's Experimental Mine Committee had met at the Research Station on 5th January 1929, in the company of Mr Herbert Smith and Mr Richardson, members of the Welfare Committee, to carry out a further inspection so that a report could be made to the Board for submission to the Welfare Committee.[22]

In April 1929, the Board considered the report of the discussions on their estimates by the Miners' Welfare Committee and the Committee's decision to allocate only £36,130 for research in 1929/30. This with the endowment income and the Exchequer contribution made a total of £50,000 against the Board's proposal for research work estimated to cost £56,242. The Welfare Committee had intimated that the Board were at liberty to rearrange their programme to provide within the £50,000 for all or part of the new work contemplated. The Committee had also asked for estimates for 1930/31 to be limited to £50,000 and to be submitted before the end of September 1929.

The Board received this decision with keen disappointment and a discussion took place on the possibility of trying to get the decision reconsidered by means of a joint meeting with the Welfare Committee, at which new proposals could be more fully explained, but the idea was dropped. Instead it was decided that a chief mining engineer should be appointed. His salary and travelling expenses in 1929/30 could be found by dropping some of the researches on coal. Once appointed, he could usefully occupy himself for several months in studying the subjects of falls of ground and haulage (both major causes of deaths and injuries to miners) and preparing programmes of the work requiring to be done and the methods to be employed. A considerable interval needed to be allowed for the preliminary negotiations for setting up the Committees in the coalfields. The Board would then be able to put before the Committee more precise particulars of their programme and the cost.

The Board continued to benefit from the co-operative work undertaken with the USA. The work on coal dusts had been particularly valuable. Mr Budge, a member of the Board and a mining engineer, considered the work on stone dust-barriers as being of great importance, especially regarding the safeguarding of the coal face. He was already using barriers composed of brattice sheets (a woven polypropylene fabric with an anti-static grid and flame-retardant coating) filled with stone dust and requested details of the barriers of the USA pattern. Dr Wheeler undertook to obtain working drawings.[23]

In September 1929, the Board considered a summary of the draft estimates for 1930/31 amounting to £54,800 as prepared by the Finance Committee, and a draft memorandum embodying the recommendations of the Programmes Committee for reducing the total to £50,000 as requested by the Welfare Committee.[24]

Mr Fudge and Mr Stedman had attended the Miners' Welfare Committee meeting on 15th October 1929, at the Committee's request. The Board had submitted certain definite proposals to confine the estimates for 1930/31 to £50,000 and the Committee wanted to offer some observations verbally rather than by way of the Committee's minutes.

The Committee agreed that the problem of reducing accidents from falls of roofs and sides in mines was so important as to demand investigation without delay, but they were doubtful whether it was right to provide any expenditure from the District Committees until the new Mining Engineer had been at work for at least a year collating the information already available within the coalfields.

The proposal to reduce the health expenditure by £2000 out of £2,200 seemed to be an altogether disproportionate reduction in that section which the Committee hardly felt able to agree with unless the proposal to find part of the money from some other source was confirmed.

The Board decided to inform the Welfare Committee that if it proved impossible to obtain financial assistance for health researches from other sources, they would provide a further grant for the Birmingham University Mine Temperature Research, which would at least ensure the effective continuance of the work in progress. Regarding the falls of ground research, it was impossible until the mining engineer had been working for two or three months to decide how soon the district investigations would be required.

An appointment of the Mining Engineer was reported to the Board in October 1929. The Treasury and the Mines Department had agreed to the release of Mr Hudspeth from the Mines Inspectorate. Concern was voiced by members of the Board that, if a Mines Inspector were appointed, he might not always receive the help at the collieries as another would. This had not been the experience of the Support Workings in Mines Committee whose investigator, although from the Inspectorate, had always been cordially received everywhere.[25]

During 1929, the Board commenced on a new series of pamphlets describing the research work undertaken by it under the title 'What every mining man should know'. The first two papers of the series drawn up in a very attractive form with numerous illustrations were published and circulated before the end of the year under the titles of 'No1 Safety in Coal Mines; Some problems of research' and 'No2 Gas and flame'.[26]

In March 1930, Professor Wheeler reported that he had received requests from Belgium and Russia for co-operation in research. The Mining Engineer in charge of the Belgium Research Station had applied formally for a scheme of co-operation similar to that between Britain and France. Two officials, the Chief Inspector of Mines and a Mining Electrical Engineer, from Russia had recently visited the Board's Research Station and Professor Dixon's laboratories. Russia was about to begin research on safety, so desired to arrange a scheme of co-operation on the same lines as that existing between Britain and America.

With Mr Hudspeth in post, in March 1930, he reported on his progress with the Falls of Ground researches. He had met with four associations of Scottish mine owners, a Committee of Monmouthshire and South Wales Coal Owners' Association, and the Support of Workings Committee of the North of England Institute of Mining Engineers. He had also been consulted about a programme of research proposed by the Lancashire and Cheshire Coal Research Association.[27]

By May 1930, the North of England and South Wales had placed advertisements for district investigators for the Falls of Ground researches. Appointments were made to both posts in June 1930.[28]

The Scottish investigator commenced work on 1st July 1930, the North of England investigator on 1st August and the South Wales investigator on 1st September. Each had a detailed programme of research to carry out.[29]

Demonstrations for miners and officials at Buxton were staged throughout the summer on Sundays. 14 parties of between 100 and 200 visited the station. Arriving at 11am, they had a short address followed by a demonstration explosion in the underground gallery or demonstrations of shot-firing. Groups were then taken round the station. After lunch, a discussion on a subject chosen by the visitors took place.

The underground gallery was not so spectacular for demonstration purposes as the surface galleries, but it did resemble mine conditions, as it could be inspected by the visitors before the explosions.[30]

By October 1930, there had been further progress with the Falls of Ground research. Dr Winstanley, the Scottish investigator, had installed two types of subsidence recorders in a mine, and observations were being taken in an area where a subjacent seam would be worked later. It was also suggested that Dr Winstanley should lecture to colliery officials on the technique of longwall roof control.

In the North of England, one of Professor Dixon's dynamometers had been temporarily lent with a view to measuring prop resistance developed in narrow workings. The colliery manager had offered to vary the width and method of working and stowing support (a method of mining in which the material is removed and the waste is packed into the space left by the working) of a particular place so that the effect of these factors could be observed.

The South Wales Committee had approved a programme proposed by their investigator, Mr Barraclough, for taking systematic subsidence observations at particular collieries where both partial and solid stowing was in practice and for observing the effects of each system of stowing at one or other collieries where the conditions were as nearly comparable as possible.

The Board had also made a grant to enable work to be commenced in the Midland Counties. An advertisement for a District Investigator was going to be placed by the Midland Counties Institution.

Mr Henshaw submitted the Report of the Committee appointed to prepare a scheme for investigating haulage accidents to the Board in October 1930. Haulage accidents had accounted for nearly a quarter of the deaths or injuries to miners in the last ten years.

The Report had proposed the appointment of district investigators, but this was considered to be premature and it was agreed instead that an assistant to Mr Hudspeth should be recruited for the haulage research, in order to carry out local investigations as recommended by the Haulage Committee.[31]

With the future of the Welfare Fund, on which the Board depended for the greater part of their income, being discussed by the Secretary for Mines and the Coal Industry, the Board had written to Mr Shinwell asking that the importance of the future research should be borne in mind. Mr Shinwell had replied expressing his readiness to consider any representations the Board wished to make. In reply, the Board submitted a memorandum to the Secretary for Mines, suggesting the establishment of a permanent fund to meet the cost of the safety research based on the present work and developments immediately in view. An annual sum of £60,000 was put forward in the memorandum.[32]

The Chairman, Mr Hudspeth and Professor Wheeler had subsequently discussed with the Secretary for Mines the Board's estimates for 1931/32, with the result that Mr Shinwell had recommended the Welfare Committee to accept the whole of the estimate. The Chairman, Dr Wheeler and Mr Stedman attended the Welfare Committee meeting on 18th November 1930. After considerable discussion, the Committee had agreed to increase the grant for safety instruction from £1,500 to £2,000, to grant the £54,000 required for research, and for future years to raise their limit for research estimates from £50,000 to £60,000, subject to certain reservations, which would be embodied in a communication with the Board in due course.[33]

In January 1931, Mr Stedman was promoted to a higher appointment and his place as Secretary to the Board was taken by Mr D. B. Woodburn.

The Board approved the purchase of twenty five subsidence recorders for the

Falls of Ground research in January 1931: twelve for Dr Winstanley in Scotland, six for the Midlands Institute and seven for other districts. The Midlands Institute of Mining Engineers had recruited their district investigator and it was hoped, subject to the Board's approval, that he would start on 1st February.

In South Wales, Mr Barraclough had designed a double leg steel arch with a transverse joint which would be stronger than a fishplate (arches were formed from two, three or four sections of joist and then connected by fish-plated joints which are still used today in railway line construction). Practical trials were planned, and the Board approved the provisional patenting of the design.[34]

Mr Hudspeth visited the Council of the South Staffordshire Institute of Mining Engineers in March 1931 to discuss proposals for research into Falls of Ground in that District. It was anticipated that they would want to proceed on similar lines to North Staffordshire.

Mr Woodburn and Mr Fowler attended the Miners' Welfare Committee meeting on the 17th March 1931 at which the estimates for 1931/32 had been considered and approved. The Miners' Welfare Committee had emphasised that the increase of the maximum limit of expenditure to £60,000 was not to be taken as implying that they would automatically consent to increases within that limit.[35]

Safe underground lighting by electricity required cables, switches, lamp holders and lamps that should be incapable of igniting firedamp. A progress report on underground lighting was presented to the Board in May 1931. Trials on a pattern of cable designed by Dr Allsop had been tried successfully at Birch Coppice Colliery and offers to experiment with cable lighting had been received from several colliery owners. Safe switches and lamp holders were already in existence, so the only outstanding issue was that of lamps.

Side movement on advancing long wall roadways was being investigated as part of the Falls of Ground researches. The gradual reduction in width occurring in advancing longwall roadways was a matter of serious concern as it frequently necessitated dangerous repair work and interfered with haulage operations. The extent and nature of the side movement had been little investigated. Since March 1930, Mr Henshaw had carried out some work on advancing longwall workings in the Barnsley seam.[36]

In June 1931, the Board considered the results of the tests on the Ringrose Firedamp Detector carried out between 7th May and 10th June 1931 at Tinsley Park and Nunnery Collieries in Yorkshire. The detectors had proved to be unreliable on two counts: inability to respond accurately to the percentage of firedamp at which it was set, and inability to be set accurately. Furthermore, the detectors failed completely at the end of the shift, owing to the running down of the batteries, and there were serious defects from the point of lighting. This information was passed onto the Secretary for Mines.

Two grants were made to Falls of Ground and Haulage research: one was made to South Staffordshire Institute of Mining Engineers, and the other to the Lancashire and Cheshire Safety in Mines Committee who had appointed a Senior Investigator.[37]

An informal meeting was held at Buxton in July 1931 to which representatives from America, Belgium, France, Germany and Czechoslovakia were invited.

At the Board's July 1931 meeting, approval was given to the appointment of an engineer for the haulage research, and the appointment of district investigators for the Falls of Ground research in North Staffordshire and South Staffordshire and Warwickshire.[38]

At their September 1931 meeting, the Safety in Mines Research Board had to consider a memorandum from the Mines Department on the reduction in inclusive salaries of the secretarial staff. The Board took a similar view to that of the Welfare Committee (see Chapter 3). The Board informed the Miners' Welfare Committee that it would be prepared to make its own proposals for the reduction in salaries, but the Board was of the opinion that any savings so effected should be applied in a reduction of the Treasury Grant.

The Chairman subsequently attended the October meeting of the Welfare Committee, where he was made aware of the Committee's decision to relieve the Exchequer of the secretarial charges. At the October 1931 meeting of the Board, the decision was taken to accept the Committee's decision.[39]

In September 1931, the Board received the report on the research in Lancashire into Falls of Ground which had been progressing along three lines. A report by Mr Faulkner on his research into 'Roof Control in the Arley Mine' had been read before the Institution of Mining Engineers. Work on the second part of the Lancashire programme, the effect on gas evolution of the rate of advance of longwall faces, had been commenced by the new Senior Investigator, Mr Hudson, and the third part, an investigation of the physical properties of coal measure strata, was being continued by Mr Phillips at Sedgwick Museum, Cambridge. Mr Phillips had delivered a lecture on this work to the mining teachers at their Buxton conference.[40]

In October 1931, Mr Hudspeth reported on the research on roof movements in advance of longwalls which was being carried out as part of the Falls of Ground research. A narrow heading six feet deep, driven in advance of the coal face, exposed an apparent forward and downward displacement of the roof, to the extent of 1½ inches approximately 3 feet 6 inches, ahead of the face line, that being within 6 inches of the usual depth of coal removed in an operation. Similar displacements, though less in extent, had been observed four yards in advance of another face by Mr Carter, working under the Midland Counties Institution of Engineers. If this tilting could be reduced by better packing, a great step would be made towards reducing breaks, which were a source of continuous danger.[41]

In December 1931, the Board received a letter from Sir Alfred Faulkner, confirming that the Secretary for Mines was glad to accept the Board's offer to repay, as from 1st October 1931, the amount expended by the Exchequer on the remuneration expenses and accommodation of the secretarial staff of the Board.

Mr Hudspeth gave the Board a short synopsis of the report on Support of Underground Roads by Steel Arches produced by the Control of Roof and Support Workings Committee of the Midland Institute of Mining Engineers. The report was based on a study of the circumstances under which steel arches were used in thirty Yorkshire collieries producing annually nearly 19,000,000 tons of coal, and having at the close of the year 1930 an aggregate length of 61 miles of roadway supported by steel arches. The work had been supported by a grant from the Board.

The issue of nystagmus was raised, as it had appeared in the minutes of the Health Advisory Committee and it was questioned as to what progress was being made for studying the effect of improved lighting on the incidence of this condition. Dr Wheeler reported that Dr Ferguson had undertaken research in several collieries and found that by using lamps of greater light intensity than that currently in use that there was a progressive diminution in the existing cases of nystagmus, and no new cases arose. In the 'control' shifts continuing with the old lamps, no cases ceased to exhibit nystagmus symptoms and new cases developed.[42]

In January 1932, Dr Wheeler reported on the recent work being undertaken at Buxton on coal dust explosions, which had built on earlier work undertaken at Eskmeals. At Buxton, they were examining the amount of stone dust required to suppress the propagation of flame under different conditions.

A considerable number of collieries were using Dr Godbert's method (a laboratory furnace developed at Sheffield by Dr Godbert) of testing flammability of road dust, and several of them had sent their chemists to Sheffield for instruction in the apparatus. As a result of the observations made with the apparatus at the collieries, the question had arisen as to the efficacy of certain stone dusts as compared with the fuller's earth used at Buxton.

Professor Dixon reported on the research undertaken at Imperial College, London, into support of workings which looked at properties of timber and steel supports. He also exhibited a new dynameter prop and demonstrated the method of using it.

Sir Edward Troup, Mr Fudge and the Secretary had attended the Miners' Welfare Committee on 19th January 1932 where the Committee had allocated £43,700 for research and £3,050 for Safety Instruction. During the discussion of the estimates 1932/3, the Committee had asked whether the Board had considered the effect of a limit of £60,000 subsequent to the Board's decision to, in future, meet the secretarial expenses which had previously been paid by the Mines Department. The Board replied that they had not considered it as the present estimate was well within the limit set by the Committee.

At the meeting on 19th January, Mr Herbert Smith had stressed the importance of finding some solution to the problem of early detection and prevention of spontaneous combustion, and he had been assured that the Board would carefully review these in the light of the recent accidents at Bentley and Frickley Collieries.

In February 1932, Mr Hudspeth reported on work carried out in Lancashire as part of the Falls of Ground researches. It had been shown that the higher the rate of face advance, the higher was the rate of subsidence. Similar results had been observed in Scotland by Dr Winstanley, but it was an important finding and it appeared that with modern intensive mining, the face advance in some pits was possibly too rapid as compared with the speed at which it was possible to follow up with efficient packing.

The Miners' Welfare Fund Committee of Inquiry wrote to the Board in April 1932 asking for their observations on the evidence given on behalf of the Mining Association, suggesting that future research should be limited to falls of ground and haulage work and the Board's views as to the future financial provision for mine safety and health research. The Board were also offered the opportunity to give evidence to the Inquiry on 1st June 1932.

In May 1932, the Board considered their draft memorandum of evidence to the Committee of Inquiry, and decided that the Chairman would give oral evidence if the Committee of Inquiry wanted to have this. The memorandum refuted the claims of the Mining Association and went on to provide evidence of the value of the Board's researches to the Mining Industry. Any curtailment of research or safety instruction would be detrimental to the Industry.

The Chairman, accompanied by Mr G. F. Anderson, Secretary to the Board, appeared before the Committee of Inquiry on 1st June to supplement the written statement of evidence submitted on behalf of the Board. The Chairman gave the Committee of Inquiry further information on the research being undertaken. As to future financial provision, the present maximum of £60,000 plus the grant for 'Safety Instruction' should stand for the next seven or ten years. He had suggested that the Board's endowment should be increased to provide an annual income of about £30,000 to be supplemented by such annual grants as might prove necessary.[44]

One of the major research projects during 1932 concerned the ignition of firedamp by explosives. The research looked at several aspects of the problem:

the methods of shot firing, method of using cooling salts, and the possibility of finding an agent to impede the explosion of firedamp under ordinary conditions.

The work on falls of ground continued to investigate the effects of subsidence, but it also began to look at the relation between subsistence and gas evolution. The impression had been that, with increasing rates of face advancement, the greater the quantity of gas evolved in a given time. However, the less the subsidence, the less the gas emission. It seemed, if the roof support could be sufficiently improved, a higher rate of face advancement might be effected without involving a higher rate of gas evolution. This was an important piece of work, and preliminary results needed to be confirmed and followed up.

The researches into haulage accidents were proceeding with metallurgical examinations of samples of broken haulage gear. Reports of the results were being given to the colliery companies concerned and sometimes, with the consent of the colliery company, to the manufacturer of the gear. Mr Henshaw had also designed a guide ramp to facilitate the transfer of full tubs to the rails at road heads. It was in use at a colliery and it enabled one man to transfer the tubs instead of two or three men. By saving labour at road heads, it was expected to reduce the risk of accidents which was greatest at this point.[45]

The 'information' service continued to develop during 1932. Over 2,800 persons, including a party of 260 from Durham, had attended the weekend demonstrations at Buxton. A transportable exhibit, illustrating the development of safe mining appliances had been shown in eight mining centres to over 5,000 mine workers. The Mining Teachers' Conference at Buxton had included a lecture on packing, mine lighting and nystagmus in relation to mine lighting.[46]

At their December 1932 meeting, the Board approved the estimates for 1933/34 amounting to £57,868 for research and £3,960 for Safety Instruction. During the discussion of the estimates, the movement in Yorkshire for the systematic instruction of boys in Mine Safety under a scheme instituted by the county education authorities in co-operation with the coal owners' association was raised. The Board expressed the opinion that the movement should be strongly encouraged and developed on a national basis and it was decided to make representation to the Miners' Welfare Committee to that effect.

On 21st November 1932, an explosion in the spontaneous combustion building in Buxton had caused such damage to the fabric that it required to be broken up and rebuilt at an estimated cost of £877 towards which it was anticipated that £400 could be recovered from the insurance of the original building and £50 for modifications was provided in the current estimates, leaving £427 to be met from other sources.

The six foot diameter steel gallery of boiler shells, transferred from Eskmeals and used for experimental work with explosives, was no longer fit for service and it was proposed that it should be replaced by a 3ft 6ins diameter, 50ft long steel tube, at a cost of £65.

It was proposed that an application should be made to the Miners' Welfare Committee for permission to draw on the sum received for the Ardeer plant to meet the expenditure on the spontaneous combustion building and the cost of the steel tube.[47]

The Chairman and Mr Fudge attended the January 1933 meeting of the Miners' Welfare Committee where the estimates for research were not challenged but the Welfare Committee found some difficulty in accepting the estimate of £3,960 for Safety Instruction in view of a recommendation by the Welfare Fund Committee of Inquiry that the annual expenditure on such work should be limited to £3,500. The Welfare Fund deferred their decision pending further examination of the Inquiry Committee's report.

In March 1933, the Welfare Committee confirmed the allocation of £3,960, subject to the condition that no expansion of Safety Instruction work would be embarked upon and agreed that the additional work could be undertaken.[48]

In January 1933, Mr Hudspeth submitted a memorandum on the use of protective equipment: hats, glasses, safety boots and goggles. In 1931, over 80,000 accidents to heads, hands, eyes and feet had been sustained. Although several British firms were attempting to manufacture suitable hats, they were unlikely to be available in the near future, so Mr Hudspeth was asking for £250 to purchase hats of an American design for those mines which were willing to experiment with them. The Board sanctioned expenditure up to £250 from the reserve of the falls of ground research.

Two collieries, one in Yorkshire and one in North Staffordshire, had put 50 hats to experimental use. Both collieries' reports in July 1933 confirmed the value of the hats as a means to reducing accidents, as not only had many minor injuries been avoided, but in at least one case in each colliery, an accident of a more serious nature had been prevented. The hats were, however, heavy and caused discomfort due to the working conditions, but it was hoped to develop lighter and better ventilated hats.

Further reports in November 1933 from North Staffordshire, South Wales, Lancashire and Nottinghamshire also gave highly satisfactory results for the use of hard hats introduced experimentally. In one of the collieries where 50 hats had been recently been put in as an experiment, 150 had been ordered at a cost of 2/9d, to be sold to the workmen at 2/- each.[49]

Throughout 1933, research into various types of stone dust continued. As early as January, the Board were in a position to make a recommendation to the Mines Department for the revision of the stone-dusting regulations as regards fineness, dispersibility and proportion of incombustible dust to be specified. However, further work continued as the Board had taken the decision to undertake further work on the prevention of explosions at the coal face. Under modern mining conditions, the man-density at the face was very high with the result that a small explosion resulted in a comparatively high casualty list.

By November 1933, an apparatus for distributing stone dust at the coal face in the event of a firedamp explosion had been constructed. It consisted essentially of an air thermometer which, when heated, completed an electrical circuit to fire a modified 'Cardox' cartridge which blew a charge of stone dust out towards the face. However, further experiments carried out on the flammability of coal dust mixtures meant that the use of stone dust could be dispensed with and the experiments into discharges of carbon dioxide only should continue which would simplify the problem of moving the apparatus forward as the face advanced.[50]

In March 1933, the Board reviewed the research programme on wire ropes being undertaken by Professor Dixon at Imperial College, London. These researches investigated the use of alternative core materials to minimise internal corrosion of the wires, corrosive properties of steels available for the manufacture of wire ropes, and the changes in the properties of wire ropes during use.

As most of the ropes which had failed in service when the lubrication had been unsatisfactory, it was suggested that Professor Dixon should draw up, for the use of colliery engineers, a specification of a lubricant suitable for application to winding ropes during their working life.

With the retirement of Professor S. M. Dixon from the Chair of Civil Engineering in December 1933, the Board considered the proposal for the transfer of the wire ropes and fall of ground researches at Imperial College from the Engineering College to the Bessemer Laboratory in the Royal School of Mines and for changes in the control and organisation of the work. Transfer of the plant would be about £400, which could be met from the savings available from 1932/33, and variations in the cost of carrying out the researches had been taken into account in framing the estimates for 1934/35. Dr Hogan would be in executive charge of the future work.[51]

Work continued on developing a safe system of main lighting in mines and improving flame safety lamps.

A trial outfit for mains lighting, designed to prevent the risk of igniting firedamp, had been used at Grange Colliery (South Yorkshire) for four months. The apparatus had functioned satisfactorily despite being moved forward as the face advanced.

The General Electric Co. Ltd. had agreed to manufacture the entire outfit, and two further trial outfits were installed free of charge for face lighting in

Grassmoor (Derbyshire) and Smithy Wood (South Yorkshire). The special bulbs had not proved quite satisfactory, tests in firedamp having resulted in ignition, with 2% of the bulbs on breakage, but attempts to make them absolutely safe continued in conjunction with the General Electric Company.

Experiments with flame safety lamps had led to a redesign which was being manufactured commercially by Messrs John Dervis and Son and Messrs Naylor's and a larger lamp of the Naylor 'Roadway' type which had not yet been manufactured for sale.[52]

H. M. Divisional Inspectors of Mines had shown that in falls of top hard seams, accident rates from falls immediately reportable were worst under sandstone, and this had also been shown to be true of compensatable accidents. As part of the falls in ground research, the movement of various kinds of roof had been studied by means of headings driven in advance of a number of faces and it had been shown that the high rate under sandstone could be attributed, at least in part, to the fact that the sandstone had less bending capacity than stone bind (interbedded layers of sandstone and shale) and required a greater measure of support, where in practice it was usually given less support.[53]

Metallurgical examination of broken haulage gear continued at Sheffield University under Professor Andrew. The examination had indicated that in many instances failure could have been avoided by different treatment of the metal, or the use of more suitable material but the cause of other failures were obscure and research appeared to be required into the effects of welding and annealing (type of heat treatment of metal) and the growth of strain hardness in service.

In December 1933, Mr Hudspeth reported on the results obtained from the haulage dynameter on measuring the loads on lashing chains, comparing steam and electric drives, computing the tractive resistance of tub bearings of various types and with different lubrication, and determining dynamic factors of safety.

North Staffordshire Committee had also issued their first safety pamphlet entitled 'An Analysis of Underground Haulage Accidents in North Staffordshire'. The analysis showed that accidents from derailments formed a relatively high percentage of the total, particularly on hand haulage.[54]

In January 1934, the Miners' Welfare Committee accepted the Boards' estimates for 1934/35: £58,438 for research and £3,155 for safety instruction.

The work on protective equipment had built up considerably. The value of hard hats had been established, and their extensive adoption could only be a matter of time. The cheap British hat had been improved, and more satisfactory reports on its wearing qualities were being received.

Different types of hand protection were required in different classes of work, the most satisfactory for general use had been found to be a string-laced fingerless leather mitt, sold by Helmets Ltd.

The Regent Boot manufacturers, who supplied boots for the iron and steel industry, had now turned their attention to the mining industry and another firm had designed 'Pitt' safety boot, of which hundreds of pairs had been sold.

Little success had been achieved with goggles, mainly due to the difficulty with diminished vision.

At a Lancashire colliery, in a thick highly inclined seam, the introduction of shin guards, costing 10d per pair, had reduced leg accidents. Over 200 pairs were currently in use at the colliery and the cost of compensation for shin injuries had been reduced by 80%. Similar protection was being experimented with in North Staffordshire.

As the work in connection with the development of the use of protective equipment was assuming large proportions, it was suggested in April 1934 that a small committee should be set up with Mr Hudspeth as Chair and Mr F. Edmond, Mr F. Lee and Sir Henry Walker as the other members.

The Treasury were approached to bear the cost of the secondment of a Mines Inspector for the work on protective equipment, but the Treasury took the view in November 1934 that the Board should bear the whole cost. The Chairman therefore wrote to Sir Alfred Faulkner, Mines Department, who reopened the matter with the Treasury. By December, the Treasury had agreed to a Junior Inspector being seconded for a period of three years and to the Mines Department bearing the cost of the normal salary. Sir Henry Walker had kindly agreed to Mr W. F. Richardson, a Junior Inspector from Durham, taking the post.[55]

In South Wales, work was being undertaken as part of the falls of ground research, into various methods of packing (loose stone built up to support the roof), the circumstances associated with large falls, and the use of wood and steel cogs.

Tests were also being carried out on packs in the 400-ton testing machine at Imperial College. The experiments emphasised the need for building the pack walls tight to the roof. The presence of well-built cross walls had been found to increase the resistance of the pack, and the quality of the filling material was important.

The Scottish Committee were undertaking research on strata movement resulting from the working of two seams in the same area. By means of an instrument in a bore hole which passed from one working to the solid coal in a seam 71 feet above, observations were made of the roof and floor movements as the upper coal face advanced towards the borehole.

It was found that in the upper seam, the roof was lowering and the floor lifting some 60 feet in advance of the coalface while at the same time the roof of the lower working was lowering proving that the intervening beds were thickening or separating.

The investigation showed the importance of taking special precautions when advancing towards an area above a worked-out seam.

In November 1934, Dr D. W. Phillips gave the Board an update on his work on the character and properties of coal measure rocks.

With the aid of the Falls of Ground District investigators, the nomenclature used in different coalfields for the rocks had been compiled. Wide differences in constitution and texture had been found even between rocks in the same class, and these differences affected their strength and their behaviour under load.

A collection of rocks of local interest, with microphotographs and descriptions, had been prepared for Nottingham University College and Chesterfield College, and another was being prepared for Sheffield University with the object of stimulating interest among students in these studies.

Tests on the effect of different rates of loading indicated that the faster the rate of loading, the greater was the load necessary to cause fracture. This would be investigated further.

Determination of the elastic moduli in bending had been made for rocks typical of the roof of coal seams. These varied widely. Under a given load, the most flexible rocks would bend five times as much as the most rigid. Elasticity was important when considering rock bursts; the fact that rocks were resilient, thus permitting 'rebound' when relieved of load, might be a source of danger. [56]

In July 1934, Dr Wheeler gave a progress report on the experimental mains lighting in mines. The lighting installed at Grange Colliery eighteen months ago had worked well and only three breakages of the outer lamp glasses had occurred.

The General Electric Company Ltd had designed a trial unit which had been installed at Steetley Colliery (Yorkshire). The trial set would only light 40 yards, and Dr Wheeler considered it necessary to install additional lamps sufficient to light a whole face so that it could be ascertained whether the plant would stand up to continuous work at full capacity under normal working conditions. [57]

Professor Andrew, of the Metallurgical Department, Sheffield University, attended the Board's May meeting to give a summary of the results of the examination during the past 2½ years of samples of broken and defective haulage gear obtained from collieries.

The faults could be considered under three headings: the use of unsatisfactory material, faults in making up the gear and defects developed in service.

The unsatisfactory material was chiefly a composite of wrought iron and steel which had been found to occur in material described as complying with BSS Grade A wrought iron.

Faults in making up the gear arose chiefly from defective welding and, in the case of wrought iron, from the plane of the piling being wrong in relation to the direction of the loading.

The most important defect that developed in service was hardening, caused in various ways, which produced brittleness.[58]

Work on coal dust and firedamp explosions continued throughout 1934, with experiments with coal dust wetting agents being undertaken at Thorpe Colliery and Hatfield Main Colliery (South Yorkshire). Experiments were also commenced at other pits on the wetting of coal dust at conveyor ends and, in the laboratory, in wetting of dust clouds.[59]

4,600 persons had attended the demonstrations at Buxton in 1934, of which just over half were boys who were attending to see the work of the Board and for the presentation of safety training badges. A large proportion of the boys were not interested in the detailed programme arranged for them, and it was suggested that their numbers might be considerably curtailed in 1935 or demonstrations limited to spectacular items which they could see as one body. The applications for still larger numbers of boys were expected for 1935. The limit of the accommodation had been reached. The matter was discussed with the Local Education Authorities concerned, who were unwilling to reduce the numbers.

It was estimated that applications would be received for about 3,800 boys, as well as a large number of men wishing to attend. It would be necessary to hold additional demonstrations for the boys on Wednesdays if the full number of applications were accepted. This would involve expenditure additional to that provided in the Board's estimates.[60]

The Chairman and Mr E. W. Ravenshear, Mines Department, had attended the Welfare Committee meeting in February 1935 in support of the estimates for 1935/36. The allocation applied for (£47,701) was approved. However, the possibility of putting a lower limit to the annual expenditure of the Board was discussed but was left in abeyance.

The Committee had expressed their interest in the Board's work on protective equipment and Mr Lawther, a member of the Committee and the MFGB, had intimated that he would submit, for the information of the Board, his personal view on his experience of its use in Durham.

In April 1935, the question of further expenditure being necessary due to the need to apply the 'government' scales of salary to the Board's scientific staff was considered by the Board.

A Sub-Committee (Mr Fudge, Dr Sinnatt and Dr Wheeler) had been set up to consider the claims of improved status and salaries which had been made by the Board's scientific staff and to advise as to the reorganisation of the staff. Their report made it obvious that if the status and salaries of the present scientific staff were raised to the levels of those of the staff at the Government Research Station, there would be a considerable increase in the Board's expenditure on salaries.

In the light of the possibility of a reduction in the Welfare Committee's grant to the Board the following year, an ad hoc Committee (Sir Edward Troup, Chair, Dr Drysdale, Mr Fudge, Mr Hudspeth, Mr Jacob, Dr Sinnatt and Dr Wheeler) was set up to consider the matter further. They would examine the Board's programmes of research in detail and report on what work could be continued and what staff could be maintained within the present limits of expenditure if the Government scales of salary were adopted by the Board.

The Board had informed the Miners' Welfare Committee of their views on the Committee's suggestion that the grant for research might have to be reduced in 1936. The Committee then asked the Board to consider whether their demands on the Welfare Fund could be reduced before 1940, and what would be the Board's plans for placing their demands on a reduced basis thereafter as recommended by the Chelmsford Committee.

The terms of reference for the Sub-Committee appointed in April 1935 had been directed towards the more immediate financial difficulties of staff reorganisation and salaries, so it was proposed that the Sub-Committee should undertake a complete review of the Board's programme and staff on the basis of reducing expenditure on research to a lower level if possible before and, in any case, after 1940. In the meantime, it was decided that no steps should be taken to fill those posts falling vacant in the Board's scientific staff, or on the staff, charged to grants made by the Board, of the District Committees and research organisations.

The report of the Sub-Committee was considered by the Board in July 1935. The pay scales proposed for the scientific staff were a substantial improvement on their current scales, but it would only be possible to adopt the new pay scale by reducing the staff and suspending certain programmes of research to comply with the Welfare Committee's request to reduce expenditure before and after 1940.

The net result of the proposed reorganisation was a reduction in the Board's expenditure, but only during the following three or four years. It was considered impossible to put forward a precise estimate of what five years hence would be the Board's annual expenditure, depending as it must on the progress of the researches and the demands of the Industry. The report of the Sub-Committee was forwarded to the Welfare Committee.

The Welfare Committee, at their meeting on 24th September 1935, considered the Board's reply to their request that the Board should consider whether their demands on the Welfare Fund could be reduced. Mr Fudge attended the meeting at the Committee's request.

Eventually, the Committee decided to explore the possibility of stabilising their grant for research for a period at a suitable figure. Mr Fudge undertook, at the Committee's request, to consider this question in consultation with the Secretaries of the Research Board and the Welfare Committee with a view to framing a proposal for discussion by the Committee at a subsequent meeting.

Mr Fudge's proposals had been considered by the Welfare Committee at their meeting on 15th October 1935. The Committee had decided to leave the question of stabilisation in abeyance but had reiterated their opinion that more determined efforts should be made to secure adequate contributions from the Exchequer and other interests. It was Mr Fudge's understanding that the Welfare Committee had decided to make representations to the Secretary for Mines.

At their meeting on 19th November 1935, the Welfare Committee decided that, in view of the appointment of the Royal Commission on Safety in Coal Mines, the Committee would continue to deal with the grants for research by way of yearly estimates under the conditions and limitations that had applied to the current year's estimates.

This decision enabled the Board to give effect to the Reorganisation Report and to prepare their estimates for 1936/37 accordingly.[61]

The results of the investigations undertaken by several districts as part of the falls of ground research into the influence of the rate of advance of the coal face on the behaviour of mine roofs were reported to the Board in July 1935.

In November 1935, the results of investigations undertaken by Mr R. Faulkner and Dr D. W. Phillips, under the auspices of the Lancashire and Cheshire Safety in Mines Committee, and in the laboratory at Sheffield into the formation of planes of weakness in shale roofs of coal seams, were presented to the Board. The evidence clearly showed that induced cleavage was not inherent but was a first result of the mining operations.

As a result of the Board's decision not to fill vacancies taken in April 1935, there were several delays in making appointments to the vacant district investigation post for the falls of ground research. In July, Mr Hudspeth had been offered a Professorship of Mining, but the Board were unable to agree to him holding this post and that of Chief Mining Engineer to the Board, as they considered his work to be of the greatest importance, demanding his whole time. However, in December 1935, the Mines Department had recalled Mr Hudspeth to take up the post as Deputy Chief Inspector of Mines. Mr Hudspeth had only been seconded to the Board, and the Board had to acquiesce to the Mines Department's request. However, Mr Hudspeth did continue his work for the Board, as well as the duties of Deputy Chief Inspector, while the Board found a successor to his position.[62]

Investigations undertaken in Yorkshire into underground haulage accidents found that the usual records of haulage accidents seldom provided information necessary for an accurate analysis of the causes of injury and that lack of uniformity of classification reduced the comparative value of information. A special record had accordingly been made of haulage accidents in six large collieries in Yorkshire during the last three months of 1933, and haulage accidents at another large colliery during two periods of twelve months before and after the introduction of underground conveyors.

The analysis had shown that accidents arising out of the manipulation of tubs frequently occurred at or near the coalface and concerned face workers. Injuries to hands constituted the largest single class of haulage injury.

Lack of clearance, improvised tracks and badly laid flat sheets (square or oblong sheets of cast iron at about ¾ inch thick which were nailed on planking at the top or bottom of a pit and formed a metal floor for the moving about of coal tubs) were important factors in haulage accidents. The use of conveyors largely eliminated these accidents.[63]

The metallurgical examination of haulage gear continued. A simple apparatus had been developed to assist colliery companies to assess the quality of the wrought iron used in haulage gear. Encouraging results had also been obtained with the use of mild steel containing 1.5% Manganese which had been suggested as an alternative to the existing materials.

A film on the use of protective equipment had been produced to promote its use and subsequently collieries had asked for posters to be produced.[64]

Progress on the investigations at Birmingham University into the use of wetting reagents for dust suppression when drilling with water-fed drills was reviewed by the Board in March 1935. It was suggested that the Imperial Chemical Industries (ICI) should be approached to see if they were prepared to assign (free of charge) the services of one of their chemists to assist in this work. By April 1935, ICI had indicated their willingness to assign one of their chemists and by May 1935, a physicist, approved by ICI and paid by them, had commenced preliminary experiments at Birmingham. A laboratory assistant had also been engaged to assist in this work, and his salary would be paid by the Board.[65]

Work had continued on the wetting of coal dust, with full scale experiments being carried out at Thorpe Colliery on 600 yards of travelling road which included 200 yards at a gradient of 1 in 3. Perminal W solution had been used to treat the dust, which was mainly stone dust, after which the roadway had been sprayed with water alone at fortnightly intervals for four months. Laboratory experiments were being undertaken on other wetting agents prior to being tried out underground.[66]

In January 1936, the Board had received a letter from the Royal Commission on Safety in Coal Mines, asking the Board to prepare, by the end of March, a memorandum of evidence which they would submit to the Commission:

witnesses would probably not be required to attend before 20th April. The Memorandum was duly forwarded to the Commission, accompanied by an invitation to the Commissioners to visit the Board's Research Stations. The Commissioners took up this invitation and visited Sheffield and Buxton on 2nd and 3rd July 1936. The Board's oral evidence would probably be held on 13th and 14th July 1936.[67]

In February 1936, the Board approved the estimates for 1936/37, amounting to £57,288 for Research and £3,260 for Safety Instruction which included a personal grant of £2,600 for 1936/37 to Professor Haldane as Director of the Mining Research Laboratory, Birmingham. The Miners' Welfare Committee approved the estimates and allocated the amount applied for of £46,382.[68]

On 14th March 1936, Professor Haldane died. He had served on the Board since 1923. In April 1936, the Chairman of the Board, accompanied by the Secretary, had discussed with Sir Evan Williams, British Colliery Owners' Research Association, and Mr A Lee, member of the Board and the Mining Association of Great Britain, the future of the research carried out under the direction of the late Professor Haldane. As the British Colliery Owners' Research Association and the Board contributed towards the cost of the research, Sir Evan Williams suggested that a small Joint Committee should be set up to consider the future scope of the work, where it should be carried out, and by whom.

By December 1936, the Mining Association had decided to transfer the laboratory from Birmingham University to Imperial College, South Kensington. The death of Professor Haldane had left the physiological side of the researches into Atmospheric Conditions in Deep and Hot Mines without the supervision of a physiologist, and the Health Advisory Committee had asked Dr C. G. Douglas to undertake this supervision. He had agreed to continue the supervision at Imperial College.

In January 1936, Dr Winstanley presented his progress report on the interaction of long wall workings. Six factors had been considered: method of working and support, order or sequence of working, the direction of advance of faces, the period allowed to elapse between workings, the inclination and depth and nature and thickness of the seam and the intervening strata. Only the first four of these factors were capable of being controlled.

By having due regard to the various factors involved and arranging the method of working accordingly, it was possible to reduce to a minimum the disturbance of the seams so that it was practicable to work seams which would otherwise have been unworkable and better roof and general conditions were obtained. However, a great deal of propaganda work had to be undertaken with the miners to dispel the idea that there was no longer any necessity for close roof support with the improved roof conditions.

In April 1936, Mr Barraclough reported on the work being carried out in South Wales mainly on packing; methods of packing, construction of packing and the petrological characteristics of packing materials. These researches had been carried out in a group of five collieries and showed that improvements in roof control were followed by a reduction in the accident rate from falls of ground.

In May 1936, Mr Hudspeth reported that there was a growing concern and complaint about the increasing noise underground, owing to the introduction of machinery. Investigations were being carried out on the use of noise-reducing materials underground in mines. Satisfactory results had been obtained in preliminary tests on a compressed air turbine driving a gate belt conveyor, and on the exhaust of a reciprocating air haulage engine, using a flexible acoustic blanket of asbestos material as a silencing medium.

By November 1936, earplugs were being tried at Chatterley Whitfield Collieries. A silencer attached to a compressed air exhaust at Askern Colliery had been very satisfactory, and an experiment was being undertaken with lining in an underground engine house at Horden Colliery.[70]

In September 1936, Professor Andrew of the Metallurgical Department, Sheffield University, updated the Board on the effects of heat treatment on wrought iron and mild steel. In a considerable number of instances, failure of haulage gear could be attributed to faults which had developed as a result of the conditions induced by service (overstrain and abrasion) and which could have been prevented by suitable heat treatment. The two simplest forms of heat treatment were annealing and normalising. The former was more commonly practised although, on scientific grounds, normalising was preferable because it tended to avoid the embrittlement of the material which was a feature of incorrect annealing. The use of 1.5% manganese steel obviated many of the difficulties associated with the use and heat treatment of wrought iron and mild steel. Examination of links and hooks made of 1.5% manganese steel after 18 months service without heat treatment had shown the absence of any appreciable deterioration during this period. The aim should be to use weldless haulage draw gear of 1.5% manganese mild steel and to avoid the necessity of annealing.[71]

At the beginning of 1937, the Miners' Welfare Committee had approved the allocation of the amount applied for, £46,169. This included £1,000 for silicosis research. The Welfare Committee made it clear that in agreeing to the £1,000, they would not commit themselves to any increase in that amount.

On 5th January 1937, the Health Advisory Committee had met to consider the decision of the Medical Research Council to turn down the schemes of investigation into pulmonary diseases among coal miners which had been proposed by their Industrial Pulmonary Disease Committee. After hearing a statement from Mr Fudge, the Health Advisory Committee decided to strongly urge the importance of investigations into the industrial and occupational conditions not being delayed while medical research was proceeding into cases of so-called 'pseudo-silicosis'.

By April 1937, the chief investigator for the medical work for investigations into pulmonary diseases among coal miners had been appointed, and the Medical Research Council proposed to hold a joint conference of representatives of the Board and the Council to discuss the programme of the investigation. Messrs Fudge and Jacobs were appointed to represent the Board.

On 4th June 1937, Mr Fudge and Mr Jacobs discussed the investigation of pulmonary diseases at coal mines in South Wales, with representatives of the Medical Research Council, and had been successful in obtaining the Council's concurrence to a study of environmental conditions to be carried out simultaneously with the investigation. Eight mines were selected for preliminary enquiry as to mining conditions and Mr Waldin, a Junior Inspector, had been seconded to carry out the work. His work would inform the selection of the mines and the investigation would start in the early Autumn. At the selected pits, every man would be examined, whether he had any symptoms or not. The South Wales Miners' Federation and the Colliery Companies had agreed full co-operation and assistance. The Council's investigators would require guidance as to the mining conditions, so it was proposed thar Mr Waldin should undertake this work under the general supervision of Mr Yates, the Senior Inspector, to ensure the strict impartiality of the investigation on the mining side.

By October 1937, it had been decided to start the intensive investigation into pulmonary diseases at the Pontyberem-Glynhebog Slant mine. This was a one steam mine with 500 employees and a high incidence of silicosis and (apparently) of other pulmonary diseases. The selection of another mine or mines for comparative purposes would be made later. It was indicated that the cost of reimbursing the workmen for the day's wage they would lose when they were examined would amount, in the case of Pontyberem, to £300-£400. It was eventually agreed that the Board would meet this cost.

Although only one day's work had been lost at Pontyberem during the past six years, owing to lack of trade with France, the colliery had been 'on stop' for a period of five weeks. It was therefore necessary to select another mine for investigation. Ammanford No. 2 mine was selected, and the examinations of the workmen commenced on 7th December.[72]

In February 1937, Mr Hudspeth had been asked to provide further evidence to the Royal Commission on Safety in Coal Mines in connection with haulage. He had been asked to submit a series of suggestions for the prevention of haulage accidents which could be converted into General Regulations, and to work out roughly a provisional scale of weights of rail with corresponding given loads.

Mr Hudspeth also drew the Board's notice to the evidence given by the Colliery Managers' Association relating to the dissemination of results of research. Mr Hudspeth's view was that the criticism was ill-founded, but he was aware that other bodies who had not yet given evidence would be advocating enlargement of the Board's activities in this matter. A memorandum, indicating in what way the Board's information service might be best developed, was sent to the Royal Commission in June 1937.[73]

The Authorities of Imperial College, having agreed to give accommodation for the work at Birmingham University to transfer to South Kensington under the administrative control of Professor Ritson, set up a Joint Committee to supervise the work. The College representatives would be Sir Frank Heath and Professor Ritson. The British Colliery Owners' Association would be represented by Sir Evan Williams, Mr J. Brass and Mr H. Eustace Mitton and the Chairman had asked Mr Hudspeth , as Chief Mining Engineer, to represent the Board. The Board would not be part owners of the Laboratory but would only make grants of a definite amount in aid of specific safety researches.[74]

At the March 1937 meeting, the Chairman was able to announce that the Selection Committee for the appointment of Chief Mining Engineer to replace Mr Hudspeth had recommended that the post be offered to Mr Foster, who was one of H. M. Inspectors of Mines. The Board approved the offer provided satisfactory arrangements could be made with the Mines Department.[75]

The Board continued to struggle with the numbers applying to attend demonstrations at Buxton. It was ultimately decided that for the year 1937, the number of visitors should be limited to a maximum of 6,000, and to give preference to parties from the more remote coalfields. Districts were given a clear intimation that the number of boys to be sent to Buxton would be considerably reduced in future years.[76]

Depth had been one of the factors listed for the attention in the scheme of research into falls of ground approved by the Board in 1930, and Mr Hudspeth was able to report on its effects in April 1937.

Theoretically, vertical pressure in undisturbed strata was proportional to depth, but experimental work indicated that lateral pressure increased at a faster rate, and moreover, this increase varied with different strata. There was greater evidence of lateral pressure in shales than in sandstone at a given depth and this was generally in accordance with observed phenomena underground.

The work undertaken by the North of England Committee on bord and pillar whole workings had shown that the nature of the roof fractures varied with depth. Bending, shear and lateral pressure, in this order of importance, were the cause of fracturing as depth increased.

It had not been possible to measure maximum loads of packs for depths greater than 200 feet, but Dr Hogan had recently designed a dynameter capable of measuring loads up to 3,000 lbs per square inch, which would enable this to be done.

In December 1937, Dr Phillips reported on an experiment that was in progress underground looking at roadside packing in longwall working. At this mine where the Silkstone seam (high quality, low sulphur coal used for coke manufacture) 2' 8" thick was being worked at a depth of 500 yards, considerable trouble had been experienced regarding the support and maintenance of haulage roads and supply gates. The roadways had all been subject to flow lift, collapse of roof and side movement. Various kinds of roadway supports were tried without success, and it was decided to carry out further experiments with road packing. The management were persuaded to adopt single packing in one tunnel (No. 7) and double packing in another tunnel (No. 8). The experiment had been going for some time, and experience had shown the benefits of adopting double packing.[77]

Underground observation of derailment of colliery tubs had not been able to identify the primary course so experiments on scale models with nine vehicular variations had been undertaken. Only two of the variations, depth of the wheel flange and the length of the wheelbase, had a considerable effect on derailment.

In October 1937, Mr Foster gave a resume of the investigations carried out during the last five years under Professor Andrew's direction concerning the quality and condition of the material of broken or defective haulage gear sent in from collieries. Over 250 samples had been examined. In most of the instances, faults contributing to failure could be classified under three headings: the material was primarily deficient, deficiency arose in the fabrication of the unit, and service caused excessive deterioration.[78]

In October 1937, after their Chairman had had a discussion with the Secretary for Mines, the Welfare Committee had decided to suggest to the Board that a joint Sub-Committee should be formed to discuss the Board's research programme 'with reference to the extent to which they dealt with problems that might have a bearing upon other questions besides that of personal safety', and nominated Mr J. T. Browne, Professor Collis and Mr Lawther to serve on the Sub-Committee. The Board accepted the Welfare Committee's suggestion and nominated Mr D. H. Currer Briggs, Mr T. Cape and Mr F. Edmond to serve on the Sub-Committee.

In January 1938, the Welfare Committee approved the allocation of £47,233 for 1938/9 subject to the report of the joint Sub-Committee of the Miners' Welfare Committee and the Board. At the request of the Chairman of the Board, Mr Hudspeth and Mr Lee had agreed to serve on the Sub-Committee in place of Major Currer Briggs and Mr Tom Cape. The first meeting was held on 15th February 1938. At the meeting, the Welfare Committee were seeking from the Board a method for reassuring the Committee on the use made of the grants. It was therefore agreed that the Joint Sub-Committee would meet to discuss the draft estimates and programmes before they were submitted to the Mines Department.[79]

More than 500 men had been examined at Ammanford Colliery as part of the research into pulmonary diseases among coal miners by March 1938. The environmental studies had been in progress for some weeks and, although the owners had decided to close down the pit, they had agreed to defer this long enough for this part of the work to be completed.[80]

In March 1938, the Board were still of the opinion that a full-time Protective Equipment Officer was essential to carry on the work. It was agreed to ask the Mines Department to second a Junior Inspector for this work for a period not exceeding three years. The Mines Department were unable to second a Junior Inspector, as they were abnormally short of experienced Junior Inspectors, but a Junior Inspector was due to retire in June. It was proposed that the post should be advertised, and this Inspector should be interviewed with any other suitable applicants. Mr Cunliffe, the investigator to the Lancashire and Cheshire Safety in Mines Research Committee, was appointed to the post and he commenced his duties on 1st September 1938.[81]

In July 1938, the Board considered its future policy on demonstrations at Buxton, particularly on the question of the visits of boys. After considerable discussion it was decided that 2,000 boys should be accepted for 1939 and that the organisers should be informed accordingly. It was also decided that parties of adults should not visit the station several years in succession.[82]

In May 1938, Mr Foster reported on the progress made on the research on 'strata' movements induced in the vicinity of the coal face. Records had been obtained showing that the rapid roof and floor convergence at the coal face, set up by cutting operations, originated well in advance of the coal cutting machine. This rapid disturbance affected the most critical part of the coal face, between the last row of props and the face. The impulsive movement set up by coal cutting was transmitted to about twenty three yards behind the coal face.[83]

In September 1938, an update on the researches on roadside packing in longwall working was given. The roadways in which the experiments had been carried out had now advanced a further 300 yards and more complete results showed that 'double packing' had been a great success except in one case.

Tests to determine the widths of packs and wastes in double packing for thin and thick seams at different depths, inclinations and roof and floor conditions were being made.

Mr Foster visited two of the pits of Messrs Bolsover Colliery Company Ltd. in October 1938, where roadways were being severely crushed. Different thicknesses of ripping (removal of the rock above the coal seam and setting rings (arches) to raise the height of the gate or the road as the coal face advances), widths of packs and methods of support had been tried but these did not fulfil the essential conditions of 'double packing' and consequently did not conflict with the evidence of success obtained in the experiments with this type of packing. Arrangements had been made to carry out experiments with 'double packing' in the Top Hard Seam at Clipstone Colliery.[84]

The Coal Mines Act 1911 required a 'back-stay or other suitable contrivance' to be provided and attached to ascending tubs, to prevent them running back, on all mechanised haulage roads, except endless rope and endless chain, where the gradient exceeded one in twelve.

The backstops in use in various coalfields varied widely in almost every detail and, as a preliminary to an experimental investigation, representative types were obtained. Seventeen examples had been obtained and grouped under four headings. Two methods of testing had been used and the preliminary results had shown the value of a full study.[85]

In November 1938, four District reports dealing with the causes of derailment of tubs in underground haulage were presented. In the North of England, where accidents to boys were of special importance, derailments in horse haulage operations were being studied.

The investigations had shown that the percentage of derailments due to the condition of the track were considerably higher on hand and horse haulage tracks than those where tubs were mechanically hauled. Good tracks were an essential requirement to satisfactory operations, and, for all classes of haulage, the use of fishplates was recommended as being necessary to maintain good points and assist alignment.

In South Wales, an analysis of derailment on direct rope haulage showed that over two-thirds of the recorded derailments occurred at points and turns. It was suggested that the principle dimensions of points and crossings should be standardised.

Tub design was also an important factor contributing to derailments. Good results had been obtained at Buxton with the use of slightly deeper wheel flanges.[86]

In July 1938, Dr Wheeler expressed his concern about the progress being made in fundamental research, particularly on explosions, owing to the reduction in staff. Whereas formerly knowledge was in advance of possible practical applications, it was now behind and the Board was not able to give the industry the information it demanded in areas of coal dust explosions, flameproof mining electrical gear, and mine lighting. Extra accommodation was required at the Sheffield station and, at Buxton, the most important need was for explosion galleries of adequate size for work on coal dust explosions.

In September 1938, Dr Wheeler presented his detailed proposals for both Research Stations. Mr Fudge pointed out that the Report of the Royal Commission would be available in the near future, and this might have a considerable effect both on the future work of the Board and also the work of the Mines Department Testing Stations. He therefore suggested that the best programme of work that could be carried out with existing facilities should be drawn up giving any additional costs and staff required. Additionally, in order to seek the solution of difficulties at certain collieries with stone dusting to the requisite standard at loading gates and other places where coal dust was made or accumulated rapidly, the Board should co-operate with the Industry in their study of these matters in the pit.

The Board were unable to come to any conclusion in October as to how to proceed with research on coal dust explosions using the current facilities at Buxton. In November 1938, the Board agreed to ask the Secretary for Mines to consider the appointment of a small committee to consider the issue.[87]

In January 1939, the Board discussed the Report of the Royal Commission on Safety in Coal Mines as far as it affected its work. There were five recommendations made by the Royal Commission to consider.

Firstly, it was recommended that a research organisation should be an integral part of the Mines Department with arrangements for interchange and close co-operation between its staff, the staff of the Department's Testing Stations and the Inspectorate. Secondly, the Board, while retaining its constitution would be consultative and advisory instead of administrative. Thirdly, the choice of subjects in the annual programme of work would fall definitely on the Secretary for Mines, who would be informed by expert staff. Fourthly, the Mines Department and the Research Board would provide, as far as possible, for co-operation and co-ordination between all the organisations engaged in research. Finally, the Board should confine its 'safety propaganda' to the 'advertisement' of its own results and should leave the business of general instructional work on accident prevention and other safety propaganda to some other organisation set up specifically for the purpose.[88]

At the Board's meeting in March, the Chairman was in receipt of a letter from the Secretary for Mines stating that he proposed to set up a Departmental Committee under the chairmanship of Sir Henry Walker with the following terms of reference:

'To review and co-ordinate the development of measure for preventing, suppressing, and/or collecting coal dust produced at mines in the mechanised working and transport of coal, to arrange for any further investigations that may be found necessary, and to recommend from time to time what measures can be effectively taken or required'.

Dr Wheeler's proposal to provide additional accommodation at Sheffield was considered in March 1939, in the light of the Royal Commission's recommendations. While it was realised that the requirements of the Mines Department Testing Station, currently housed in the same building, might be increased as a result of the recommendations of the Royal Commission, there was an urgent need for an additional storey of the existing building. It was agreed that Dr Wheeler's proposal should be forwarded to the Welfare Committee with a view to obtaining a grant of about £5,000 to cover the cost of the proposed extension.

The proposal was considered with the Board's estimates for 1939/40 at the Miner's Welfare Committee's meeting held on 21st March 1939. The Miners' Welfare Committee agreed to allocate £48,834 to cover the balance of the expenditure of the Board up to the limit of £63,000 after allowing for the income received from other sources. However, the Welfare Committee were not able to make grants from the Welfare Fund to cover expenditure in excess of £63,000 so the application for £5,000 to meet the cost of an extension to the Sheffield Research Station was refused.[89]

Work had continued on roof movements involving machine mining. Convergence records had been obtained at the coal face for complete cycles of work showing relative movements set up by each face operation. One rather persistent feature was the much greater and more rapid convergence taking place during cutting than during coal filling, inferring that the roof had been deprived during coal cutting of most of the support offered by the uncut coal. If this proved accurate, two major points would have to be considered: a method of support to cover the cutter tract which could be further reinforced immediately after cutting had ceased, and the method of extracting the cut coal and loading it into conveyors. South Staffordshire Committee had been studying the problem of the influence of packing in strata movement set up by coal cutting,and had concluded that cutting before packing resulted in a greater height reduction than cutting afterwards.[90]

Following on from the preliminary work undertaken in 1938 on back-stays or drags, a report on an investigation to determine why back-stays used in mines in compliance with the Coal Mines Act were sometimes inefficient and failed to arrest runaway tubs was presented in April 1939. Drags currently in use with a pin and forked end for attachment to the drawbar hole were found to be superior to the three other groups of drags, as they could not be over-ridden without fracture of the drawbar or back-stay, which needed to be robust to avoid bending or fracture. A back-stay had been designed, applying the knowledge gained from observing the four groups of back-stay which coupled to the drawbar so as to project beneath the tubs, so preventing over-riding. Satisfactory results had been obtained with the new back-stay.[91]

In June 1939, Sir Edward Troup resigned as Chairman for reasons of ill health. He consented to continue until after the summer recess, pending the appointment of his successor. Sir Malcolm Delevingne was invited to be Chairman of the Board by the Secretary for Mines, and he took up the Chairmanship in September 1939.[92]

With the outbreak of the War in September 1939, the Secretary for Mines had found it necessary, after consultation with the members individually, to transfer the services of four of the District Investigators and the Protective Equipment Officer to work of urgent importance with the Mine Department in maintaining essential supplies for carrying on the work at the collieries.

The Board took the view that it would be unwise to permit their highly experienced and expert organisation to be dispersed. There were three kinds of service the organisation might be able to render during the war: continuance of the work bearing directly on safety in mines, research into practical problems raised by the war in connection with the coal mining industry, and research into war problems not connected with the industry. However, it was recognised that there would be individual applications from staff to join the forces or take up other war work.[93]

At the end of October 1939, Professor Wheeler died. This was a huge loss to the Board, as Professor Wheeler had been Director of Research since 1923. It was felt inadvisable to attempt to make an appointment of a full-time Director of Research, in view of the difficulties and uncertainties created by the war. The Board accordingly decided that, for the time being, Dr Coward, Mr Foster and Mr Poulton should be in charge of their respective spheres of work under the general direction of a Governing Committee of the Board. The Governing Committee's function would be to see that the decisions and policy of the Board were effectively carried out, and it would not trespass upon the general authority and control of the Board itself. The Board appointed the Chairman, Mr Edmond and Mr Hudspeth to be on the Governing Committee and decided that the Committee should meet monthly either at Sheffield or Buxton.[94]

The Board seems to have only met twice in 1940. At the February 1940 meeting, they considered the matters dealt with by the Governing Committee, which had met on 29th December 1939 and 31st January 1940, and gave approval to the decisions taken at these meetings.

An Advisory Research Council of the Chemical Society were able to disseminate problems of national importance to universities and technical

Schools , which owing to pressure of work, could not be undertaken by official research bodies; Professor Rideal, one of the Board's members, suggested Dr Coward might seek assistance through this source for the coal dust programmes such as the research on wetting agents.

The proposed electrical research programmes, drawn up by Drs Coward and Allsop in consultation with Mr Horsley of the Mines Department and Mr Bell of the Wigan Coal Corporation, had been agreed by the Governing Committee at their last meeting and were then endorsed by the Board.

The Miners' Welfare Commission had decided to dispense with detailed estimates for the financial year 1940/41, and to permit savings effected during the year 1939/40 and 1940/41 to be retained by the Board as a reserve fund towards later meeting the cost of the developments held up because of the war.

The estimates for 1940/41 came to a total of £63,000, with the Miners' Welfare Committee making a grant of £45,222 to bring the income of the Board up to this figure.

In December 1940, the Board considered the report of the Governing Committee for the period February to November 1940. It emerged that there was no specific co-ordination of the coal dust programmes, but Mr J. Iron Graham was collecting information for the Colliery Owners' Research Association and Captain P. S. Hay was doing likewise for the Mines Department.[95]

The Board met twice in 1941. At the first meeting in April, the Board considered the future of Buxton Research Station. The Welfare Commission architects had reported on the bad condition of the existing building, which it had been suggested should be repaired pending a general scheme of rebuilding after the war.

The Governing Committee had expressed a view that a field research station was a permanent necessity and there were good reasons why the Buxton site should be retained. However, the Committee considered that Buxton should be purely a field research station and that the remainder of the research work should be relocated elsewhere. The Board agreed that it would be preferable for the laboratory work to be continued at Sheffield.

The Governing Committee had had to make changes to staff arrangements following the retirement of Mr H. T. Foster, the Chief Mining Engineer. The Committee were mindful of the Board's decision to appoint a Director when circumstances permitted. Dr Phillips had been appointed in the interim as liaison officer with the District Committees, and to co-ordinate the reduced work that was being undertaken.

In July 1941, Dr Douglas attended the Board's meeting to give a brief account of the 'silicosis' investigation in the South Wales coalfield by the Industrial Pulmonary Disease Committee.

The South Wales coalfield had been selected for the investigation, as it was an area where silicosis was a cause of various and widespread disability, more particularly in the anthracite regions. The pulmonary condition found in South Wales' mines differed from the 'classical' silicosis met with in the coal mines, in the potteries and sand blasters.

The cause of the silicosis apparently lay in the type of dust breathed in by the workers. It did not necessarily follow that the coal dust was harmful, but it might well be that the mineral constituents other than the coal, both in the coal mass itself and in the adjacent strata might prove to be the main cause of the trouble.[96]

The Board met only once in 1942. The Board heard an account of the Governing Committee's administration of the research station since the last meeting in July 1941.

The draft of the Special Report on Coal Dust Explosions called for by the Secretary for Mines was discussed at length.

The Miners' Welfare Commission were only able to make a grant of £31,980 for safety in mines research for 1942/43. The Commission regretted that they were prevented from making a larger grant but the estimate of the receipts of the Welfare General Fund showed a continuation of the heavy reduction which had been experienced progressively during the last three years.[97]

The Board continued to receive annual grants from the Miners' Welfare Fund (£33,800 in 1943, and £20,000 in 1944 and 1945) but there are no further minutes of the Board's meetings after May 1942.

The Coal Industry Nationalisation Act 1946 specifically placed the responsibility for safety and health research under the Ministry of Fuel and Power, and provided for the funds for such researches to be wholly met out of the monies provided by Parliament.[98]

SEVEN

EDUCATION

The Central Committee, early after it was established, recognised that they would need assistance in identifying the then current availability of mining education, and where the Fund could be most effectively spent. They therefore consulted with the Board of Education and the University Grants Committee and, as a result of this consultation, the University Grants Committee appointed a Mining Sub-Committee (see Chapter 2).

The Mining Sub-Committee was appointed on 27th April 1922, and completed its report on 17th November 1922. They had been asked to enquire into the existing facilities for mining education at Universities and Technical Schools, and then to recommend the principles on which future spending might be made.

They held six meetings where they considered comprehensive statements indicating the nature and scope of the complete organisation of mining education provided by Local Education Authorities, at technical schools, colleges, universities and university colleges, which were submitted by the Board of Education, the Scottish Education Department and the University Grants Committee. Nine representatives of Institutions and of Authorities concerned in existing educational work in mining areas attended meetings of the Sub-Committee in order to assist them with their intimate knowledge of the organisation and aims of mining education. Mr W. G. Nott-Bower, the Secretary of the Miners' Welfare Committee, also attended some of the meetings in order to preserve a connection with the body ultimately responsible for the administration of the Miners' Welfare Fund.

The general result of the Sub-Committee's survey of the then position of mining education was that better and wider facilities were called for in every grade of mining education.

In making their recommendations, they dealt with them in relation to the existing educational facilities for coal miners. These facilities varied in different areas, as in some counties the scheme was more comprehensive than in others. The more complete and better organised type of scheme was taken as a standard to which it was hoped, with the help of the Miners' Welfare Fund, would become general. Their recommendations were made under nine headings.

Junior part-time courses combined general education and culture with matters bearing on coal mining and were intended for boys who had just left school. The courses usually extended over two years and the ages of the students ranged from 14 to 16 or 17. Subjects included English, Practical Mathematics and Drawing (treated as one subject), and Elementary Science. The classes were usually conducted in elementary school premises, which was not considered to be ideal. In well-organised areas, suitable apparatus was provided for demonstration purposes. In some places, classes of Junior Course standard were provided for older students.

The instruction in Junior Courses prepared the students to proceed to the Senior part-time courses held at senior centres which served a group of Junior Course schools. The course would extend over three years and was intended to prepare the ground for the study of technical subjects in the Advanced Courses.

Schemes of technical education in well-organised areas usually included part-time courses of instruction for girls and women. In addition to subjects of a cultural character intended to widen the interest and outlook of the girls, practical instruction was provided in subjects directly connected with the home such as home-management, cookery, sick-nursing and different kinds of needlecraft.

Although many Local Education Authorities provided facilities as outlined above, the Sub-Committee recognised that the funds available to Local Authorities and grants through the Board of Education or Scottish Education Department were not such as to enable them to adequately and efficiently maintain and develop these part-time courses of instruction. District Welfare Committees had already recommended grants for such educational purposes, and the Sub-Committee saw this source of funding to be the most appropriate. However, they did discuss the possibility of grants being made from the General Fund to enable Local Authorities to build and equip small mining schools at centres where they were much needed.

Advanced part-time courses were intended normally for students from 19 or 20 to 23 or over. For such students, free admission to the Advanced courses was provided in many areas, together with a travelling allowance where necessary.

Though not of University standard, these courses required accommodation and equipment suitable for advanced instruction and individual practical work, and were usually held at well-equipped technical or mining schools. Schools of this type prepared candidates for the statutory examinations for Mine Managers 1st and 2nd Class Certificates for Competency. Students could also be able to proceed to a University or Technical College doing work of University standard. Advanced part-time schools were linked up with Senior part-time schools and, sometimes, individual schools provided Senior and Advanced courses.

Whole-time courses of University standard were provided by existing institutions in ten areas. Mining Degrees and Diplomas were awarded as a result of satisfactory attendance and passing examinations. Both the degrees and diplomas of an institution approved for this purpose by the Mines Department were accepted in lieu of two of the five years of practical experience otherwise required of the candidates for Mine Managers' Certificates (subject to the condition that a certain amount of time in each year of the course was spent at a colliery).

The institutions which then provided mining education of university standard fell into two categories: institutions which granted degrees (Durham University, Leeds University, Sheffield University, Manchester University, Birmingham University, Edinburgh University, Herriot-Watt College, Edinburgh, Glasgow University and the Royal Technical College, Glasgow and University College of South Wales and Monmouthshire, University of Wales) and institutions which did not themselves grant degrees but where the students presented themselves for the External Degree of London University (University College, Nottingham and Wigan and District Mining and Technical College).

The Wigan and District Mining and Technical College was not directly controlled by a Local Education Authority, but was subsidised by Lancashire County Council and Wigan County Borough Council whose representatives formed a majority of the Governing Body. Its students predominantly came from all parts of the Lancashire and North Wales coalfields. The South Wales and Monmouthshire School of Mines (at Treforest and Crumlin) carried a full-time diploma course in conjunction with the University College of South Wales and Monmouthshire. The School of Mines had been established and was managed by the principle coal owners in the South Wales and Monmouthshire coalfield, at whose sole expense it was supported and maintained.

The Sub-Committee were of the opinion that financial support for both Advanced part-time courses and full-time courses of University standard ought to come from the General Fund. As the future of the Fund, at that time, was not guaranteed beyond the statutory five years, it was suggested that any grant made should be for buildings and equipment.

There were two main categories of teachers engaged in organised schemes of mining education. The first included the person who was primarily a teacher by profession working in the daytime either in a local elementary or secondary school. Part-time courses for these teachers had, from time to time, been provided by various County Education Authorities for their own areas or by the Board of Education.

The second category of teacher included those who were teachers of mining technology. These part-time teachers often worked in some official capacity during the day at a local colliery. With the growth of part-time and whole-time courses of mining education, the demand for whole-time teachers with suitable practical training and experience would increase. The provision of residential or summer courses for teachers of this second category was recommended as suitable for aid from the General Fund.

Unfortunately, only a minority of the mining community availed themselves of the facilities offered. The majority received no further education than that of elementary school. This was regrettable as, so long as boys and men employed in the mines were ignorant of the elementary principles which underlay the precautions taken to guard against danger, the ever-present dangers of the mines would never be entirely overcome.

Mining communities were often segregated, and the miners did not come into contact with workers in other industries. This all tended towards an outlook which was narrow in comparison with the general body of workers in and about large towns, where there was a variety of occupations. The Sub-Committee believed that the provision of suitable lectures in mining areas would not only reach large numbers of miners who might not otherwise be exposed to any kind of educational influence, but would tend to lead many to seek the benefits to be derived from attendance at regular organised classes. It was felt that the District Committees and Local Education Authorities had a role to play in the provision of these lectures.

The Sub-Committee did consider the question of recommending a grant from the General Fund for the provision of scholarships and exhibitions for miners. They were aware that several Local Education Authorities offered scholarships tenable at a University for degree and diploma courses to all types of technical students, including mining, but there were also scholarships open to mining students only. However, considerable development and improvement in the general education of miners was needed to be secured before any increase in the provision of university scholarships should be considered. The Sub-Committee were aware that the allowances attached to Local Authority university scholarships in some districts were insufficient, although the number was satisfactory.

In mining departments of universities and institutions of university rank, research work was undertaken into matters that had an intimate connection with the problems of the mining industry. The Sub-Committee understood that such work would be subsidised by the Miners' Welfare Committee from another part of the General Fund, so they offered no recommendation under this heading.[1]

Although the Central Committee had received the Sub-Committee's report at the end of 1922 and copies had been circulated to District Committees and Local Education Authorities, the Central Committee had chosen to wait until they had all the facts before them before making the decisions about how the money earmarked from the General Fund might be allocated.

In Chapter 2 (pp41–42, 47–49), an outline has been given as to how the Committee set up the mechanisms by which allocations for Mining Education were to be made in 1924, but a more detailed description is given here.

The twenty-five districts had been grouped into eight geographical groups. Each group contained both districts and educational authorities as follows:

Group I. North-Eastern Area
Districts: Northumberland and Durham
Education Authorities: Armstrong College (University of Durham)
                                 Counties of Northumberland and Durham
                                 County Boroughs of Newcastle, Gateshead,
                                 South Shields and Sunderland

Group II. North Western Area
Sub-Group A:
District: Cumberland
Education Authority: County of Cumberland
Sub-Group B:
District: Lancashire and Cheshire
Education Authorities: University of Manchester
                                 Counties of Lancashire and Cheshire
                                 City of Manchester
                                 County Boroughs of Bolton, Burley, St Helens and
                                 College)
Sub-Group C:
District: North Wales
Education Authorities: Counties of Denbigh and Flint

Group III. North-Midland Area
Districts: West Yorkshire, South Yorkshire, Nottinghamshire, Derbyshire, South Derbyshire (part)
Education Authorities: Universities of Leeds and Sheffield, Nottingham
                                 University College
                                 Counties of West Riding of Yorkshire,
                                 Nottinghamshire and Derbyshire
                                 County Boroughs of Barnsley, Dewsbury,
                                 Huddersfield, Leeds, Rotherham,
                                 Sheffield, Wakefield and Nottingham

Group IV. South Midland Area
   Sub-Group A:
   Districts: South Derbyshire (part), Leicestershire
   Education Authority: County of Leicestershire
   Sub-Group B:
   Districts: North Staffordshire, Cannock Chase, South Staffordshire
   (including East Warwickshire)
   Education Authorities: University of Birmingham
                         Counties of Staffordshire and Worcestershire
                         County Boroughs of Stoke-on-Trent, Walsall and
                         Dudley
Sub-Group C:
   District: Warwickshire
   Education Authorities: University of Birmingham
                         County of Warwickshire
Sub-Group D:
   District: Shropshire
   Education Authorities: University of Birmingham
                         County of Shropshire

Group V. Western Area
   Sub-Group A:
   District: Forest of Dean
   Education Authority: County of Gloucestershire
   Sub-Group B:
   Districts: Bristol, Somerset
   Education Authorities: Merchant Venturers' Technical College, Bristol,
                         County of Somerset
                         County Borough of Bristol
   Sub-Group C:
   Districts: South Wales and Monmouthshire
   Education Authorities: University of Wales, University of South Wales and
                         Monmouthshire,
                         Cardiff, South Wales School of Mines
                         Counties of Brecon, Carmarthen, Glamorgan and
                         Monmouth
                         County Boroughs of Swansea and Merthyr Tydville
                         Urban District of Rhondda

Group VI. South Eastern
    District: Kent
    Education Authority: County of Kent

Scotland
Group VII. West Scotland
    Districts: Lanarkshire (less Linlithgowshire), Ayr
    Education Authorities: University of Glasgow, Royal Technical College,
                Glasgow
                County Authorities of Ayr, Dunbarton, Dumfries,
                Lanark, Renfrew and Stirling
                Urban Authority of Glasgow

Group VIII. East Scotland
    Districts: Fife and Clackmannan, The Lothians, Lanark (Linlithgowshire)
    Education Authorities: University of Edinburgh, Heriot-Watt College
                County Authorities of Clackmannan, Edinburgh,
                Fife, Haddington, Kinross and Linlithgow
                Burgh Authority of Edinburgh

No allocations were made in Northumberland and Durham (Group I) in 1924, as not much progress had been made in the direction of formulating a comprehensive scheme. The number of working miners in this coalfield was very nearly one-fifth of the total number in the country, so approximately £88,565 was available for mining education in this area. However, the provision for the lower rungs needed careful reorganisation and extensive improvements and developments were needed before definite allocations could be made from the General Fund for educational purposes in this area.

In Cumberland (Group II, Sub-Group A), there was no organised scheme of mining education so the education authority needed to take steps to organise lower-rung centres before any assistance could be given to establish a suitable senior centre.

A general report on the Lancashire Coalfield (Group II, Sub-Group B) had been published by the Board of Education in which a lack of definite organisation for mining education had been identified. A condition for their allocation was that steps had to be taken to reorganise the provision for lower rungs to the satisfaction of the Board of Education. The condition was accepted, and the Board confirmed that Lancashire had made satisfactory arrangements for the future.

The total amount of the allocation for this sub-group was £38,920.4s.6d, of which £1,420.4s.6d had been confirmed for the improvement of equipment at Burnley Technical School. The provisional allocations were for an extension and equipment of the Technical School at Leigh, an extension and equipment at Wigan Mining and Technical School, the establishment and equipment for the proposed mining school at St Helens and assistance in the equipping of the mining department of the Manchester Municipal College.

In the special report published by the Board of Education, the two authorities in North Wales (Group II, Sub-Group C) were urged to co-operate with a view to establishing an advanced centre available for both, to be fed from suitable senior centres. The application that was received did not indicate any prospect of co-operation on these lines.

In Group III (West Yorkshire, South Yorkshire, Nottingham, Derbyshire and South Derbyshire (part)), the standard of the organisation of mining education was very high, with very good co-operation between county authorities. This was not so for the County Boroughs.

Two confirmed allocations were made to the University of Leeds (additional apparatus and equipment) and University College, Nottingham (additional equipment) and a provisional allocation to Sheffield University towards building new laboratories. The allocation to Leeds was approved, with some reluctance. The Central Committee thought that it was a pity that two universities as close to one another as Leeds and Sheffield should maintain independent mining departments. The centre of the coalfield in this area was moving further and further away from Leeds, so Sheffield was the obvious centre for university work.

£101,000 was the total amount allocated to the local authorities in Group III, of which £8,000 had been confirmed for the provision of additional equipment at the Technical School at Batley, West Riding of Yorkshire Education Authority (£2,000) and the provision of equipment for the mining department at the new Technical School at Chesterfield, Derbyshire Education Authority (£6,000).

The senior and advanced work in Group IV, Sub-Group A was concentrated at Coalville, Leicestershire and a confirmed allocation of £4,298.6s was made towards the establishment and equipping of a new mining institute at that centre. The first portion of the centre had been opened by Mr Shinwell, Secretary for Mines, on 5th July 1924 and was the first new educational centre opened under the Miners' Welfare Scheme. The preliminary allocation of £3,200 for the building at Coalville was originally made from the District Funds of Leicestershire (£3,000) and South Derbyshire (£200). The £3,200 had been reimbursed back to the Districts from the General Fund.

Mining education in North Staffordshire and South Staffordshire (Group IV, Sub-Group B) were separately organised with North Staffordshire requiring some reorganisation and improvement of the lower rungs. This was now in

The Mining Institute at Coalville, Leicestershire

progress so a provisional allocation of £10,000 had been made towards the extension of the mining department of the Central School of Science and Technology at Stoke-on-Trent to be made available at the beginning of 1926. In South Staffordshire, a provisional allocation of £12,000 had been made for the immediate erection of one wing of the proposed technical institute at Hednesford and a confirmed allocation of £500 for additional equipment at the Technical College, Dudley, which had previously been made from South Staffordshire District Fund.

In Warwickshire (Group IV, Sub-Group C), a confirmed allocation of £5,733 was made for the building and equipping of the County Mining School at Nuneaton. An allocation of £3,000 for building the extension was originally made from the District Fund on the recommendation of Warwickshire District Committee so the £3,000 represented a transfer from the General Fund to the District Fund.

The Salop Education Committee (Group IV, Sub-Group D) had obtained funds for the erection of a technical institute at Oakengate so a provisional allocation of £1,500 was made towards the equipment of the mining department of the proposed institute.

In the Forest of Dean (Group V, Sub-Group A) there was a pressing need for a centre for senior and advanced work, so a confirmed allocation of £6,000 was made for the establishment and equipment of a Mining School at Cinderford.

The County Mining School, Nuneaton, Mechanical and Electrical Engineering Laboratory

This allocation exceeded considerably the proportion of the amount (£2,710) to this district for mining education based on number of miners so the allocation was supplemented by a grant from the Reserve (see Chapter 2, p48).

No allocations were made in Bristol and Somerset (Group V, Sub-Group B) as facilities for mining education had not yet been organised.

A special report on mining education in South Wales and Monmouthshire had been published by the Board of Education in May 1924, which made it clear that the money available to be spent in Group V, Sub-Group C from the General Fund should be concentrated on the provision of buildings suitable for the accommodation of senior courses. Until there was evidence of reorganisation being undertaken along the lines of recommendations made in the special report, only one confirmed allocation of £3,000 could be made to Monmouthshire Education Authority for purchasing an existing building at Pontlanfraith, for conversion into a senior centre.

The Kent coalfield (Group VI) had hardly developed sufficiently for any special provision for higher education for miners, and their proportion of the money designated for mining education only amounted to £710.

Shortly before the end of 1923, the District Welfare Committees of Fife, Lothian and Lanark had recommended that a sum of £50,000 should be provided from the General Fund and invested to establish a scholarship scheme in Scotland. During the early part of 1924, the Committee considered this proposal alongside the applications they had received from universities, technical colleges and local authorities in Scotland for grants towards buildings and equipment. The total for Scotland would not be more than £50,000 and the priority was buildings and equipment.

In West Scotland (Group VII), the Committee were disappointed to find duplication of staff and equipment and no practical co-operation between the University of Glasgow and the Royal Technical College, Glasgow. There was little hesitation in making a confirmed allocation of £2,250 for the equipment of the mining department at the Royal Technical College, which appeared to cater particularly for the needs of the working miner, being the normal centre of advanced work to which students proceeded from the local authority centres in the western parts of the Scottish coalfield. The confirmed allocation of £1,520 to the University of Glasgow for equipment for the mining department was viewed as barely justified, but it did result in very definite progress being made in the direction of extending co-operation with the Royal Technical College.

A confirmed allocation of £980 was also made to Hamilton Academy Technical School, County of Lanark. Higher courses at the School had temporarily been suspended due to a lack of suitable apparatus and this allocation would make good this deficiency.

In the East of Scotland (Group VIII), a very satisfactory system of co-operation had developed between the University of Edinburgh, the Heriot Watt College and the local education authorities. Three provisional allocations were made in this Group. £8,000 was allocated to the Heriot Watt College towards the building and equipment of a new mining laboratories at the College subject to an equal sum being raised locally. A second allocation of £8,000 was made to Fifeshire Education Authority for the extension and equipment of the Technical Schools at Kirkcaldy and Buckhaven. The third allocation of £5,000 was made to Linlithgowshire Education Authority for the establishment and equipment of the mining department of the proposed Technical School at Bathgate.[2]

Slower progress was made in 1925 in allocating the money that had been earmarked for education from the General Fund, but the Committee were able to increase the amount earmarked from £475,000 to £500,000 (see Chapter 2, p55). The Committee however were disappointed in the slow progress in converting provisional allocations made in 1924 into confirmed allocations.

In Group I (North-Eastern Area), Northumberland Authority had proposed establishing four or five senior centres, starting with one in Ashington district. They were informed that grants would be available for at least two centres, but they decided later in the year that the depression in the industry made it inopportune to proceed. On the other hand, Durham Authorities expressed a definite intention of establishing six or eight senior centres, starting probably with West Stanley, Bishop Auckland and Wellfield districts. A provisional allocation of £6,000 for the West Stanley centre was made.

There was no development in Cumberland, Lancashire and Cheshire or North Wales (Group II, North-Western area).

In Group III (North Midland Area), the authorities had been very active but the money available was far from sufficient to meet the applications received. The Committee were therefore unable to promise any assistance to the County Borough of Rotherham towards the mining department at the technical college, which they proposed to erect at a total cost of £56,000. The County Borough of Barnsley had already been promised a provisional allocation of £15,000 in 1924, and pending the preparation of final plans for the proposed new building, a sum of £960 had been spent on buying equipment for the existing centre which would be available for transfer for the new building later.

In West Riding of Yorkshire Authority, the extension of the technical school at Mexborough was already in progress, the Authority having added £600 from their own funds to meet the excess cost over the allocation of £2,250. Plans were well forward for the comprehensive centre at Dinnington, and subject to the approval of the Board of Education, the Authority proposed to make a substantial contribution, as the estimated cost of the building and equipment was £25,000 compared with an allocation of £17,500.

However, the Committee were unable to promise any assistance for the erection of permanent premises at Wombwell similar to those at Dinnington, or for equipment for the proposed extension at Doncaster due to lack of funds.

In Nottinghamshire, it had been decided to proceed with the new building at Mansfield on a much more ambitious scale increasing the total cost to £44,000. The Committee increased the original allocation of £9,700 by making a contribution of £500 towards the cost of the gymnasium (£5,000), provided the Board of Education agreed to the inclusion of the gymnasium in the approved plan. The cost of the senior centre planned for Worksop had increased so the provisional allocation was raised to £9,800 (increase of £4,500).

In Group IV (South Midland Area) the principal new development was the building of the coal-treatment laboratory and provision of suitable heavy equipment at Birmingham University. £1,692 was allocated for erecting the building and £4,700 for equipment.

The provisional allocation for the extension of the mining department of the Central School of Science and Technology at Stoke-on-Trent (County of Staffordshire) was increased to £12,000, on the understanding that a common room and mess room for students was added to the original plan.

Coal-Treatment Laboratory, Birmingham University

In Warwickshire, the total cost of the extension to the County Mining School at Nuneaton exceeded the estimate by nearly £1,160, owing to unforeseen expenditure mainly in connection with the foundations for the heavy machinery. £900 was added to the original allocation.

In Group V (Western Area), the Mining School at Cinderford in the Forest of Dean Sub-Group was completed in the autumn, and opened by Lord Chelmsford in November 1925.

In South Wales, numerous joint meetings of the authorities concerned at last resulted in some measure of agreement so it was hoped that it would be possible to make definite progress in deciding on the most suitable senior centres to meet the immediate needs of the coalfield. However, the sum available, after allowing for work of university standard, was barely sufficient for the erection and equipment of 15 centres. The Board of Education Inspectors in South Wales had put forward recommendations for the most useful distribution of centres, and this was being considered by the joint committee of authorities.

In Group VII (West Scotland), the most important provisional allocation was for the development of the mining department of the proposed new technical school at Coatbridge in Lanarkshire. The estimated cost for the whole building was £81,000 and £19,000 for equipment. No part of the building was to be solely for mining students, but it was expected that one quarter of the total

The Forest of Dean Mining School (Cinderford)

attending would be mining students. The sum available to the Committee for allocation would not allow for more than £20,000, and that was only if no other development in mining education in the county was contemplated.

In Dumfries, £600 was provisionally allocated for adding suitable laboratory accommodation to the secondary school at Sanquhar, together with £150 for providing the necessary permanent equipment. This allocation was made on the understanding that provision would be made for third year courses to be affiliated with the Royal Technical College, Glasgow.

In 1924, the Committee had promised to provide for the new mining laboratory at Heriot-Watt College, Edinburgh, a sum equal to that contributed locally subject to a maximum limit of £8,000. Sufficient money had been raised locally in 1925 for this promise to be confirmed as soon as the plans for the new laboratories had been approved by the Scottish Education Department. 3

In 1926, with the extension of the Fund for a further five years, the Committee were able to set aside a further £250,000 for buildings and equipment and to establish an endowment fund of £150,000 to establish the Miners' Welfare Fund Scholarship Scheme.

Progress had not been as rapid as the Committee could have hoped either in the submission of new proposals or in the confirmation of provisional schemes. This was due largely to the financial stringency and the resulting measures of economy pursued by the Board of Education for 1926–7, which had the effect of suspending, for a period of twelve months, the majority of the Local Authority schemes in England and Wales where new capital expenditure was involved. In preparing their programmes of future development for the three financial years, 1927-1930, the Board had warned all Local Authorities that any proposals for which assistance had been provisionally granted, or was likely to be sought, must be included in their programme or they would be postponed until after 1930. It was hoped that once these programmes received the Board's approval, progress would probably be more rapid. The Committee were not disposed to keep their offers of assistance from the Fund open if there were delays beyond 1930.

In Group I (Northumberland and Durham), progress was made in securing the co-operation of the local authorities in the establishment of a scheme covering the coalfield and the county boroughs of Sunderland and Newcastle had agreed with the County Authorities to provide centres which would serve the surrounding county area. A technical college at Sunderland was being extended to provide more suitable accommodation for the mining department and £7,550 was allocated towards the cost of the building and equipment. In Durham, it was now intended that the advanced centres should be established at West Stanley and Durham and senior centres at Ryton-Crookhill, Bishop Auckland, Houghton or Hetton and Wellfield or Easington. The Authority proposed to proceed at once with West Stanley and Bishop Auckland so the provisional allocation for West Stanley made in 1925 was raised to £9,000, while a new allocation of £6,000 was made for Bishop Auckland. The Northumberland Authority had also submitted similar comprehensive proposals involving the establishment of centres at Ashington, Seaton Delaval, Newburn and Broomhill. Plans for the centres were being prepared. The university work would be undertaken by Armstrong College who had submitted proposals for building a new department of mining. A provisional allocation of £20,000 had been made for this proposal. The principal developments in the North-Western Area (Group II) were at Wigan in Lancashire and Wrexham in North Wales.

The Mining and Technical College at Wigan served a wide area in the county as a senior centre, as well as being the advanced centre for the coalfield. The original scheme proposed in 1924 was delayed due to the retirement of the principal, but early in 1926, a more ambitious scheme was put forward for dealing with the whole of the available site and for erecting a permanent instead of a temporary building. This was approved on the understanding that an early start would be made and the allocation of £25,000 was raised to £37,000. The building was started in 1926.

In North Wales, co-operation between the counties of Denbigh and Flint had been secured and a grant was made for the purchase and adaptation of a

New Mining Department at Armstrong College

valuable site and building at Wrexham for use as a senior and advanced centre. Later, the building would be incorporated in a new technical college which the Denbighshire Authority proposed to erect on the site.

In Group III (North Midland Area), further progress was made in Yorkshire consolidating the co-operation between the West Riding Authority and the County Boroughs, in particular Rotherham and Wakefield. At Rotherham, a new technical college was proposed and assistance to the extent of £9,000 (representing the actual cost of the building and equipping the portion to be used as a mining department) was provisionally allocated. Progress for extending the existing mining department of the technical school at Wakefield as a senior and advanced centre was also provisionally approved, but was temporarily held up by the Board of Education. Instead of the originally proposed development at Castleford and Normanton, West Riding had decided on a senior and advanced centre at Whitwood instead. In Nottinghamshire, the revised plans for Mansfield had been approved by the Board of Education (allocation of £10,200 confirmed).

In Group IV, further assistance was given to the University of Birmingham for additional equipment for the new coal-treatment laboratory and for building

Denbighshire Technical Institute at Wrexham

an annexe to an analysis laboratory. The new laboratory was opened by Lord Chelmsford in November 1926.

In South Derbyshire, the development of the Newhall Memorial Hall as a senior and advanced centre was commenced and the provisional allocation of £5,000 was confirmed to the extent of £1,615 for the adaptation of the Hall. The building of extensions would follow. In Shropshire, the grant of £1,500 for the provision of equipment for the technical institute at Oakengates was confirmed and £750 was provisionally allocated for equipping the mining laboratory at the technical institute at Oswestry, to serve as a senior centre for that part of the county. There were four coal areas in Shropshire, and it was difficult to provide effectively for the scattered mining populations with the small amount of money available.

In Group V (Western Area), there still were no developments in Bristol or Somerset. In South Wales, the revised coalfield scheme, based on the Board of

Senior Mining Centre, Pontllanfraith, Physics and Chemistry Laboratory and Drawing Classroom

Education report, provided for the establishment of senior centres at Abersychan, Abertilley, Ebbw Vale and Pontllanfraith in Monmouthshire; Bargoed, Caerphilly, Pontardawe, Bridgend and Neath (together with existing centres at Pontypridd and Aberdare) in Glamorganshire; Pentre and Porth in the Rhondda Urban District Council area; Quaker's Yard and the existing centre in Merthyr in the

Merthyr County Borough area; Ystradgynlan in Breconshire; Ammanford in Carmarthenshire and the Swansea Technical College in the Swansea County Borough area. A provisional allocation of £58,000 was made and the authorities continued to act jointly. They had plans and specifications drawn up which provided for the inclusion in each centre of suitably equipped laboratory for physics and chemistry, a small dark room, two classrooms, a room for drawing, a staffroom and appropriate lavatory and cloakroom accommodation. The centre at Pontllanfraith was the first to be completed and was opened in the autumn of 1926.

The scheme also provided for the establishment of a joint advisory committee of which the eight education authorities, the South Wales Miners' Federation, the South Wales Mining Association, the Travelling Teachers Association, each advanced centre and the University of Wales were all to have appropriate representation. The committee commenced its activities in 1926.

£8,985 was provisionally allocated towards the erection of a mining department at Swansea Technical College to enable it to become the advanced centre for Pembrokeshire, Carmarthenshire, West Glamorganshire and the accessible parts of Breconshire. £1,015 had already been confirmed for the purchase of new equipment.

In 1924, a sum of £3,000 had been provisionally allocated for the provision of better accommodation and equipment at Ayr and Kilmarnock (Group VII, West Scotland). The Ayrshire Education Authority had since decided, after a thorough examination of the whole question by a special committee, to make Kilmarnock the principle mining centre in the county. This involved the adaptation of parts of the existing technical school at Kilmarnock, the erection of a new building as an extension in an adjoining site and the provision of suitable apparatus and equipment. The total estimated cost was £12,500 so the provisional allocation was increased to £7,450 subject to the authority finding the balance.

In East Scotland (Group VIII), the plans for the new mining laboratories at Heriot-Watt College, Edinburgh, were approved. The new building at Buckhaven in Fifeshire was completed during the year and opened in the autumn. The Fund had contributed £4,000 towards the total cost of £8,000.

By 1929, the Fund had provided either the whole or part of the cost of building or enlarging five university mining departments, and 55 advanced or senior course mining centres of which all the university departments and 34 of the other centres were complete and in use, while fourteen more were in the course of erection. In addition, equipment had been provided for three university mining departments and eight senior or advanced centres.

The twenty centres planned for South Wales and Monmouthshire had been provided and only four awaited completion.

In Northumberland (Group I, North Eastern Area), only one centre

Buckhaven Technical School

(Ashington) had been started out of the four planned. In Durham, the allocation for the first of the senior centres was confirmed for West Stanley. The new mining department at Armstrong College was opened on 14th May 1929 by HRH the Prince of Wales. £20,000 was granted from the General Fund as well as £10,000 from the Northumberland District Fund.

In Group II (North Western Area) the extension of Wigan Mining Technical College which was provided by an allocation from the Fund was opened by Lord Chelmsford on 13th June 1929. A grant of £1,253 was made to Burnley Technical School for equipment and another of £2,162 for a new senior centre at Shotten in Flintshire.

In Group III (North Midland Area), an additional allocation of £4,000 was made for a gymnasium at Worksop senior centre. The allocation for the new senior centre at Clowne (£6,000) and for the equipment for the new advanced centre at Whitwood (total cost of building and Equipment £21,250) were confirmed. A grant of £1,000 was made to Nottingham University for equipment.

In Group IV (South Midland Area) a grant (£2,750) was made to Birmingham University to enable them to erect a mining machinery laboratory where students could take to pieces and assemble used machinery. The equipment in this building was provided free of charge by the manufacturers. It was opened on 13th November 1929. The new senior centre at Cannock was opened by Lord Chelmsford on 22nd October.

In Group V (Western Area), the allocation of £6,808 for the Neath senior centre was confirmed. The centres at Ammanford, Bridgend and Quaker's Yard were opened early in 1929 and that at Bargoed later. Good progress was made towards the completion of the remaining centres at Pentre, Abertillery and Ebbw Vale. An allocation was made for an extension to the Forest of Dean Mining School at Cinderford by the addition of an engineering laboratory and a science room.

In Group VII (Western Scottish Area), the centres at Falkirk (cost £6,510) and Kilmarnock (cost £7,450) were completed and a grant for equipment at Falkirk was confirmed and increased.

Quakers' Yard Mining Centre, Merthyr Tydfil

Bargoed Mining Centre, Glamorgan

In Group VIII (Eastern Scottish Area), the new mining department in the new technical school at Kirkcaldy (£4,000) was completed and opened. An allocation was made for the provision of apparatus at the Fife Mining School at Cowdenbeath and a small sum was granted to the West Lothians Education Authority to purchase an optical lantern for use in connection with lectures arranged by the mining students' association.[5]

By the end of 1932, £689,418 of the original £750,000 set aside for mining education had been allocated. Forty-one allocations amounting to £24,331 were made for educational purposes during 1932. Only one allocation was made during the year for a new centre at Alloa in Clackmannan (£1,700). Four allocations amounting to £21,300 were made for extensions to existing centres.

In Group I (North-Eastern Area), there had been no progress made in Durham in providing mining education at senior and advanced level. In Northumberland, nothing had been done since Ashington had been provided.

In Group II (North-Western Area), there had had to be some modification necessitated by the economic situation in the plans for the projected mining centre at Workington. The Technical Institute at Wrexham had officially opened on 2nd November 1932.

In Group III (North Midland Area), the new mining department at Sheffield University was opened on 14th June by Mr Benton Jones, Chairman of the South Yorkshire Coal Trade Association and the new Barnsley Mining and Technical College was opened on 10th October 1932. A sum of £5,300 was provisionally allocated towards the cost of the extension to the mining department at

New Mining Department at Sheffield University

Chesterfield Technical College which, although only opened in 1927, had already proved inadequate in size. £5,000 was allocated towards extending the mining school at Heanor (Derbyshire) and £2,872, previously allocated for an extension at Newhall, which had been dropped, was transferred to Heanor.

In Group V (Western Area), a grant of £1,000 was made for the provision of a metal workshop and woodwork room at Bridgend senior centre. The provision of facilities for a certain amount of manual instruction of this kind was seen as a valuable adjunct to the normal provision for a senior centre, but as the sum set aside for mining education purposes was approaching exhaustion, this allocation was an exceptional case and no further allocations elsewhere would be made for a similar purpose.

The senior centre at Pontardawe (Glamorgan) was ready for use and marked the completion of the original building programme for the joint scheme of mining education agreed in 1925 with all the local authorities in South Wales coalfield. An additional new senior centre at Tredegar was under construction.

The negotiations over the recognition of Treforest by the University of Wales as the advanced centre for Eastern Glamorgan were still ongoing; until these had been concluded, it was not possible to bring the facilities at the mining departments at Treforest or Cardiff University College up to the current standard required for mining education.

The extension to the Forest of Dean Mining School at Cinderford was opened on 15th September by Mr G. H. Winstanley.

In Group VI (Kent), the Welfare Fund was able to make its first allocation to this group. The Kent Education Authority had made excellent progress in handling the new educational problem introduced by the increase in importance of this county in recent years as a mining district. An allocation of £300 was made for the provision of equipment at the small centres that had been established at Aylsham, Deal, Dover, Elvington and Ramsgate.

In addition to the sum of £6,665.10s allocated in previous years towards non-vocational lectures in Yorkshire, Nottinghamshire, Derbyshire, the Forest of Dean and the Lothians, a further sum of £1,265 was allocated in 1932 for the continuance of these schemes except the last. In all these cases, four-fifths of the cost was provided by the District Funds and one-fifth from the General Fund.

Two allocations, one of £59.8s and one of £60 were made in respect of a day added for the discussion of mining education subjects to the annual conference of mining teachers and organisers at Buxton under the auspices of the Safety in Mines Research Board. The former allocation was in respect of the 1931 conference.[6]

The grants for mining schools during 1933 amounted to £24,770 from the General Fund. The largest grant was £11,710 for a new mining school at

Nuneaton in Warwickshire, which would replace the current school which was inadequate for present requirements. A grant of £4,000 was made for a new mining school at Freston in East Lothian where mining classes for senior work had hitherto been carried out in a secondary school building.

The remaining grants, five in England and Wales and two in Scotland, were supplementary. £1,062 was allocated to complete the senior centre at Pontardowe which was opened in January 1934. It was the last senior centre to be completed under the original building programme for South Wales and Monmouthshire which had commenced in 1926. A grant of £3,227 was made for a proposed reorganisation of the mining department at Nottingham University College. Supplemental grants were made to Cowdenbeath Mining School, the advanced centre in Fifeshire (£1,500) and the new mining department at Clackmannan (£500) whose costs, on revised plans, were more than originally anticipated.

During 1933, grants were made to 127 students to assist them in their studies. 73 of them had not previously received a grant, the remainder wanted a further year. The total sum granted was £4,195, of which £3,625 was from the District Funds and £570 from the General Fund.

The number of small grants made on the recommendation of the Selection Committee of the Miners' Welfare National Scholarship Scheme to students who had not be successful in their application but were highly meritorious and required assistance in 1933 was twenty-seven and the total sum allocated was £1,140.

Following the example of the two Yorkshire districts in 1931 and of Nottingham in 1932, safety instruction courses for pit boys had been arranged in four other Districts. Northumberland, Durham and Derbyshire received grants of £20, £40 and £50 respectively from District Funds in 1933 to provide badges for boys who satisfactorily passed through a safety instruction course. Courses were being conducted in Lancashire without a grant from the General Fund at St Helens and Leigh mining instruction centres.

Schemes of technical education for persons employed in the coal mining industry had always included dangers associated with coal mining and their mitigation. Unfortunately, only a small proportion of the total number of persons employed in the industry took advantage of these educational facilities. This was partly because of the poor response on the part of boys employed in the mining industry. Therefore, the local authorities in the Yorkshire coalfields, acting through the Yorkshire Council for Further Education, conceived the idea of the award of a 'Safety Badge' as an inducement to attend the courses of instruction provided for them in the evening institutes.

The experiment which began in the autumn of 1931 took the form of a modification of the existing evening institute courses in the mining areas. A new subject called 'Safety Principles' was introduced as one of the obligatory subjects to which 1 ½ hours was devoted weekly. The other obligatory subject, occupying an hour in the same evening, was 'Calculations'. On a second evening there was a choice of optional subjects. The course extended over a period of 24 to 26 weeks from September to March.

Courses on these lines were provided at between 40 and 60 centres in premises which were provided for the normal evening institute classes. The teachers were mainly officials employed at the local collieries and most were experienced as part-time teachers.

Boys who entered as soon as possible after leaving school were admitted without a fee. On the completion of the course, oral examinations were held in the presence of assessors. The Safety Badges were awarded as the result of these examinations.

The Yorkshire scheme was the only one in which instruction in Safety Principles was an integral part of the normal institute courses. In the other areas, there were variations, but attention was concentrated upon safety instruction.

Grants of £240 and £120 were made to Farm Training for Pit Boys scheme from the Fifeshire and West Yorkshire District Funds, respectively. A report on the scheme showed that 33 boys had been selected for training and 21 had completed the training and 20 were at work.[7]

In July 1931, the Committee had considered an outline of a scheme for making grants to enable students to attend part-time day courses in advanced mining and technical schools. Most of the classes were held in the evening, a time when students who had been working during the day were physically tired. It would be an advantage to such students if they could attend for a whole day a week.

This proposal, in principle, was approved by the Committee but the scheme had to be worked out in detail. If it were decided to establish an endowment similar to that of the Scholarship Scheme, a capital sum of possibly £100,000 would be required. At the end of 1931, £58,877 in the General Fund was unassigned so the scheme would not make a heavy demand on the General Fund in the third period.

The matter was referred to the Departmental Inquiry on the Miners' Welfare Fund chaired by Lord Chelmsford whose Report was presented to Parliament in January 1933. In Chapter 13, the Committee of Inquiry remarked on the progress made in the provision of mining classes but there was still a further step which could be taken by the provision, on a larger and wider scale of part-time day courses. The Committee of Inquiry were aware that the Miners' Welfare Committee had approved in principle a proposal to allocate a large sum to endow a new scholarship scheme to provide a number of scholarships for part-time day advanced courses in mining at approved institutions, the award in each case covering fees, travelling expenses, books and some compensation for loss of time.

In Chapter 13, it was mentioned that 'Some £75,000 might be required, though the amount would naturally depend on the number of awards to be awarded annually'.

At the November 1934 meeting of the Welfare Committee, Mr Winstanley presented proposals for the scholarship scheme for part-time day advanced mining courses.

While the specially planned and equipped premises provided for advanced mining courses by the Miners' Welfare Fund were fully occupied in the evenings, they were only used to a very limited extent during the day. To ensure more regular and more profitable use of the premises, two alternatives were suggested: full-time day mining courses or the development of part-time day courses for mineworkers. The first could be dismissed as students would not be able to support themselves and very few institutions were in the position to conduct full-time day courses.

Part-time day courses in printing, engineering and building were growing in popularity and becoming more and more successful with younger workers being encouraged and assisted by their employers to attend. It was therefore proposed that a scholarship scheme intended to encourage the development of part-time day mining courses therefore making it possible for a number of suitably qualified students who were workers in or about the mines to avail themselves of the existing facilities.

Part-time day mining courses already established usually extended over four years. Based on an endowment fund of £75,000, it would be possible to maintain an annual average of 120 scholarships (30 per year over the 4-year period) of the value of £20 each. £10 per annum would enable the student to attend on one day weekly and an average of £10 per annum would cover the cost of fees, books, instruments and travelling expenses.

As only 30 new scholarships would be available for award each year, it was essential to ensure that awards were only tenable where the institution was a mining school or technical school with a mining department recognised by the Board of Education or the Scottish Education Department in Scotland with well-equipped and adequate accommodation for teaching mining subjects and subjects allied to mining.

To be eligible for scholarships, candidates would have to be wage-earning workers, dependent on their earnings, and employed in or about mines and so employed for at least eighteen months prior to the award of a scholarship. They should have attended and satisfactorily completed an approved part-time senior course. Candidates would need to have reached the age of 18 years at or before the date of the award. All awards would be reviewed annually and were liable to be withdrawn in the event of unfavourable reports of progress or conduct.

Applications for scholarships would be made to the approved institutions to which the candidate sought admission and each candidate would be required to produce a report from the Principal of the institution in which he attended classes in the Senior Mining Course. The scholarships would be awarded on the results of examinations held annually in June, in the subjects of the Senior Course. The papers would be set, and scripts marked by the approved institutions. The examination papers would be subject to moderation and the marked scripts reviewed by an external assessor or assessors appointed by the Miners' Welfare Committee.

The scheme was terminated in 1948 as its need had been removed by the introduction of the National Coal Boards' scheme for students attending part-time day courses.[8]

By December 1936, £762,649 had been allocated from the General Fund and £21,425 from the Districts Fund for mining education. £663,284.17s.4d had been allocated to Education Authorities and £99,364.15s.5d to seven universities.

However, in two instances, the allocations were not taken up until 1950. The plans for a new college at Nuneaton, Warwickshire, had been approved in 1930 but the proposals were shelved in 1942 due to war time building restrictions and the provisional grant of £10,000 suspended. In February 1950, the grant of £10,000 was again approved for revised plans. The new Mining Department at Cardiff University College had also originally been proposed in 1930 and a provisional grant of £28,000 made. Proposals were put forward in 1947 but it was not until March 1950 that all the conditions attached to the grant by the Commission had been fulfilled.[9]

From the very beginning recreation schemes, funded from the Districts Fund, proved very popular with 85% of the schemes funded in the first five years of the Miners' Welfare Fund coming under this heading. In monetary terms, this represented 66.7% of the Districts Fund so, from the start, the Central Committee were very anxious that the schemes were planned properly and gave value for money (see Chapter 2).

The Industrial Welfare Society became involved with the Miners' Welfare Fund as early as 1921. The Society came into existence in 1919 with the purpose of improving the relationship between employer and employed by introducing carefully planned welfare developments. It was already dealing with Welfare developments of a few colliery companies before the Mining Act, 1920. Mr Charles Mason, South Wales Organiser for the Industrial Society, had been active in promoting Welfare Schemes in the South Wales Industries, including the coal industry, since 1919. In January 1922, he had submitted a statement to the Central Committee explaining his role within the South Wales Welfare District.

EIGHT

RECREATION

In 1923, the Industrial Welfare Society offered to establish an advisory centre which would be available for Local Committees to obtain assistance with individual schemes. The centre commenced operations in March 1923. In order to make the Local Committees aware of what the advisory centre could offer, a reference guide was produced listing its activities. As the centre gained experience in what might be of value to mining communities, it published circulars dealing with children's playgrounds, recreation grounds, libraries, children's corners, maintenance and the upkeep of recreation schemes.[1]

With the transfer of Cdr. Coote and his staff to the new Advisory Branch under the direct control of the Committee and the Secretary of Mines in March 1925, Cdr. Coote was appointed as an Advisor to the Committee and became more proactive in shaping recreational schemes with the assistance of his staff.[2]

In 1925, the Committee were still concerned that a large number of the proposals for recreation grounds had been made with no complete plan for full development of the area available or the facilities that could be provided for each section of the community concerned. Similarly, in the case of buildings, plans sometimes showed a lack of practical knowledge of the space required for various activities. The lack of adequate specifications and contracts without reasonable safeguards and guarantees were also of concern to the Committee who were now promoting the Advisory Branch as a resource for District and Local Committees to call upon.[3]

A revised reference guide was issued by the Advisory Branch in May 1925 to bring the District and Local Committees up to date with the services that could be provided by the Branch. Cdr. Coote also began to produce circulars and specimen plans starting with the establishment of a library and specimen plans for institutes.[4]

Although there had been widespread recognition, by 1925, that adequate facilities for children (ten years and under) and for young people (10-16), the provision of separate facilities for young people was not being fully realised, because the need for indoor recreational facilities for these age groups had not been fully grasped. Cdr. Coote duly produced a specification for clubs for boys and girls which was reproduced in the 4th Annual Report of the Miners'

Welfare Fund and dealt with what sort of building was necessary, what rooms it should contain, how it should be furnished and how it might be controlled. The club could either be for boys or girls alone or for both combined. A T-shaped building was envisaged with a reading room and library, parlour games room, committee and classrooms, swimming bath with a floor for the winter (gymnasium and hall), billiard and bagatelle room, buffet and separate workshops, lavatories and dressing rooms.[5]

By 1925, there were eleven schemes devoted entirely to covered swimming baths, but there were many other schemes which had swimming baths as part of an institute building or open-air swimming baths alone or occupying part of a recreation ground. The Committee had been particularly struck by the Lambton 'D' Swimming Baths in Durham which had cost only £4,300, in comparison to other schemes that had cost over three times as much. The total capital cost of £4,300 had been met from the Durham District Fund and the building stood on a site provided at a nominal rental by Lambton and Hetton Collieries Ltd. Taking the experience gained from Lambton in its first year, the Advisory Branch produced a model plan which might be followed by any welfare committee proposing a scheme for a swimming bath.[6]

As 1926 marked the end of the first quinquennium, the Central Committee had taken the opportunity to review the first period of the Fund. The Advisory Branch had subsequently produced several papers for publication in the 5th Annual Report of the Miners' Welfare Fund to help local Welfare Committees to avoid the pitfalls that could befall new recreation schemes.

Based directly on the system that the Advisory Branch staff followed when they were invited to assist directly in drawing up a scheme, the sequence of technical stages which a local welfare committee, either starting a scheme or extending an existing scheme, were presented logically so no stage of constructing either a building or outdoor recreation scheme could be overlooked. The local committee needed to know exactly what they wanted but the position of services (sewer, water, electricity and gas) had to be considered. Sketch plans and rough cost estimates for buildings allowed various designs to be considered. Comprehensive layout and approximate costings for outdoor recreation grounds would enable a local committee to decide what they could afford to develop at any one time without prejudicing the overall plan. Tendering was one of the most important stages and needed to be examined closely and advice sought, as necessary. As the work was carried out, periodic visits were advised. It was flagged up that the Advisory Branch were able to obtain special discounts on furniture and equipment for miners' welfare schemes.

Football and cricket grounds were popular but, where local committees wanted to provide both these facilities, there might not be sufficient space

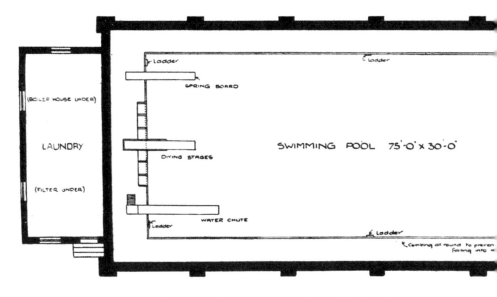

Proposed Swimming Baths, design for Miners' Welfare Schemes

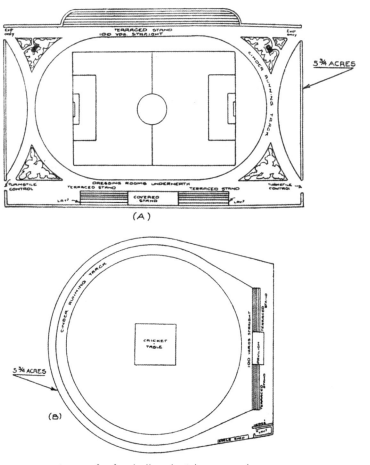

Layout for football and cricket grounds

RECREATION

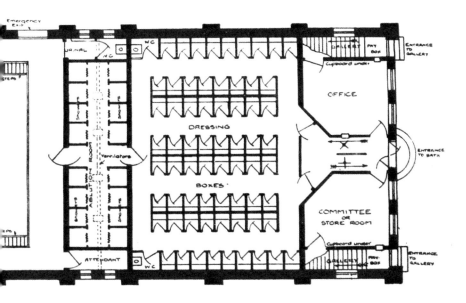

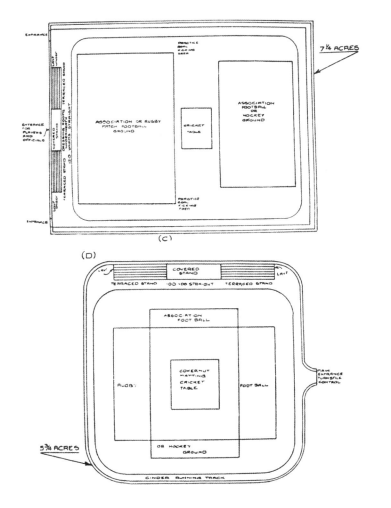

Example of a comprehensive plan for a partial development
at Ryhill and Havercroft Recreation Ground

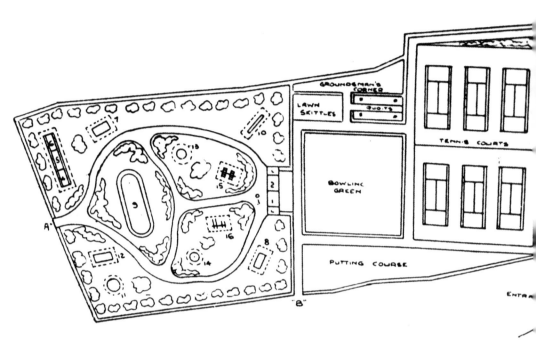

available through the lack of suitable sites or owing to insufficient funds. 5¾ acres were required separately for Association football or cricket. The Advisory Branch showed on the same scale how less than double this area could be made to serve both. They had hesitated to make this suggestion, but several important clubs already did this. An arrangement of 7¼ acres incorporating pitches for Association rugby, Association football and cricket already existed on the Sheffield ground where test matches were played.

Ryhill and Havercroft Recreation Ground (South Yorkshire) was given as an example of the development of a recreation scheme where sufficient funds were not available to undertake the whole of it at the outset. The local committee were in a position to obtain an allocation of £2,950 to include the purchase of a site of eight acres. The Central Advisory Branch produced a complete layout which included a football and cricket section, park section, adult section and children's section which was estimated to cost £4,714 for the whole scheme. On the advice of the Central Advisory Branch, the local committee chose to make a start on the children's section, the adult section (bowling green and three hard tennis courts), the park section (bandstand and paths) and preparing the ground and equipment for the football and cricket section. With the purchase of the land and fencing,

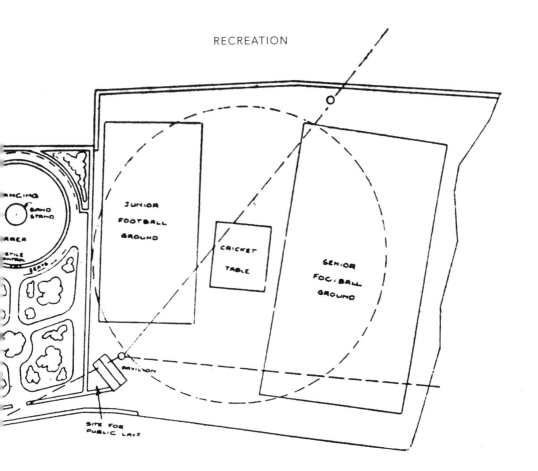

the total cost came to £2,950 for which the local committee were in a position to apply. The accepted tender for the bowling green and tennis courts was £90 less than the approximate estimate so it had been possible to include for the original figure, the quoit pitches, putting course and lawn skittles areas.

Cdr Coote also chose to introduce the concept of evening play centres. Children's playgrounds for outdoor recreation were then generally recognised by local committees as part and parcel of a recreation scheme but there was an equal need for indoor play centres in the winter. Cdr. Coote had visited several evening play centres in London. The Evening Play Centres Committee leased school buildings with their playgrounds from the London County Council every evening from 3 to 7pm for the benefit of the children of the neighbourhood who would otherwise have no place to play except the streets. There were 33 Play Centres scattered all over London, which took in over 12,000 children every evening for games, dancing, handicrafts, painting, gymnastics and similar occupations. Each centre was under the direction of a paid superintendent who was responsible to the Play Centres Committee. The classes were held by trained teachers with a sprinkling of volunteers. The idea of the 'Play Centre' was much more than play. It gave boys and girls the opportunity of to do better things than spending time under the risk of bad influences in the streets.

The Advisory Branch had also circulated a paper to local committees recommending that children's playgrounds should be for the greater part of the area surfaced with grass instead of ash. Ash was still to be used under each piece of apparatus as hard surfaces such as concrete or asphalt could only be used where there was no risk of falls. The children's playground at Newtongrange Park, Lothians (see Chapter 3) was mainly grass and trees, and flower beds had been freely used to make the playground beautiful. In addition to the sandpit, there were twenty-three pieces of apparatus together with a large shelter with lavatory accommodation and several drinking fountains.[7]

The First District Organisers' Conference was held in London on 17th November 1926 at the Mines Department in London. The meeting was chaired by Cdr. Coote and Captain J. D. O'Kelly and Mr R. W. Parker from the Advisory Branch and Mr E. W. Ravenshear, Secretary to the Miners' Welfare Committee were present. There were four District Organisers attending: Mr D. Thomson Kennedy (Fife), Mr R. Prince (Lanarkshire), Mr W. A. Bates (South Yorkshire) and Mr C. S. Mason (South Wales).

The rationale behind this conference and the subsequent ones seemed to have been threefold: an opportunity to meet with members of the Advisory Branch, a forum to discuss the many aspects of recreational schemes and pool experience, and possibly as a means of overcoming the isolation that District Organisers must have experienced working alone.

The Second District Organisers' Conference took place the following year in London on 17th March 1927. Again, there were only 4 District Organisers present. Mr Mason had been prevented from attending by South Wales District Committee, but Mr H. Fisher attended as District Organiser for the Forest of Dean. The conference's discussion on Institutes was wide ranging and covered internal activities, ventilation and cleanliness, lighting, sanitation, accounts, caretakers and fire extinguishers. With the stoppage in 1926, maintenance and upkeep of schemes was an issue and various suggestions were put forward to overcome the situation. A discussion about competitions as a means of encouraging greater interest in recreation among the community led Cdr. Coote to introduce a warning note as to the effect of over-specialisation. It was generally agreed that friendly matches between neighbouring Institutes was a good thing, with the majority able to take part rather than the specialised minority. The District Organisers were given information on the Pithead Baths Section, and they paid a visit to Mr Forshaw's room where he and Mr Rayner explained the plans of the first experimental installation which was put up at Pooley Hall in Warwickshire.[8]

The Third District Organisers Conference took place in Glasgow on 13th and 14th July 1927. Cdr. Coote asked for opinions as to the wisdom of leaving any scheme without some assistance from the Fund. The general view seemed to be that if the local committees were led to expect yearly allocations , it might prevent self-help and that, where there was a District Organiser, local committees were given every opportunity to progress and keep in touch with new ideas. Cdr. Coote then updated the meeting on 'Pit Welfare', as this came within the sphere of the District Organiser's duties. The conference went on to discuss employers' liability and caretakers, equipment discounts, various aspects of compiling specifications, insurance of playgrounds and intoxicants in institutes. The second day was spent visiting schemes in the local area.[9]

The Fourth District Organisers Conference took place in the Mines Department, London, on 16th November 1927. Cdr. Coote updated the conference on experimental canteens then Mr Naish, Finance Branch, explained details of a comprehensive policy of 'All-In' insurance which he had discussed with Lloyds to cover all the risks mentioned by the Organisers at the last conference. Captain O'Kelly explained a draft pamphlet which he had compiled on the maintenance and treatment of tennis courts, hard and grass, and bowling greens, sea-washed, local turf or 'sown'. A pamphlet on 'Precautions found necessary in compiling specifications' was in hand.

Cdr. Coote was keen to obtain more information about construction, control, upkeep and maintenance of cinemas which were being run in Miners' Welfare Institutes by local committees in various parts of the coalfield. Mr Parker detailed several points in connection with construction which required attention in advance of building and addressed local authorities' requirements and safety. Mr Prince reported that Lanarkshire had 23 cinemas in operation which were valuable for generating income. He went on to supply useful information on purchase of machines and hire of film and how a weekly programme could be organised as a paying proposition.

There was a long discussion about the relationship of football clubs to the Miners' Welfare Committees. Cdr. Coote mentioned that in his tours with the Secretary, he had come across some very elaborate provisions for football including covered and terraced stands. In some instances, the football teams were being paid to play and all the gate money went to the football club. It was agreed that football grounds should be retained primarily for the use of the general community, and miners should not get payment for playing.

The Organisers received an explanation of the method which the Miners' Welfare Committee adopted in investigating the 'pros and cons' of plans sent in support of applications. It made all the difference to local committees to have all the preliminary work of planning and estimating costs done for them before making their application.

Cdr. Coote also returned to the subject of children's playgrounds, as he was still looking for the ideal playground. He then went on to explain what he meant by an 'ideal' playground. After the meeting, Mr Mason received permission from the Joint Committee in South Wales to include in the 1928 programme the development of an ideal children's playground in South Wales.[10]

The Fifth District Organisers' Conference was held in Cardiff from 21st to 23rd May 1928. Only three District Organisers attended, as Mr Thomson Kennedy (Fifeshire) was unable to attend due to illness at home and Mr Bates (South Yorkshire) had received instructions from his District Welfare Committee not to attend. The meeting was updated on experimental canteens, the pamphlet on precautions found necessary in compiling specifications, training of groundsmen, special discount terms, relation of football clubs to local welfare committees and plans in support of applications. They then went on to discuss the best type of surface for hard tennis courts and types of turf used for bowling greens. The duties, responsibilities and wages of caretakers were discussed as it was clear that there were variations not only between districts but also within districts. In normal times, the Central Committee would suggest that money should be set aside for periodical repair of miners' welfare buildings but, with the then state of wages, this seemed impossible. The last item was subsequently taken up by the Central Committee.[11]

Prior to 1925, no grants had been made for the maintenance expenses of any scheme, except in the case of Talygarn Convalescent Home which was allowed to have the annual deficit met by direct grants pending the completion of an endowment fund.

In 1925, the South Wales District Welfare Committee sent up a deputation to urge the Miners' Welfare Committee to address the serious position of some schemes as a result of colliery closures and the difficulties of a possible stoppage. The Committee agreed to make direct grants from the District Fund to keep schemes going subject to certain stringent conditions, the most important being that all the supporting collieries must be temporarily closed. In 1926, after the general stoppage, Ayr, Lanark, Fife, South Yorkshire, West Yorkshire, South Staffordshire and South Wales did take advantage of this decision to a small extent.

In 1926, the Committee notified Districts that, in making allocations from the Fund during the second quinquennium, they would not object to extending somewhat the definition of what might be regarded as 'capital' outlay.

The matter was discussed at the Conference of Representatives from District Committees in November 1927 and the Committee agreed to consider applications if submitted by Districts, provided the total amount so allocated did not exceed in any year 5% of the normal district income.

Later in 1928, the Committee became alarmed at the gradual extension of applications of this kind. In South Wales, for instance, the concession, originally intended to apply only to recreational schemes, was regarded as also including certain hospitals which had been dependent almost entirely on the contribution of coal miners for their support. At the July 1928 meeting of the Central Committee, it was agreed that the matter should be raised again at the Annual Conference. In the interim, it was decided to first review the whole situation in order to settle the basis on which any further extension of the concession might be limited.

There were a number of difficulties about the proposal that each district might establish a fund available for paying maintenance grants by setting aside a sum equal to 5% of each allocation for local schemes, leading to the conclusion that it would not be practicable under the existing system of local administration.

It was therefore suggested that a committee composed largely of district representatives be set up with the terms of reference:

'To consider to what extent, if any, local welfare schemes should be assisted from the Miners' Welfare Fund in meeting their current or periodic expenditure; to examine any proposals which might be made for dealing with the question in a comprehensive manner and to make recommendations regarding the conditions or safeguards to be imposed or required with the event of one or more proposals being considered practicable and desirable.'

At the November 1928 meeting of the Central Committee it was agreed to set up a sub-committee consisting of Sir A. Lowes Dickinson, Mr Lesley Wright and Mr A. Cook to consider the above. The issue was also discussed at the 7th Conference of Representatives of District Committees.[12]

The sub-committee obtained written information on how all schemes were maintained and what had been abandoned or were likely to be abandoned. After consideration of this information, the sub-committee produced their report which was presented at the Central Committee's meeting in October 1929.

As a result of their report, the Central Committee drew up fresh rules for the guidance of District Committees in making recommendations for maintenance and for certain non-capital purposes in connection with recreation schemes.

The local committees were still encouraged to set aside a sum of money each year to form a reserve which would enable schemes to tide over temporary periods of embarrassment. District Committees were also recommended to consider the setting up of Area Committees to receive all colliery levies for a particular area and to see that every man's deductions were paid to the scheme nearest the place in which he lived.

The Rules of Guidance were sent out on 26th November 1929, and covered allocations to meet annual expenditure of schemes, allocations to meet periodic expenditure of schemes, allocations to provide games and sports equipment for schemes and allocations to meet provision of trophies or expenses for competitions. (The Rules of Guidance made it clear that the Committee were not prepared to consider further allocations for this last item).[13]

The Eighth District Organisers' Conference was held from 11th to 13th June 1930 at the South Yorkshire District Welfare Committee's Offices, Royal Victoria Station Hotel, Sheffield. The number of District Organisers had increased to seven.

Reference was made to the circular on the Rules and Guidance on upkeep and maintenance of recreation schemes issued to district committees to inform them in making their recommendations. At that time, the Fund was not permanent, so the Miners' Welfare Committee did not want to be put in a position of meeting periodical expenditure for a year or two and then not be able to continue.

The Conference looked at the construction of buildings and the design of institutes. Local committees generally wanted more than the money would provide for the scheme, so good strong useful materials were to be used for construction of the building. The design of billiard rooms, reading rooms, hall, heating and ventilation, lavatories, baths and wash basins and ladies' accommodation were discussed. Slipper baths were considered a waste of money and space. This also applied to lavatory basins as soap and towels were rarely supplied.

It had proved more economical in designing pavilions to have as many activities as possible under one roof, but children still needed a separate shelter in their playground.

As there had been requests for grants to re-erect buildings which had been wholly or partly demolished by fire, the Central Committee had issued a circular on comprehensive insurance of institutes and recreation grounds at the beginning of January 1929. The District Organisers attending the Conference were reminded of the need to ascertain whether buildings in their districts were insured for their proper amounts.

A report was given on the model children's playground at Llanbradach, which had been opened by Lord Chelmsford. The maintenance and upkeep of children's playgrounds was discussed and Cdr. Coote expressed his wish for the opportunity of developing a model, organised playground for young people, both boys and girls who were too old for children's playgrounds and too young for the adult section.

The upkeep and maintenance costs of swimming baths was discussed. Emley Moor was used as an example of a scheme which raised a profit of £300-£400 per year through a combination of a grant from the education committee, a levy (2d per man per week), charges for non-members, season ticket holders and hire of the hall for dances and concerts. The latter had been made possible by providing a floor that converted the building into a hall in the winter months.

During the second and third day of the Conference, visits were made to sixteen schemes in the South Yorkshire District.[14]

The Ninth District Organisers' Conference was held in Derbyshire. The first day of the Conference was held in the Welfare Institute, Chesterfield on 24th June 1931 with the following two days being spent visiting recreation schemes in Derbyshire. Representatives from eight districts who did not have District Organisers attended in addition to seven District Organisers. Cdr. Coote was joined by Captain O'Kelly, Mr R. W. Parker and Miss E. Stocker from the Central Technical Staff.

Following the last Conference, a questionnaire had been sent out to the Secretaries of all local schemes to gather information on wages and duties of caretakers in Miners' Welfare buildings. Very few questionnaires had been returned but, by analysing those that had been returned and notes made by Mr Parker on his visits to institutes in various parts of the country, Mr Parker was able to give a report.

Caretakers varied greatly with regard to appearance, age, fitness and ability. The average weekly wage varied from £2 to £4.10s depending on the capital cost of the institute. Smaller institutes had part-time caretakers who were paid 7/6d or 10/- a week for evening work. The hours appeared excessive (10–12 hours a day), in addition to the time spent in superintending the cleaning, which had to be done before the institute opened. Mr Parker felt that it was essential to appoint a man who could set an example and sustain discipline.

The model playground at Llanbradach (South Wales) which had been opened in May 1930 by Lord Chelmsford was well used, with an average of 250 children using it on a fine evening. The expense of upkeep was borne by the Llanbradach Association as part of their non-profit activities. Other model playgrounds had been started, and South Yorkshire were being asked to consider one at Bolton-on-Deane.

The layout and construction of Miners' Welfare buildings was again discussed as two fundamental errors were still arising: the minimum cue space for billiard tables and ventilation.

There were still problems in some areas with finding money for maintenance of schemes. The Central Committee's memorandum No. 136 on maintenance definitely stated that the Central Committee were not prepared to consider making grants for internal repair and redecoration.

Upkeep of bowling greens and football grounds, children's playgrounds and basketball pitches were revisited. The county wide organisation of games in Derbyshire was presented and the suggestion made to extend the county scheme nationally.

The first day finished with Cdr. Coote reminding the Conference that the welfare of children and young people had so far received little or no attention.[15]

In January 1931, Cdr. Coote presented his paper on boys' club finance to the Central Committee. As a result of the Chairman's promise made at the July 1930 committee meeting of the Central Committee to explore the possibility of encouraging the boy club movement, Cdr. Coote had met with Mr C. S. Mason, District Organiser for South Wales, and Captain Glynn Jones, Welfare Supervisor of the Ocean Coal Company, to whose initiative was owed the existence of seven boys' clubs. They served the Districts of Ton Pentre, Nantymoel, Treharris, Wattstown, Treorchy, Llwnpia and Newbridge. The first three had permanent premises and the latter only temporary accommodation. The membership totalled 1,061.

It was agreed that 200 boys were as many as one club leader could handle satisfactorily and a club building costing £5,000, to include £500 for equipment, would cater for all the activities that boys might require.

By comparing the expenses of the existing clubs, £600 a year was required to run a club for 200 boys and included the cost of a trained club leader and cleaner.

In the existing clubs, a boy paid 3d a week as his membership subscription on joining the club. It was estimated that a club could generate an income of £250 a year. The deficit at Treharris and Nantymoel, as neither had a recreation scheme attached, was met by the Ocean Area Recreation Union who allocated a certain sum of money yearly from the local welfare levy to each club. At the other clubs, the income was swallowed up by the ground expenses. At Ton Pentre, where there was an extensive recreation scheme, the ground expenses took all the yearly sum so they could not afford a club leader.

Cdr. Coote estimated that an endowment fund of £9,000 would relieve all boys' clubs from financial difficulties.

The Central Committee supported Cdr. Coote's recommendations and a draft circular to all District Committees was discussed at the February meeting of the Central Committee and circulated on 25th February 1931.[16]

The 10th Conference of District Organisers was held in Birmingham between 25th and 27th May 1932. Sixteen districts were represented, and those present were concerned with 82% of the Districts Fund. The agenda was sufficiently varied to be of special interest to those who were not District Organisers.

Mr Parker dealt with minor troubles with the maintenance of the fabric in Miners' Welfare Buildings. He suggested these were bound up with the appointment of an efficient caretaker and the adoption of some system of training caretakers so that they maintained the fabric of the buildings. This training needed to include instruction in heating and ventilation and recognition of dry rot.

Problems met with in isolated buildings were included on the agenda so that the four chief difficulties (sanitation, heating, artificial light and water) with buildings could be discussed. Earth closets would never be allowed in Miners' Welfare schemes, so the use of septic tanks, disposable systems and chemical closets were described. Wells had been sunk to obtain water or rainwater collected and stored. Where electricity was not laid on, a gas plant or lamp could be installed.

Treatment of sea-washed turf, mole drainage in grounds, surrounds for football pitches and tennis courts and materials for tennis courts were included for general discussion. Mr Herbert Robinson, of Messrs Ransome, Simms and Jefferies Ltd. attended to give a lantern lecture on the cutting of lawns.

The next two days of the Conference were spent visiting recreation schemes in Warwickshire and Cannock Chase.[17]

The Eleventh District Organisers' Conference was held in Dunfermline and Edinburgh from 27th to 29th June 1933. Fifteen out of the twenty-five districts had sent representatives and those present were concerned with over 80% of the money in the Districts Fund.

Cdr. Coote expressed the hope that the Conference would provide a means for the interchange of new ideas in welfare developments on up-to-date lines, and an opportunity for the exchange of opinions and discussion of experiences.

Attendees not only visited recreational schemes in Fife, Clackmannan, Kinross and the Lothians but were able to discuss the problems and difficulties met with in the various districts for the benefit of all attending the Conference.

The rest of the Conference was devoted to various aspects of indoor recreation: heating, flooring, colour schemes, internal wall coverings and wood rot. Cdr. Coote also took the opportunity to discuss boys' clubs.[18]

A joint meeting of the Central Staff with District Organisers and District Secretaries was held in London on 19th and 20th June 1935. The meeting was opened by the Chairman of the Central Committee, Major-General the Right Honourable Sir Frederick Sykes, who assured the meeting that it was not the wish of the Central Committee to lessen in any way the functions of the District Committees. The aim of the Central Committee was to co-operate with them more closely and to offer all possible help to the District Committees and, through them, to the local committees when help of any sort might be of value.

The general object of the meeting was to co-ordinate the work in London with the Districts and to discuss the work of District Organisers so that the District Committees' Organisers and the Central Committee's Organisers (employed in other districts) might, as far as possible, agree upon uniform practice and have the assistance of each other's experience. Co-ordination would be assisted by the Central Committee's Districts Branch, which was intended to form a permanent link between the Districts and the Central Staff.

The District Organiser would have three functions in the District: applications for new grants, management of existing local welfare schemes and future progressive development of miners' welfare in the district. Each of these functions was discussed and procedures agreed under the three headings. The assistance available from the central technical staff was explained.[19]

Conferences of District Miners' Welfare Organisers (renamed District Miners' Welfare Officers in 1942) were held twice a year from 1935 to September 1942 and were not resumed until May 1946. Pressure of work in the Districts and at Headquarters and travel restrictions compelled the Commission to suspend these conferences.[20]

Although advice continued to be produced centrally on construction and proposed programmes of work, such as various types of hard tennis courts and upkeep of schemes, by the issuing of pamphlets and lectures, District Committees and Local Committees were being encouraged to work more closely with Local Authorities and the National Advisory Council for Physical Training to provide recreational facilities.[21]

By the end of 1945, the Miners' Welfare Fund had made grants for recreation and leisure-time occupation to 1,523 centres amounting to £5,994,879 (25.8 % of all grants from the Fund). Although the outbreak of war had put a stop to the building and constructional work, a stage had been reached at which all principal communities in most coalfields had some sort of accommodation for recreational activities. With a few exceptions, no great effort had been made to organise a variety of purposeful activities.

The Commission, therefore, welcomed the provision of the Education Act 1944, which charged local education authorities with the provision of further education in co-operation with other bodies whose objects included the provision of facilities or organisation of educational activities.

The Miners' Welfare Commission thought that admission of local residents other than miners would be a condition of assistance from the local authorities but saw such a move as a means to strengthen membership, to breakdown social prejudice and to afford opportunities for mine workers to meet people with fresh interests. At the suggestion of the Commission, the Coal Industry Nationalisation Act 1946 included a provision to legalise the admission of non-miners to membership of Miners' Welfare schemes by empowering the Minister of Fuel and Power to make the necessary variation of the trusts of miners' welfare schemes in suitable instances.

This led, the Commission, in February 1945, to recommend to District Committees in 'Miners' Welfare Looks Forward' to prepare short-term and long-term plans.

The short-term plans, proposed in 1945, aimed at the immediate development of additional activities at Miners' Welfare Centres and the long -term plans related to necessary developments when building again became practicable.

In February 1945, with the aim of developing additional activities at institutes, the Commission added a District Officer to headquarters to give the matter special attention.

Meanwhile, the Commission decided upon arranging courses for training voluntary leaders. Owing to consideration of staff and the experimental nature of the project, the first approach was made to the Scottish Districts and South Wales because the District Committees and the Local Education Authorities were likely to be responsive. The District Committees, when consulted by the District Officers, convened conferences of representatives of the miners' welfare schemes, at which the proposals for training leaders and developing new activities at the institutes were fully explained and assurances of local support were received.

Courses for management committees and secretaries were held over three weekends in March and May 1946 in three districts (Fife, Lanarkshire and Lothians), and were attended by both men and women. The courses took the form of demonstrating activities which could be undertaken in any Miners' Welfare Institute including physical recreation, music, discussion groups, creative activities, adult education lectures, the library, drama, art, the place of women in the institute, the relationship of the institute to other community activities, a social evening, the running of a tea bar or canteen, problems of finance, committees and publicity.

Since 1936, the Central Council of Physical Recreation had annually organised training courses for men and women following other occupations or professions who wished to fit themselves to act as leaders of outdoor recreation activities. A few members of the Miners' Welfare Centres had taken advantage of these courses and had been instrumental in introducing fresh sports and games into Centres. From 1943 onwards, arrangements were made to include mine workers in CCPR holiday camp schemes.

In 1938, the Commission embarked upon a special effort to foster boys' clubs. Warwickshire responded first, appointing a full-time club leader and arranged for a pioneer club at Dordon out of which grew an organisation including thirteen boys' clubs and three mixed clubs.

In 1940 and 1941, Miners' Welfare Youth Schemes were formed in Nottinghamshire and Fife. By 1946, fifteen clubs, including seven girls' clubs, had been set up in Nottinghamshire and twenty six clubs clubs in Fife. The Commission had also decided that Youth Schemes should be under the general government of District Miners' Youth Councils, appointed by the Commission, composed of representatives of the District Miners' Welfare Committee, Local

Authority, voluntary organisations and club representatives and charged with the duties of administering the Welfare Fund grants, appointing salaried leaders and promoting new clubs.

Later youth schemes were formed in West Yorkshire, the Lothians, Derbyshire North, North Staffordshire, Shropshire and Cannock Chase.

The policy in setting up these clubs was directed towards integrating them with parent Miners' Welfare Recreation Centres. To avoid segregation, club membership was open to non-mining youth, but emphasis was laid on contact with colliery personnel. In general, the aim was to develop social education in parallel with technical mining training and to provide a useful means of graduation to adult activities of the parent Miners' Welfare Centre.

A number of clubs were connected with other organisations including the Young Men's and Women's Christian Associations, the National Association of Girls and Mixed Clubs, the National Association of Boys' Clubs, the Scottish National Association of Boys' Clubs, the Carnegie Trust, the Co-operative Movement, Boy Scouts, Boys' Brigade and Girl Guides.

The normal age limits of the clubs were 14 to 18 years. Both outdoor and indoor activities were organised including outdoor and indoor sports, rambling, camping, holiday visits, crafts, music, drama and ambulance work. Most clubs had libraries, and some had their own cine-projector.

From September 1943 until 1946, the Entertainments National Service Association (ENSA) parties toured in all the coalfields giving musical, dramatic and variety entertainment in welfare halls.

From 1940, with the help of the Commission's staff, the Council for the Encouragement of Music and the Arts (CEMA) had arranged tours in the mining districts. These were both educational and recreational: ranging from full philharmonic orchestras and repertory companies to small concert parties of two or three performers. There was a change of policy when the Art Council took the place of CEMA with the Art Council supporting and encouraging entertainment rather than taking the initiative.

While dramatic and musical societies already existed at some miners' welfare institutes in a number of Districts, particularly South Wales, the ENSA and CEMA entertainments stimulated the formation of others.[22]

In 1947, the development of Miners' Welfare schemes into community centres continued. District Officers were being encouraged to concentrate on developing activities and social lives around existing schemes rather than starting new projects as neither materials nor labour were available.

Training courses in the Administration and Management of Miners' Welfare Centres to serve local communities were being more widely organised in 1947. Courses in Northumberland and South Wales were held in the early part of

1947. Glamorgan held a third series of training courses in November 1947 and Monmouth held a preliminary conference of representatives in October 1947.

Considerable deterioration in recreational schemes had occurred during the war so in 1947, the Commission was looking to district surveys to identify these schemes and rehabilitate them as rapidly as possible.[23]

In 1949, Women's Welfare Committees were beginning to be set up. In the East Midlands Division, eight women's sections were formed in the No. 6 Area. Their activities included handicrafts, Music, Drama, lectures and discussion groups. Women's groups were also being formed in Derbyshire.

By the beginning of 1950, Nottinghamshire (East Midlands Division) had fourteen women's groups with an active membership of 720. Their activities, arranged in conjunction with the Local Education Authority, included classes, craft groups, film and puppet shows, education and social visits.[24]

The Joint Council, at their October 1949 meeting, took the decision that Divisional and Sub-Divisional Welfare Committees were to ensure that all applications from the local schemes for 50% grant towards the cost of post war reconditioning must be submitted to the Council by 31st January 1950.

The approximate cost of the proposals for all the Divisions came to £236,612, towards which grant-aid amounting to about £31,200 was expected from the Ministry of Education. This left a balance of £205,412 to be attracted from grants from the Miners' Welfare Fund, less any assistance that might be forthcoming from the Scottish Home Department.[25]

On 1st July 1952, all recreational schemes, designated as social welfare, were transferred to the Coal Industry Social Welfare Organisation as set out in the Miners' Welfare Act 1952.

NINE

HEALTH

In the 1920s, miners were still working in an extremely dangerous industry. Between 1920 and 1929, 1,587,330 miners were either killed or injured in and about mines. 543,826 (34.3%) deaths or injuries were due to falls of ground. Miscellaneous accidents underground (including explosives, suffocation by natural gases, underground fires, eruptions of water, electricity and machinery) were responsible for 515,691 (32.5%) of deaths or injuries. Haulage (ropes or chains breaking, run over or crushed by trains or tubs, mechanical haulage, horse haulage or hand haulage) accounted for 387,993 (24.4%) of deaths or injuries. The remaining 8.8% of deaths or injuries were due to shaft or surface accidents and explosions of firedamp or coal dust.[1]

This high level of mortality and morbidity of miners prompted the Safety in Mines Research Board to initiate research in the coalfield into falls of ground and haulage in 1930 (see Chapter 6).

Special treatment for seriously injured miners attracted grants from the Welfare Fund as early as 1925, and continued at District level until the Commission were asked to set up a miners' rehabilitation service nationally in 1942.

The Nottinghamshire District Committee had first applied for funding for their scheme of special treatment for those seriously injured in colliery accidents in 1925, and it was considered at the Central Committee's meeting in May. Nottinghamshire had proposed that instead of investing a capital sum, they should be authorised to utilise an annual sum to be applied to payment of specialist fees, nursing, institution charges, railway fares and clothing, particularly in the cases of injuries to the spine. This was not a capital expenditure, so the proposal was turned down. At the next meeting of the Central Committee, the District Committee made an application for £200 to treat a case of spinal injury arising from an accident at the pit. In principle, the Committee were still unwilling to make an allocation until after the passage of the Bill extending the life of the Fund but, in the meanwhile, they would consider whether arrangements could be worked out for giving assistance to such cases consistent with their general policy. In December 1925, Nottinghamshire wrote to the Committee to inform them that they no longer needed the £200, as the Duchess of Portland had provided the money to send the man, Flint, to London for special treatment which had been entirely satisfactory, and he had been able to return to his previous occupation.

With the extension of the Fund at the end of 1925, and the Committee now open to considering non-capital expenditure, the Nottinghamshire District Committee chose to present a resume of what their sub-committee had achieved with seriously injured miners at the 5th Conference of District Committees Representatives in November 1926 in the hope that some part of the money might be spent in this direction in other counties and other districts. They presented a report on ten cases treated at the National Hospital, Queen's Square, London. At least five miners were back in work. They had had their failures, but they were very careful in the selection of the right class of case. They had been assisted by the Duchess of Portland, who was able to put the District Committee in touch with doctors who could make assessments. Only cases with a reasonable certainty of some improvement as a result of the treatment were included in the scheme. No case that could be treated locally was accepted into the scheme.[2]

In September 1927, Nottinghamshire District Miners' Welfare Sub-Committee for dealing with serious colliery accidents presented their report for the half-year ending 30th June 1927. It had been very difficult to single out the most urgent cases for treatment with many of them being longstanding cases. Fourteen cases were presented: four were still undergoing treatment, two were hopeless, and the rest had shown various degrees of improvement.

Since their last report, arrangements had been made for convalescent patients to go to the Seaside Convalescent Hospital, Sussex. With Fund money, they had been able to buy a spinal carriage at a cost of £24.12s.6d. The total costs including specialist fees, convalescent home subscription and maintenance charges, travelling expenses, hospital charges and the spinal carriage was £234.12s.6d.[3]

The Sub-Committee presented two reports during 1928. Reports were made for twenty-one men. Eleven of these sustained fractured spines, two had injuries to their backs and three had compound fractures. One had lost a limb, but after two operations and the provision of a special limb, he had returned to light work. One was a survivor of the Bilsthorpe Shaft disaster. This man's life had been saved by being tied to a pump for about six hours, with his right arm broken in many places. He was being given special treatment, but it was feared he would have to lose his arm; however, he was much improved by the special treatment.

One case with a fractured spine received special treatment but had to be brought home as the case was hopeless; however, the Committee continued to give careful nursing and best attention.

One case had lost both arms in an accident at Welbeck Colliery. He had been in Mansfield hospital for five months, then sent to the Roehampton Hospital for Limbless Soldiers and Sailors. After having one artificial arm fitted, he was discharged. He was awaiting an operation to the other stump of his arm before being fitted with an artificial one. The Welfare Fund met the cost of special treatment, and the indemnity company had agreed to bear the cost of the artificial limbs.

Four cases of fractured spines appeared in both reports to illustrate the aftercare being undertaken once these patients had been brought back to their homes.[4]

At the 8th Conference of Representatives of District Committees in October 1929, the Sub-Committee presented a resume of their work since June 1926. They had dealt with 41 cases; nineteen of which were spinal injuries, the remaining twenty-two had serious injuries. Out of the nineteen spinal cases, eight were either able to get about or were at work. Eight of them were still under treatment, two had died and one was a hopeless case. Of the twenty-two other injuries, three were greatly improved, twelve were at work or up and about, five were under treatment, one died, and one was a hopeless case. A further seventeen cases were considered outside the purview of the scheme and could be treated in local hospitals.

The work of the Sub-Committee had given hope to men where none existed, who were lying on their backs without any prospect except waiting to die.[5]

In North Staffordshire, since 1926, 57 cases of miners with fractured spines had been treated over a period of four years at the North Staffordshire Royal Infirmary, the principal hospital in the district. In the majority of the cases, treatment had been so successful as to at least enable the men to return home and live their lives in some degree of comfort. There were, however, seven or eight cases where the men were completely paralysed from the waist downwards and had no control over their bowels or bladder, with the result that they required regular nursing attention. They could not be kept indefinitely in the hospital as beds were badly needed for other injured miners for whom something could be done. If they were sent home, they would not live long. Although there were two institutions in the country where they could be sent if payment for maintenance was made, it would have been inhuman to send them away from their relatives and friends who would not have been able to afford to visit them.

The District Committee put forward a suggestion that a small home should be established in the District for the accommodation of such cases, which differed from the cases dealt with in Nottinghamshire, Derby and the Forest of Dean, as they were incurable.

In April 1930, the Central Committee considered North Staffordshire's application and decided that Professor Collis should visit the District. He met with the Chairman and Secretary of the District Committee as well as

Drs Allardice and Young from the infirmary. There was no suitable nursing organisation in existence so it was proposed that accommodation at the District Convalescent Home might be provided on the understanding that Mr Parker (Advisory Branch) would draw up suitable plans enabling the District to decide how much they would need to apply for in the way of capital cost and endowment. £22,000 was thought to be sufficient to which the Central Committee agreed in May 1930.[6]

The Forest of Dean had an arrangement with the local hospital committee for treatment of injured miners whereby, if the patient could not get to the hospital, arrangements would be made for treatment to be provided at the injured miner's home. In February 1931, the Central Committee allocated £300 for treatment for eight cases over twelve months.[7]

Colliery companies had a statutory liability to provide an ambulance for colliery accident cases so, when a District made an application for an ambulance, they had to state that the scheme would not relieve the mine owners of their statutory obligations.

Grants from the Miners' Welfare Fund for ambulances had been made as early as 1922 and by 1931, grants for 63 ambulances had been made at a total cost to the Fund of £53,673.13s.2d.

Durham and Northumberland had 29 ambulances (22 in Durham and 7 in Northumberland) in 1931. The greatest part of the mileage undertaken by the ambulances was on behalf of mineworkers although there was evidence that they were used for colliery accidents. The average annual mileage in Northumberland was 7,152 and in Durham 4,193.

In Northumberland, the ambulances were mainly supported by colliery levies but there was nothing allowed for depreciation and most had no reserve fund. Only four colliery companies made contributions to the ambulance schemes.

In Durham, there was a weekly levy in most cases. In nine of the schemes, an annual sum was put aside for depreciation. Many of the Durham schemes had reserve funds varying from £50 to £300. Twelve colliery companies made no contribution, even though there was evidence that the welfare ambulance had been used in colliery accidents in five collieries.

South Wales took a different approach to ambulance provision. The coalfields in South Wales covered a similar area to Northumberland and Durham and employed about the same number of men, although geographical conditions and inter-communication was more difficult in South Wales. The South Wales allocation for ambulances contributed to a co-ordinated scheme unlike Northumberland and Durham which was entirely individual.

Altogether, sixteen ambulances had been provided in South Wales, the grants having been made in every case to the St John Ambulance Service.

In 1930, the St John Ambulance Service in South Wales dealt with 3,291 mineworker cases of which 1,377 were colliery accidents. The average annual mileage for the 16 ambulances was 7,305 of which 1,341 were for colliery accidents.

The existing St John's ambulance stations were situated within a distance of six to ten miles of each other. The ambulances had full-time drivers providing a 24-hour a day service and could be called by telephone to the driver's house or through a local police station, the whole service being under headquarters' administration.

Other ambulance services were provided in Whitburn and District (Lanarkshire), Tilmanstone and Snowdon (Kent), Kippax (West Yorkshire), Cudworth (South Yorkshire), Somerset and Lochgelly, Alloa, Cowdenbeath (Fifeshire). All Scottish schemes had arrangements for co-operation with other ambulance schemes.[8]

There had been rehabilitation facilities for miners before 1942. Outpatient clinics had been established in 1935 by the Lanarkshire Orthopaedic Association, financed by the district Colliery Owners and Mineworkers Association. The Emergency Medical Schemes set up in 1939, primarily to meet the needs of air raid casualties and services, was extended to workers in war industries including mining and aimed to cover fracture services and rehabilitation. In 1940, Berry Hill Hall, Mansfield, became a miners' residential rehabilitation centre under the Midland Colliery Owners' Mutual Indemnity Company and an outpatient department was started in Wigan by the Northern Mutual Indemnity Company.

However, by June 1942, the Government White Paper had recognised the need for a nationwide medical facility for miners. By September 1942, it was confirmed that existing hospital services to meet the miners' particular needs were required and it was recommended that the Miners' Welfare Commission should set up special rehabilitation centres. In mid-December 1942, rehabilitation had been added to the Commission's other activities.

Although the Ministry of Fuel and Power's intention was to conserve manpower in the industry, in the interests of miners, the Commission widened its programme as it could not withhold treatment from an injured man merely because it was considered that he could not return to the industry.

Broad principles were laid down in the early planning of the service. Overlapping with established or projected rehabilitation services would be avoided. Surgical treatment would be through specialist fracture departments. As far as possible, the same surgeon would see the miner through all stages of his rehabilitation to ensure continuity of treatment. A system would therefore be evolved whereby surgeons at key hospitals had direct contact with the rehabilitation centres and members of staff. For the miners' centre and post-centre needs, facilities were required to implement resettlement into the industry.

Centres would need to have residential facilities in pleasant surroundings. With these principles in mind, the Commission started acquiring centres.

Berry Hill Hall, standing in ninety acres of private park above Mansfield, Nottinghamshire, was taken over by the Commission from the Midland Colliery Owners' Indemnity Company in January 1943.

Talygarn, Pontyclun, Glamorganshire, was acquired by the Miners' Welfare Commission in December 1943 from the South Wales District Miners' Welfare Committee who had used it from 1922 as a convalescent home. The 100-acre estate was said to contain every known specimen of tree which grew in the UK.

Hartford Hall, Bidington, Northumberland, was officially opened as a centre in June 1944 and had over thirty rooms. Its lawns and woodland ran down to the River Blyth.

Higham Grange, near Nuneaton, became a convalescent home for miners in 1924 and was taken over by the Commission in 1944. Built in 1887, with an estate of 126 acres, it had beautiful views over Leicestershire and Warwickshire.

The Hermitage, Chester-le-Street, Co. Durham, was built in the early nineteenth century. Shortly after the outbreak of war, it had been requisitioned by the military authorities. The Miners' Welfare Commission opened it as a rehabilitation centre in 1944

Oakmere Hall, Sandiway, Cheshire, on the fringe of the Delamere Forest, stood in large grounds with extensive lawns and lakes. It was opened as a rehabilitation centre by the Miners' Welfare Commission in October 1944.

Uddingston Centre, Lanarkshire, was previously a Miners' Welfare Institute when nearby collieries were in production. It was converted and enlarged to provide outpatient facilities and was opened in 1945.

Firbeck Hall, sixteen miles east of Sheffield, was of Elizabethan origin and had become an exclusive country club in 1936. It was converted into a centre by the Commission and received its first patients on 4th April 1947.

Each residential centre had to be adapted to provide an indoor gymnasium. There also had to be some form of outside terracing for physical training and remedial games.

Accommodation had to be made for the requirements of the physiotherapist and occupational therapy. Indoor provision was made for lighter crafts (weaving, pottery, carpentry, metal work, basket making) while outside there was an opportunity for heavier work. Facilities for running were arranged wherever possible.

Each centre had to have first-class kitchens, since there were no extra rations available. Kitchen gardens and greenhouses were exploited to supplement and vary the diet.

Each centre had its Surgeon-in-Charge whose appointment was part-time, so that he could continue to be active in orthopaedic surgery in the hospitals in the District. In view of the importance of securing the interest of all surgeons who had handled a substantial number of patients, subordinate appointments of visiting or assistant surgeons were made according to status and the relative number of miners they had as patients.

Each patient was examined upon admittance and subsequently at frequent intervals by the surgeon who, in consultation with the Chief of Treatment staff, prescribed the treatment. His progress was noted, treatment was varied, as necessary. In this way, surgeons were able to continue responsibility for the patients who received hospital treatment at their hands.

When the surgeon discharged each patient, he graded the miner according to his capacity for work. Rehabilitation was incomplete until the patient was not only back at work, but back at the highest possible level of work. His discharge classification was passed to the colliery manager and the miners' agent as part of the welfare service follow-up system.

To facilitate the all-round co-operation, the surgeon held regular clinics which were attended by the centre's Chief of Treatment staff and the Social Welfare Workers.

Each rehabilitation centre was linked with specific hospitals and surgeons' conferences were held twice yearly to exchange information of mutual interest.

A matron was employed in each centre. Matron was responsible for the efficient running of the centre and for all domestic arrangements, the food, fuel, laundry and linen. She also had to be an amateur publican as each miner got one free pint of beer every day. She also dealt with any complaints or suggestions which reached her through the centre's Captain, who was a miner elected by his fellow patients to perform such duties and to assist the chief-of-staff in organising recreational activities.

There was a weekly menu, Monday to Saturday morning, providing four meals a day: breakfast, dinner, tea and supper. Cocoa was provided at 10.10am each day. No meals were served on Sundays as the Miners' Welfare Commission made it a part of policy that each miner went home at the weekend, travel expenses being paid by the Welfare Fund.

The Chief of Treatment at a centre was generally a certified physiotherapist, under whom there were one or two qualified gymnasts and, as a rule, an assistant physiotherapist.

The fundamental principle behind the rehabilitation given in the centres was that the patient should learn or re-learn muscle control. He, therefore, had to be an active participant in his treatment as, without his co-operation and confidence, the treatment was ineffective. The psychological element of the treatment was also important.

Each miner got individual attention, and there was careful planning of his daily programme. Competitive games were encouraged and there were also cycle rides and other activities designed to encourage muscular activity. There was no rigid rule as to the sex of the remedial staff. During the war, with the shortage of manpower, the tendency was to employ women.

While remedial gym and games formed the basis of the patient's activities, heat and massage, electrical and similar treatment were used to give comfort and alleviate pain.

Occupational therapists planned a full programme for patients, both indoor and out. These activities were so arranged that there was something to suit the patient at all stages of his recovery.

As the miner neared the completion of his rehabilitation programme at the centre, the medico-social worker came into action. Each medico-social worker would have undertaken a course of study which included physiology, psychology, ethics, economics, legislation and social work.

Each social worker was present every time the patient was seen by the surgeon and made herself familiar with all the miners' difficulties. She had the medical knowledge necessary to appreciate the implications of each disability and sufficient knowledge of the industry and its processes to be able to decide whether available work was suitable for the patient.

In co-operation with the secretary of the centre and the colliery manager, the social worker would see the miner safely returned to his house and to industry and watch over him for many months after he had left the centre.

2406 patients were discharged from rehabilitation centres as fit for work of some kind during 1947. 89% returned to the mining industry, 61% to pre-accident work and 28% to light work. These figures were based on follow-up results of patients six months after their discharge. Additionally, 450 patients were re-admitted to hospital or went into permanent retirement immediately after they were discharged from the centres.

The success of the Miners' Welfare Commission rehabilitation schemes for trauma cases raised the possibility of similar schemes for miners who were disabled due to other causes directly related to their working conditions.

For rheumatism, the Commission established a clinic at Walkden in Lancashire, at which the latest forms of treatment were given under supervision of a specialist expert and where a survey of the incidence and causes of rheumatism amongst miners was started. Preliminary results were reported but the survey was curtailed when the clinic was transferred to the National Health Service in 1951.

For pneumoconiosis, nystagmus and paraplegia, the Commission's Advisory Medical Committee had done extensive preparatory work which was handed over to the National Health Service on 1st April 1951.[9]

TEN

PITHEAD WELFARE

Provision was made in Section 77 of the Coal Mines Act, 1911, for the compulsory establishment of washing and drying accommodation if demanded by a two-third majority of the workmen employed provided that, among other conditions, the estimated total cost of maintenance did not exceed 3d per head per week, and on the understanding that the workmen agreed to contribute to the cost of maintenance a sum not exceeding half that amount. This section proved to be virtually inoperable due to the high cost of construction and maintenance. In 1923, the cost of maintenance could have been as much as 1s per workman per week.

The position was somewhat modified by Section 20(5) of the Mining Industry Act, 1920, which provided that the cost of maintenance should not be deemed to include any interest on capital expenditure so far as that expenditure was met out of the money allocated from the Fund. Even so, the estimated cost of maintenance at 1923 prices exceeded the limit beyond which colliery companies could be compelled to establish accommodation. Accordingly, such pithead baths that were provided before 1926, wholly or partly from the Miners' Welfare Fund, had been the subject of mutual agreement between the owners and the workmen so far as the arrangements for meeting the cost of maintenance were concerned and, in most cases, the workmen agreed to contribute a weekly sum in excess of the statutory limit of 1½d per head.

The majority of the pithead baths built before 1923 were of the type that had been recommended by the Department Committee appointed by the Home Office who reported in 1913 and whose recommendations were incorporated into the General Regulations, dated 29th August 1913, as the Accommodation and Facilities for taking Baths and drying Clothes, and as to the Constitution, Powers and Duties of the Committees of Management. The main feature of this type of bath was the provision of arrangements for suspending separately in the roof of the building the clothes of each workman using it.[1]

The lack of pithead baths had serious consequences for both miners and their families. Lt-Colonel G. R. Lane-Fox MP, Secretary for Mines, was well aware of this issue when he stated in the House of Commons on 24th July 1923:

'I look at it from the point of view of its value to the women and children. We often hear people say 'Think what it means if there are two or three men who work in the mines bringing their wages into the same house', but we never hear people talk about what else they are bringing in. When it comes to three or four people in pit clothes, which are, perhaps, wringing wet, when some of them wear pit boots and when very many of them require baths in a very small house with limited accommodation, it is obvious that it must be extremely difficult for the woman who runs the house to keep it clean as she would like under such conditions'.[2]

The women of the house were also responsible for heating the water for the miners' baths and cleaning and drying their clothes. They were subjected to never-ending backbreaking work, exhaustion and physical strain often leading to serious health problems, and in some cases to miscarriages or premature births.

The sheer quantity of hot water used in the miners' homes was also very dangerous in itself. One South Wales coroner claimed, 'Every winter I hold more inquests on miners' children who die from scalds or burns than I do on miners who are killed underground'.[3]

During the first five years of the Fund, other aspects of industrial welfare had developed on different lines for coal mines and factories. For factories, advances had been determined by the powers taken under the Police, Factories etc (Miscellaneous Provisions) Act 1916, under which orders, for securing the welfare of factory workers, may be made, applying to 'arrangements for preparing or heating and taking meals; the supply of drinking water; the supply of protective clothing; ambulance and first aid arrangements; the supply and use of seats in work rooms; facilities for washing; accommodation for clothing; arrangements for supervision of workers.'

These powers had been extensively used. First aid provision, called for by Order had become part of the Workmen's Compensation Act, 1923 (which applied to coal mines) while drinking water had to be supplied in all factories.

For coal mines there was nothing to limit the scope of welfare activities. Ambulances and first aid arrangements had already been adequately provided under the Mines Act. Miners provided their own working clothes and facilities for washing and accommodation for clothing had been, in principle, adopted when provision was being made for pithead baths.

In coal mines, drinking water was only supplied to pit ponies. Mining work was laborious and often carried out in hot and humid atmospheres. A miner could lose as much as 18lbs weight (about 12 pints of water) in one shift, but 6 to 8lbs was more usual. Pure water should be available a short distance away from the working face, as well as at the pithead and other fluids such as tea should be available at the pithead. Reports of outbreaks of enteric fever due to polluted water having been drawn on the way to the pit or underground existed.

Unlike factory workers who had canteens, the miners still carried with them cold and unappetising food to be consumed daily under uncongenial surroundings. The colliery population suffered from enteric fever to a greater extent than any other section of workers, partly due to eating below ground. The atmosphere of the pit was not one in which eating was to be encouraged. The air was filled with spores from the mould covering timbers and from the stables where horses were kept. There were also sources of excremental pollution of human origin and the danger of fouling of hands in this way was great. Any provision for furnishing meals below ground would have to be supplemented by ablution or by supplying cold food in a 'wrapped' form from the pithead so that it could be eaten without being touched by the hands.

Great value was already gained in factories from the voluntary employment of Welfare Supervisors, particularly in the case of boys. The extent to which boys were employed in coal mines suggested that consideration should be given for establishing trained welfare supervisors at collieries where it was decided to provide pithead baths, kitchens and drinking water.[4]

Miner washing in front of the range

Drying clothes in front of the fire

The Mining Industry Act 1926 finally placed the responsibility of providing pithead baths at all coal mines on the Miners' Welfare Fund, but, as has been seen previously (see Chapter 3), the Fund did receive an extra contribution in the form of a levy on mineral rights.

No applications for pithead baths had been received from the District Committees in 1926 except for a proposal from Warwickshire District Welfare Committee that the General Fund should assist in erecting an experimental installation of the new type. The District Welfare Committee had received an application from the Pooley Hall Colliery Company asking the District Committee to recommend an allocation of £6,000 for the provision of pithead baths. Mr Stuart of the Pooley Hall Colliery Company had been in communication with Cdr. Coote, who had suggested that instead of the continental type, an experimental design of pithead baths should be tried. As such an experiment would be for the benefit not only of Warwickshire but everyone else who wished to adopt pithead baths, Warwickshire asked for the Central Committee to provide half of the allocation requested, as it would hardly be fair for the Warwickshire funds to bear the cost, and for the Pooley Hall Colliery to be landed with a method which might not work.[5]

Even when the royalties levy was instituted and the Baths Fund established, there was no great inclination to embark on baths schemes. In 1927, it was not easy to find collieries that were willing to receive installations. Some of this reluctance emanated from the mineworkers. A majority had to give their approval to the bath scheme at their pit. There were a number of reasons for this.

Each miner would be expected to have a weekly deduction from their wages. The list of off-takes on a miner's payslip was larger than in most industries, and represented a heavy burden when wages were low. Besides the contribution for National Health and Unemployment Insurance, there were weekly deductions for medical benefits for the wives and children of the workmen, for explosive tools, pick-sharpening, check weighmen (representatives elected by the coal miners to check the findings of the mine-owner's weight of coal mined) and occasional levies for various purposes such as infirmaries, the local nursing association or football team.

The older miners were reluctant to change their habit of never washing their whole body. Some objected to the pithead baths on the grounds that they were unsanitary or that there was insufficient privacy. Another reason given was there was a possibility of catching a cold as a result of coming from a hot pit to the baths and from the baths into the cold. Another objection was that if men stayed to bathe, they might be late home for their meals and might upset domestic arrangements.

There was very little experience of baths to demonstrate their benefits, the cost of running them and how costs could be met. Many of the colliery owners were under the erroneous impression that the provision of baths involved them in heavy financial liabilities. The construction and subsequent management of the baths presented new and complex problems.

From the outset, the Central Committee took the decision to undertake the building programme and to give guidance to the colliery pithead committees on how to manage the baths and the expenses of maintaining them.[6]

Of the 296 offers of baths made by the Welfare Committee between 1927 and 1929, only 102 (34%) were accepted. After 1929, the pithead baths movement gathered momentum and a remarkable change occurred in the attitude of both owners and men. In 1930 and 1931, out of 100 offers, 63 were accepted and in 1932 and 1933, 62 offers were made and 46 (74%) accepted.

Uninvited applications provided still more direct evidence of the demand for baths. Before 1931, uninvited applications were received from only eleven collieries (nine from the men and two from the owners). Between 1931 and 1932, applications were received from 70 collieries (twenty-nine on behalf of the men, twenty-two by the owners and nineteen from both sides jointly).[7]

The baths had proved to have a distinct benefit to the mine workers. There was a decrease in time lost, as the miners no longer stole ten or fifteen minutes at the end of the shift knowing that they had before them the long walk home, probably in wet clothes, and the slow and laborious process of washing in a confined space with few facilities. Now that the baths were in use, there was not the necessity to rush away at the end of the shift because the men were speedily washed and could go home on the bus in clean, dry clothes which they had left in their clean lockers, while they wore their pit clothing during their shift. Being able to use the bus had the advantage of men arriving at work unfatigued, which probably was one of the chief factors affecting the fall in the accident rates in the pits.

Another beneficial factor was the first aid room. Previously, small cuts and bruises had been ignored, but wounds that were neglected could turn septic. It became compulsory for every man with a scratch of any kind to go to the first aid room where it was reported, treated and subsequently redressed until the wound was healed.[8]

In 1933, the Committee had adopted the aim, when building pithead baths, to achieve some general improvement of pithead amenities. During 1934, there was a growing response of colliery companies to the suggestion by the Committee's architects in this direction. Well-arranged and well-kept surface buildings, apart from their effect on operating efficiency, aroused a psychological response in the miners resulting from the improved environment at the workplace.

Two speeches, one given in November 1933, by HRH, the Prince of Wales at the Centenary Celebration Banquet of the Royal Institute of Architects, and the other given by Sir Giles Gilbert Scott at the Inaugural Meeting of the Centenary Conference of the Institute, had reminded the Committee of the growing concern about working conditions and environment of workers and gave it encouragement to continue with their policy of using its influence towards improvements in the mining industry and to hope for increasing co-operation from colliery companies.

The Committee's policy also demanded that it built baths with regard to architectural values in the buildings themselves, as well as in their siting and arrangement. Good design and craftmanship induced respect and care for the completed work.

During the previous decade, the intensification of the demand for more hygienic conditions had resulted in a new approach to the problem of design and construction and in employment of new materials. This advance was reflected in some of the work of the Committee's architects which had attracted occasional criticism. Brightly-coloured paint and tiled surfaces were unusual and unexpected at pithead baths and, erroneously, thought of as expensive or extravagant. Brightly- coloured paint was no more expensive than dull colours. Good and durable surfaces and fittings were needed in order to reduce the burden of the maintenance.

During 1934, the Committee's met with high commendation in professional circles with the inclusion of Sherwood Pithead Baths and Swimming Baths in the Centenary Exhibition of 'International Architecture 1924–1934' organised by the Royal Institute of British Architects.

It was quite impracticable to cheapen the work of providing pithead baths by standardising the plan and design and to construct the buildings in units. The choice of site was generally very restricted because the baths had to be fitted into the lay-out of a working colliery. The plan had to be adapted not only to the site but had to take account of variations of level, the varying scale of bath cubicle provision according to the rate of winding and the direction of arrival of men at the baths when going to and leaving work.

Other problems of the site had to be taken into consideration. The type of foundations to be used on made-up ground or on ground subject to movement, the accessibility of water, electricity and steam supplies and the arrangement for the treatment and disposal of bath waste and sewage. The Committee's architects and engineers were also called upon to design many of the standard fittings and items of equipment amongst which were lockers, cold water mixing valves and other cubicle fittings, and boot brushing and greasing apparatus.[9]

Further additional facilities began to appear in the 1930's. At Fryston Colliery in West Yorkshire, there were artificial sunlight and radiant heat treatment rooms near the baths, under the supervision of the colliery doctors. The District Nursing Association also co-operated in the treatment of women patients. The annual running costs of £100 was paid by the colliery company, all of whose employees were treated free. At Mainsforth Pithead Baths, in Durham, apparatus was provided in 1933 at a cost of £125 out of the income of the baths. Artificial sunlight apparatus had also been installed at the baths at Kingshill No. 1 and Whitrigg Collieries in Lanarkshire and at Sherwood Colliery in Nottinghamshire at their own expense, and had been in use for a long time.

While treatment by artificial sunlight was in suitable cases beneficial, the apparatus was not provided out of the central Baths Fund.

In May 1938, the Committee received several requests from pithead baths for information on artificial sunray treatment following press reports on a solarium

Sherwood Pithead Baths and Swimming Baths, Nottinghamshire

at a mine in Sweden. At that time there were four pithead baths (see above) in Britain where lamps had been fitted without advice or assistance from the Welfare Fund. Dr Ferguson offered to obtain information on the Kingshill and Whitrigg baths and Dr Quinn arranged to visit Mainsforth and Mansfield.

At the June meeting of the Central Committee, it was decided to consult the Ministry of Health for their opinion on artificial light installations. They replied that there was no direct or specific evidence of a beneficial effect on the average person, but suggested that the Welfare Committee should investigate the question themselves by arranging actual experiments under medical supervision.

The Baths Committee at Whitburn Colliery, Durham, had submitted proposals for an installation with a view to applying for a grant from the District Fund to meet the cost of providing it.

The Committee decided to ask the Ministry of Health whether they would assist the Welfare Committee in making the necessary medical arrangements for instituting and controlling the experiment and observing the results and what expenditure was likely. If the Ministry were unable to do this, the Health Advisory Committee would be approached.

By January 1939, the Mines Department Health Advisory Committee had replied to the Committee that, based on existing scientific evidence, treatment was in its infancy and they were not prepared to recommend or undertake the arrangements for an experiment. The Committee therefore decided not to proceed further on considering grants from the Baths Fund or the General Fund.

The blackout conditions of the war years brought renewed attention to the possibilities of artificial sunlight. In October 1941, Leicestershire District Committee submitted recommendations for installations at their chief collieries as a means of stimulating production of coal. The Ministry of Health was asked to consider the matter again but were unable to support the proposal of arranging a scientific investigation.

Several Leicestershire colliery owners, the Manvers Main Colliery (South Yorkshire) and two or three other companies, installed the apparatus at their own expense in the hope that it would increase the output of coal. Initially the installations were well used but then attendance fell.

Request for installations continued to come in and the Commission continued its efforts to arrange an authoritative test for the use of artificial sunlight.

In 1944, the Industrial Health Research Board of the Medical Research Council reconsidered its position, and decided to carry out a controlled and relatively large-scale inquiry.

At about the same time, Nottinghamshire District Committee, impressed by the results claimed for the Butterley Company's clinic at Kirkby Colliery, strongly urged the Commission to make grants from the District Fund for solaria at Blidworth and Silverhill collieries, under the supervision of the Kirkby doctor who had specialised in this type of treatment. The Commission gave its approval in principle.

The Industrial Health Research Board trials were conducted during the winter months of 1944 and 1945 at the South Kirkby Colliery (Yorkshire), Vauxhall Motors Ltd (Luton) and the Admiralty (London) and the numbers taking part were 1,314 miners (including 1,137 underground workers), 1042 male day-shift workers and 1,043 women clerks respectively. The routine dosage was two minutes exposure twice weekly.

At the colliery, the solarium was situated in the pithead baths between the showers and the clean locker room. During the first eight-week period, attendance was good but by the end of the second period, a fairly heavy drop in numbers had occurred.

The effects of the light treatment were judged according to sickness absence in each of the three communities, injury and total absence among the miners and the duration of the colds of the factory and clerical workers.

The Research Board's report (issued in May 1946) summarised the results by saying that using an accepted technique of irradiation, there was in these trials no evidence whatsoever that the benefits claimed for artificial sunlight on people in normal health were in fact produced.[10]

The problem of drying overcoats and trousers had been an issue for a number of pithead baths and it was discussed in detail at a meeting held at Oakdale Colliery, South Wales, on 4th November 1937. Based on these discussions, Mr Tait, one of the agents for the Powell Duffryn Association Collieries Ltd., produced recommendations which were considered by the Central Committee.

Oakdale pithead baths used the plenum system, whereby warm air was forced through the lockers by a fan which gave 40 to 50 air changes an hour. The temperature of the air was kept at about 85F, but if the room was long, the temperature could reach 95F in the first nest of lockers. These conditions would dry an ordinary suit of pit clothes in sixteen hours, but they might not dry a very wet overcoat inside a clean locker in eight hours (the length of the shift). Hooks outside the clean lockers provided for overcoats and warm air could be passed through the lockers on wet days, the flow being regulated by the attendant. Wet mackintoshes and oil skins were not put in the lockers as they would be damaged by the heat.

Home boots, left in clean lockers, were not observed to deteriorate if heated on wet days for eight hours. Pit boots were greased once or twice a week, which assisted the longer exposure to warm air.

Pilfering of boots and overcoats left outside the lockers could be reduced by firm action being taken by the Baths Management Committee. At Silverwood in South Yorkshire, pilfering had taken place at the outset but had been stamped out by firm action taken by the Management Committee and the Bath Superintendent. Boots there were stored on racks under the seats as well as in the lockers.

If overcoats were dried in lockers, the dimensions of the lockers would have to be increased as well as the heating plant. As not every miner came to work in an overcoat, it was suggested that it would be more economical to either provide a separate drying or cloak room or a separate drying cabinet in the locker room.[11]

In 1939, reports were made by Mr Bradley of the British Boot, Shoe and Allied Trades Research Association to the Central Committee. Twenty-four-hour tests had been carried out by the Committee's Engineering Staff at the baths at two hot and dry pits, Parsonage (Lancashire) and Shelton Deep (North Staffordshire). Mr Bradley had examined the thermographic charts and sample clogs and boots and found that boots had suffered no ill effects from storage in lockers. Those examined only showed deterioration as a consequence of foot perspiration or from slow burning in the high temperatures in the pits plus perspiration. There was no evidence of excess heat scorching in the lockers, so there was no necessity for any modification of the system of lockers and heating in the pithead baths.

Complaints continued to be made that boots became over-dry in the lockers, and some even refused to keep their boots in the lockers and either placed them on racks under the lockers or wore their pit boots to and from home.

In September 1947, the Comrie Pithead Baths Management Committee asked the Commission to consider meeting the cost of a proposed modification to the existing lockers, to provide storage space for boots which would isolate them from the heat system. There had been detailed discussions between the National Coal Board, the Boot, Shoe and Allied Trades Research Association and Comrie Pithead Baths Management Committee who had, at their own expense, modified 4 lockers. The Boot, Shoe and Allied Trades Research Association were confident that they could carry out the experiment to show that boots stored in the new lockers design were less affected by heat.

In May 1948, a new type of locker was approved by the National Miners' Welfare Joint Council. This locker had a boot storage space in the bottom of the locker with an insulated container to hold the boots. This type of locker was to be installed at all standard pithead baths when existing contracts for lockers ran out.[12]

In dusty pits, men made a practice of 'dadding' their clothes. Through the 1930's, requests were made from a number of Districts (6 from Durham, 3 from Northumberland, one from Lanark, one from Derby and one from North Staffordshire) for de-dusting apparatus. Three Local Committees, Ellington (Northumberland), Eppleton and Elsmore (Durham) had installed apparatus themselves.

The apparatus at Ellington, provided in 1938, consisted of wire panels clamped to a metal suction chamber with an electrically-driven fan. The apparatus alone cost £30 but it was housed in a separate room. This was found to be satisfactory at Ellington which was a hanger type-bath. For baths with lockers, however, it would not be possible to ensure that the men would use a separate room. Without an unrestricted view which a hanger installation afforded, the attendants would not be able to prevent men from using the walls or lockers, if so inclined.

At Eppleton, wire mesh panels were fitted to the wall at the gangway and of the pithead lockers. There were 8 panels costing £8 each. There was no suction apparatus and consequently, there was a fair amount of fine dust in the atmosphere, but the men did not object to this as the dadding was done when they were going on shift. Approximately 86% of the bathers used the apparatus which had been installed in 1931.

At Elsmore, one wire mesh panel, at the end of the pit locker room on each floor, was installed in 1926. The panel was clamped to a metal suction chamber and an electrically driven fan on the first floor was used to extract the dust not only from the panels but from the boot cleaning machines. The cost of the apparatus was approximately £90. It was used by only about 13% of the bathers, the majority of whom still 'dadded' their clothes on the walls.

The men at Ashington and New Moor (Northumberland) and Beamish (Durham) had requested that de-dusting equipment to be installed at the sketch plan stage of their pithead baths. The sketch plans for all three installations had been submitted to the Local Committees in 1938.

All the systems in use for de-dusting were considered but it was concluded that an alternative solution was needed. It was suggested that the de-dusting might be made part of the vacuum plant by substitution of a central plant for a portable plant. This would enable piping to be fitted along the length of the pit locker room and a number of branch hoses with bristle brush mouthpieces to be placed in convenient positions where the men could either brush their clothes whilst wearing them or while pulled taut on some form of coat rack. The extra cost of these proposals over a portable vacuum cleaning plant was approximately £70 in January 1940.

The Central Committee approved the provision of de-dusting apparatus from a central vacuum plant at Beamish, Ashington, New Moor and West Sleekburn experimentally, with a view to assisting consideration of the question of all pits where the workings were dusty and the workmen made a practice of 'dadding' their clothes.[13]

In January 1940, the Committee considered a recommendation from South Yorkshire District Committee for a grant of £250 to provide a second Aerotone Therapeutic bath at Manver Main Pithead Baths. A decision was deferred pending further inquiries from the Empire Rheumatism Council and the Medical Research Council.

The Aerotone Therapeutic Bath was a patented apparatus invented by Professor William Oliver, Professor of Organisation of Industry and Commerce, University of Edinburgh. The Committee endeavoured to ascertain whether the claims made for the Bath could be supported by authoritative medical opinion and made enquiries with H. M. Inspector of Mines, Ministry of Health, the Empire Rheumatism Council and the Medical Research Council. The replies revealed that considerable doubt prevailed as to whether the Bath was capable of curing any but temporary disorders but, on the other hand, the Commission understood that many patients who had used the Bath had felt the benefit from it. In the circumstances, the Commission decided not to refuse the District's recommendation but, at the same time, the Commission would try to arrange an investigation by the appropriate medical authority of the therapeutic value of the treatment by the Aerotone Bath.

On 24th April, a letter was addressed to the Health Advisory Committee of the Mines Department, asking if such an investigation could be instigated by the Committee. Replying on 1st June, Dr Fisher, the Secretary of the Health Advisory Committee, had stated that his members had been consulted, but their view was 'that a thorough investigation would entail a great amount of work over a long period of time, and they further felt that the need for it is not a matter of such urgency as to justify, in present conditions, an extensive investigation into the possible therapeutics of the bath. They suspend expressing any opinion as to the beneficial results the bath might give in certain cases.'

On 27th May 1940, the South Yorkshire Committee had written that applications had been received from several other Committees in South Yorkshire for Aerotone Baths installations. On 21st May, a deputation of the District Committee discussed this subject amongst other matters with the Commission saying that they had five further applications for assistance in hand. The deputation was asked to take no action until investigations had taken place. The District Committee would be informed as to progress made in the matter.

At the May 1940 meeting of the Commission, a recommendation from West Yorkshire District Committee for a grant of £500 for an Aerotone Bath at Glass Houghton Pithead Baths was considered.

At their June 1940 meeting, the Committee decided to ask the District Committees to postpone their recommendations until a more favourable time, as there were wartime restrictions on building and materials and the Commission had been unable to obtain an authoritative medical opinion.

In July 1940, the Commission reconsidered West Yorkshire's application for an Aerotone Bath at Glass Houghton Pithead Baths. West Yorkshire's District Organiser had written to explain the reason that had led the West Yorkshire District to make the recommendation. The Aerotone Bath at Glass Houghton was to be an experiment, and not an indication that the District Committee intended to make numerous recommendations of a similar nature.

In the light of this new information and with the Commission unable to obtain the means to conduct such an experiment themselves for the time being, the Commission approved a grant of £500 subject to a number of conditions including those related to the installation of the bath, the conduct of the experiment including the need for qualified medical advice and doctor's reports, one before, one after and one six months after treatment, on the patients included in the experiment.14

A six-month experimental laundry service was instituted by the Moseley Common Pithead Baths Committee in co-operation with the Co-operative Laundries Association in the first half of 1950. A minimum of 250 participants was required to run the service but not more than 75 used it. There was insufficient accommodation for the collection and delivery necessary for a laundry service as the baths were used to capacity due to the transfer of men from Mosten Colliery during the experimental period.

Although the experiment had been disappointing in terms of the number of participants, it had provided valuable experience. The Co-operative Laundries Association and the British Launderer's Association were willing to co-operate where the prospects were good so preliminary enquiries were made in four Divisions.

An experiment to test the value of footbaths as a preventative against epidermophytosis (athlete's foot), which took place at the Dean and Chapter Pithead Baths in Durham, proved inconclusive. This was initiated in 1945 by the Mines Medical Service, Ministry of Fuel and Power, and financed by the Miners' Welfare Commission at a cost of £115.13s.4d. The cost included the supply of a disinfectant (£66.16s.8d) and turnstile (£67.12s.6d) designed to ensure that bathers used the footbath. The experiment was discontinued in 1948, the Divisional Medical Officer, reporting that he had introduced a method of individual treatment which was proving effective.

In 1951, the East Midland Divisional Medical Officer had suggested that all new pithead baths should be equipped with footbaths as a means of drawing the attention of the men to the importance of adequate care of their feet.

Discussions had taken place between HM Chief Mines Medical Officer, the Board's Chief Medical Officer, representatives of the Ministry of Fuel and Power and of the Welfare Sub-Department on the problem of epidermophytosis and controlled research was seen as desirable. The appropriate body to conduct this research was the Medical Research Council.

Pending the outcome of this research, the Joint Council recommended that the East Midland Divisional Welfare Committee restrict the number to three experimental footbaths where results should be carefully observed. 16

Under the Miners' Welfare Act, 1952, all pithead welfare was transferred to the National Coal Board on 1st July 1952.

ELEVEN

THE FINAL YEARS
1946–1952

When the Commission held its first meeting in 1946, the Coal Industry Nationalisation Bill had already been presented in Parliament on 19th December 1945. The Bill proposed the nationalisation of the entire British Coal Industry and the establishment of the National Coal Board who would have sole responsibility for managing and running the industry.

Sir Patrick Abercrombie and Mr Lawther had resigned from the Commission and their places were taken by Miss M. Herbison MA, MP, and Mr J Bowman. Miss Herbison was the daughter of a Lanarkshire coalminer who had died in the mine in which he had been employed near Shotts. Mr Bowman was the nominee of the NUM.

Although the Secretary had prepared notes on the provision of the Coal Industry Nationalisation Bill, in relation to the Miners' Welfare Fund, the Commission decided to defer this item to their next meeting as the Bill was going through its Second Reading in Parliament.

The Commission had finally received a reply, dated 14th January 1946, from the Minister of Fuel and Power to the questions put by the Commission at the meeting on 13th November 1945 and the Commission's letter dated 28th November 1945.

The Minister confirmed that the Commission should proceed on the basis of a seven-year baths programme subject to the necessary funding being provided and sufficient building labour and materials being available.

Staff salaries would be examined and considered by the Establishment Division of the Ministry. If staff were transferred to the National Coal Board, there was no reason to believe that they would not be retained by the Board as long as the work was required. The Department was in the process of negotiating the return of the Commission's staff from the Forces who were required for the baths building programme.

The Minister accepted, in principle, the desirability of a return to London from Ashstead of the Headquarters' staff and the Commission were authorised to find accommodation on their own account, subject to certain conditions which had been communicated separately.

The existing practice when acquiring sites for building pithead baths, whereby sites of buildings were vested in local trustees or charitable trusts, would continue unchanged for the present. Medical treatment centres would be included in all new pithead baths and funded on the same basis as the pithead baths.

The Commission decided to submit further observations on the answers that the Minister had given. The Commission had agreed to include medical centres in all pithead baths on the understanding that the cost would not be chargeable to the Welfare Fund. The temporary departure from the principles hitherto followed (the employer was responsible for the first-aid rooms) did not seem very desirable.

The Commission wanted to bring to the notice of the Ministry the need for defining the constitution and functions of the District Miners' Welfare Committees which came together in 1921 on an informal and temporary basis pending the appointment of the District Committees provided by Part II of the Mining Industry Act 1920. Part II had never come into operation. The Minister was asked to consider including a provision in the Nationalisation Bill similar to that of Part II of the Mining Industry Act 1920.

The Secretary had submitted a memorandum on the question of legalising the admission of non-miners to membership of the miners' welfare institutes and recreation grounds where it had hither to been restricted in law (though not always in practice) to mineworkers. The Secretary had taken advice from the Charity Commission on the legal position regarding the trust deed of the miners' welfare schemes permitting the admission of the general public.

In view of the need to legalise the policy declared by the Commission in 'Miners' Welfare Looks Forward' and to enable persons in the employment of the National Coal Board to be eligible for membership of the Miners' Welfare Schemes, the Commission decided to propose to the Minister that it was desirable to legalise the position by including a provision in the Coal Industry Nationalisation Bill or by some other means and that admission of non-mineworkers should be conditional upon the recommendation being adopted by a majority of the current members at a general meeting.

At a special meeting in February 1946, the Commission considered the Secretary's notes on the Coal Industry Nationalisation Bill as it related to the Miners' Welfare Fund.

The output levy and the principles under which sums from it were appropriated remained unchanged, excepting the provision of the £20,000 a year to safety and health research which was repealed. The Minister would assume the responsibility for safety and health research and the cost would be charged to the Ministry Vote. The Mining Research (Safety and Health) Endowment Fund (representing grants totalling £259,528 from the Welfare Fund) and the Research Board's Reserve Fund (which amounted to £65, 238) on 31st March

1945 (and had also been derived from grants from the Welfare Fund) were, when the Treasury so directed, to be sold and the cash paid into the Exchequer. The Ministry would also take over the Research Stations of the Safety in Mines Research Board at Sheffield and Buxton. The future of the Research Board was not explained.

The mineral rights duty (and consequently the royalties welfare levy) might, it was understood, be abolished by other legislation.

The purposes to which the Welfare Fund was applied, and the persons entitled to the benefits were not altered. The statutory duties and powers of the Fund were not changed except the Minister was empowered to give the Commission direction in respect of the exercise and performance of their functions. Additional duties might be given to the Commission which would empower it to act as an agent of the National Coal Board at the Board's expense.

The Commission would be reconstituted. Members were to vacate office at the commencement of the Act. The number of members was to remain unchanged at 10. The chairman would be appointed by the Minister instead of by the Commission itself.

There were two provisions in the Bill concerning pithead baths, canteens and other pithead welfare that would affect the Commission's interests. Contracts entered into with colliery companies to supply steam, electricity or water or to lease land or to provide facilities for the pithead baths or other welfare schemes would be taken over by the Coal Board and would be binding on them. Any sum devoted by a colliery company after 1st August 1945 to the provision of owner's additions to pithead baths such as a statutory first-aid room would be refunded in cash.[1]

On 12th July 1946, Royal Assent was given to the Coal Industry Nationalisation Act 1946. On 29th August, the Minister of Fuel and Power formally advised the Commission's office of the appointments to the new Commission which met for the first time on 11th September 1946.

The new Commission was chaired by Rt. Hon. Lord Citrine. Sir Ronald Adam and Mr A. M. Bryan were appointed in place of Lord Abercrombie and Mr F Llewellin Jacob.

Mr Steadman had retired on 30th June 1946. Lord Citrine had approached the Minister of Fuel and Power with the proposal that Mr Steadman should be appointed as his Personal Advisor until he had learnt more about the Commission's past. This appointment was approved by the Ministry of Fuel and Power for a period of one year. It had been decided at the April meeting of the previous Commission that the two Assistant Secretaries (Mr Bennett and Mr Freston) would be Acting Joint Secretaries on the retirement of Mr Steadman, pending another appointment by the new Commission.

At their first meeting in September 1946, the new Commission considered the provision of the Act with particular reference to the Commission and the Miners' Welfare Fund.

No definite indication had so far been given as to how and when the assurance made by the previous and present Minister of Fuel and Power regarding the money required for pithead baths would be implemented.

The Commission decided that a Finance Sub-Committee, consisting of the Chairman, Professor Collis, Mr Drummond and Mr Horner, should be appointed to examine the question of the financial position of the Miners' Welfare Fund in all its aspects, including the refund of money expended from the Fund on canteens and rehabilitation centres with a view to placing the subject before the National Coal Board for their consideration.

The Act had now made provision giving the Minister power to vary the trusts of any property provided out of the Miners' Welfare Fund and consideration was being given by the Ministry of Fuel and Power and the Commission's officials to the drawing up of the necessary regulations and form of Order for giving administrative and legal effect to this provision. Although the original objective of the Commission was to secure the use of local recreation and leisure-time schemes as community centres by other persons other than mineworkers and their dependents, the provision in the Act extended this objective to all classes of Miners' Welfare property which were subject to trusts, as well as persons.

On 30th October 1946, a joint meeting of principal officers of the Commission and the Manpower and Welfare Department of the National Coal Board was held under the chairmanship of Lord Citrine. An interesting and comprehensive discussion about co-ordination with the Board regarding miners' welfare work took place. It was agreed that there was an overwhelming case for central co-ordination and that a further meeting should be held as soon as possible to consider how this could be satisfactorily achieved.

A further meeting of the officers took place prior to the Commission's meeting on 18th December 1946. Although the Commission's officers had stressed the need for defining the functions of each body, the National Coal Board's officers had expressed the view that the problem of integration of the two forms of organisation was more urgent and consequently, the discussion had been confined to this subject. It was hoped that a detailed report would be available for the January 1947 meeting of the Commission.

Mr Bennett had submitted a memorandum on the subject of co-ordination with the National Coal Board for consideration by the Commission at its meeting in December 1946, but it had been published before this latest meeting with the Coal Board. The memorandum did additionally contain proposals for the seconding of seven District Officers to act as Divisional Officers of the National Coal Board.

The Divisional Coal Boards were offering these appointments to the District Officers at a higher salary than they were receiving from the Commission. The Commission agreed to the secondment subject to a number of conditions.[2]

The effect of the Minister of Fuel and Power 's assurances on the Baths Fund and his approval of the Commission's proposal to complete their Baths programme within a period of seven years led the Commission to assume the amount of money to be found for the Baths Fund would be regulated according to the rate at which it was possible to build baths rather than, as in the past, by the amount of money available. Each District's share in the Baths Fund was therefore no longer an appropriate basis for the regulation of the provision of baths between Districts. It was therefore decided at the Commission's meeting on 15th January 1946 that, in future, each District's share of the number of baths to be provided in any one year's programme should be proportionate to that District's share of the miners working at unprovided collieries.

With the obligation of the Commission to provide 'medical treatment centres' and cycle stores as part of future pithead baths, provided out of the Baths Fund, in January 1945, the Commission had agreed that prototype 'medical treatment centres' should be planned for erection at six existing pithead baths so that experience could be gained. In February 1946, the Chief Architect presented proposals for four types of cycle stores and their approximate costings.

By March 1946, it had become necessary to defer three baths from the programme of tenders for pithead baths from 1946 to 1947, in order to make room for five experimental medical treatment centres required by the Ministry of Fuel and Power.

By June 1946, the priority lists for pithead baths had been received from all but two District Committees, Ayr and Cannock Chase.

The Ministry of Supply still had not cleared the premises at Denaby Main (South Yorkshire). Until this had happened, the District Valuer could not issue the de-requisition notice. It had been agreed at the March meeting of the Commission that the pithead baths at Denaby Main should be completed to ground floor level, the shell having already been built, in view of the fact the number of men employed at the colliery had been halved.

There were delays in the pithead baths programme chiefly due to obtaining deliveries of essential materials and manufactured articles when required. The shortage of bricks had created a demand for substitute walling materials which in turn were in short supply. The position was generally so serious that the Ministry of Works had introduced a scheme for priorities in distribution of a large range of building materials, for which contract certificates had to be obtained for all materials and components which were covered by the scheme. As pithead baths did not carry the highest priority for labour, there was doubt whether all applications for certificates to enable the purchase of materials would be successful.

The possibility of completing the tender programme for 1946 of thirty-three baths and one extension was in doubt. Nineteen baths and one extension now appeared to be the maximum number which could be tendered for in 1946, leaving fourteen jobs to be carried forward into 1947. The chief reasons for falling short of the original target were that twenty-one of the thirty-three schemes needed revised sketch plans due to changes of site or change of accommodation required, and the lack of staff due to a lack of suitable office space.

In September 1946, the Chief Architect had to inform the new Commission that lack of accommodation and the consequent impossibility of securing the necessary technical and other staff, together with the considerable additional work on planning the five experimental protype Medical Treatment Centres for the Ministry of Fuel and Power, had prevented any prospect of the fulfilment of the whole of the 1946 programme and it would be necessary to carry eleven jobs forward to the 1947 programme. The 1947 programme therefore would have to be reduced from the planned number of 60 to 40 so that it was likely that, by the end of 1947, the building programme would be thirty-one baths behind schedule unless a full staff could be recruited.

The Commission therefore agreed that approval should be sought from the Minister of Fuel and Power for the recruitment of the complement of staff proposed by the Chief Architect and recruitment then started as soon as possible.

The Commission also agreed that a sub-committee comprising Lord Citrine (ex officio), Mr Bowman, Mr Drummond, Mr Hall and Mr Horner should be appointed to consider the whole question of the pithead baths programme and to meet the Minister on the question of priority for office accommodation, staff, building labour, materials and plant.

The sub-committee met on 2nd October. It asked Mr Kemp to provide additional information which might be useful when the deputation from the Commission met the Minister. They also recommended that the Commission should give the Chief Architect full authority to employ outside architects at his discretion and to permit overtime to be worked by his staff for a limited period.

The sub-committee also considered the Fife proposal for a second programme for small installations to run parallel with the main programme but advised against the proposal.

The 1946 and 1947 instalments of the 'Seven Year Plan' made provision for placing contracts for 90 installations. Only 19 contracts would be placed by the end of 1946. The placing of work with local architects had been agreed at the Commission's October meeting so, at the November meeting of the Commission, Mr Kemp proposed giving out 51 installations to local architects.

Delays in delivery of equipment continued throughout November and December causing delays in the opening of installations so it was decided that the Commission's officers should meet representatives of the Mining Supplies Division to discuss the problem, and Lord Citrine agreed to be present at the meeting.[3]

The Commission was informed in April 1946 that the Government had again found itself unable to give miners extra rations at home. It had been decided that a new drive should be made to increase the service of extra food through their canteens. Grants on a substantial scale would be made to improve facilities which the committees were unable to make from their own resources.

The Ministry did not expect the Miners' Welfare Fund to find the money for the grants, and the Ministry was willing to relieve the Fund of all further obligation for canteens except for the cost of erecting canteens where a form of provision had yet to be made from the Fund.

By June 1946, the procedure for handing over the grant-aiding and supervision of the colliery canteens to the Ministry of Fuel and Power was being hammered out in the Ministry in consultation with the Commission's staff. It was not likely that the handover would take place earlier than 1st August and quite possibly not until 1st September 1946.

It was finally agreed with the Ministry that it would take over the full range of responsibilities for the upkeep of the canteens as from 1st September. The Ministry had already made a preliminary survey of the canteens to determine those in the most urgent need of alterations, improvements or redecoration. The Ministry had appointed a number of catering officers and canteen executive officers to their Regional Staff. As a result of these arrangements, the functions of District Welfare Officers and Divisional Architects would cease but they would continue to be available to give advice.

The Ministry had issued a memorandum setting out these arrangements which had been sent to all District Miners' Welfare Committees and Colliery Canteen Committees. They had also issued a statement to the press setting out the arrangements and stating the Ministry's great appreciation of the work done by the Commission in establishing canteen facilities for approximately 98% of miners.

After 1st September, the canteen section of the Ministry of Fuel and Power had frequent consultations with the Commission's Headquarter Staff related to structural alterations to existing canteens and plans for new canteens. The Ministry had also sent particulars of half a dozen 'black spot' canteens, mostly in South Wales, which they suggested would need replacing by new buildings.

The Commission continued to receive applications for new canteens. Between 1st September and the end of November 1946, twenty-two applications had been received.[4]

At the March 1946 meeting of the Commission, it had been reported that six experimental medical treatment centres were to be built, but a survey of Parsonage Colliery had revealed that there was no suitable site so the scheme had been dropped. Progress on the remaining five prototypes was reported to the June meeting of the Commission. It had taken more time than anticipated to decide on requirements and to obtain estimates for items of medical equipment with a consequent delay of one month in obtaining tenders.

Five types of plans, designed to meet the requirements of collieries of various sizes, had been settled with the Ministry of Fuel and Power. At the request of the Ministry, five prototype treatment centres were being erected at collieries with existing pithead baths, selected by the Chief Mines Medical Officer in consultation with the Commission. By October 1946, four of the treatment centres were under construction at New Harrington and Vane Tempest (Durham). Markham Main (South Yorkshire) and Western (South Wales).

The Commission had agreed that all the plans for new pithead baths would include medical centres. The Ministry hoped to have 50 nurses working at collieries in the near future and had requested the Commission's architects' assistance in identifying space in existing premises so that these nurses could be recruited.[5]

At the beginning of 1946, seven rehabilitation centres were in full operation, providing 317 beds and 150 places for outpatients. The only major coalfield not provided for was Yorkshire but Firbeck Hall had been acquired and would start to take patients during 1946. A second centre to serve the Sunderland area, had been approved for Durham. A new centre had been proposed for Fife to take both residential and non-residential cases. In Kent and Cumberland, non-residential schemes attached to hospitals were being assisted and developed. Other schemes not under the control of the Miners' Welfare Rehabilitation Scheme existed at Gleneagles, Pathill (West Midlands), Betley Court (North Staffordshire) Pinderfields (Yorkshire) and Wigan. Some of these schemes were dependent on mine owners, so were likely to be affected by the nationalisation of the coal mines (Wigan and Betley Court) while Pinderfields and Gleneagles were both regarded as temporary.

On 3rd December 1945, Mr Nicoll, Consulting Surgeon had visited Talygarn Rehabilitation Centre to investigate why a high percentage of men discharged (30%) in category 'A' (return to full-time work) were still unemployed after three months. The surgeon-in-charge had admitted that the policy was deliberate as there was an absolute shortage of light work. This had been Mr Nicoll's experience as well.

On the same day, Mr Nicoll and a deputation from the Talygarn Rehabilitation Centre met with representatives of the Welsh Board of Health to discuss the lack of co-operation on the part of the medical fraternity in South Wales and expressed the hope that the Welsh Board of Health could exercise its influence to induce local practitioners to pass suitable cases on either to the Prince of Wales Hospital for primary treatment or to Talygarn for rehabilitation. The representatives of the Welsh Board of Health admitted that they had no powers of compulsion and, while agreeing personally that the provision of an orthopaedic hospital, linked with a number of peripheral hospitals with a specialist fracture department, should be made in the future National Health Service, the Board could not anticipate the National Health Service.

Subsequently, the Chairman of the District Rehabilitation Committee had written to ask if an approach to the Minister of Health might be a suitable next move.

The Medical Committee held their meeting at Talygarn on 25th January 1946. In addition, they made a tour of inspection of the treatment accommodation and they also met members of the South Wales and Monmouthshire Rehabilitation Committee together with the South Wales surgeons. A particularly useful discussion on the general problem of rehabilitation of miners in South Wales was held.

Mr A. J. Pratt, agent of the National Union of Mineworkers at Hedworth, had written to the West Midland Rehabilitation Committee following his discussion on Miners' Nystagmus with Dr D. R. Campbell, who was working on behalf of the Colliery Association and whose patients were attending Coventry Hospital for a kind of rehabilitation treatment which was only given intermittently. Mr Pratt had suggested that rehabilitation for these patients could be given at Higham Grange. The Executive of the Miners' Rehabilitation Medical Committee considered the question at its meeting on 26th July, but did not feel that it was in their terms of reference to advise on the rehabilitation of miners suffering from nystagmus and recommended that such cases should not be undertaken in existing rehabilitation centres which were designed to provide treatment for miners who had suffered injury.

Nystagmus was discussed by the Commission at their October 1946 meeting. Nystagmus (involuntary eye movements) was acknowledged to be a condition associated with poor lighting, but neurosis was a large factor in the disease. The Chairman questioned whether the Commission could afford to wait for the National Health Service to be in a position to deal with these cases. It was therefore agreed that steps should be taken to collate information on the research being conducted at Oxford, Coventry and elsewhere and that a committee should be set up to consider the matter and report back to the Commission. The following were appointed to this committee, with powers to co-opt others, particularly an ophthalmic specialist: Professor Collis, Mr Hall, Dr Fisher and Mr Hartwell. The Chairman suggested co-opting Sir Charles Ellis, the scientific member of the National Coal Board.

The question of research into the causes and incidence of rheumatism was also raised at the October meeting. The Empire Rheumatism Council had asked Mr Freston to meet them to explore the possibility of the Commission sponsoring some 'pilot' surveys into diseases popularly known as 'rheumatism'. Although the Empire Rheumatism Council had left the field of research, the Association of Industrial Medical Officers had suggested the mining industry as the most suitable industry for an early survey.

The Durham District Miners' Association had accepted the gift of Dene House, near Seaham, from Lord Londonderry for a clinic for the treatment of rheumatism. Lord Londonderry had also met the cost of the decoration and furnishing of the clinic and was prepared to provide the equipment.

Although the Ministry of Health had gone some distance with organising diagnostic and research centres in the provinces, Lord Citrine suggested that the Commission could not wait until the medical professionals had eliminated all possible chances of error in their advice as to the appropriate treatment of rheumatic conditions.

The Commission therefore approved the maintenance grant of £1,500 recommended by the Durham District Committee for Dene House, Durham Rheumatism Treatment Centre and decided to obtain the views of the Medical Advisory Committee on the project. It was also decided that the scheme must be able to fit in with any National Health schemes which might be established.

Dr W. S. C. Copeman, representing the Empire Rheumatism Council attended the Medical Advisory Committee meeting on 19th October 1946 to explain the idea of the Council for a 'pilot' survey in connection with rheumatism amongst miners. The Committee agreed to recommend the suggested pilot survey but were unanimously agreed that the Commission should be advised not to give its blessing to a 'rheumatism clinic' which was not linked with diagnostic and investigative facilities and which could only be resourced at a general hospital with expert staff. Dr Copeman pointed out that the clinic at Seaham would be developed as a peripheral clinic linked closely with the Newcastle diagnostic centre.

It was agreed that the practical possibilities of linking the pilot survey suggested by the Empire Rheumatism Council to the treatment clinic proposed by the Durham miners would be considered by an ad hoc committee.

At the same meeting, the Medical Advisory Committee discussed the rehabilitation of miners with permanent paraplegia. In peace time, 90% of cases of paraplegia due to spinal injuries were incurred by miners working underground. The management of these patients was complex, so a sub-committee (Mr F. W. Holdsworth, Mr E. Nicoll and Professor Platt) was set up to examine the whole problem and report back to the Executive Committee.

Mr Freston and Messrs Nicoll and Holdsworth visited Stoke Mandeville Hospital on 5th December 1946, and saw Dr Guttman and the work being done with paraplegic patients. Of the 175 cases handled by Dr Guttman at Stoke Mandeville, only 7% had died within two years. Mr Nicoll had investigated his figures on paraplegic miners in the Mansfield area and 75% were dead within two years (twelve out of sixteen cases). Mr Holdsworth had found that out of twenty-two cases, fifteen had died within two years.

Dr Guttman gave the sub-committee members details of treatment, rehabilitation, resettlement and aftercare. The British Legion in Aylesbury had provided a home in which men could experiment in the problems of living at home with their families or other carers.

By December 1946, the Medical Advisory Committee's ad hoc committee on rheumatism had met in Newcastle to examine the facilities available and then their conclusions were presented to the Commission for its consideration at their December meeting. One of the committee's conclusions involved the reversal of the Commission's previous refusal to take over full responsibility of the Dene House Clinic as an integral part of a general scheme for the treatment of rheumatism in miners.

The Commission therefore decided to set up a Rheumatism Committee, comprising Lord Citrine, Professor Collis, Mr J. Hall, Dr Fisher, Dr Conybeare, Mr Hartwell, Dr W. S. C. Copeman, a nominee of Sir Charles Ellis, Mr E. A. Nicoll, Dr G. Laughton-Scott, and Mr E. A. Shearing, with the power to co-opt, to keep under review the facilities available for miners, to stimulate hospitals and other organisations into making provisions in mining areas, and to advise the Commission on any concrete proposals which might arise.[6]

In December 1946, the Commission were given a progress report on the Finance Sub-Committee, appointed at the September 1946 meeting, which met on 19th November. The Sub-Committee had considered a memorandum prepared by Mr Bennett which included the historical financial data for the Baths, General and Districts Fund up to 31st December 1945. This comprised the estimated amounts available for allocation up to 31st March 1952, when the receipts of the output levy were due to cease, an estimate of the financial needs of the Miners' Welfare Fund up to 31st March 1952 and an estimate of the financial position at that date.

A supplementary statement was also submitted to the meeting showing that the estimated payments would exceed the estimated receipts of the Fund at 31st March 1952 by £7½ million and that the General Fund would be overspent by the end of 1948, whilst the Baths Fund would commence to be overspent by the second half of 1948. Mr Bennett further reported verbally at the December meeting that, since the memorandum had been prepared in October 1946, proposals had been put forward involving further expenditure of £2 ¼ million on additional rehabilitation facilities.

In addition, as a result of the deliberations of the Youth Welfare Sub-Committee, it was estimated that approximately £387,000 more would be required for youth welfare than previously estimated. This would bring the total deficit at March 1952 to over £10 million.

It was therefore essential to share this financial information with the Ministry of Fuel and Power and the National Coal Board so that the Commission would be clear as to the future funding and responsibilities. Clarification was also needed on the probable length of life of the Defence Regulation 60BA and the position on the proposed repeal of the Royalties Welfare Levy.

The Sub-Committee decided that a draft case for submission to the Minister of Fuel and Power be prepared for consideration by the Commission. The draft case would be supported by graphs showing the movement of the trends of the receipts and expenditure of the Fund and rises in costs. A statement of alternative methods of meeting the estimated deficit of £7½ million at 31st March 1952 would be included.

At the January 1947 meeting of the Commission, Mr Bennett reported on the case for submission to the Minister of Fuel and Power, but in view of the subsequent developments in connection with the integration of the work of the National Coal Board with the work of the Commission and their implications on financial issues, a number of points on which advice was sought from the Minister were no longer applicable. It was felt that the final form of the case be deferred until the scheme of integration had been settled. As far as the actual receipts and payments estimates were concerned, the addition of a voluntary output levy of 1d a ton to the statutory output levy of 1d a ton would relieve the immediate anxiety, especially as the rate of expenditure would probably not be as rapid as was originally contemplated. When the baths building programme reached its zenith, an income equivalent to the product of at least 3d output levy would be needed, but this was not a problem for immediate consideration because, if the Board contributed a 1d levy to the common fund, this could be used for baths, leaving the statutory income to be used for the purposes of the General and Districts Fund. The Commission therefore agreed to reconsider the subject at its March meeting.

At the March 1947 meeting, it was decided to defer the submission of the case on the financial position of the Miners' Welfare Fund to the Minister of Fuel and Power so that it could be coupled with the submission to the Minister of the scheme of co-ordination between the Commission and the National Coal Board.[7]

The issue of co-ordination between the Miners' Welfare Commission and the National Coal Board dominated the proceedings of the Welfare Commission throughout 1947.

Following a proposal made at the Commission's December 1946 meeting to discuss the subject of co-ordination, the Chairman had submitted a memorandum detailing the statutory position of the Board and the Commission in the field of welfare and the possible solutions to the problem of avoiding overlapping, duplication and waste in this field.

There were 5 possible alternatives. Three of these involved the virtual disappearance of the welfare field of either the Board or the Commission and therefore were impracticable.

One possible alternative was a division of functions between the Board and the Commission whereby the Board would be responsible for all pit and pithead welfare and the Commission for all extra-mural welfare. This would involve grave disadvantages, so the only alternative was integration.

There were 3 essentials of integration: joint authority at the national level, a common welfare fund and an integrated staff working as one team. Integration at Divisional level would be achieved by the replacement of the existing District Committees by Divisional Committees. It was for consideration whether similar arrangements were required at area level, in view of the existence of the Board's Area Executive Committees and Area Consultative Committees.

Lord Citrine had started having discussions with the officials of the Commission and the Board to see if co-ordination between the two Authorities could be achieved. It had emerged from these discussions that there were two principal ways in which the problem might be solved, either by division of functions or by co-ordination.

Lord Citrine's memorandum contemplated a complete integration of the staffs of both organisations, although his immediate and specific recommendation on this point was that the field officers of the Commission should be absorbed into the staffs of the Divisional Coal Boards. A common fund should be created which would be jointly administered subject to the statutory obligations of the Commission being adequately protected. Lord Citrine thought that this could be most easily achieved by the appointment of a joint committee composed of the members of the Commission, including assessors, and perhaps two additional members of the Board.

Lord Citrine's proposals were approved by the Commission and it was agreed that a sub-committee consisting of Lord Citrine, Mr A. M. Bryan, Professor E. L. Collis and Mr Horner be appointed to meet a sub-committee of the National Coal Board with a view to presenting an agreed scheme to the two parent bodies.

At the Commission's February 1947 meeting, Lord Citrine presented the report of the joint sub-committee appointed to prepare the agreed scheme of co-ordination between the Commission and the Board. The essence of the scheme was that there would be:

a) A joint authority consisting of the Commission and two members of the Board to be known as 'The National Miners' Welfare Joint Council'
b) Two funds, to comprise the Miners' Welfare Fund and a contribution from the Board, both to be administered by the joint authority, subject to keeping separate accounts
c) A transfer of the Commission's staff, except the staff of the rehabilitation centres, to the Board, but carrying out the approved recommendations of the joint authority
d) A divisional and area organisation conforming to the geographical organisation of the Board, neighbourhood and local welfare committees.

It was hoped that the report would be adopted by the Board and the Commission and endorsed by the Minister of Fuel and Power in time to bring the approved scheme into operation as from 31st March 1947.

The Commission amended sections relating to divisional, area and neighbourhood committees and then adopted the amended report and then gave the Commission's representatives on the sub-committee plenary powers to complete the arrangements envisaged in the report, obtain the approval of the Minister of Fuel and Power and to bring the scheme into operation as from 31st March 1947.

Without the staff present, the Commission also decided that the proposed integration of some of its staff with the National Coal Board's staff would result in a reduction of the duties and responsibilities of the Secretaryship which could no longer be envisaged on the level of the post advertised. In these circumstances, the Commission concluded that it did not seem necessary to look for candidates outside the present staff.

The Commission considered the revised report of the joint sub-committee of the Coal Board and the Commission at their March meeting. The main endeavour had been to ensure that there would be adequate representation of all interests at each level of the organisation, although this had involved a considerable increase in the size of the Divisional Committees to allow the

National Union of Mineworkers to have adequate representation on each Conciliation Board Area and also to enable each Area Welfare Committee to be represented on the Divisional Committee.

The Commission agreed that once the amended report had been submitted to the National Union of Mineworkers and the National Association of Colliery Managers for their observations and the sub-committee had considered these observations, the scheme would be submitted to the Minister of Fuel and Power for approval.

In July 1947, the Minister of Fuel and Power appointed a new Miners' Welfare Commission for a period of three years under the Chairmanship of Sir Joseph Hallsworth who, like Lord Citrine, was a trade unionist. Lord Citrine had asked Mr Stedman to continue as Personal Advisor to the Chairman for a further year.

The proposal for co-ordination between the Miners' Welfare Commission and the National Coal Board as approved by the joint sub-committee had been sent to the Minister of Fuel and Power on 8th July 1947 with a suggestion in a covering letter that the Minister should meet the sub-committee for a discussion of the main principles of the co-ordination scheme prior to the discussion of details between the sub-committee and the officials of the Ministry.

The co-ordination sub-committee had met Sir Donald Ferguson, Secretary of the Ministry of Fuel and Power, on 29th July 1947 and the proposed scheme of co-ordination was discussed at considerable length. Sir Donald did not oppose co-ordination in principle, but he saw strong objections on constitutional grounds to the proposed setting up of a joint welfare authority.

On 21st August 1947, the Minister of Fuel and Power (Mr Shinwell) wrote to the Chairman of the Commission admitting that he had always felt serious misgivings about the proposals during the course of their development and that he was unable to abandon his strong conviction that it would be contrary to the spirit of the statutory provisions (both in the Miners' Welfare Acts and the Coal Industry Nationalisation Act) and inconsistent with his responsibilities as Minister for the Commission to be put in the position of merely endorsing the decisions of some other non-statutory body or for its staff to be transferred to the National Coal Board.

He would be happy, however, if the Board so desired, for the Commission to act as the Board's agent. If this suggestion was adopted, he would be willing to re-arrange the membership of the Commission in such a way as to give the Board in effect a fifty percent representation. If, however, this solution was not acceptable, and if the Board was not willing for the Commission to be its agent, the Minister could see no alternative but to leave things as they were. In this case, the Board would have to make its own arrangements for spending the money assigned to welfare purposes.

In September 1947, the Commission considered the Minister's letter. The National Coal Board had already considered the implications and held the view that the Minister should be informed that both the Commission and the Board felt that he had made an unfortunate decision. The National Coal Board was opposed to the idea of using the Commission as its agent for all welfare purposes.

After a very long discussion as to the way forward, the Commission resolved that a joint meeting of the Commission and representatives of the National Coal Board should be held during the afternoon of 15th October 1947 to consider what arrangement should be made to co-ordinate the welfare work of the bodies following the Minister's rejection of the integration proposals and that the Minister of Fuel and Power should be requested to appoint representatives to be present at that meeting as assessors.

The Chairman wrote to Mr Shinwell on 23rd September regarding the observations of both the Commission and the National Coal Board on the rejection by the Minister of the integration proposals. He had had no reply, but he did not press the issue as there were impending changes in Ministerial offices. After Mr Gaitskell's appointment as Minister of Fuel and Power, the Chairman had an interview with Sir Donald Ferguson, Secretary to the Ministry, who judged the revised proposals, involving a division of functions or activities, were not as satisfactory as the original scheme which had been proposed after close consultation between the Commission, the Board and the National Union of Mineworkers.

Sir Donald Ferguson had undertaken to put this point of view to the new Minister, so the joint meeting for the afternoon of 15th October was cancelled. The Minister had written back on 13th October indicating that he had had an opportunity to study the original and revised proposals and that, after careful consideration, he was willing to accept, in principle, whichever of the proposals were recommended jointly as a result of further discussion and agreement between the National Coal Board and the Miners' Welfare Commission.

The Chairman had had an opportunity of discussing the letter with the National Coal Board at its meeting on 14th October, and the unanimous choice of the Board was in favour of the original integration proposals. At its meeting on 15th October 1947, the Commission were of the same mind and the Minister was informed accordingly.

The Minister had written back on 29th October 1947, accepting this recommendation in principle, and agreeing, in order to give effect to it, that the consultation should proceed at official level between the Ministry, the National Coal Board and the Commission in order that the details incidental to the operation of the scheme could be examined.

A working party had, therefore, been constituted of officials of the Ministry of Fuel and Power, the Acting Joint Secretaries of the Commission and officials of the National Coal Board. The first meeting was held on 14th November 1947 at which considerable progress on accounting and staff arrangements had been made but there was still a big question concerning the Architects' Branch awaiting a decision.

During these protracted negotiations over co-ordination, it was essential that the District Welfare Committees continued in office. The decision was taken at the March meeting of the Commission to ask the current District Committees, including the Joint Secretaries, to continue in office after 31st March pending a definite conclusion in the negotiations. By May 1947, twenty-one replies had been received and eighteen had intimated their willingness to continue in office. No replies had been received from Cumberland, North Wales, Warwickshire or Somerset District Committees.

At the November meeting of the Commission, the Chairman referred to a memorandum which had been circulated to the Commission from the Miners' Welfare Commission Staff Committee requesting an audience with the Commission in order to bring its notice to 'the present very strong feelings of the staff regarding the way in which the integration proposals have been managed'.

The memorandum did not represent the up-to-date position as the Chairman, immediately after his appointment as Manpower and Welfare member of the National Coal Board and Chairman of the Commission, had met the Chairman and Secretary of the Staff Committee in company of the Acting Joint Secretaries and a representative of the Establishment Directorate of the National Coal Board. Negotiations were being conducted by the Board with various trade unions throughout the country. In the case of the Commission's staff, there was a further complication in that not only was there a Staff Committee but there were also four Trade Unions which continued to represent the interests of different sections of the staff.

The Chairman had already given his personal assurance to the representatives of the staff that he would do his utmost to ensure that the terms of transfer were equitable but he would not agree either that the Staff Committee had the right to discuss the policy of integration or on the allocation of individual staff to the various departments or sections of the National Coal Board.[8]

In January 1947, there continued to be delays in the pithead baths building programme with supplying material and equipment. There was a prospect of increasing the output of schemes in 1947 by 34 schemes and 2 extensions as a result of obtaining further office accommodation and some additional staff for the Architects' Branch and working overtime.

There were still difficulties in ascertaining the future life of pits in the current circumstances. Lord Citrine had circulated to all Divisional Boards details of the Commission's proposed building programme, but they had only identified one or two pits.

A deputation of the Commission's officers had met with Mr Lebeter, Director of Mining Supplies, on 27th January 1947. He had stressed how extremely serious were the shortages of materials, particularly steel, timber and, amongst components, electric motors, the time of the latter being not less than 84 weeks. The Ministry had recently submitted a considerable memorandum to the Lord President's Committee, complaining that the coal mining industry was not obtaining sufficient priority.

Although the steel shortage was such that the production of sheet steel would be cut by 50% during 1947, priority for pithead lockers had been promised by Sankey-Sheldon, who were using their own bulk allocation of steel sheeting.

Such was the seriousness of the shortage problem that a special officer with the rank of Architect had been deputed to deal with it as well as the general progressing of the pithead baths programme.

By March 1947, the Divisional Labour Directors of the National Coal Board had visited the priority lists for the provision of pithead baths at all unequipped collieries in their Divisions and provided the Commission with their revised lists which included reports on collieries whose future life was uncertain. The Commission therefore took the decision to temporarily drop these from the current building programme (2 from the 1946 programme and 20 from the 1947 programme). 22 alternative schemes and one extension were identified as replacements for schemes that had been dropped.

The Commission thought it inadvisable at this stage to inform the men at the collieries which had been removed from the current programme. In any case, where temporary suspension became permanent, the men would be taken into the confidence of the National Coal Board as to the cause and as to the arrangements for future employment in due course.

The Pithead Baths Sub-Committee meeting, held on 12th March 1947, had discussed a report by Mr Kemp on forms of construction for pithead baths which did not involve the use of labour required for housing purposes.

Bricks were certainly the cheapest and probably the quickest method. They permitted the employment of small local contractors. Bricks were made in the coalfield and the 70 contracts for the proposed baths would only entail the use of 1.6% of the bricks produced by the National Coal Board itself. The 1947 programme would entail the employment of only 0.4% of the total number of bricklayers in the country. The Architects' Branch had therefore prepared detailed specifications and working drawings for a standardised unit of construction based on brickwork.

In March 1947, the Commission decided to proceed on the basis that the 1947 and 1948 pithead baths building programme would be in brick, but alternative methods of construction would be explored with some experimental installations in the 50–250 accommodation group with at least one of these installations to be sited in Fife.

There was a pressing need for drawing office staff to cope with the currently planned programme. Of the 96 asked for by the Chief Architect and sanctioned at the September 1946 meeting of the Commission, there were only twenty-seven at Headquarters and twenty-three in the provinces with forty-five vacancies, the bulk at Headquarters. There had been difficulties in recruitment because draughtmen had not been in training during the war. In March 1947, the Commission decided that additional highly qualified staff might be temporarily appointed for work performed by less qualified staff.

On 21st August 1947, the Minister of Fuel and Power wrote to the Chairman of the Commission about the pithead baths building programme expressing 'his great concern and anxiety that I learn of the serious delays which have already taken place in the two earlier years, resulting in only nineteen baths being started in 1946, and up to the present none in 1947 which means that a large proportion of the 71 that were intended to be started before the end of 1947 will in fact have to be added to the already heavy programme in 1948.'

The letter was considered by the Commission at their meeting on 17th September 1947. In their reply, the difficulties which led to this situation were listed: lack of office accommodation and of technical and other staff, lack of definite information on the probable numbers employed and site difficulties on which to select collieries for baths, projected life and additional work for medical centres, canteens and colliery buildings in connection with baths extensions.

The office accommodation situation was improving with offices leased in Old Queen Street in September 1946 and other accommodation in Great Portland Street coming into use by the end of the year, but this still was not enough. Staff were still being recruited and private architects were being engaged to assist in making up the deficiency.

The Commission regretted that adverse circumstances outside their control had prevented them from attaining the accelerated programme in 1946 and 1947 but the Chief Architect had assured the Commission that he expected to achieve the target for 1948.

The target of 120 installations for 1948 involved incurring commitments in excess of the current unallocated balance of the Baths Fund by March 1948 and an estimated deficit at the end of 1948 of £4½ million (including £515,000 for rehabilitation centres).

The Commission had received a reassurance that this deficit would be met both from the Minister's predecessor and Mr Fudge on the Minister's behalf in January 1946. The Commission felt that the time had arrived for the Minister to state clearly how these assurances would be implemented.

At the Commission's October meeting, the Chairman reported that he had received a reply from the Minister of Fuel and Power to the letter which had been sent to him on 18th September 1947. The Minister had indicated that it was difficult for him to reply fully to that letter until the Commission and the Coal Board had notified him of joint proposals about co-ordination and he had considered the recommendations in the report of the Investment Programmes Committee, so far as they related to the Commission's building plans for 1948. He reaffirmed the view that the balance of the money required to complete the baths building programme during the next seven years would have to come from the industry and that no contribution could be expected from the Exchequer.

By July 1947, following negotiations with the Ministry of Fuel and Power, it had been ascertained that the National Coal Board had agreed to accept responsibility for expenditure on medical treatment centres, of which it was estimated that approximately 500 would be required at a cost of £2,000,000. The Board proposed to raise the matter at a convenient meeting of the National Miners' Welfare Joint Council when instructed in order to clear the future procedure to be followed regarding the authorisation of such expenditure. In the interim, the Commission confirmed that it would finance the building and equipment of these centres on the understanding that the expenditure involved would be refunded to the Miners' Welfare Fund by the National Coal Board.

In October 1947, it was reported that the prototype medical treatment centres were nearing completion. Vane Tempest and New Herrington (both in Durham) and Western (South Wales) were due to be completed in November. Difficulties in obtaining delivery of electrical equipment had delayed the completion of Markham Main (South Yorkshire) and Devon (Fifeshire) by about 3 months.

Nine sketch plans had been prepared by the Architects' Branch containing proposals for providing Medical Treatment accommodation at collieries with pithead baths where it had not been found possible to provide adaptations. At a meeting at the Ministry of Fuel and Power, it had been agreed that these proposals did not meet the needs of a satisfactory medical service. Subsequently, accommodation in the form of a 'Medical Treatment Unit' had been agreed with the Ministry. The medical treatment unit would be a new building, similar to the appropriate standard type of medical treatment centre, but excluding the separate nurse's room, bathroom and stretcher entrance lobby and would not, it was estimated, involve any greater expenditure of the architect's time and building labour and materials than the average form of adaptation it replaced.[9]

The Miners' Welfare Rehabilitation Service had begun to attract interest from other countries. On 13th and 14th January 1947, a party from France had visited Hartford Hall and the Hermitage. Mr J. Novotny of the Czech Ministry of Social Welfare had met with Mr Freston and suggested that a party might be sent by the Czech Government next year to study what was being done in the field of rehabilitation by the Miners' Welfare Commission.

In Cumberland, the Commission were informed in January 1947, that the hut offered by the Ministry of Health for Whitehaven was unsuitable so it was proposed that a purpose-built gymnasium should be built which might slightly exceed the £7,000 already agreed by the Commission.

The Nystagmus Committee had meet on the afternoon of 15th January 1947 and arranged that experts in the field should be invited to a discussion under the Chairmanship of Professor Collis on 19th February.

The Pneumoconiosis Committee met on 23rd January 1947 and agreed that an institution of at least 100 beds was required in South Wales in which the most recent techniques of treatment, as advised by the Research Unit of the Medical Research Council, would be practiced on a large scale. An experimental rehabilitation centre for pneumoconiotics should be established in South Wales to be controlled by a suitable physician under the advice of Research Unit. It was recognised that the service of a medico-social worker was necessary to cover the needs of the pneumoconiotics in South Wales.

Having considered the note of the discussion of the experts in nystagmus that had taken place in February, the Nystagmus Committee decided to recommend to the March 1947 meeting of the Commission to approve, in principle, the provision of rehabilitation facilities at Higham Grange and at Buxton for sufferers of nystagmus. The position at Higham Grange was that it had never yet been occupied to capacity, and Dr Dorothy Campbell was in practice at Coventry within convenient reach and had the assistance of a psychiatrist in Dr Stern at Warwick. An experiment at Higham Grange was a feasible proposition.

The Nystagmus Committee also thought that it would be possible to have an experiment of a slightly different sort at Buxton if the acquisition of the Empire Hotel went through. Dr Wellwood Ferguson of Sheffield might be prepared to supervise rehabilitation at Buxton.

Firbeck Hall (Yorkshire) received its first patients on 14th April 1947. It had been hoped that Firbeck Hall would have opened on 1st February, but there had been delays in the delivery of medical equipment from the Ministry of Works and appointments of staff. However, a medico-social worker had been appointed before the opening of Firbeck Hall which enabled her to spend a period of training with Mrs Miller, the Commission's Chief Social Worker at Uddingston.

Mr Freston had a discussion at Higham Grange on 10th April 1947 and it had been agreed that 10 cases of nystagmus would be accepted in the Trauma Centre as an experiment. In the light of this decision, the Medical Advisory Committee would be asked to reconsider their objection to the inclusion of nystagmus suffers in Trauma Centres.

The other recommendation of the discussion at Higham Grange was that the services of a suitably trained medico-social worker should be obtained as early as possible to make the preliminary contacts with the nystagmus suffers in the West Midlands.

On 27th March, Mr Nicoll and Mr Freston met Dr Fletcher in Cardiff. On 29th March 1947 there was a special meeting of the Monmouthshire and South Wales Rehabilitation Committee to discuss the provision in South Wales of an experimental centre for the rehabilitation of pneumoconiosis cases which was attended by Mr Horner, Mr Nicoll and Dr Fletcher. Having heard Mr Horner's explanation of the origin of the proposal and Mr Nicoll's account and Dr Fletcher's views, the Committee agreed that something must be done. A centre within convenient reach of Llandough with about 100 beds in an existing building which could be rapidly adapted was recommended.

At the Commission's May 1947 meeting, Mr Nicoll presented the Annual Report of the Consulting Surgeon for 1946. The Commission's arrangements for rehabilitation had achieved 84% coverage for miners and, when the plans being worked on had been completed, it would be 90%. However, there were still certain pockets of miners not covered by any scheme sponsored by the Commission, one being Ayrshire.

The collection of cases for rehabilitation had posed a difficult problem early on but this had been solved and, as a by-product of that solution, a keen group of surgeons had been formed who met twice yearly to exchange information. These surgeons were becoming a very valuable and almost unique team.

Trauma cases having been provided for, other classes of disability were coming under review.

In considering the percentage of men returning to pre-accident work, it had to be remembered that the average age of miners at the Centre was 40 years and that these had sustained severe injuries. 34% of the men were back to pre-accident work and 50% went back into the industry.

The proposal for a centre and settlement for paraplegic patients was considered by the Commission at their May 1947 meeting. The incidence of paraplegia in miners was 11.4 cases per annum per 100,000 as against 0.3 cases amongst non-miners, i.e. thirty-three cases among miners to every one person among the rest of the community. Mr Nicoll had estimated the number of new cases per annum from the whole of the mining industry would be 80, of which an estimated 56 were likely to survive the first critical three weeks. On the assumption that the average duration of treatment in a Rehabilitation Centre would be two years, 112 beds would be required.

The condition of paraplegia carried ever present possibilities of critical complications therefore highly skilled treatment and nursing was required and one centre was recommended. A proportion of the cases would need to be flown by air ambulance. For psychological reasons, it was further recommended that there should be a 'settlement' in the same grounds of the rehabilitation centre where the men could be with their families yet have immediate access to specialised medical treatment.

The capital cost of such a centre would be substantial (£125,000) and maintenance costs were estimated to be £21,000 per annum to which would be added £6,500 in nursing and other support staff costs. No attempt had been made to cost the settlement.

The Commission agreed in principle to both the centre and the settlement, and Messrs Bennett and Freston were asked to examine the question of responsibility of the various Ministries in respect of the treatment and care of paraplegics with a view to representation being made, in due course, for grant aid towards both capital and maintenance costs.

The Rheumatism Committee had met on 18th March 1947 and agreed that, for the present at least, the Commission's activities ought to be limited to the establishment of a clinic from which a pilot survey might be conducted, and at which treatment would be carried out in accordance with the advice of a diagnostic centre.

The Medical Clinic at Walkden, which had for some years provided physiotherapy and remedial gymnastics to the men of Manchester Collieries Ltd., had been identified as an ideal place for providing the treatment which was essential to attract human material for any survey. It was proposed that when the treatment clinic had been established, the Director of Rheumatism, who was being appointed to Manchester University under the Nuffield Benefaction, should, in collaboration with the Scientific Department of the National Coal Board, plan and supervise a survey to be based on the clinic. There would be a technical committee to advise on the whole project comprising the Professors of the University most nearly interested in the matter, the Director of Rheumatism when appointed, Mr Nicoll and Mr Cullen, the Supervising Surgeon for Lancashire, and Dr Cope, Director of Research (Human Problems), National Coal Board.

It was proposed that the Walkden Clinic should be taken over from the North Western Coal Board, perhaps on a lease, and one Chief of Treatment Staff and four or five assistants would be required for the treatment of rheumatic cases. As soon as the survey became possible, the services of a social worker and clerical staff would be required. At its May meeting, the Commission agreed that the project should proceed as described and that the whole cost of the treatment and survey should be borne by the Miners' Welfare Commission.

Lanelay Hall had been selected as a suitable place for a rehabilitation centre for pneumoconiosis. The Commission at its May meeting agreed that Lanelay Hall should be purchased (vendor price £25,000) and that a medico-social service for work amongst pneumoconiosis suffers should be organised in South Wales. Lanelay Hall was subsequently purchased for £23,000.

The Nystagmus Committee had met the previous day to the Commission's May meeting and had decided to recommend to the Commission that 10 nystagmus cases should be admitted on an experimental basis to Higham Grange and that a psychiatric social worker should be appointed to the Staff at Higham Grange to work among the nystagmus cases in the West Midlands as well as amongst the trauma patients in the Centre.

At the April meeting of the Commission, Mr Bennett was asked to undertake negotiations to acquire Herrington Hall estate for the second rehabilitation centre in Durham. Mr Bennett had managed to purchase the property for £12,000.

The County Borough of Sunderland had reacted very strongly to the news that the Commission had completed the negotiations for the purchase of Herrington Hall and estate because the Borough had been on the point of purchasing it through the District Valuer. The County Borough had issued a Compulsory Acquisition order and had involved the intervention of the Ministry of Education who had taken it up with the National Coal Board. Before resorting to litigation, Mr Freston suggested a meeting in London on 3rd June to discuss the matter.

At the meeting in London, representatives of Sunderland Borough Council accepted that the Commission had a prior claim to Herrington Hall and agreed to recommend the Council to withdraw its Compulsory Acquisition Order and leave the estate for the Miners' Rehabilitation Centre.

In July 1947, the Commission confirmed that the projected centre at Aberdour for Fife should be able to provide accommodation for 50 inpatients and 50 outpatients. It was also agreed that, in view of the comparatively small number of miners in Ayrshire (12,700) scattered over a wide area, the establishment of a Miners' Rehabilitation Centre in the District was not warranted but that provision for Ayrshire miners should be made by adding hostel accommodation for twenty-five patients at Uddingston Centre (Lanarkshire).

In November 1947, the sketch plans for the purpose-built centre at Aberdour were nearly ready and Mr Freston hoped to meet the District Committee early in December to discuss them. There had been some question of the Fife County Council raising an objection to the proposed centre but, following a visit from Mr Bennett, an assurance had been given that there would be no objections subject to the Council's formal approval of the plans.

A meeting had been held on 23rd October 1947 at which representatives were present of all those concerned in the scheme for a rheumatic treatment clinic and survey at Walkden (Lancashire). Subsequently, Mr Freston was asked to draw up a draft document incorporating the arrangements for consideration by Manchester University on 14th November and the Commission on 19th November.[10]

The Commission, in March 1947, considered a memorandum submitted by Mr Bennett on the provisions of the National Health Service Act, 1946, in so far as they appeared, either directly or indirectly, to relate to miners' welfare health schemes and/or grants from the Miners Welfare Fund for health purposes. The Commission decided that there should be a full examination of the implications of the Act in relation to the miners' welfare property used for health purposes and the making of grants in future from the Miners' Welfare Fund for such purposes and a report produced. The Chairman was authorised to call a special meeting, if necessary, of available members of the Commission to consider such a report, including the legal, financial and other implications.

Preliminary talks were held with the administrative side of the Ministry of Health, who strongly advised that the Commission's legal advisor should consult the Ministry's legal adviser.

The Commission needed to be advised on the legal position with regard to the extent that:

a) existing welfare property (including endowments) provided for health purposes were affected by the Act and
b) the provision of health purposes which, in the past had been provided by the Miners' Welfare Fund would, in future, be the responsibility of the State (under the Act).

Mr Bennett therefore sent a memorandum to the solicitor of the Ministry of Fuel and Power which was then informally discussed between the legal advisors of the Ministry of Fuel and Power and the Ministry of Health when it was concluded that the wording of the Act was so wide that, in order to decide what welfare schemes might or might not be vested in the Ministry of Health, each scheme would have to be considered and its activities examined under its appropriate group.

Apart from hospitals, rehabilitation centres and medical treatment centres, it was the general opinion of the legal advisers that the Miners' Welfare Health Schemes would not be liable to vest in the Ministry. However, the services provided by these Miners' Welfare Schemes would be the responsibility of the Minister of Health through the Regional Health Authorities.

The Solicitor of the Ministry of Fuel and Power had, therefore, suggested that, in order to clarify the position as soon as possible, a meeting at a high level should be held with officials of the Ministry of Health to decide on the detailed application of the Act in specific cases. The Commission agreed to this proposal at their May 1947 meeting.

A meeting between officials of the Commission and the Ministry of Health took place on 17th June 1947 at which the implications of the National Health Service Act 1946, in relation to the Miners' Welfare Fund Health purposes and schemes were discussed.

It was generally agreed that, apart from Hospital, Hospital Trust Funds and possibly Rehabilitation Centres, all Miners' Welfare Schemes were excluded from the provisions of the 1946 Act but there was no real need for the Miners' Welfare Fund to be called to make grants for any of these purposes in the future, since the objects (except the miners' welfare convalescent homes) could be achieved by or in co-ordination with the Regional Hospital Boards and the Local Health Authorities.

The Commission at its July 1947 meeting considered the report of the meeting and decided to set up a sub-committee consisting of Professor E. L. Collis, Mr J. A. Hall and Miss Herbison to consider the subject and report with recommendations. No further grants would be made in the case of hospitals and hospital endowments but recommendations for other District Fund health schemes would be considered on their merits and District or Divisional Committees would be provisionally advised of the position regarding the National Health Service Act 1946 and Miners' Welfare health schemes. 11

On 19th March 1947, the Ministry of Education sent to local education authorities in England and Wales a circular (No. 133) which directed them to prepare schemes of further education providing for educational and leisure-time needs of all who had left school. They were asked at the same time to prepare their plans for county colleges for the compulsory part-time education of young people up to the age of 18, since, in many areas, a simple college of further education would be used for voluntary as well as compulsory studies. Schemes and plans were to be submitted to the Ministry by 31st March 1948. This circular reflected the duties of the local education authorities laid down in Section 41 of the Education Act 1944.

A joint Consultative Committee of the Ministry of Education and the Miners' Welfare Commission had been established in December 1944 (the

Commission's current representatives were Mr T. A. Bennett, Mr Whitfield Parker, Mr J. D. Herd and Mr R. D. Roberts) to consider the problems incidental to the development of recreative and leisure-time activities and the provision of community centres in mining areas in England and Wales. Similar arrangements had been established with the Scottish Education Department. At the last meeting of the Committee held on 1st October 1946, it had been agreed to issue procedures notes for the guidance of District Welfare Officers and Mining Education Inspectors.

At their May 1947 meeting, the Commission thought that the Local Education Authorities in mining areas were certain to consider the Miners' Welfare Centres in their District in preparing their plans , and it was important, therefore that there should be consultation and co-operation between the Miners' Welfare interests and the Education Authorities. Fruitful co-operation was already taking place in Scotland, the North East Coast and South Wales where training courses for representatives of the Miners' Welfare Centres had been held.

Mr Whitfield Parker urged that sufficient staff should be appointed immediately if the work started at the courses were to be consolidated and developed. The lack of staff also applied to furtherance of Youth work. The Commission therefore agreed to the immediate appointment of two officers to specialise in Community work (one of which would assist in developing Miners' Welfare Centres in Scotland) and two officers to specialise in Youth work.

The Commission also gave general approval to the short-term and long-term proposals for the development of recreational, social and cultural activities of the Miners' Welfare Centres.

The short-term plan included the completion of the Miners' Welfare survey of all welfare and recreational facilities in mining communities, reconditioning of Miners' Welfare Centres which had deteriorated during the war, stimulating new activities and developing established activities, the establishment of leagues and competitions, development of women's activities and interests and providing and extending the formation of boys, girls and mixed Youth clubs in co-operation with Local Authorities. In addition to increasing the amount and efficiency of collection from usual sources, the Local Authority might, in some cases, want to contribute towards the maintenance of suitable centres.

The long-term plan would consist of the formulation and implementation of a plan based on the Miners' Welfare Commission (National Miners' Joint Council) for the future development of adequate facilities for the recreation and leisure-time occupation of the mining community. The long-term plan would include the establishment of joint consultative machinery to secure co-operation between the Local Education Authorities and the Divisional and Area Miners'

Welfare Committees, the provision of suitable up-to-date accommodation for recreation, social and cultural pursuits to be prepared in consultation with the Local Education Authorities , increased quality and variety of suitable activities in the Miners' Welfare Centres and the employment of wardens and trained leaders at all suitable Miners' Welfare Centres.[12]

The search for office space had continued throughout 1947. The Commission had taken a 21-year lease on 10/21 Great Portland Street in March 1947 and alterations and redecoration had commenced in June. 18 members of the Engineers Section of the Architects' Branch were moved to the fourth floor of the new premises from the Queen Street Office in September, and more staff were to be moved to Great Portland Street when the work on the remaining floors was completed.

The search for further accommodation to house the staff at Ashstead had been suspended pending consideration of the revised proposals for co-ordination between the Commission and the National Coal Board.[13]

In January 1948, the National Miners' Welfare Joint Council superseded the Commission. Sir Joseph Hallsworth remained as Chairman. Two new members had been appointed to represent the Coal Board: Sir Geoffrey Vickers VC and Mr L. H. H. Lowe. The four Assessors were Mr H. R. Hartwell (Ministry of Health), Mr J. Lambie (Scottish Education Department), Mr E. A. Shearing (Ministry of Fuel and Power) and Mr H. J. Shelley (Ministry of Education). Mr Stedman continued as Advisor to the Chairman and Mr J. B. Longmuir attended in his role as Director of Welfare. It was hoped that meetings would be held in Hobart House unless members had other suggestions.

Following this first meeting of the Council, the members and staff of the Council had the opportunity of meeting the Minister of Fuel and Power, his Parliamentary Secretary and permanent officials, the Chairman, Deputy Chairman and other members of the National Coal board and members of the Coal Board staff at a luncheon which was held in the Goring Hotel.

The scheme for co-ordination had been approved by both the Commission and the National Coal Board so would now be submitted to the Minister of Fuel and Power.

Proposed staff arrangements had been discussed at a meeting held on 1st January 1948 with representatives of the National Coal Board, the Miners' Welfare Commission, the Ministry of Fuel and Power and the Miners Welfare Commission Staff Committee. These staff arrangements had been agreed in general terms by the Establishments Directorate of the National Coal Board.

The memorandum of arrangements for co-ordination provided for the Joint Council to arrange the formation of a Divisional Welfare Committee to replace the District Welfare Committee or Committees within Divisions. The Council, at their first meeting decided that arrangements should be put in hand for the establishment of these Divisional Committees.

It was confirmed at the February 1948 meeting of the Council that the Ministry of Fuel and Power had approved the appointment of Mr T. A. Bennett to the post of Secretary to the Commission as of 1st January 1948.

Following the previous meeting, two letters had been sent out to each of the twenty-five District Miners' Welfare Committees from the Chairman to the Chairman of each District Miners' Welfare Committee setting out the process of disbandment of the District Committees and the formal handing over of the District Committee's affairs to the Divisional Committee. The operative date of 31st March 1948 had been fixed for the disbandment, to allow a reasonable time for handing over their functions and duties to Divisional Committees and to avoid the appearance of indecent haste in this matter after twenty-seven years' service given by these Committees to the Commission.

Two letters had been sent to each Divisional Coal Board. The first from the Chairman to the Chairman of each Divisional Coal Board inviting the Board, in consultation with the Divisional Consultative Council, to set up a Divisional Welfare Committee and convene it not later than 1st April 1948. The second, from the Secretary to the Secretaries of each Divisional Coal Board giving detailed information on the necessary arrangements to be made in setting up Divisional, Area and Group Welfare Committees.

It was arranged that a standard letter would be sent to the Commission's staff being transferred to the Board, thanking them for their past service and giving formal notice, to meet legal requirements, terminating their employment with the Commission before 28th February concurrently with the Board's letter offering an appointment to the Board's staff as from 1st March 1948. The Staff Committee continued to be aggrieved about the way the staff transfers were being conducted. The Chairman had tried to explain to the Chairman and Secretary of the Staff Committee that the most sympathetic consideration had been given to an endeavour to ensure that staff transferring to the Board were placed in suitable jobs on protected salaries, if appropriate.

The Council received a memorandum and chart, submitted by the Chairman, of the names and duties of the officers showing that it was proposed to constitute seven sections to deal with: Secretarial; Canteens and Catering services; General Social Welfare initiated at Divisional and Area level; Colliery Welfare, benevolent funds, welfare committees, suggestion schemes, saving schemes etc.; Pithead Baths and Ancillary Services; Architects Services; Rehabilitation and Health Schemes. The Chief Officer (Mr Longmuir) of the Council would be solely responsible to the Chairman for all matters affecting the Council. The Secretary of the Commission would have direct access to the Chairman on all matters that concerned the Commission only and would continue to administer the Commission's educational activities until the education policies of the Board and the Commission had been co-ordinated.

The Architects' Department would move from Old Queen Street to Great Portland Street and the other staff would move to Old Queen Street on 23rd February. Old Queen Street would house the Secretary, Administrative Sections and the Quantity Surveyors, pending the provision of accommodation for the Secretary at Lansdowne House and the provision for the latter welfare staff at Hobart House. The lease of Ashley Court, Ashstead, was to be surrendered.

At the Council meeting on 31st March 1948, it was reported that the disbanding of the District Committees and handing over of office to Divisional Welfare Committees was progressing to the timetable, with the exception of South Wales District Committee where it was alleged that lack of information or instruction received by the men's side of the Committee from the National Union of Mineworkers' Executive had led to a delay. There had been local interests and circumstances that produced proposed deviations from the pattern laid down in the scheme of co-ordination for setting up the various Welfare Committees in the Divisions.

At their March meeting, the Council agreed to the recommendation made by the Northern Division, North Western Division and East Midland Division. However, in South Western Division, the first meeting called by the Divisional Board to arrange the formation of the Divisional Welfare Committee had ended in an impasse despite the presence of Mr Whitfield Parker. The Divisional Board intended to call a second meeting at which Mr Longmuir, Mr Bennett and Mr Whitfield Parker might present any further information that might be required.

Advice and guidance was given to the District Committees on many points of detail which attended the change over to the new organisation. By May 1948, 16 out of the 25 District Miners' Welfare Committees had disbanded.

Progress continued to be slow, with no Division having entirely completed the formation of all welfare committees by July 1948. It was in the case of Area and Group Welfare Committees that most remained to be done. Queries continued to be received from Divisional Welfare Committees at Headquarters for the rest of 1948.[14]

At the October meeting of the Council, Sir Geoffrey Vickers reported that with the concurrence of Sir Joseph Hallsworth, the Board had approved the reorganisation of the Welfare Branch which would in future become a Sub-Department of the Manpower and Welfare Department under the Controller of Welfare with two branches; one for welfare services and the other for welfare buildings under Directors and a Secretariat of the Joint Council. The Board had appointed Mr Carver, Controller of the Welfare Sub-Department and Mr Longmuir would in future be Director of Welfare Services.

A detailed statement of the Sub-Department as reorganised was presented to the Council's December 1948 meeting. Mr Carver, as Chief Officer of the Council, explained that the responsibilities of the Commission's Secretary now related only to the duties of the staff retained by the Commission; presenting accounts and financial matters relating to Rehabilitation Centres and the Commission's Education schemes. The setting up of the Joint Council implied recognition of the fact that welfare interests of the Board and the Commission covered very largely the same field and would be co-ordinated by Mr Carver as Chief Officer of the Council.[15]

The Chairman submitted a memorandum to the February meeting of the Council setting out the proposed constitution and terms of reference of a Finance Sub-Committee. The Manpower and Welfare Department, in association with the Finance Department, had been examining the subject of finance in relation to the total commitments of the Board. The estimated expenditure on welfare purposes (excluding the Board's expenditure on safety and health, maintenance of pithead baths, rehabilitation of canteens etc) between the 1st January 1948 and 31st March 1952 was in the region of £27 ½ million, towards which it was estimated that the income during that period of the Miners' Welfare Fund would be about £5 ½ million, leaving £22 million to be found by the Board.

The Sub-Committee were to review the probable expenditure on the whole of the field of welfare to be covered by the Joint Council, both on capital and revenue accounts, to ascertain the funds available to meet this expenditure and to submit recommendations as to the allocation of commitments between the various sources of funds. Miss Herbison, Mr Horner, Mr Lowe, Mr Shearing and Mr Iestyn Williams were appointed members of the Sub-Committee with the Chairman of the Council, the Chief Officer and the Secretary as ex-officio members.

The Sub-Committee's progress report was considered at the Council's April 1948 meeting. In the report it was indicated that, apart from the penny statutory levy, the Board was prepared to meet expenditure on the pithead baths programme up to £6 ½ million in the next four years, 1948-1951, an average of about £1,625,000 or the equivalent of 2d per ton on the output of saleable coal. This contribution would include the Board's voluntary contribution of 1d per ton under the scheme of co-ordination. The Board would expect the Council to finance all expenditure on the pithead baths programme out of the statutory income plus the Board's additional contribution of 2d per ton. This contribution would not be available for other welfare activities. The subject of the financial provision of new expenditure on rehabilitation centres would be considered at a future meeting of the Committee. The subject of the repayment of the

Commission's expenditure already incurred or commitments entered into, in respect of erecting and equipping medical centres was under consideration by the Board's legal advisers.

The Board had also agreed to bear the cost of pithead baths maintenance, medical centres and the staff taken over from the Miners' Welfare Commission which it was estimated would, in all, amount to the equivalent of a further 2d per ton. The Board was, therefore, paying the statutory levy plus a voluntary contribution of 4d a ton, making 5d in all for welfare purposes.

Separately, the Council appointed a Miners' Welfare Convalescent Homes Committee in July 1948 to review the problem of the future of the Convalescent Homes established by grants from the Miners' Welfare Fund, then to report and make recommendations to the Council. Professor E. L. Collis, Mr J. A. Hall, Mr H. R. Hartwell, Dr R. J. Peter and Mr J. Stanleigh Turner were appointed members of the Committee. The Chairman of the Council, the Chief Officer and the Secretary were to be ex-officio members of the Committee.[16]

The Pithead Baths programme would account for a significant part of the Board's spending on welfare. The January 1948 meeting of the Council considered the Pithead Baths Programme in 1948, with a view to the Architects' Department being instructed to concentrate during the first three months of 1948 upon planning the maximum number of contracts with large scale builders capable of giving completion in 1948. It was also suggested that a Pithead Baths Sub-Committee should be appointed with a first reference to consider whether the present planning of baths was satisfactory. It was agreed that the Sub-Committee would also consider and report on the whole subject of Pithead Baths. Mr Horner, Mr Lowe, Mr Shearing and Mr Iestyn Williams were appointed members of the Sub-Committee with the Chairman of the Joint Council, the Director of Welfare and the Secretary as ex-officio members. Co-opted members could be authorised by the Chairman for the consideration of special aspects of the problem as they arose.

In February 1948, the Pithead Baths Sub-Committee's interim report was considered by the Council. They had met twice and had visited three pithead baths (Calverton, Limby and Bentinck) near Nottingham.

The Sub-Committee had recommended the Council to adopt the principle of the employment of the Architects' Department on professional services for all Departments of the National Coal Board, subject to the parameter that pithead baths and other welfare work would not be restricted. The Chairman had already discussed this recommendation with the Board so, after a long discussion, the Council concurred with the decision of the Board that the services of the Architects' Department should, for the time being, be confined to welfare projects only and that the Department should remain the responsibility of the

Board for Manpower and Welfare. The Board's Establishment Branch would examine the staff requirements of the Architects' Department in relation to the building programme coming within the purview of the Joint Council.

The Council also endorsed the recommendation of the Sub-Committee of the provision at short-life collieries, at an estimated cost of £100,000, of one experimental baths incorporating the Hy-gard-all system of hangers instead of lockers, with a prefabricated building in each of the National Coal Board Divisions.

In April 1948, the Council endorsed the recommendation of the Pithead Baths Sub-Committee that the number of cubicles should be limited to 10% of the number of showers, subject to the provision being made for an increase later on if the men desired.

By May 1948, no fewer than thirty schemes for pithead baths had had to be aborted since 1st January 1948, as the information originally obtained had proved to be unreliable. The current practice was to obtain information from the Divisional Labour Director who should consult with the Divisional Planning Officer of the Board, but the information supplied was unsatisfactory and was frequently altered in many cases. A disturbing feature of this was that this was often the men's first intimation that their colliery had a doubtful life.

As the Council had decided upon a firm building programme of 90 baths a year, the Council, at their May meeting, requested that the Pithead Baths Sub-Committee should meet representatives of the Production Department of the Board to discuss the procedure to be followed for obtaining definite information about the life of collieries and accommodation to be provided in pithead baths. Thereafter, the Divisional Boards and Divisional Welfare Committees should be informed of that procedure in order that it might be followed in the future.

In June 1948, the Commission took the decision to terminate the authority to appoint associate architects in the name of the Commission as from 31st May. The authority for future appointments of associate architects was to be regarded as one for decision by the National Coal Board.

In October 1946, the Chief Architect had been authorised by the Commission to appoint associate architects as a step to overcoming the shortage of experienced staff for the bath programme and it had been agreed that the fees should be charged to administration expenses. Up to the end of May 1948, 108 such appointments had been made, with more contemplated, but, as the Chief Architect had ceased to be employed by the Commission on 29th February 1948 and the Board had taken over the responsibility for meeting the administrative expenses of the Commission, it had been arranged between the Commission's Secretary and the Chief Architect, that, as from the end of May 1948, no more appointments would be made in the name of the Commission. A review of the work of the architects was in process in June 1948.

The Pithead Baths Committee put forward a number of recommendations for economies to the Council at its July meeting. These included the restrictions of cubicles to 10% and a reduction in height of the partitions to 5', a proposal to revert to in situ concrete frames, a reversion to steam plenum from water plenum, omitting covered ways to canteens and restriction of paths and approach roads to immediate necessities.

In December 1948, the Council and the Commission considered a draft Omnibus Agreement which had been prepared and agreed at official level. It provided that the Board would, in future, undertake the construction of all pithead baths canteens and ancillary buildings, recouping from the Commission the cost in the cases where allocations had been made from the Miners' Welfare Fund. The Council made some amendments and approved the Agreement as amended.

The Council and the Commission also approved arrangements for placing contracts for pithead baths and ancillary building programmes, which had been agreed at official level, in which the Board took over all responsibilities for the contracts except the payment of those contracts already placed in the name of the Commission, which the Commission would make direct to the contractors.[17]

Appointments of staff had usually been made by the Rehabilitation Committees of the Centres concerned but, in February 1948, the Ministry of Fuel and Power wanted future appointments made by the Commission.

The Ministry of Fuel and Power had recently shown much concern about the apparently elaborate staffing of the Commission's rehabilitation centres, and were examining the position with a view to an approval of overall grading, complements and scales of pay. All rehabilitation staff matters were to be handled by the Commission's Secretary in future.

By May 1948, the Ministry of Fuel and Power, as Accounting Officer of the Miners' Welfare Fund, had decided that the staffing of the centres should be examined by the Ministry's Organisation and Methods Branch, commencing with a visit to Talygarn Rehabilitation Centre.

At their February meeting, the Commission decided to authorise the West Midlands Miners' Rehabilitation Committee to provide spectacles for nystagmus cases under the same conditions as surgical appliances might be applied. The recommendation had not been referred to the Nystagmus Committee before submission to the full meeting of the Commission and Professor Collis, as Chairman of the Nystagmus Committee, pointed out this anomaly.

The Council had under consideration at their May meeting, the proposal to replace the existing Winter Gardens at Talygarn with an Exercise Hall and the question as to whether it was still necessary to provide a second rehabilitation centre in South Wales. As the Finance Committee were still looking at the future expenditure on rehabilitation centres, the Council deferred its decision on both items, pending the Finance Committee's report.

Professor Collis pointed out at the May meeting of the Council that Dr Dorothy Campbell's report on the progress of the experiment with nystagmus at Higham Grange had suggested that the experiment should continue. He also questioned whether there would be a possibility of providing an 80-bed home for such patients instead of the ten beds then available. It was suggested that the position under the National Health Service should be investigated. Attention was also drawn to the fact that, under the provision of Section 40(4) of the Coal Industry Nationalisation Act, 1946, the Commission was prevented from spending Miners' Welfare Fund money on research. If the present experiment was to be extended, the matter would have to be examined by the Ministry of Fuel and Power.

Following the May meeting of the Council, Mr Freston had again discussed the question of contributions from the Ministry of Health towards the cost of motor-propelled chairs and, apparently the Ministry would not assist in 'contribution to appliances supplied by others'. On the other hand, as from 5th July 1948, when the National Health Service would come into operation, the Ministry of Pensions would be responsible for the provision of invalid chairs, artificial limbs and certain surgical appliances. There was no assurance as to the date of delivery if the order were placed with the Ministry of Pensions which already had a long waiting list and these fourteen people awaiting invalid chairs would have to take their turn with others. Consequently, the Council agreed at their June meeting to place an order directly with the manufacturer but all future recommendations for invalid chairs for paraplegics would, in the first instance, be submitted to the Ministry of Health.

The Finance Committee had appointed a deputation to meet the Minister of Health for a personal discussion on the future of the Commission's rehabilitation centres for miners in relation to the national service. The Chairman, Sir Geoffrey Vickers, Mr Shearing, Mr Longmuir, Mr Bennett and Mr Freston had met the Minister on 21st September 1948 for an exploratory discussion with neither side being committed. The Minister had expressed the view that industrial health services should be integrated with the national health service and should not duplicate State services. He was of the opinion that the burden of rehabilitation should not fall upon the mining industry as such. He would, therefore, welcome the transfer of the Commission's centres to the State on the basis that there would be no compensation paid for capital expenditure undertaken in the past by the Commission but the Minister would satisfy the Commission that the industry would have the necessary services and facilities developed where needed.

The Minister was not able to give definite assurances that the high standards of the rehabilitation centres would be maintained or that new centres which were planned by the Commission would be immediately provided by the State as these would be added to the Regional Hospital Boards' planning arrangements.

There were currently ten rehabilitation centres, seven providing residential treatment and three providing outpatient treatment. The Chairman pointed out at the Council's September meeting that nobody could pretend that the provision could continue to be made and that the other capital development visualised by the Commission could be financed on the current basis of available funds, which were only at the disposal of the Commission because of Defence Regulations.

Under the terms of the finance programme, approved by the Council, provision had been made for an expenditure of £150,000 a year on rehabilitation for the next four years and, if that expenditure was exceeded, then the amount available for building pithead baths and ancillary buildings would be correspondingly reduced. There was nearly £1,000,000 worth of rehabilitation work held in abeyance because there were no available funds with which to finance any immediate programme of development. The Board could not devote any more money to welfare, so, if this work was to proceed, the State would have to accept the responsibility.

There then followed a very long discussion of the issues surrounding the handing over of the rehabilitation centres to the National Health Service. In the end, the Chairman decided that the discussion on the question of whether this was the right moment to hand over the centres would have to be resumed at a future meeting. In the meantime, he with Sir Geoffrey Vickers and the officers of the Council would hold further discussions with the Ministry of Health as further information needed to be obtained before any decision could be taken.

As a result of the discussions that had taken place at official level with the Ministry of Health, the Council were able to continue the debate on the future arrangements for rehabilitation centres at their October meeting. The Minister would prefer to see the centres incorporated into the National Health Service but, if it was decided not to transfer the centres to the Ministry, it would be possible to make contractual arrangements with the Regional Health Boards whereby the latter would pay the cost of all patients who had moved into the centres from a hospital. Under these arrangements, there would be no interference with the management of the centres. Regional Hospital Boards had authority to pay £8.8s.0d per patient per week, the exact amount being based upon ascertained costs.

As to the new developments which were envisaged by the Commission, the Ministry recommended that they should assume responsibility for them which would ensure that the new centres would have an appropriate place in the Ministry's plans for the development of the National Health Service.

After another long debate, the Council and the Commission decided that the Ministry of Health should be informed that it had been decided not to transfer the centres to the National Health Service. Negotiations would be opened with the Regional Hospital Boards, in consultation with the Ministry of Health, whereby contractual arrangements would be made for the cost of all patients who had moved into Centres from hospital, to be paid by the National Health Service, on the understanding that these arrangements would not confer any right to interfere in the management of the centres other than the right to satisfy themselves that the treatment provided was to a certain standard. Negotiations would be opened with the object of ensuring that the new centres proposed by the Commission would be included in the Regional Hospital Boards' planning programmes and be given a high priority.

At the November meeting of the Council, Mr Nicoll presented the Consulting Surgeon's Report for 1947. The rehabilitation centres had shown 93% capacity usage. Only cases of major injury were being systematically recruited and very few cases of minor injuries were being admitted. 57% of patients returned to their pre-accident work. 30% returned to light permanent work. 4.2% were able to undertake work outside the mining industry. Only 4.2% discharged from the centres were unemployed at the end of six months after their discharge.

Sir Reginald Watson-Jones also attended the meeting and said that he hoped the Council and the Commission recognised the value of the rehabilitation service it had established. It was a pioneering development, and the only organised scheme of rehabilitation which existed in this or any other country in the world.

At their December meeting, the Council were in receipt of a further letter from the Ministry of Health enquiring whether the Commission would re-consider the transfer of its rehabilitation centres to the National Health Service, on the understanding that the Minister would ensure that each centre, with the possible exception of the outpatient clinics, should have its own management committees. He would also obtain binding assurance from the Regional Hospital Boards concerned that each Hospital Management Committee would include a substantial representation of the present managements (at least a majority), and that in all centres priority should be given to the needs of mineworkers unless and until alternative facilities were available.

At the request of Mr Hall (member of the Council and nominated by the NUM) the council deferred consideration of this matter in order that the representatives of the National Union of Mineworkers might submit their observations on these new proposals.[18]

In January 1949, the Council needed to consider its future spending on rehabilitation. They had before them the tenders for the adaptation of the existing buildings and the addition of a new gymnasium at Herrington Hall (Durham) and the provision at Lanelay Hall (South Wales) of an experimental rehabilitation centre for pneumoconiosis cases which together amounted to about £105,000. It was also necessary to make a provisional allocation of £34,300 to cover the estimated maintenance costs for the centres for the next two to three months.

The Executive Council of the National Union of Mineworkers had discussed whether rehabilitation centres should be transferred to the Minister of Health, and had decided that a decision should be deferred for twelve months to allow for time to see how the provision of facilities for rehabilitation of injured persons were delivered under the National Health Service.

As far as the expenditure on new rehabilitation facilities were concerned, the Council saw this as the responsibility of the National Health Service, but that the Council should ensure as far as possible that the rate of providing these facilities was not diminished under State responsibility. A fresh approach should be made to the Minister of Health.

The £34,300 was approved, and it was agreed that the South Wales Rehabilitation Committee should be consulted over Lanelay Hall.

The South Wales Rehabilitation Committee met on 29th January 1949 and the meeting was attended by Mr Horner. The Committee concluded that there was a need for a pneumoconiosis treatment centre in South Wales and, as the treatment to be given was past the research stage, it qualified for a grant from the Miners' Welfare Fund.

It was therefore decided that a deputation (Sir Joseph Hallsworth, Mr Bowman, Professor Collis, Mr Hall, Mr Horner and Mr Shearing) should meet the Minister of Health on 2nd March 1949 to discuss maintenance of existing miners' welfare centres, capital and maintenance expenditure on new projects and the provision of facilities for the rehabilitation treatment of suffers from pneumoconiosis.

The deputation met with the Minister of Health who expressed the view that there was no reason why the transfer of the rehabilitation centres to the National Health Service on the conditions already offered should be postponed for a period of 12 months as suggested by the National Union of Mineworkers. The Minister subsequently met the Executive Committee of the National Union of Mineworkers on 3rd March and apparently had succeeded in persuading them to withdraw their objections to the immediate transfer of the centres.

It was therefore decided at the Council's March 1949 meeting that, subject to the concurrence of the Minister of Fuel and Power, its rehabilitation centres would be transferred to the National Health Service on the conditions offered by the Minister of Health in his letter of 30th November 1948.

The Minister of Fuel and Power had expressed the view that the Acts establishing the Miners' Welfare Fund would not permit the transfer unless the Ministry of Health was prepared to guarantee that the centres would continue to be available primarily for mineworkers, so at the Council's April meeting, it was proposed that there should be a meeting with the legal side of the Ministry of Health to seek a satisfactory formula that met the requirements of the Acts.

The Chairman had also visited Talygarn Rehabilitation Centre and Lanelay Hall with the Minister of Health. The Minister did not consider Lanelay Hall a suitable place for a centre for pneumoconiosis but had undertaken to see what other arrangements could be made. The Secretary was therefore authorised to commence negotiations for the sale of Lanelay Hall as soon as confirmation that the property would not be required as a Rehabilitation Centre was obtained from the Ministry of Health.

A meeting with the Ministry of Health's solicitor was held on 11th May 1949 at the Ministry of Fuel and Power, at which general agreement had been reached in principle as to the legal basis for the transfer of the centres to the National Health Service, and it was left to the Ministry of Fuel and Power's solicitors to prepare a 'Heads of Trusts' for consideration by the Ministry of Health on 16th May 1949.

It was proposed to effect the transfer of the centres by means of a trust deed which would, as far as possible, embody the general principles governing the protection of property owned by the Miners' Welfare Fund, and would also ensure the main conditions of transfer which had been agreed with the Minister of Health.

Sir Reginald Watson-Jones presented the Consulting Surgeon's Report for 1948 to the May meeting of the Council, as Mr Nicoll was indisposed. Over 11,000 patients had been treated in the centres to the end of 1948, of these, over 95% had been resettled either in their own or lighter work in the mining industry, or some other form of employment. All the patients who received treatment were suffering from major fractures or dislocations. Not only did the industry benefit from the high proportion of injured men who returned to work, but the knowledge of the existence of an efficient rehabilitation and resettlement service was an important influence in maintaining the morale of mineworkers as a whole.

Sir Reginald Watson-Jones pointed out that the transfer of the Rehabilitation Service to the Ministry of Health meant a change from a centrally-controlled service to one organised on a regional basis. His doubts about this change had arisen from his recent experience connected with paraplegia. Paraplegia had been thoroughly studied by the Rehabilitation Medical Committee over the past two years, and a plan for treatment had been prepared for a protype paraplegic unit at the Wharncliffe Hospital in Sheffield.

A representative of the Ministry had attended the last meeting of the Committee on 18th March and had stated that the problem was being studied. One of the reasons given for not implementing the Committee's plan immediately was that the Ministry was only a co-ordinator and did not control the Regional Boards. It appeared that the difficulty in the way of the Sheffield scheme was not so much the expenditure, which was small, but the fact that it involved co-ordination between three organisations.

The Council at its May meeting, in consequence, instructed the Secretary to inform the Ministry of Health of the Council's concern over the delay in the setting up of the protype centre at Sheffield for the treatment of paraplegic miners and also instructed the officers to examine the possibility of the Miners' Rehabilitation Medical Committee functioning within the provisions of the National Health Service Act 1946.

In June 1949, the Commission's booklet 'Learning at Every Step' had been published and had received good notices in the press, particularly as a result of the rapid recovery of a patient at Talygarn.

The surgeons controlling the Miners' Rehabilitation Centres in Great Britain met at Berry Hill Hall, Mansfield, on 30th June under the Chairmanship of Sir Reginald Watson-Jones. They recognised that the medical rehabilitation of miners did not differ fundamentally from the medical rehabilitation of other industrial workers, and that sooner or later such services should be part of a National Health Service. Nevertheless, after careful thought and discussion, they agreed unanimously 'That the special rehabilitation service that had been organised and developed by the Miners' Welfare Commission will be seriously jeopardised and perhaps even destroyed if, at this stage, it is handed over to the National Health Service.'

Sir Reginald Watson-Jones prepared a memorandum based on the views expressed by the members of the meeting which was considered at a meeting held on 11th July 1949 at the Ministry of Health prior to its submission to the Joint Council meeting on 20th July. The meeting on 11th July was attended by representatives of the Ministry of Health, the Ministry of Fuel and Power and the National Miners' Welfare Joint Council, Sir Reginald Watson-Jones and Mr E. A. Nicoll.

A number of points were discussed. The surgeons were afraid that many difficulties would arise, that miners would not receive the priority of treatment they had hitherto enjoyed, and that rehabilitation would not receive the attention that it deserved since the Ministry of Health had a large number of pressing problems to solve in the early days of the new National Health Service. Many of the fears that the surgeons had expressed were allayed by the meeting at the Ministry of Health.

However, at the Council's meeting on 20th July, Sir Reginald Watson-Jones had to point out that there was still one important difficulty to overcome. No fewer than 75% of the surgeons serving the Commission's rehabilitation centres had made it clear that they would find it necessary to resign if the rehabilitation service was taken over by the National Health Service, because their hospital commitments were such that they were already serving the maximum number of part-time sessions permitted by the Ministry of Health. If the surgeons continued to attend the rehabilitation centres after the transfer to the Ministry of Health, it would not only be in a voluntary, unpaid capacity but also at the expense of the limited time that remained for private practice and this they were unwilling to countenance. The Ministry had indicated that similar problems had arisen in other directions and, although they were investigating it, no solution had yet been found.

In September, the Joint Council considered a draft conveyance of a rehabilitation centre by the Miners' Welfare Commission to the Minister of Health, and a statement of assurance which would be required from the Minister of Health as forming the basis of an agreement to transfer the centres to him.

These assurances included alterations to Herrington Hall (Durham), the need for a second centre in South Wales, and accepting the responsibility for the provision of all rehabilitation services for miners including silicosis, pneumoconiosis paraplegia, rheumatism and nystagmus.

It was reported to the Council at their October 1949 meeting that the draft model conveyance and the amended draft Statement of Assurance approved at their September 1949 meeting had been referred to the top level of the Ministry of Health. In November 1949, the Council had been informed that the two documents were still under active consideration and that the Minister of Health had written a personal letter to the Minister of Fuel and Power who wished to discuss its contents with the Chairman before referring it to the Council for their observations. Mr Horner informed the Council at their November meeting that the Minister of Health had informed him that the delay in bringing this matter to a conclusion was entirely due to the attitude of the Council's officials.[19]

109 pithead baths, 60 canteens and 64 ancillary buildings had been awarded priority by Divisional Boards and Divisional Welfare Committees by 31st January 1949. The Joint Council had already approved the four-year (1948-1951) programmes for Scottish, North Western and East Midlands Divisions

and interim lists for inclusion in the four-year programme of Northern and South Western Divisions.

At the February 1949 meeting, Mr Kemp, Chief Architect, had explained that difficulties were occurring in the completion of pithead baths due to delays in obtaining fittings and equipment. Mr Longmuir, therefore, had taken this up with the Production Department (Supplies Sub-Department) and a new procedure had been designed for Divisional Architects, Area Supplies Managers and the Supplies Sub-Department to follow to overcome the difficulties in obtaining fittings and equipment.

Although the Council had approved the Scottish Divisional programme at their December 1948 meeting, the Divisional Welfare Committee submitted a list of additions to their programme (fifteen modified type pithead baths with canteens, four extensions to existing baths, three separate new canteens and five schemes of sundry work at existing baths). These additions, despite amendments to the cost of schemes in the original programme had brought the expenditure to £19,411 in excess of the Divisional Apportionment of funds. The revised programme was approved at the Council's April meeting as well as the South Western Division's amendments and additions to their interim 1948/51 programme. This left South Western Divisional apportionment with a balance of £269,724.

By June 1949, six of the experimental pithead baths (Kirkford, Scottish; Howroyd, North Eastern, Salterford, North Western; Lodge, East Midlands; Yew Tree, West Midlands and Lucy Thomas, South Western) were in use. The installation at Tilley's Drift, Northern, was nearing completion. A feature of these baths had been the speed of their construction. The average time taken to complete each of the six schemes had been 8 months from commencement of building work.

Divisional Boards were also providing modified pithead baths. Mr Kemp visited two in June 1949 at Kenhall Colliery (West Midlands) and Oakwood Grange. At Kenhall, an existing building had been adapted to accommodate 240 men using chiefly colliery labour and took twelve months to complete. Clothes were stored on hangers rather than in lockers.

Oakwood Grange had been provided without any reference to the Welfare Building Branch. Clean and dirty changing rooms were equipped with clothes hangers. The baths accommodated 120 men and took approximately ten months to build. The bath waste was discharged directly into a stream without treatment. In Mr Kemp's opinion, the savings in time and money was not sufficient to justify the expedients employed at the two collieries.

At the September meeting of the Council, Sir Geoffrey Vickers presented a memorandum on a Supplementary Pithead Baths Programme. At the May 1949 meeting of the Council, a request from the Scottish Divisional Committee for additional funds for building baths at new small mines had been considered and Mr Horner had pointed out that it was the responsibility of the Board, as a good employer to see that baths were provided for the men working at pits developed by the Board in their efforts to secure coal quickly. This opinion was supported by the Council, and Sir Geoffrey Vickers was invited to bring it to the attention of the Board.

The Board took the decision to undertake a secondary programme of baths or extensions to existing baths at all new or reconstructed pits, in addition to the programme already initiated. The cost would be borne by the Board independently of the Divisional allocation under the four-year programme. As a result of this decision, certain baths that featured in the four-year programme were transferred to the Board's secondary programme.

However, the Board, having made the decision to make this offer, had been required to curtail the total amount of their capital expenditure in 1950. In September 1949, they were revising their programme but did not have sufficient details to forecast the effect this restriction would have on welfare building, including the principal baths-building programme.[20]

In April 1949, the Joint Council received reports from the Selection Committee of the Miners' Welfare National Scholarship, the Student Exhibition Scheme and the Special Committee appointed to consider recommendations made by the Moderating and Examining Committees of the Miners Welfare National Part-time Day Advanced Mining Scholarship Scheme.

At their November 1948 meeting, the Selection Committee of the Miners' Welfare National Scholarship and Students' Exhibition Scheme had been asked to consider the future of the schemes in view of the substantial increase that had taken place in recent years in the financial assistance available from national and local sources to students taking university and other educational courses.

There had been no appreciable reduction in the annual number of awards of new scholarships and the high standard of the candidate receiving the awards was being well maintained. The Joint Council therefore agreed that the scheme should continue.

The Moderating and Examining Committees for the Miners' Welfare National Part-time Day Advanced Mining Scholarship scheme had reached the conclusion that, whilst the Commission's Scheme had served an invaluable purpose, the need for its continuance in its existing form had, in the main, been removed by the introduction of the National Coal Board's scheme covering loss of wages etc. for students attending part-time courses. A Special Committee had been appointed at the November 1948 meeting of the Joint Council; they had recommended that no further scholarships should be awarded, and that consideration should be given to the establishment of a Travelling Mining Scholarship in substitution for the current scheme.[21]

At the end of October 1949, the Minister of Fuel and Power appointed Viscount Hyndley as Chairman of the Miners' Welfare Commission until 12th July 1950. Sir Joseph Hallsworth had chaired his last meeting of the Council in April 1949 and, in the intervening months, Professor Collis had been elected as acting Chairman.

In November 1949, the Council considered a resolution passed by the East Midlands Divisional Welfare Committee at their meeting on 29th September. The Committee considered that the present functions of the National Miners' Welfare Joint Council should as far as possible be decentralised. The functions of the Council should be to give general guidance and instruction to all Miners' Welfare Councils or Committees and that Divisional Miners' Welfare Committees should be given full power to administer the Miners' Welfare Funds allocated to them by the National Joint Council in accordance with the principles laid down by them. The Council agreed that an investigation into the working of the Scheme of Co-ordination should be made.[22]

In January 1950, the Council confirmed the appointment of Mr Saise as Chief Architect as Mr Kemp had accepted employment with the British Electricity Authority. Mr Bowman also resigned as he had been appointed as Chairman of the Northern Divisional Coal Board. At the invitation of the Minister of Fuel and Power, the National Union of Mineworkers nominated Mr J. H. Southall to fill the vacancy.

In July 1950, the Minister of Fuel and Power decided to reappoint the members of the Miners' Welfare Commission, with the exception of Professor Collis and Mr J. Stanleigh Turner whose places would be filled by Dr S. W. Fisher and Sir Geoffrey Vickers.

The Chairman informed the Council at their January 1950 meeting that he had been consulted by the Minister of Fuel and Power about the letter from the Minister of Health reporting that negotiations for the transfer of the centres had reached a deadlock, and inviting the Minister of Fuel and Power to assist in resolving it.

There had, however, been some development in providing paraplegic units. In Sheffield, the current premises at Wharncliffe Hospital were to be used temporarily as a paraplegic unit and plans produced for building a new unit at the City General Hospital or elsewhere. In Southport, 20 beds were currently in use as a paraplegic unit with a proposal to increase the unit to about 50 beds. This unit would serve the Manchester region as well as the Liverpool region.

At their February meeting, the Council agreed in principle to the proposal that assurances which the Commission wished to obtain should be covered by an exchange of letters between the Minister of Fuel and Power and the Minister of Health but, before any final decision was reached, Mr Horner would consult the National Executive Committee of the National Union of Mineworkers.

The National Executive Committee met on 9th March 1950 and had raised four points concerning the proposed assurances: representation of mineworkers on the management committees, outpatient clinics at Uddingston (Scotland), Walkden and Wigan, the disclosure of medical records and the recent forecast in Parliament of the National Health Service's economics. On the latter, reassurance was required that such economics would not affect the undertaking of the Minister of Health to accept responsibility for the provision of all kinds of rehabilitation for miners, particularly pneumocoiotics.

As a result of the points raised by the National Union of Mineworkers, it was decided that further consultation with the Ministry of Health was needed.

At their March meeting, the Council were made aware of the difficulty being experienced at the Wharncliffe Hospital over the arrangements promised by the Ministry of Health for the treatment of paraplegics. Certain equipment had been on order for a considerable period and there appeared to be no hope of immediate delivery. The lack of progress appeared to be down to the Management Committee.

In June 1950, the Council were informed that the Minister of Health had written to the Minister of Fuel and Power agreeing to a meeting with representatives of the Council and the Commission to discuss the points which had been recently raised on the proposed transfer of the rehabilitation centres to the National Health Service.

This meeting between the Minister of Health and the deputation from the Council took place on 17th July. The Minister had given assurances on the constitution of the new Management Committees, the management of the clinics at Walkden and Wigan by the Oakmere Hall Committees and that medical records would be made available for medical purposes to other hospitals but not to the Ministry of National Insurance. However, the future development of the rehabilitation services for miners might not take the precise form which the Miners' Welfare Commission had contemplated, but the Minister did propose to develop the service, particularly pneumoconiosis, if the current uncertainty as to the future of the rehabilitation centres could be cleared up. He would undertake a review of the position and inform the Board and the Commission by mid -September whether Lanelay Hall and Herrington Hall would be required and, if not, of the alternative proposals he had in mind for dealing with the pneumoconiosis problem.

Sir Reginald Watson-Jones, Mr A. Miller and Mr E. A. Nicoll attended the June meeting of the Council to present the Consulting Surgeon's Annual Report for 1949. Of the patients discharged, 94% had been resettled in employment; of these, 91% had been resettled in the mining industry and 3% in other industries. These results were indicative not only of the excellence of the treatment which the men received at the centres, but also of the value of the medico-social work being done for them.

However, Mr Nicoll concluded his report by pointing out that, during the last two years of uncertainty about the future of the centres, there had been some effect upon the enthusiasm of the people working in them. He hoped that, for the rehabilitation service, something could be decided in the near future.

The Council received an update on the transfer of the rehabilitation centres to the Ministry of Health. The effective date of transfer would be 1st April 1951. The Minister had decided, following a report by his medical officer that there was clearly an urgent need for a residential rehabilitation centre for pneumoconiosis, but he would prefer to use a completely new and specially planned building. Lanelay Hall had been offered for sale. The Minister was still considering Herrington Hall.

A meeting had been held on 12th October 1950 between officials of the Council and the Department of Health for Scotland to discuss Uddingston. As it was not residential, the Department did not feel able to give all the assurances that Mr Bevan had given in respect of the rehabilitation centres in England and Wales, particularly on the question of management. The Secretary of State for Scotland would be writing to the Council.

The Council were informed that the Ministry of Health were not prepared to meet any expenditure, either capital or maintenance, incurred or due for payment before 1st April 1951, although they would accept responsibility for expenditure still to be incurred on that date on commitments entered into by the Commission prior to 1st April in consultation with the Ministry. There were six urgent projects which had been recommended by management committees on which decisions were outstanding.

The Chairman was therefore asked to discuss with the Minister of Health the pneumoconiosis proposal and the question of responsibilities for capital or other abnormal expenditure which might be incurred before 1st April 1951.

The Ministry of Health accepted responsibility for any work on the six urgent projects that had not been completed by 31st March 1951, but the Chairman had not been able to arrange a meeting prior to the Council's November meeting to discuss Mr Bevan's pneumoconiosis proposals and the responsibility for capital expenditure incurred before 1st April 1951.[23]

The Council considered, at their January 1950 meeting, the apportionment of the Miners' Welfare Baths Fund for Pithead Baths and ancillary buildings. The current policy was to apportion the Baths Fund to the twenty five Coal

Districts on a 'fair shares' basis. If this was to continue, it would be difficult to fit in allocations from the Commission's Baths Fund with those to be charged to the Board's contribution for building pithead baths. The difficulty could be overcome if the apportionment was made on a Divisional instead of a District basis. It was therefore agreed to discontinue the apportionment of the Baths Fund on a District basis.

The Pithead Baths Committee in April decided that no further aluminium prefabricated baths should be erected. This decision was based on the report on the seven experimental prefabricated pithead baths erected following the decision taken by the Council in February 1948. Although the experiment was not complete, the interim conclusions drawn showed that the cost of a conventional brick and concrete shell would not be more expensive than the prefabricated aluminium hull, and the time taken to build in brick would probably not be longer.

At the May meeting of the Council, the summary of adjustments to the approved pithead baths building programme reported by the Divisions for the first quarter of 1950 suggested that a number of cases of alterations involved pithead baths which would be financed from the Miners' Welfare Fund, for which authority to proceed should be subject to approval by the Commission prior to any commitments being entered into by the Divisions.

The Council had delegated to the Divisions the responsibility for planning and executing the 1948/51 programme within the limits of the Divisional apportionment of funds. In the case of baths finance from the Board's 2d, changes in the financial details could be authorised at Divisional level but would have to be reported to the Council at quarterly intervals.

The Council decided that all proposed extensions or deviations from the approved programme which involved projects being paid by the Miners' Welfare Fund should be approved by the Commission in advance of commitments being entered into.

In June 1950, the Welfare Service Branch reported to the Council that there was evidence that pegging of food subsidies, together with the plentiful supplies of food available had resulted in the reduction of the number of men using colliery canteens (specially for full meals service) and this made it increasingly difficult for canteens to pay their way.

The Northern Welfare Committee had agreed that future canteens should be constructed to serve only a snap and snack service, and that canteens committees experiencing financial difficulties should be advised to provide a similar limited service. In the North-Eastern and North-Western Divisions, many of the canteens had closed down.

The Council at their June 1950 meeting agreed that no further canteens should be erected and that, wherever practicable, work should be suspended on those canteens now under construction. They also invited Pithead Baths Committees to review the use of existing canteens.

At their November 1950 meeting, it was reported that Divisional Committees and Divisional Boards were generally agreed that the need for a main meal service was unlikely to continue and that the demand would probably be for snap and snacks of a rather better standard than before the war. The Welfare Building Branch was therefore asked to prepare a new set of standards for the Commission's canteens.[24]

In January 1950, the Council were made aware that the Ministry of Education, in accordance with the Governments proposals to deal with the economic situation, were obliged to curtail (at least temporarily) the financial help which they had been giving to the miners' welfare schemes (normally 50% of the expenditure involved) under the Physical Training and Recreation Act 1937, and had advised Local Education Authorities to act similarly in respect of their activities under the terms of the Education Act 1944. A similar course had been taken by the Scottish Home Department and the Scottish Education Department in respect of the 1937 Act and the Education (Scotland) Act 1946.

Based on the experience of the first two or three weeks of January 1950, this had meant that grant-aid was limited to a maximum expenditure of about £1,500 and, in the case of the purchase of a site or existing building, no grant-aid would be given where the price that the local committee was prepared to pay exceeded the valuation placed on that building or site by the District Valuer.

The Minister of Fuel and Power had also written to the Chairman inviting him to exercise restraint and to economise wherever possible to reduce the inflationary pressure on the national economy.[25]

Warwickshire County Council Authority had asked for confirmation of the provisional grant of £10,000 which was made before the war from the General Fund of the Miners' Welfare Fund towards the cost of erecting and equipping a mining department of a new College of Technology and Art at Nuneaton subject to the approval of the plans by the Ministry of Education and completion of an agreement protecting the grant, between the Commission and the Authority.

Grants totalling £9,073 had previously been made from the Fund during the period 1923 to 1940, to provide and equip a laboratory and lecture room in an extension adjoining the existing County Mining and Technical School and also for a mining library and additional equipment and apparatus.

The preliminary plans for the new college were approved by the Ministry in 1930, but owing to the war and restrictions on building, the proposals were shelved and, in 1942, the Commission suspended the provisional grant of £10,000 for the time being.

The plans had been entirely revised, in consultation with the Ministry of Education, to meet the Education Authority's obligations to provide for Further Education under the Education Act 1944. The mining department would occupy approximately one-eighth of the teaching accommodation in the new building, but the students would have access to other facilities in the new building.

The grant was supported by Mr H. J. Shelley, Ministry of Education, and the grant was approved by the Council at their February 1950 meeting, together with a retransfer from the General Endowment Fund of £10,000 to the General Fund.[26]

Cardiff University College sought confirmation of a provisional grant of £28,000 from the General Fund of the Miners' Welfare Fund towards the cost of erecting and equipping a new University Mining Department block and had asked that consideration might be given to increasing the grant by a further £2,000.

The new Mining Department was originally proposed in 1930 but, owing to local complications of finance and control followed by conditions arising from the war, the proposal did not reach a concrete form until 1947, when the Commission approved in principle, its offer of the grant, subject to assurances that sufficient funds would be forthcoming from other sources to meet the balance of the capital cost, that satisfactory arrangements had been made for organisation and maintenance of the new department when completed, that building would commence within a reasonable time and that an agreement between the college and the Commission to protect the grant would be completed.

The college authorities were further required to consult the National Coal Board with a view to ascertaining whether the proposed new Mining Department fitted in with the Board's plans for mining education and to what extent (if any) the Board were willing to assume responsibility for an offer originally made by the South Wales Coal Owners' Association to contribute a sum of £5,000 a year towards maintenance of the department when completed.

The new building was due to commence in July 1950 and the new block would be completed by 1953. Consultation was taking place between the college and the National Coal Board who, while welcoming the new Department, were not prepared to commit themselves as to the form or amount of assistance until their long-term policy for support of universities was in place.

The University Grants Committee was prepared to proceed with its capital allocation, so it was for the Commission at its March 1950 meeting to say whether they were prepared to proceed with their grant. A grant of £30,000 was confirmed at the meeting as funds were available.[27]

The Miners' Welfare National Scholarship Committee had recommended that the maximum value of the awards under the scholarship should be increased to bring them in line with the value of the State Scholarships with effect from

1st October 1949. The revised values were approved by the Council at their September 1949 meeting. The financial implications, however, had not been calculated. In May 1950, the Miners' Welfare National Selection Committee had therefore recommended to the Council that sufficient funds should be provided to enable a normal average of 15 new scholarships to be awarded annually for the next three years, on their assurance that they would continue to maintain high standards of selection and that they would submit a report on the long term policy as soon as the effects on the scheme of the increased number of State University awards had become apparent.

The Council agreed to a grant of between £2,500 and £3,000 from the General Fund as this was the sum requested by the Selection Committee but instructed the Secretary to prepare a full report on the income and expenditure of the Miners' Welfare National Scholarship Endowment Fund.

The Secretary's report was presented to the June meeting of the Council. It suggested that not more than nine or ten new scholarships should be recommended for award in 1950 and that a further review of the financial position of the Scheme would need to be made at the end of 1950. 28

In October 1950, it was suggested that a committee should be appointed to make recommendations on the future organisation of miners' welfare after the end of 1951, when the output levy was due to terminate.

In March 1951, the Chairman made a statement to the Council that the ad hoc committee's agreed proposals for the future of miners' welfare after the end of 1951 were still under discussion, but would probably be submitted to their May meeting.

It was not until the Council's June 1951 meeting that the Chairman reported that the ad hoc committee had reached their final conclusions, which had provisionally been accepted by the Board and the National Executive Committee of the National Union of Mineworkers and embodied in a Memorandum of Agreement. It still needed to be accepted by the Lodges, however. A formal resolution in favour of the proposal would be put forward at the NUM Annual Conference in July 1951.

The Memorandum of Agreement was signed on 24th July by Lord Hyndley and Sir Geoffrey Vickers on behalf of the Board, and Will Lawther and Mr A. L. Horner on behalf of the National Union of Mineworkers.

The Agreement set up the responsibilities for the welfare of persons employed in or connected with the coal industry, and all other persons employed by the Board from 1st April 1952 with the cessation of the output payments which were paid into the Miners' Welfare Fund.

Welfare in the coal industry was divided into two categories: Colliery Welfare and Social Welfare. Colliery Welfare included pithead baths, canteens, cycle stores, medical treatment centres, vocational and training for employment in the coal industry, attention to individual needs of workers affecting their work and the welfare of workers absent from work through sickness or accident and their resettlement at work on their return. Social Welfare included the provision of recreational, social and cultural facilities and activities through recreation grounds, recreation or community centres, youth clubs and camps, holidays and holiday camps. Social welfare also included assistance of sick or disabled persons and the provision, maintenance or support of convalescent homes and funds and education in all fields other than vocational training in the Industry.

The Board would assume responsibility for Colliery Welfare, and would maintain consultation at all levels on questions relating to Colliery Welfare with representatives through the consultative machinery set up in accordance with the Agreement.

The responsibility for Social Welfare would be placed upon a newly constituted body to be known as the Coal Industry Social Welfare Council. The Council would be an independent body incorporated under the Companies Act 1948 and would be constituted as a Private Company limited by shares, having the Board and a representative of the NUM as members. In each Division of the Board, the Council would establish a Divisional Welfare Committee to which the Council would annually allocate sums available for Social Welfare purposes and supervise the activities of the Committees.

The functions, assets and liabilities of the Miners' Welfare Commission would be transferred by legislation to the Board or the Council. The National Miners' Welfare Joint Council would be abolished.

The Board would make available to the Council, as and when required, sums amounting in aggregate to one million pounds to provide welfare schemes. Once this sum had been reduced to four hundred thousand, the Council could apply for further funding.

The Miners' Welfare National Scholarship Endowment Fund and the Fund established in connection with the Miners' Welfare National Student Exhibition Scheme would be transferred to the Council but should continue to be applied for the purpose for which those funds had been established. The Miners' Welfare National Mining Education Scholarship Fund would be disposed of or applied elsewhere.[29]

The National Health Service had made redundant many miners' welfare schemes, such as ambulances and nursing schemes, which had been established with charitable trusts. The Council at their February 1951 meeting were informed that the Charity Commissioners had approved the transfer of the trust funds of seventeen ambulance and nursing schemes in South Yorkshire to the South Yorkshire Miners' Welfare Convalescent Treatment Fund. Four other similar transfers were expected to be approved. When the transfers were completed, the endowment of the Convalescent Treatment Fund scheme would be increased to £41,152, yielding an additional income of £1,400 a year, thus relieving to that extent the need for grants from the District Fund towards deficits on the maintenance account for the scheme.[30]

The formal exchange of letters between the Minister of Fuel and Power and the Minister of Health embodying the agreed arrangements for the transfer of the rehabilitation centres to the National Health Service had been duly concluded by a letter dated 26th January 1951 from the Minister of Health to the Minister of Fuel and Power accepting the conditions under which the Miners' Welfare Commission would formally transfer to the Minister of Health their rehabilitation centres and clinics for inclusion in the National Health Service as from 1st April 1951.

The Chairman had raised with the Minister four consequential questions arising out of the agreed arrangements for the transfer of the centres. At the February 1951 meeting of the Council, Lord Hyndley reported that he was in receipt of a letter dated 19th February 1951 from the Minister of Health dealing with three of these questions. Herrington Hall was too small to convert into an efficient residential rehabilitation centre, and too dilapidated to be worth reconditioning with a view to extending it. The Minister requested evidence of the urgency of the need for rehabilitation facilities for the Swansea area. He confirmed that a separate rehabilitation unit for pneumoconiosis would be provided at Llandough Hospital as originally suggested.

The Chairman, Sir Arthur Street, Sir Geoffrey Vickers and Mr Horner had met with the Minister of Health on 19th February to discuss the fourth question. Mr Marquand, Minister of Health, had promised to reconsider his previous decision against continuing the payment of fares or the provision of free transport for patients attending the centres.

The Secretary of State for Scotland, however, had not yet seen his way to agree to the transfer of the Uddingston Centre, pending approval by parliament of the sum to be provided for the National Health Service in Scotland.

In March 1951, the Joint Council were made aware that the Minister of Health had written on 14th March 1951, stating that he was unable to accept the payment of fares of miners travelling to and from the centres. The Commission therefore agreed to pay such fares or the cost of transport pending further representation by the Council to the Minister.

Negotiations were proceeding between the surgeons to the centres and the Regional Hospital Boards with a view to continuing their service under the new set up, but it appeared that difficulties were being experienced in coming to an arrangement acceptable to the surgeons. The Commission's Rehabilitation

Medical Committee had met on 13th March, and had recommended that the centres should not be transferred on 1st April 1951 unless continuation of the payment of surgeons was first assured. The Commission agreed at the March meeting of the Council that surgeons should continue their work at the centres which was an essential part of the agreement for transfer. If the surgeons, in continuing to work at the centres suffered loss of fees, the Commission would make good any such loss.

The transfer of the seven centres and three clinics in England and Wales had taken place on and with effect from 1st April and the administrative arrangements had in general proceeded satisfactorily.

However, the Sheffield Regional Hospital Board, responsible for Firbeck Hall, Berry Hill Hall and Higham Grange Centres had incorporated 'Hospital' into the title of the Management Committee. The Sheffield Board had also decided to appoint the Chairman of the Hospital Management Committee for a period of 3 years unlike the practice under the Commission when the appointment was made annually in consultation with the Management Committee.

The Manchester Regional Hospital Board had appointed an independent Chairman of the new Management Committee. A meeting of the Committee had been prevented in view of the opposition of the National Union of Mineworkers' representatives to this action. A meeting was being arranged between the Chairman of the Regional Hospital Board, Mr W. J. Drummond, representing the National Coal Board, and Mr E. Hull, representing the NUM, to resolve the difficulty.

Ten out of thirty surgeons employed at the rehabilitation centres held maximum part-time contracts with their Regional Hospital Boards, and it was not possible to include service to the centres in their contracts without displacing other duties and responsibilities which were impracticable.

Acting on the suggestion made by the Minister of Health with the approval of the Chairman, Sir Reginald Watson-Jones had been invited to discuss with Sir John Charles, Chief Medical Officer of the Ministry of Health, how a mutually acceptable settlement with the surgeons might be reached.

Mr E. A. Nicoll had accepted an appointment as Consulting Adviser on Rehabilitation to the Ministry of Health but the Commission at the Council's meeting in May had agreed that Mr Nicoll's appointment as Consulting Surgeon to the Commission should be continued in an honorary capacity subject to the agreement of the Ministry of Health for such period as the Commission deemed appropriate.

As a result of the meeting on 10th May 1951, held in Edinburgh between the representatives of the Department of Health for Scotland, the Scottish Divisional Welfare Committee and the Lanarkshire Miners' Rehabilitation

Committee, arrangements for the transfer of the Uddingston Rehabilitation Centre to the National Health Service were being put in place.

The Scottish Divisional Welfare Committee and the Uddingston Rehabilitation Centre Management Committee were invited to make observations on the proposals for the transfer of the centre and they raised four points; payment of travelling expenses including meals, management, priority use of the Centre and the transfer of the property. As the Commission had already agreed in principle to pay travelling expenses of patients, at the June meeting of the Council, the Commission agreed that, subject to approval of the Secretary of State for Scotland, negotiations with the Department of Health should be concluded with a view to the transfer of the Uddingston Centre to the National Health Service on 1st July 1951.

Confirmation had been received in June 1951 from the Birmingham Regional Hospital Board that arrangements had been made for the continuation of the clinical work carried out by Dr Dorothy Campbell on miners' nystagmus in the West Midlands, and for the necessary alteration in Dr Campbell's contract with the Hospital Board.

Following the decision taken at the June meeting of the Council that transfer of the Uddingston centre should take place on 1st July, the Commission's Secretary had met representatives of the Department of Health for Scotland to discuss the arrangements for implementing the Commission's decision. For administrative reasons, the Department proposed that the takeover should take place on 1st October, but it was eventually agreed to aim for 1st September as the effective date.

The Scottish Area of the National Union of Mineworkers wrote to the Commission protesting against the decision to transfer the Uddingston Rehabilitation Centre to the National Health Service, and asked for reconsideration of this decision.

On 2nd August 1951, the Secretary had attended a meeting between representatives of the Department of Health for Scotland, the Western Regional Hospital Board, the Management Committee of the Uddingston Centre, the Glasgow Victoria Hospital Management Committee and the Scottish Divisional Welfare Committee for the intended purpose of settling the consequential administrative arrangements for putting the transfer of the Centre into effect on 1st September.

As there was an apparent dissension concerning procedure and detail on the National Health side, the only outcome of the meeting was that the Department of Health agreed to examine once again the legal position in regard to setting up a Hospital Management Committee instead of a Centre Committee, and to hold a further meeting when the decision of the Secretary of State on this point was available.

As the law stood, the Secretary for State was unable to appoint a hospital committee so the decision for the centre to have a Centre Committee was confirmed. Meanwhile, following the meeting on 2nd August, the Divisional Welfare Committee and the Scottish Area of the National Union of Mineworkers again expressed their dissatisfaction with the procedure adopted for the transfer of the Uddingston Centre to the National Health Service.

The Chairman, together with Mr Drummond, Sir Geoffrey Vickers and Mr Bennett, met representatives of the Scottish Area of the National Union of Mineworkers following the September 1951 meeting of the Council. Mr Moffat had subsequently intimated that, provided a Hospital Management Committee was set up instead of a Centre Committee, the Union were prepared to accept the transfer of the centre. The Chairman therefore decided to defer the proposed transfer and, after discussing this with the Council at their 28th November 1951 meeting, he and Mr Horner sought an interview with the Secretary of State on the specific question of substituting a hospital management committee for the centre committee.

In September 1951, the Council were made aware that deductions were being made from the sickness benefits of injured miners after 8 weeks at the Rehabilitation Centres. This was a logical result of the transfer of the centres to the Ministry of Health. The Commission agreed that they would make good any deductions from sickness benefits from miners attending the Commission's former centres until 31st March 1952.

Although the position of provision of facilities for paraplegics at Wharncliffe Hospital had improved, it was reported that the facilities were in September 1951 less than those three years ago and consequently nursing staff were leaving and the medical officer, Dr Hardy, who had done so much for paraplegic miners was on the point of resignation. Similar evidence of the state of affairs had been reported by the Yorkshire Branch of the National Union of Mineworkers and Dr Holdsworth. The Ministry of Health had been asked for their observations and they had called for a full report from the Senior Regional Medical Officer of the Sheffield Regional Hospital Board. This report was still unavailable at the end of 1951.

In September, the Minister of Health advised that a special committee had been set up by the Board of Governors of Llandough Hospital to consider the precise scope of facilities to be provided in the pneumoconiosis centre. It appeared that the immediate need was not for a rehabilitation centre but for a therapeutic hospital unit equipped for the full investigation and treatment both for bed and ambulant cases with effective liaison with the local industrial rehabilitation units and the Ministry of Labour and National Service. It was therefore proposed to provide a treatment unit only as an extension of the Llandough Hospital to accommodate 50 patients.

By September, Mr E. A. Nicoll, the Commission's Consulting Surgeon, had had two meetings with representatives of the Ministry of Health about the arrangements for the continuation of surgeons' services following the transfer of the centres in England and Wales to the National Health Service. It had been established that there was no method whereby the Ministry of Health could continue to pay those surgeons who were on maximum part-time contracts, and that it had accordingly been necessary to formulate proposals for future medical staffing of the centres. It would be necessary for the Surgeon-in-Charge and visiting surgeons of all centres to be replaced by other surgeons who could include the duties in their contract under the National Health Service. As it might be some time before this change materialised, Mr Nicoll asked for a decision as to the amount of ex-gratia payments that could be made to surgeons who were to be replaced in consideration of their continuing to serve until satisfactory arrangements were made. In September 1951, the Commission agreed to ex-gratia payments of one year's salary in recognition of the services rendered to the centres, whilst not receiving remuneration for this work from the National Health Service in lieu of notice terminating their appointments with the Commission.

Mr Nicoll presented the Annual Report of the Consulting Surgeon for the year ending 31st December 1950 to the meeting of the Council held on 28th November 1951. This would be the last such report, and Sir Reginald Watson-Jones, Chairman of the Medical Advisory Committee to the Miners' Welfare Commission had written a foreword:

'Yet again over ninety per cent of miners with grave and severe injuries have been so restored that they went back to work in the mines; over seventy per cent have gone back to their full pre-accident work. No less brilliant achievements have been recorded year by year in former reports of our Consulting Surgeon, but on this occasion – on the occasion of the last report of its kind - I am anxious to add a comment.

None must accept such astonishing success with complacency. Least of all the Ministry of Health must not accept with complacency the very remarkable service they have gained. If its high standard is not maintained a trust will have been betrayed. If the plan for resettlement of paraplegic miners- a plan that was quite complete and would have been accomplished by now if it had not been for the nationalisation of medicine- is not established soon, the betrayal of trust will be tragic.'[31]

In March 1951, serious shortages were being reported in supplies for pithead baths and equipment for miners. The South-Western Divisional Welfare Committee had written to the Council to bring their attention to the shortages especially of constructional steel which would affect the pithead baths programme. They had referred the matter to London and the Divisional Board had referred it to the National Board.

The Board of Trade had called a meeting on 9th March 1951 to discuss the shortage of pit-drawers, hose and utility towels. Representatives of the Ministry of Fuel and Power and the National Union of Mineworkers were also present. Difficulties in the supply position had been admitted by the Board of Trade. The Board of Trade were prepared to grant facilities to manufacturers of pit-drawers. Further meetings had taken place to examine the position of safety and heavy pit boots. The position here was more serious as representations were to be made at Ministerial level if supplies of materials could not be guaranteed. Shortage of tin plate for the manufacture of snap-tins and water bottles had been overcome.[32]

In April 1951, the National Miners' Welfare Joint Council Finance Committee were given details by the Head of the Welfare Building Branch, of four standard types of pithead baths providing accommodation for 120, 180, 240 and 360 men respectively, and each with appropriate first aid accommodation, which had been designed for the North-Western Division who intended to erect them at small collieries having an anticipated life of not more than ten years. These baths, eight of which were to be built immediately, were of simplified traditional construction, including the usual provisions on a modified scale, new standard lockers and low-pressure hot water plenum systems heated by hot water boilers with mechanical stokers. Standard drawings and bills of quantities had also been prepared for small 'snap and snack' canteens for use with these baths.[33]

The May meeting of the Council was held in the Institute of Engineers, Cardiff. This enabled the Council to hold a joint meeting with the South-Western Divisional Welfare Committee. The Committee wished to discuss the organisation of welfare and the shortage of materials required for building pithead baths.

A sum of approximately £160,000 would be required to complete the rehabilitation of existing miners' welfare schemes in the South-Western Division, whilst a further expenditure of £500,000 was visualised in their survey of requirements to complete the development of existing schemes and the provision of new schemes which had been held up for the past 10 years. These figures did not allow for any grant-aid either from the Ministry of Education or the local authorities. Their present income of £20,000 a year from the District Fund needed to be augmented if they were to proceed with their urgently needed developments and, at the same time, provide the minimum expenditure on their convalescent homes, St Athan's Boys' Camp and other activities of a social welfare character. The Divisional Welfare Committee were anxious to know as soon as possible what their responsibilities under the new organisation would be and how much money would be available for expenditure on social welfare. Until they knew these things, they could not plan their programme, nor could they have a sound basis on which to approach grant-aiding authorities.

Lord Hyndley outlined the proposals for the future of miners' welfare which had been agreed by the ad hoc committee but stressed that had not yet been fully approved (The Memorandum of Agreement was signed on 24th July 1951, see page 407).

Lord Hyndley gave reassurances about the Board being fully alive to the need for providing bathing facilities for all miners at the earliest possible moment and, following a statement by the Minister of Fuel and Power on 11th May 1951, that the necessary labour and materials would be made available for the Board's essential need.

The Board would press on with the provision of medical centres. This work had been held up pending the outcome of the Dale Committee of Enquiry on Industrial Health Services. Although the ban on providing medical centres had been lifted, there were still difficulties to be overcome, particularly in obtaining the necessary materials and the professional services of doctors and nurses. 34

On 25th July 1951, the Minister of Fuel and Power appointed a new Chairman of the Miners' Welfare Commission, Sir Hubert Houldsworth KC, as from 1st August 1951, who would also be the Chairman of the Council. The Board had appointed Sir Andrew Bryan and Sir Charles Ellis to be their representatives in place of Sir Lionel Lowe and Sr Geoffrey Vickers.

At the May 1951 meeting of the Council, Lord Hyndley had suggested that Divisional Welfare Committees should be invited to submit proposals for the future organisation of welfare when the new arrangements came into operation in 1952. They were asked to indicate how Committees for Welfare should be set up below Divisional level. By way of guidance, committees were told how new Divisional Welfare Committees would be constituted, as recommended in the Memorandum of Agreement and had been advised that the same principle should be applied in establishing subordinate committees.

The September meeting of the Council had the various proposals made by the six Divisional Welfare Committees for the future organisation of welfare in their Division to consider. The Scottish, North Western and East Midlands Divisions had still to submit their proposals. South Western and South Eastern Divisional Welfare Committees were asked to supply further details of their proposed arrangements. The Council also agreed to invite all Divisional Committees to submit, by 31st October 1951, detailed plans for staff, office accommodation and other relevant matters affecting new Divisional and Area Committees. 35

The Council held their meeting on 1st November 1951 at the Victoria Hotel, Wolverhampton. Following their meeting they met with the West Midlands

Divisional Welfare Committee to discuss whether the Board of the new Social Welfare Council were responsible for organising boys' camps, the cost of first aid and rescue competitions, the cost of inter-colliery and inter-area cricket, football and other competitions held exclusively for miners, and who would be expected to deal with the money.

During the discussion, some of the members of the Divisional Welfare Committee expressed their concern lest the financial and other assistance which had hitherto been forthcoming from the Board should be withheld under the new setup, particularly in connection with the organisation of camps and competitions. Moreover, by making these activities primarily the responsibility of the new Council, additional burdens would be thrown upon the Divisional Committees.

The general conditions of ambulance and rescue competitions would be a matter of colliery welfare, but the Social Welfare Organisation would give assistance in many directions. Similarly, while the Social Welfare Organisation would be primarily responsible for such activities as camps and sports competitions, the Board, the colliery consultative committees and others would be interested, and it would be part of their duties to help in seeing that they were properly organised.

As to financial arrangements for social welfare, it would be for the Divisional Welfare Committees to administer the funds subject to the approval of budgets in accordance with the policy of the new Organisation which would be an independent body, appointing and paying their own officers.

In preparing their plans, Divisional Welfare Committees should ensure that the voluntary spirit and experience of miners' welfare were retained and that local efforts were not stultified.[36]

At their September 1951 meeting, the Council received a report on the Northumberland and Durham Divisional Mining Degree Scholarship scheme for the 1951/52 session and awards completed. Special grants were made from the Northumberland and Durham District Funds. Four scholarships had been renewed for 1951/52.

Since the inception of the Schemes in 1938 (Northumberland) and 1939 (Durham), forty-two scholarships in all had been awarded. Thirty-seven had been successfully completed (each scholar obtaining the ordinary BSc degree) and fifteen had been terminated for various reasons.

Both these schemes had been discontinued, except for the provision necessary to enable scholarship holders to complete their courses. [37]

The Ministry of Education, acting for the Charity Commissioners, had expressed that trusts for the Miners' Welfare National Mining Education Scholarship Fund might be deemed to have failed. They saw no objection to the endowment monies (including accumulated income) being transferred to the Coal Industry Joint Welfare Organisation and that such transfer might be most conveniently effected by means of the proposed legislation for dealing with the future of the miners' welfare.

The Council, at its meeting on 1st November 1951, agreed to the winding up of the Miners' Welfare National Mining Education Scholarship Fund and that it should be dealt with under the proposed Miners' Welfare Bill. [38]

No further minutes or agendas are available, although the agenda for the Joint Council's meeting on 1st November 1951 included a proposal for a meeting on 23rd January 1952 in London.

The Miners' Welfare Act 1952 was given Royal Assent on 30th April 1952. The Act discontinued the royalties welfare levy from 31st March 1952, and dissolved the Miners' Welfare Commission on 1st July 1952.

All property, rights, liabilities, obligations and functions vested in the Commission would be transferred on 1st July 1952 and divided between the National Coal Board or the Coal Industry Social Welfare Organisation as set out in the Act.

A luncheon was given by Sir Hubert Houldsworth, Chairman of the Miners' Welfare Commission, on 28th May 1952 for members of the Commission and the Commission's staff. The luncheon was also attended by the Minister of Fuel and Power, past Chairmen, past Secretaries and officials of the Ministry of Fuel and Power.

The Coal Industry Social Welfare Organisation still exists today. It became a charity in 1995, providing free support to former coal miners and their families. The Organisation also works to secure the future of recreational facilities in former coal mining communities and works with local mining charities to ensure their service continues.

APPENDICES

SECRETARIES FOR MINES 1921–1942, MINISTERS OF FUEL AND POWER 1942–1952

Mr W. C. Bridgeman	22 August 1920 – 6 November 1922
Lt-Col. G. R. Lane-Fox	6 November 1922 – 23 January 1924
Manny Shinwell	23 January 1924 – 11 November 1924
Lt-Col. G. R. Lane-Fox	11 November 1924 – 13 January 1928
Douglas King	13 January 1928 – 1 June 1929
Ben Turner	1 June 1929 – 5 June 1930
Manny Shinwell	5 June 1930 – 3 September 1931
Isaac Foot	3 September 1931 – 30 September 1932
Ernest Brown	30 September 932 – 18 June 1935
Harry Crookshank	18 June 1935 – 21 April 1939
George Lloyd	21 April 1939 – 15 May 1940
David Grenfell	15 May 1940 – 3 June 1942
Gwilym Lloyd-George	3 June 1942 – 26 July 1945
Emanuel Shinwell	3 August 1945 – 7 October 1947
Hugh Gaitskell	7 October 1947 – 28 February 1950
Philip Noel Baker	28 February 1950 – 31 October 1951
Geoffrey Lloyd	31 October 1951 – 20 December 1955

APPENDIX 2 **CHAIRMAN OF THE MINERS' WELFARE COMMITTEE AND COMMISSION**

Lord Gorell	January 1921 – September 1921
Lord Chelmsford	September 1921 – 26 February 1924
Sir William Walker	26 February 1924 – 20 January 1925
Lord Chelmsford	21 January 1925 – 21 July 1931
Lord Noel-Buxton	22 July 1931 – 4 June 1934
Sir Frederick Sykes	2 August 1934 – June 1946
Lord Citrine	September 1946 – 13 July 1947
Sir Joseph Hallsworth	13 July 1947 – April 1949
Professor E L Collis (Acting)	October 1948 – February 1949
	May 1949 – November 1949
Lord John Hyndley	November 1949 – July 1951
Sir Hubert Houldsworth	1 August 1951 – 1 July 1952

APPENDIX 3 SECRETARIES TO THE MINERS' WELFARE COMMITTEE AND COMMISSION

William Guy Nott-Bower	1921 – 1923 (Acting until May 1922, then permanent)
Ewart Watson Ravenshear	1923 – 1932
A. D. Stedman	3 June 1932 – 30 June 1946
T. A. Bennett and T. A. Freston	30 June 1946 – 1 January 1948 (Joint Acting Secretaries)
Thomas Albert Bennett	1 January 1948 – 1 July 1952

APPENDIX 4 REPRESENTATIVES OF MINERS' UNIONS ON THE COMMITTEE AND COMMISSION

Miners' Federation of Great Britain

Mr Brace	January 1921 – October 1921
Herbert Smith	21 November 1921 – 1938 (deceased)
Arthur Cook	January 1926 – 2 November 1931
William Richardson	December 1926 – 8 August 1930 (deceased)
Ebby Edwards	16 October 1930 – August 1936
Peter Lee	25 January 1932 – 12 October 1934
William Lawther	12 October 1934 – 1945
Joseph Jones	August 1936 – 1942
Andrew Clarke	1938 – February 1940 (deceased)
W. Ernest Jones	1940 – 1942

Nation Union of Mineworkers

James Bowman	1946 – 1950
J. A. Hall CBE, JP	1942 – 1952
Arthur Lewis Horner	1942 – 1952
J. H. Southall	1950 – 1952

ACKNOWLEDGEMENTS

I would like to thank Paul Darlow, Archivist at the National Union of Mineworkers, Barnsley, for answering my technical questions and Tessa Card and Jacky Statham for proofreading my manuscript.

ABBREVIATIONS

Deb	Debate
DMM	Durham Mining Museum
HC	House of Commons
HL	House of Lords
MFGB	Miners' Federation of Great Britain
MWC	Miners' Welfare Committee
NA	The National Archives, Kew
NUM	National Union of Mineworkers

ENDNOTES

1 THE MINERS' WELFARE FUND IS CONCEIVED 1919–1920

1. Page Arnot, R: *The Miners, A History of the Miners' Federation of Great Britain from 1910 onwards, Years of Struggle*: published by George Allen and Unwin Ltd 1953: pp 184–185
2. Page Arnot, R: *Facts from the Coal Commission*: published by the MFGB 1919: p 5
3. Page Arnot, R: *The Miners' A History of the Miners' Federation of Great Britain from 1910 onwards, Years of Struggle*: published by George Allen and Unwin Ltd 1953: p 185
4. NA: Meeting of the War Cabinet held at 10 Downing Street, 31/1/1919: p 3: CAB/23/9
5. NA: Cabinet Memorandum, Miners' claim for advance on wages and reduction in hours etc, 4th February 1919: CAB/24/74
6. NA: Meeting of the War Cabinet held at 10, Downing Street, 7th February 1919: pp 2–6: CAB/23/9
7. Page Arnot, R: 1953: pp 185–6
8. Page Arnot, R: 1953: pp 5–6
9. Hansard 1803–2005: HC Deb 24th February 1919 vol 112 cc1474–1545: HC Deb 25th February 1919 vol 112 cc1635-1708: HL Deb 26th February 1919 vol 33 cc339-347
10. Coal Industry Commission, Vol I, Reports and Minutes of Evidence of the First Stage of the Inquiry: 1919: p iv
11. Page Arnot, R: 1953: pp 188–189
12. ibid: 1953: p 189
13. ibid: 1953: p 194
14. ibid: 1953: p 195
15. Coal Industry Commission, Vol I, Reports and Minutes of Evidence of the First Stage of the Inquiry: 1919: pp 320–345
16. ibid: pp ix, 345–354
17. Page Arnot, R: 1953: p 197
18. ibid: 1953: p 198
19. Coal Industry Commission, Vol I, Reports and Minutes of Evidence of the First Stage of the Inquiry: 1919: p xiii
20. ibid: pp vii–viii
21. ibid: p ix
22. ibid: p viii
23. ibid: pp xxi–xxiii
24. Page Arnot, R: 1953: p 201

25. NA: War Cabinet meeting held at 10 Downing Street, 25th March 1919, The Labour Situation: The miners' Demands: CAB/23/9
26. Page Arnot, R: 1953: pp 201–2
27. ibid: pp 203–207
28. ibid: p 209
29. Ives, Martyn: *Reform, Revolution and Direct Action amongst British Miners. The Struggle for the Charter in 1919*: Published by British Academics: 2016: p 232
    War Cabinet (589), 8th July 1919: CAB 23/11/14/15
    Hansard: House of Commons: Deb: Vol 117: c1817: 9th July
30. Ives, Martyn: 2016: pp 253–254
31. ibid: p 227
32. A: War Cabinet 598, Meeting held at 10 Downing Street, 23rd July 1919, Nationalisation: CAB/23/11
33. Hansard: HC Deb 18th August 1919 vol 119 cc 2001–4
34. Hansard: HC Deb 30th June 1920 vol 131 cc 477–595
    Hansard: HL Deb 3rd August 1920 vol 41 cc 674–711
35. Hansard: HL Deb 16th August 1920 vol 41 cc 1242
36. The Mining Industry Act 1920: legislation. gov.uk

2 FIRST QUINQUENNIUM 1921–1926

1. NA: POWE 1/1: Minutes of meeting of Miners' Welfare Committee 3/2/1921, POWE 1/47: 1st Annual Report of the Miners' Welfare Fund 1921–1922: p 5
2. https:/en.m. Wikipedia.org/wiki/Ronald_ Barnes, 3rd Baron_Gorell
3. http://en.n.wikipedia.org/wiki/William_Brace
4. *British Medical Journal*: Occupational and Environmental Medicine: Vol. 15: Issue 1: p 71
5. DMM: *The Science and Art of Mining*: 6th September 1930: p 51: column 2
6. NA: POWE1/47: 2nd Report of the Miners' Welfare Fund 1923: p 23
7. Page Arnot, R: *The Miner, A history of the Miners' Federation of Great Britain from 1910 onwards*: published by George Allen and Unwin Ltd: 1953: pp 278–339

8. NA: POWE 1/1: Minutes of meetings of the Miners' Welfare Committee 3/2/1921, 15/2/1921

9. NA: POWE 1/45: Miners' Welfare Fund Circulars to District Committees and others: MWF 2

10. NA: POWE 1/47: 1st Annual Report of the Miners' Welfare Fund 1921–22: p 5

11. NA: POWE 1/1: Minutes of meeting of Miners' Welfare Committee 27/7/1921

12. *Australian Dictionary of Biography*: Vol 7: 1979

13. NA: POWE 1/47 1st Annual Report of the Miners' Welfare Fund: p 5

14. NA: POWE 1/1: Minutes of Miners' Welfare Committee 5/10/21

15. NA: POWE 1/45: Miners' Welfare Fund Circular to District Committees and others: MWF 18

16. ibid: MWF 18(a)

17. NA: POWE 1/47: 1st Annual Report of the Miners' Welfare Fund 1921–22: pp 6–7

18. ibid: NA: POWE 1/45: Miners' Welfare Fund Circulars to District Committees and others: MWF 18

19. NA: POWE 1/47: 1st Annual Report of the Miners' Welfare Fund 1921–22: p 6

20. NA: POWE 1/1: Minutes of the meeting of the Miners' Welfare Committee 17/1/1922

21. ibid: Meetings 22/8/1922 and 28/11/1922
NA: POWE 1/47: 1st Annual Report of the Miners' Welfare Fund 1921–22: pp 11–14

22. ibid p 26
NA: POWE 1/1: Minutes of meeting of the Miners Welfare Committee 25/4/1922

23. NA: POWE 1/47: 1st Report of the Miners' Welfare Fund 1921–22: pp 14,25

24. NA: POWE 1/46: Conference Papers of the 1st District Committee Conferences 28/11/1922

25. NA: POWE 1/47: 2nd Report of the Miners' Welfare Fund 1923: p 5

26. NA: POWE 1/45: Miners' Welfare Fund Circulars to District Committees and other: MWF 40

27. NA: POWE 1/47: 2nd Report of the Miners' Welfare Fund 1923: pp 8–9

28. NA: POWE 1/45: Miners' Welfare Fund Circulars to District Committees and others: MWF 45 (a)

29. NA: POWE 1/47: 2nd Report of the Miners' Welfare Fund 1923: pp 22–23,37
NA: POWE 1/1: Minutes of meeting of the Miners' Welfare Committee 23/10/1923
NA: POWE 1/18: Agenda paper MWC 113 for meeting 27/11/1923

30. NA: POWE 1/1: Minutes of meetings of the Miners' Welfare Committee 26/2/1924, 9/4/1924, 24/6/1924

31. NA: POWE 1/47: 2nd Annual Report of the Miners' Welfare Fund 1923: pp 10–12

32. NA: POWE 1/1: Minutes of meetings of the Miners' Welfare Committee 26/6/1923 and 29/8/1923

33. NA: POWE 1/47: 2nd Annual Report of the Miners' Welfare Fund 1923: pp 13–22

34. NA: POWE 1/46: 2nd Conference of Representatives of District Committees 27/11/1923

35. NA: POWE 1/47: 3rd Annual Report of the Miners' Welfare Fund 1924: pp 5–15

36. NA: POWE 1/1: Minutes of meeting of the Miners' Welfare Committee 21/3/1924
NA: POWE 1/18: Agenda Paper MWC 131, SB Papers 225 and 227

37. NA: POWE 1/47: 3rd Annual Report of the Miners' Welfare Fund 1924: pp 22–24

38. NA POWE 1/18: Agenda paper MWC 119
NA: POWE 1/1: Minutes of meeting of the Miners' Welfare Committee 26/2/1924

39. NA: POWE 1/47: 3rd Annual Report of the Miners' Welfare Fund 1924: pp 25–27, 52–57

40. NA: POWE 1/47: 4th Annual Report of the Miners' Welfare Fund 1925: p 6

41. ibid p7
NA: POWE 1/1: Minutes of meetings of the Miners' Welfare Fund 27/1/1925 and 24/3/1925

42. ibid 27/10/1925
NA: POWE 1/47: 4th Annual Report of the Miners' Welfare Fund 1925: pp 7–9

43. ibid pp 10–12
NA: POWE 1/45: Miners' Welfare Fund Circulars to District Committees and others: MWF 40, MWF 65
NA: POWE 1/1: Minutes of meeting of the Miners' Welfare Committee 24/3/1925

44. ibid 26/5/1925, 24/7/1925

45. ibid 23/6/1925
NA: POWE 1/47: 4th Annual Report of the Miners' Welfare Fund: pp 13–14

46. ibid pp16–20

47. ibid pp22–23

48. ibid pp 23–26

49. NA: POWE 1/47: 2nd Annual Report of the Miners' Welfare Fund 1923: pp 24–25
3rd Annual Report of the Miners' Welfare Fund 1924: pp 16–17
NA: POWE 1/18: Agenda paper MWC 165
NA: POWE 1/1: Minutes of meeting of Miners' Welfare Committee 29/7/1924

50. NA: POWE 1/47: 4th Annual Report of the Miners' Welfare Fund 1925: pp 26–27

51. ibid p24

52. ibid pp26, 39

53. ibid pp6, 38

3 SECOND QUINQUENNIUM 1926–1931

1. NA: POWE 1/47: 5th Report of the Miners' Welfare Fund 1926: pp 7–23

2. ibid pp 24–25

3. NA: POWE 1/20: Agenda papers for meetings 40–48 1926: MWC 287 for 41st meeting 16/2/1926 and MWC 341 for 48th meeting 16/11/1926

4. ibid MWC 308: POWE 1/1: Minutes of meeting 18/5/1926

5. NA: POWE 1/20: Agenda paper for 47th meeting 19/10/1926 MWC 330(a)

6. ibid Agenda paper for 48th meeting 16/11/1926 MWC 341

7. NA: POWE 1/21: Agenda paper for 49th meeting 18/1/1927

8. NA: POWE 1/47: 5th Report of the Miners' Welfare Fund 1926: pp 26–32

9. ibid pp 36–39
POWE 1/1: Minutes of meetings 41st 16/2/1926, 44th 18/5/1926, 46th 20/7/1926 and 47th 19/10/1926
POWE 1/20: Agenda paper for 41st meeting MWC291 (a)(b)(c)(d), 46th meeting and 47th meeting MWC 334

10. NA: POWE 1/47: 5th Report of the Miners Welfare Fund 1926: pp 39–46
POWE 1/20: Agenda paper 45th meeting MWC 328
POWE 1/45: MWF 101: 25/10/1926
POWE 1/1: Minutes of 45th meeting 23/6/1926

11. NA: POWE 1/47: 5th Report of the Miners' Welfare Fund: pp 21–23
Report of the Royal Commission on the Coal Industry (1925) Vol 1 pix–x, pp 163–4
The Miners' Years of Struggle by R Page Arnott; *A History of the Miners' Federation of Great Britain*; published by George Allen and Unwin Ltd: 1953; pp 362–506

12. NA: POWE 1/21: Agenda paper for 49th meeting 18/1/1927 and for 51st meeting 23/3/1927
POWE 1/45: Circulars to District Committees MWF 106 4/4/1927 and MWF 113 19/10/1927
POWE 1/22: Agenda paper for 55th meeting 6/7/1927

POWE 1/2: Minutes 57th meeting 20/9/1927

13. NA: POWE 1/22: Agenda paper for 58th meeting 18/10/1927

14. NA: POWE 1/21: Paper for 51st meeting MWC 374 and 53rd meeting MWC 381
POWE 1/1: Minutes 50th meeting 2/3/1927
POWE 1/2: minutes 51st meeting 29/3/1927 and 54th 17/5/1927

15. NA: POWE 1/1: Minutes 49th meeting 18/1/1927
POWE 1/21: Agenda paper for 49th meeting MWC 357

16. NA: POWE 1/2: Minutes 51st meeting 23/3/1927
POWE 1/22: Agenda paper 51st meeting

17. NA: POWE 1/2: Minutes 54th meeting 17/5/1927
POWE 1/22: Agenda paper for 54th meeting 17/5/1927 and 56th meeting 19/7/1927 MWC 399

18. NA: POWE 1/2: Minutes 55th meeting 6/7/1927
POWE 1/22: Agenda paper 55th meeting

19. NA: POWE 1/2: Minutes of 57th meeting 29/9/1927 and 59th meeting 15/11/1927
POWE 1/22: Agenda paper 57th meeting MWC 410

20. ibid Minutes 58th meeting 18/10/1927 and agenda paper 58th meeting MWC 421

21. ibid Minutes 59th meeting 15/11/1927 and agenda paper 59th meeting MWC 428

22. ibid Minutes of 55th meeting 6/7/1927, 57th meeting 20/9/1927, 59th meeting 15/11/1927 and agenda papers for 55th meeting MWC 394, 57th meeting MWC 412 and 59th meeting MWC 429

23. ibid Minutes of 54th meeting 17/5/1927, 56th meeting 19/7/1927, 59th meeting 15/11/1927 and agenda paper 54th meeting MWC 387
POWE 1/20: Agenda paper for meeting 47 October 1926 MWC 314

24. NA: POWE 1/22: Agenda paper for 59th meeting MWC 427

25. NA: POWE 1/2: Minutes of 53rd meeting 13/4/1927

26. ibid Minutes 54th meeting 17/5/1927

27. ibid Minutes 51st meeting 23/3/1927
POWE 1/21: Agenda paper 51st meeting MWC 369

28. NA: POWE 1/2: Minutes 56th meeting 19/7/1927
POWE 1/22 Agenda paper for 56th meeting

29. ibid Minutes 57th meeting 20/9/1927

30. NA: POWE 1/23: Agenda papers for 60th meeting 17/1/1928, 61st meeting 21/2/1928

MWC 444 and 63rd meeting 17/4/1928
MWC 460

31. NA: POWE 1/2: Minutes 60th meeting
17/1/1928, 61st meeting 21/2/1928 and 62nd
meeting 20/3/1928
POWE 1/23: Agenda paper for 60th meeting
MWC 437, 61st meeting MWC 447 and 62nd
meeting MWC 456

32. ibid Minutes for 63rd meeting 17/4/1928,
64th meeting 18/5/1928, 65th meeting
15/6/1928, Agenda paper for 63rd meeting
MWC 463, 64th meeting MWC 468 and 65th
meeting MWC 474

33. ibid Minutes for 66th meeting 13/7/1928,
67th meeting 11/9/1928, agenda papers for
66th meeting MWC 482 and 67th meeting
MWC 490

34. Ibid Minutes for 68th meeting 16/10/1928,
69th meeting 20/11/1928 and agenda papers
for 68th meeting
MWC 493 and 69th meeting MWC 503

35. ibid Minutes of 61st meeting 21/2/1928 and
agenda paper 60th meeting MWC 439

36. NA: POWE 1/23: Agenda paper for 65th
meeting MWC 471 Appendix A

37. NA: POWE 1/2: minutes of 66th meeting
13/7/1928, 68th meeting 16/10/1928 and
70th meeting 15/1/2929
POWE 1/23: agenda paper for 66th meeting
MWC 479 Appendix B

38. ibid Minutes 66th meeting and agenda paper
MWC 479

39. ibid Minutes of 62nd meeting 20/3/1928 and
agenda paper 62nd meeting MWC 452

40. NA: POWE 1/23: Agenda paper for 64th
meeting MWC 470

41. NA: POWE 1/2: Minutes of 62nd meeting
20/3/1928 and 63rd meeting 17/4/1928
POWE 1/23: Agenda paper 60th meeting
Allocation, 62nd meeting SB Paper no 547 and
63rd meeting Allocations from General Fund

42. NA: POWE 1/23: Agenda paper for 69th
meeting MWC 504

43. ibid Agenda paper for 62nd meeting
20/3/1928

44. ibid Agenda paper for 64th meeting
18/5/1928

45. ibid Agenda paper for 65th meeting
15/6/1928

46. ibid Agenda paper for 67th meeting
11/9/1928

47. NA: POWE 1/2: Minutes of meetings 70–79,
1929

48. NUM: 8th Report of the Miners' Welfare
Fund 1929: pp 10–11

49. NA: POWE 1/2: Minutes of meeting 70–79,
1929

50. NUM: 8th Report of the Miners' Welfare
Fund: pp 8–13

51. NA: POWE 1/2: Minutes of 72nd meeting
19/3/1929 and 73rd meeting 16/4/1929

52. NUM: 8th Report of the Miners' Welfare
Fund 1929: p16

53. ibid p 13 and p 18

54. NA: POWE 1/25: Agenda paper for 82nd
meeting MWC 590, *4th meeting MWC 608
and 87th Meeting MWC 626

55. ibid Agenda paper for 80th meeting MWC
583

56. NA: POWE 1/2: Minutes of 81st meeting
18/2/1930
POWE 1/25: Agenda paper for 81st meeting
MWC 591

57. NA: POWE 1/2: Minutes of meetings 80–89.
1930

58. ibid Minutes 86th meeting 15/7/1930
POWE 1/25: Agenda paper 86th meeting
MWC 619

59. ibid Minutes of 87th meeting 16/9/1930 and
agenda paper 87th meeting MWC 626

60. ibid Minutes of 88th meeting 21/10/1930,
90th meeting 26/11/1930 and agenda paper
for 90th meeting MWC 643

61. ibid Minutes of 86th meeting 15/7/1930,
87th meeting 16/9/1930, 88th meeting
21/10/1920, 90th meeting 26/11/1930 and
agenda papers 86th meeting MWC 620, 87th
meeting MWC 627 and 90th meeting MWC
642

62. ibid Minutes 80th meeting 21/1/1930, 81st
meeting 18/2/1930, 82nd meeting 18/3/1930
and agenda papers 81st meeting MWC 588,
82nd meeting and 85th meeting MWC 612

63. ibid Minutes of 85th meeting 17/6/1930 and
agenda paper 85th meeting MWC 610

64. NA: POWE 1/25: Agenda paper 97th
meeting MWC 623 Appendix A

65. ibid Agenda paper for 88th meeting MWC
630

66. NA: POWE 1/2: Minutes 82nd meeting
18/3/1930
POWE 1/25: Agenda paper for 82nd meeting
SB Paper 738

67. ibid Minutes 89th meeting 18/11/1930 and
agenda paper 89th meeting

68. NA: POWE 1/25: Agenda paper for 83rd
meeting

69. ibid Agenda paper 84th meeting MWC 609

70. NA: POWE 1/2: Minutes for 80th meeting
21/1/1930

POWE 1/25: Agenda paper for 80th meeting MWC 584

71. ibid Minutes of 89th meeting 18/11/1930 and agenda papers for 81st meeting, 82nd meeting MWC 594, 85th meeting MWC 614, 88th meeting, 89th meeting

72. NA: POWE 1/25: Agenda paper for 82nd meeting

73. ibid Agenda paper 87th meeting

74. ibid Agenda paper for 89th meeting

75. NA: POWE 1/2: Minutes for 96th meeting 16/6/1931 and 97th 21/7/1931
POWE 1/26: Agenda paper 97th meeting MWC 672
Hansard: 8th February 1934: Vol 285: cc1397–1459

76. NA: POWE 1/2: Minutes for 91st meeting 30/1/1931
POWE 1/26: Agenda paper for 91st meeting MWC 650

77. ibid Minutes for 92nd meeting 17/2/1931 and agenda paper for 92nd meeting MWC 656

78. ibid Minutes for 93rd meeting 17/3/1931 and agenda paper for 93rd meeting MWC 661

79. ibid Minutes for 94th meeting 21/4/1931 and agenda paper for 94th meeting MWC 667

80. ibid Minutes for 95th meeting 19/5/1931 and agenda paper for 95th meeting MWC 671

81. ibid Minutes for 96th meeting 16/6/1931 and agenda paper for 96th meeting MWC 675

82. ibid Minutes for 97th meeting 21/7/1931 and agenda paper for 97th meeting MWC 682

83. NA: POWE 1/2: Minutes for 98th meeting 15/9/1931

84. NA: POWE 1/26: Agenda paper for 101st meeting MWC 705

85. ibid Agenda paper for 100th meeting 20/10/1931

86. ibid Agenda paper for 91st meeting MWC 647

87. NA: POWE 1/2: Minutes 92nd meeting 17/2/1931, 94th meeting 21/4/1931 and 97th meeting 21/7/1931
POWE 1/26: Agenda paper for 92nd meeting MWC 659, agenda paper for 94th meeting MWC 664 and agenda paper for 97th meeting
POWE 1/46: Minutes of 10th Conference of District Representatives 17/11/1931

88. ibid Minutes 93rd meeting 17/3/1931 and agenda paper for 93rd meeting

89. NA: POWE 1/26: Agenda paper for 97th meeting MWC 681

90. NA: POWE 1/2: Minutes for 91st meeting 20/1/1931

POWE 1/26: Agenda paper for 91st meeting

91. ibid Minutes for 91st meeting 20/1/1931, 92nd meeting 17/2/1931, 94th meeting 21/4/1931 and agenda papers for 91st meeting and 94th meeting MWC 664

92. NA: POWE 1/26: Agenda paper for 93rd meeting 93 and101st meeting

93. ibid Agenda papers for 94th meeting and 101st meeting

94. NA: POWE 1/2: Minutes of 99th meeting 12/10/1031
POWE 1/26: Agenda paper for 99th meeting MWC 698

4 THE COMMITTEE BECOMES THE COMMISSION 1932–1939

1. NA: POWE 1/49 11th Report of the Miners' Welfare Fund 1932: p5
2. ibid pp 7–9
3. ibid pp 10–12
4. ibid pp 9–10, 18–21
5. ibid pp 17–18
6. ibid pp 13–14, 16–17
7. NA: POWE 1/49: 12th the Report of the Miners' Welfare Fund 1933: pp 5–6
8. ibid pp 10–12
9. ibid pp 15–18
10. ibid pp 19–24
11. ibid pp26–28
12. ibid pp 18, 29, 32
13. ibid p33
14. NA: POWE 1/49: 13th Report of the Miners' Welfare Fund 1934: pp 5–7
15. ibid pp 8–11
16. NA: POWE 1/29: Agenda paper for meeting 25/9/1934 MWC 888 and agenda paper for Meeting 15/10/1934 no 897
17. NA: POWE 1/49: 13th Report of the Miners' Welfare Fund 1934: pp 11–20
18. ibid pp 20–22
19. ibid pp 22–26
POWE 1/29: Agenda paper for meeting 20/3/1934 MWC 843, meeting 27/4/1934 MWC 844, meeting 15/5/1934 MWC 649 and meeting 19/6/1934 MWC 861
20. NA: POWE 1/49: 13th Report of the Miners' Welfare Fund 1934: p 27
21. ibid p 28
POWE 1/29: Agenda paper for meeting 16/1/1934 MWC 823
22. NA: POWE 1/6: Minutes of meetings 15/1/1935 and 19/2/1935, POWE 1/30: Agenda papers for meetings 15/1/1935 MWC 918 and 19/2/1935 MWC 934

23. ibid Minutes of meetings 15/1/1935, 19/2/1935 and 19/3/1935. Agenda papers for meetings 19/2/1935 Paper 942 and 19/3/1935

24. NA: POWE 1/49: 14th Report of the Miners Welfare Fund 1935: pp 7–21
POWE 1/30: Agenda paper for meeting 15/10/1935 Paper 1042

25. NA: POWE 1/6: Minutes of meeting 19/2/1935
POWE 1/30: Agenda paper meeting 18/6/1935 paper 994 and meeting 23/7/1935 Paper 1007

26. NA: POWE 1/49: 14th Report of the Miners' Welfare Fund 1935: pp 22–24

27. NA: POWE 1/6 Minutes of meetings 19/2/1935, 21/5/1935, 24/9/1935, 15/10/1935 and 19/11/1935
POWE 1/49: 14th Report of the Miners' Welfare Fund 1935: pp 24–25

28. NA: POWE 1/49: 15th Report of the Miners' Welfare Fund 1936: pp 5, 9–35

29. NA: POWE 1/7: minutes of meetings 21/4/1936, 22/9/1936
POWE 1/32: Agenda paper for meeting 19/1/1937

30. NA: POWE 1/49: 15th Report of the Miners' Welfare Fund 1936: pp 36–51

31. NA: POWE 1/7 Minutes of meeting 18/2/1936

32. NA: POWE 1/49: 15th Report of the Miners' Welfare Fund 1936: pp 38, 51–62

33. NA: POWE 1/32: Agenda papers meeting 16/3/1937, letter to District Committees 10/3/1937

34. NA: POWE 1/8: Minutes of meeting 19/1/1937
POWE 1/32: Agenda paper for meeting 19/1/1937 Paper 11, meeting 16/2/1937 paper 1 and 10, meeting 16/3/1937 paper 12 and 13, meeting 20/4/1937 paper 1

35. NA: POWE 1/32: Agenda paper for meeting 16/3/1937 paper 10

36. ibid Agenda paper for meeting 20/7/1937paper 1

37. ibid Agenda paper for meeting 22/6/1937 paper 11, meeting 20/7/1937 paper 13

38. ibid Agenda paper for meeting 19/10/1937 paper 11

39. ibid Agenda paper for meeting 21/9/1937 paper 1
POWE 1/33: agenda paper for meeting 18/1/1938 paper 1

40. NA: POWE 1/32 Agenda paper for meeting 19/1/1937 paper 12, meeting 16/2/1937 paper 9

41. ibid Agenda paper for meeting 16/3/1937 paper 2

42. ibid Agenda paper for meeting 20/4/1937 paper 2, meeting 20/7/1937 paper 2

43. ibid Agenda paper for meeting 25/5/1937 paper 2, meeting 22/6/1937 paper 2

44. ibid Agenda paper for meeting 20/7/1937 paper 2

45. NA: POWE 1/8: Minutes of meeting 20/7/1937
POWE 1/32: Agenda paper for meeting 25/5/1937 paper 7 appendix 1, meeting 20/7/1937 Paper 8
POWE 1/33: Agenda paper for meeting 168, May 1938

46. NA: POWE 1/8: Minutes for meeting 20/7/1937
POWE 1/32: Agenda paper for meeting 20/7/1937 paper 7

47. NA: POWE 1/32: Agenda paper for meeting 21/9/1937 paper 3

48. ibid Agenda paper for meeting 19/1/1937

49. ibid Agenda paper for meeting 16/3/1937

50. NA: POWE 1/33: Agenda paper for meeting 165, February 1938, letter to District Committees 5/2/1938

51. NA: POWE 1/34 Agenda papers for meeting 24/1/1939 paper 17

52. NA: POWE 1/33 Agenda paper for meeting 165, February 1938 paper 11

53. ibid Agenda paper for meeting 165, February 1938

54. ibid Agenda paper for meeting January 1938 paper 1 and meeting May 1938 paper 1

55. ibid Agenda paper for April meeting paper 8, May meeting paper 10, June meeting paper 11

56. ibid Agenda paper for November 1938 paper 5A

57. ibid Agenda paper for meeting 164, January 1938 paper 9

58. ibid Agenda paper for meeting 164, January 1938 paper 2, meeting 165, February 1938 paper 2, Meeting 167, April 1938 paper 2

59. ibid Agenda paper for meeting 165, February 1938 paper 15, meeting 172, October 1938 paper 10

60. NA: POWE 1/32: Agenda paper meeting 162, 19/10/ 1937
POWE 1/33: Agenda paper for meeting 165, February 1938 paper 16

61. NA: POWE 1/33: Agenda paper for meeting 166, March 1938 paper 13, meeting 173, November 1938 paper 7

62. ibid Agenda paper for meeting 168, May 1938 paper 2, meeting 170, July 1938 paper 2,

meeting 171, September 1938 paper 2

63. ibid Agenda paper for meeting 168, May 1938 paper 1, meeting 170, July 1938 paper 1, meeting 171, September 1938 paper 1, meeting 173, November 1938 paper 1

64. ibid Agenda paper for meeting 170, July 1938 paper 7

65. ibid Agenda paper for meeting 173, November 1938 paper 5

66. ibid Agenda paper for meeting 164, January 1938, meeting 166, March 1938

67. ibid Agenda paper for meeting 172, October 1938 paper 1

68. NA: POWE 1/10: Minutes of 1st meeting of the Commission 21/11/1939
POWE 1/34: Agenda paper for meeting 174, January 1939 paper 3 and 4, meeting 182 item 3 (c)

69. ibid Minutes for meeting 174, 24/1/1939
Agenda paper for meeting 174 and meeting 175 paper 11

70. NA: POWE 1/10: Minutes of meeting 175, 21/3/1939 and 176, 18/4/1939

71. ibid Minutes of meeting 176, 18/4/1939 and meeting 179, 18/7/1939
POWE 1/34: Agenda paper meeting 175, March 1939 paper 13, meeting 176, April 1939 paper 8, meeting 179, July 1939 paper 6

72. NA: POWE 1/10: Minutes of meeting 174, 24/1/1939, meeting 176, 18/4/1939

73. ibid Minutes of meeting 174, 24/1/1939
POWE 1/34: Agenda paper for meeting 174 paper 9

74. NA: POWE 1/34: Agenda paper for meeting 174, January 1939 paper 13, meeting 176, April 1939 paper 6

75. ibid Agenda paper for meeting 175, March 1939 paper 11A

76. ibid Agenda paper for May 1939 meeting paper 7, June 1939 meeting paper 11
POWE 1/10: Minutes of meeting 178, 20/6/1939

77. NA: POWE 1/10: Minutes meeting 178, 20/6/1939
Hansard HL Deb 2/3/1939: Vol 111: cc 1065–9

78. NA: POWE 1/10: Minutes of meeting 174, 24/1/1939, meeting 177, 16/5/1939, meeting 178, 20/6/1939
POWE 1/34: Agenda paper for meeting 177, May 1939 papers 10, 11 and 14, meeting 178, June 1939 paper 5

79. ibid Minutes of meeting 176, 18/4/1939, 1st meeting of Commission 21/11/1939
Agenda paper for meeting 176, April 1939

paper 11, meeting 180, September 1939

80. NA: POWE 1/10 Minutes of meeting 179, 18/7/1939
POWE 1/33: Agenda paper meeting 169, June 1938 paper 3, meeting 170, July 1938 paper 3
POWE 1/34: Agenda paper for 180, September 1939

81. NA: POWE 1/10: Minutes of meeting 180, 19/9/1939, meeting 181, 17/10/1939. 1st meeting of the Commission, 21/11/1939
DMM: The Science and Art of Mining: 13th July 1940: page 10: Column 1: 'Miners' Welfare: Forging Steadily Forward'

5 THE WAR YEARS 1940–1945

1. NA: POWE 1/11: Minutes of 9th meeting 19/11/40
NUM: Miners' Welfare in Wartime: pp 5–7

2. NUM: Miners' Welfare in Wartime: p 67

3. ibid Miners' Welfare in Wartime: p 9
NA: POWE 1/35: Agenda paper for 2nd meeting 16/1/1940 paper 2, 3rd meeting 19/3/1940 paper 3

4. NA: POWE 1/11: Minutes of 4th meeting 16/4/1940
POWE 1/35: Agenda papers for 4th meeting paper 4 item 5

5. ibid Minutes of 5th meeting 21/5/1940, 6th meeting 18/6/1940 and 9th meeting 19/11/1940
Agenda paper 5th meeting Item 4 (c), 7th meeting Item 4, 9th meeting Item 6
NUM: Miners' Welfare in Wartime: p10

6. NA: POWE 1/11: Minutes of 9th meeting 19/11/1940
POWE 1/35: Agenda paper for 9th meeting Item 4 (a)

7. ibid Minutes for 3rd meeting 19/3/1940
Agenda paper for 3rd meeting Item 3 (c)

8. ibid Minutes for 2nd meeting 16/1/1940, 3rd meeting 19/3/1940
Agenda for meeting 2nd June 1940 Item 6 (a) 3 afternoon session, 8th meeting September 1940, Item 10 (b)

9. ibid Minutes for 8th meeting 17/9/1940
Agenda paper for 8th meeting Item 3

10. ibid Minutes for 8th meeting 17/9/1940
Agenda paper for 8th meeting Item 4

11. ibid Minutes for 2nd meeting 16/1/1940
Agenda paper for 2nd meeting Item 5 (b)

12. ibid Minutes for third meeting 19/3/1940
Agenda paper for 3rd meeting Item 2 (a)

13. ibid Minutes for 3rd meeting 19/3/1940

Agenda paper for 3rd meeting Item 2(a)

14. ibid Minutes for 9th meeting 19/11/1940
Agenda paper for 9th meeting Item 3(d)
POWE 1/36: Agenda paper for 10th meeting
Item 2(b)

15. NUM: Miners' Welfare in Wartime: p67

16. NA: POWE 1/12: Minutes for 10th meeting
21/1/1941, 11th meeting 18/3/1941, 12th
meeting 20/5/1941, 13th meeting 22/7/1941,
15th meeting 21/10/1941
POWE 1/36: Agenda paper for 10th meeting
Item 2 (a), 11th meeting Item 2(a), 12th
meeting Item 2(a), 13th meeting Item 2(a),
15th meeting Item 8(a)

17. ibid Minutes for 10th meeting 21/1/1941,
12th meeting 20/5/1941
Agenda paper for 10th meeting Item 2(b),
12th meeting Item 2(b)

18. NUM: Miners' Welfare in Wartime: pp 20–23

19. NA: POWE 1/12: Minutes for 12th meeting
20/5/1941
POWE 1/36: Agenda paper 13th meeting
Item 3(a), 15th meeting Item 8(a)
NUM: Miners' Welfare in Wartime: p 25

20. NA: POWE 1/12: Minutes for 16th meeting
26/11/1941
NUM: Miners Welfare in Wartime: pp 23,
26–27

21. NA: POWE 1/12: Minutes for 10th meeting
21/1/1941, 11th meeting 18/3/1942, 12th
meeting 20/5/1941
POWE 1/36: Agenda paper for 10th meeting
Item 3

22. ibid Minutes for 11th meeting 18/3/1941
Agenda paper for 11th meeting Item 4 (d)
(1), Item 2(a)

23. NA: POWE 1/12: Minutes for 10th meeting
21/1/1941

24. Hansard: HL Debate 11/6/1942: Vol 123:
cc 311–359

25. NUM: Miners' Welfare in Wartime: p 67

26. ibid pp 23–24
NA: POWE 1/12: Minutes for 17th meeting
29/1/1942, 18th meeting 23/4/1942

27. NA: POWE 1/12: Minutes for 16th meeting
26/11/1941, 18th meeting 23/4/1942

28. ibid Minutes for 18th meeting 23/4/1942,
19th meeting 17/6/1942, 20th meeting
18/8/1942, 21st meeting 20/10/1942, 22nd
meeting 15/12/1942

29. ibid Minutes for 17th meeting 29/1/1942,
18th meeting 23/4/1942, 20th meeting
18/8/1942, 21st meeting 20/10/1942, 22nd
meeting 15/12/1942
NUM: Miners' Welfare in Wartime: p 45

30. NA: POWE 1/12: Minutes for 19th meeting
17/6/1942

31. NUM: Miners' Welfare in Wartime: p 67

32. NA: POWE 1/12: Minutes of 23rd meeting
12/2/1943, 24th meeting 24/4/1943, 25th
meeting 26/6/1943, 26th meeting 17/8/1943

33. ibid Minutes of 23rd meeting 16/2/1943,
24th meeting 22/4/1943, 25th meeting
22/6/1943, 27th meeting 19/10/1943, 28th
meeting 14/12/1943

34. ibid Minutes for 21st meeting 20/10/1942,
22nd meeting 15/12/1942, 24th meeting
22/4/1943, 25th meeting 22/6/1943,
26th meeting 17/8/1943, 27th meeting
19/10/1943, 28th meeting 14/12/1943
Mansard: HL Deb 7/12/1943: Vol 130: cc
102–105

35. NA: POWE 1/12: Minutes for 24th meeting
22/4/1943

36. NUM: Miners' Welfare in Wartime: pp 8, 67

37. NA: POWE 1/13: Minutes of 29th meeting
15/2/1944
POWE 1/38: Agenda paper for 29th meeting
Item 8, 34th meeting Item 7

38. ibid Minutes for 29th meeting 15/2/1944,
30th meeting 18/4/1944, 34th meeting
5/12/1944
Agenda papers for 29th meeting Item 4 (a),
30th meeting Item 5 (a), 31st meeting Item
5(a), 34th meeting Item 4(a)

39. ibid Minutes for 32nd meeting 19/9/1944,
33rd meeting 24/10/1944
Agenda paper for 32nd meeting Item 2
(Addendum), 33rd meeting

40. NUM: Miners' Welfare in Wartime: p 67

41. NA: POWE 1/13: Minutes for 35th meeting
6/2/1945, 36th meeting 20/3/1945, 37th
meeting 15/5/1945, 38th meeting 17/7/1945,
39th meeting 18/9/1945, 40th meeting
16/10/1945, 41st meeting 13/11/1945
POWE 1/38: Agenda paper for 35th
meeting Item 3, 36th meeting Item 2, 38th
meeting Item 2(a), 39th meeting Item 2(a)
(Addendum), 40th meeting Item 3, 41st
meeting Item 3

42. NUM: Miners' Welfare in Wartime: p27

43. NA: POWE 1/13: Minutes for 37th meeting
15/5/1945, 39th meeting 18/9/1945,
40th meeting 16/10/1945, 41st meeting
13/11/1945
POWE 1/38: Agenda paper for 39th meeting
Item 3, 40th meeting Item 2

44. ibid Minutes of 37th meeting 15/5/1945, 41st
meeting 13/11/1945
Agenda paper for 35th meeting Item 4(b),

36th meeting Item 3(b), 37th meeting Item 2(a), 38th meeting Item 3 (a)(d)(f), 39th meeting Item 4(a)(b), 41st meeting Item 4(b)

45. ibid Minutes of 37th meeting 15/5/1945 Agenda paper for 37th meeting Item 5(a)

46. NA: POWE 1/38: Agenda paper for 39th meeting Item 7

6 SAFETY IN MINES RESEARCH BOARD

1. NA: POWE 1/1: Minutes of 5th meeting 17/1/1922

2. NA: POWE 59/1: Minutes 1st meeting of Board 21/9/1921

3. NA: POWE 1/47: 1st Report of the Miners' Welfare Fund 1922: p 10

4. ibid p 14

5. ibid pp 25–26

6. ibid 2nd Report of the Miners' Welfare Fund 1923: p 14
   NA: POWE 59/1: Minutes of meetings 13 and 14

7. NA: POWE 1/47: 2nd Report of the Miners Welfare Fund 1923: pp 37–37

8. NA: POWE 1/18: Agenda paper for 27th meeting 29/7/1924
   The Miner's Elbow: Bulletin of the History of Medicine: Vol 18:no 8 (October 1940): pp 1249–51

9. NA: POWE 1/18: Agenda paper for Committee meeting 12/3/1924 SB Paper 227

10. NA: POWE 59/1: Minutes of 27th meeting of Board 23/5/1924, 30th meeting 18/9/1924/ 31st Meeting 23/10/1924, 33rd meeting 21/1/1925

11. NA: 1/47: 3rd Report of the Miners' Welfare Fund 1924: pp 18–19, 50–51

12. ibid pp 52–53
    NA: POWE 59/1: Minutes of 33rd meeting of Board 22/1/1925

13. NA: POWE 1/47: 5th Report of the Miners' Welfare Fund 1926: pp 69–70

14. NA: POWE 1/21: Agenda paper for 51st meeting of Committee 23/3/1927 MWC 369

15. NA: POWE 59/2: Minutes for 54th meeting of Board 6/5/1927, 55th meeting 13/6/1927 POWE 1/22: Agenda paper for 56th meeting of the Committee 19/7/1927

16. NA: POWE 1/22: Agenda paper for 59th meeting of the Committee 15/11/1927

17. NA: POWE 59/2: Minutes of 54th meeting of Board 6/5/1927, 55th meeting 13/6/1927, 56th Meeting 18/7/1927, 57th meeting 23/9/1927

18. ibid Minutes of 60th meeting of the Board 20/1/1928

19. NA: POWE 1/23: Agenda paper for 62nd meeting of the Committee SB Paper No 547

20. NA: POWE 59/2: Minutes of 63rd meeting of the Board 22/5/1928

21. ibid Minutes of 66th meeting of the Board 15/9/1928
    NA: POWE 1/23: Agenda paper for 67th meeting of the Committee

22. NA: POWE 59/2: Minutes of 67th meeting of Board 26/10/1928, 68th meeting 23/11/1928, 70th meeting 14/1/1929, 80th meeting 7/2/1930

23. ibid Minutes of 73rd meeting of the Board 19/4/1929

24. ibid Minutes of 76th meeting of the Board 20/9/1929

25. ibid Minutes of 77th meeting of the Board 18/10/1929

26. NUM: 8th Report of the Miners' Welfare Fund 1929: p 15

27. NA: POWE 59/3: Minutes of 81st meeting of the Board 7/3/1930

28. ibid Minutes of 83rd meeting of the Board 9/5/1930, 84th meeting 26/6/1930

29. ibid Minutes of 85th meeting of the Board 25/7/1930

30. ibid Minutes of 86th meeting of the Board 19/9/1930

31. ibid Minutes of 87th meeting of the Board 24/10/1930

32. ibid Minutes of 87th meeting of the Board 24/10/1930

33. ibid Minutes of 88th meeting of the Board 20/11/1930

34. ibid Minutes of 89th meeting of the Board 9/1/1931

35. ibid Minutes of 91st meeting of the Board 27/3/1931

36. ibid Minutes of 92nd meeting of the Board 1/5/1931

37. ibid Minutes of 93rd meeting of the Board 20/6/1931

38. ibid Minutes of 94th meeting of the Board 30/7/1931

39. ibid Minutes of 96th meeting of the Board 30/10/1931

40. ibid Minutes of 95th meeting of the Board 30/9/1931

41. ibid Minutes of 96th meeting of the Board 30/10/1931

42. ibid Minutes of 97th meeting of the Board 9/12/1931

43. ibid Minutes of 98th meeting of the Board 21/1/1932, 99th meeting 26/2/1932, 100th

meeting 15/4/1932

44. ibid Minutes of 101st meeting of the Board 12/5/1932, 102nd meeting 17/6/1932

45. ibid Minutes of 104th meeting of the Board 30/9/1932

46. ibid Minutes of 102nd meeting of the Board 17/6/1932, 103rd meeting 19/7/1932, 104th meeting 30/9/1932, 105th meeting 7/11/1932

47. ibid Minutes of 106th meeting of the Board 14/12/1932

48. ibid Minutes of 107th meeting of the Board 27/1/1933, 108th meeting 10/3/1933

49. ibid Minutes of 107th meeting of the Board 27/1/1933, 112th meeting 27/7/1933, 114th meeting 7/11/1933

50. ibid Minutes of 107th meeting of the Board 27/1/1933, 109th meeting 27/4/1933, 114th meeting 7/11/1933, 115th meeting 15/12/1933

51. ibid Minutes of 108th meeting of the Board 10/3/1933, 115th meeting 15/12/1933

52. ibid Minutes of 108th meeting of the Board 10/3/1933, 110th meeting 26/5/1933

53. ibid Minutes of 108th meeting of the Board 10/3/1933

54. ibid Minutes of 107th meeting of the Board 27/1/1933, 115th meeting 15/12/1933

55. ibid Minutes of 116th meeting of the Board 21/1/1934, 117th meting 8/3/1934, 118th meeting 12/4/1934
NA: POWE 59/4: Minutes of 123rd meeting of the Board 2/11/1934, 124th meeting 18/12/1934

56. ibid Minutes of 117th meeting of the Board 6/3/1934, 118th meeting 12/4/1934, 121st meeting 26/7/1934, 123rd meeting 2/11/1934

57. NA: POWE 59/3: Minutes of 121st meeting of the Board 26/7/1934

58. NA: POWE 59/4: Minutes of 122nd meeting of the Board 27/9/1934

59. NA: POWE 59/3: Minutes of 120th meeting of the Board 29/6/1934
POWE 59/4: Minutes of 123rd meeting of the Board 2/11/1934, 124th meeting 18/12/1934

60. NA: POWE 59/4: Minutes of 125th meeting 25/1/1935, 126th meeting 6/3/1935

61. ibid Minutes of 126th meeting 6/3/1935, 127th meeting 10/4/1935, 128th meeting 23/5/1935, 130th meeting 26/3/1935, 131st meeting 4/10/1935, 132nd meeting 6/11/1935, 133rd meeting 20/12/1935

62. ibid Minutes of 130th meeting of the Board 26/7/1935, 131st meeting 4/10/1935, 132nd meeting 6/11/1935, 133rd meeting 20/12/1935

63. ibid Minutes of 126th meeting of the Board 6/3/1935, 132nd meeting 6/11/1935

64. ibid Minutes of 131st meeting of the Board 4/10/1935, 132nd meeting 6/11/1935

65. ibid Minutes of 126th meeting of the Board 6/3/1935, 127th meeting 10/4/1935, 128th meeting 23/5/1935

66. ibid Minutes of 127th meeting of the Board 10/4/1935

67. ibid Minutes of 134th meeting of the Board 24/1/1936, 136th meeting 18/3/1936, 137th Meeting 22/4/1936

68. ibid Minutes of 135th meeting of the Board 20/2/1936, 136th meeting 18/3/1936

69. ibid Minutes of 136th meeting of the Board 18/3/1936, 137th meeting 22/4/1936, 142nd meeting 10/12/1936

70. ibid Minutes of 134th meeting of the Board 24/1/1936, 137th meeting 22/4/1936, 138th meeting 26/5/1936, 141st meeting 4/11/1936

71. ibid Minutes of 140th meeting of the Board 29/9/1936

72. ibid Minutes of 143rd meeting of the Board 2/2/1937, 145th meeting 22/4/1937, 147th meeting 23/7/1937, 148th meeting 8/10/1937, 149th meeting 12/11/1937, 150th meeting 17/12/1937

73. ibid Minutes of 143rd meeting of the Board 2/2/1937, 145th meeting 22/4/1937, 146th meeting 3/6/1937

74. ibid

75. ibid Minutes of 144th meeting of the Board 11/3/1937

76. ibid Minutes of 144th meeting of the Board 11/3/1937

77. ibid Minutes of 145th meeting of the Board 22/4/1937, 150th meeting 17/12/1937

78. ibid Minutes of 147th meeting of the Board 23/7/1937, 148th meeting 8/10/1937

79. ibid Minutes of 148th meeting of the Board 8/10/1937, 151st meeting 1/2/1938, 152nd meeting 10/3/1938

80. ibid Minutes of 152nd meeting of the Board 10/3/1938

81. Ibid Minutes of 152nd meeting of the Board 10/3/1938, 153rd meeting 27/4/1938, 155th meeting 24/6/1938, 156th meeting 26/7/1938

82. ibid Minutes of 156th meeting of the Board 26/7/1938

83. ibid Minutes of 154th meeting of the Board 26/5/1938

84. ibid Minutes of 157th meeting of the Board 21/9/1938, 158th meeting 18/10/1938

85. ibid Minutes of 155th meeting of the Board 24/6/1938

86. ibid Minutes of 159th meeting of the Board 16/11/1938
87. ibid Minutes of 156th meeting of the Board 26/7/1938, 157th meeting 21/9/1938, 158th meeting 18/10/1938, 159th meeting 16/11/1938
88. ibid Minutes of 160th meeting of the Board 24/1/1939
89. ibid Minutes of 161st meeting of the Board 1/3/1939, 162nd meeting 27/4/1939
90. ibid Minutes of 161st meeting of the Board 1/3/1939
91. ibid Minutes of 162nd meeting of the Board 27/4/1939
92. ibid Minutes of 163rd meeting of the Board 8/6/1939
    NA: POWE 59/5: Minutes of 165th meeting of the Board 28/9/1939
93. NA: POWE 59/5: Minutes of 165th meeting of the Board 28/9/1939
94. ibid Minutes of 166th meeting of the Board 29/11/1939
95. ibid Minutes of 167th meeting of the Board 15/2/1940, 168th meeting 11/12/1940
    NUM: Miners' Welfare in Wartime: p 73
96. NA: POWE 59/5: Minutes of 169th meeting of the Board 22/4/1941, 170th meeting 31/7/1941
97. ibid Minutes of 171st meeting of the Board 7/5/1942
98. NUM: Miners' Welfare in Wartime: pp64–65

7 EDUCATION

1. NA: POWE 1/45: Circulars to District Committees 1921–1931 MWF 44 1923
2. NA: POWE 1/47: 3rd Report of the Miners' Welfare Fund 1924: pp 27–37, 52–58
3. NA: POWE 1/47: 4th Report of the Miners' Welfare Fund 1925: pp 30–34
4. NA: POWE 1/47: 5th Report of the Miners' Welfare Fund 1926: pp 28–29, 31–39
5. NUM: 8th Report of the Miners' Welfare Fund 1929: pp 16–18
6. NA: POWE 1/49: 11th Report of the Miners' Welfare Fund 1932: pp 14–17
7. ibid 12th Report of the Miners' Welfare Fund 1933: pp 29–32
    NA: POWE 1/29: Agenda paper for Committee meeting 30/3/1934 MWC 843
8. ibid Agenda paper for Committee meeting 20/11/1934
    NA: POWE 1/15: Minutes of meeting 27/4/1949 Item 13 and 14
9. NA: POWE 1/49: 15th Report of the Miners'

Welfare Fund 1936: pp 54–55, 94–95
NA: POWE 1/16: Minutes of Council meeting 15/2/1950
NA: POWE 1/43: Agenda paper for February 1950 meeting (50) 19, March 1950 meeting (50) 33

8 RECREATION

1. NA: POWE 1/46: 3rd Conference of District Committees 1924
2. NA: POWE 1/47: 4th Report of the Miners' Welfare Fund 1925: pp 15–16
3. NA: POWE 1/45: Circulars to District Committees MWF83 18/5/1925
4. NA: POWE 1/1: Minutes of Committee meeting 23/6/1925
5. NA: POWE 1/47: 4th Report of the Miners' Welfare Fund 1925: pp 16–17, 46–47
6. ibid pp 19–19, 44
7. ibid 5th Report of the Miners' Welfare Fund 1926: pp 55–62
8. NA: POWE 1/21: Agenda paper for 49th meeting 18/1/1927, 53rd meeting 13/4/1927
9. NA: POWE 1/22: Agenda paper for 57th meeting 20/9/1927
10. NA: POWE 1/23: Agenda paper for 60th meeting 17/1/1928
11. NA: POWE 1/23: Agenda paper for 66th meeting 13/7/1928
12. ibid Agenda paper for 68th meeting 16/10/1928 MWC 496, 69th meeting 20/11/1928
    NA: POWE ½: Minutes of 69th meeting 20/11/1928
    NA: POWE 1/46 Minutes of 7th Conference of District Committees 20/11/1928
13. NA: POWE 1/45: Circulars to District Committees MWF 136
14. ibid
    NA: POWE 1/25: Agenda paper for 86th meeting 15/7/1930
15. NA; POWE 1/26: Agenda paper for 97th meeting 21/7/1931 MWC 672
16. ibid Agenda paper 91st meeting 30/1/1931, 92nd meeting 17/2/ 1931 MWC 653
    NA: POWE 1/45: Circulars to District Committees MWF 143
17. NA: POWE 1/45 Circulars to District Committees
18. ibid MWF 161
19. NA: POWE 1/30: Agenda paper for meeting 23/7/1935 paper 1008
20. NUM: Miners' Welfare in Wartime: p7
21. NA: POWE 1/32: Agenda paper for

158th meeting Sixth District Organisers'
Conference 27/4/1937
NA: POWE 1/33: Agenda paper for 171st
meeting 1938, Nineth Conference of District
Organisers 12–13 July 1938
NA: POWE 1/34: Agenda paper for 178th
meeting June 1939, Tenth Conference of
District Organisers 1–3 May 1939

22. NUM: Miners' Welfare in Wartime: pp 32–42
23. NA: POWE 1/40: Agenda paper for 51st
meeting 15/1/1947, 53rd meeting 19/3/1947,
60th meeting 19/11/1947
NA: POWE 1/43: Agenda paper for 81st/21st
meeting (50)15
24. NA: POWE 1/42: Agenda paper for 72nd
meeting 12/2/1949
POWE 1/43: Agenda paper 81st /21st
meeting 18/1/1950 (50)15
25. ibid Agenda paper for meeting 18/10/1950
(50)90

9 HEALTH

1. NA: POWE 1/25: Agenda paper for 89th
meeting 18/11/1930
2. NA: POWE 1/1: Minutes of 35th meeting
26/5/1925, 37th meeting 24/7/1925
POWE 1/20: Agenda paper for 40th meeting
19/1/1926
POWE 1/46: 5th Conference of District
Committees 16/11/1926
3. NA: POWE 1/22: Agenda paper for 50th
meeting 15/11/1927
4. NA: POWE 1/23: Agenda paper for 64th
meeting MWC 465, 68th meeting MWC 492
5. NA: POWE 1/46: 8th Conference of District
Committees 15/10/1929
6. NA: POWE 1/2: Minutes of 83rd meeting
15/4/1930, 84th meeting 20/5/1930
POWE 1/25: Agenda paper for 83rd meeting
7. NA: POWE 1/26: Agenda paper for 91st
meeting February 1931
8. ibid Agenda paper for 97th meeting 21/7/1931
MWC 684
9. British Library: Learning at Every Step,
Rehabilitation by the Miners' Welfare
Commission. 1949

10 PITHEAD WELFARE

1. NA: POWE 1/47: 2nd Report of the Miners'
Welfare Fund 1923: pp11–12
2. Hansard: 5th Series: Vol 167: CC 339–340
3. The Pithead Baths Story published by National
Museum of Wales Books, 2010: pp 6–9

4. NA: POWE 1/20: Agenda paper 45th
meeting 23/6/1926 MWC 314
5. NA: POWE 1/47: 5th Report of the Miners'
Welfare Fund 1926
POWE 1/20: Agenda paper for 43rd
meeting 20/4/1926 MWC 304, 44th meeting
18/5/1926 MWC 311
6. NA: POWE 1/49: 12th Report of the Miners'
Welfare Fund 1933: pp 9–10, 81–82, 84
7. ibid p 9
8. ibid p82–85
9. NA: POWE 1/49: 13th Report of the Miners'
Welfare Fund 1934: pp 15–17
10. NA: POWE 1/49: 15th Report of the Miners
Welfare Fund 1936: p 26
POWE 1/33: Agenda paper for 168th
meeting May 1938, 171st meeting 1938
POWE 1/10 Minutes of 174th meeting
24/1/1939
NUM: Miners' Welfare in Wartime: pp 16–17
11. NA: POWE 1/33: Agenda paper for 164th
meeting January 1938
12. NA: POWE 1/10: Minutes of 179th meeting
18/7/1939
13. NA: POWE 1/35: Agenda paper for 2nd
meeting 16/1/1940
POWE 1/11: Minutes of 2nd meeting of the
Commission 16/1/1940
14. NA: POWE 1/11: Minutes of 2nd meeting
16/1/1940, 4th meeting 16/4/1940, 6th
meeting 18/6/1940, 7th meeting 18/7/1940
NA: POWE 1/35: Agenda paper 4th meeting
Item 5(a), 6th meeting Item 4(d), 7th
meeting Item 1
15. NA: POWE 1/43: Agenda paper for June
1950 meeting (50) 73
16. NA: POWE 1/44: Agenda paper for
September 1951 meeting (51) 57
POWE 1/16: Minutes meeting 19/9/1951

11 THE FINAL YEARS 1946–1952

1. NA: POWE 1/13: Minutes of 42nd meeting
15/1/1946
POWE 1/39: Agenda paper for 42nd meeting
Items 4 and 5, 43rd meeting
Item 2
2. ibid Minutes of 45th meeting 20/4/1946, 47th
meeting 11/9/1946, 50th meeting 18/12/1946
Agenda paper for 47th meeting Items 1 and 4,
49th meeting Item 6, 50th meeting Item 6
3. ibid Minutes for 42nd meeting 15/1/1946,
44th meeting 19/3/1946, 47th meeting
11/9/1946 50th meeting 18/12/1946
Agenda paper for 42nd meeting Items 6(a)

and (b), 43rd meeting Item 7, 46th meeting Item 2(a), 47th meeting Item 6(a), 48th meeting Item 3(a), 49th meeting Item 3(a), 50th meeting Item 2(c)

4. ibid Minutes of 45th meeting 30/4/1946, 46th meeting 18/6/1946
   Agenda paper for 46th meeting Item 3, 46th meeting Item 3(e), 47th meeting Item 6(a), 50th meeting Item 2(a)

5. NA: POWE 1/39: Agenda paper for 46th meeting Item 2(a), 48th meeting Item 3(a)

6. ibid Agenda paper for 42nd meeting Item 9, 44th meeting Item 2(a), 47th meeting Item 7(a), 48th meeting Items 4(a) and (b)
   NA: POWE 1/13: Minutes 0f 48th meeting 16/10/1946

7. NA: POWE 1/14: Minutes for 51st meeting 15/1/1947, 53rd meeting 19/3/1947
   POWE 1/40: Agenda paper for 53rd meeting Item 3

8. ibid Minutes for 51st meeting 15/1/1947, 52nd meeting 19/2/1947, 53rd meeting 19/3/1947, 57th meeting 16/7/1947, 58th meeting 19/9/2947, 59th meeting 15/10/1947, 60th meeting 19/11/1947
   Agenda papers for 51st meeting Item 2, 55th meeting Item 7, 58th meeting Item 2, 59th meeting Item 2, 60th meeting Item 2(b)

9. ibid Minutes for 51st meeting 15/1/1947, 52nd meeting 19/2/1947, 53rd meeting 19/3/1947, 57th meeting 16/7/1947, 58th meeting 17/9/1947, 59th meeting 15/10/1947
   Agenda paper for 51st meeting Item 5(a), 52nd meeting Item 5(a), 53rd meeting Item 4(a), 58th meeting Item 4a(i), 59th meeting Item 4 (a)

10. ibid Minutes for 51st meeting 15/1/1947, 53rd meeting 19/3/1947, 54th meeting 16/4/1947, 55th meeting 21/5/1947, 56th meeting 19/6/1947, 57th meeting 16/7/1947
    Agenda paper for 51st meeting Item 6, 52nd meeting Item 3, 53rd meeting Item 5, 55th meeting Items 2 (a, b, c, d, e, f, g), 60th meeting Item 3(c)

11. ibid Minutes for 53rd meeting 19/3/1947, 55th meeting 21/5/1947, 57th meeting 16/7/1947
    Agenda paper for 53rd meeting Item 6, 55th meeting Item ^, 57th meeting Item 4

12. ibid Minutes for 55th meeting 21/5/1947
    Agenda paper for 55th meeting Item 5(a)

13. NA: POWE 1/40: Agenda paper for 59th meeting Item 4

14. NA: POWE 1/15: Minutes for 61/1st meeting

7/1/1948, 62/2nd meeting 18/2/1948, 63/3rd meeting 31/3/1948, 64/4th meeting 21/4/1948, 65/5th meeting 26/5/1948, 67/7th meeting 28/7/1948, 70/10th meeting 15/12/1948

15. ibid Minutes for 69/9th meeting 20/10/1948, 70/10th 15/12/1948

16. ibid Minutes for 62/2nd meeting 18/2/1948, 64/4th 21/4/1948, 67/7th 28/7/1948

17. ibid Minutes 61/1st meeting 7/1/1948, 62/2nd meeting 18/2/1948, 64/4th meeting 21/4/1948 65/5th meeting 26/5/1948, 66/6th meeting 30/6/1948, 67/7th meeting 28/7/1948, 70/10th meeting 15/12/1948

18. ibid Minutes for 62/2nd meeting 18/2/1948, 65/5th meeting 26/5/1948, 66/6th meeting 30/6/1948, 68/8th meeting 22/9/1948, 69/9th meeting 20/10/1948, 70/10th meeting 17/11/1948 and 15/12/1948

19. NA: POWE 1/15: Minutes for 71/11th meeting 19/1/1949, 72/12th meeting 16/2/1949, 73/13th meeting 16/3/1949, 74/14th meeting 27/4/1949, 75/15th meeting 18/5/1949, 77/17th meeting 20/7/1949, 78/18th meeting 21/9/1949, 79/19th meeting 19/10/1949, 80/20th meeting 16/11/1949
    POWE 1/42: Agenda paper for 71/11th meeting Item 3(a), 73/13th meeting Item 6, 75/15th meeting Item 4, 76/16th meeting, 77/17th meeting Item 2(a) Appendix, 78/18th meeting Item 2, 79/19th meeting Item 3, 80/20th meeting Item 4

20. ibid Minutes for 73/13th meeting 16/3/1949
    Agenda paper for 72/12th meeting Item 6(a), 73/13th meeting Item 2(f), 74/14th meeting, 76/16th meeting, 77/17th meeting, 78/18th meeting

21. ibid Minutes for 74/14th meeting27/4/1949
    Agenda paper for April meeting Items 13 and 14

22. ibid Minutes for 74/14th meeting 27/4/1949, 75/15th meeting 18/5/1949
    Agenda paper for 78/18th meeting

23. NA: POWE 1/16: Minutes for meeting 18/1/1950, meeting 15/2/1950, meeting 15/3/1950, meeting 21/6/1950, meeting 19/7/1950, meeting 18/10/1950, meeting 15/11/1950
    POWE 1/43: Agenda paper January meeting (50) 15, February meeting (50) 2, March meeting (50) 30 and 31, June meeting (50) 61, October meeting (50) 79

24. ibid Minutes for meeting 18/1/1950, meeting 17/5/1950, meeting 21/6/1950, meeting 15/11/1950

Agenda paper for January Meeting (50)3,
April meeting (50)11, May meeting (50)58,
June meeting (50)73

25. NA: POWE 1/43: Agenda paper for January
meeting (50)7

26. NA: POWE 1/16: Minutes of meeting
15/2/1950
POWE 1/43: Agenda paper for February
meeting (50)19

27. NA: POWE 1/43: Agenda paper for March
meeting (50) 33

28. NA: POWE 1/16: Minutes for meeting
17/5/1950, meeting 21/6/1950
POWE 1/43: Agenda paper for February
meeting (50)21, May meeting (50)52, June
meeting (50)70

29. NA: POWE 1/16: Minutes of meeting
18/10/1950, meeting 14/3/1951, meeting
20/6/1951
NUM: Memorandum of Agreement

30. NA: POWE 1/16: Minutes of meeting
21/2/1951
POWE 1/44: Agenda paper for February
meeting (51)2

31. ibid Minutes of meeting 21/2/1951, meeting
14/3/1951, meeting 16/5/1951, meeting
20/6/1951, meeting 18/7/1951, meeting
19/9/1951, meeting 1/11/1951, meeting
28/11/1951

Agenda paper for February meeting (51)8,
March meeting (51) 15,21, May meeting
(51)23, June meeting (51) 33, July meeting
(51)42, September meeting (51) 53, 1st
November meeting (51) 67, 28th November
meeting (51) 72

32. ibid Minutes for meeting 14/3/1951
Agenda paper for March meeting (51)18

33. NA: POWE 1/44: Agenda paper for May
meeting (51)22

34. NA: POWE 1/16: Minutes for meeting
16/5/1951

35. NA: POWE 1/16: Minutes for meeting
19/9/1951
POWE 1/44: Agenda item for September
meeting (51)52

36. NA: POWE 1/16: Minutes for meeting
1/11/1951

37. NA: POWE 1/44: Agenda paper for
September meeting (51)60

38. NA: POWE 1/16: Minutes for meeting
1/11/1951
POWE 1/44: Agenda paper for November
meeting (51)68

LIST OF ILLUSTRATIONS

8 **RECREATION**

10 **PITHEAD WELFARE**

INDEX